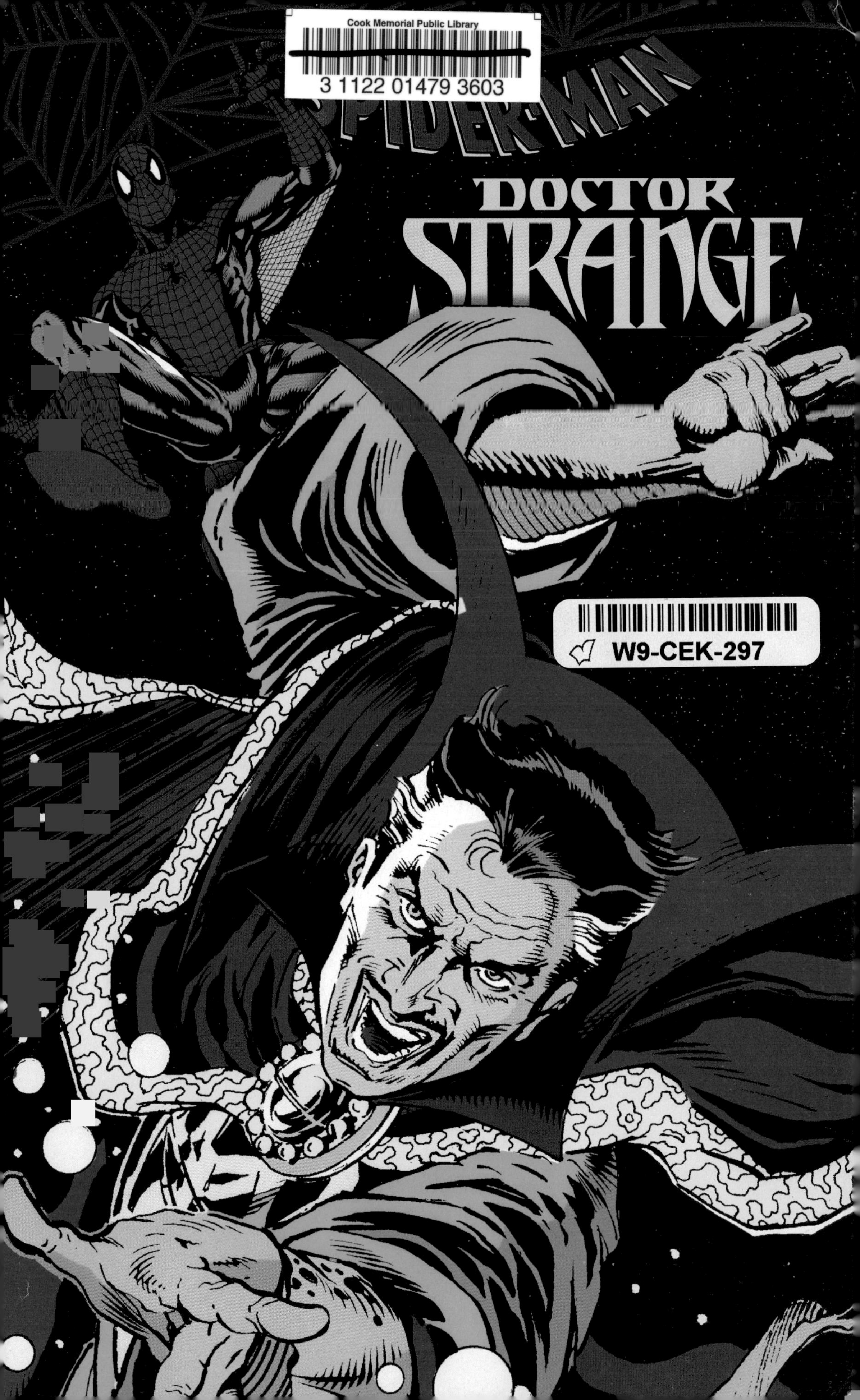
SPIDER-MAN
DOCTOR STRANGE

SPIDER-MAN

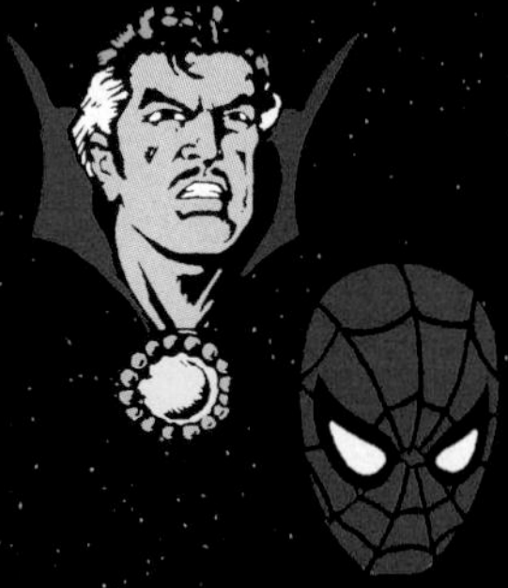

DOCTOR STRANGE

THE WAY TO DUSTY DEATH

LEN WEIN, ROY THOMAS, BILL MANTLO, CHRIS CLAREMONT, DENNY O'NEIL, KURT BUSIEK & ROGER STERN WITH STEVE DITKO, STAN LEE, MIKE W. BARR, SANDY PLUNKETT & GERRY CONWAY
WRITERS

STEVE DITKO, SAL BUSCEMA, SANDY PLUNKETT, MICHAEL BAIR, HOWARD CHAYKIN, MIKE VOSBURG, FRANK MILLER & NEIL VOKES
PENCILERS

STEVE DITKO, P. CRAIG RUSSELL, MICHAEL BAIR, MIKE ESPOSITO, JEFF ACLIN, JUAN ORTIZ, GENE DAY, STEVE LEIALOHA, TOM PALMER & JAY GELDHOF WITH FRANK GIACOIA, DAVE HUNT, MARK BEACHUM & MARK TEXEIRA
INKERS

GLYNIS WEIN, PETRA GOLDBERG, BOB SHAREN, JANICE COHEN, CARL GAFFORD, MARIO SEN, BEN SEAN & MATT HOLLINGSWORTH
COLORISTS

SAM ROSEN, DAVE HUNT, JIM NOVAK, JOE ROSEN, RICK PARKER, KAREN MANTLO, IRV WATANABE, DENISE WOHL AND RICHARD STARKINGS & COMICRAFT
LETTERERS

ANN NOCENTI, DAN CUDDY, MARY JO DUFFY & GREGG SCHIGIEL
ASSISTANT EDITORS

STAN LEE, ROY THOMAS, AL MILGROM, ROB TOKAR, DANNY FINGEROTH, ARCHIE GOODWIN, BOB HALL & TOM BREVOORT
EDITORS

MICHAEL BAIR
FRONT COVER ARTIST

GIL KANE
BACK COVER ARTIST

SPIDER-MAN AND DOCTOR STRANGE CREATED BY STAN LEE & STEVE DITKO

COLLECTION EDITOR MARK D. BEAZLEY
ASSISTANT EDITOR CAITLIN O'CONNELL
ASSOCIATE MANAGING EDITOR KATERI WOODY
ASSOCIATE MANAGER, DIGITAL ASSETS JOE HOCHSTEIN
SENIOR EDITOR, SPECIAL PROJECTS JENNIFER GRÜNWALD

VP PRODUCTION & SPECIAL PROJECTS JEFF YOUNGQUIST
RESEARCH & LAYOUT JEPH YORK
PRODUCTION COLORTEK & JOE FRONTIRRE
BOOK DESIGNER ADAM DEL RE
SVP PRINT, SALES & MARKETING DAVID GABRIEL

EDITOR IN CHIEF AXEL ALONSO
CHIEF CREATIVE OFFICER JOE QUESADA
PRESIDENT DAN BUCKLEY
EXECUTIVE PRODUCER ALAN FINE

SPECIAL THANKS TO MIKE HANSEN

INTRODUCTION

BY RALPH MACCHIO

Those of you discerning Marvelites who've purchased this colorful collection are in for a double treat. I say that because each of these titanic tales features two of Stan Lee and Steve Ditko's great creations: the Amazing Spider-Man and the Master of the Mystic Arts, Doctor Strange! Somehow, despite the vast differences between these two in terms of powers, personality and the nature of their respective enemies, they work together like hand in glove. When you think about it, though, the more memorable team-ups in any medium seem to occur between dissimilar characters. Spidey and the good doctor are definitely the odd couple of comics, let's face it. Spider-Man is the acrobatic, wisecracking youth, hounded by police, unappreciated by the public and haunted by personal guilt. Stephen Strange is the former surgeon, now the secretive, spell-casting sorcerer whose very existence is unknown to the general public. You'd imagine there's no threat that could possibly unite these two disparate do-gooders. Well, this carefully assembled trade paperback is out to prove you wrong. Within these pages, spanning more than 30 years of published material, are many powerful pairings of the web-spinner and ol' Doc by some of the top talents in comicdom. So, let's dive right in and test the waters.

The initial meeting of our two heroes occurred in *Amazing Spider-Man Annual #2*. It's a genuine classic by Stan and Steve, introducing an evil sorcerer named Xandu, whose malign presence permeates the pages of this collection. Little did we awestruck readers at the time know, but the sinister saga of Xandu was just beginning, as you'll see. Let me say that while I am a sucker for those dark Ditko-esque cityscapes, I'm even more of a devotee of Steve's utterly unique take on other spatial dimensions. Luckily, there's an abundance of both in "The Wondrous World of Doctor Strange." And isn't that a title to conjure with.

I recall in one of the many conversations I've had with the incomparable Mr. Ditko through the years that I asked him what sources he'd used to illustrate Nightmare's realm or Dormammu's Dark Dimension. He replied that it all came out of his head; every single crazy quilt panel that has transfixed *Doctor Strange* readers. All of that illustrative brilliance accomplished minus the use of any hallucinogens, I might add. Although,

speaking of magic mushrooms and the like, journalist Tom Wolfe in his book *The Electric Kool-Aid Acid Test* had numerous mentions of those singular Ditko dimensions and their effect on the book's protagonist, Ken Kesey and his Merry Pranksters. Steve's otherworldly graphics mightily influenced every penciler who succeeded him on *Doctor Strange*.

I mentioned that the zany Xandu was just beginning his villainous escapades in that second Spidey annual. Obviously, there is something highly intriguing about this mystical menace because he popped up again and again, for example, in our reprinted *Marvel Team-Up #21*. Therein we learn there is more to Xandu than a man on a quest for unlimited magical power. Yes, he desperately wants to be the baddest sorcerer on the block. He also wants to use that mystical might to save the life of his beloved Melinda. So, knowing that, our sympathies shift toward him. We can all identify with someone who would go to extremes to save a loved one. This deepening of Xandu's motivation would play out significantly in upcoming stories. Kudos to writer Len Wein and penciler Sal Buscema for crafting this emotional tale.

The spider and the sorcerer joined forces once again in the pages of *Marvel Team-Up #50* and *#51*. A 50th issue is a landmark for any comic, and *Team-Up* was no exception. Bill Mantlo had been handling the scripting duties on a regular basis for more than a year, and he introduced a new baddie called the Wraith in issue #48, who stayed around to bedevil our dynamic duo in their issues.

There's a particularly harrowing sequence in issue #51. Stephen Strange must perform surgery once again, years after abandoning it when an automobile accident irreparably damaged his nerves. You can sense the internal struggle as this former surgical master questions whether he can do the operation. This is a complex story, pulled off with aplomb by Misters Mantlo and Buscema.

Chris Claremont of *X-Men* fame also took a crack at the *Team-Up* title and turned in some masterful tales, including four that we've reprinted here for your enjoyment. The first two from issues #76 and #77 are illustrated by a comics great: Howard Chaykin. The villain of the piece is Silver Dagger, who became an instant sensation when he was introduced by Steve Englehart and Frank Brunner in their much-lauded tenure on Doctor Strange. It was a gutsy move by Claremont to revisit Silver Dagger, because when a particular villain becomes deeply associated with a certain creative team, that character's return can pose problems for the subsequent writer. I was a huge fan of the groundbreaking Englehart/Brunner run and I feel that Chris handled Silver Dagger exceptionally well. He was just as malevolent in *Team-Up* as he had been in Doc's own title. And that's saying something. His scheme to steal the soul of

Strange's beloved Clea was effectively portrayed. Once again, the mystic master and the web-spinner worked together beautifully. Something about these two characters in tandem clicked both creatively and with the readers. I thoroughly enjoyed Chaykin's rendition of Strange and Spider-Man, which borrowed from no other penciler and was captivating.

Mr. Claremont followed up with another highly readable two-parter, this time with artist Mike Vosburg, featuring our friendly neighborhood web-slinger, the master mage and his lady, Clea. I found myself enjoying these issues most because of the appearance of a favorite femme fatale of mine: Satana, the Devil's Daughter. She plays a key role in the story, in which Chris so effectively exploits the dichotomy of her character. She is indeed the offspring of Satan, but her mother was human. To Mr. C's credit, he zeroes in on that crucial aspect of her personality to show that the human side of her fighting to bring forth her better nature. The life of Stephen Strange depends on the outcome of that struggle in the climax.

Another unforgettable Marvel female is featured in the Marvel Fanfare tale written by Mike Barr and penciled and co-plotted by Sandy Plunkett. This one stars the stunning Scarlet Witch who teams with Spidey against— you guessed it—Xandu himself, back for a rematch. Some 20 years after his first showdown in *Amazing Spider-Man Annual #2*, he's back. Mike Barr is a truly fine writer who's done far too little for the House of Ideas. Here, he picks up on plot threads left over from Xandu's prior outings and shows us a dangerous Scarlet Witch who isn't in her right mind—and I mean that literally. The Plunkett art is something to savor. Once you get into it, you will wish this entry was twice as long.

Let's take a break from the Xandu chronicles and delve into *Amazing Spider-Man Annual #14*, by Denny O'Neil and Frank Miller. Frank brought elements of the classic Steve Ditko art, mixed with Miller's own energetic penciling style, to create a visual tour de force that will absolutely blow you away. His collaborator, Denny O'Neil, is one of the finer talents ever to darken our doorway and he shows his Marvel chops here, big time. His interpretation of both Dormammu and Doctor Doom and what draws them together is at once startling and disturbing. This is a tale you'll be rereading many times, not only for the visual feast, also for the philosophical nuggets embedded in the storyline.

Like a bad penny, our malign mystic, Xandu, takes his final bow in "The Way to Dusty Death" by those masters of the Marvel Method, Roy Thomas and Gerry Conway. The highly talented Mike Bair supplies the illustrations. This wondrous one-shot delves deeply into the haunted relationship between Xandu and his lover Melinda. Once again, Spidey and Doc Strange are drawn into the diabolical doings of their emerald-clad enemy, and the results are incredible. Perhaps no other Xandu episode probed so unforgivingly into his true motivations and primal fears. Xandu must finally accept the fragility of life and the finality of death in this fitting capstone. Not an easy thing to do when you've possessed almost limitless power.

Our final entry is "Strange Encounter" from *Untold Tales of Spider-Man* by Kurt Busiek and Roger Stern, both of whom have made innumerable contributions to the Marvel mythos. Here, they hearken back to the very early days of both Spidey and Strange. What a kick to see our favorite mage in his first magical attire, complete with square amulet and purple cloak. If you remember Doc from his first appearances in *Strange Tales*, you'll definitely get a nostalgic twinge. They face off against Baron Mordo, who all Strangeophiles know has been trying to take down the mystic master since 1963. Some guys never give up. The art by Neil Vokes has a charm that's undeniable. And his take on those Ditko-esque dimensions is not to be missed.

This volume you hold in your hands is a true chest of wonders. Story gems of every facet abound. The art ranges from the stunning to the sublime. And what better place to begin the magic than with the evil Xandu's first time upon the Marvel stage? Be prepared to voyage from the garbage-strewn streets of Manhattan to other dimensions at the farthest reaches of human imagination. All you have to do is take that first all-important step. We'll be with you all the way.

Enjoy,

Ralph Macchio

RALPH MACCHIO

Ralph Macchio spent over 35 years at Marvel, starting as an assistant editor and later writing *Avengers*, and many others. As editor, he oversaw books across the Marvel line, including shepherding the Ultimate line into existence, and editing all of Stephen King's Marvel adaptations.

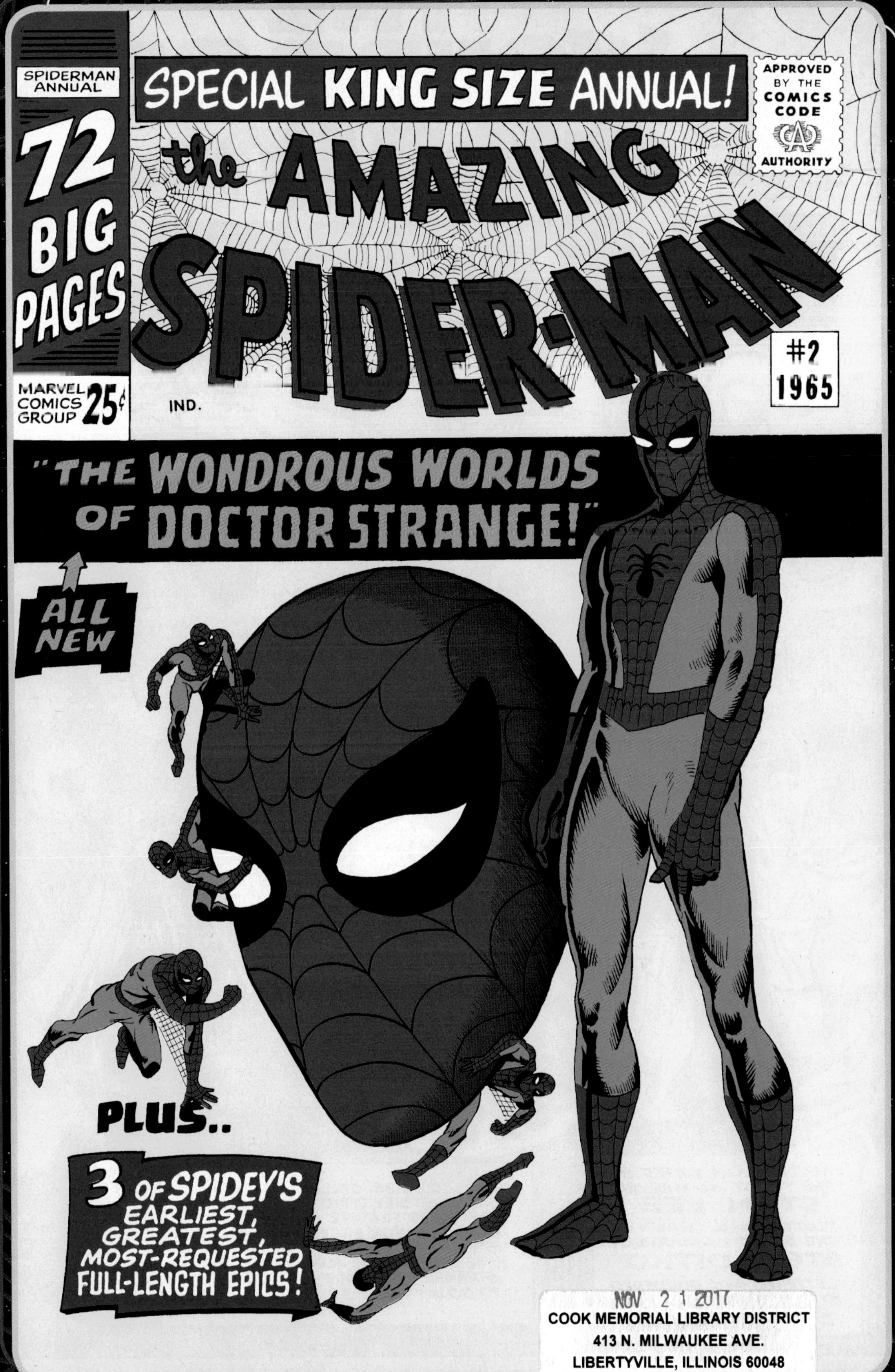
SPIDERMAN ANNUAL
SPECIAL KING SIZE ANNUAL!
APPROVED BY THE COMICS CODE AUTHORITY
72 BIG PAGES
the AMAZING SPIDER-MAN
#2
1965
MARVEL COMICS GROUP 25¢
IND.
"THE WONDROUS WORLDS OF DOCTOR STRANGE!"
ALL NEW
PLUS..
3 OF SPIDEY'S EARLIEST, GREATEST, MOST-REQUESTED FULL-LENGTH EPICS!

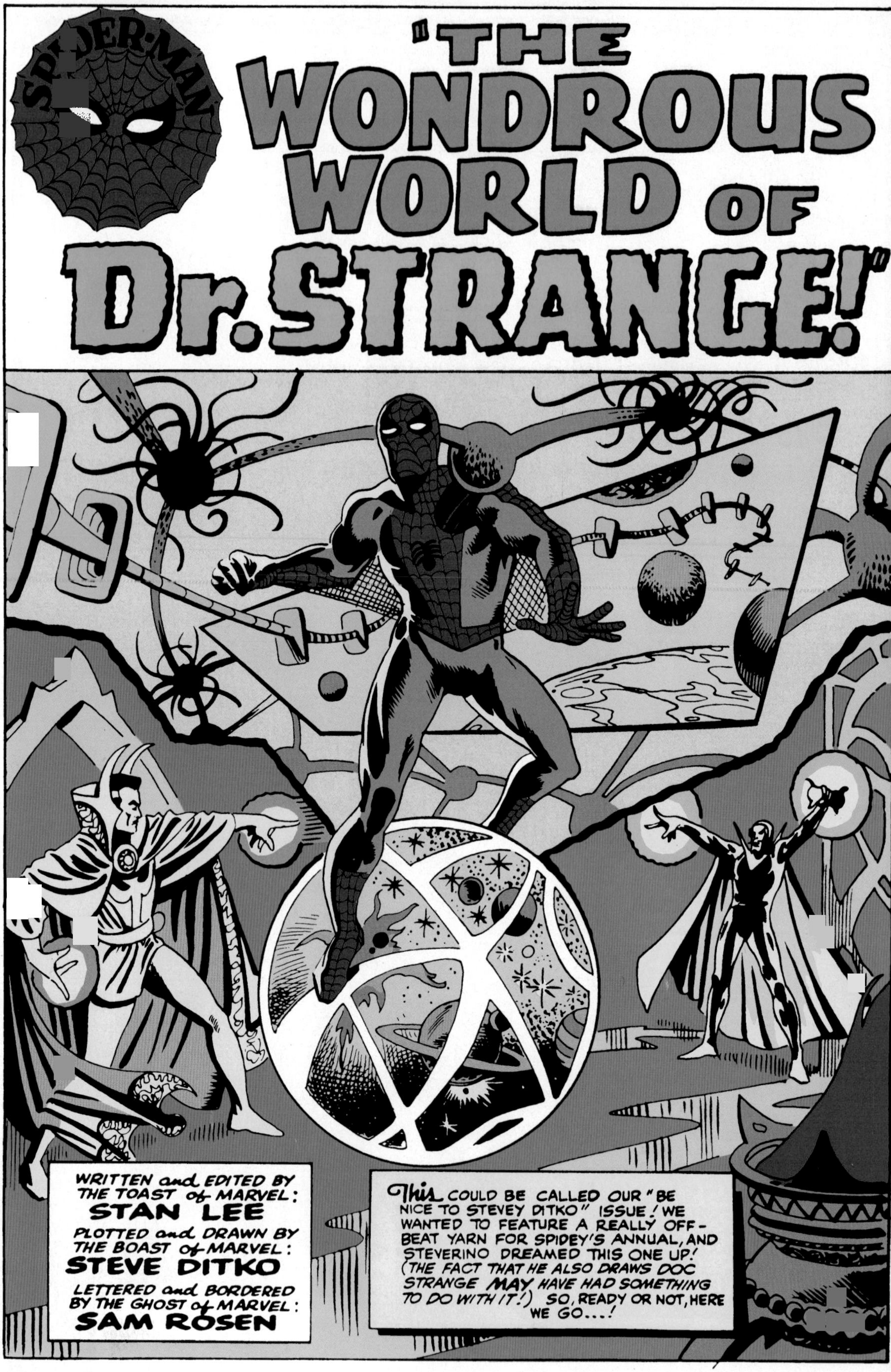
SPIDER-MAN
"THE WONDROUS WORLD OF Dr. STRANGE!"
WRITTEN and EDITED BY THE TOAST of MARVEL: STAN LEE
PLOTTED and DRAWN BY THE BOAST of MARVEL: STEVE DITKO
LETTERED and BORDERED BY THE GHOST of MARVEL: SAM ROSEN
This COULD BE CALLED OUR "BE NICE TO STEVEY DITKO" ISSUE! WE WANTED TO FEATURE A REALLY OFF-BEAT YARN FOR SPIDEY'S ANNUAL, AND STEVERINO DREAMED THIS ONE UP! (THE FACT THAT HE ALSO DRAWS DOC STRANGE MAY HAVE HAD SOMETHING TO DO WITH IT!) SO, READY OR NOT, HERE WE GO...!

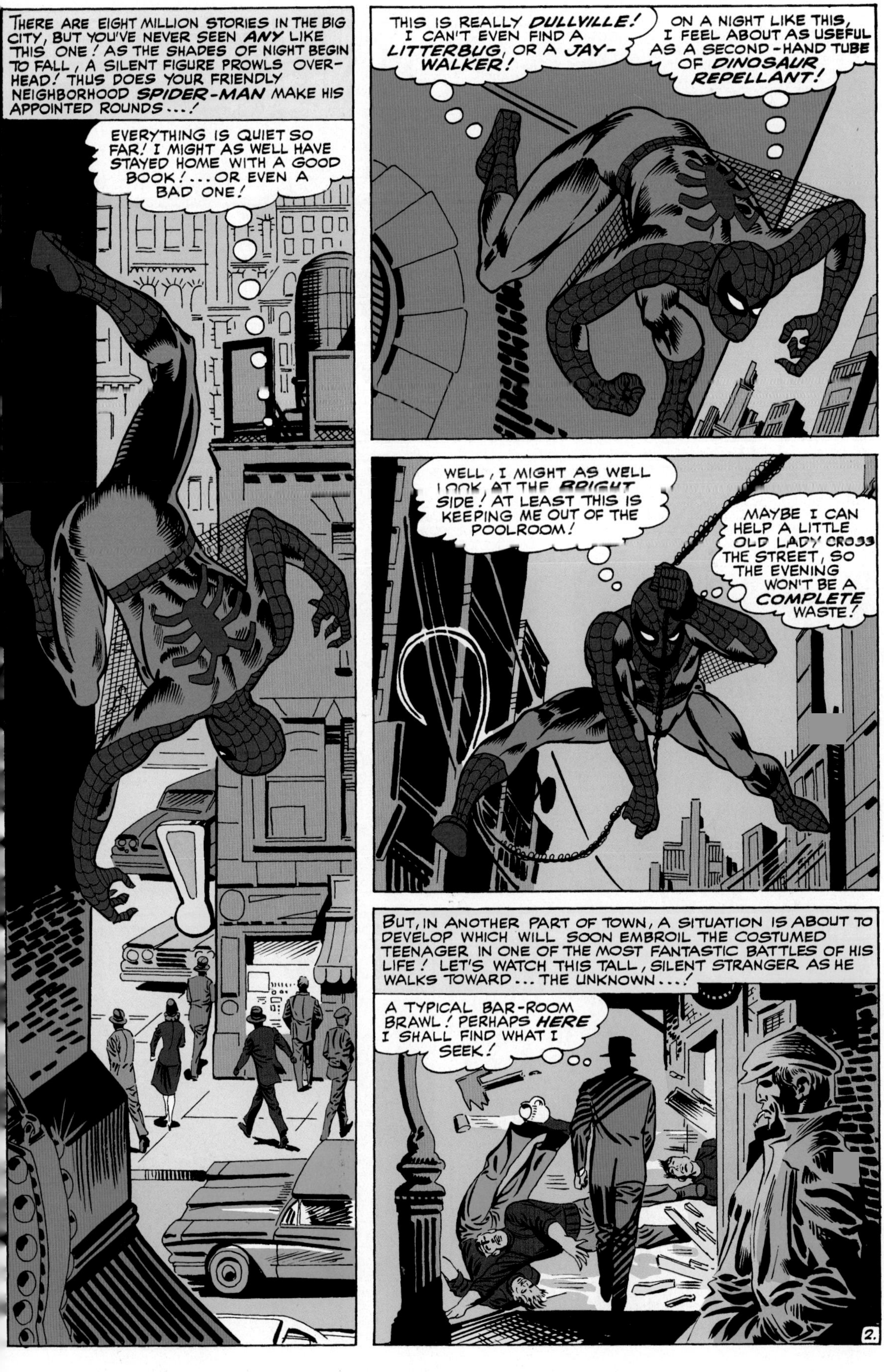
THERE ARE EIGHT MILLION STORIES IN THE BIG CITY, BUT YOU'VE NEVER SEEN ANY LIKE THIS ONE! AS THE SHADES OF NIGHT BEGIN TO FALL, A SILENT FIGURE PROWLS OVERHEAD! THUS DOES YOUR FRIENDLY NEIGHBORHOOD SPIDER-MAN MAKE HIS APPOINTED ROUNDS...!
EVERYTHING IS QUIET SO FAR! I MIGHT AS WELL HAVE STAYED HOME WITH A GOOD BOOK!...OR EVEN A BAD ONE!
THIS IS REALLY DULLVILLE! I CAN'T EVEN FIND A LITTERBUG, OR A JAY-WALKER!
ON A NIGHT LIKE THIS, I FEEL ABOUT AS USEFUL AS A SECOND-HAND TUBE OF DINOSAUR REPELLANT!
WELL, I MIGHT AS WELL LOOK AT THE BRIGHT SIDE! AT LEAST THIS IS KEEPING ME OUT OF THE POOLROOM!
MAYBE I CAN HELP A LITTLE OLD LADY CROSS THE STREET, SO THE EVENING WON'T BE A COMPLETE WASTE!
BUT, IN ANOTHER PART OF TOWN, A SITUATION IS ABOUT TO DEVELOP WHICH WILL SOON EMBROIL THE COSTUMED TEENAGER IN ONE OF THE MOST FANTASTIC BATTLES OF HIS LIFE! LET'S WATCH THIS TALL, SILENT STRANGER AS HE WALKS TOWARD... THE UNKNOWN...!
A TYPICAL BAR-ROOM BRAWL! PERHAPS HERE I SHALL FIND WHAT I SEEK!
2.

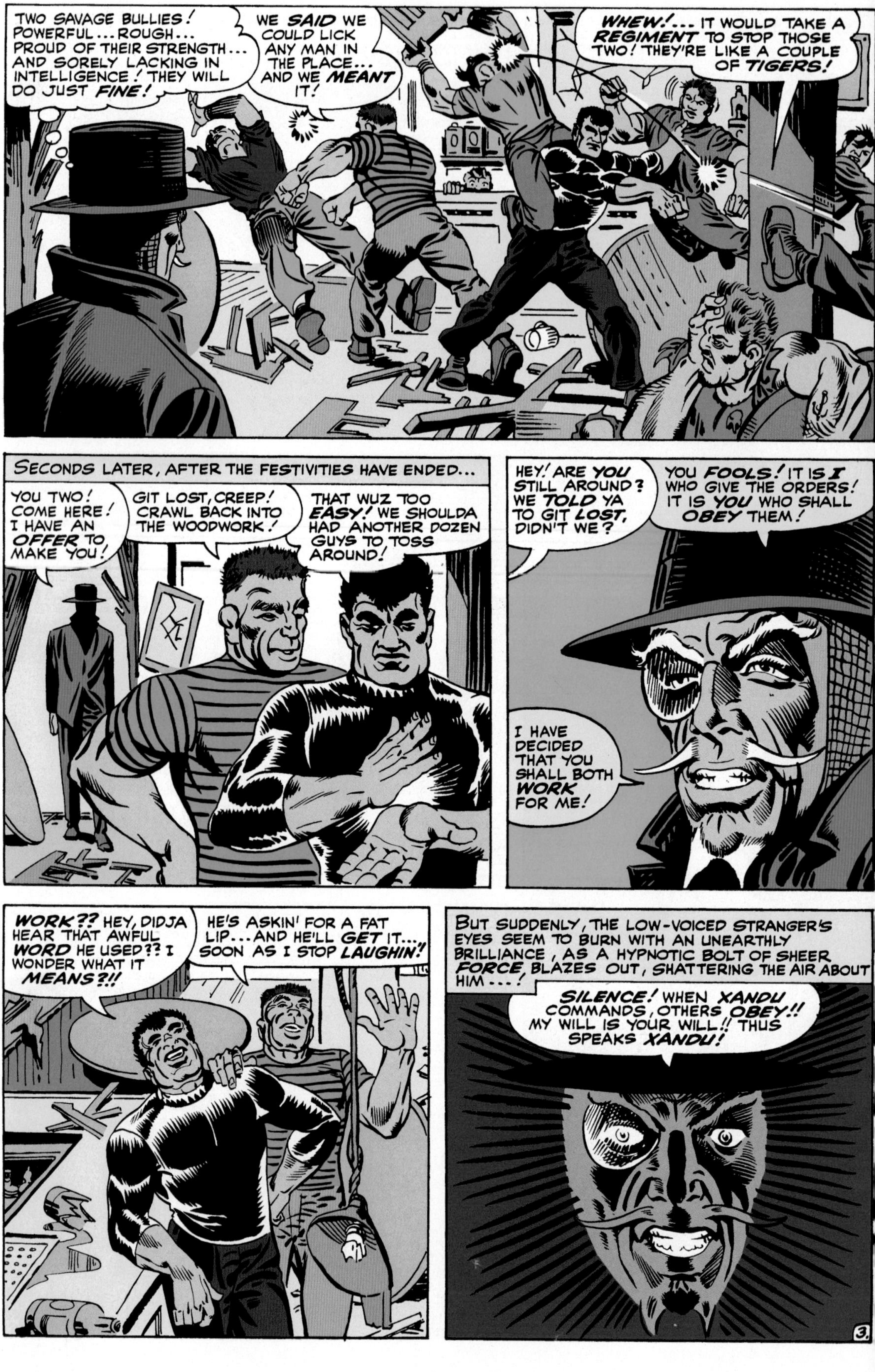
TWO SAVAGE BULLIES! POWERFUL... ROUGH... PROUD OF THEIR STRENGTH... AND SORELY LACKING IN INTELLIGENCE! THEY WILL DO JUST FINE!
WE SAID WE COULD LICK ANY MAN IN THE PLACE... AND WE MEANT IT!
WHEW!... IT WOULD TAKE A REGIMENT TO STOP THOSE TWO! THEY'RE LIKE A COUPLE OF TIGERS!
SECONDS LATER, AFTER THE FESTIVITIES HAVE ENDED...
YOU TWO! COME HERE! I HAVE AN OFFER TO MAKE YOU!
GIT LOST, CREEP! CRAWL BACK INTO THE WOODWORK!
THAT WUZ TOO EASY! WE SHOULDA HAD ANOTHER DOZEN GUYS TO TOSS AROUND!
HEY! ARE YOU STILL AROUND? WE TOLD YA TO GIT LOST, DIDN'T WE?
YOU FOOLS! IT IS I WHO GIVE THE ORDERS! IT IS YOU WHO SHALL OBEY THEM!
I HAVE DECIDED THAT YOU SHALL BOTH WORK FOR ME!
WORK?? HEY, DIDJA HEAR THAT AWFUL WORD HE USED?? I WONDER WHAT IT MEANS?!!
HE'S ASKIN' FOR A FAT LIP... AND HE'LL GET IT... SOON AS I STOP LAUGHIN'!
BUT SUDDENLY, THE LOW-VOICED STRANGER'S EYES SEEM TO BURN WITH AN UNEARTHLY BRILLIANCE, AS A HYPNOTIC BOLT OF SHEER FORCE BLAZES OUT, SHATTERING THE AIR ABOUT HIM...!
SILENCE! WHEN XANDU COMMANDS, OTHERS OBEY!! MY WILL IS YOUR WILL!! THUS SPEAKS XANDU!
3

YOUR-WILL-IS-OUR-WILL!

XANDU-MUST-BE-OBEYED!

I SHALL GIVE YOU *POWER*, GREATER THAN YOU HAVE EVER DREAMED OF! AND, IN RETURN, YOU SHALL SERVE ONLY *ME*!

UNDER MY HYPNOTIC SPELL, YOU WILL FEEL NO PAIN...YOU WILL FEAR NO FOE!! AND NOW, TO TEST MY CONTROL OVER YOU...!

STRIKE...WITH ALL YOUR MIGHT! *GOOD!* *GOOD!*

YOU OBEYED *INSTANTLY!* AND UNDER MY SPELL, HE FELT *NOTHING!* THE BLOW DID NOT AFFECT HIM!

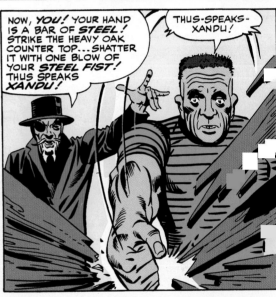

NOW, *YOU!* YOUR HAND IS A BAR OF *STEEL!* STRIKE THE HEAVY OAK COUNTER TOP...SHATTER IT WITH ONE BLOW OF YOUR *STEEL FIST!* THUS SPEAKS *XANDU!*

THUS-SPEAKS-XANDU!

THEN, SATISFIED WITH THE RESULT OF HIS HYPNOTIC HANDIWORK, THE MAN CALLED *XANDU* WALKS BACK FROM WHENCE HE CAME...FOLLOWED BY TWO POWERFUL, HULKING BEINGS WHOSE ONLY WILL IS *XANDU'S* WILL...!

MOMENTS LATER, IN A STRANGE, CANDLE-LIT CHAMBER, XANDU HOLDS ALOFT A SHIMMERING, GLEAMING OBJECT..!

AT LAST! I HAVE TWO SERVANTS WHO WILL OBTAIN THE *OTHER* HALF OF THIS WAND FOR ME!

FOR, HE WHO POSSESSES *BOTH* HALVES OF THE *WAND OF WATOOMB*, POSSESSES THE GREATEST POWER OF ALL!

4

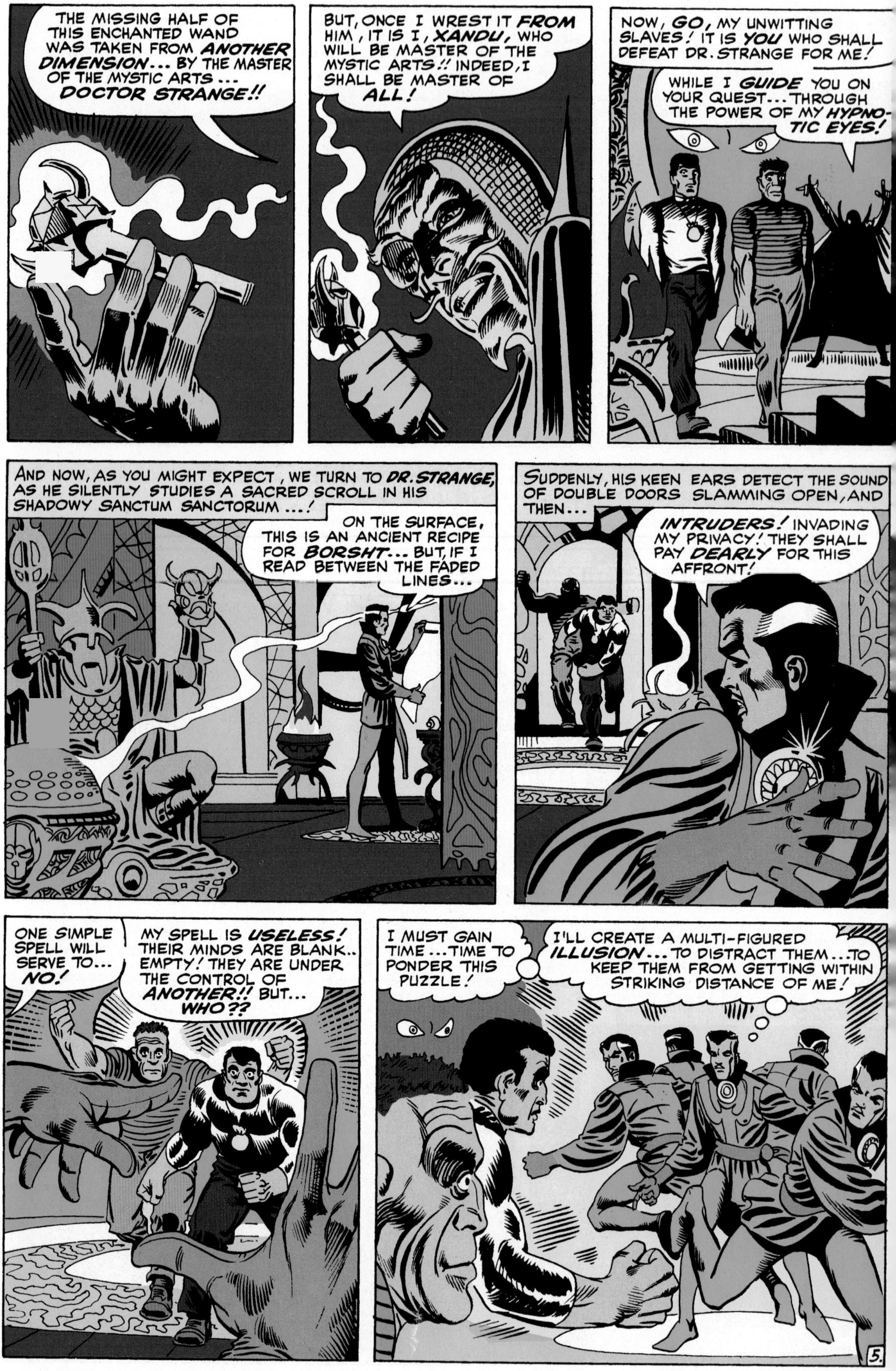
THE MISSING HALF OF THIS ENCHANTED WAND WAS TAKEN FROM ANOTHER DIMENSION... BY THE MASTER OF THE MYSTIC ARTS... DOCTOR STRANGE!!
BUT, ONCE I WREST IT FROM HIM, IT IS I, XANDU, WHO WILL BE MASTER OF THE MYSTIC ARTS!! INDEED, I SHALL BE MASTER OF ALL!
NOW, GO, MY UNWITTING SLAVES! IT IS YOU WHO SHALL DEFEAT DR. STRANGE FOR ME!
WHILE I GUIDE YOU ON YOUR QUEST... THROUGH THE POWER OF MY HYPNO-TIC EYES!
AND NOW, AS YOU MIGHT EXPECT, WE TURN TO DR. STRANGE, AS HE SILENTLY STUDIES A SACRED SCROLL IN HIS SHADOWY SANCTUM SANCTORUM...!
ON THE SURFACE, THIS IS AN ANCIENT RECIPE FOR BORSHT... BUT, IF I READ BETWEEN THE FADED LINES...
SUDDENLY, HIS KEEN EARS DETECT THE SOUND OF DOUBLE DOORS SLAMMING OPEN, AND THEN...
INTRUDERS! INVADING MY PRIVACY! THEY SHALL PAY DEARLY FOR THIS AFFRONT!
ONE SIMPLE SPELL WILL SERVE TO... NO!
MY SPELL IS USELESS! THEIR MINDS ARE BLANK.. EMPTY! THEY ARE UNDER THE CONTROL OF ANOTHER!! BUT... WHO??
I MUST GAIN TIME... TIME TO PONDER THIS PUZZLE!
I'LL CREATE A MULTI-FIGURED ILLUSION... TO DISTRACT THEM... TO KEEP THEM FROM GETTING WITHIN STRIKING DISTANCE OF ME!
5.

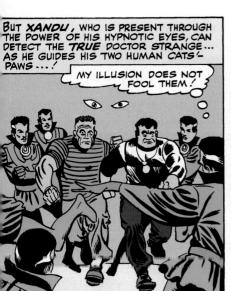

BUT XANDU, WHO IS PRESENT THROUGH THE POWER OF HIS HYPNOTIC EYES, CAN DETECT THE TRUE DOCTOR STRANGE... AS HE GUIDES HIS TWO HUMAN CATS'-PAWS...!

MY ILLUSION DOES NOT FOOL THEM!

THERE IS NO TIME FOR FURTHER EVASIVE ACTION! I MUST DO BATTLE! BUT..THEIR STRENGTH IS INCONCEIVABLE!! ...UHHHH!

WITHIN SECONDS, THE VALIANT MASTER OF THE MYSTIC ARTS IS DOWNED LAPSING INTO UNCONSCIOUSNESS, AS HIS ENCHANTED AMULET PROTECTS HIS STILLED FIGURE FROM FURTHER HARM!

WELL DONE! BUT NOW HE IS OF NO FURTHER INTEREST TO US! IT IS THE WAND! YOU MUST FIND THE OTHER HALF OF THE WAND OF WATOOMB!

IT MUST BE LOCKED SOMEWHERE! SMASH OPEN EVERY CABINET UNTIL IT IS FOUND! THUS SPEAKS XANDU!

WHUMP!

WAIT! SEARCH NO LONGER! THE FATES HAVE SMILED UPON ME! THERE IT IS! WE'VE FOUND IT!

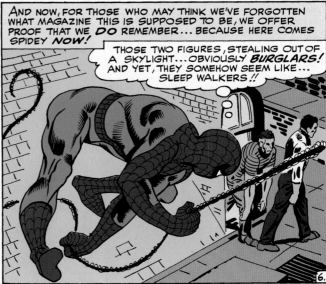

AND NOW, FOR THOSE WHO MAY THINK WE'VE FORGOTTEN WHAT MAGAZINE THIS IS SUPPOSED TO BE, WE OFFER PROOF THAT WE DO REMEMBER... BECAUSE HERE COMES SPIDEY NOW!

THOSE TWO FIGURES, STEALING OUT OF A SKYLIGHT...OBVIOUSLY BURGLARS! AND YET, THEY SOMEHOW SEEM LIKE... SLEEP WALKERS!!

6.

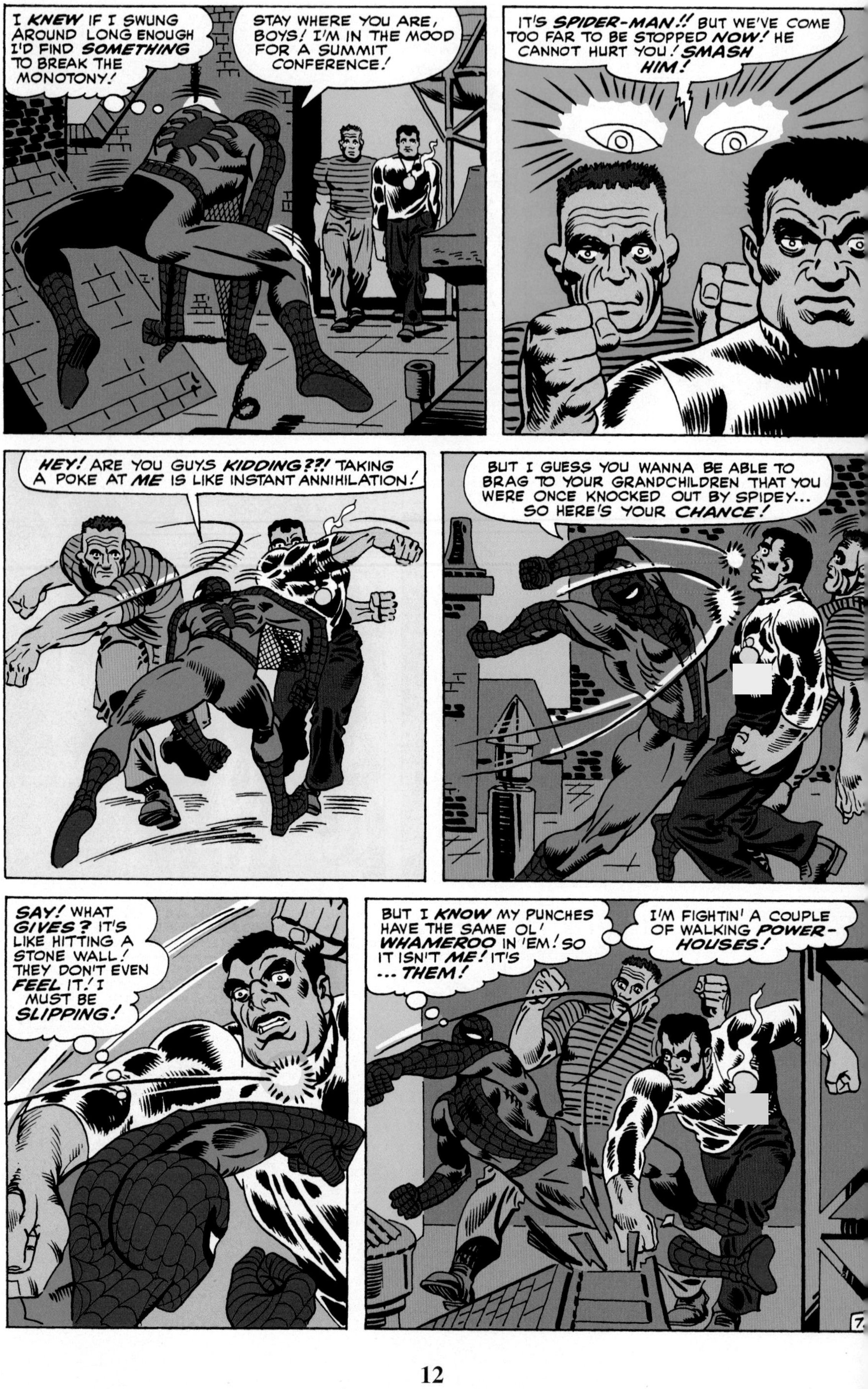
I KNEW IF I SWUNG AROUND LONG ENOUGH I'D FIND SOMETHING TO BREAK THE MONOTONY!
STAY WHERE YOU ARE, BOYS! I'M IN THE MOOD FOR A SUMMIT CONFERENCE!
IT'S SPIDER-MAN!! BUT WE'VE COME TOO FAR TO BE STOPPED NOW! HE CANNOT HURT YOU! SMASH HIM!
HEY! ARE YOU GUYS KIDDING??! TAKING A POKE AT ME IS LIKE INSTANT ANNIHILATION!
BUT I GUESS YOU WANNA BE ABLE TO BRAG TO YOUR GRANDCHILDREN THAT YOU WERE ONCE KNOCKED OUT BY SPIDEY... SO HERE'S YOUR CHANCE!
SAY! WHAT GIVES? IT'S LIKE HITTING A STONE WALL! THEY DON'T EVEN FEEL IT! I MUST BE SLIPPING!
BUT I KNOW MY PUNCHES HAVE THE SAME OL' WHAMEROO IN 'EM! SO IT ISN'T ME! IT'S ...THEM!
I'M FIGHTIN' A COUPLE OF WALKING POWER-HOUSES!
7

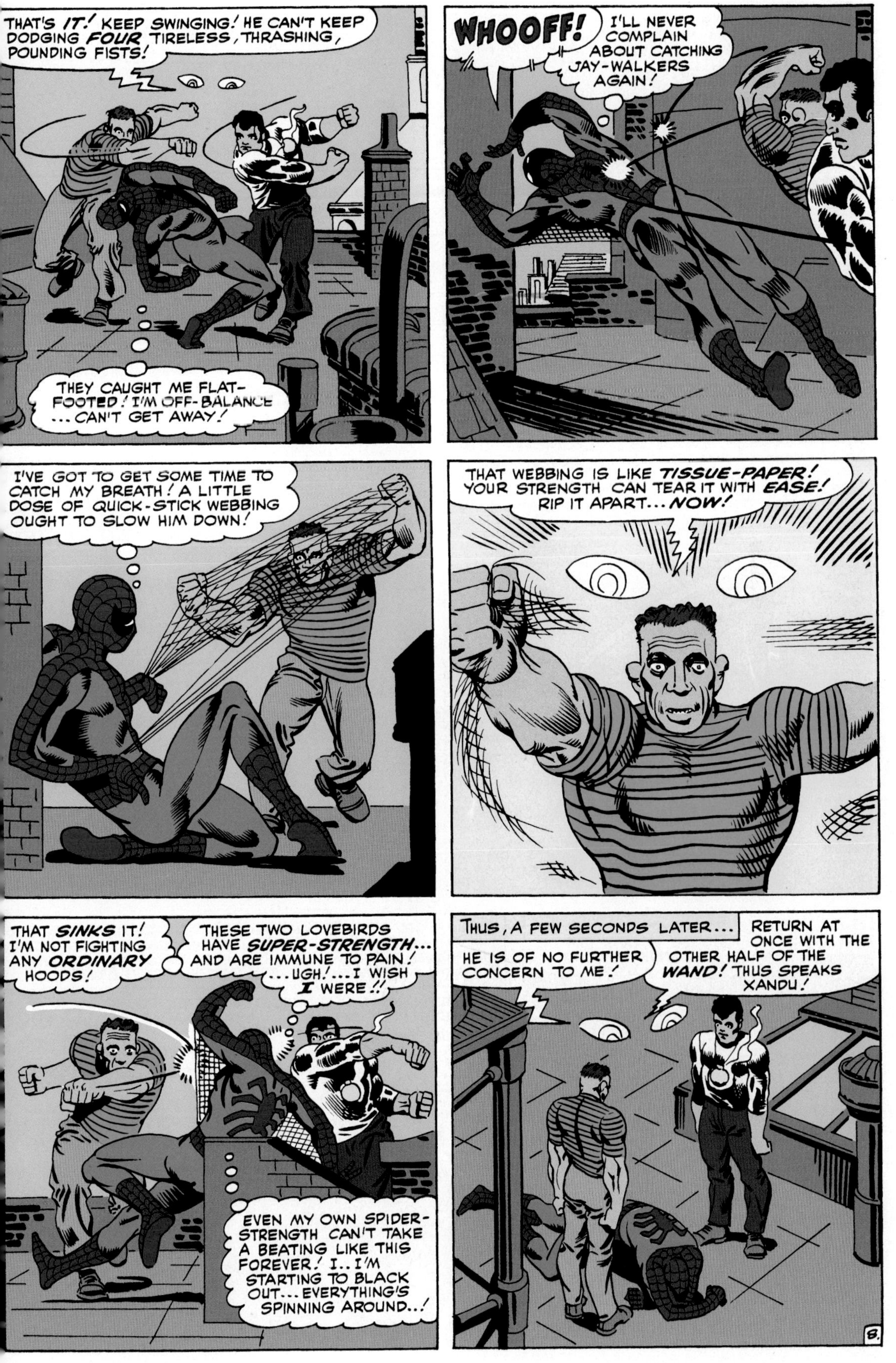
THAT'S IT! KEEP SWINGING! HE CAN'T KEEP DODGING FOUR TIRELESS, THRASHING, POUNDING FISTS!
THEY CAUGHT ME FLAT-FOOTED! I'M OFF-BALANCE ...CAN'T GET AWAY!
WHOOFF!
I'LL NEVER COMPLAIN ABOUT CATCHING JAY-WALKERS AGAIN!
I'VE GOT TO GET SOME TIME TO CATCH MY BREATH! A LITTLE DOSE OF QUICK-STICK WEBBING OUGHT TO SLOW HIM DOWN!
THAT WEBBING IS LIKE TISSUE-PAPER! YOUR STRENGTH CAN TEAR IT WITH EASE! RIP IT APART...NOW!
THAT SINKS IT! I'M NOT FIGHTING ANY ORDINARY HOODS!
THESE TWO LOVEBIRDS HAVE SUPER-STRENGTH... AND ARE IMMUNE TO PAIN! ...UGH!...I WISH I WERE!!
EVEN MY OWN SPIDER-STRENGTH CAN'T TAKE A BEATING LIKE THIS FOREVER! I..I'M STARTING TO BLACK OUT...EVERYTHING'S SPINNING AROUND..!
THUS, A FEW SECONDS LATER...
HE IS OF NO FURTHER CONCERN TO ME!
RETURN AT ONCE WITH THE OTHER HALF OF THE WAND! THUS SPEAKS XANDU!
8.

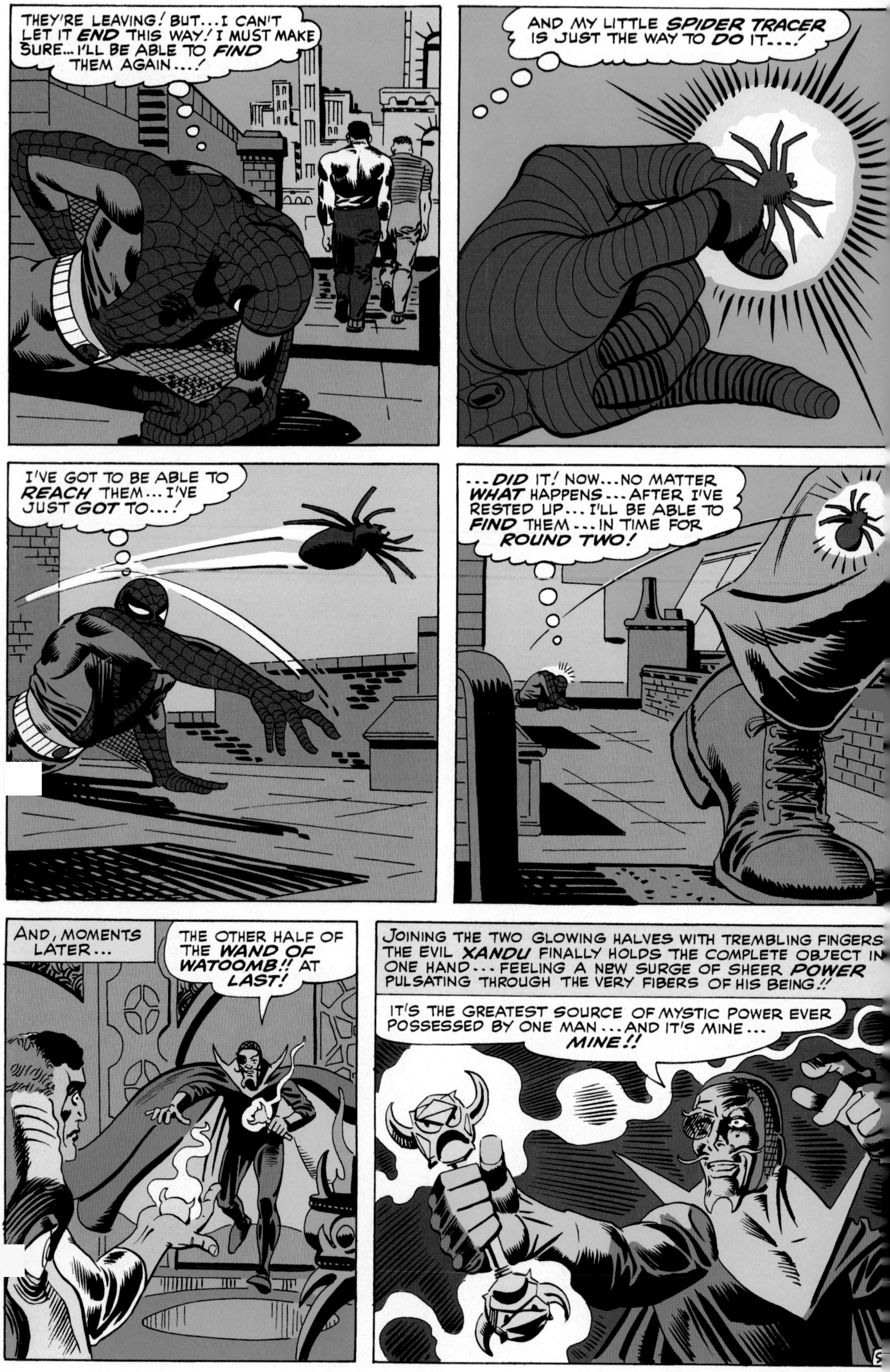
THEY'RE LEAVING! BUT... I CAN'T LET IT END THIS WAY! I MUST MAKE SURE... I'LL BE ABLE TO FIND THEM AGAIN...!
AND MY LITTLE SPIDER TRACER IS JUST THE WAY TO DO IT...!
I'VE GOT TO BE ABLE TO REACH THEM... I'VE JUST GOT TO...!
...DID IT! NOW...NO MATTER WHAT HAPPENS... AFTER I'VE RESTED UP... I'LL BE ABLE TO FIND THEM... IN TIME FOR ROUND TWO!
AND, MOMENTS LATER...
THE OTHER HALF OF THE WAND OF WATOOMB!! AT LAST!
JOINING THE TWO GLOWING HALVES WITH TREMBLING FINGERS THE EVIL XANDU FINALLY HOLDS THE COMPLETE OBJECT IN ONE HAND... FEELING A NEW SURGE OF SHEER POWER PULSATING THROUGH THE VERY FIBERS OF HIS BEING!!
IT'S THE GREATEST SOURCE OF MYSTIC POWER EVER POSSESSED BY ONE MAN... AND IT'S MINE... MINE!!

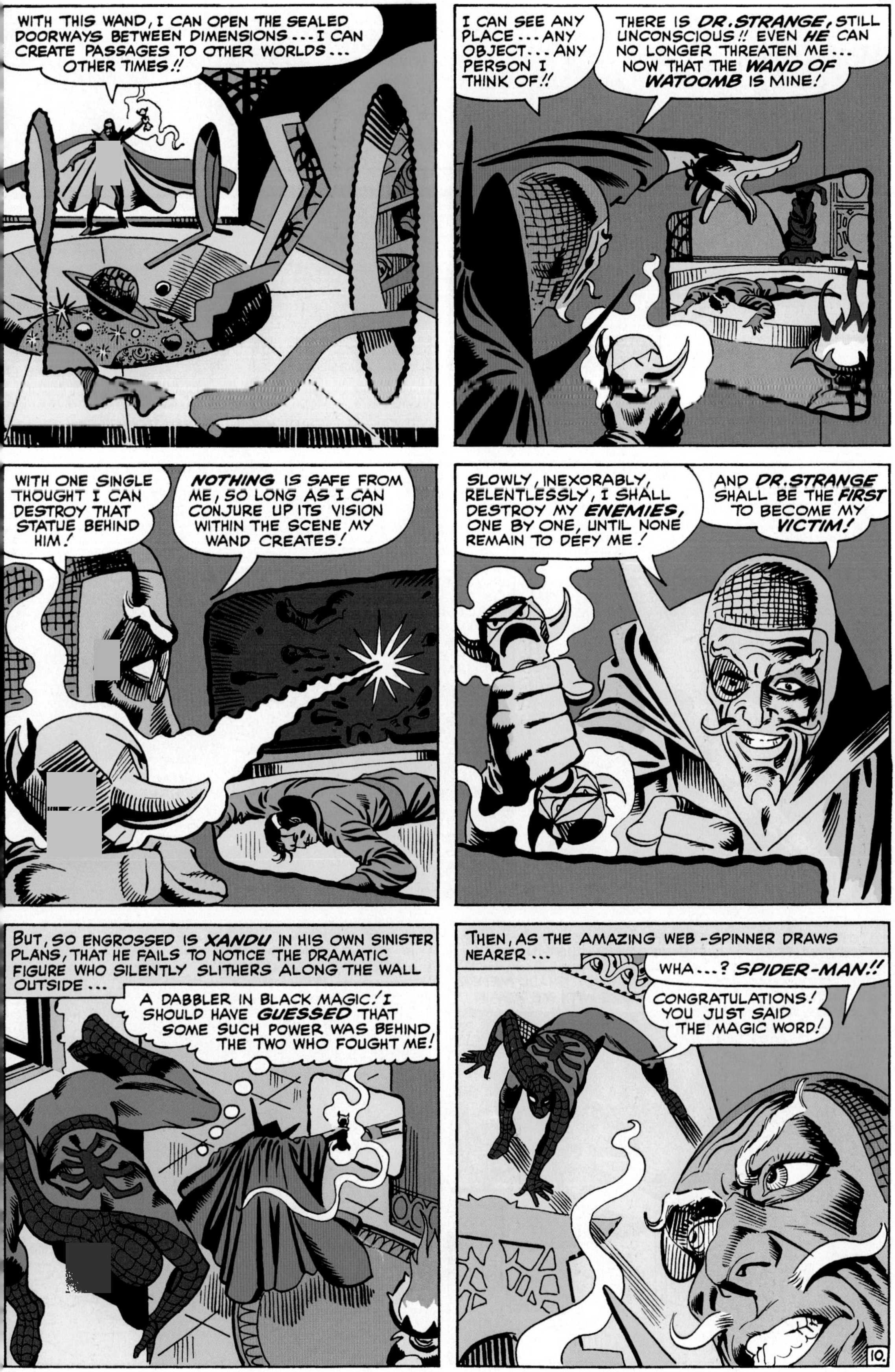
WITH THIS WAND, I CAN OPEN THE SEALED DOORWAYS BETWEEN DIMENSIONS... I CAN CREATE PASSAGES TO OTHER WORLDS... OTHER TIMES!!
I CAN SEE ANY PLACE... ANY OBJECT... ANY PERSON I THINK OF!!
THERE IS DR. STRANGE, STILL UNCONSCIOUS!! EVEN HE CAN NO LONGER THREATEN ME... NOW THAT THE WAND OF WATOOMB IS MINE!
WITH ONE SINGLE THOUGHT I CAN DESTROY THAT STATUE BEHIND HIM!
NOTHING IS SAFE FROM ME, SO LONG AS I CAN CONJURE UP ITS VISION WITHIN THE SCENE MY WAND CREATES!
SLOWLY, INEXORABLY, RELENTLESSLY, I SHALL DESTROY MY ENEMIES, ONE BY ONE, UNTIL NONE REMAIN TO DEFY ME!
AND DR. STRANGE SHALL BE THE FIRST TO BECOME MY VICTIM!
BUT, SO ENGROSSED IS XANDU IN HIS OWN SINISTER PLANS, THAT HE FAILS TO NOTICE THE DRAMATIC FIGURE WHO SILENTLY SLITHERS ALONG THE WALL OUTSIDE...
A DABBLER IN BLACK MAGIC! I SHOULD HAVE GUESSED THAT SOME SUCH POWER WAS BEHIND THE TWO WHO FOUGHT ME!
THEN, AS THE AMAZING WEB-SPINNER DRAWS NEARER...
WHA...? SPIDER-MAN!!
CONGRATULATIONS! YOU JUST SAID THE MAGIC WORD!
10.

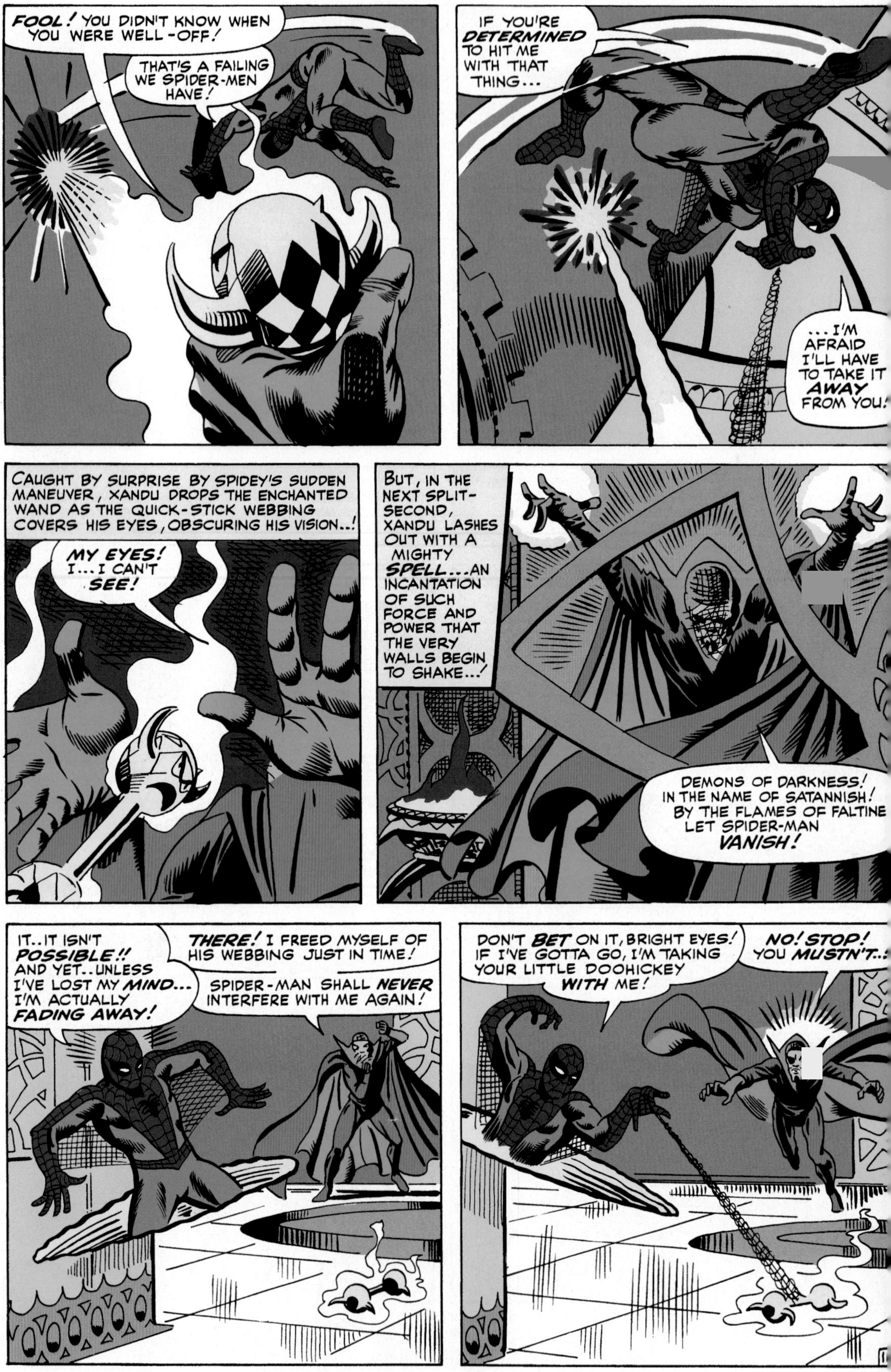
FOOL! YOU DIDN'T KNOW WHEN YOU WERE WELL-OFF!
THAT'S A FAILING WE SPIDER-MEN HAVE!
IF YOU'RE DETERMINED TO HIT ME WITH THAT THING...
...I'M AFRAID I'LL HAVE TO TAKE IT AWAY FROM YOU!
CAUGHT BY SURPRISE BY SPIDEY'S SUDDEN MANEUVER, XANDU DROPS THE ENCHANTED WAND AS THE QUICK-STICK WEBBING COVERS HIS EYES, OBSCURING HIS VISION..!
MY EYES! I...I CAN'T SEE!
BUT, IN THE NEXT SPLIT-SECOND, XANDU LASHES OUT WITH A MIGHTY SPELL...AN INCANTATION OF SUCH FORCE AND POWER THAT THE VERY WALLS BEGIN TO SHAKE...!
DEMONS OF DARKNESS! IN THE NAME OF SATANNISH! BY THE FLAMES OF FALTINE LET SPIDER-MAN VANISH!
IT..IT ISN'T POSSIBLE!! AND YET..UNLESS I'VE LOST MY MIND... I'M ACTUALLY FADING AWAY!
THERE! I FREED MYSELF OF HIS WEBBING JUST IN TIME!
SPIDER-MAN SHALL NEVER INTERFERE WITH ME AGAIN!
DON'T BET ON IT, BRIGHT EYES! IF I'VE GOTTA GO, I'M TAKING YOUR LITTLE DOOHICKEY WITH ME!
NO! STOP! YOU MUSTN'T..

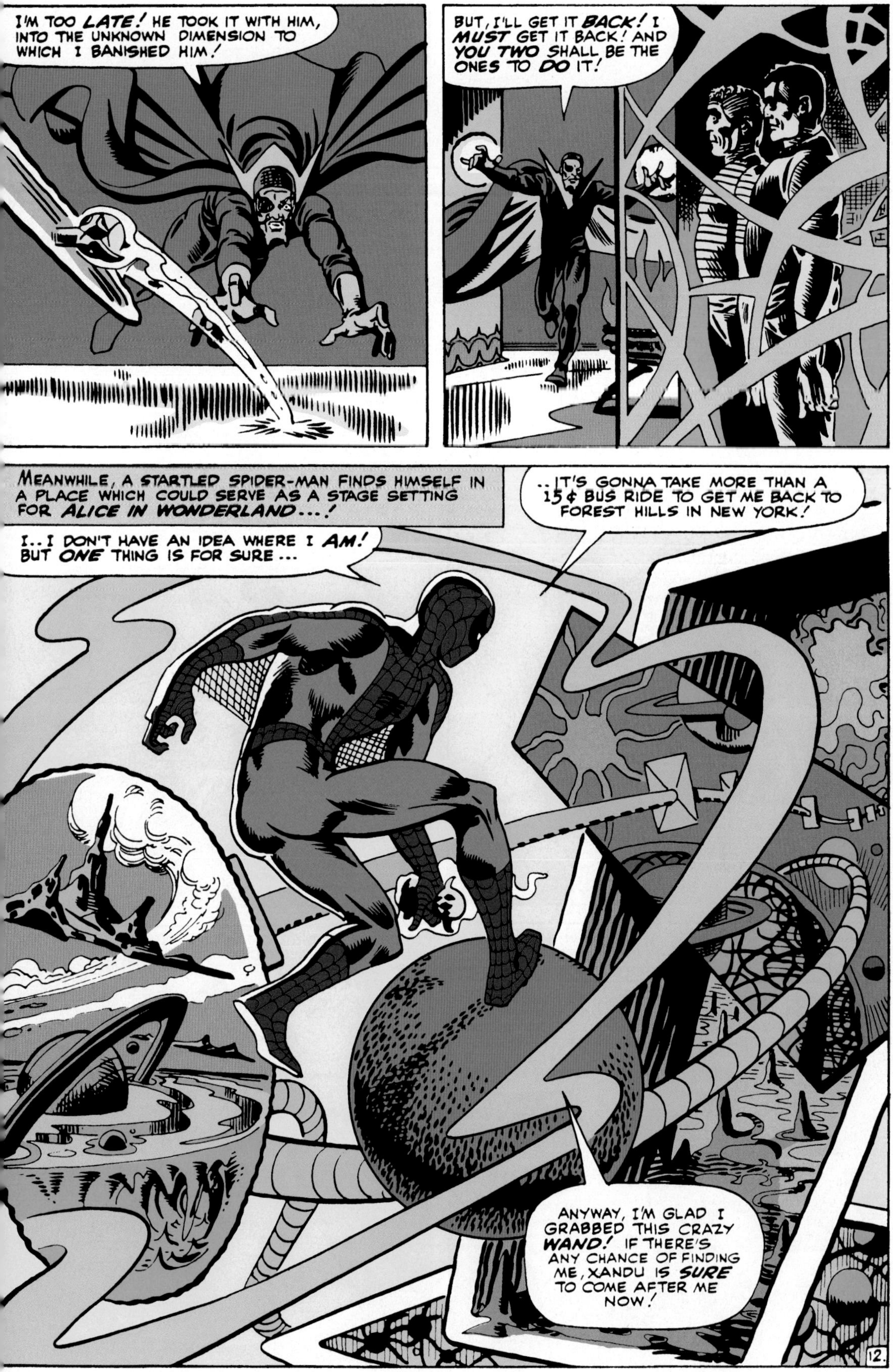
I'M TOO LATE! HE TOOK IT WITH HIM, INTO THE UNKNOWN DIMENSION TO WHICH I BANISHED HIM!
BUT, I'LL GET IT BACK! I MUST GET IT BACK! AND YOU TWO SHALL BE THE ONES TO DO IT!
MEANWHILE, A STARTLED SPIDER-MAN FINDS HIMSELF IN A PLACE WHICH COULD SERVE AS A STAGE SETTING FOR ALICE IN WONDERLAND...!
I.. I DON'T HAVE AN IDEA WHERE I AM! BUT ONE THING IS FOR SURE...
..IT'S GONNA TAKE MORE THAN A 15¢ BUS RIDE TO GET ME BACK TO FOREST HILLS IN NEW YORK!
ANYWAY, I'M GLAD I GRABBED THIS CRAZY WAND! IF THERE'S ANY CHANCE OF FINDING ME, XANDU IS SURE TO COME AFTER ME NOW!
12.

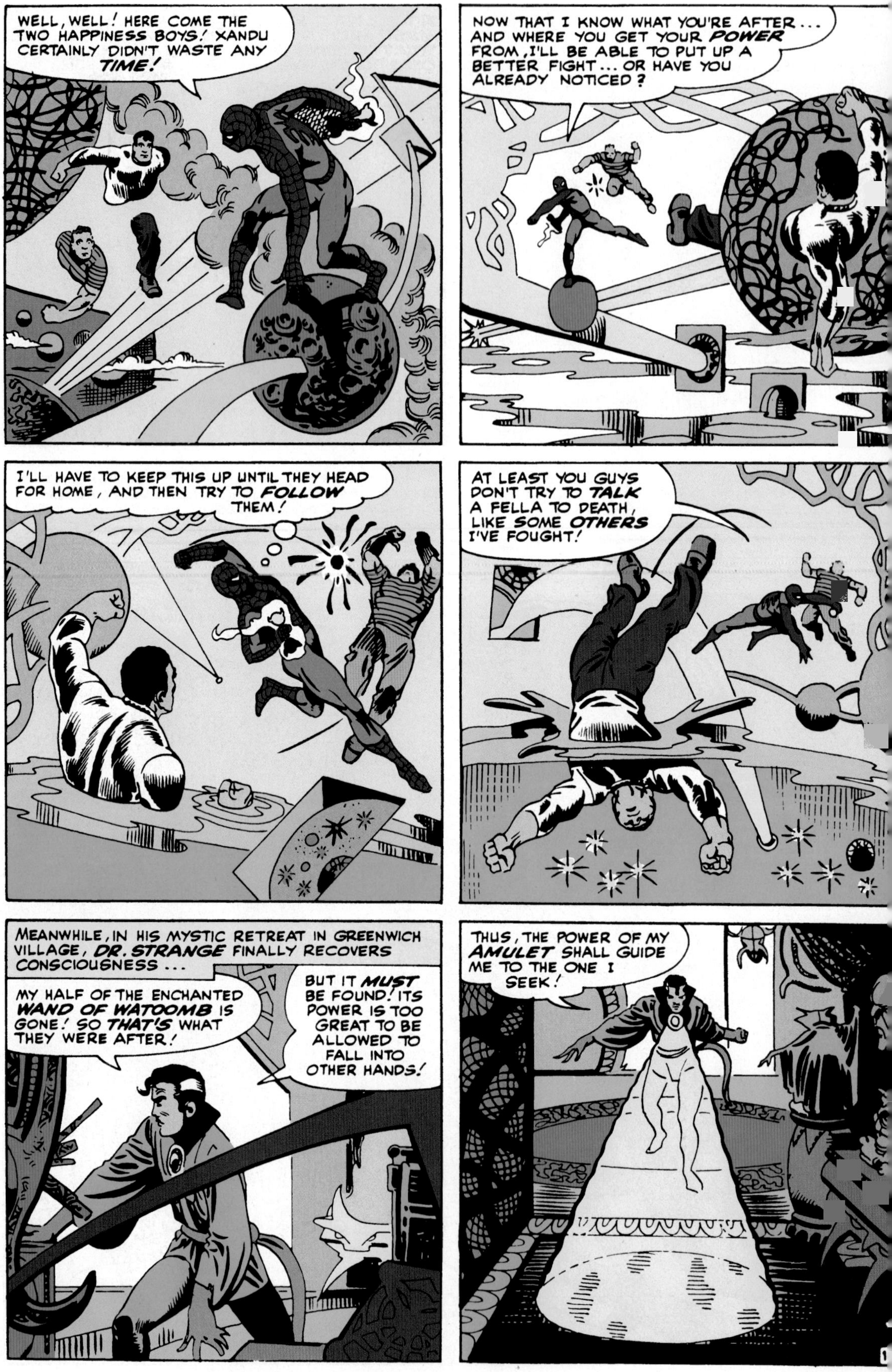
WELL, WELL! HERE COME THE TWO HAPPINESS BOYS! XANDU CERTAINLY DIDN'T WASTE ANY TIME!
NOW THAT I KNOW WHAT YOU'RE AFTER... AND WHERE YOU GET YOUR POWER FROM, I'LL BE ABLE TO PUT UP A BETTER FIGHT... OR HAVE YOU ALREADY NOTICED?
I'LL HAVE TO KEEP THIS UP UNTIL THEY HEAD FOR HOME, AND THEN TRY TO FOLLOW THEM!
AT LEAST YOU GUYS DON'T TRY TO TALK A FELLA TO DEATH, LIKE SOME OTHERS I'VE FOUGHT!
MEANWHILE, IN HIS MYSTIC RETREAT IN GREENWICH VILLAGE, DR. STRANGE FINALLY RECOVERS CONSCIOUSNESS...
MY HALF OF THE ENCHANTED WAND OF WATOOMB IS GONE! SO THAT'S WHAT THEY WERE AFTER!
BUT IT MUST BE FOUND! ITS POWER IS TOO GREAT TO BE ALLOWED TO FALL INTO OTHER HANDS!
THUS, THE POWER OF MY AMULET SHALL GUIDE ME TO THE ONE I SEEK!

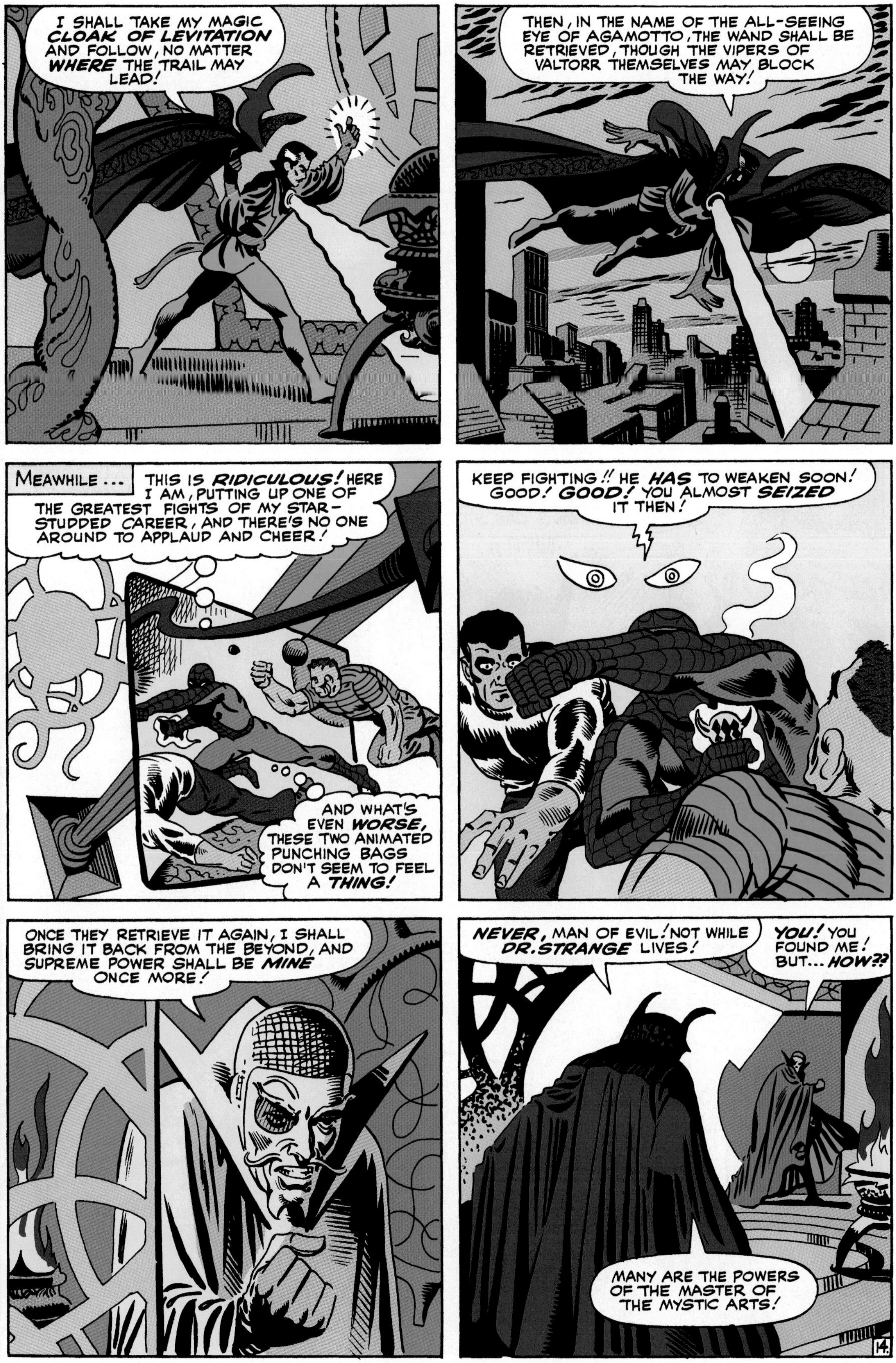
I SHALL TAKE MY MAGIC CLOAK OF LEVITATION AND FOLLOW, NO MATTER WHERE THE TRAIL MAY LEAD!
THEN, IN THE NAME OF THE ALL-SEEING EYE OF AGAMOTTO, THE WAND SHALL BE RETRIEVED, THOUGH THE VIPERS OF VALTORR THEMSELVES MAY BLOCK THE WAY!
MEAWHILE ...
THIS IS RIDICULOUS! HERE I AM, PUTTING UP ONE OF THE GREATEST FIGHTS OF MY STAR-STUDDED CAREER, AND THERE'S NO ONE AROUND TO APPLAUD AND CHEER!
AND WHAT'S EVEN WORSE, THESE TWO ANIMATED PUNCHING BAGS DON'T SEEM TO FEEL A THING!
KEEP FIGHTING!! HE HAS TO WEAKEN SOON! GOOD! GOOD! YOU ALMOST SEIZED IT THEN!
ONCE THEY RETRIEVE IT AGAIN, I SHALL BRING IT BACK FROM THE BEYOND, AND SUPREME POWER SHALL BE MINE ONCE MORE!
NEVER, MAN OF EVIL! NOT WHILE DR. STRANGE LIVES!
YOU! YOU FOUND ME! BUT... HOW??
MANY ARE THE POWERS OF THE MASTER OF THE MYSTIC ARTS!
14.

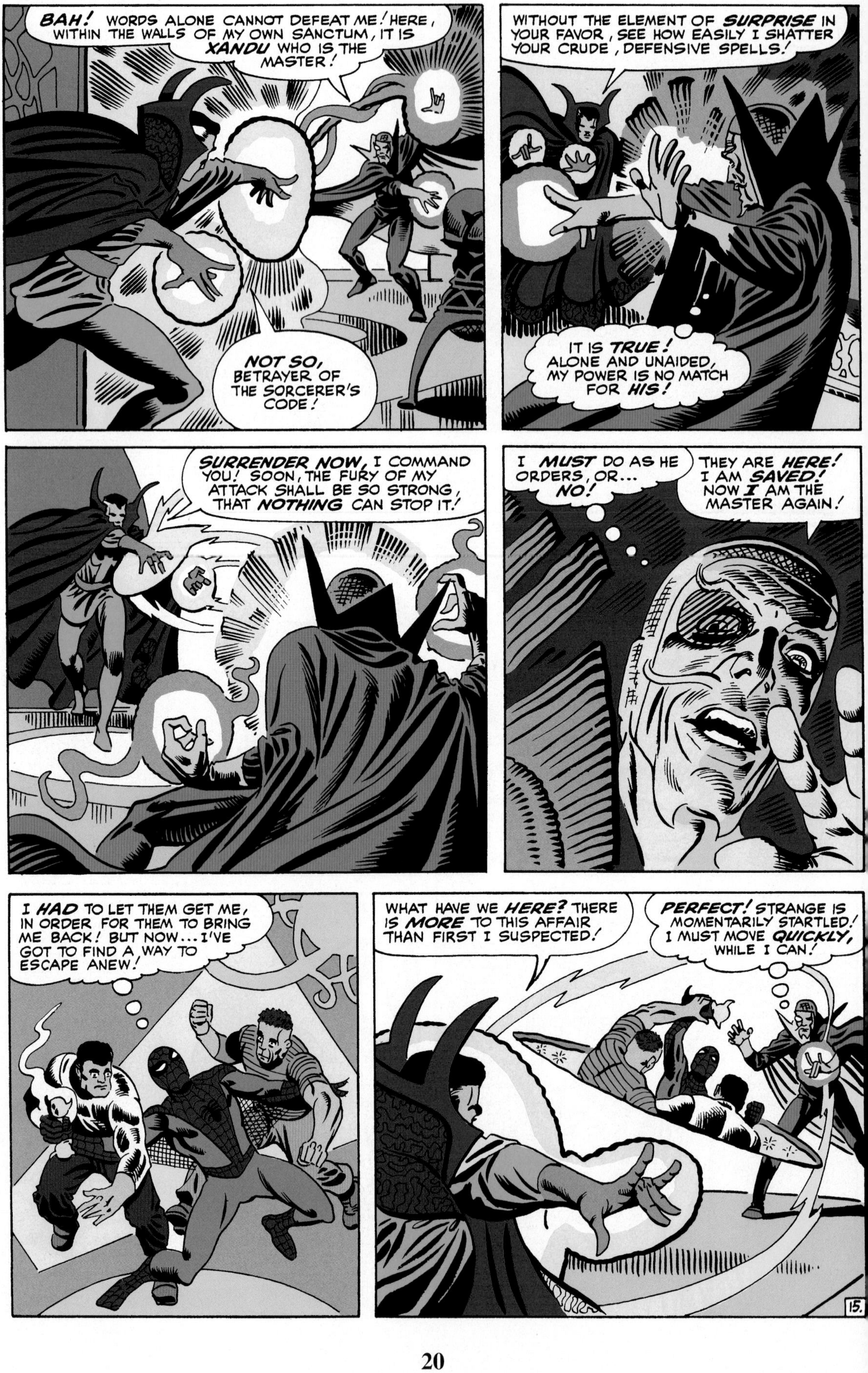
BAH! WORDS ALONE CANNOT DEFEAT ME! HERE, WITHIN THE WALLS OF MY OWN SANCTUM, IT IS XANDU WHO IS THE MASTER!
NOT SO, BETRAYER OF THE SORCERER'S CODE!
WITHOUT THE ELEMENT OF SURPRISE IN YOUR FAVOR, SEE HOW EASILY I SHATTER YOUR CRUDE, DEFENSIVE SPELLS!
IT IS TRUE! ALONE AND UNAIDED, MY POWER IS NO MATCH FOR HIS!
SURRENDER NOW, I COMMAND YOU! SOON, THE FURY OF MY ATTACK SHALL BE SO STRONG, THAT NOTHING CAN STOP IT!
I MUST DO AS HE ORDERS, OR... NO!
THEY ARE HERE! I AM SAVED! NOW I AM THE MASTER AGAIN!
I HAD TO LET THEM GET ME, IN ORDER FOR THEM TO BRING ME BACK! BUT NOW... I'VE GOT TO FIND A WAY TO ESCAPE ANEW!
WHAT HAVE WE HERE? THERE IS MORE TO THIS AFFAIR THAN FIRST I SUSPECTED!
PERFECT! STRANGE IS MOMENTARILY STARTLED! I MUST MOVE QUICKLY, WHILE I CAN!
15.

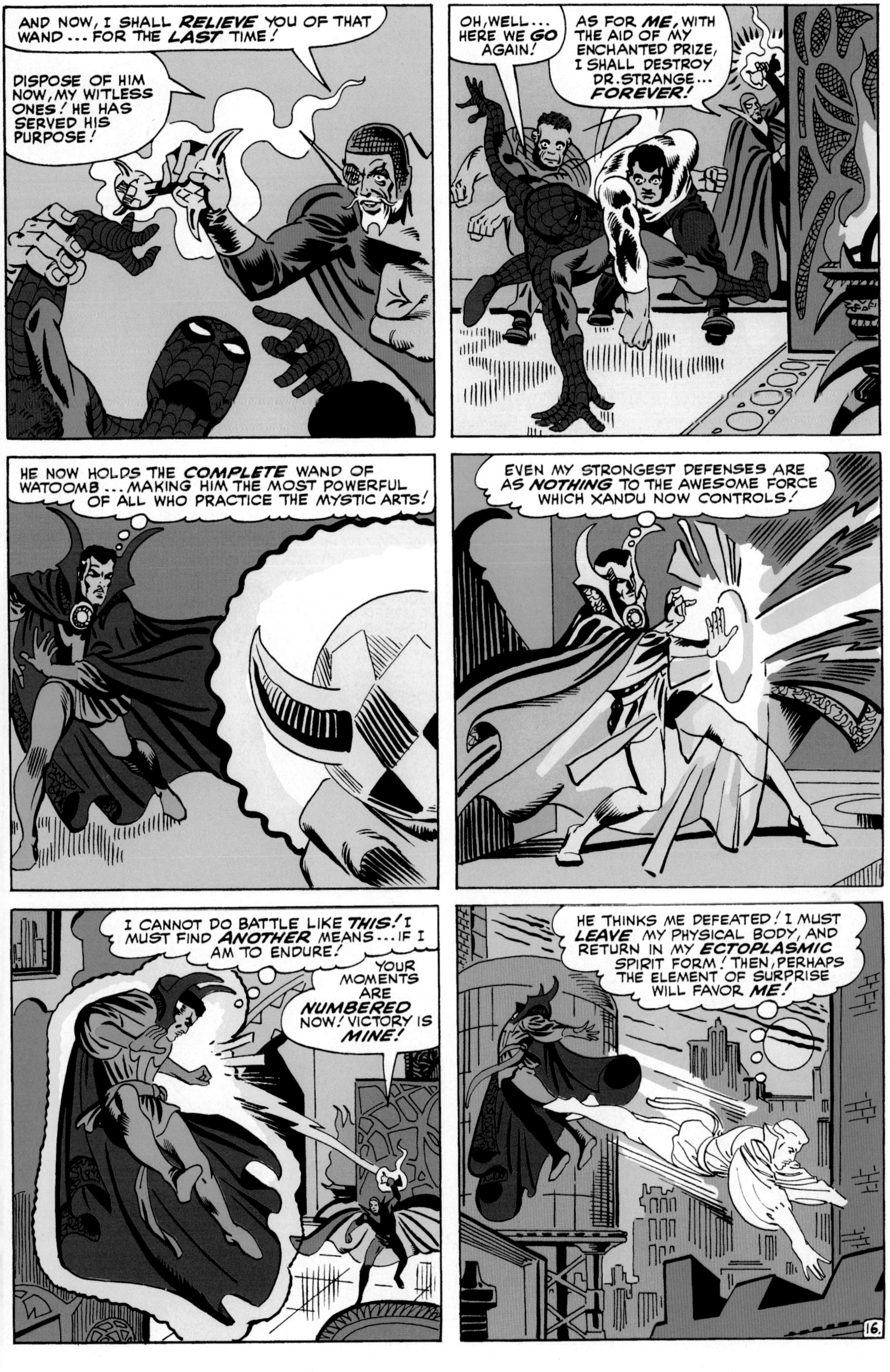

AND NOW, I SHALL RELIEVE YOU OF THAT WAND ... FOR THE LAST TIME!
DISPOSE OF HIM NOW, MY WITLESS ONES! HE HAS SERVED HIS PURPOSE!
OH, WELL... HERE WE GO AGAIN!
AS FOR ME, WITH THE AID OF MY ENCHANTED PRIZE, I SHALL DESTROY DR. STRANGE... FOREVER!
HE NOW HOLDS THE COMPLETE WAND OF WATOOMB ... MAKING HIM THE MOST POWERFUL OF ALL WHO PRACTICE THE MYSTIC ARTS!
EVEN MY STRONGEST DEFENSES ARE AS NOTHING TO THE AWESOME FORCE WHICH XANDU NOW CONTROLS!
I CANNOT DO BATTLE LIKE THIS! I MUST FIND ANOTHER MEANS... IF I AM TO ENDURE!
YOUR MOMENTS ARE NUMBERED NOW! VICTORY IS MINE!
HE THINKS ME DEFEATED! I MUST LEAVE MY PHYSICAL BODY, AND RETURN IN MY ECTOPLASMIC SPIRIT FORM! THEN, PERHAPS THE ELEMENT OF SURPRISE WILL FAVOR ME!
16.

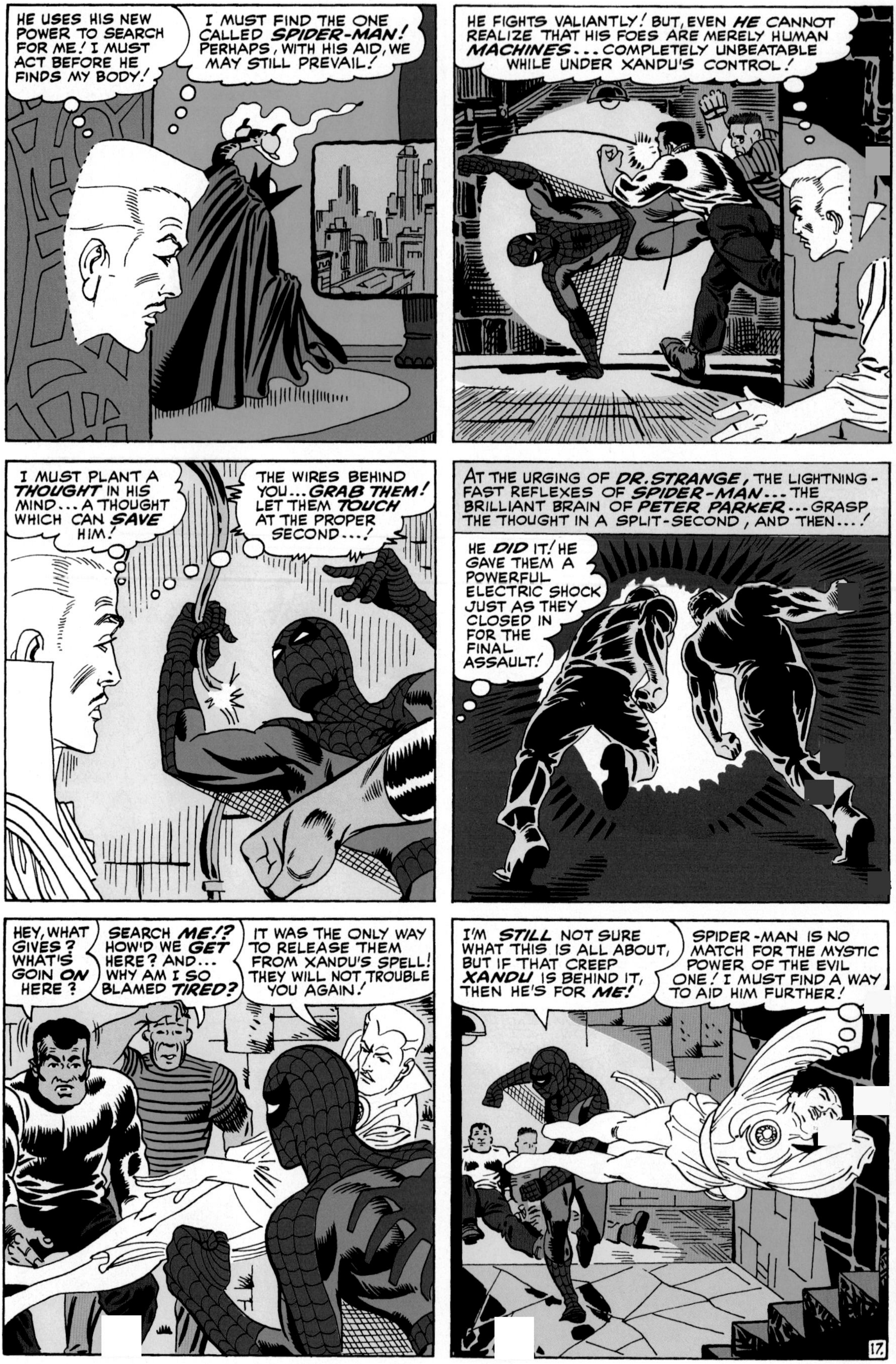
HE USES HIS NEW POWER TO SEARCH FOR ME! I MUST ACT BEFORE HE FINDS MY BODY!
I MUST FIND THE ONE CALLED SPIDER-MAN! PERHAPS, WITH HIS AID, WE MAY STILL PREVAIL!
HE FIGHTS VALIANTLY! BUT, EVEN HE CANNOT REALIZE THAT HIS FOES ARE MERELY HUMAN MACHINES... COMPLETELY UNBEATABLE WHILE UNDER XANDU'S CONTROL!
I MUST PLANT A THOUGHT IN HIS MIND... A THOUGHT WHICH CAN SAVE HIM!
THE WIRES BEHIND YOU... GRAB THEM! LET THEM TOUCH AT THE PROPER SECOND...!
AT THE URGING OF DR. STRANGE, THE LIGHTNING-FAST REFLEXES OF SPIDER-MAN... THE BRILLIANT BRAIN OF PETER PARKER... GRASP THE THOUGHT IN A SPLIT-SECOND, AND THEN...!
HE DID IT! HE GAVE THEM A POWERFUL ELECTRIC SHOCK JUST AS THEY CLOSED IN FOR THE FINAL ASSAULT!
HEY, WHAT GIVES? WHAT'S GOIN ON HERE?
SEARCH ME!? HOW'D WE GET HERE? AND... WHY AM I SO BLAMED TIRED?
IT WAS THE ONLY WAY TO RELEASE THEM FROM XANDU'S SPELL! THEY WILL NOT TROUBLE YOU AGAIN!
I'M STILL NOT SURE WHAT THIS IS ALL ABOUT, BUT IF THAT CREEP XANDU IS BEHIND IT, THEN HE'S FOR ME!
SPIDER-MAN IS NO MATCH FOR THE MYSTIC POWER OF THE EVIL ONE! I MUST FIND A WAY TO AID HIM FURTHER!
17.

FIRST, I MUST ASSUME MY *PHYSICAL* SELF AGAIN... WITHOUT A SECOND TO SPARE!

IF I DO NOT REACH SPIDER-MAN'S SIDE IN TIME, IT COULD BE *FATAL!*

OKAY, XANDU! NOW IT'S JUST YOU AND ME!!

BUT NOT FOR *LONG!* WHEN I FINISH USING MY MYSTIC WAND, IT SHALL BE ONLY *ME!!*

BUT AT THAT SPLIT-SECOND, *ANOTHER* SPELL IS HURLED BETWEEN THE TWO ANTAGONISTS!

THIS CAN ONLY BE THE WORK OF *STRANGE!* HE STILL *LIVES!*

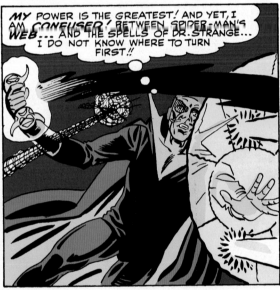

MY POWER IS THE GREATEST! AND YET, I AM *CONFUSED!* BETWEEN SPIDER-MAN'S *WEB....* AND THE SPELLS OF DR. STRANGE... I DO NOT KNOW WHERE TO TURN FIRST!!

THAT'S *IT*, SPIDER-MAN! KEEP MOVING *FAST!* KEEP HIM OFF-BALANCE...IT'S OUR ONLY CHANCE AGAINST HIS DEADLY *WAND!*

I HEAR YA TALKIN', DOC! THIS IS BEGINNING TO FEEL LIKE OLD TIMES!

18.

23

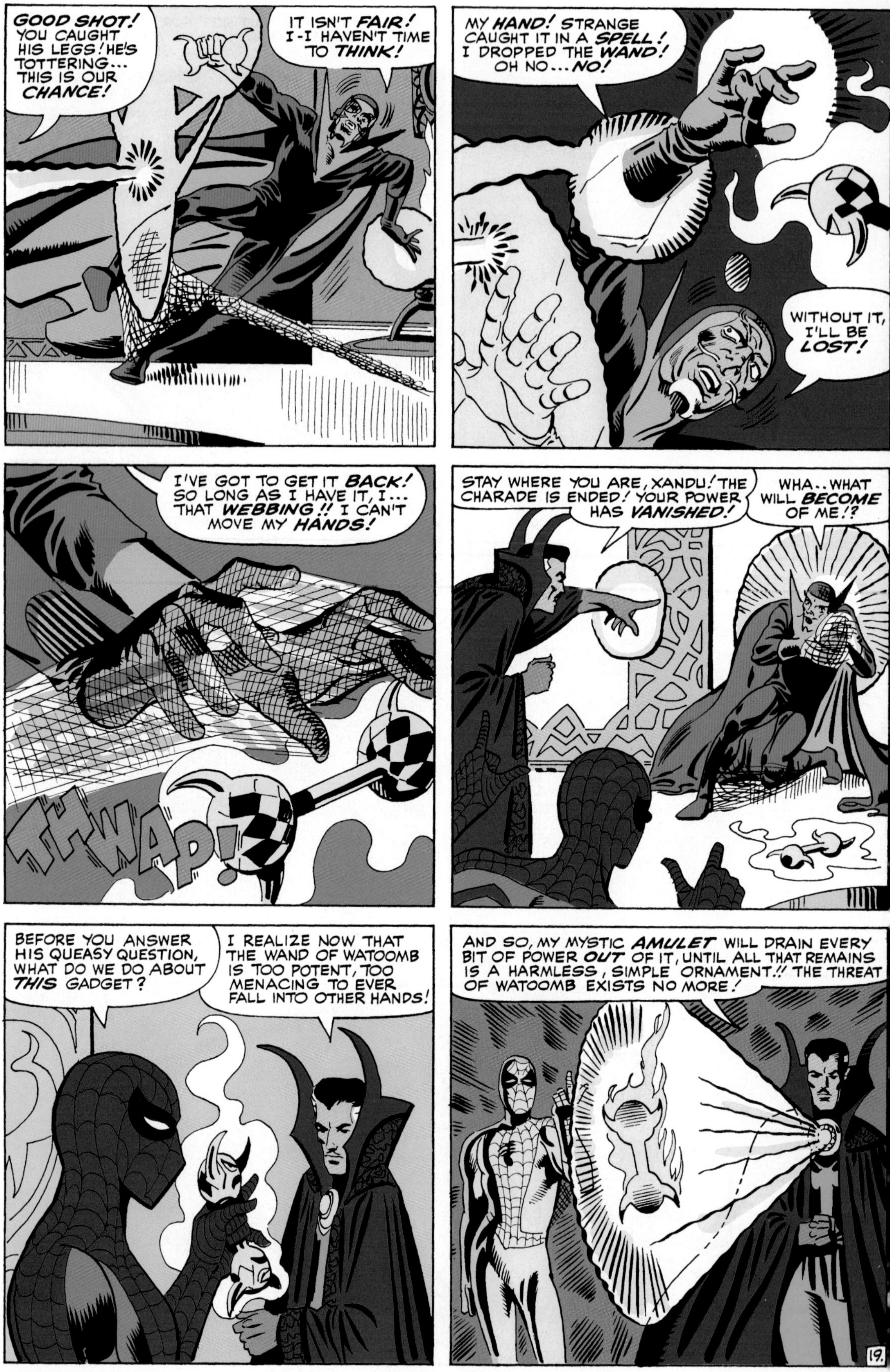
GOOD SHOT! YOU CAUGHT HIS LEGS! HE'S TOTTERING... THIS IS OUR CHANCE!
IT ISN'T FAIR! I-I HAVEN'T TIME TO THINK!
MY HAND! STRANGE CAUGHT IT IN A SPELL! I DROPPED THE WAND! OH NO... NO!
WITHOUT IT, I'LL BE LOST!
I'VE GOT TO GET IT BACK! SO LONG AS I HAVE IT, I... THAT WEBBING!! I CAN'T MOVE MY HANDS!
THWAP!
STAY WHERE YOU ARE, XANDU! THE CHARADE IS ENDED! YOUR POWER HAS VANISHED!
WHA.. WHAT WILL BECOME OF ME!?
BEFORE YOU ANSWER HIS QUEASY QUESTION, WHAT DO WE DO ABOUT THIS GADGET?
I REALIZE NOW THAT THE WAND OF WATOOMB IS TOO POTENT, TOO MENACING TO EVER FALL INTO OTHER HANDS!
AND SO, MY MYSTIC AMULET WILL DRAIN EVERY BIT OF POWER OUT OF IT, UNTIL ALL THAT REMAINS IS A HARMLESS, SIMPLE ORNAMENT!! THE THREAT OF WATOOMB EXISTS NO MORE!
19.

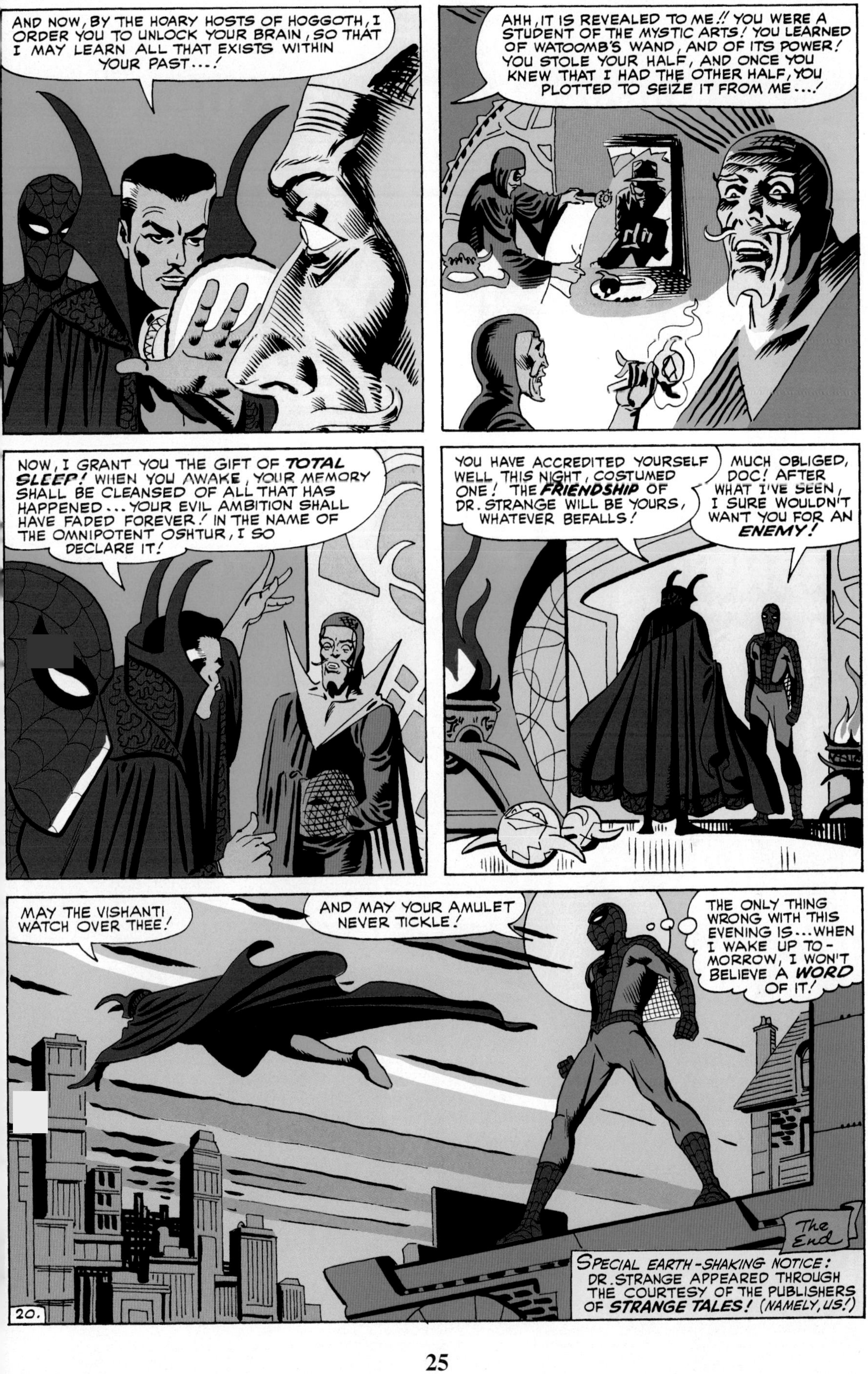
AND NOW, BY THE HOARY HOSTS OF HOGGOTH, I ORDER YOU TO UNLOCK YOUR BRAIN, SO THAT I MAY LEARN ALL THAT EXISTS WITHIN YOUR PAST...!
AHH, IT IS REVEALED TO ME!! YOU WERE A STUDENT OF THE MYSTIC ARTS! YOU LEARNED OF WATOOMB'S WAND, AND OF ITS POWER! YOU STOLE YOUR HALF, AND ONCE YOU KNEW THAT I HAD THE OTHER HALF, YOU PLOTTED TO SEIZE IT FROM ME...!
NOW, I GRANT YOU THE GIFT OF TOTAL SLEEP! WHEN YOU AWAKE, YOUR MEMORY SHALL BE CLEANSED OF ALL THAT HAS HAPPENED... YOUR EVIL AMBITION SHALL HAVE FADED FOREVER! IN THE NAME OF THE OMNIPOTENT OSHTUR, I SO DECLARE IT!
YOU HAVE ACCREDITED YOURSELF WELL THIS NIGHT, COSTUMED ONE! THE FRIENDSHIP OF DR. STRANGE WILL BE YOURS, WHATEVER BEFALLS!
MUCH OBLIGED, DOC! AFTER WHAT I'VE SEEN, I SURE WOULDN'T WANT YOU FOR AN ENEMY!
MAY THE VISHANTI WATCH OVER THEE!
AND MAY YOUR AMULET NEVER TICKLE!
THE ONLY THING WRONG WITH THIS EVENING IS... WHEN I WAKE UP TO-MORROW, I WON'T BELIEVE A WORD OF IT!
The End
SPECIAL EARTH-SHAKING NOTICE: DR. STRANGE APPEARED THROUGH THE COURTESY OF THE PUBLISHERS OF STRANGE TALES! (NAMELY, US!)
20.

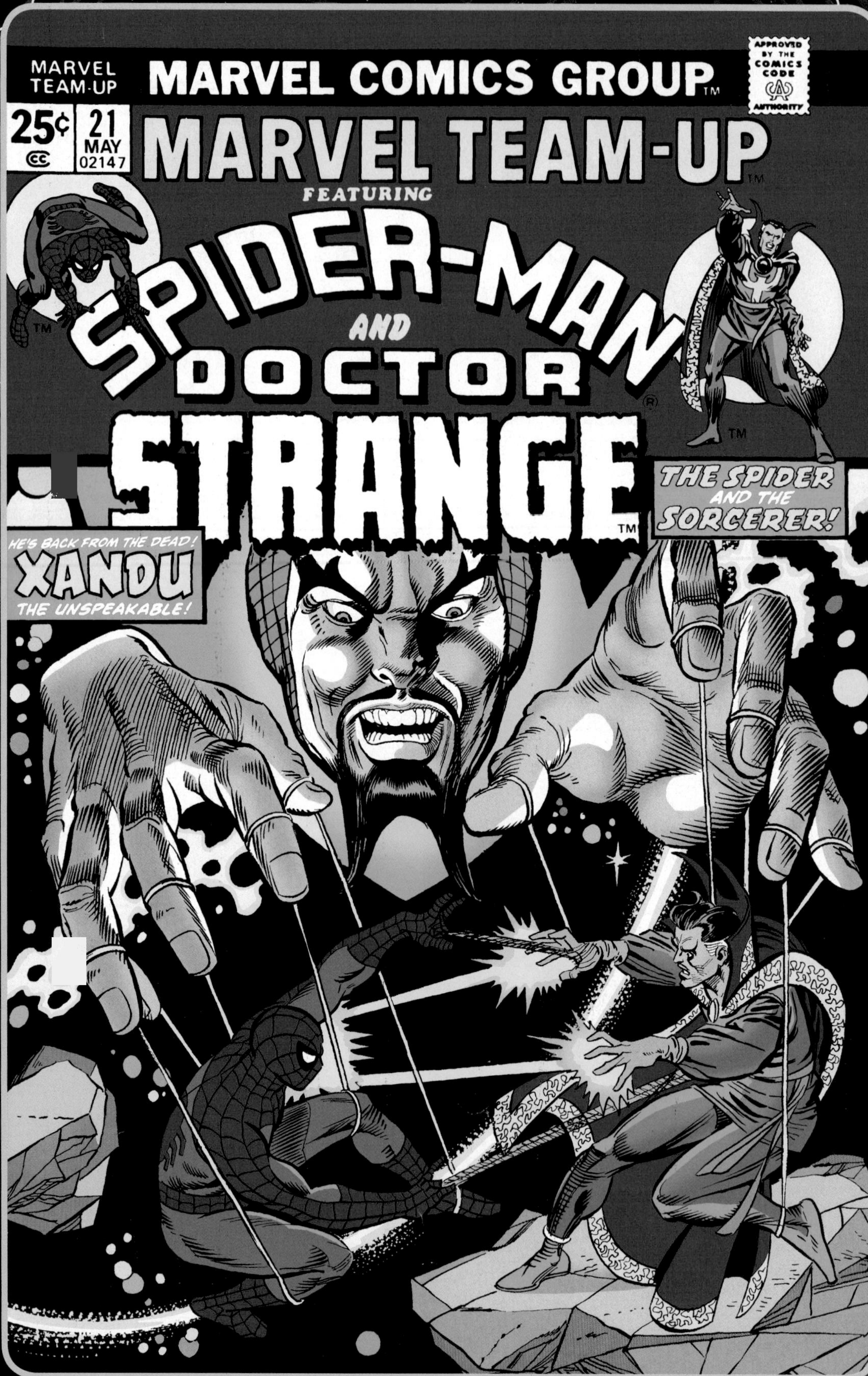

MARVEL TEAM-UP
MARVEL COMICS GROUP
25¢
21 MAY 02147
APPROVED BY THE COMICS CODE AUTHORITY
MARVEL TEAM-UP
FEATURING
SPIDER-MAN AND DOCTOR STRANGE
THE SPIDER AND THE SORCERER!
HE'S BACK FROM THE DEAD! XANDU THE UNSPEAKABLE!

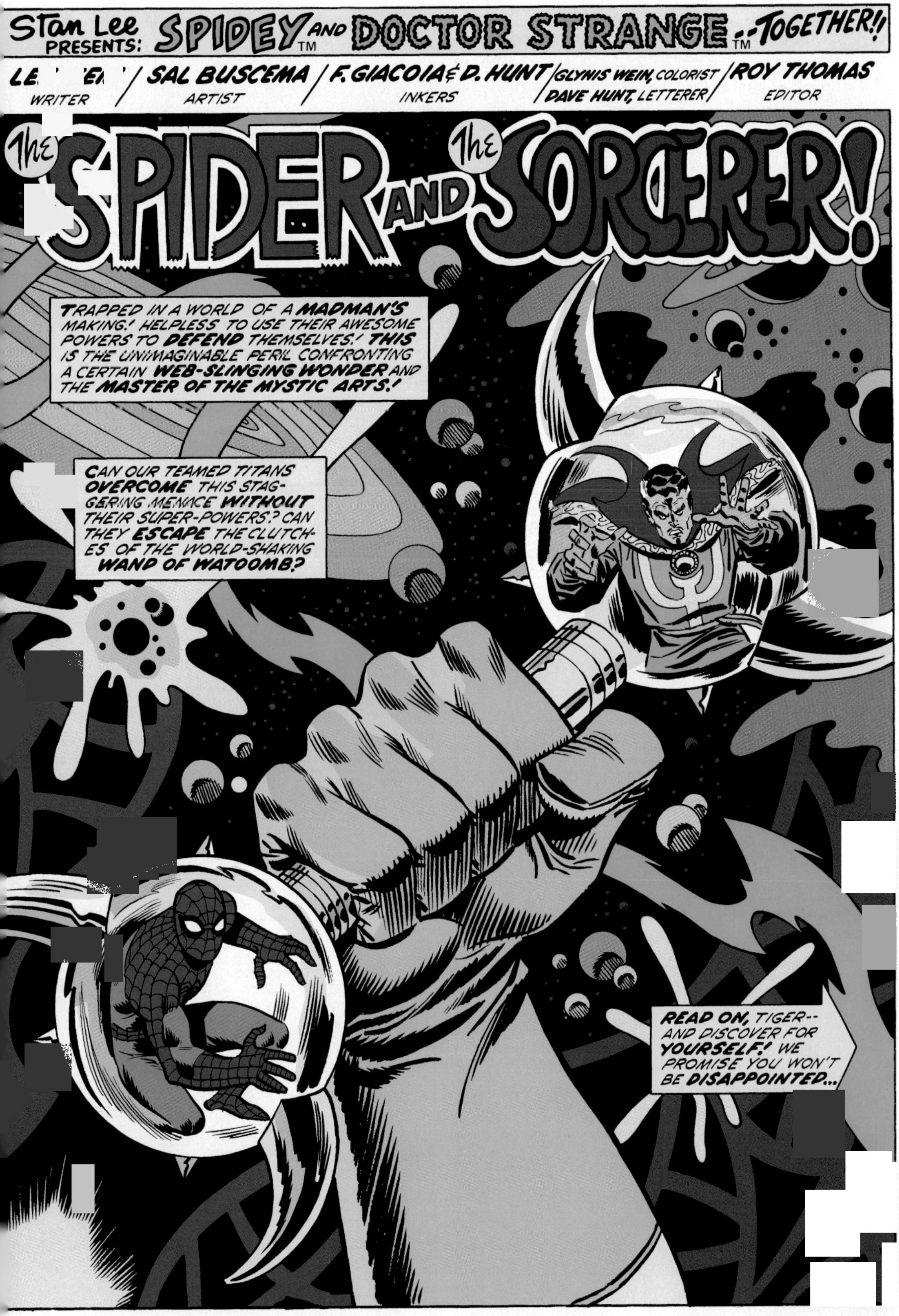

Stan Lee PRESENTS: SPIDEY™ AND DOCTOR STRANGE™ --TOGETHER!!
WRITER
SAL BUSCEMA ARTIST
F. GIACOIA & D. HUNT INKERS
GLYNIS WEIN, COLORIST
DAVE HUNT, LETTERER
ROY THOMAS EDITOR
The SPIDER AND The SORCERER!
TRAPPED IN A WORLD OF A MADMAN'S MAKING! HELPLESS TO USE THEIR AWESOME POWERS TO DEFEND THEMSELVES! THIS IS THE UNIMAGINABLE PERIL CONFRONTING A CERTAIN WEB-SLINGING WONDER AND THE MASTER OF THE MYSTIC ARTS!
CAN OUR TEAMED TITANS OVERCOME THIS STAGGERING MENACE WITHOUT THEIR SUPER-POWERS? CAN THEY ESCAPE THE CLUTCHES OF THE WORLD-SHAKING WAND OF WATOOMB?
READ ON, TIGER-- AND DISCOVER FOR YOURSELF! WE PROMISE YOU WON'T BE DISAPPOINTED...

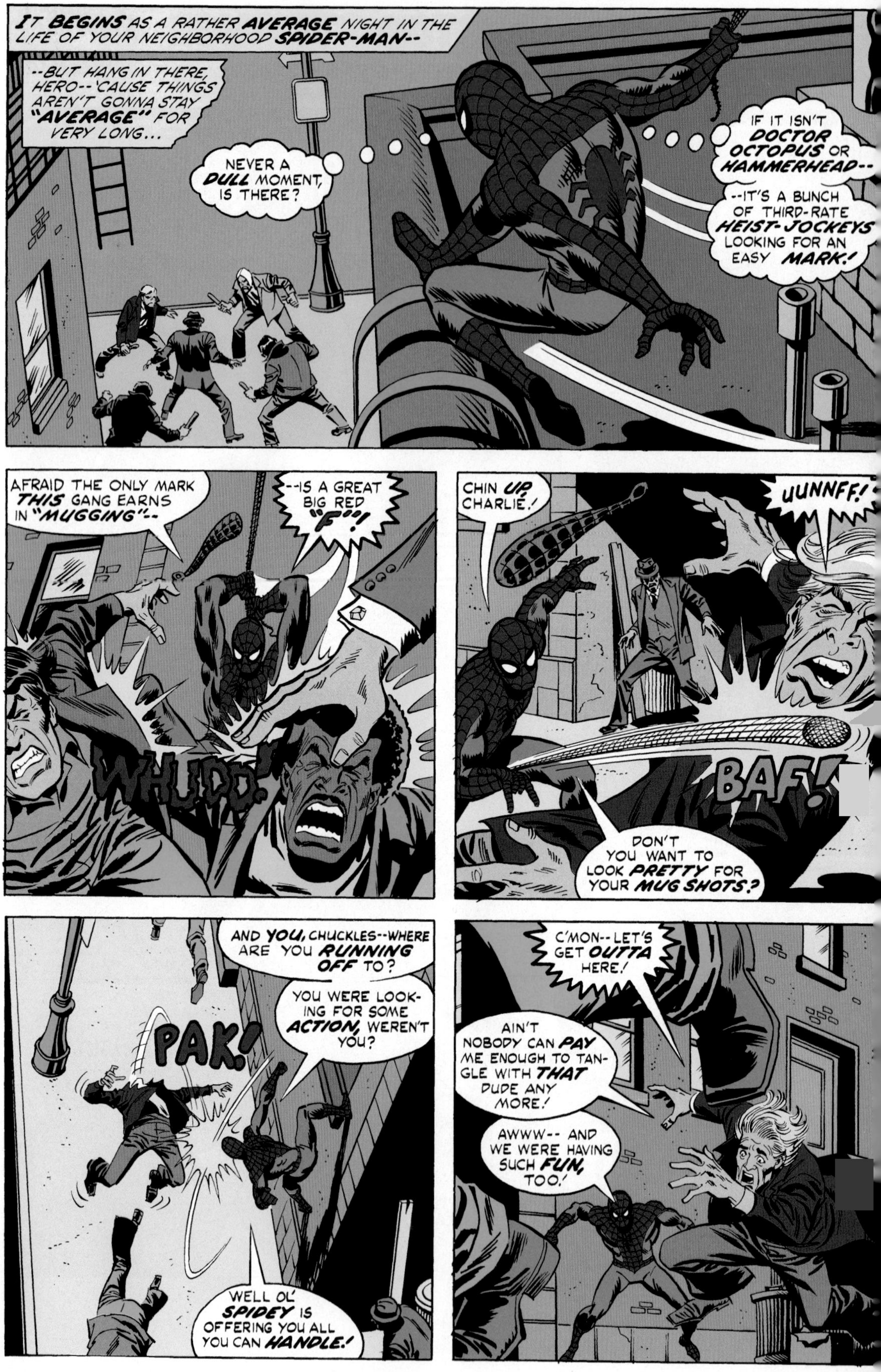
IT BEGINS AS A RATHER AVERAGE NIGHT IN THE LIFE OF YOUR NEIGHBORHOOD SPIDER-MAN--
--BUT HANG IN THERE, HERO--'CAUSE THINGS AREN'T GONNA STAY "AVERAGE" FOR VERY LONG...
NEVER A DULL MOMENT, IS THERE?
IF IT ISN'T DOCTOR OCTOPUS OR HAMMERHEAD--
--IT'S A BUNCH OF THIRD-RATE HEIST-JOCKEYS LOOKING FOR AN EASY MARK!
AFRAID THE ONLY MARK THIS GANG EARNS IN "MUGGING"--
--IS A GREAT BIG RED "F"!
WHUDD!
CHIN UP, CHARLIE!
UUNNFF!
BAF!
DON'T YOU WANT TO LOOK PRETTY FOR YOUR MUG SHOTS?
AND YOU, CHUCKLES--WHERE ARE YOU RUNNING OFF TO?
YOU WERE LOOKING FOR SOME ACTION, WEREN'T YOU?
PAK!
WELL OL' SPIDEY IS OFFERING YOU ALL YOU CAN HANDLE!
C'MON--LET'S GET OUTTA HERE!
AIN'T NOBODY CAN PAY ME ENOUGH TO TANGLE WITH THAT DUDE ANY MORE!
AWWW-- AND WE WERE HAVING SUCH FUN, TOO!

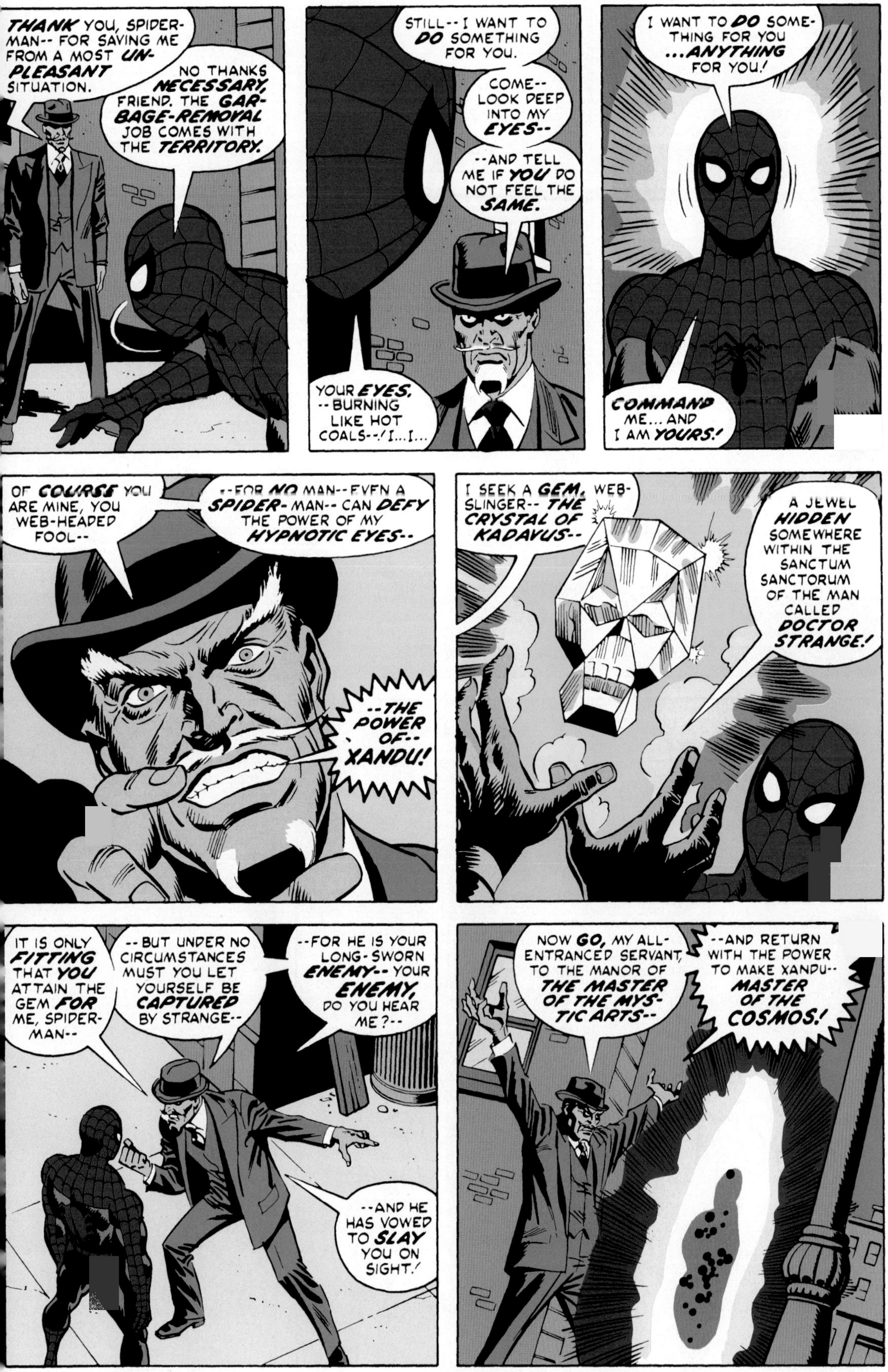
THANK YOU, SPIDER-MAN-- FOR SAVING ME FROM A MOST UN-PLEASANT SITUATION.
NO THANKS NECESSARY, FRIEND. THE GAR-BAGE-REMOVAL JOB COMES WITH THE TERRITORY.
STILL--I WANT TO DO SOMETHING FOR YOU.
COME-- LOOK DEEP INTO MY EYES--
--AND TELL ME IF YOU DO NOT FEEL THE SAME.
YOUR EYES, --BURNING LIKE HOT COALS--! I...I...
I WANT TO DO SOME-THING FOR YOU ...ANYTHING FOR YOU!
COMMAND ME... AND I AM YOURS!
OF COURSE YOU ARE MINE, YOU WEB-HEADED FOOL--
--FOR NO MAN--EVEN A SPIDER-MAN--CAN DEFY THE POWER OF MY HYPNOTIC EYES--
--THE POWER OF-- XANDU!
I SEEK A GEM, WEB-SLINGER-- THE CRYSTAL OF KADAVUS--
A JEWEL HIDDEN SOMEWHERE WITHIN THE SANCTUM SANCTORUM OF THE MAN CALLED DOCTOR STRANGE!
IT IS ONLY FITTING THAT YOU ATTAIN THE GEM FOR ME, SPIDER-MAN--
--BUT UNDER NO CIRCUMSTANCES MUST YOU LET YOURSELF BE CAPTURED BY STRANGE--
--FOR HE IS YOUR LONG-SWORN ENEMY-- YOUR ENEMY, DO YOU HEAR ME?--
--AND HE HAS VOWED TO SLAY YOU ON SIGHT!
NOW GO, MY ALL-ENTRANCED SERVANT, TO THE MANOR OF THE MASTER OF THE MYS-TIC ARTS--
--AND RETURN WITH THE POWER TO MAKE XANDU-- MASTER OF THE COSMOS!

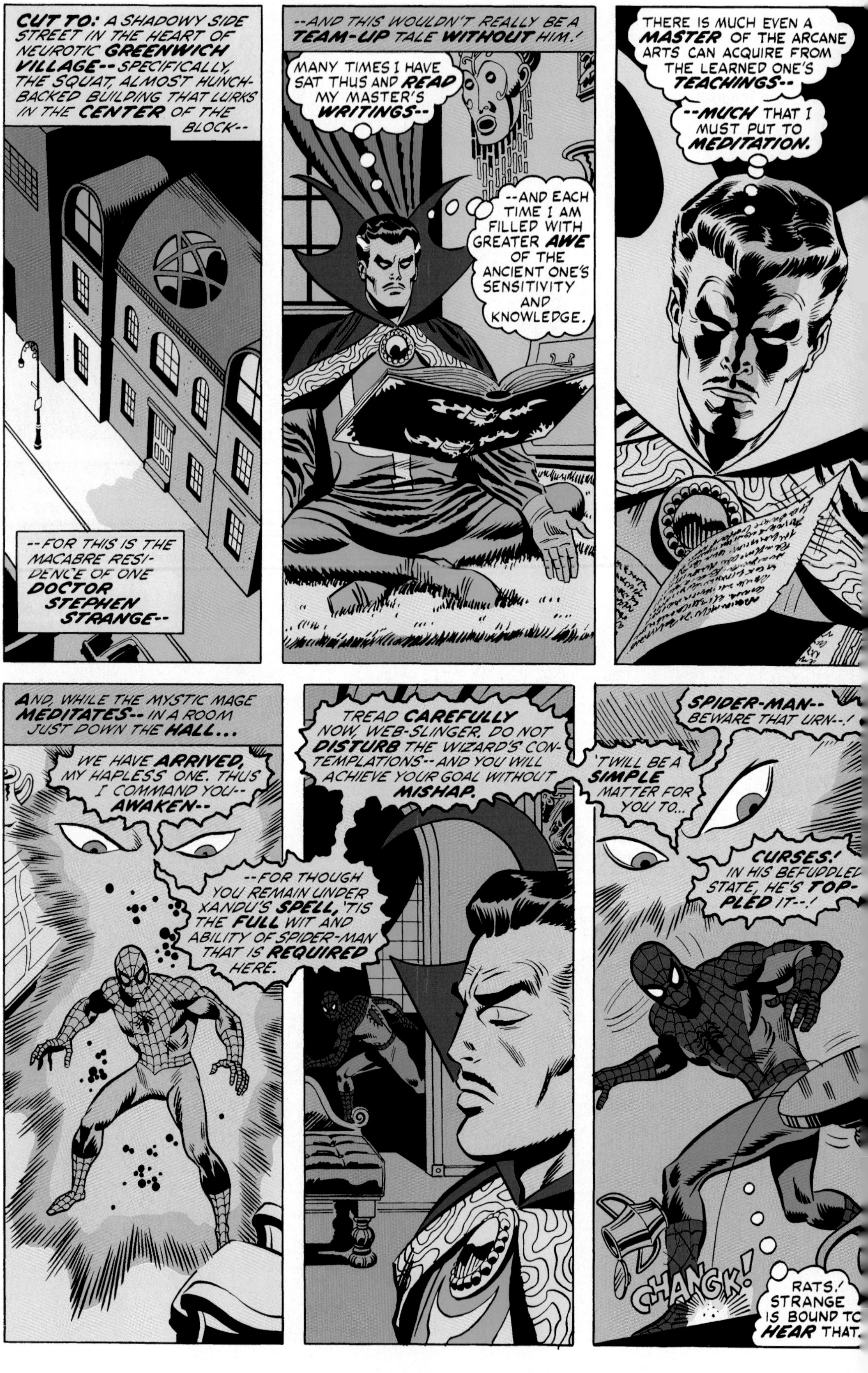
CUT TO: A SHADOWY SIDE STREET IN THE HEART OF NEUROTIC GREENWICH VILLAGE-- SPECIFICALLY, THE SQUAT, ALMOST HUNCH-BACKED BUILDING THAT LURKS IN THE CENTER OF THE BLOCK--
--FOR THIS IS THE MACABRE RESI-DENCE OF ONE DOCTOR STEPHEN STRANGE--
--AND THIS WOULDN'T REALLY BE A TEAM-UP TALE WITHOUT HIM.!
MANY TIMES I HAVE SAT THUS AND READ MY MASTER'S WRITINGS--
--AND EACH TIME I AM FILLED WITH GREATER AWE OF THE ANCIENT ONE'S SENSITIVITY AND KNOWLEDGE.
THERE IS MUCH EVEN A MASTER OF THE ARCANE ARTS CAN ACQUIRE FROM THE LEARNED ONE'S TEACHINGS--
--MUCH THAT I MUST PUT TO MEDITATION.
AND, WHILE THE MYSTIC MAGE MEDITATES-- IN A ROOM JUST DOWN THE HALL...
WE HAVE ARRIVED, MY HAPLESS ONE. THUS I COMMAND YOU-- AWAKEN--
--FOR THOUGH YOU REMAIN UNDER XANDU'S SPELL, 'TIS THE FULL WIT AND ABILITY OF SPIDER-MAN THAT IS REQUIRED HERE.
TREAD CAREFULLY NOW, WEB-SLINGER. DO NOT DISTURB THE WIZARD'S CON-TEMPLATIONS-- AND YOU WILL ACHIEVE YOUR GOAL WITHOUT MISHAP.
SPIDER-MAN-- BEWARE THAT URN--!
'TWILL BE A SIMPLE MATTER FOR YOU TO...
CURSES! IN HIS BEFUDDLED STATE, HE'S TOP-PLED IT--!
CHANGK!
RATS! STRANGE IS BOUND TO HEAR THAT.

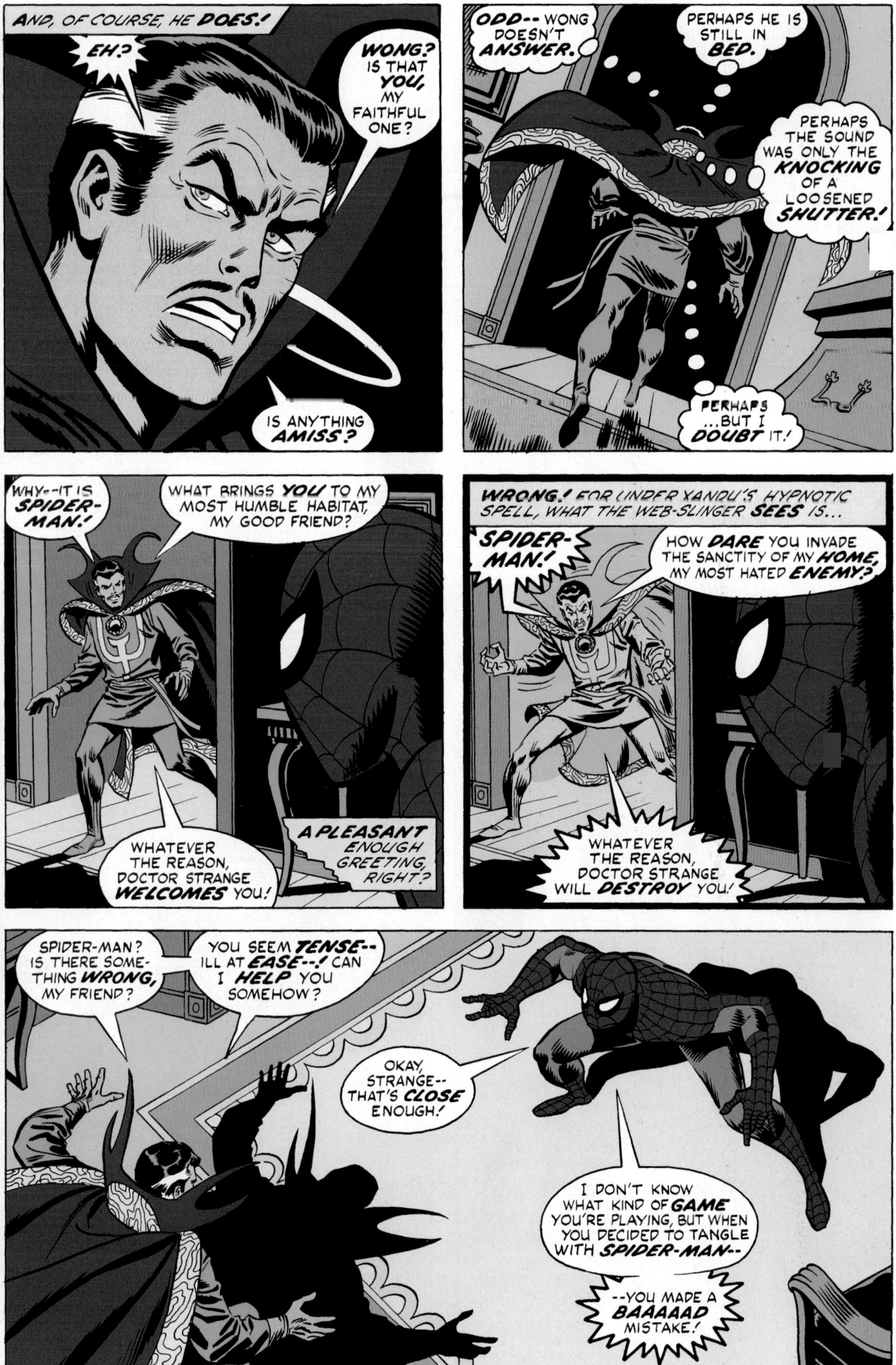

AND, OF COURSE, HE DOES!
EH?
WONG? IS THAT YOU, MY FAITHFUL ONE?
IS ANYTHING AMISS?
ODD-- WONG DOESN'T ANSWER.
PERHAPS HE IS STILL IN BED.
PERHAPS THE SOUND WAS ONLY THE KNOCKING OF A LOOSENED SHUTTER!
PERHAPS ...BUT I DOUBT IT!
WHY--IT IS SPIDER-MAN!
WHAT BRINGS YOU TO MY MOST HUMBLE HABITAT, MY GOOD FRIEND?
WHATEVER THE REASON, DOCTOR STRANGE WELCOMES YOU!
A PLEASANT ENOUGH GREETING, RIGHT?
WRONG! FOR UNDER XANDU'S HYPNOTIC SPELL, WHAT THE WEB-SLINGER SEES IS...
SPIDER-MAN!
HOW DARE YOU INVADE THE SANCTITY OF MY HOME, MY MOST HATED ENEMY?
WHATEVER THE REASON, DOCTOR STRANGE WILL DESTROY YOU!
SPIDER-MAN? IS THERE SOMETHING WRONG, MY FRIEND?
YOU SEEM TENSE-- ILL AT EASE--! CAN I HELP YOU SOMEHOW?
OKAY, STRANGE-- THAT'S CLOSE ENOUGH!
I DON'T KNOW WHAT KIND OF GAME YOU'RE PLAYING, BUT WHEN YOU DECIDED TO TANGLE WITH SPIDER-MAN--
--YOU MADE A BAAAAAD MISTAKE!

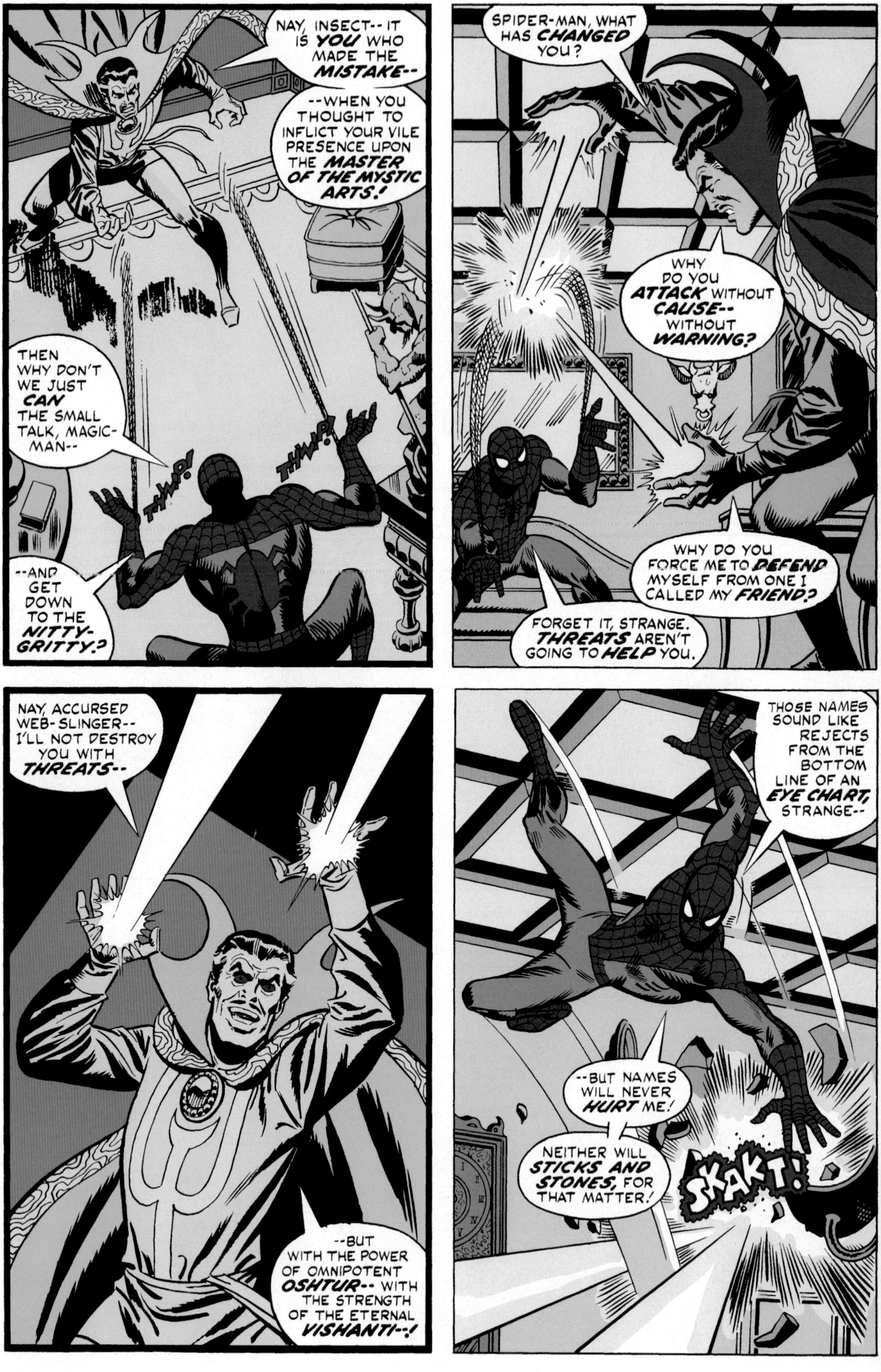
NAY, INSECT-- IT IS YOU WHO MADE THE MISTAKE--
--WHEN YOU THOUGHT TO INFLICT YOUR VILE PRESENCE UPON THE MASTER OF THE MYSTIC ARTS!
THEN WHY DON'T WE JUST CAN THE SMALL TALK, MAGIC-MAN--
THWIP!
THWIP!
--AND GET DOWN TO THE NITTY-GRITTY?
SPIDER-MAN, WHAT HAS CHANGED YOU?
WHY DO YOU ATTACK WITHOUT CAUSE-- WITHOUT WARNING?
WHY DO YOU FORCE ME TO DEFEND MYSELF FROM ONE I CALLED MY FRIEND?
FORGET IT, STRANGE. THREATS AREN'T GOING TO HELP YOU.
NAY, ACCURSED WEB-SLINGER-- I'LL NOT DESTROY YOU WITH THREATS--
--BUT WITH THE POWER OF OMNIPOTENT OSHTUR-- WITH THE STRENGTH OF THE ETERNAL VISHANTI--!
THOSE NAMES SOUND LIKE REJECTS FROM THE BOTTOM LINE OF AN EYE CHART, STRANGE--
--BUT NAMES WILL NEVER HURT ME!
NEITHER WILL STICKS AND STONES, FOR THAT MATTER!
SKAKT!

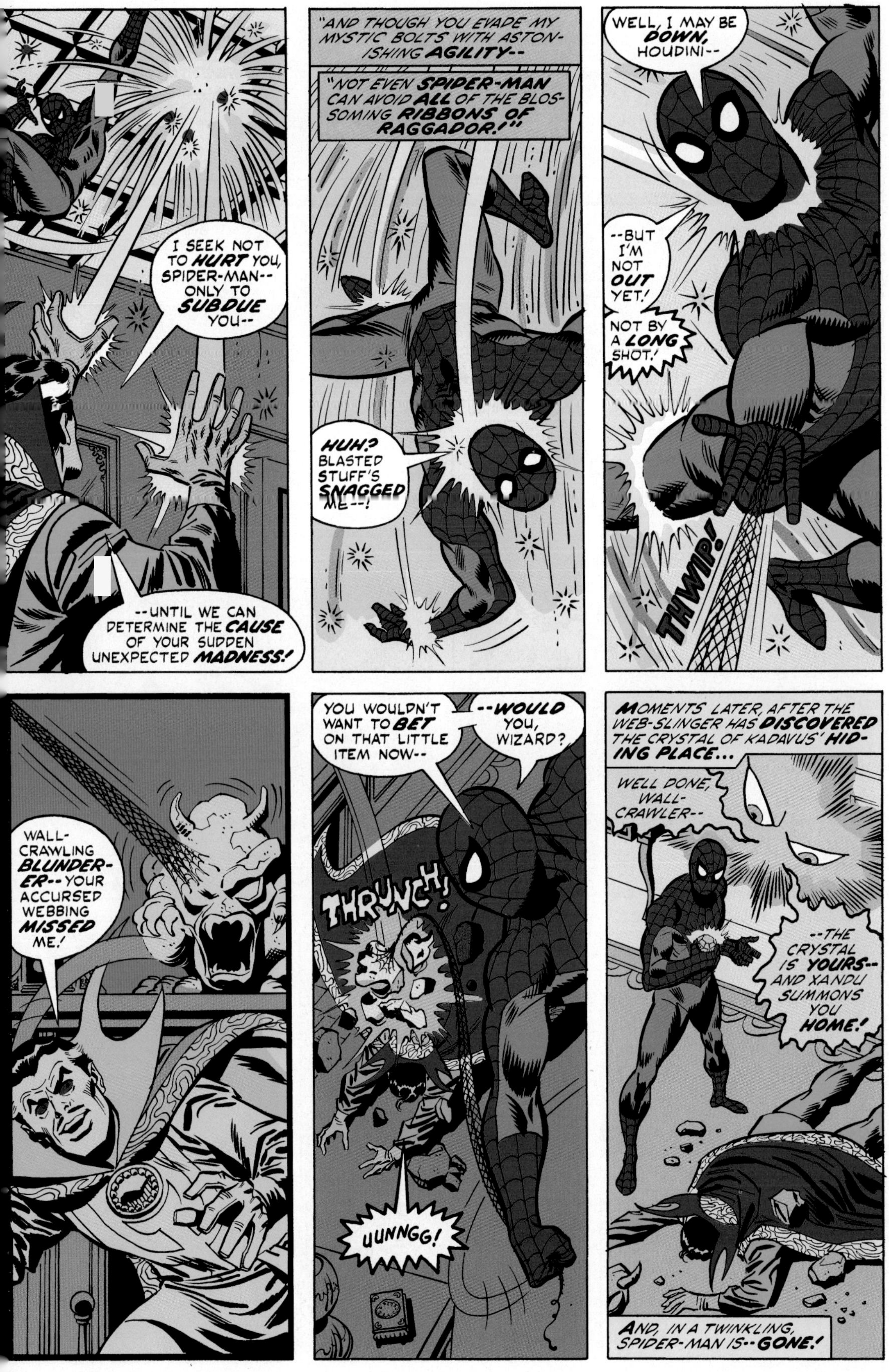
I SEEK NOT TO HURT YOU, SPIDER-MAN-- ONLY TO SUBDUE YOU--
--UNTIL WE CAN DETERMINE THE CAUSE OF YOUR SUDDEN UNEXPECTED MADNESS!
"AND THOUGH YOU EVADE MY MYSTIC BOLTS WITH ASTONISHING AGILITY--
"NOT EVEN SPIDER-MAN CAN AVOID ALL OF THE BLOSSOMING RIBBONS OF RAGGADOR!"
HUH? BLASTED STUFF'S SNAGGED ME--!
WELL, I MAY BE DOWN, HOUDINI--
--BUT I'M NOT OUT YET!
NOT BY A LONG SHOT!
THWIP!
WALL-CRAWLING BLUNDERER-- YOUR ACCURSED WEBBING MISSED ME!
YOU WOULDN'T WANT TO BET ON THAT LITTLE ITEM NOW--
--WOULD YOU, WIZARD?
THRUNCH!
UUNNGG!
MOMENTS LATER, AFTER THE WEB-SLINGER HAS DISCOVERED THE CRYSTAL OF KADAVUS' HIDING PLACE...
WELL DONE, WALL-CRAWLER--
--THE CRYSTAL IS YOURS-- AND XANDU SUMMONS YOU HOME!
AND, IN A TWINKLING, SPIDER-MAN IS-- GONE!

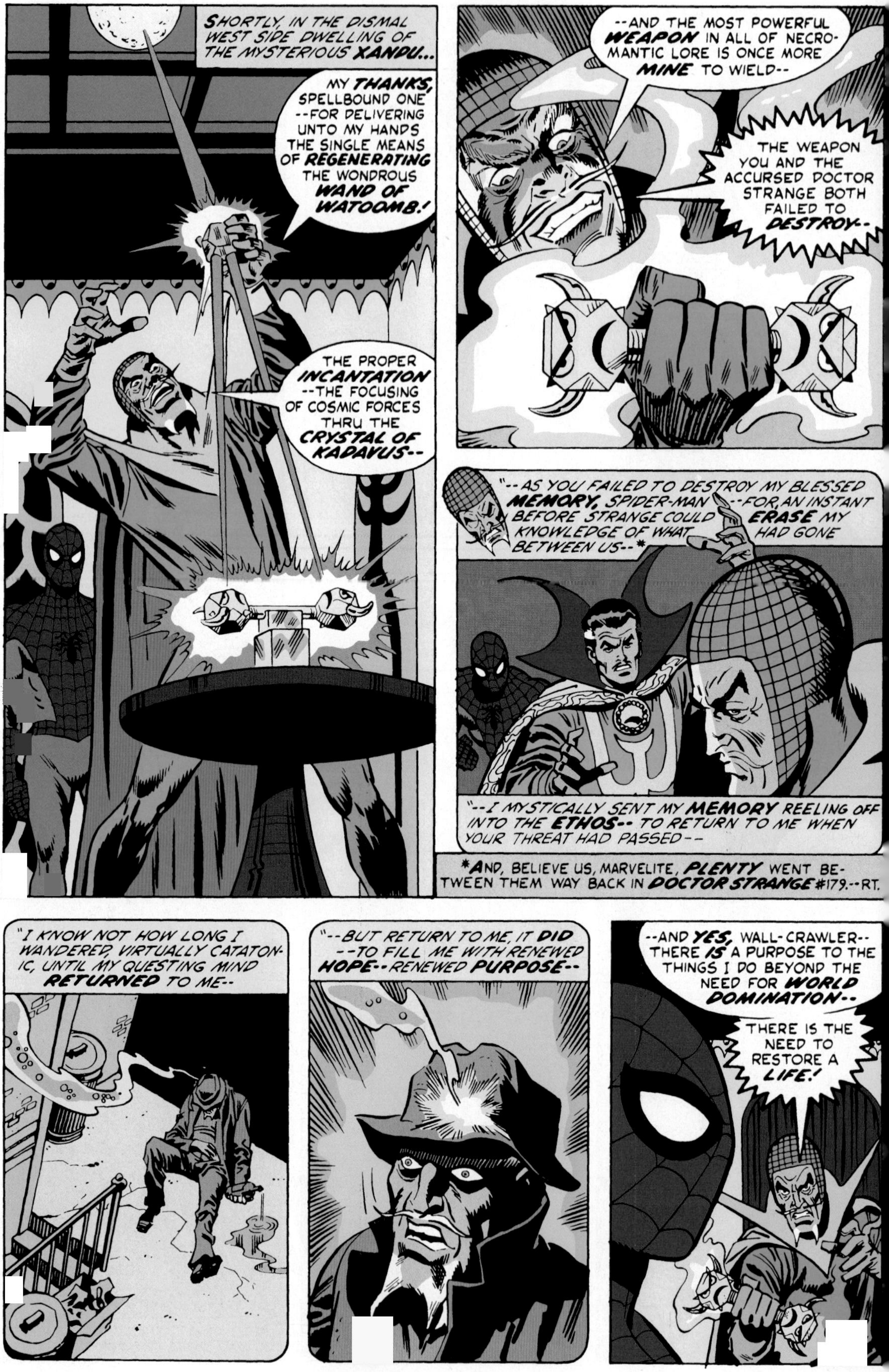

SHORTLY, IN THE DISMAL WEST SIDE DWELLING OF THE MYSTERIOUS XANDU...
MY THANKS, SPELLBOUND ONE --FOR DELIVERING UNTO MY HANDS THE SINGLE MEANS OF REGENERATING THE WONDROUS WAND OF WATOOMB!
THE PROPER INCANTATION --THE FOCUSING OF COSMIC FORCES THRU THE CRYSTAL OF KADAVUS--
--AND THE MOST POWERFUL WEAPON IN ALL OF NECROMANTIC LORE IS ONCE MORE MINE TO WIELD--
THE WEAPON YOU AND THE ACCURSED DOCTOR STRANGE BOTH FAILED TO DESTROY--
"--AS YOU FAILED TO DESTROY MY BLESSED MEMORY, SPIDER-MAN --FOR, AN INSTANT BEFORE STRANGE COULD ERASE MY KNOWLEDGE OF WHAT HAD GONE BETWEEN US--*
"--I MYSTICALLY SENT MY MEMORY REELING OFF INTO THE ETHOS-- TO RETURN TO ME WHEN YOUR THREAT HAD PASSED--
*AND, BELIEVE US, MARVELITE, PLENTY WENT BETWEEN THEM WAY BACK IN DOCTOR STRANGE #179.--RT.
"I KNOW NOT HOW LONG I WANDERED, VIRTUALLY CATATONIC, UNTIL MY QUESTING MIND RETURNED TO ME--
"--BUT RETURN TO ME, IT DID --TO FILL ME WITH RENEWED HOPE--RENEWED PURPOSE--
--AND YES, WALL-CRAWLER-- THERE IS A PURPOSE TO THE THINGS I DO BEYOND THE NEED FOR WORLD DOMINATION--
THERE IS THE NEED TO RESTORE A LIFE!

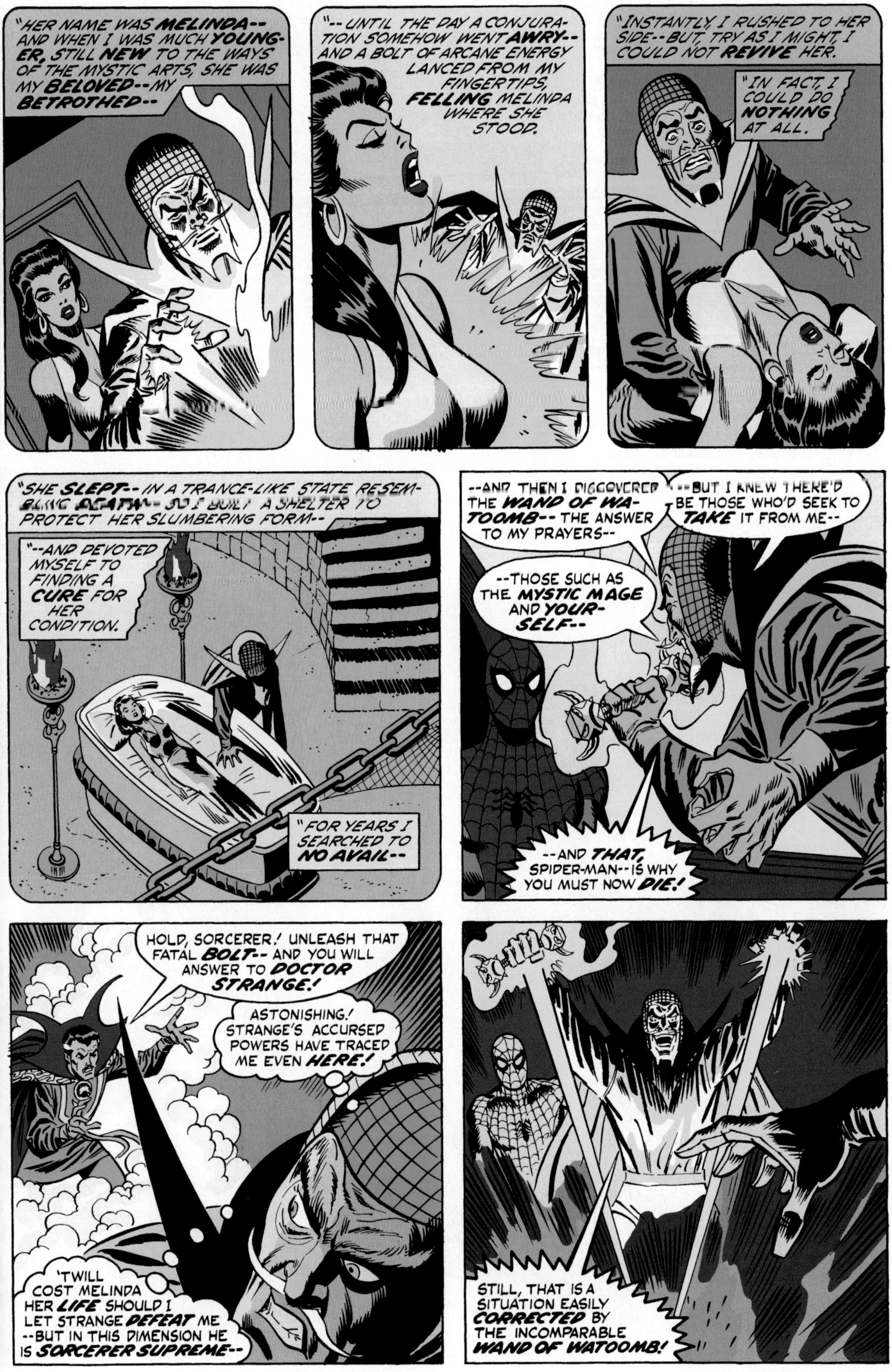
"HER NAME WAS MELINDA-- AND WHEN I WAS MUCH YOUNGER, STILL NEW TO THE WAYS OF THE MYSTIC ARTS, SHE WAS MY BELOVED--MY BETROTHED--
"--UNTIL THE DAY A CONJURATION SOMEHOW WENT AWRY-- AND A BOLT OF ARCANE ENERGY LANCED FROM MY FINGERTIPS, FELLING MELINDA WHERE SHE STOOD.
"INSTANTLY, I RUSHED TO HER SIDE--BUT, TRY AS I MIGHT, I COULD NOT REVIVE HER.
"IN FACT, I COULD DO NOTHING AT ALL.
"SHE SLEPT-- IN A TRANCE-LIKE STATE RESEMBLING DEATH-- SO I BUILT A SHELTER TO PROTECT HER SLUMBERING FORM--
"--AND DEVOTED MYSELF TO FINDING A CURE FOR HER CONDITION.
"FOR YEARS I SEARCHED TO NO AVAIL--
--AND THEN I DISCOVERED THE WAND OF WATOOMB-- THE ANSWER TO MY PRAYERS--
--BUT I KNEW THERE'D BE THOSE WHO'D SEEK TO TAKE IT FROM ME--
--THOSE SUCH AS THE MYSTIC MAGE AND YOURSELF--
--AND THAT, SPIDER-MAN--IS WHY YOU MUST NOW DIE!
HOLD, SORCERER! UNLEASH THAT FATAL BOLT-- AND YOU WILL ANSWER TO DOCTOR STRANGE!
ASTONISHING! STRANGE'S ACCURSED POWERS HAVE TRACED ME EVEN HERE!
'TWILL COST MELINDA HER LIFE SHOULD I LET STRANGE DEFEAT ME --BUT IN THIS DIMENSION HE IS SORCERER SUPREME--
STILL, THAT IS A SITUATION EASILY CORRECTED BY THE INCOMPARABLE WAND OF WATOOMB!

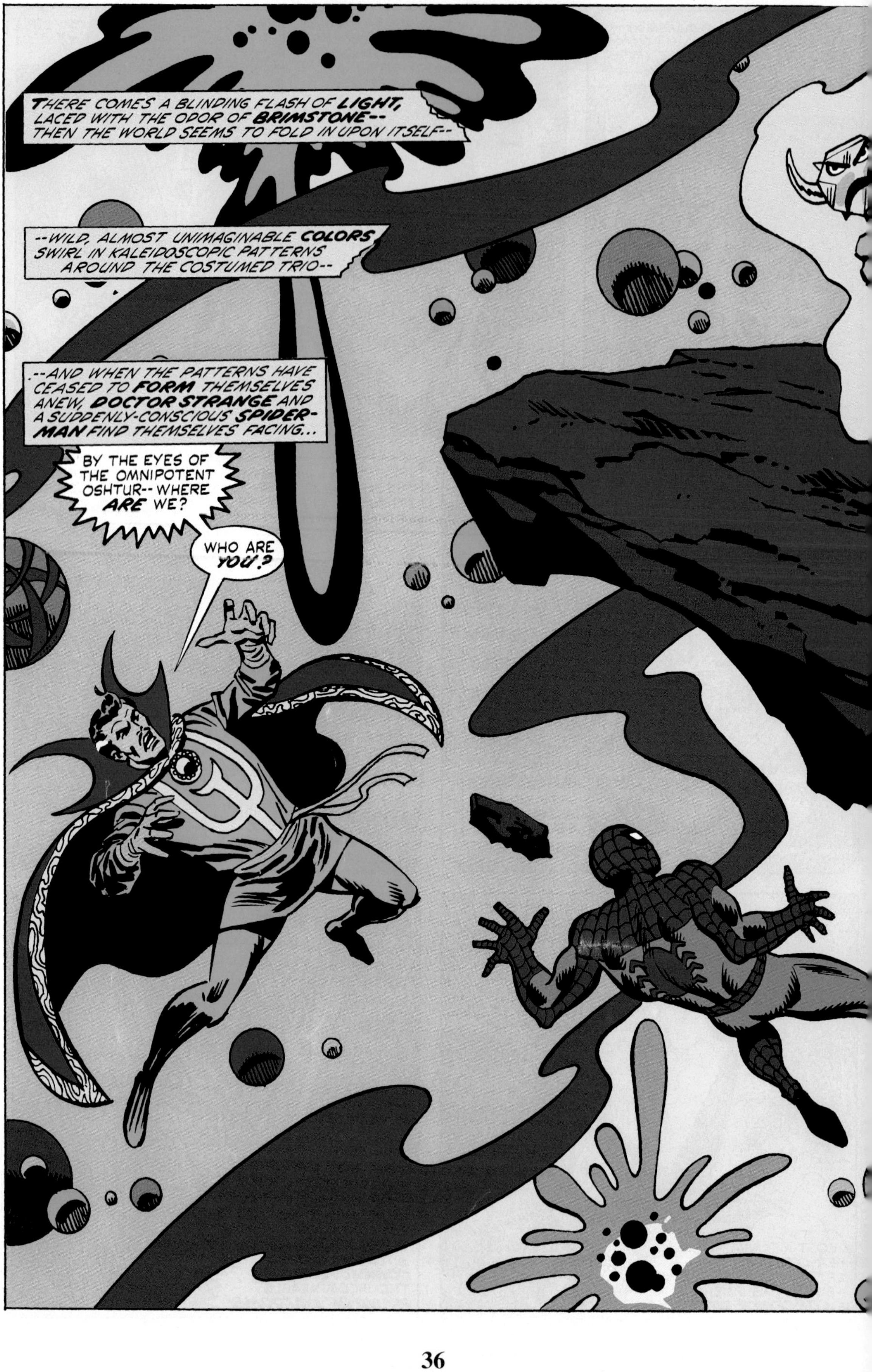
THERE COMES A BLINDING FLASH OF LIGHT, LACED WITH THE ODOR OF BRIMSTONE-- THEN THE WORLD SEEMS TO FOLD IN UPON ITSELF--
--WILD, ALMOST UNIMAGINABLE COLORS SWIRL IN KALEIDOSCOPIC PATTERNS AROUND THE COSTUMED TRIO--
--AND WHEN THE PATTERNS HAVE CEASED TO FORM THEMSELVES ANEW, DOCTOR STRANGE AND A SUDDENLY-CONSCIOUS SPIDER-MAN FIND THEMSELVES FACING...
BY THE EYES OF THE OMNIPOTENT OSHTUR-- WHERE ARE WE?
WHO ARE YOU?

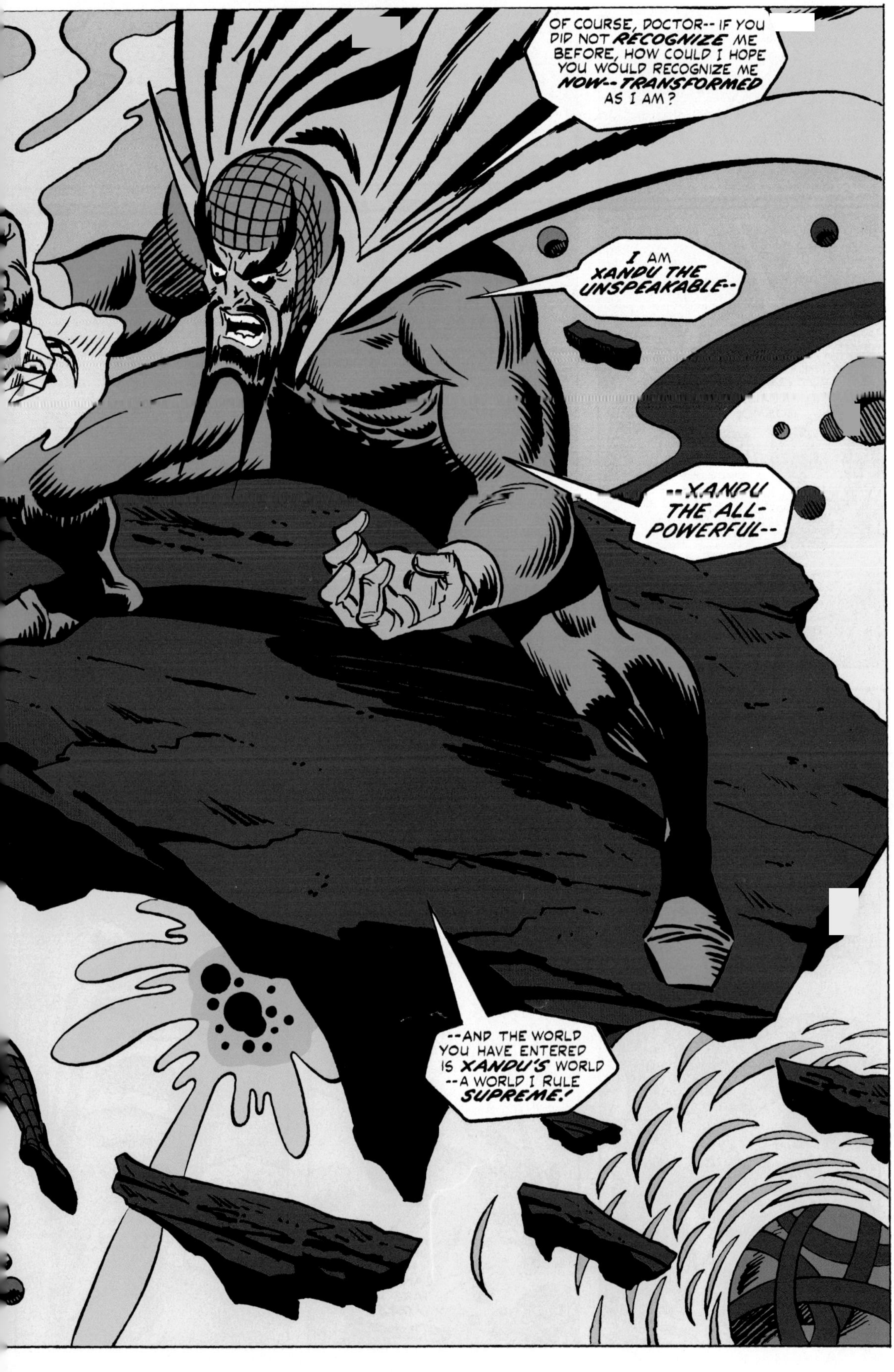
OF COURSE, DOCTOR-- IF YOU DID NOT RECOGNIZE ME BEFORE, HOW COULD I HOPE YOU WOULD RECOGNIZE ME NOW--TRANSFORMED AS I AM?
I AM XANDU THE UNSPEAKABLE--
--XANDU THE ALL-POWERFUL--
--AND THE WORLD YOU HAVE ENTERED IS XANDU'S WORLD --A WORLD I RULE SUPREME!

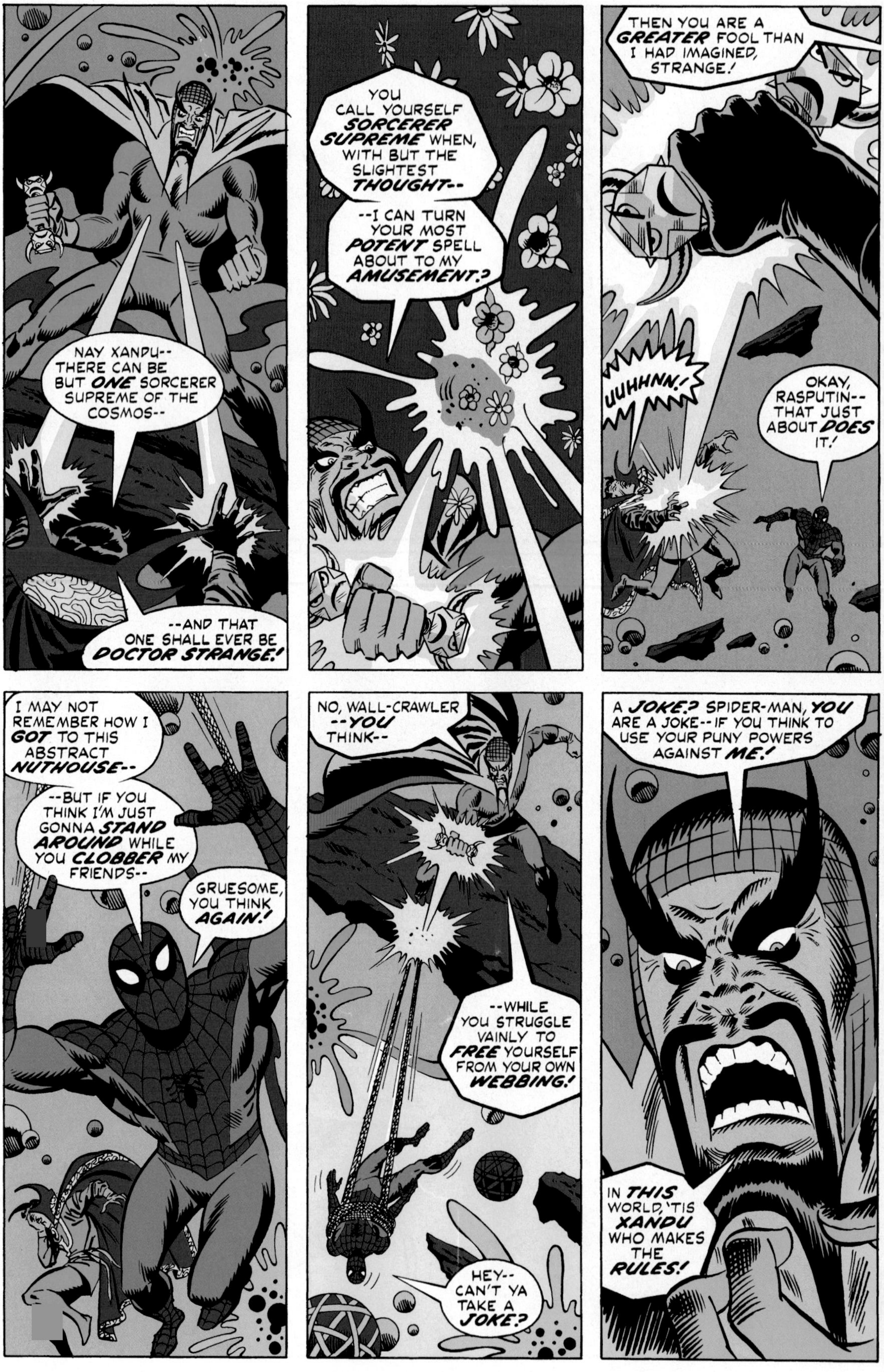
NAY XANDU--
THERE CAN BE BUT ONE SORCERER SUPREME OF THE COSMOS--
--AND THAT ONE SHALL EVER BE DOCTOR STRANGE!
YOU CALL YOURSELF SORCERER SUPREME WHEN, WITH BUT THE SLIGHTEST THOUGHT--
--I CAN TURN YOUR MOST POTENT SPELL ABOUT TO MY AMUSEMENT?
THEN YOU ARE A GREATER FOOL THAN I HAD IMAGINED, STRANGE!
UUHHNN!
OKAY, RASPUTIN--THAT JUST ABOUT DOES IT!
I MAY NOT REMEMBER HOW I GOT TO THIS ABSTRACT NUTHOUSE--
--BUT IF YOU THINK I'M JUST GONNA STAND AROUND WHILE YOU CLOBBER MY FRIENDS--
GRUESOME, YOU THINK AGAIN!
NO, WALL-CRAWLER--YOU THINK--
--WHILE YOU STRUGGLE VAINLY TO FREE YOURSELF FROM YOUR OWN WEBBING!
HEY--CAN'T YA TAKE A JOKE?
A JOKE? SPIDER-MAN, YOU ARE A JOKE--IF YOU THINK TO USE YOUR PUNY POWERS AGAINST ME!
IN THIS WORLD, 'TIS XANDU WHO MAKES THE RULES!

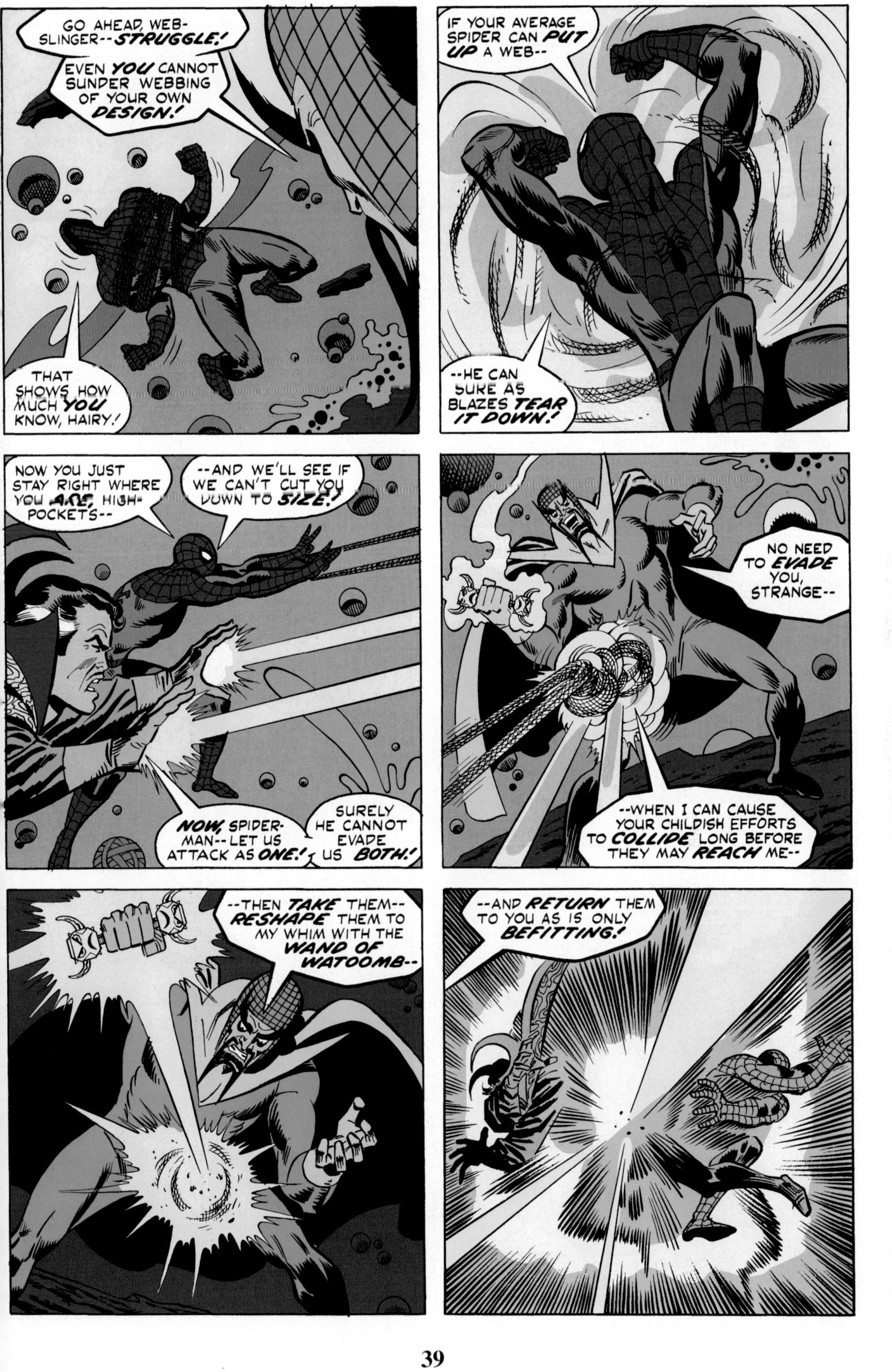
GO AHEAD, WEB-SLINGER--STRUGGLE!
EVEN YOU CANNOT SUNDER WEBBING OF YOUR OWN DESIGN!
THAT SHOWS HOW MUCH YOU KNOW, HAIRY!
IF YOUR AVERAGE SPIDER CAN PUT UP A WEB--
--HE CAN SURE AS BLAZES TEAR IT DOWN!
NOW YOU JUST STAY RIGHT WHERE YOU ARE, HIGH-POCKETS--
--AND WE'LL SEE IF WE CAN'T CUT YOU DOWN TO SIZE!
NOW, SPIDER-MAN--LET US ATTACK AS ONE!
SURELY HE CANNOT EVADE US BOTH!
NO NEED TO EVADE YOU, STRANGE--
--WHEN I CAN CAUSE YOUR CHILDISH EFFORTS TO COLLIDE LONG BEFORE THEY MAY REACH ME--
--THEN TAKE THEM--RESHAPE THEM TO MY WHIM WITH THE WAND OF WATOOMB--
--AND RETURN THEM TO YOU AS IS ONLY BEFITTING!

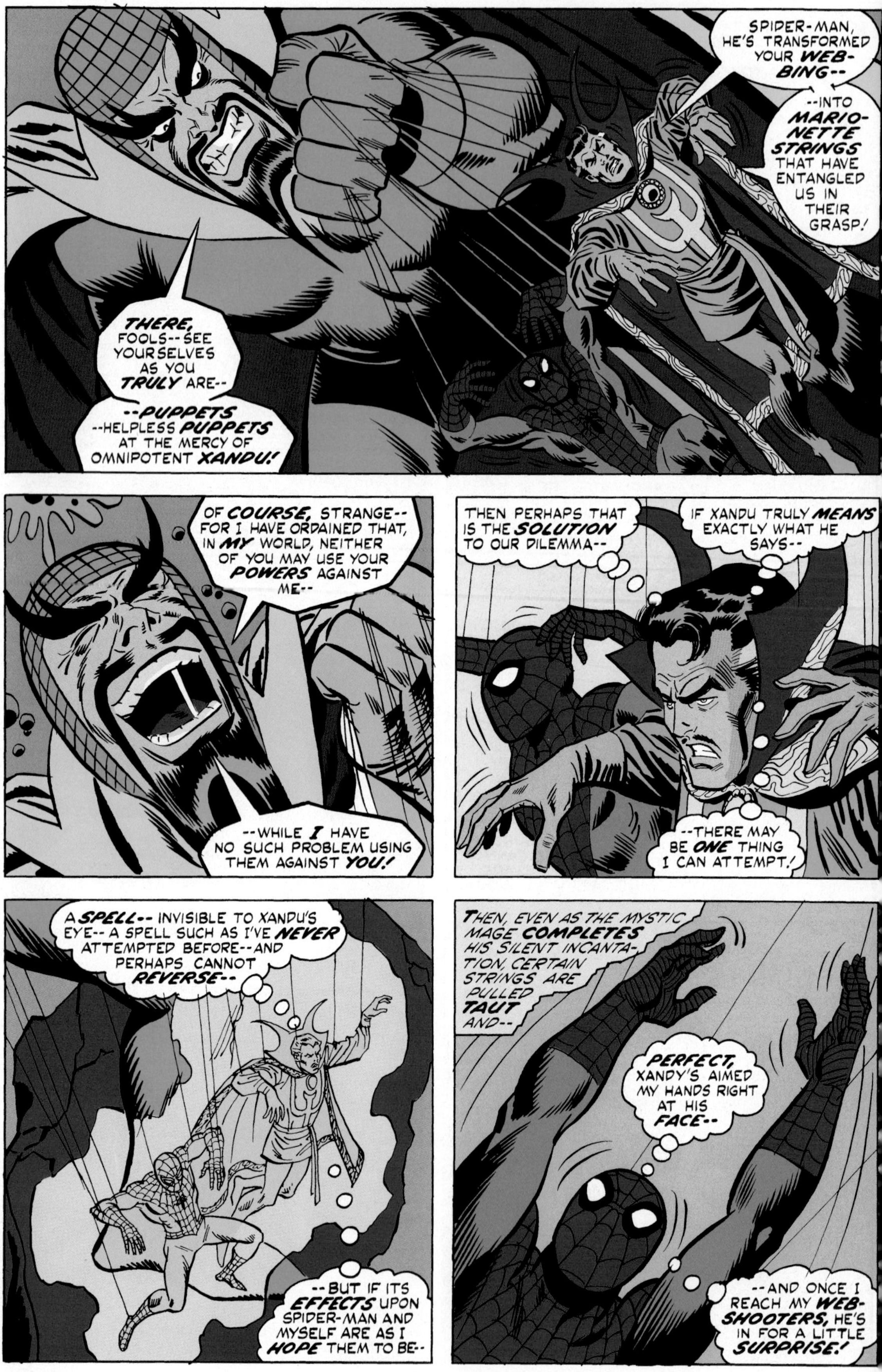
SPIDER-MAN, HE'S TRANSFORMED YOUR WEB-BING--
--INTO MARIO-NETTE STRINGS THAT HAVE ENTANGLED US IN THEIR GRASP!
THERE, FOOLS--SEE YOURSELVES AS YOU TRULY ARE--
--PUPPETS --HELPLESS PUPPETS AT THE MERCY OF OMNIPOTENT XANDU!
OF COURSE, STRANGE--FOR I HAVE ORDAINED THAT, IN MY WORLD, NEITHER OF YOU MAY USE YOUR POWERS AGAINST ME--
--WHILE I HAVE NO SUCH PROBLEM USING THEM AGAINST YOU!
THEN PERHAPS THAT IS THE SOLUTION TO OUR DILEMMA--
IF XANDU TRULY MEANS EXACTLY WHAT HE SAYS--
--THERE MAY BE ONE THING I CAN ATTEMPT!
A SPELL-- INVISIBLE TO XANDU'S EYE-- A SPELL SUCH AS I'VE NEVER ATTEMPTED BEFORE--AND PERHAPS CANNOT REVERSE--
--BUT IF ITS EFFECTS UPON SPIDER-MAN AND MYSELF ARE AS I HOPE THEM TO BE--
THEN, EVEN AS THE MYSTIC MAGE COMPLETES HIS SILENT INCANTATION, CERTAIN STRINGS ARE PULLED TAUT AND--
PERFECT, XANDY'S AIMED MY HANDS RIGHT AT HIS FACE--
--AND ONCE I REACH MY WEB-SHOOTERS, HE'S IN FOR A LITTLE SURPRISE!

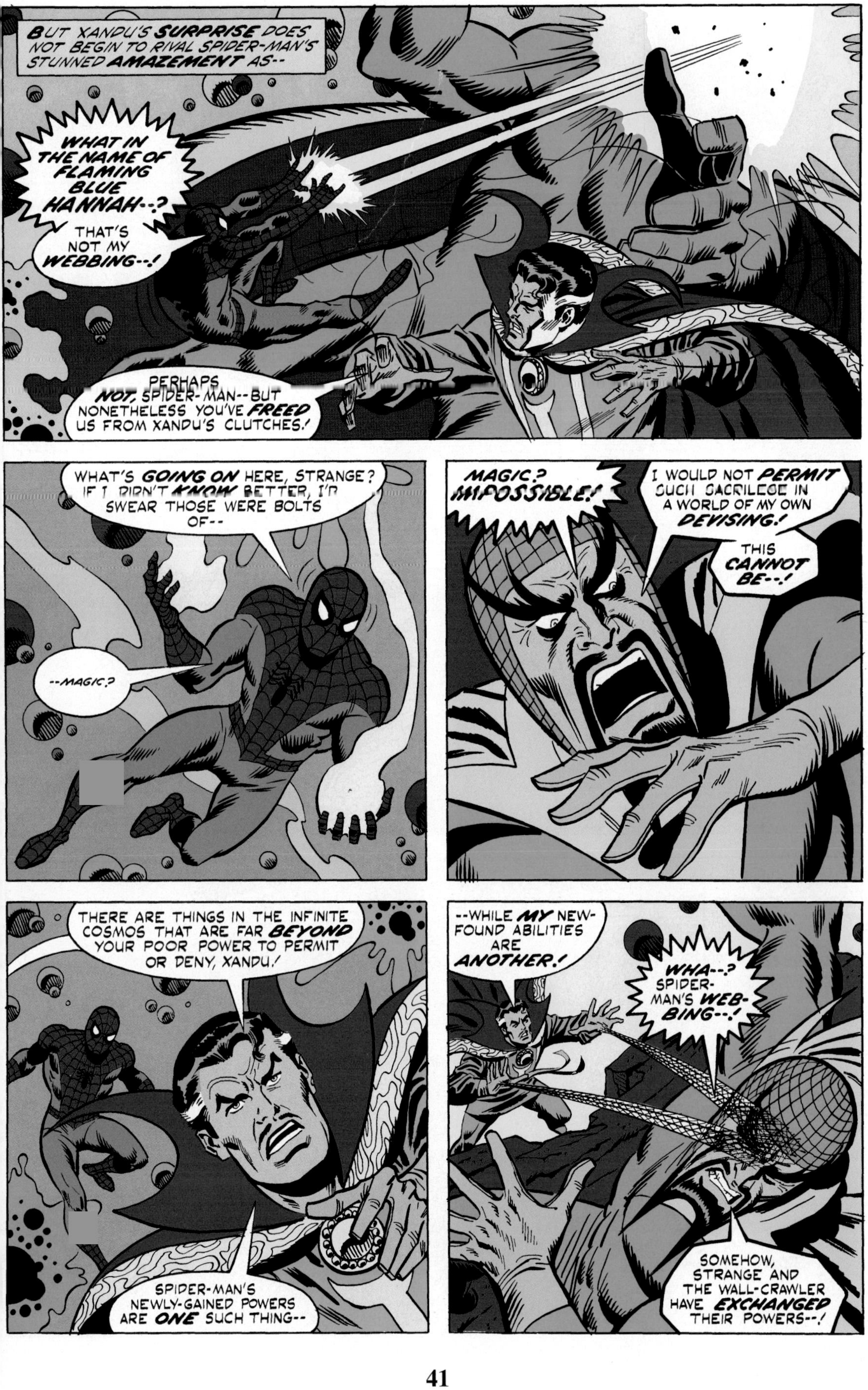
BUT XANDU'S SURPRISE DOES NOT BEGIN TO RIVAL SPIDER-MAN'S STUNNED AMAZEMENT AS--
WHAT IN THE NAME OF FLAMING BLUE HANNAH--?
THAT'S NOT MY WEBBING--!
PERHAPS NOT, SPIDER-MAN--BUT NONETHELESS YOU'VE FREED US FROM XANDU'S CLUTCHES!
WHAT'S GOING ON HERE, STRANGE? IF I DIDN'T KNOW BETTER, I'D SWEAR THOSE WERE BOLTS OF--
--MAGIC?
MAGIC? IMPOSSIBLE!
I WOULD NOT PERMIT SUCH SACRILEGE IN A WORLD OF MY OWN DEVISING!
THIS CANNOT BE--!
THERE ARE THINGS IN THE INFINITE COSMOS THAT ARE FAR BEYOND YOUR POOR POWER TO PERMIT OR DENY, XANDU!
SPIDER-MAN'S NEWLY-GAINED POWERS ARE ONE SUCH THING--
--WHILE MY NEW-FOUND ABILITIES ARE ANOTHER!
WHA--? SPIDER-MAN'S WEB-BING--!
SOMEHOW, STRANGE AND THE WALL-CRAWLER HAVE EXCHANGED THEIR POWERS--!

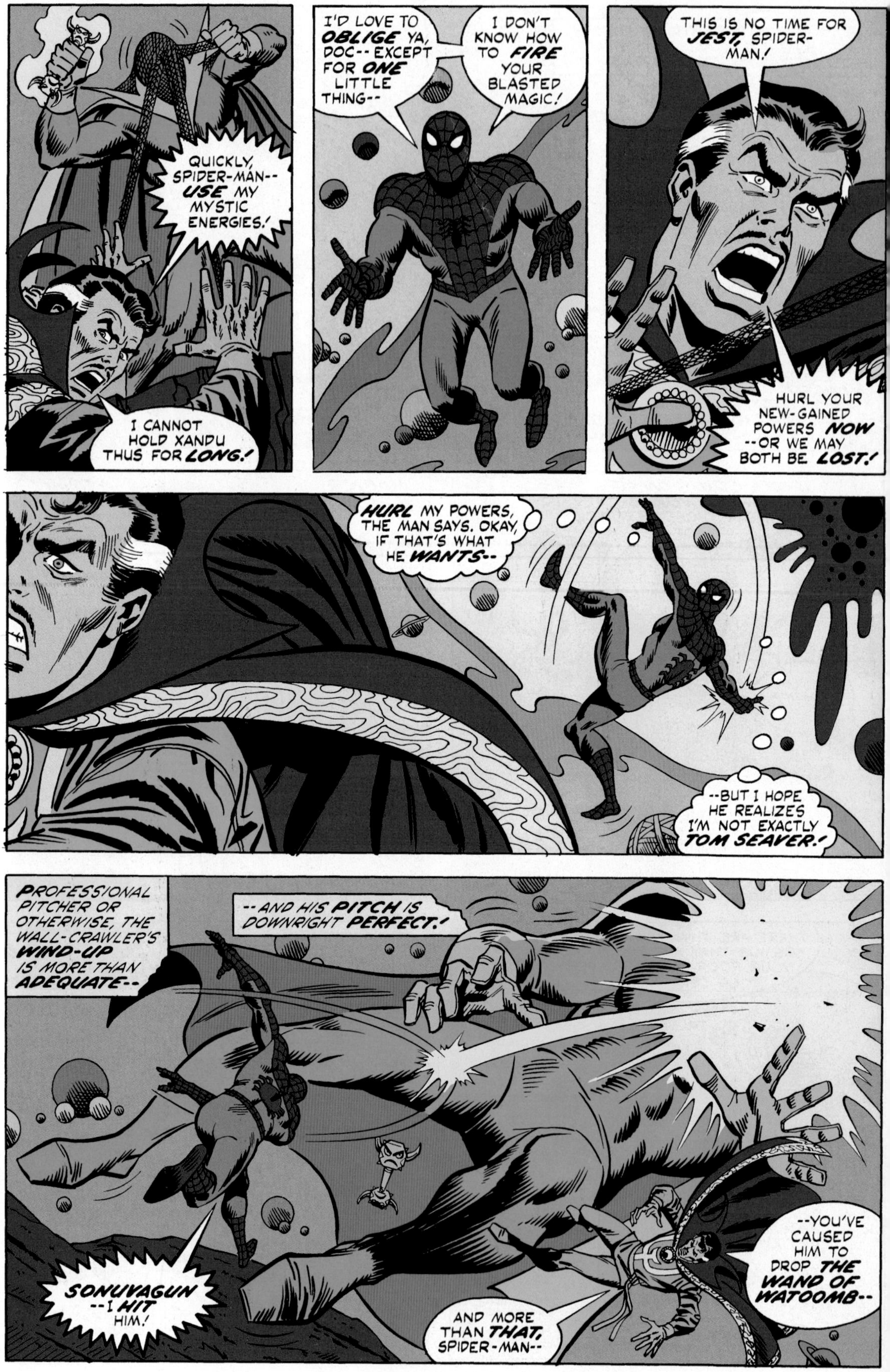
QUICKLY, SPIDER-MAN-- USE MY MYSTIC ENERGIES!
I CANNOT HOLD XANDU THUS FOR LONG!
I'D LOVE TO OBLIGE YA, DOC--EXCEPT FOR ONE LITTLE THING--
I DON'T KNOW HOW TO FIRE YOUR BLASTED MAGIC!
THIS IS NO TIME FOR JEST, SPIDER-MAN!
HURL YOUR NEW-GAINED POWERS NOW --OR WE MAY BOTH BE LOST!
HURL MY POWERS, THE MAN SAYS. OKAY, IF THAT'S WHAT HE WANTS--
--BUT I HOPE HE REALIZES I'M NOT EXACTLY TOM SEAVER!
PROFESSIONAL PITCHER OR OTHERWISE, THE WALL-CRAWLER'S WIND-UP IS MORE THAN ADEQUATE--
--AND HIS PITCH IS DOWNRIGHT PERFECT!
SONUVAGUN --I HIT HIM!
AND MORE THAN THAT, SPIDER-MAN--
--YOU'VE CAUSED HIM TO DROP THE WAND OF WATOOMB--

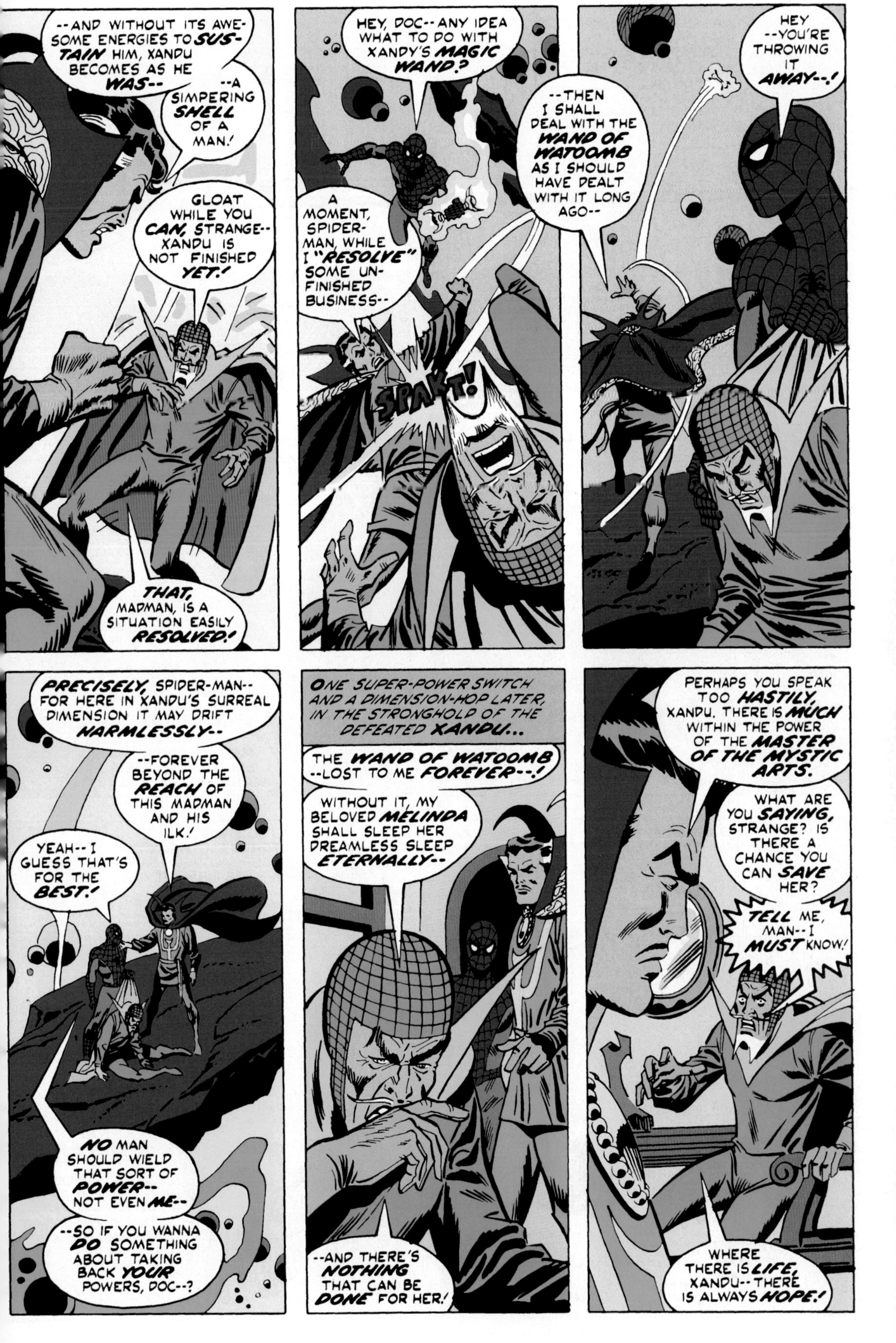
--AND WITHOUT ITS AWESOME ENERGIES TO SUSTAIN HIM, XANDU BECOMES AS HE WAS--
--A SIMPERING SHELL OF A MAN.!
GLOAT WHILE YOU CAN, STRANGE-- XANDU IS NOT FINISHED YET.!
THAT, MADMAN, IS A SITUATION EASILY RESOLVED!
HEY, DOC--ANY IDEA WHAT TO DO WITH XANDY'S MAGIC WAND?
A MOMENT, SPIDER-MAN, WHILE I "RESOLVE" SOME UNFINISHED BUSINESS--
SPAKT!
--THEN I SHALL DEAL WITH THE WAND OF WATOOMB AS I SHOULD HAVE DEALT WITH IT LONG AGO--
HEY --YOU'RE THROWING IT AWAY--!
PRECISELY, SPIDER-MAN-- FOR HERE IN XANDU'S SURREAL DIMENSION IT MAY DRIFT HARMLESSLY--
--FOREVER BEYOND THE REACH OF THIS MADMAN AND HIS ILK.!
YEAH--I GUESS THAT'S FOR THE BEST.!
NO MAN SHOULD WIELD THAT SORT OF POWER-- NOT EVEN ME--
--SO IF YOU WANNA DO SOMETHING ABOUT TAKING BACK YOUR POWERS, DOC--?
ONE SUPER-POWER SWITCH AND A DIMENSION-HOP LATER, IN THE STRONGHOLD OF THE DEFEATED XANDU...
THE WAND OF WATOOMB --LOST TO ME FOREVER--!
WITHOUT IT, MY BELOVED MELINDA SHALL SLEEP HER DREAMLESS SLEEP ETERNALLY--
--AND THERE'S NOTHING THAT CAN BE DONE FOR HER!
PERHAPS YOU SPEAK TOO HASTILY, XANDU. THERE IS MUCH WITHIN THE POWER OF THE MASTER OF THE MYSTIC ARTS.
WHAT ARE YOU SAYING, STRANGE? IS THERE A CHANCE YOU CAN SAVE HER?
TELL ME, MAN--I MUST KNOW!
WHERE THERE IS LIFE, XANDU--THERE IS ALWAYS HOPE!

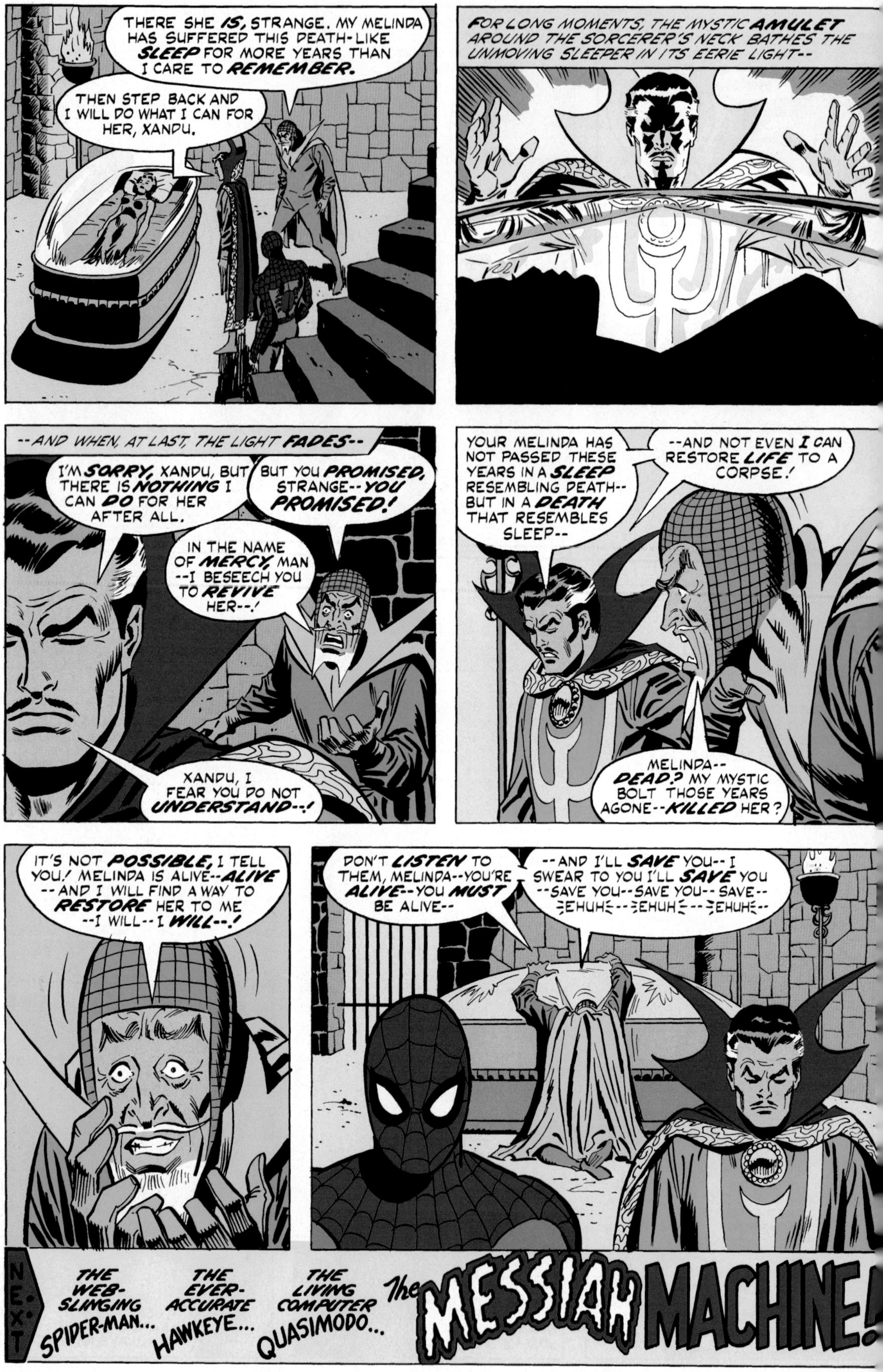
THERE SHE IS, STRANGE. MY MELINDA HAS SUFFERED THIS DEATH-LIKE SLEEP FOR MORE YEARS THAN I CARE TO REMEMBER.
THEN STEP BACK AND I WILL DO WHAT I CAN FOR HER, XANDU.
FOR LONG MOMENTS, THE MYSTIC AMULET AROUND THE SORCERER'S NECK BATHES THE UNMOVING SLEEPER IN ITS EERIE LIGHT--
--AND WHEN, AT LAST, THE LIGHT FADES--
I'M SORRY, XANDU, BUT THERE IS NOTHING I CAN DO FOR HER AFTER ALL.
BUT YOU PROMISED, STRANGE--YOU PROMISED!
IN THE NAME OF MERCY, MAN --I BESEECH YOU TO REVIVE HER--!
XANDU, I FEAR YOU DO NOT UNDERSTAND--!
YOUR MELINDA HAS NOT PASSED THESE YEARS IN A SLEEP RESEMBLING DEATH-- BUT IN A DEATH THAT RESEMBLES SLEEP--
--AND NOT EVEN I CAN RESTORE LIFE TO A CORPSE!
MELINDA-- DEAD? MY MYSTIC BOLT THOSE YEARS AGONE--KILLED HER?
IT'S NOT POSSIBLE, I TELL YOU! MELINDA IS ALIVE--ALIVE --AND I WILL FIND A WAY TO RESTORE HER TO ME --I WILL--I WILL--!
DON'T LISTEN TO THEM, MELINDA--YOU'RE ALIVE--YOU MUST BE ALIVE--
--AND I'LL SAVE YOU-- I SWEAR TO YOU I'LL SAVE YOU --SAVE YOU--SAVE YOU-- SAVE-- EHUH--EHUH--EHUH--
NEXT
THE WEB-SLINGING SPIDER-MAN...
THE EVER-ACCURATE HAWKEYE...
THE LIVING COMPUTER QUASIMODO...
The MESSIAH MACHINE!

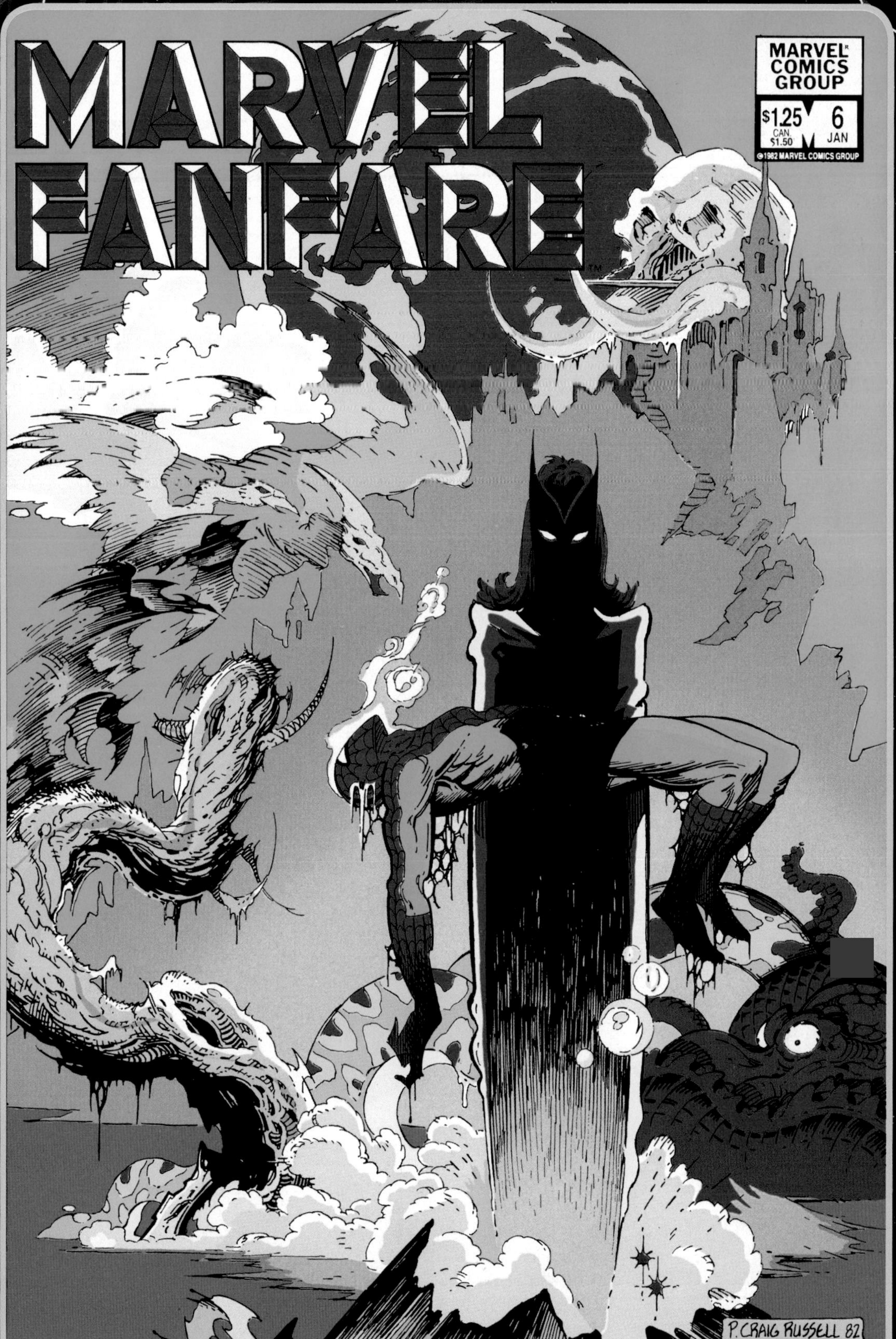
MARVEL FANFARE
MARVEL COMICS GROUP
$1.25 CAN. $1.50
6 JAN
©1982 MARVEL COMICS GROUP
P. CRAIG RUSSELL 82

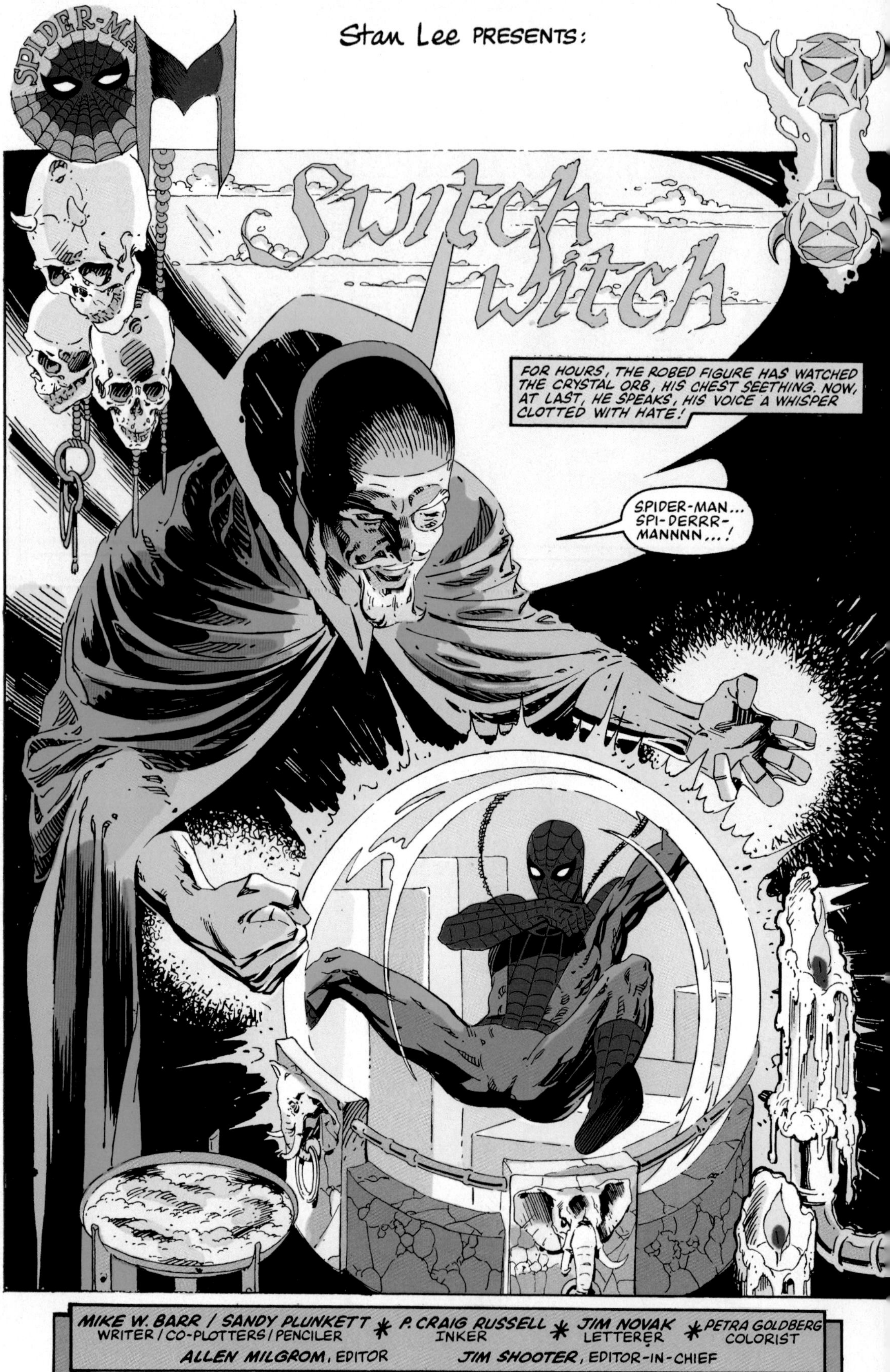
Stan Lee PRESENTS:
SPIDER-MAN
Switch witch
FOR HOURS, THE ROBED FIGURE HAS WATCHED THE CRYSTAL ORB, HIS CHEST SEETHING. NOW, AT LAST, HE SPEAKS, HIS VOICE A WHISPER CLOTTED WITH HATE!
SPIDER-MAN... SPI-DERRR-MANNNN...!
MIKE W. BARR / SANDY PLUNKETT WRITER / CO-PLOTTERS / PENCILER * P. CRAIG RUSSELL INKER * JIM NOVAK LETTERER * PETRA GOLDBERG COLORIST
ALLEN MILGROM, EDITOR JIM SHOOTER, EDITOR-IN-CHIEF

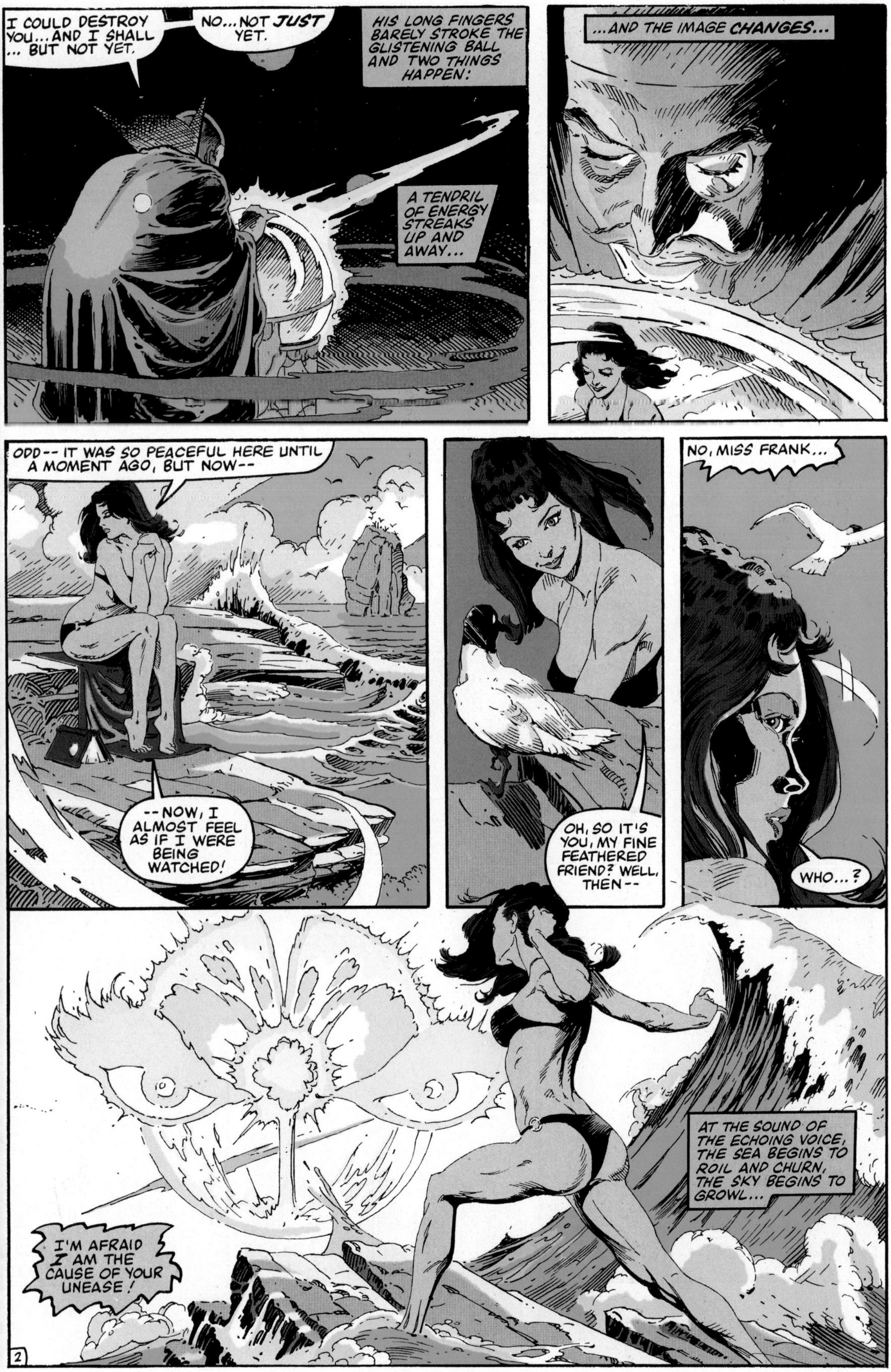
I COULD DESTROY YOU... AND I SHALL ... BUT NOT YET.
NO... NOT JUST YET.
HIS LONG FINGERS BARELY STROKE THE GLISTENING BALL AND TWO THINGS HAPPEN:
A TENDRIL OF ENERGY STREAKS UP AND AWAY...
...AND THE IMAGE CHANGES...
ODD-- IT WAS SO PEACEFUL HERE UNTIL A MOMENT AGO, BUT NOW--
--NOW, I ALMOST FEEL AS IF I WERE BEING WATCHED!
OH, SO IT'S YOU, MY FINE FEATHERED FRIEND? WELL, THEN--
NO, MISS FRANK...
WHO...?
AT THE SOUND OF THE ECHOING VOICE, THE SEA BEGINS TO ROIL AND CHURN, THE SKY BEGINS TO GROWL...
I'M AFRAID I AM THE CAUSE OF YOUR UNEASE!
2

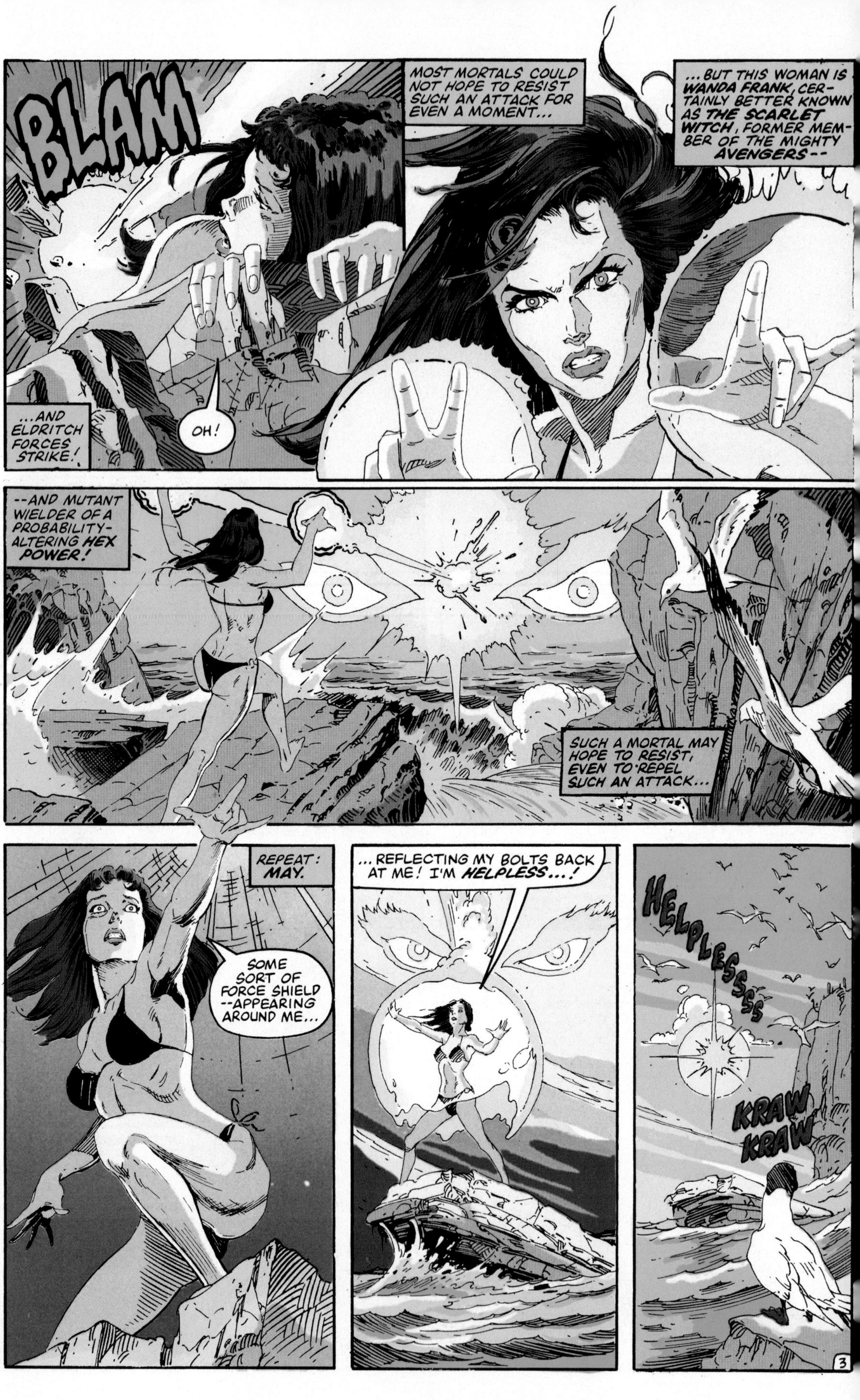
BLAM
...AND ELDRITCH FORCES STRIKE!
OH!
MOST MORTALS COULD NOT HOPE TO RESIST SUCH AN ATTACK FOR EVEN A MOMENT...
...BUT THIS WOMAN IS WANDA FRANK, CERTAINLY BETTER KNOWN AS THE SCARLET WITCH, FORMER MEMBER OF THE MIGHTY AVENGERS--
--AND MUTANT WIELDER OF A PROBABILITY-ALTERING HEX POWER!
SUCH A MORTAL MAY HOPE TO RESIST, EVEN TO REPEL SUCH AN ATTACK...
REPEAT: MAY.
SOME SORT OF FORCE SHIELD --APPEARING AROUND ME...
...REFLECTING MY BOLTS BACK AT ME! I'M HELPLESS...!
HELPLESSSSS
KRAW KRAW
3

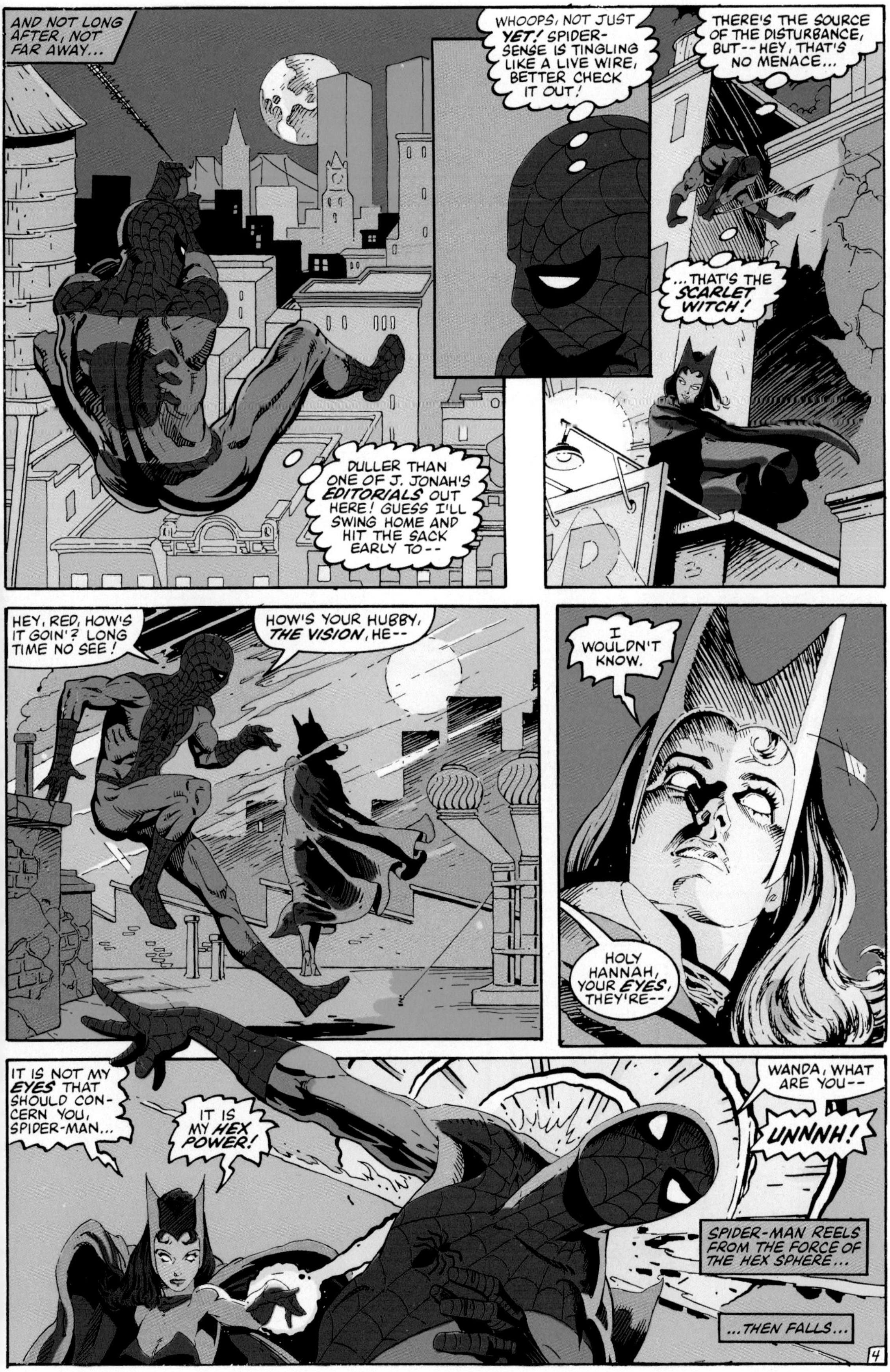
AND NOT LONG AFTER, NOT FAR AWAY...
DULLER THAN ONE OF J. JONAH'S EDITORIALS OUT HERE! GUESS I'LL SWING HOME AND HIT THE SACK EARLY TO--
WHOOPS, NOT JUST YET! SPIDER-SENSE IS TINGLING LIKE A LIVE WIRE, BETTER CHECK IT OUT!
THERE'S THE SOURCE OF THE DISTURBANCE, BUT--HEY, THAT'S NO MENACE...
...THAT'S THE SCARLET WITCH!
HEY, RED, HOW'S IT GOIN'? LONG TIME NO SEE!
HOW'S YOUR HUBBY, THE VISION, HE--
I WOULDN'T KNOW.
HOLY HANNAH, YOUR EYES, THEY'RE--
IT IS NOT MY EYES THAT SHOULD CONCERN YOU, SPIDER-MAN...
IT IS MY HEX POWER!
WANDA, WHAT ARE YOU--
UNNNH!
SPIDER-MAN REELS FROM THE FORCE OF THE HEX SPHERE...
...THEN FALLS...
4

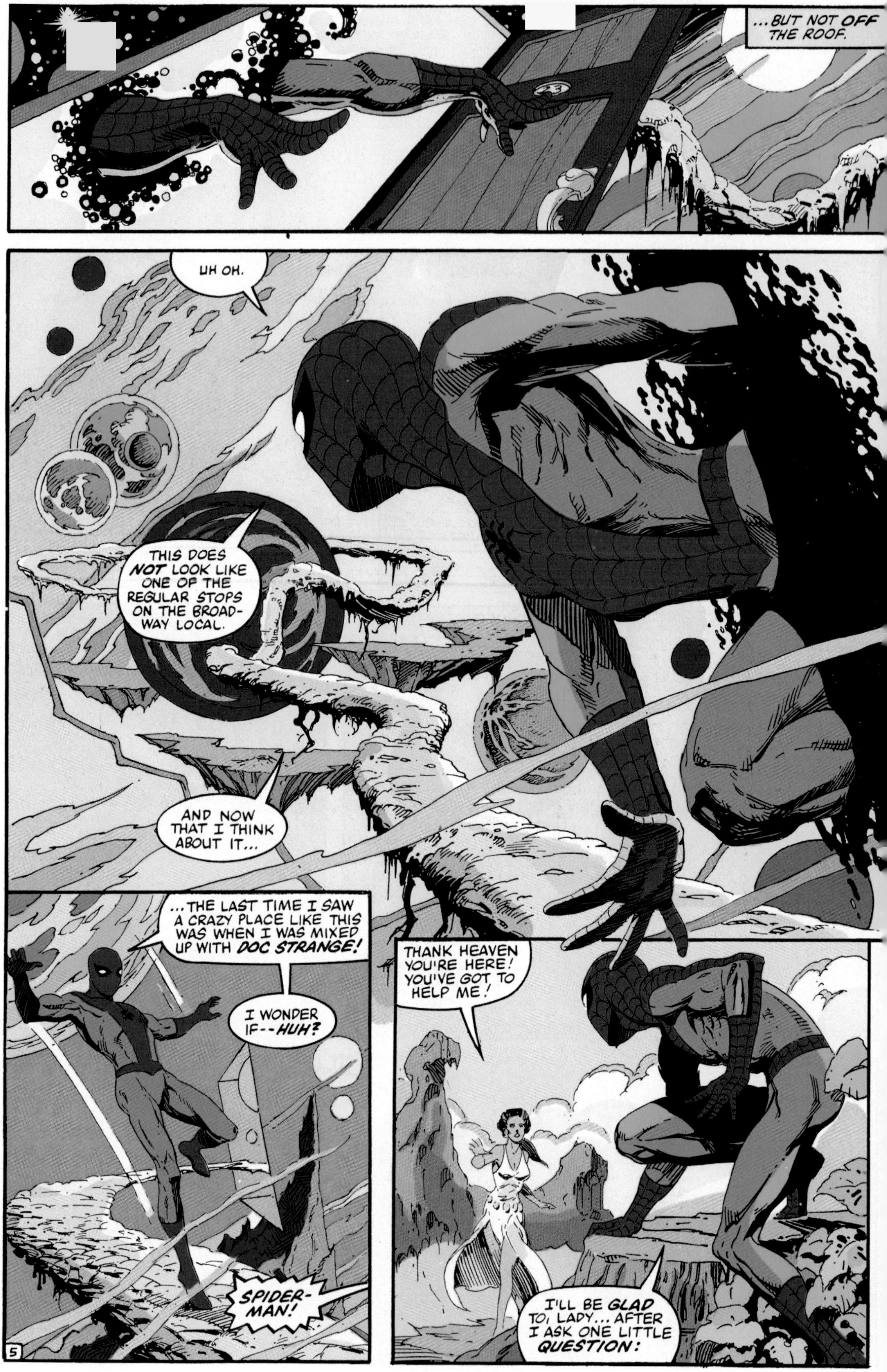
...BUT NOT **OFF** THE ROOF.
UH OH.
THIS DOES **NOT** LOOK LIKE ONE OF THE REGULAR **STOPS** ON THE BROADWAY LOCAL.
AND NOW THAT I THINK ABOUT IT...
...THE LAST TIME I SAW A CRAZY PLACE LIKE THIS WAS WHEN I WAS MIXED UP WITH **DOC STRANGE!**
I WONDER IF--**HUH?**
SPIDER-MAN!
THANK HEAVEN YOU'RE HERE! YOU'VE GOT TO HELP ME!
I'LL BE **GLAD** TO, LADY... AFTER I ASK ONE LITTLE **QUESTION:**
5

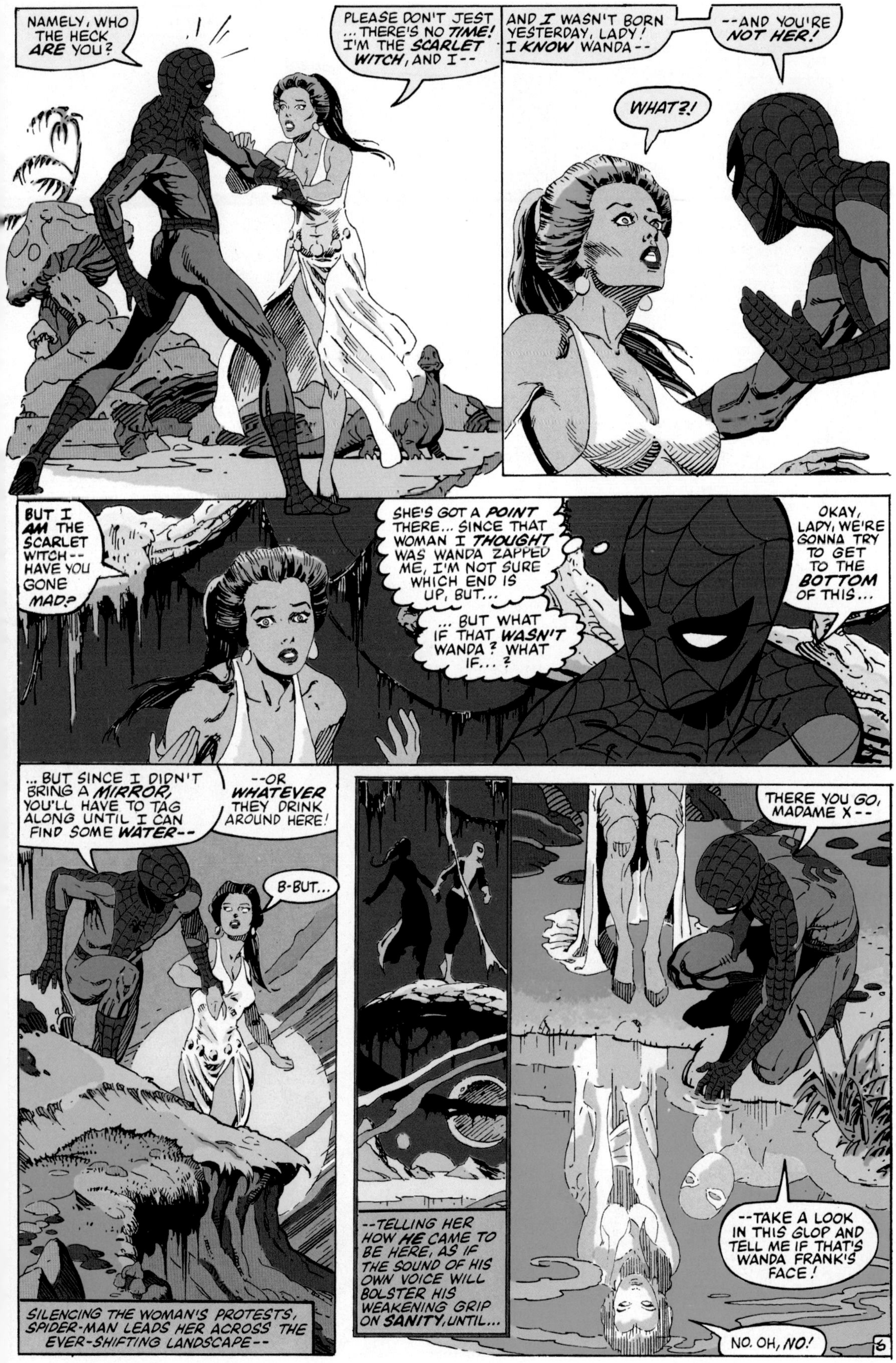
NAMELY, WHO THE HECK ARE YOU?
PLEASE DON'T JEST ...THERE'S NO TIME! I'M THE SCARLET WITCH, AND I--
AND I WASN'T BORN YESTERDAY, LADY! I KNOW WANDA--
--AND YOU'RE NOT HER!
WHAT?!
BUT I AM THE SCARLET WITCH--HAVE YOU GONE MAD?
SHE'S GOT A POINT THERE... SINCE THAT WOMAN I THOUGHT WAS WANDA ZAPPED ME, I'M NOT SURE WHICH END IS UP, BUT...
... BUT WHAT IF THAT WASN'T WANDA? WHAT IF...?
OKAY, LADY, WE'RE GONNA TRY TO GET TO THE BOTTOM OF THIS...
... BUT SINCE I DIDN'T BRING A MIRROR, YOU'LL HAVE TO TAG ALONG UNTIL I CAN FIND SOME WATER--
--OR WHATEVER THEY DRINK AROUND HERE!
B-BUT...
SILENCING THE WOMAN'S PROTESTS, SPIDER-MAN LEADS HER ACROSS THE EVER-SHIFTING LANDSCAPE--
--TELLING HER HOW HE CAME TO BE HERE, AS IF THE SOUND OF HIS OWN VOICE WILL BOLSTER HIS WEAKENING GRIP ON SANITY, UNTIL...
THERE YOU GO, MADAME X--
--TAKE A LOOK IN THIS GLOP AND TELL ME IF THAT'S WANDA FRANK'S FACE!
NO. OH, NO!
6

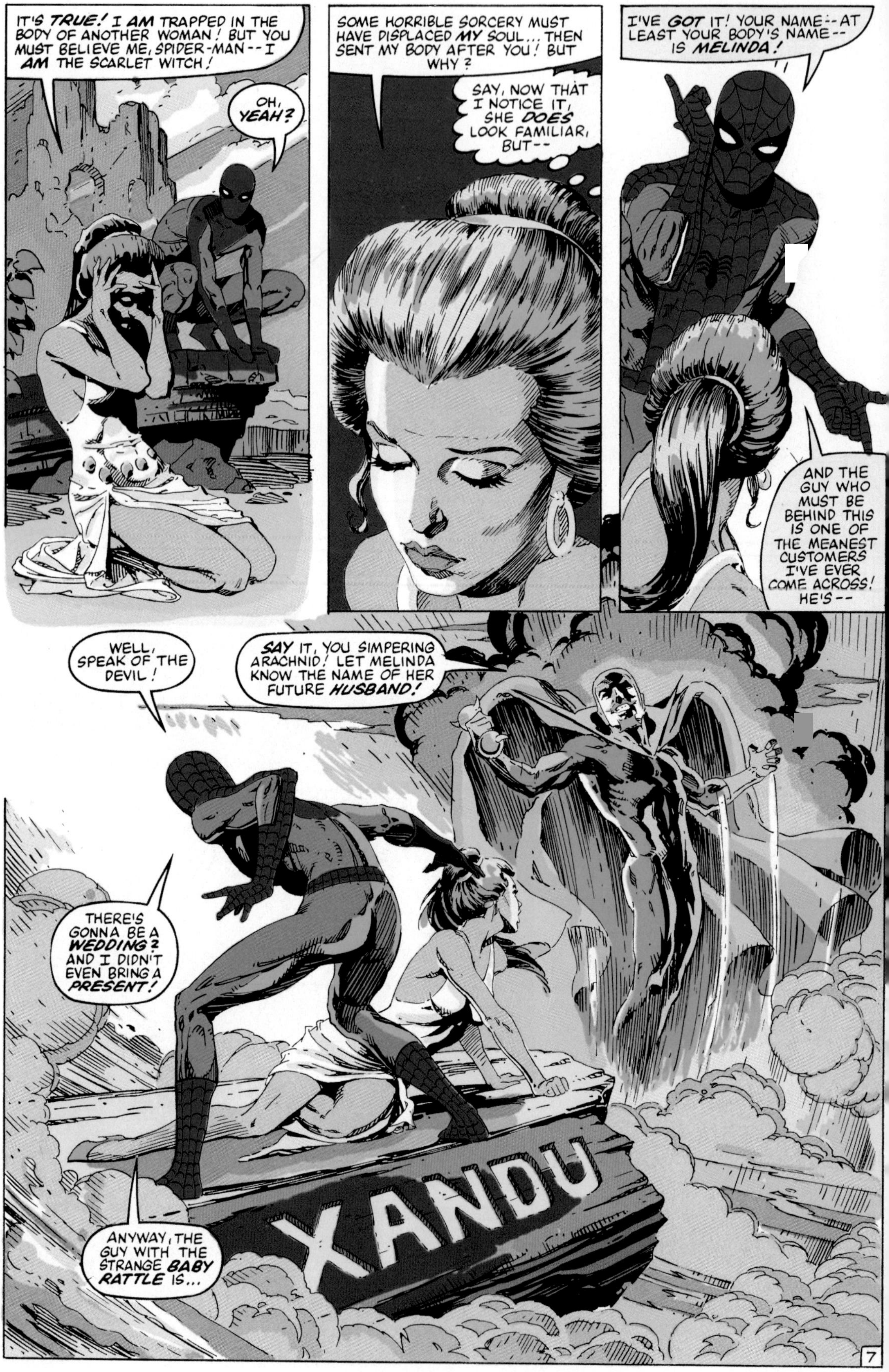

IT'S TRUE! I AM TRAPPED IN THE BODY OF ANOTHER WOMAN! BUT YOU MUST BELIEVE ME, SPIDER-MAN--I AM THE SCARLET WITCH!
OH, YEAH?
SOME HORRIBLE SORCERY MUST HAVE DISPLACED MY SOUL... THEN SENT MY BODY AFTER YOU! BUT WHY?
SAY, NOW THAT I NOTICE IT, SHE DOES LOOK FAMILIAR, BUT--
I'VE GOT IT! YOUR NAME--AT LEAST YOUR BODY'S NAME--IS MELINDA!
AND THE GUY WHO MUST BE BEHIND THIS IS ONE OF THE MEANEST CUSTOMERS I'VE EVER COME ACROSS! HE'S--
WELL, SPEAK OF THE DEVIL!
SAY IT, YOU SIMPERING ARACHNID! LET MELINDA KNOW THE NAME OF HER FUTURE HUSBAND!
THERE'S GONNA BE A WEDDING? AND I DIDN'T EVEN BRING A PRESENT!
ANYWAY, THE GUY WITH THE STRANGE BABY RATTLE IS...
XANDU
7

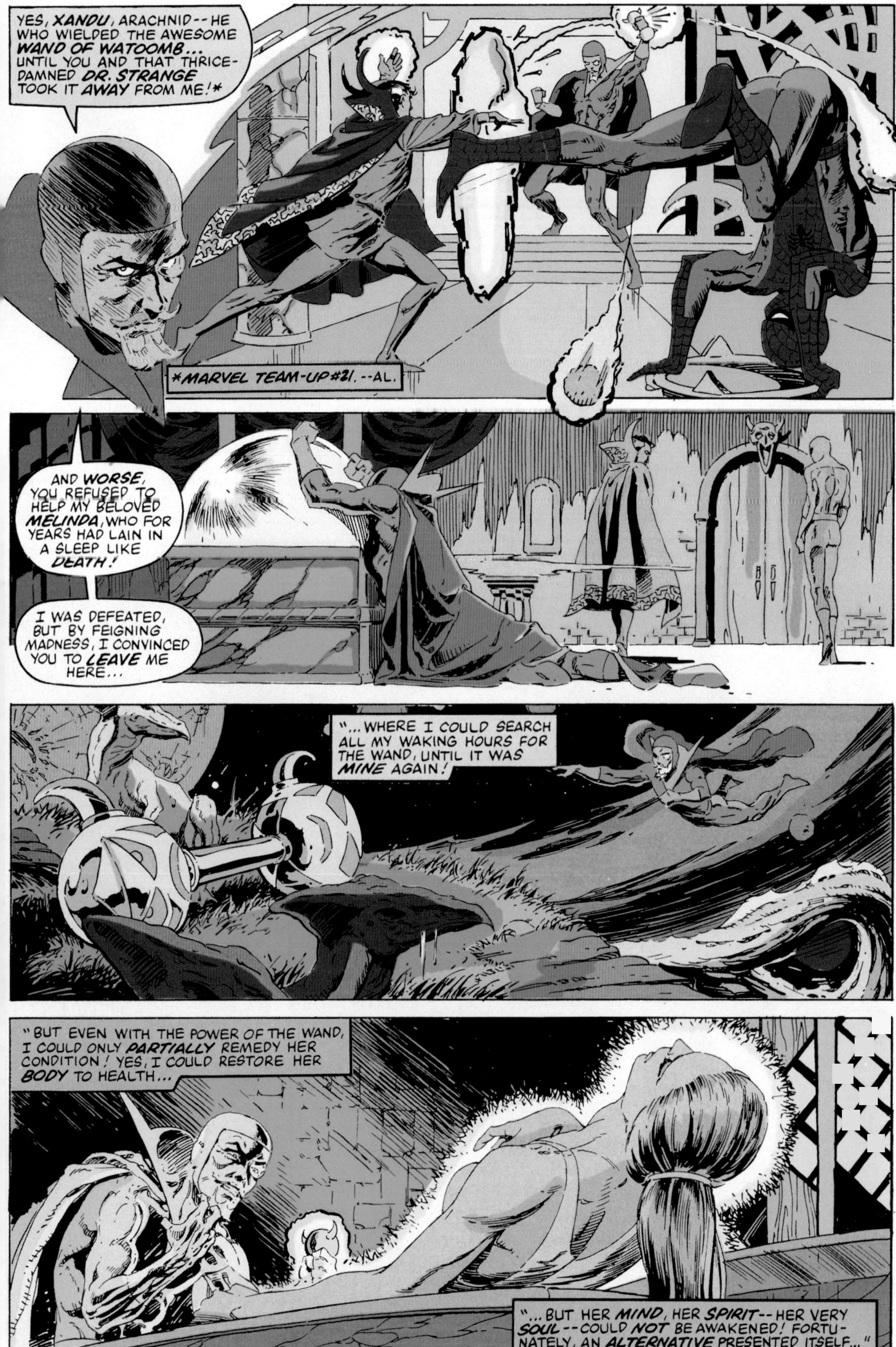
YES, XANDU, ARACHNID--HE WHO WIELDED THE AWESOME WAND OF WATOOMB... UNTIL YOU AND THAT THRICE-DAMNED DR. STRANGE TOOK IT AWAY FROM ME!*
*MARVEL TEAM-UP #21. --AL.
AND WORSE, YOU REFUSED TO HELP MY BELOVED MELINDA, WHO FOR YEARS HAD LAIN IN A SLEEP LIKE DEATH!
I WAS DEFEATED, BUT BY FEIGNING MADNESS, I CONVINCED YOU TO LEAVE ME HERE...
"...WHERE I COULD SEARCH ALL MY WAKING HOURS FOR THE WAND, UNTIL IT WAS MINE AGAIN!
"BUT EVEN WITH THE POWER OF THE WAND, I COULD ONLY PARTIALLY REMEDY HER CONDITION! YES, I COULD RESTORE HER BODY TO HEALTH...
"...BUT HER MIND, HER SPIRIT--HER VERY SOUL--COULD NOT BE AWAKENED! FORTU-NATELY, AN ALTERNATIVE PRESENTED ITSELF..."
8

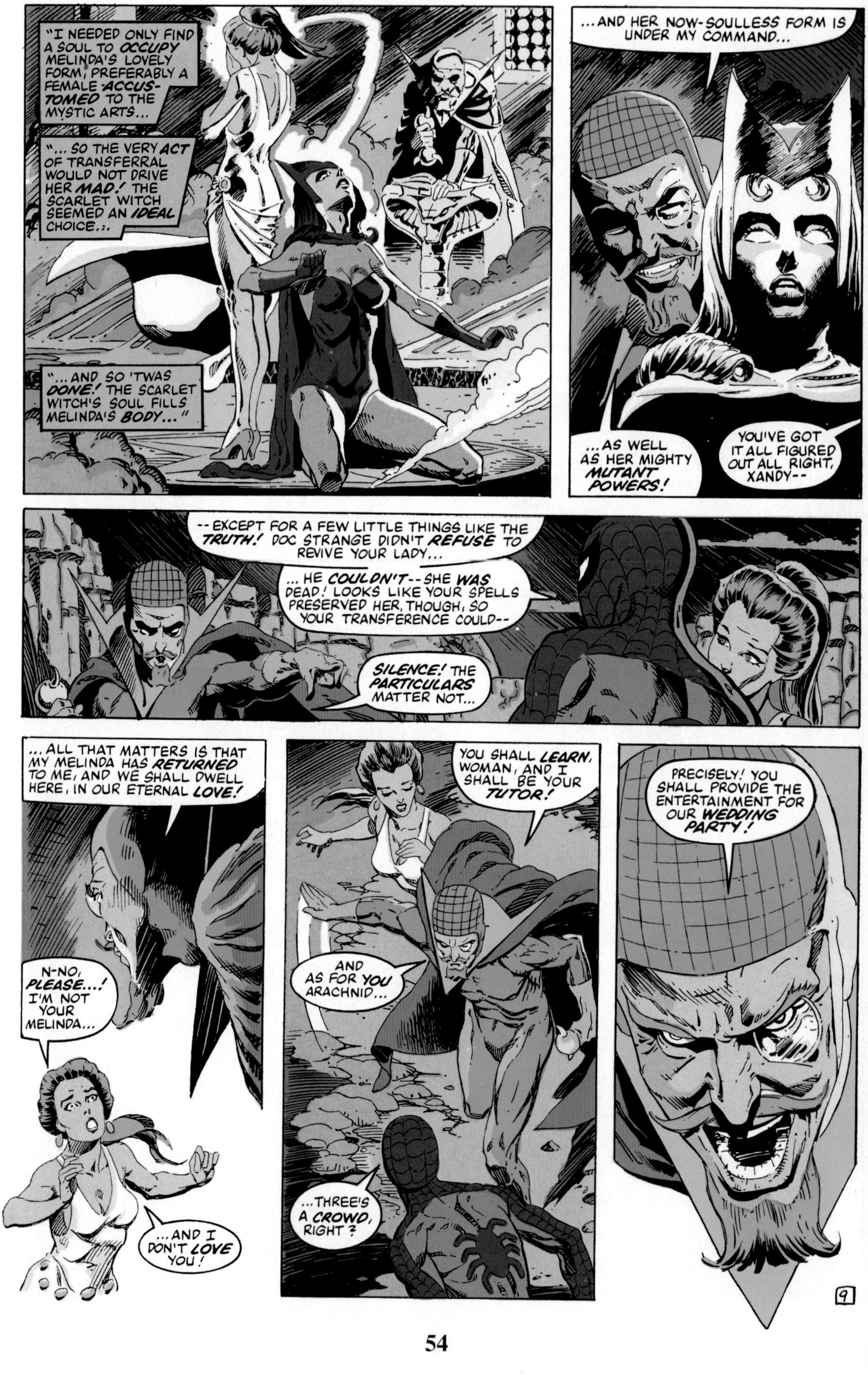
"I NEEDED ONLY FIND A SOUL TO OCCUPY MELINDA'S LOVELY FORM, PREFERABLY A FEMALE ACCUSTOMED TO THE MYSTIC ARTS...
"...SO THE VERY ACT OF TRANSFERRAL WOULD NOT DRIVE HER MAD! THE SCARLET WITCH SEEMED AN IDEAL CHOICE...
"...AND SO 'TWAS DONE! THE SCARLET WITCH'S SOUL FILLS MELINDA'S BODY..."
...AND HER NOW-SOULLESS FORM IS UNDER MY COMMAND...
...AS WELL AS HER MIGHTY MUTANT POWERS!
YOU'VE GOT IT ALL FIGURED OUT ALL RIGHT, XANDY--
--EXCEPT FOR A FEW LITTLE THINGS LIKE THE TRUTH! DOC STRANGE DIDN'T REFUSE TO REVIVE YOUR LADY...
...HE COULDN'T--SHE WAS DEAD! LOOKS LIKE YOUR SPELLS PRESERVED HER, THOUGH, SO YOUR TRANSFERENCE COULD--
SILENCE! THE PARTICULARS MATTER NOT...
...ALL THAT MATTERS IS THAT MY MELINDA HAS RETURNED TO ME, AND WE SHALL DWELL HERE, IN OUR ETERNAL LOVE!
N-NO, PLEASE...! I'M NOT YOUR MELINDA...
...AND I DON'T LOVE YOU!
YOU SHALL LEARN, WOMAN, AND I SHALL BE YOUR TUTOR!
AND AS FOR YOU ARACHNID...
...THREE'S A CROWD, RIGHT?
PRECISELY! YOU SHALL PROVIDE THE ENTERTAINMENT FOR OUR WEDDING PARTY!
9

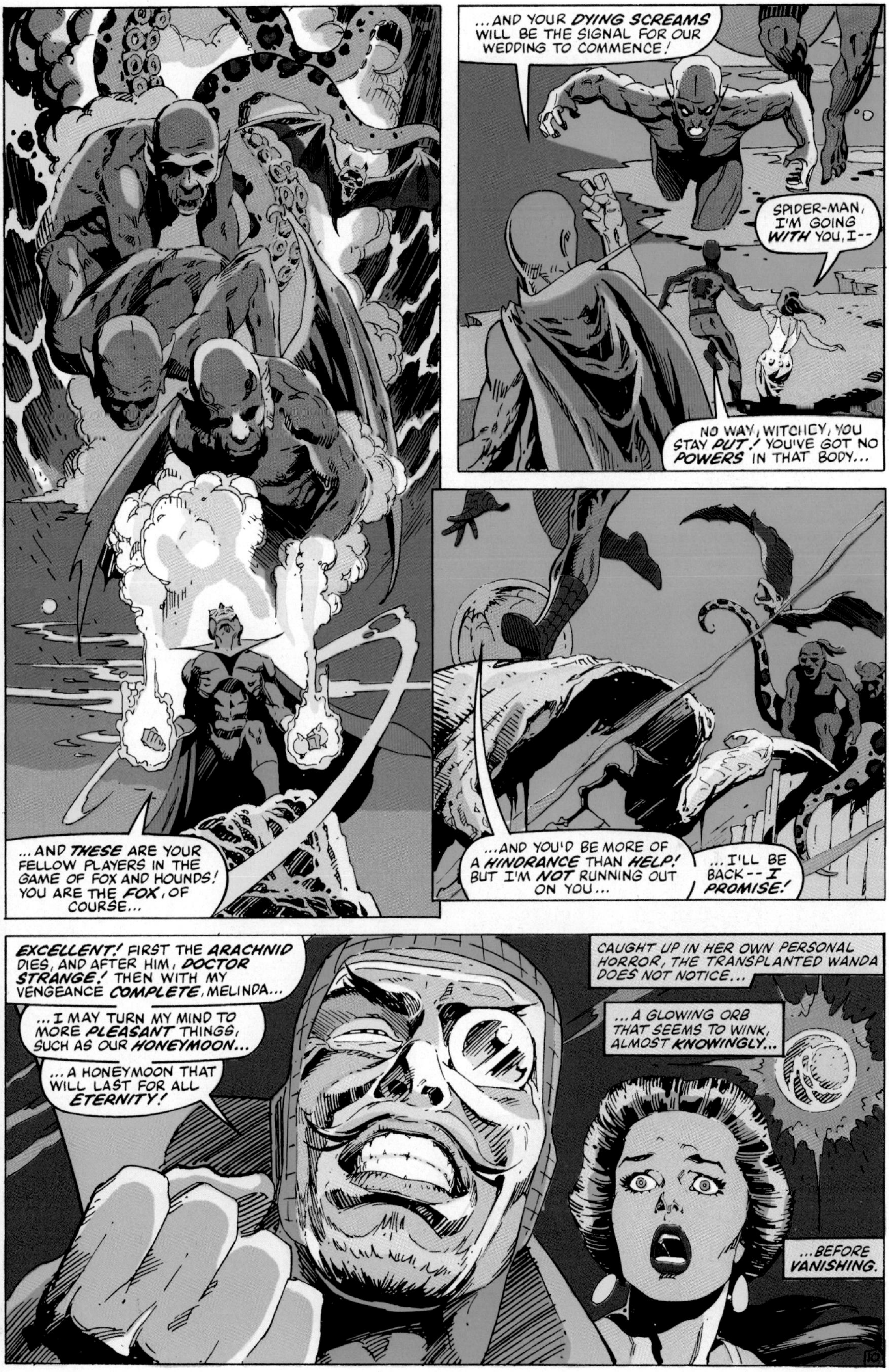
...AND YOUR DYING SCREAMS WILL BE THE SIGNAL FOR OUR WEDDING TO COMMENCE!
SPIDER-MAN, I'M GOING WITH YOU, I--
NO WAY, WITCHCY, YOU STAY PUT! YOU'VE GOT NO POWERS IN THAT BODY...
...AND THESE ARE YOUR FELLOW PLAYERS IN THE GAME OF FOX AND HOUNDS! YOU ARE THE FOX, OF COURSE...
...AND YOU'D BE MORE OF A HINDRANCE THAN HELP! BUT I'M NOT RUNNING OUT ON YOU...
...I'LL BE BACK -- I PROMISE!
EXCELLENT! FIRST THE ARACHNID DIES, AND AFTER HIM, DOCTOR STRANGE! THEN WITH MY VENGEANCE COMPLETE, MELINDA...
...I MAY TURN MY MIND TO MORE PLEASANT THINGS, SUCH AS OUR HONEYMOON...
...A HONEYMOON THAT WILL LAST FOR ALL ETERNITY!
CAUGHT UP IN HER OWN PERSONAL HORROR, THE TRANSPLANTED WANDA DOES NOT NOTICE...
...A GLOWING ORB THAT SEEMS TO WINK, ALMOST KNOWINGLY...
...BEFORE VANISHING.

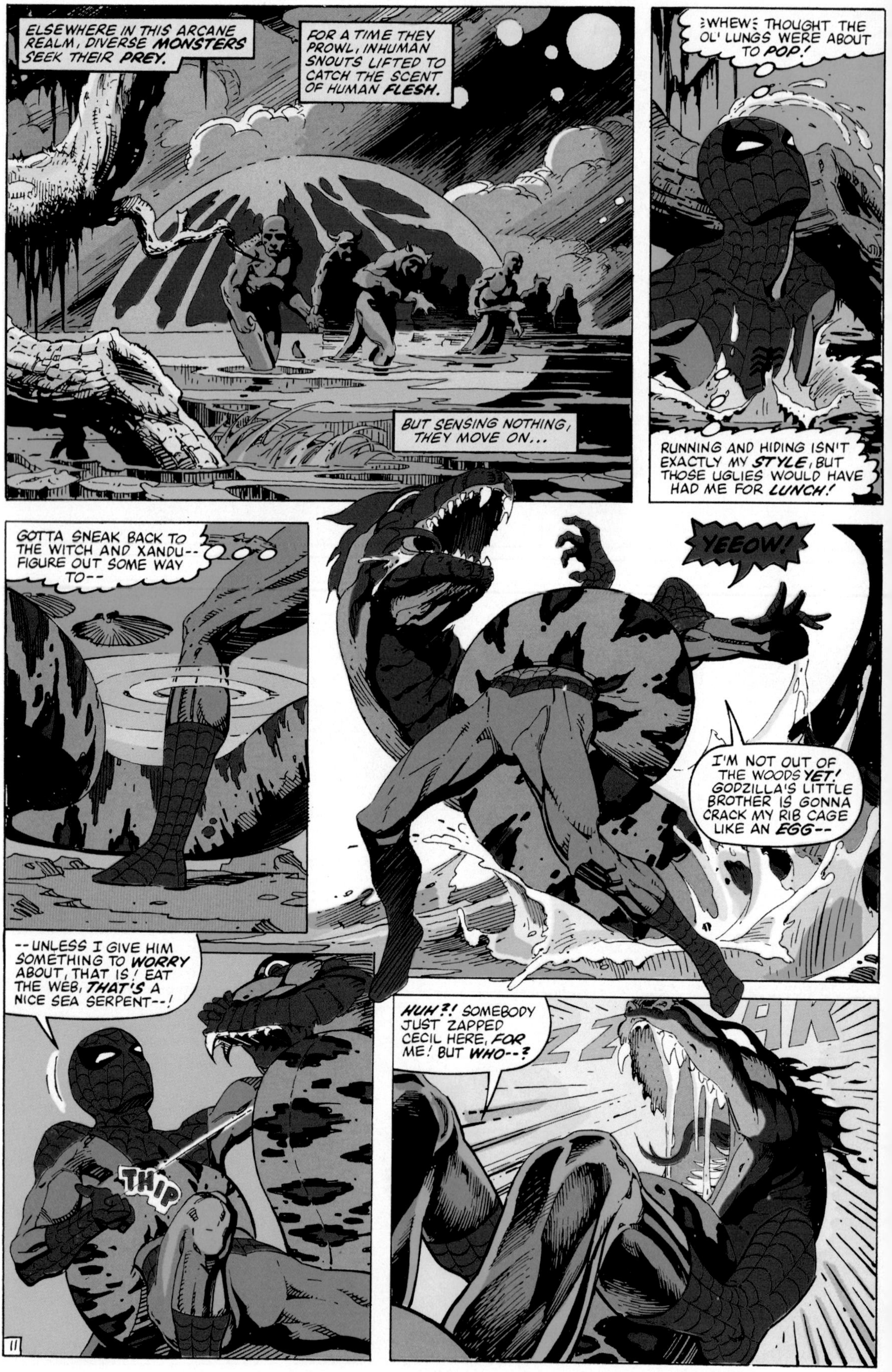
ELSEWHERE IN THIS ARCANE REALM, DIVERSE MONSTERS SEEK THEIR PREY.
FOR A TIME THEY PROWL, INHUMAN SNOUTS LIFTED TO CATCH THE SCENT OF HUMAN FLESH.
BUT SENSING NOTHING, THEY MOVE ON...
WHEW! THOUGHT THE OL' LUNGS WERE ABOUT TO POP!
RUNNING AND HIDING ISN'T EXACTLY MY STYLE, BUT THOSE UGLIES WOULD HAVE HAD ME FOR LUNCH!
GOTTA SNEAK BACK TO THE WITCH AND XANDU-- FIGURE OUT SOME WAY TO--
YEEOW!
I'M NOT OUT OF THE WOODS YET! GODZILLA'S LITTLE BROTHER IS GONNA CRACK MY RIB CAGE LIKE AN EGG--
--UNLESS I GIVE HIM SOMETHING TO WORRY ABOUT, THAT IS! EAT THE WEB, THAT'S A NICE SEA SERPENT--!
THIP
HUH?! SOMEBODY JUST ZAPPED CECIL HERE, FOR ME! BUT WHO--?
11

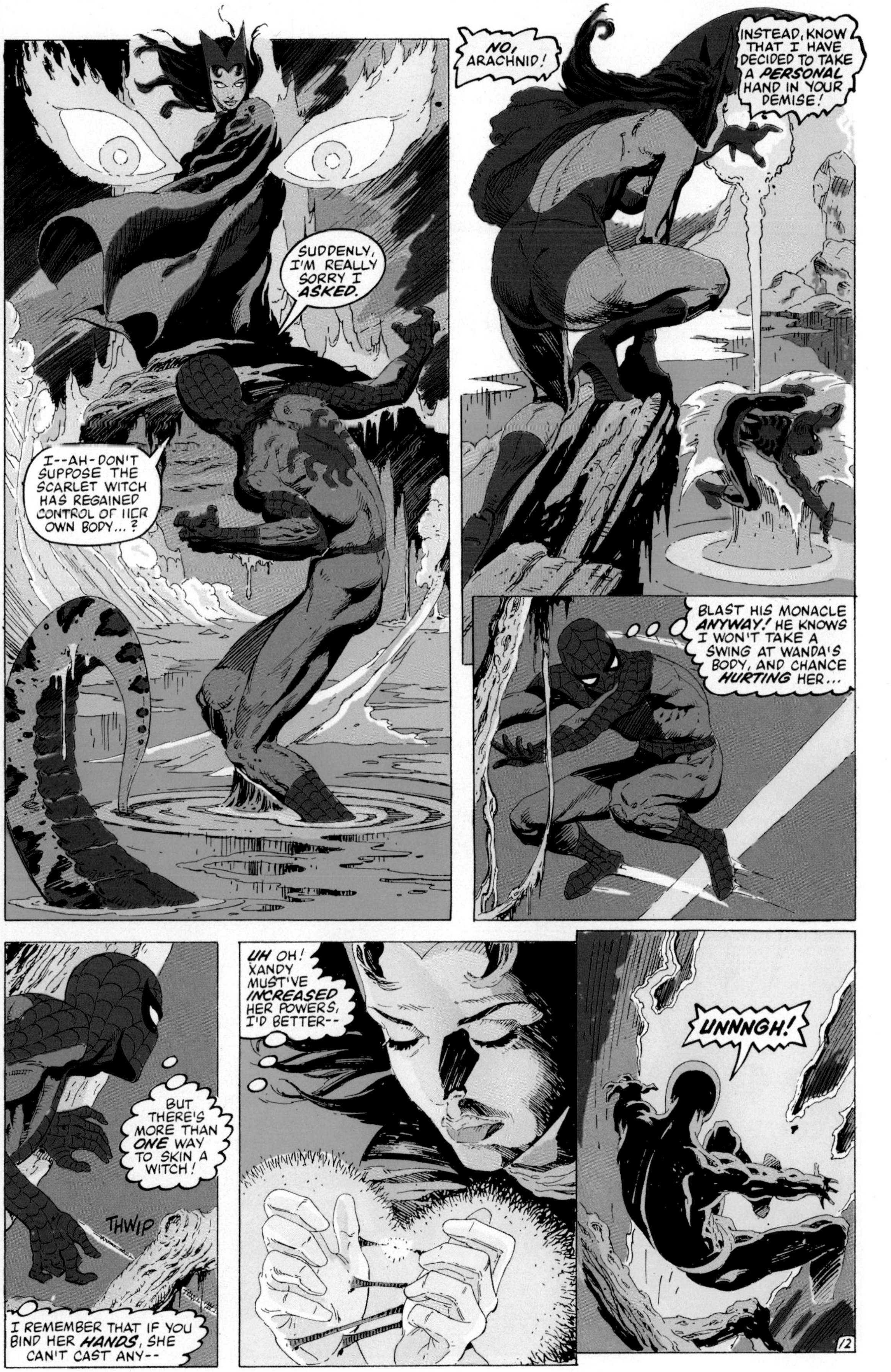
SUDDENLY, I'M REALLY SORRY I ASKED.
I--AH-DON'T SUPPOSE THE SCARLET WITCH HAS REGAINED CONTROL OF HER OWN BODY...?
NO, ARACHNID!
INSTEAD, KNOW THAT I HAVE DECIDED TO TAKE A PERSONAL HAND IN YOUR DEMISE!
BLAST HIS MONACLE ANYWAY! HE KNOWS I WON'T TAKE A SWING AT WANDA'S BODY, AND CHANCE HURTING HER...
BUT THERE'S MORE THAN ONE WAY TO SKIN A WITCH!
THWIP
I REMEMBER THAT IF YOU BIND HER HANDS, SHE CAN'T CAST ANY--
UH OH! XANDY MUST'VE INCREASED HER POWERS, I'D BETTER--
UNNNGH!
12

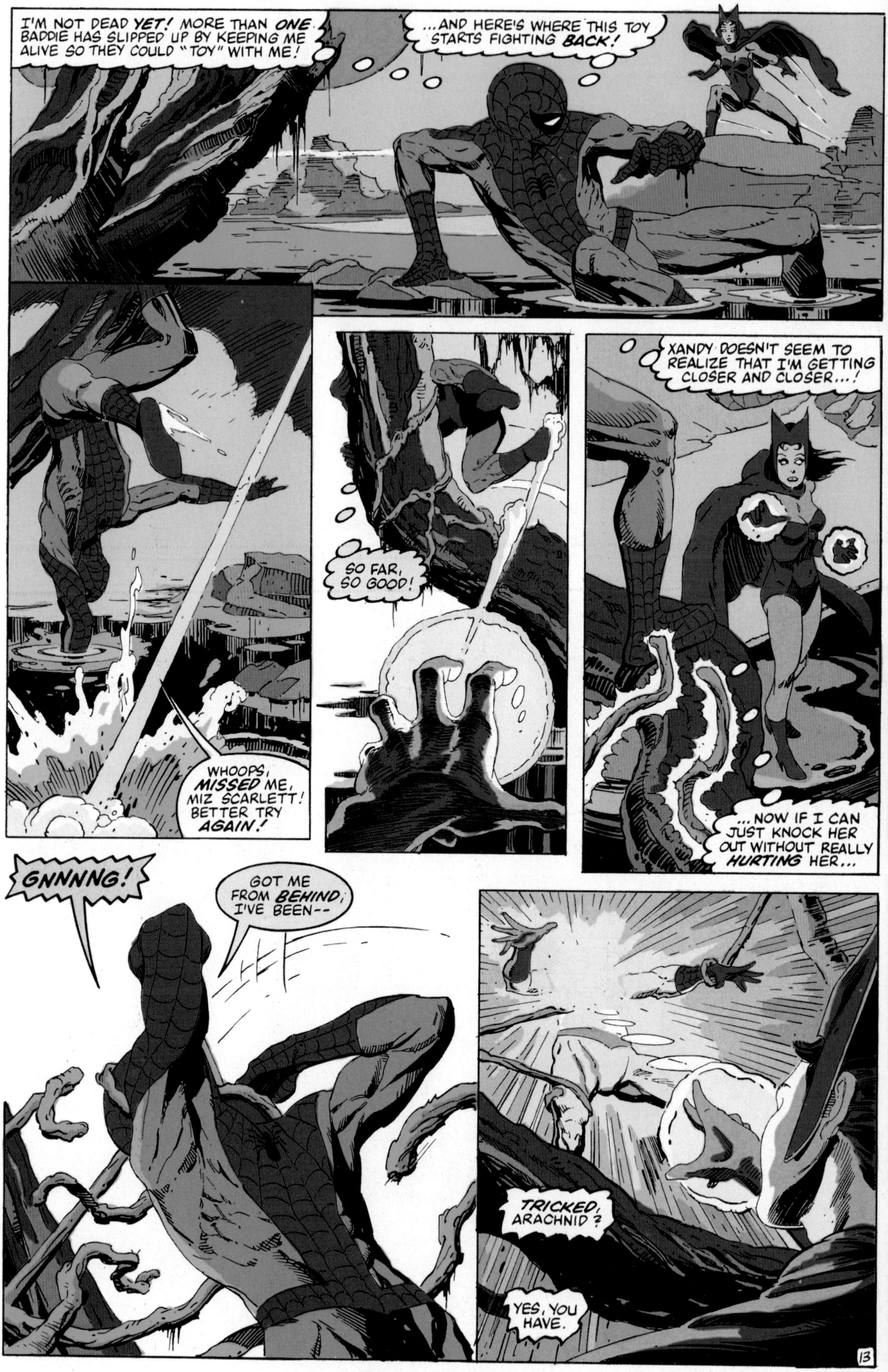

I'M NOT DEAD YET! MORE THAN ONE BADDIE HAS SLIPPED UP BY KEEPING ME ALIVE SO THEY COULD "TOY" WITH ME!
...AND HERE'S WHERE THIS TOY STARTS FIGHTING BACK!
WHOOPS, MISSED ME, MIZ SCARLETT! BETTER TRY AGAIN!
SO FAR, SO GOOD!
XANDY DOESN'T SEEM TO REALIZE THAT I'M GETTING CLOSER AND CLOSER...!
...NOW IF I CAN JUST KNOCK HER OUT WITHOUT REALLY HURTING HER...
GNNNNG!
GOT ME FROM BEHIND; I'VE BEEN--
TRICKED, ARACHNID?
YES, YOU HAVE.
13

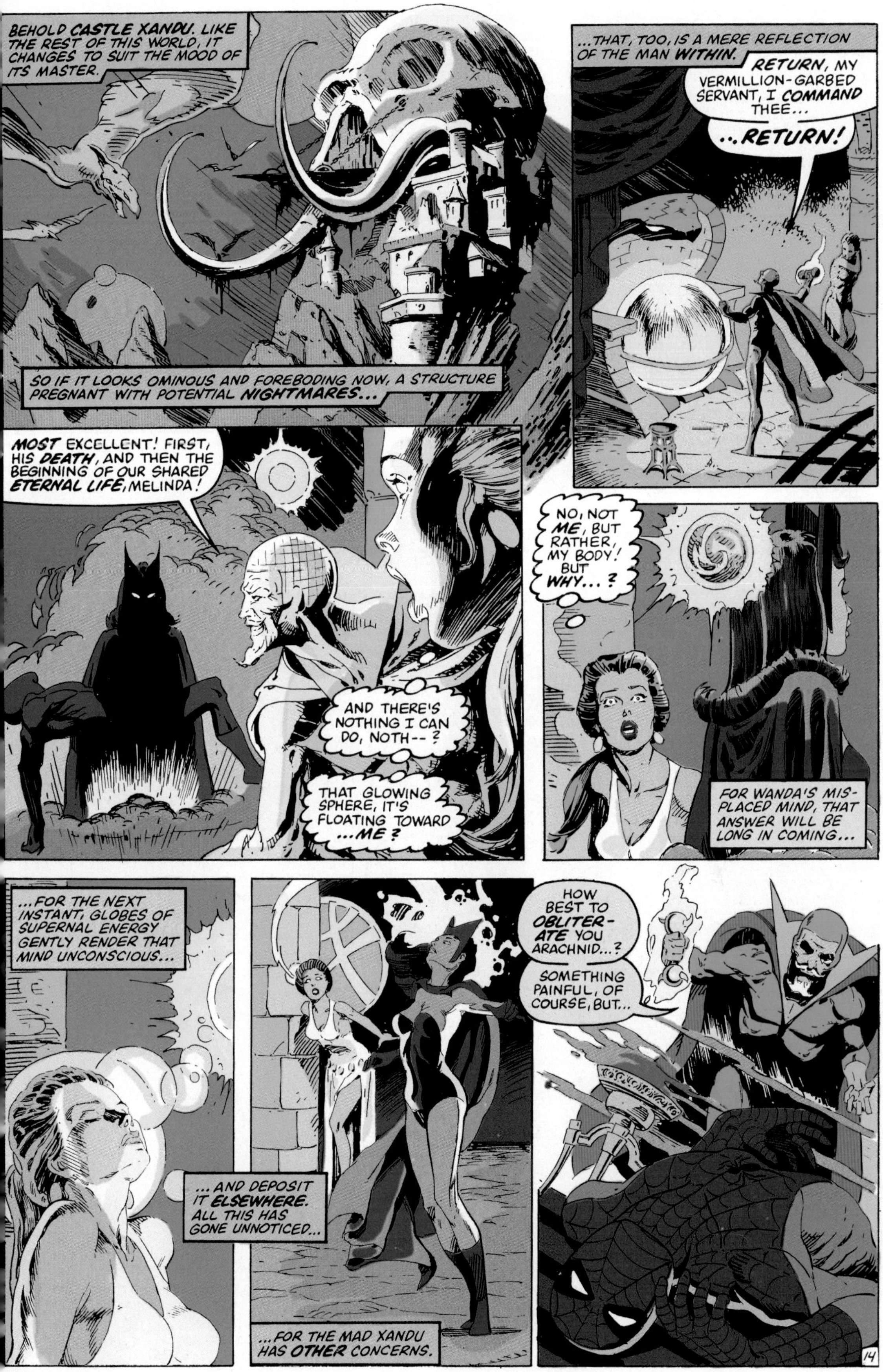
BEHOLD CASTLE XANDU. LIKE THE REST OF THIS WORLD, IT CHANGES TO SUIT THE MOOD OF ITS MASTER.
SO IF IT LOOKS OMINOUS AND FOREBODING NOW, A STRUCTURE PREGNANT WITH POTENTIAL NIGHTMARES...
...THAT, TOO, IS A MERE REFLECTION OF THE MAN WITHIN.
RETURN, MY VERMILLION-GARBED SERVANT, I COMMAND THEE...
...RETURN!
MOST EXCELLENT! FIRST, HIS DEATH, AND THEN THE BEGINNING OF OUR SHARED ETERNAL LIFE, MELINDA!
AND THERE'S NOTHING I CAN DO, NOTH-- ?
THAT GLOWING SPHERE, IT'S FLOATING TOWARD ...ME ?
NO, NOT ME, BUT RATHER, MY BODY! BUT WHY... ?
FOR WANDA'S MISPLACED MIND, THAT ANSWER WILL BE LONG IN COMING...
...FOR THE NEXT INSTANT, GLOBES OF SUPERNAL ENERGY GENTLY RENDER THAT MIND UNCONSCIOUS...
... AND DEPOSIT IT ELSEWHERE. ALL THIS HAS GONE UNNOTICED...
...FOR THE MAD XANDU HAS OTHER CONCERNS.
HOW BEST TO OBLITERATE YOU ARACHNID...?
SOMETHING PAINFUL, OF COURSE, BUT...
14

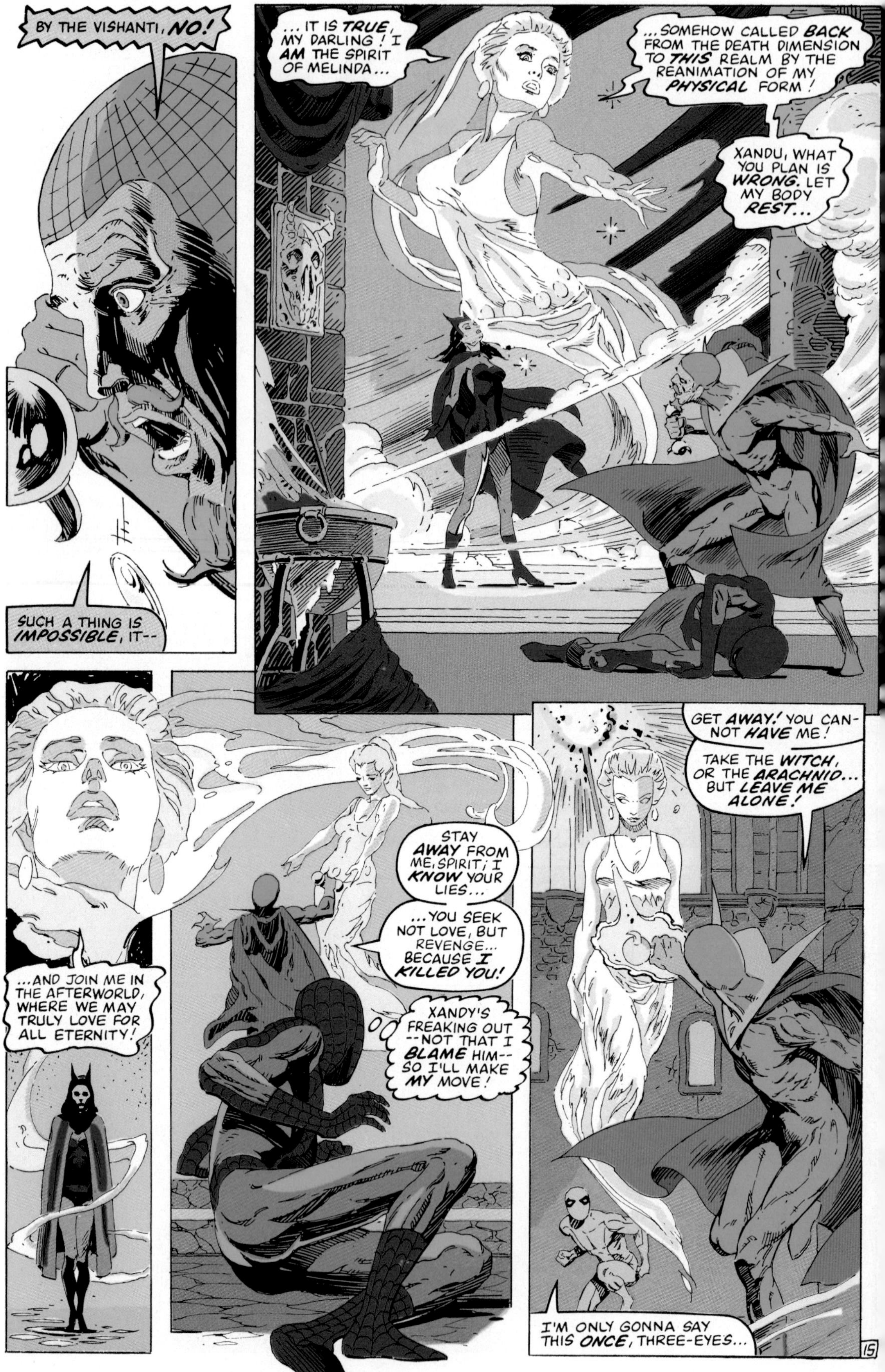

BY THE VISHANTI, NO!
SUCH A THING IS IMPOSSIBLE, IT--
...IT IS TRUE, MY DARLING! I AM THE SPIRIT OF MELINDA...
...SOMEHOW CALLED BACK FROM THE DEATH DIMENSION TO THIS REALM BY THE REANIMATION OF MY PHYSICAL FORM!
XANDU, WHAT YOU PLAN IS WRONG. LET MY BODY REST...
...AND JOIN ME IN THE AFTERWORLD, WHERE WE MAY TRULY LOVE FOR ALL ETERNITY!
STAY AWAY FROM ME, SPIRIT; I KNOW YOUR LIES...
...YOU SEEK NOT LOVE, BUT REVENGE... BECAUSE I KILLED YOU!
XANDY'S FREAKING OUT --NOT THAT I BLAME HIM-- SO I'LL MAKE MY MOVE!
GET AWAY! YOU CANNOT HAVE ME!
TAKE THE WITCH, OR THE ARACHNID... BUT LEAVE ME ALONE!
I'M ONLY GONNA SAY THIS ONCE, THREE-EYES...
15

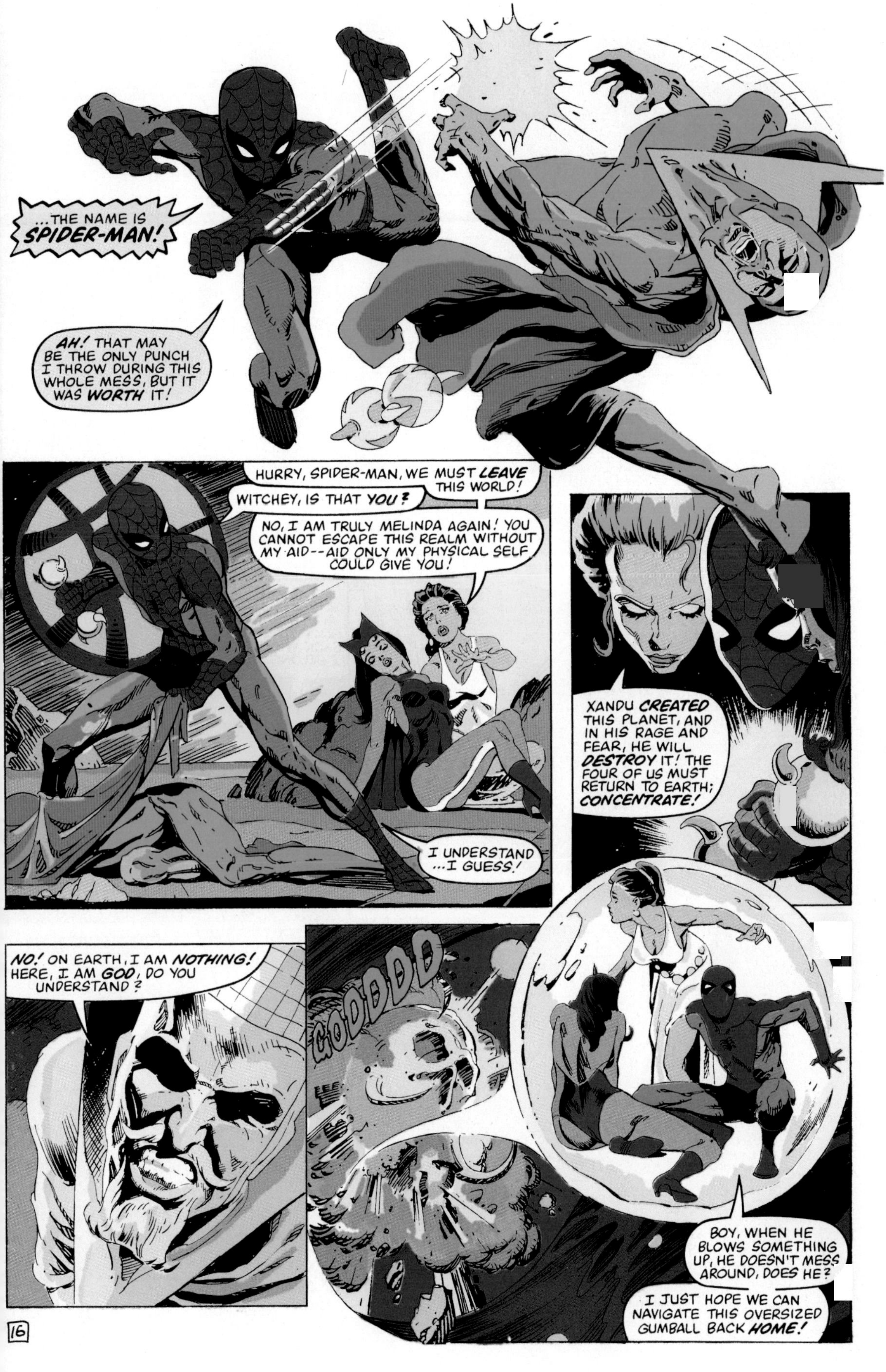
...THE NAME IS SPIDER-MAN!
AH! THAT MAY BE THE ONLY PUNCH I THROW DURING THIS WHOLE MESS, BUT IT WAS WORTH IT!
HURRY, SPIDER-MAN, WE MUST LEAVE THIS WORLD!
WITCHEY, IS THAT YOU?
NO, I AM TRULY MELINDA AGAIN! YOU CANNOT ESCAPE THIS REALM WITHOUT MY AID--AID ONLY MY PHYSICAL SELF COULD GIVE YOU!
I UNDERSTAND ...I GUESS!
XANDU CREATED THIS PLANET, AND IN HIS RAGE AND FEAR, HE WILL DESTROY IT! THE FOUR OF US MUST RETURN TO EARTH; CONCENTRATE!
NO! ON EARTH, I AM NOTHING! HERE, I AM GOD, DO YOU UNDERSTAND?
GODDDD
BOY, WHEN HE BLOWS SOMETHING UP, HE DOESN'T MESS AROUND, DOES HE?
I JUST HOPE WE CAN NAVIGATE THIS OVERSIZED GUMBALL BACK HOME!
16

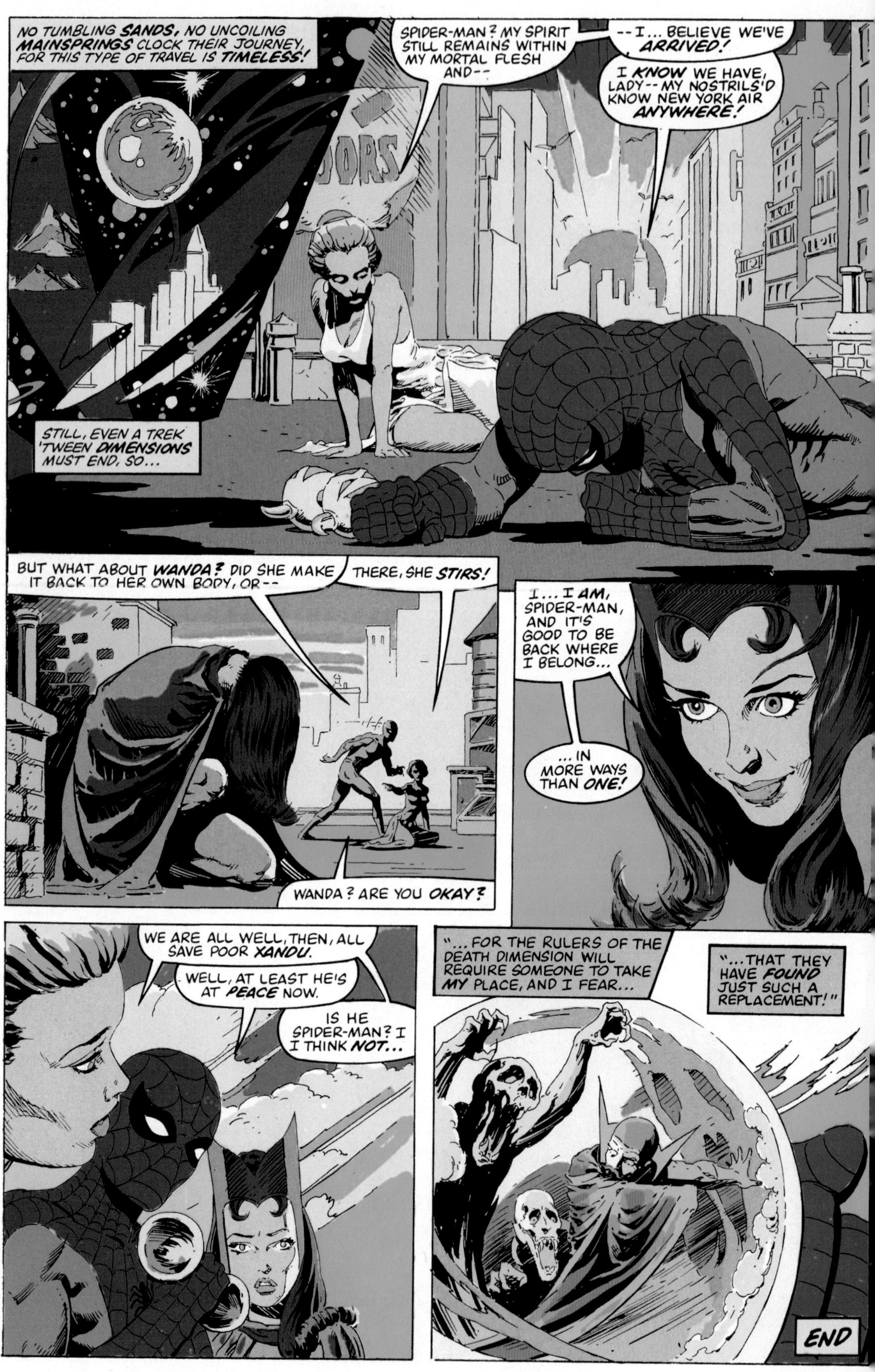
NO TUMBLING SANDS, NO UNCOILING MAINSPRINGS CLOCK THEIR JOURNEY, FOR THIS TYPE OF TRAVEL IS TIMELESS!
SPIDER-MAN? MY SPIRIT STILL REMAINS WITHIN MY MORTAL FLESH AND--
--I... BELIEVE WE'VE ARRIVED!
I KNOW WE HAVE, LADY--MY NOSTRILS'D KNOW NEW YORK AIR ANYWHERE!
STILL, EVEN A TREK 'TWEEN DIMENSIONS MUST END, SO...
BUT WHAT ABOUT WANDA? DID SHE MAKE IT BACK TO HER OWN BODY, OR--
THERE, SHE STIRS!
WANDA? ARE YOU OKAY?
I... I AM, SPIDER-MAN, AND IT'S GOOD TO BE BACK WHERE I BELONG...
... IN MORE WAYS THAN ONE!
WE ARE ALL WELL, THEN, ALL SAVE POOR XANDU.
WELL, AT LEAST HE'S AT PEACE NOW.
IS HE SPIDER-MAN? I I THINK NOT...
"...FOR THE RULERS OF THE DEATH DIMENSION WILL REQUIRE SOMEONE TO TAKE MY PLACE, AND I FEAR...
"...THAT THEY HAVE FOUND JUST SUCH A REPLACEMENT!"
END

DR. STRANGE #179 REPRINTED AMAZING SPIDER-MAN ANNUAL #2.
COVER ART BY BARRY WINDSOR-SMITH.

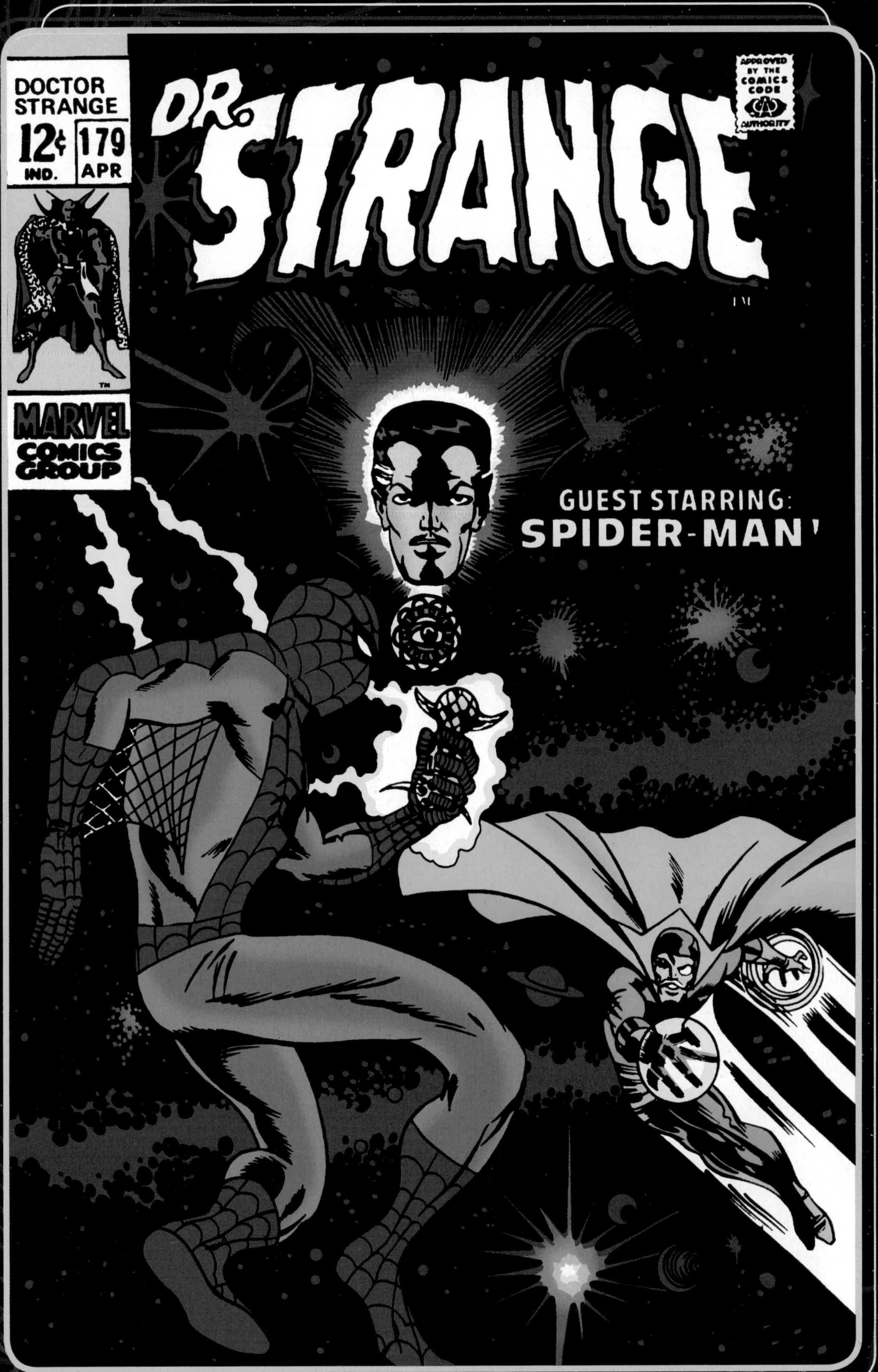
DOCTOR STRANGE
12¢ IND.
179 APR
DR. STRANGE
APPROVED BY THE COMICS CODE AUTHORITY
MARVEL COMICS GROUP
GUEST STARRING:
SPIDER-MAN!

WELCOME TO THE DEATH DIMENSION

Somewhere beyond time and space is a phantasmagoric landscape populated by demons, evil wizards and damsels in dis-
tress. A netherworld where the forces of darkness rule supreme.
A nightmare realm where Spider-Man and Doctor Strange must
wage a very personal battle, with the fate of the entire universe at
stake. Welcome to the Death Dimension. No one gets out alive.

ISBN: 0-87135-960-X

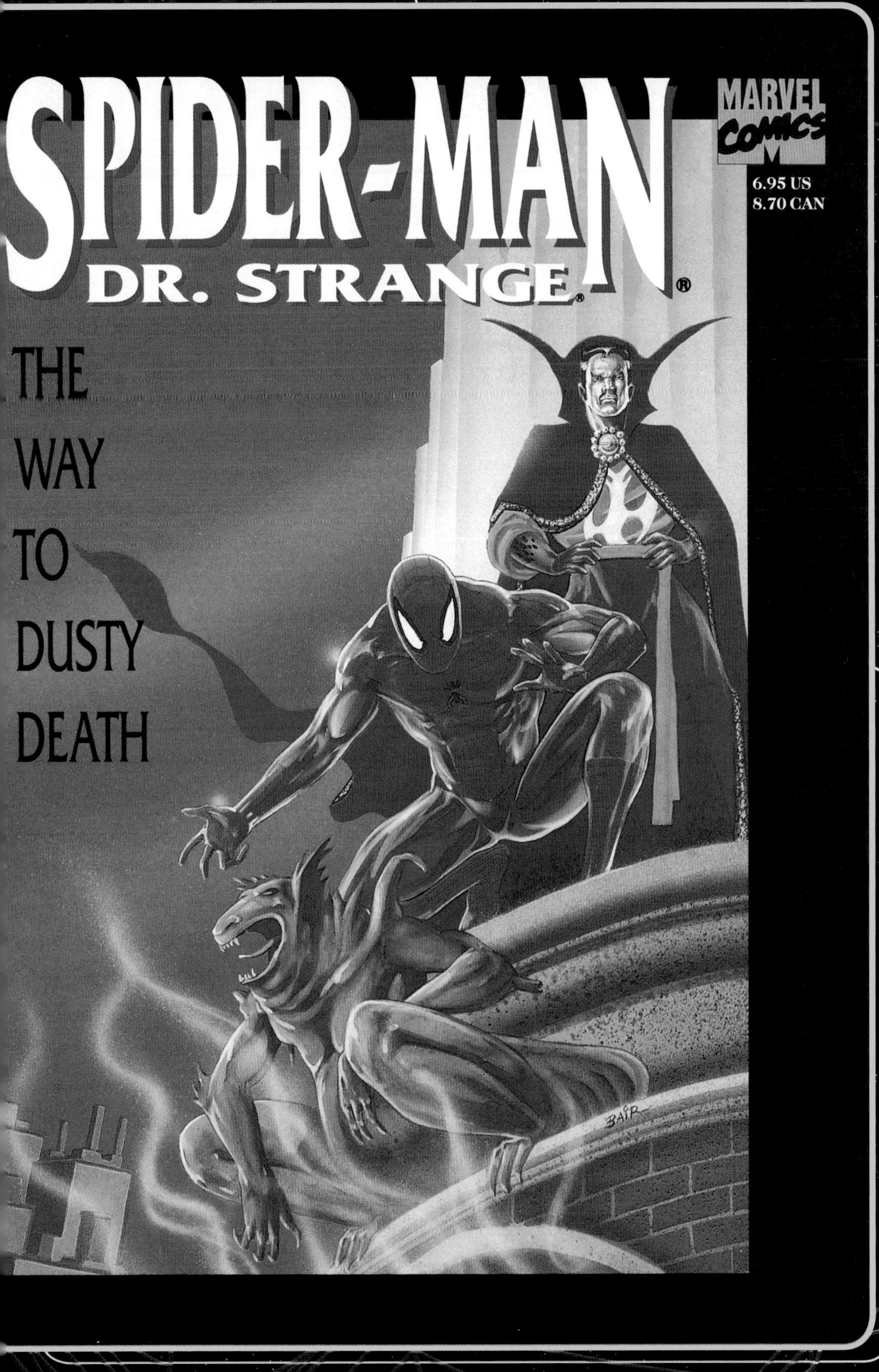

SPIDER-MAN
DR. STRANGE®
®
MARVEL COMICS
6.95 US
8.70 CAN
THE WAY TO DUSTY DEATH
BAIR

SPIDER-MAN
DR. STRANGE

THE WAY TO DUSTY DEATH

ROY THOMAS

co-plotter/scripter

GERRY CONWAY

co-plotter

MICHAEL BAIR

penciler

MARK BEACHUM

inker/MELINDA

MARK TEXEIRA

inker/XANDU

MICHAEL BAIR

inker

JOE ROSEN
RICK PARKER

letterers

BOB SHAREN

colorist

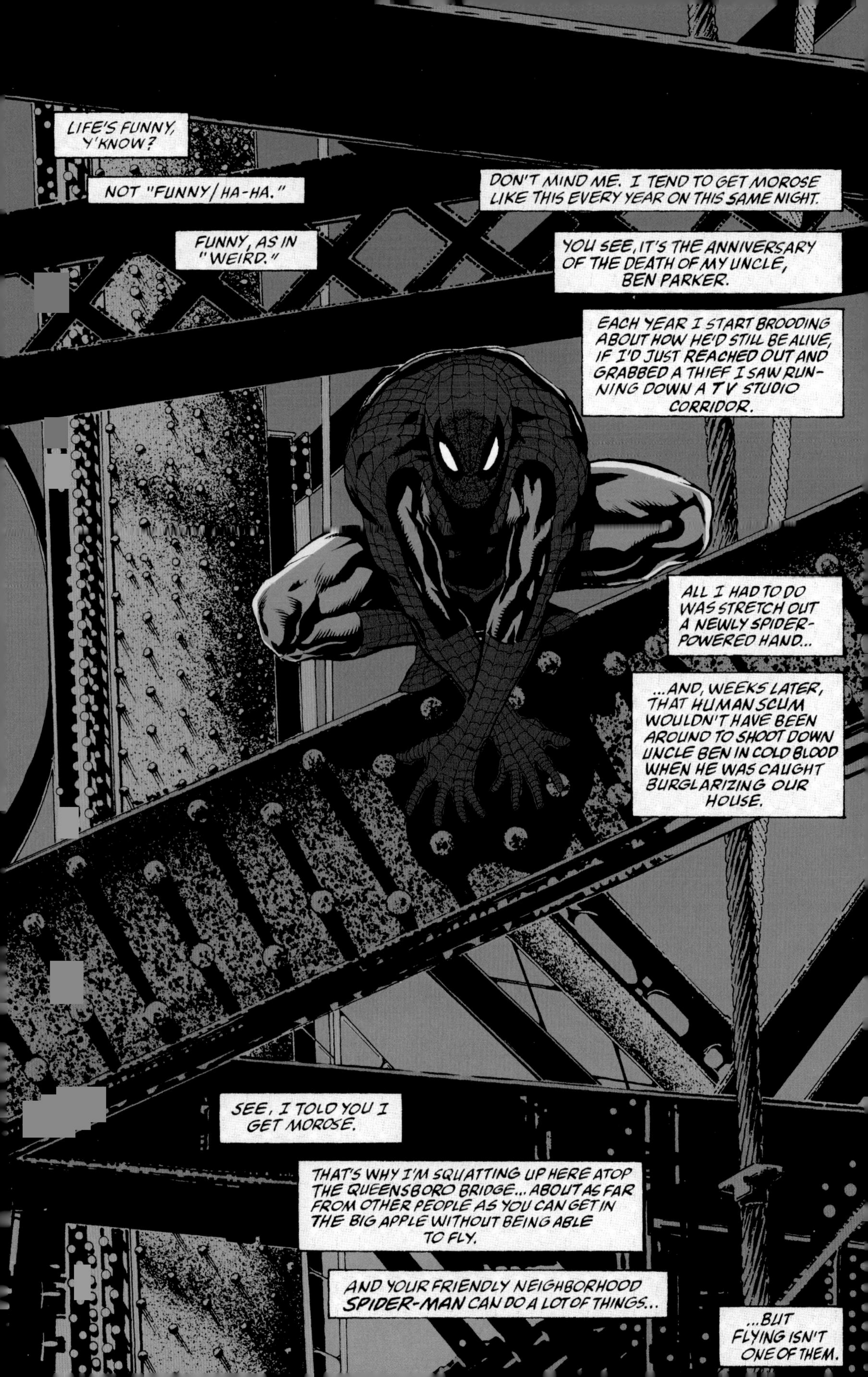
LIFE'S FUNNY, Y'KNOW?
NOT "FUNNY/HA-HA."
FUNNY, AS IN "WEIRD."
DON'T MIND ME. I TEND TO GET MOROSE LIKE THIS EVERY YEAR ON THIS SAME NIGHT.
YOU SEE, IT'S THE ANNIVERSARY OF THE DEATH OF MY UNCLE, BEN PARKER.
EACH YEAR I START BROODING ABOUT HOW HE'D STILL BE ALIVE, IF I'D JUST REACHED OUT AND GRABBED A THIEF I SAW RUNNING DOWN A TV STUDIO CORRIDOR.
ALL I HAD TO DO WAS STRETCH OUT A NEWLY SPIDER-POWERED HAND...
...AND, WEEKS LATER, THAT HUMAN SCUM WOULDN'T HAVE BEEN AROUND TO SHOOT DOWN UNCLE BEN IN COLD BLOOD WHEN HE WAS CAUGHT BURGLARIZING OUR HOUSE.
SEE, I TOLD YOU I GET MOROSE.
THAT'S WHY I'M SQUATTING UP HERE ATOP THE QUEENSBORO BRIDGE... ABOUT AS FAR FROM OTHER PEOPLE AS YOU CAN GET IN THE BIG APPLE WITHOUT BEING ABLE TO FLY.
AND YOUR FRIENDLY NEIGHBORHOOD SPIDER-MAN CAN DO A LOT OF THINGS...
...BUT FLYING ISN'T ONE OF THEM.

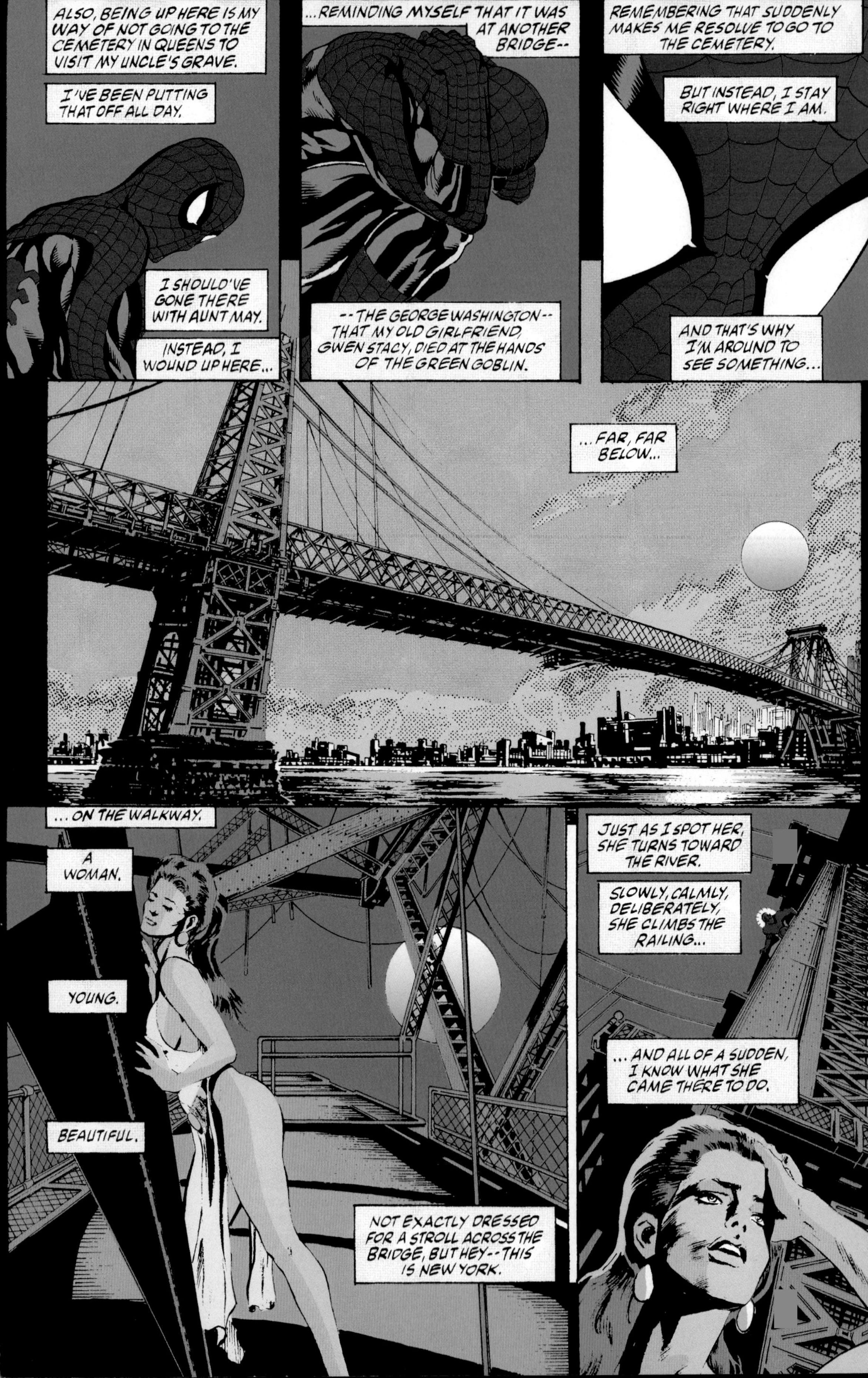
ALSO, BEING UP HERE IS MY WAY OF NOT GOING TO THE CEMETERY IN QUEENS TO VISIT MY UNCLE'S GRAVE.
I'VE BEEN PUTTING THAT OFF ALL DAY.
I SHOULD'VE GONE THERE WITH AUNT MAY.
INSTEAD, I WOUND UP HERE...
...REMINDING MYSELF THAT IT WAS AT ANOTHER BRIDGE--
--THE GEORGE WASHINGTON--THAT MY OLD GIRLFRIEND, GWEN STACY, DIED AT THE HANDS OF THE GREEN GOBLIN.
REMEMBERING THAT SUDDENLY MAKES ME RESOLVE TO GO TO THE CEMETERY.
BUT INSTEAD, I STAY RIGHT WHERE I AM.
AND THAT'S WHY I'M AROUND TO SEE SOMETHING...
...FAR, FAR BELOW...
...ON THE WALKWAY.
A WOMAN.
YOUNG.
BEAUTIFUL.
NOT EXACTLY DRESSED FOR A STROLL ACROSS THE BRIDGE, BUT HEY--THIS IS NEW YORK.
JUST AS I SPOT HER, SHE TURNS TOWARD THE RIVER.
SLOWLY, CALMLY, DELIBERATELY, SHE CLIMBS THE RAILING...
...AND ALL OF A SUDDEN, I KNOW WHAT SHE CAME THERE TO DO.

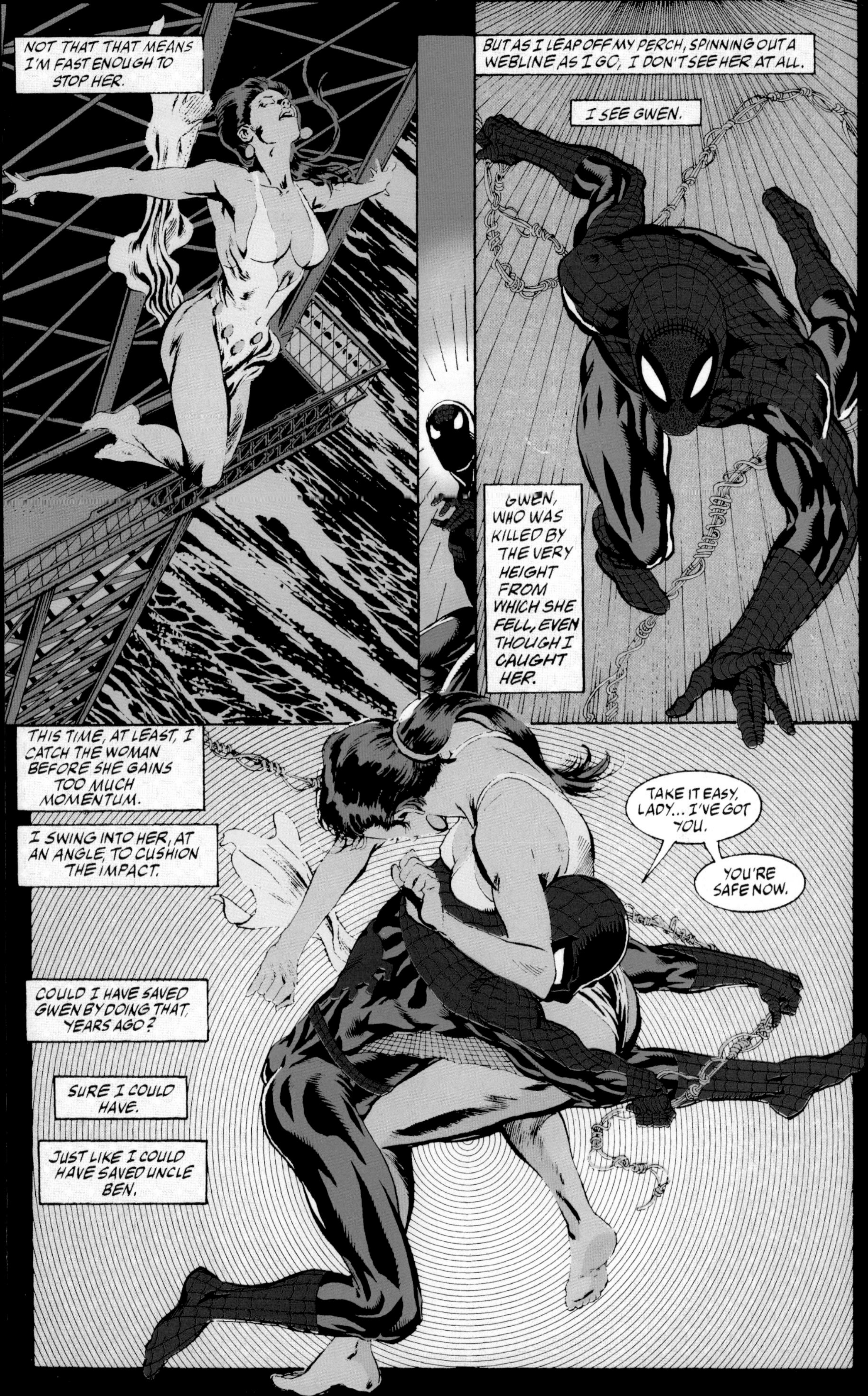
NOT THAT THAT MEANS I'M FAST ENOUGH TO STOP HER.
BUT AS I LEAP OFF MY PERCH, SPINNING OUT A WEBLINE AS I GO, I DON'T SEE HER AT ALL.
I SEE GWEN.
GWEN, WHO WAS KILLED BY THE VERY HEIGHT FROM WHICH SHE FELL, EVEN THOUGH I CAUGHT HER.
THIS TIME, AT LEAST, I CATCH THE WOMAN BEFORE SHE GAINS TOO MUCH MOMENTUM.
I SWING INTO HER, AT AN ANGLE, TO CUSHION THE IMPACT.
TAKE IT EASY, LADY... I'VE GOT YOU.
YOU'RE SAFE NOW.
COULD I HAVE SAVED GWEN BY DOING THAT, YEARS AGO?
SURE I COULD HAVE.
JUST LIKE I COULD HAVE SAVED UNCLE BEN.

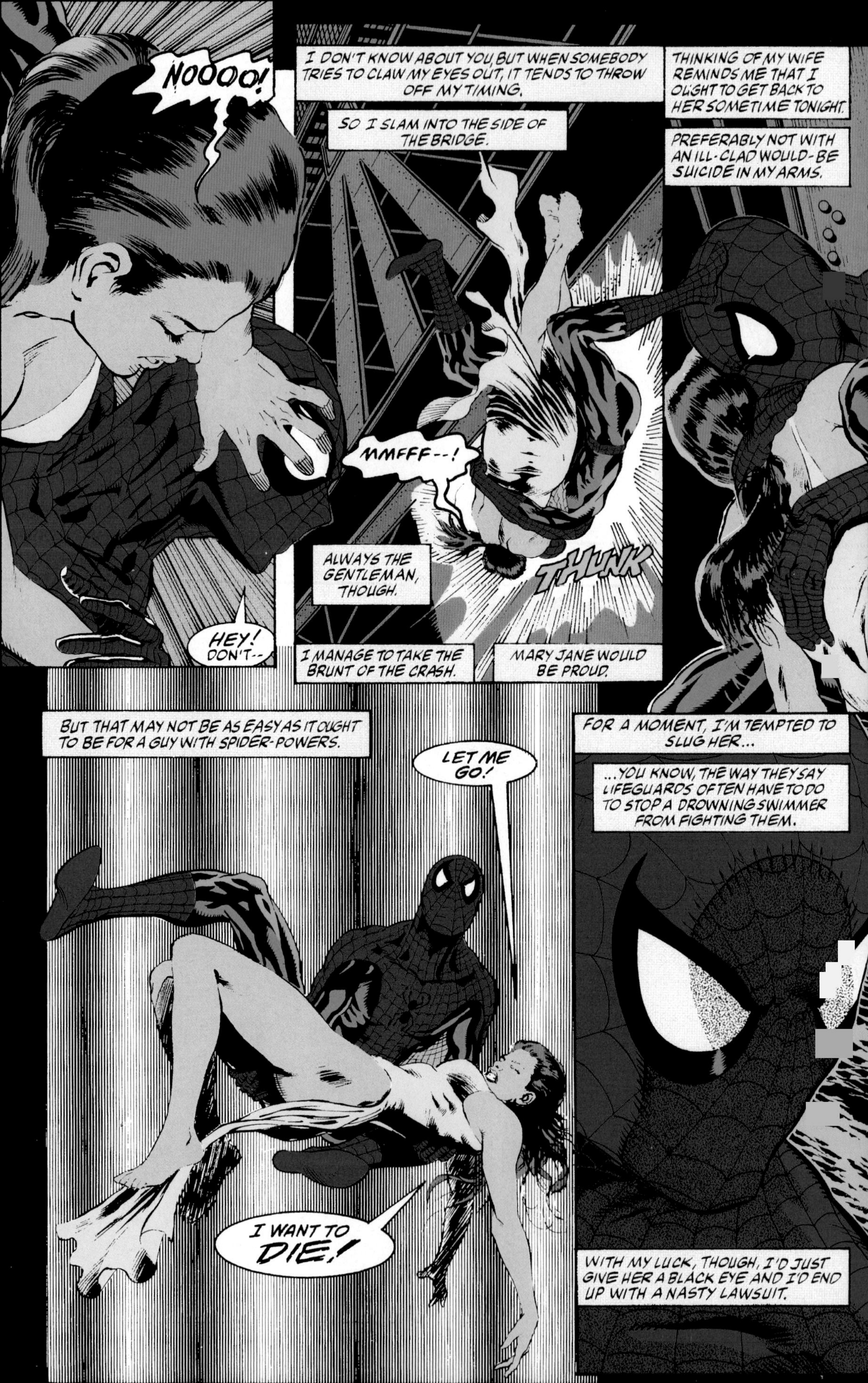
NOOOO!
HEY! DON'T--
I DON'T KNOW ABOUT YOU, BUT WHEN SOMEBODY TRIES TO CLAW MY EYES OUT, IT TENDS TO THROW OFF MY TIMING.
SO I SLAM INTO THE SIDE OF THE BRIDGE.
MMFFF--!
ALWAYS THE GENTLEMAN, THOUGH.
THUNK
I MANAGE TO TAKE THE BRUNT OF THE CRASH.
MARY JANE WOULD BE PROUD.
THINKING OF MY WIFE REMINDS ME THAT I OUGHT TO GET BACK TO HER SOMETIME TONIGHT.
PREFERABLY NOT WITH AN ILL-CLAD WOULD-BE SUICIDE IN MY ARMS.
BUT THAT MAY NOT BE AS EASY AS IT OUGHT TO BE FOR A GUY WITH SPIDER-POWERS.
LET ME GO!
I WANT TO DIE!
FOR A MOMENT, I'M TEMPTED TO SLUG HER...
...YOU KNOW, THE WAY THEY SAY LIFEGUARDS OFTEN HAVE TO DO TO STOP A DROWNING SWIMMER FROM FIGHTING THEM.
WITH MY LUCK, THOUGH, I'D JUST GIVE HER A BLACK EYE AND I'D END UP WITH A NASTY LAWSUIT.

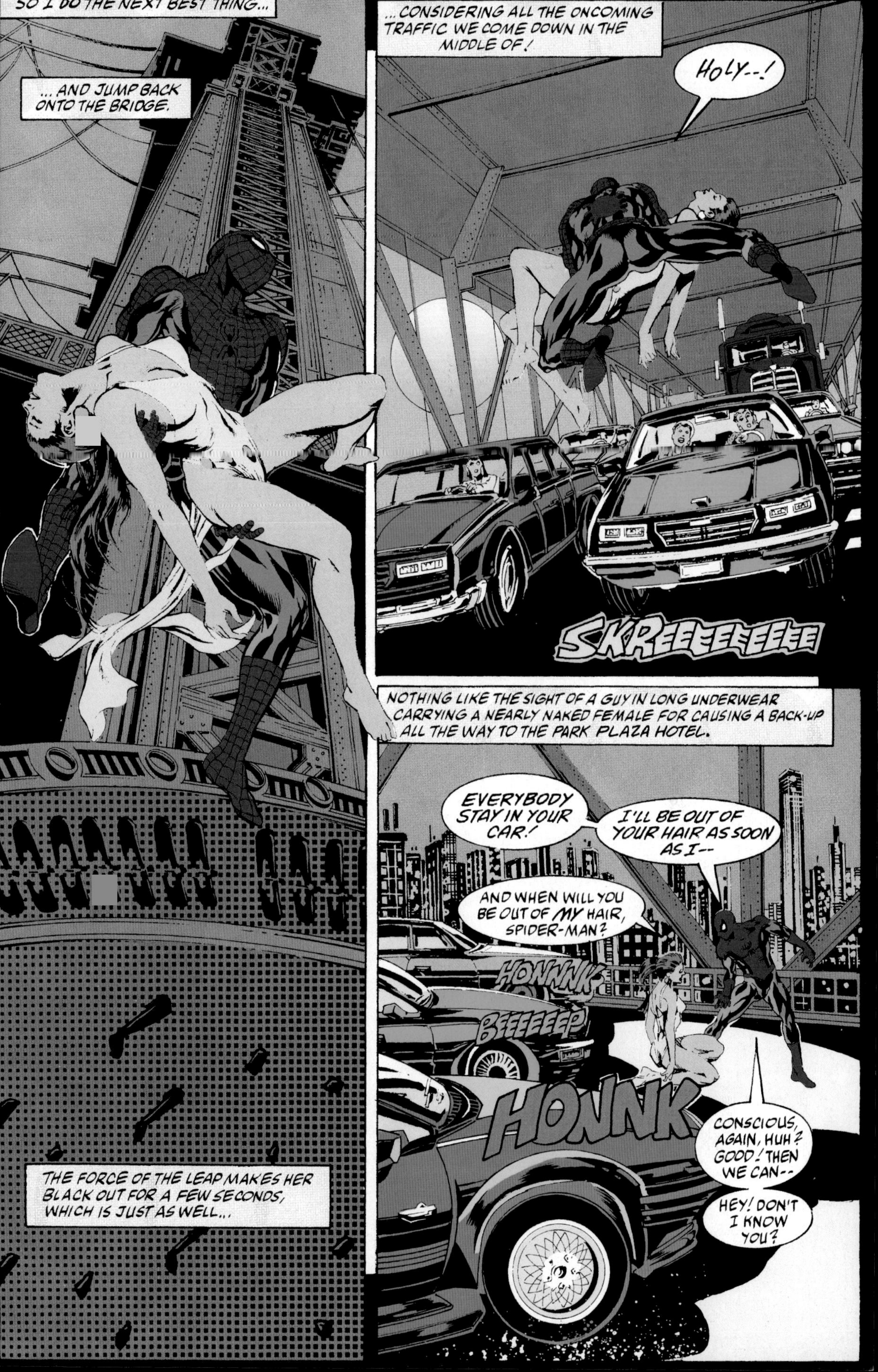

SO I DO THE NEXT BEST THING...
...AND JUMP BACK ONTO THE BRIDGE.
THE FORCE OF THE LEAP MAKES HER BLACK OUT FOR A FEW SECONDS, WHICH IS JUST AS WELL...
...CONSIDERING ALL THE ONCOMING TRAFFIC WE COME DOWN IN THE MIDDLE OF!
HOLY--!
SKREEEEEEEEE
NOTHING LIKE THE SIGHT OF A GUY IN LONG UNDERWEAR CARRYING A NEARLY NAKED FEMALE FOR CAUSING A BACK-UP ALL THE WAY TO THE PARK PLAZA HOTEL.
EVERYBODY STAY IN YOUR CAR!
I'LL BE OUT OF YOUR HAIR AS SOON AS I--
AND WHEN WILL YOU BE OUT OF MY HAIR, SPIDER-MAN?
HONNNK
BEEEEEP
HONNK
CONSCIOUS, AGAIN, HUH? GOOD! THEN WE CAN--
HEY! DON'T I KNOW YOU?

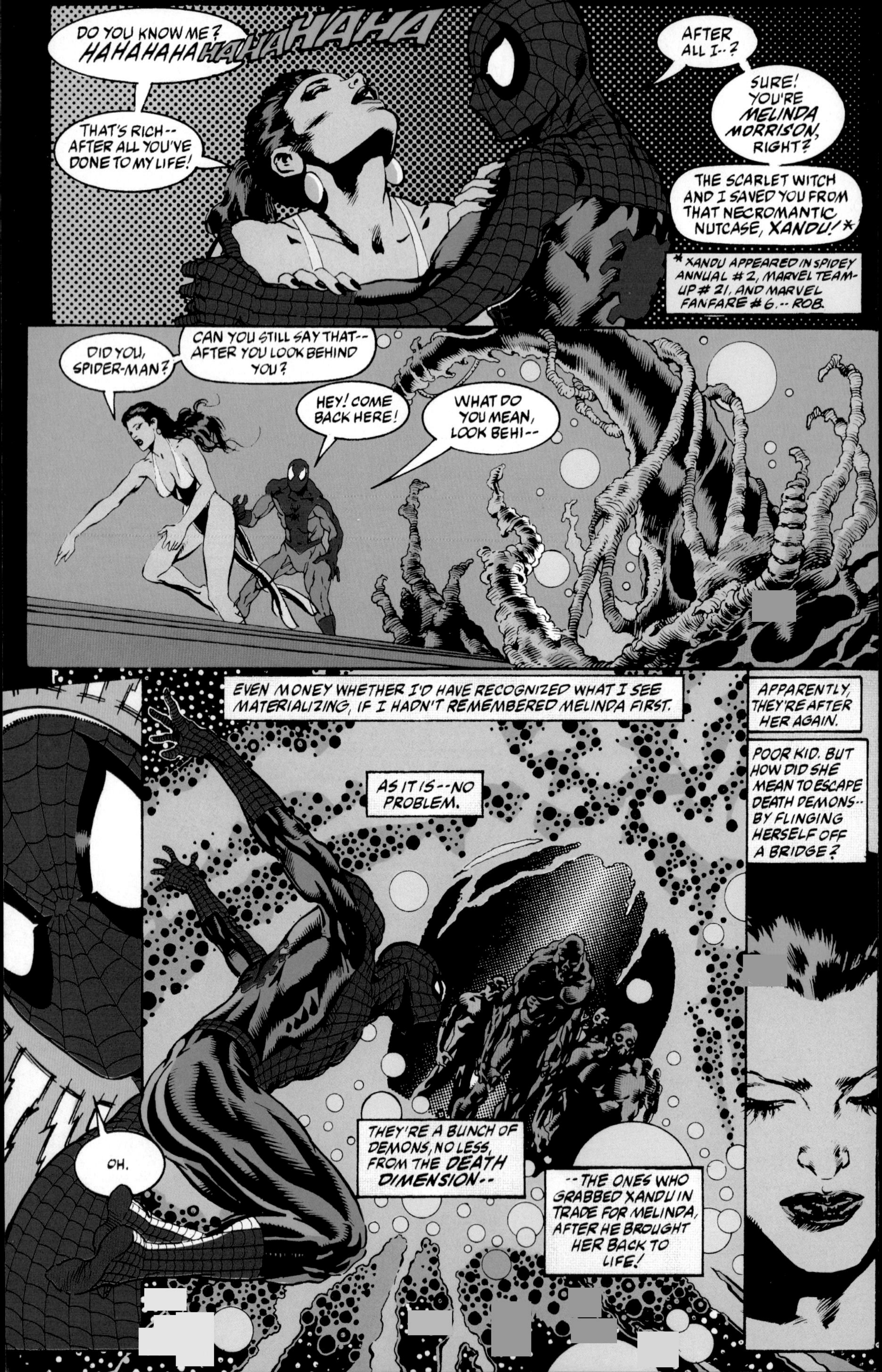
DO YOU KNOW ME? HAHAHAHAHAHAHAHAHA
THAT'S RICH--AFTER ALL YOU'VE DONE TO MY LIFE!
AFTER ALL I--?
SURE! YOU'RE MELINDA MORRISON, RIGHT?
THE SCARLET WITCH AND I SAVED YOU FROM THAT NECROMANTIC NUTCASE, XANDU!*
* XANDU APPEARED IN SPIDEY ANNUAL #2, MARVEL TEAM-UP #21, AND MARVEL FANFARE #6.--ROB.
DID YOU, SPIDER-MAN?
CAN YOU STILL SAY THAT--AFTER YOU LOOK BEHIND YOU?
HEY! COME BACK HERE!
WHAT DO YOU MEAN, LOOK BEHI--
OH.
EVEN MONEY WHETHER I'D HAVE RECOGNIZED WHAT I SEE MATERIALIZING, IF I HADN'T REMEMBERED MELINDA FIRST.
AS IT IS--NO PROBLEM.
APPARENTLY, THEY'RE AFTER HER AGAIN.
POOR KID. BUT HOW DID SHE MEAN TO ESCAPE DEATH DEMONS--BY FLINGING HERSELF OFF A BRIDGE?
THEY'RE A BUNCH OF DEMONS, NO LESS, FROM THE DEATH DIMENSION--
--THE ONES WHO GRABBED XANDU IN TRADE FOR MELINDA, AFTER HE BROUGHT HER BACK TO LIFE!

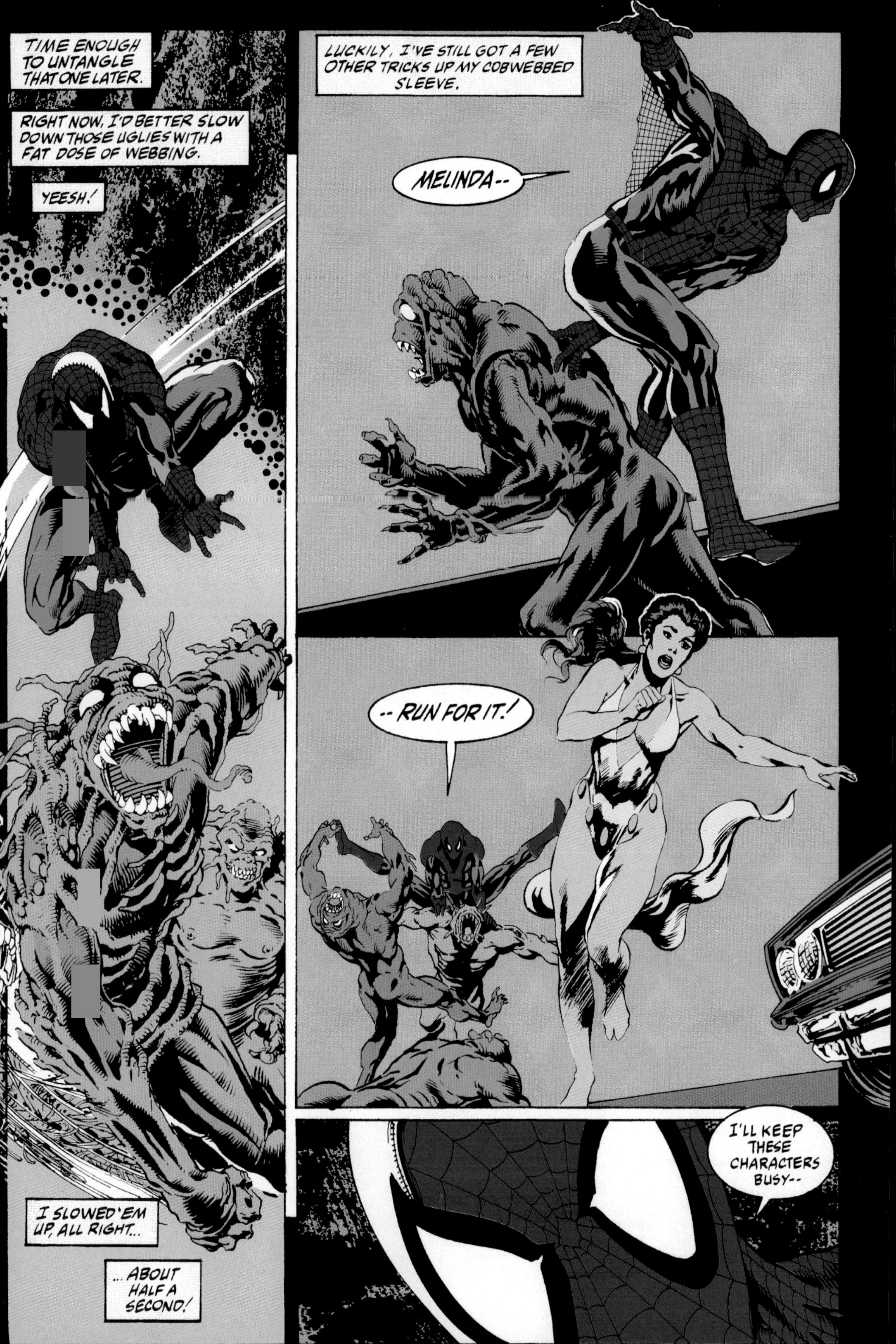
TIME ENOUGH TO UNTANGLE THAT ONE LATER.
RIGHT NOW, I'D BETTER SLOW DOWN THOSE UGLIES WITH A FAT DOSE OF WEBBING.
YEESH!
I SLOWED 'EM UP, ALL RIGHT...
...ABOUT HALF A SECOND!
LUCKILY, I'VE STILL GOT A FEW OTHER TRICKS UP MY COBWEBBED SLEEVE.
MELINDA--
--RUN FOR IT!
I'LL KEEP THESE CHARACTERS BUSY--

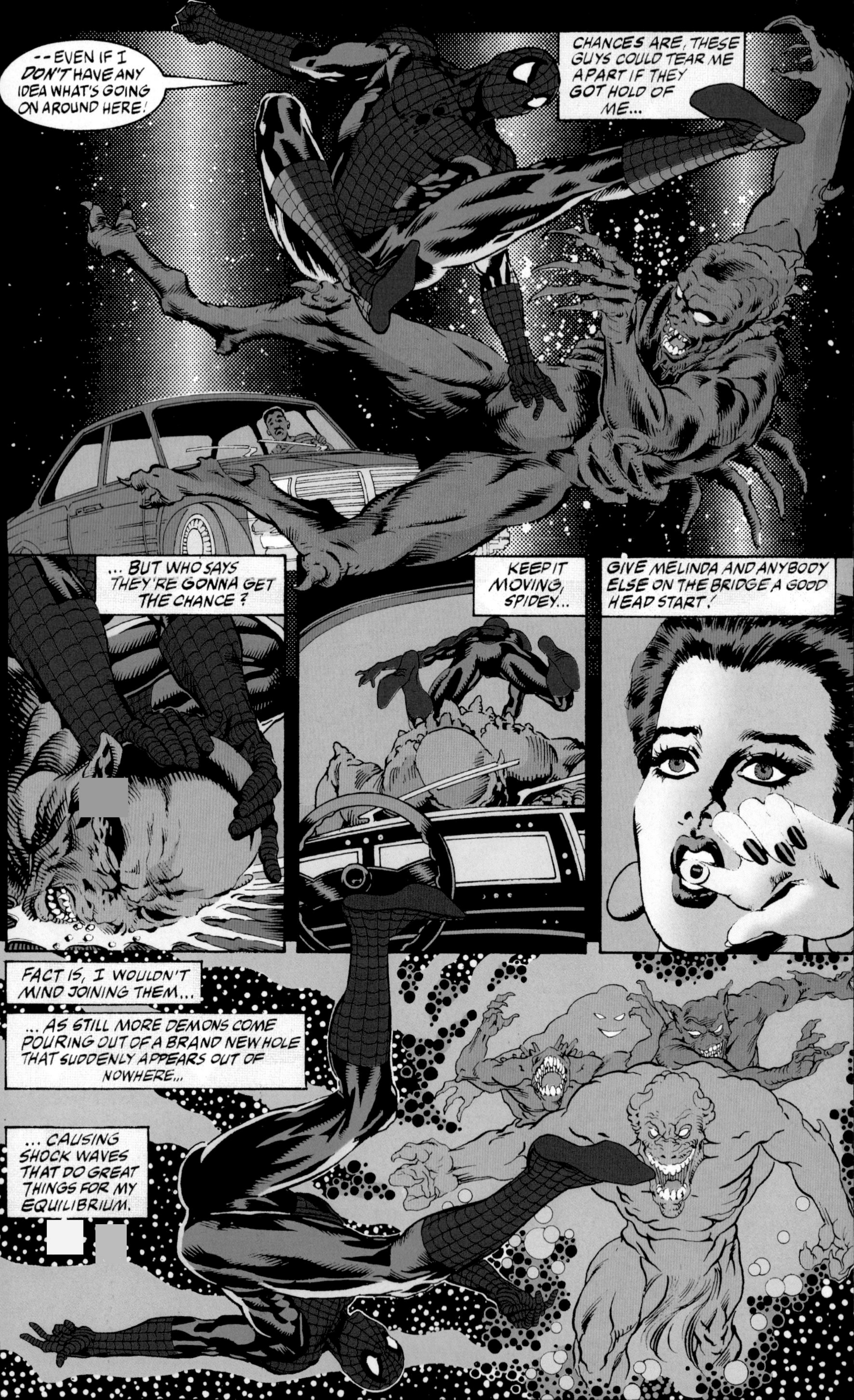
--EVEN IF I DON'T HAVE ANY IDEA WHAT'S GOING ON AROUND HERE!
CHANCES ARE, THESE GUYS COULD TEAR ME APART IF THEY GOT HOLD OF ME...
...BUT WHO SAYS THEY'RE GONNA GET THE CHANCE?
KEEP IT MOVING, SPIDEY...
GIVE MELINDA AND ANYBODY ELSE ON THE BRIDGE A GOOD HEAD START!
FACT IS, I WOULDN'T MIND JOINING THEM...
...AS STILL MORE DEMONS COME POURING OUT OF A BRAND NEW HOLE THAT SUDDENLY APPEARS OUT OF NOWHERE...
...CAUSING SHOCK WAVES THAT DO GREAT THINGS FOR MY EQUILIBRIUM.

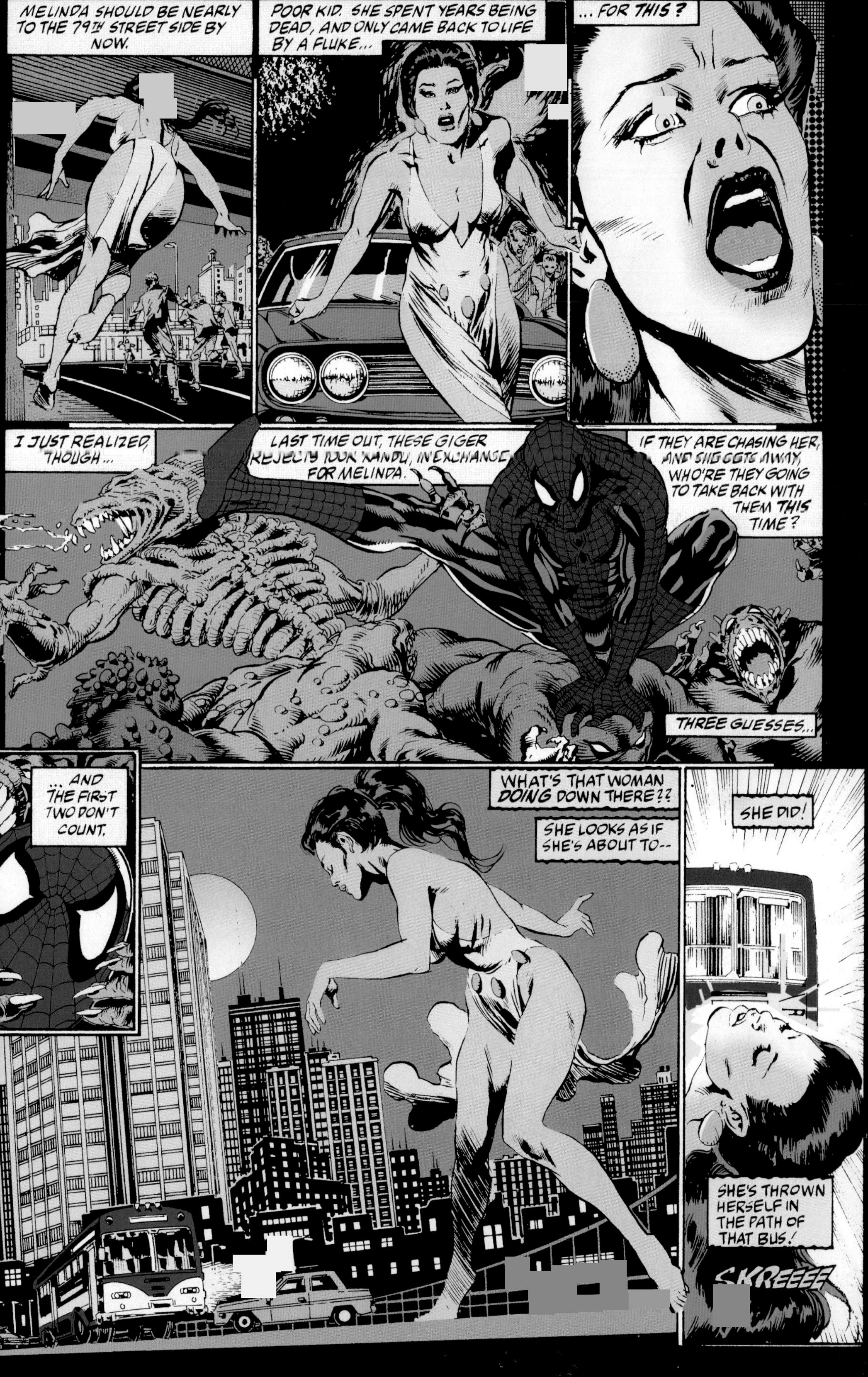
MELINDA SHOULD BE NEARLY TO THE 79TH STREET SIDE BY NOW.
POOR KID. SHE SPENT YEARS BEING DEAD, AND ONLY CAME BACK TO LIFE BY A FLUKE...
... FOR THIS?
I JUST REALIZED, THOUGH...
LAST TIME OUT, THESE GIGER REJECTS TOOK XANDU, IN EXCHANGE FOR MELINDA.
IF THEY ARE CHASING HER, AND SHE GETS AWAY, WHO'RE THEY GOING TO TAKE BACK WITH THEM THIS TIME?
THREE GUESSES...
... AND THE FIRST TWO DON'T COUNT.
WHAT'S THAT WOMAN DOING DOWN THERE??
SHE LOOKS AS IF SHE'S ABOUT TO--
SHE DID!
SHE'S THROWN HERSELF IN THE PATH OF THAT BUS!
SKREEEEE

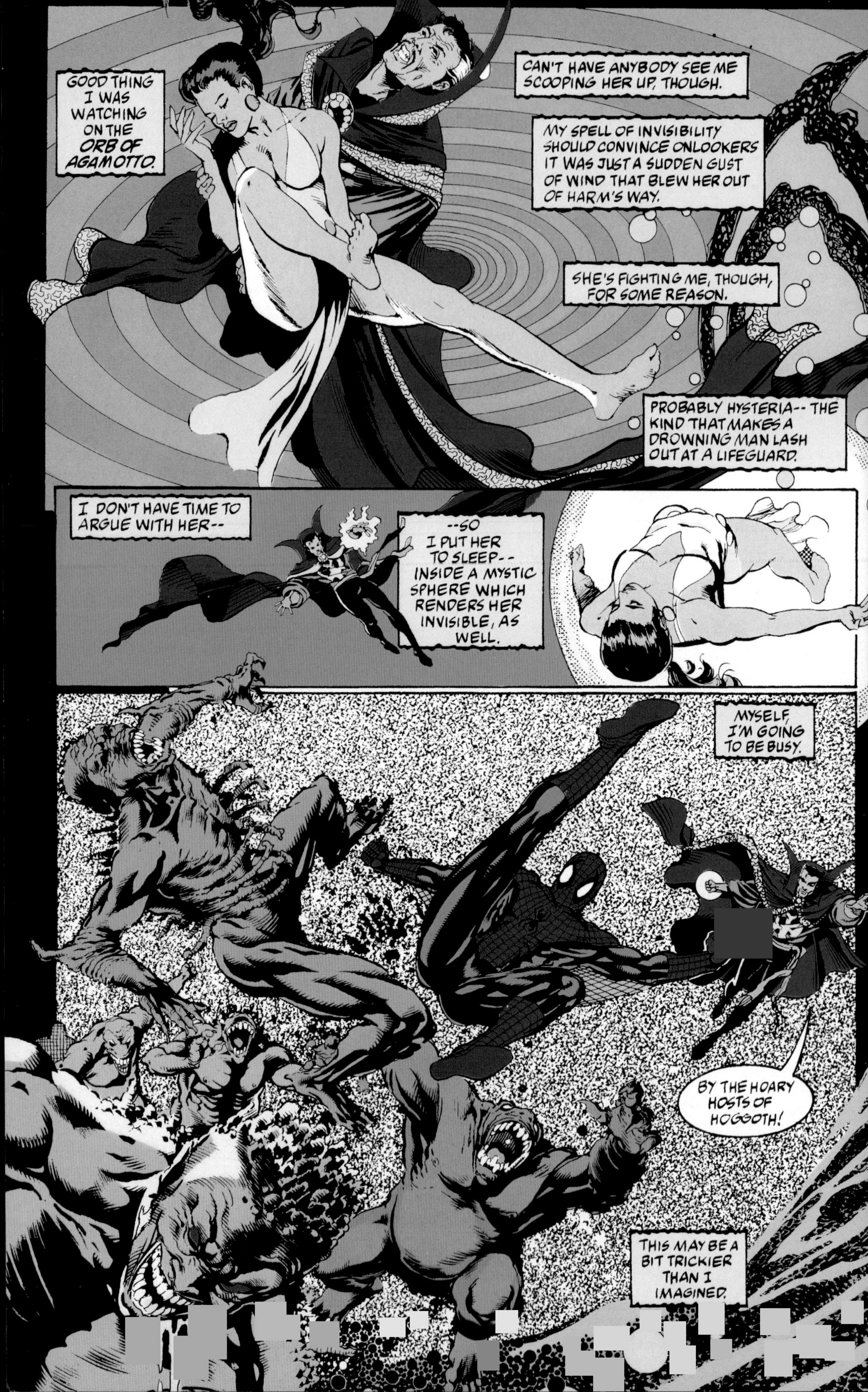
GOOD THING I WAS WATCHING ON THE ORB OF AGAMOTTO.
CAN'T HAVE ANYBODY SEE ME SCOOPING HER UP, THOUGH.
MY SPELL OF INVISIBILITY SHOULD CONVINCE ONLOOKERS IT WAS JUST A SUDDEN GUST OF WIND THAT BLEW HER OUT OF HARM'S WAY.
SHE'S FIGHTING ME, THOUGH, FOR SOME REASON.
PROBABLY HYSTERIA-- THE KIND THAT MAKES A DROWNING MAN LASH OUT AT A LIFEGUARD.
I DON'T HAVE TIME TO ARGUE WITH HER--
--SO I PUT HER TO SLEEP-- INSIDE A MYSTIC SPHERE WHICH RENDERS HER INVISIBLE, AS WELL.
MYSELF, I'M GOING TO BE BUSY.
BY THE HOARY HOSTS OF HOGGOTH!
THIS MAY BE A BIT TRICKIER THAN I IMAGINED.

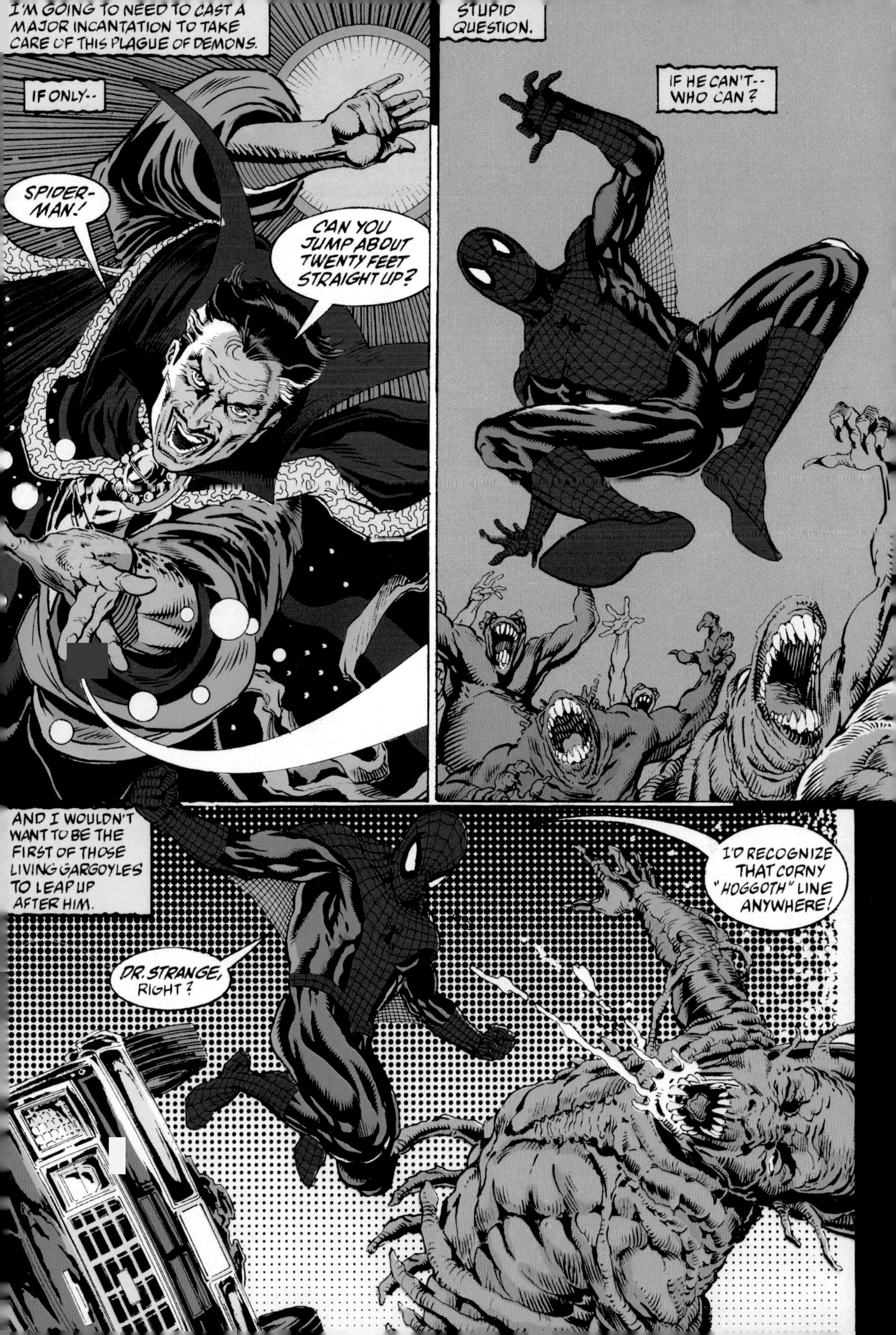
I'M GOING TO NEED TO CAST A MAJOR INCANTATION TO TAKE CARE OF THIS PLAGUE OF DEMONS.
IF ONLY--
SPIDER-MAN!
CAN YOU JUMP ABOUT TWENTY FEET STRAIGHT UP?
STUPID QUESTION.
IF HE CAN'T-- WHO CAN?
AND I WOULDN'T WANT TO BE THE FIRST OF THOSE LIVING GARGOYLES TO LEAP UP AFTER HIM.
I'D RECOGNIZE THAT CORNY "HOGGOTH" LINE ANYWHERE!
DR. STRANGE, RIGHT?

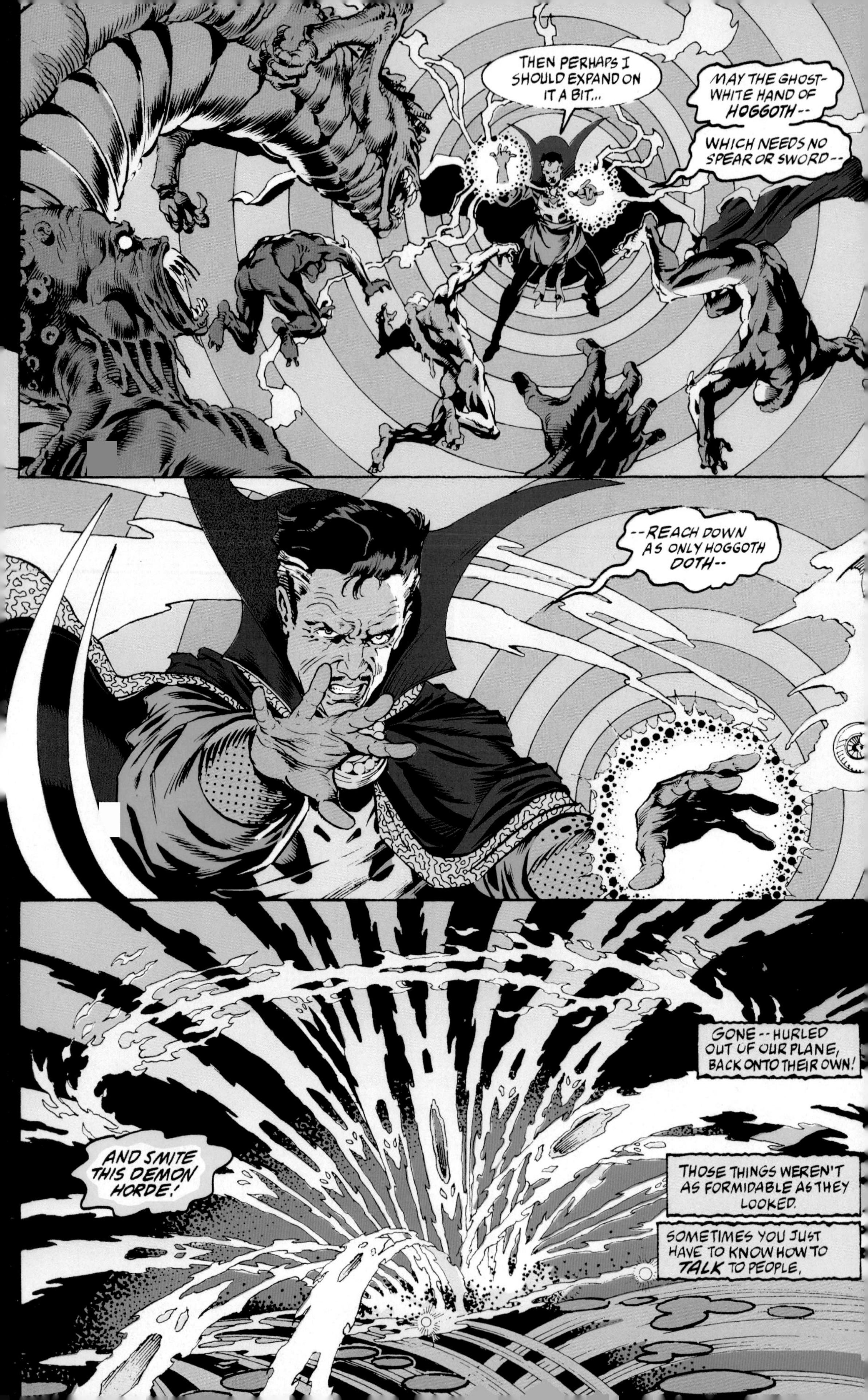
THEN PERHAPS I SHOULD EXPAND ON IT A BIT...
MAY THE GHOST-WHITE HAND OF HOGGOTH--
WHICH NEEDS NO SPEAR OR SWORD--
--REACH DOWN AS ONLY HOGGOTH DOTH--
AND SMITE THIS DEMON HORDE!
GONE--HURLED OUT OF OUR PLANE, BACK ONTO THEIR OWN!
THOSE THINGS WEREN'T AS FORMIDABLE AS THEY LOOKED.
SOMETIMES YOU JUST HAVE TO KNOW HOW TO TALK TO PEOPLE.

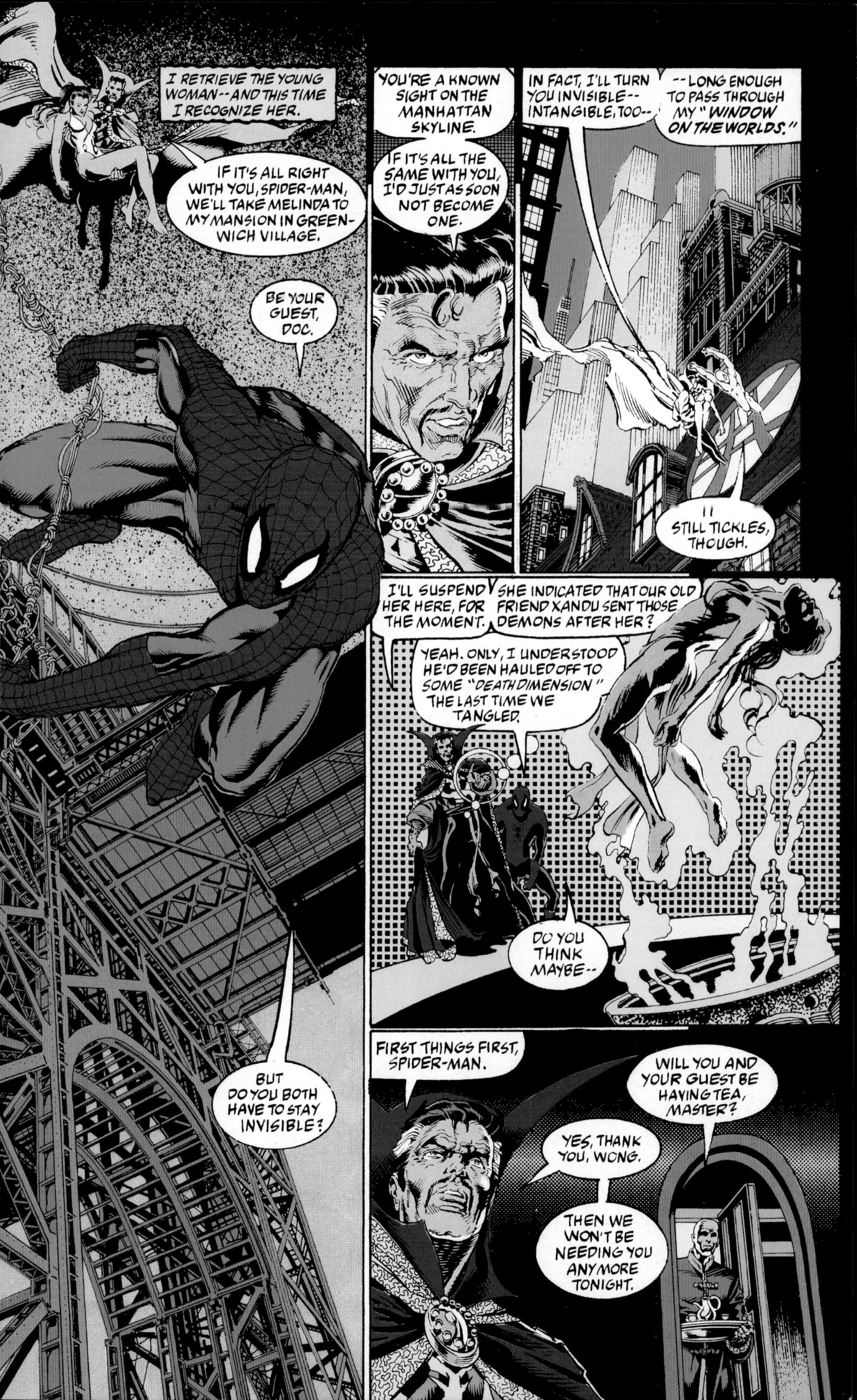

I RETRIEVE THE YOUNG WOMAN--AND THIS TIME I RECOGNIZE HER.
IF IT'S ALL RIGHT WITH YOU, SPIDER-MAN, WE'LL TAKE MELINDA TO MY MANSION IN GREENWICH VILLAGE.
BE YOUR GUEST, DOC.
BUT DO YOU BOTH HAVE TO STAY INVISIBLE?
YOU'RE A KNOWN SIGHT ON THE MANHATTAN SKYLINE.
IF IT'S ALL THE SAME WITH YOU, I'D JUST AS SOON NOT BECOME ONE.
IN FACT, I'LL TURN YOU INVISIBLE--INTANGIBLE, TOO--
--LONG ENOUGH TO PASS THROUGH MY "WINDOW ON THE WORLDS."
STILL TICKLES, THOUGH.
I'LL SUSPEND HER HERE, FOR THE MOMENT.
SHE INDICATED THAT OUR OLD FRIEND XANDU SENT THOSE DEMONS AFTER HER?
YEAH. ONLY, I UNDERSTOOD HE'D BEEN HAULED OFF TO SOME "DEATH DIMENSION" THE LAST TIME WE TANGLED.
DO YOU THINK MAYBE--
FIRST THINGS FIRST, SPIDER-MAN.
WILL YOU AND YOUR GUEST BE HAVING TEA, MASTER?
YES, THANK YOU, WONG.
THEN WE WON'T BE NEEDING YOU ANYMORE TONIGHT.

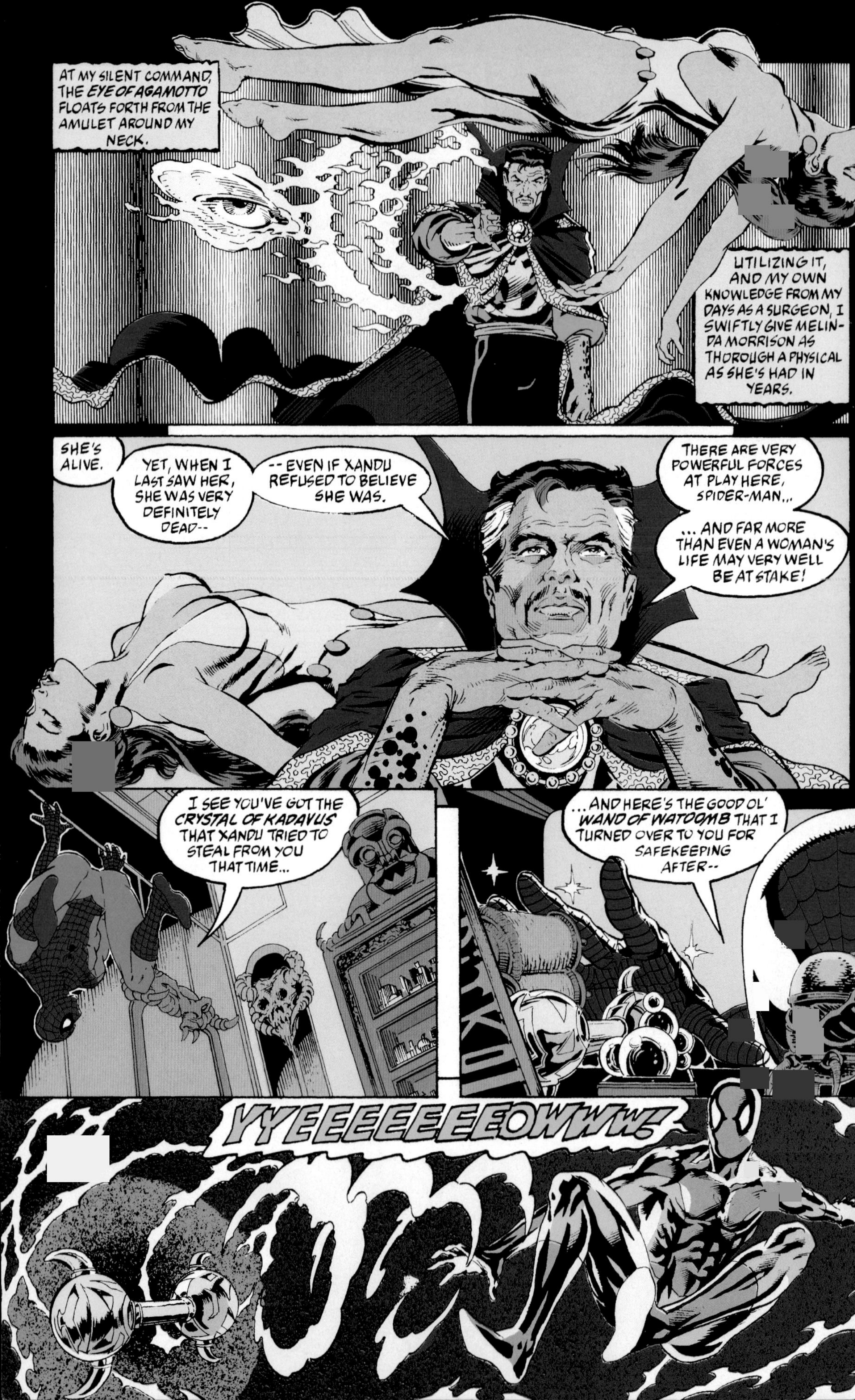
AT MY SILENT COMMAND, THE EYE OF AGAMOTTO FLOATS FORTH FROM THE AMULET AROUND MY NECK.
UTILIZING IT, AND MY OWN KNOWLEDGE FROM MY DAYS AS A SURGEON, I SWIFTLY GIVE MELINDA MORRISON AS THOROUGH A PHYSICAL AS SHE'S HAD IN YEARS.
SHE'S ALIVE.
YET, WHEN I LAST SAW HER, SHE WAS VERY DEFINITELY DEAD--
-- EVEN IF XANDU REFUSED TO BELIEVE SHE WAS.
THERE ARE VERY POWERFUL FORCES AT PLAY HERE, SPIDER-MAN...
... AND FAR MORE THAN EVEN A WOMAN'S LIFE MAY VERY WELL BE AT STAKE!
I SEE YOU'VE GOT THE CRYSTAL OF KADAVUS THAT XANDU TRIED TO STEAL FROM YOU THAT TIME...
...AND HERE'S THE GOOD OL' WAND OF WATOOMB THAT I TURNED OVER TO YOU FOR SAFEKEEPING AFTER--
YYEEEEEEEEOWWW!

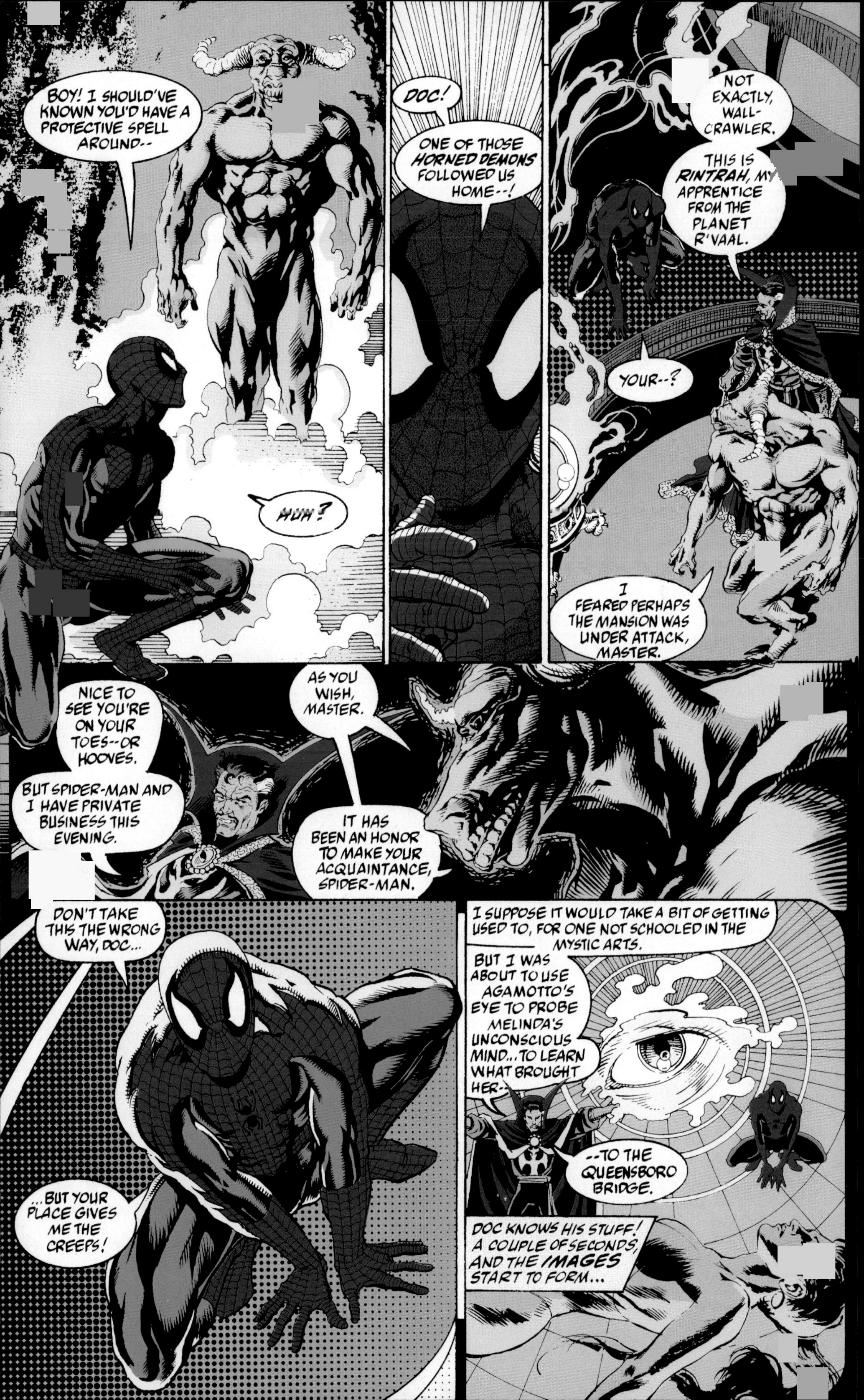
BOY! I SHOULD'VE KNOWN YOU'D HAVE A PROTECTIVE SPELL AROUND--
HUH?
DOC!
ONE OF THOSE HORNED DEMONS FOLLOWED US HOME--!
NOT EXACTLY, WALL-CRAWLER.
THIS IS RINTRAH, MY APPRENTICE FROM THE PLANET R'VAAL.
YOUR--?
I FEARED PERHAPS THE MANSION WAS UNDER ATTACK, MASTER.
NICE TO SEE YOU'RE ON YOUR TOES--OR HOOVES.
BUT SPIDER-MAN AND I HAVE PRIVATE BUSINESS THIS EVENING.
AS YOU WISH, MASTER.
IT HAS BEEN AN HONOR TO MAKE YOUR ACQUAINTANCE, SPIDER-MAN.
DON'T TAKE THIS THE WRONG WAY, DOC...
...BUT YOUR PLACE GIVES ME THE CREEPS!
I SUPPOSE IT WOULD TAKE A BIT OF GETTING USED TO, FOR ONE NOT SCHOOLED IN THE MYSTIC ARTS.
BUT I WAS ABOUT TO USE AGAMOTTO'S EYE TO PROBE MELINDA'S UNCONSCIOUS MIND...TO LEARN WHAT BROUGHT HER--
--TO THE QUEENSBORO BRIDGE.
DOC KNOWS HIS STUFF! A COUPLE OF SECONDS, AND THE IMAGES START TO FORM...

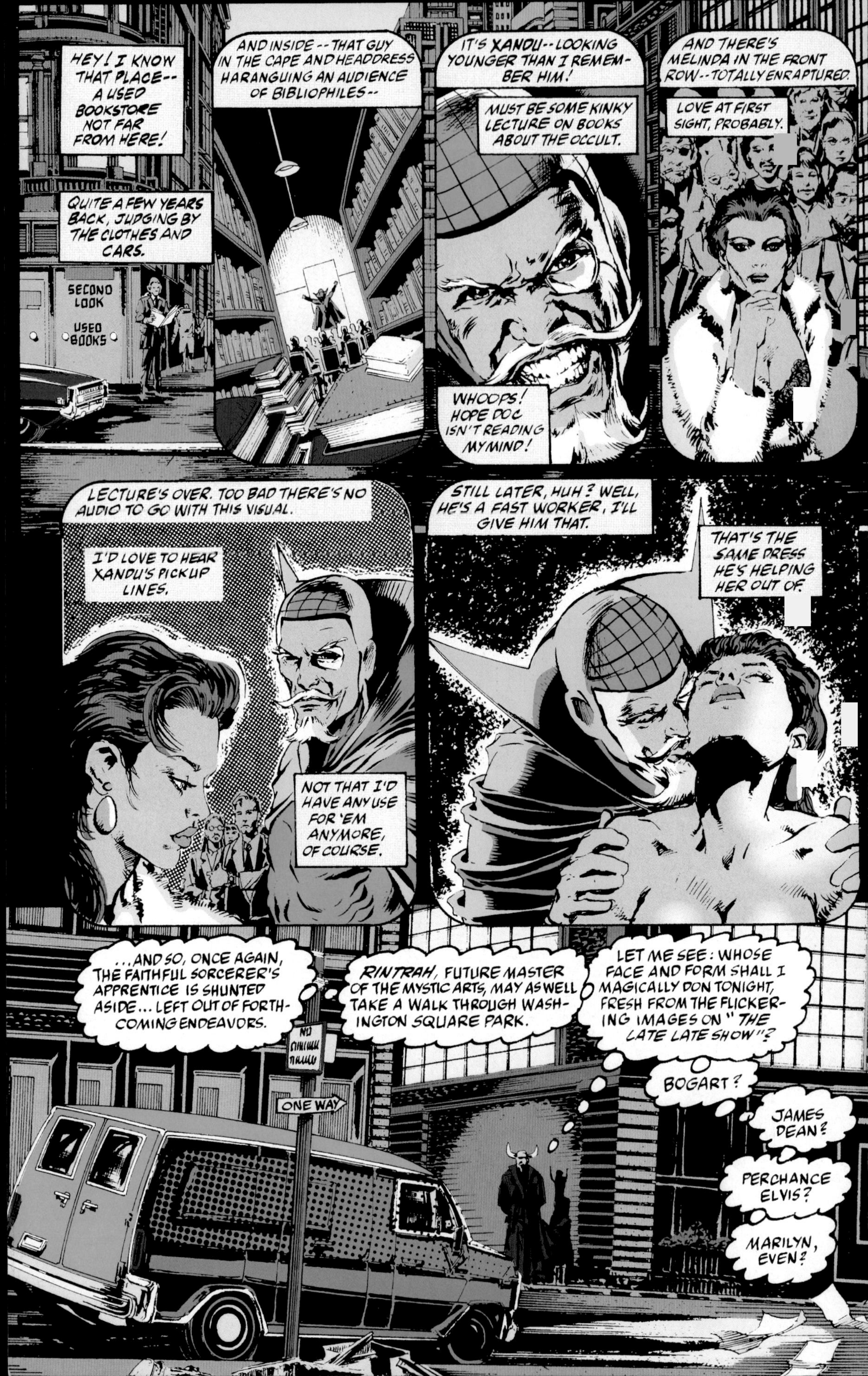
HEY! I KNOW THAT PLACE-- A USED BOOKSTORE NOT FAR FROM HERE!
QUITE A FEW YEARS BACK, JUDGING BY THE CLOTHES AND CARS.
SECOND LOOK
USED BOOKS
AND INSIDE -- THAT GUY IN THE CAPE AND HEADDRESS HARANGUING AN AUDIENCE OF BIBLIOPHILES --
IT'S XANDU -- LOOKING YOUNGER THAN I REMEMBER HIM!
MUST BE SOME KINKY LECTURE ON BOOKS ABOUT THE OCCULT.
WHOOPS! HOPE DOC ISN'T READING MY MIND!
AND THERE'S MELINDA IN THE FRONT ROW -- TOTALLY ENRAPTURED.
LOVE AT FIRST SIGHT, PROBABLY.
LECTURE'S OVER. TOO BAD THERE'S NO AUDIO TO GO WITH THIS VISUAL.
I'D LOVE TO HEAR XANDU'S PICKUP LINES.
NOT THAT I'D HAVE ANY USE FOR 'EM ANYMORE, OF COURSE.
STILL LATER, HUH? WELL, HE'S A FAST WORKER, I'LL GIVE HIM THAT.
THAT'S THE SAME DRESS HE'S HELPING HER OUT OF.
...AND SO, ONCE AGAIN, THE FAITHFUL SORCERER'S APPRENTICE IS SHUNTED ASIDE... LEFT OUT OF FORTHCOMING ENDEAVORS.
RINTRAH, FUTURE MASTER OF THE MYSTIC ARTS, MAY AS WELL TAKE A WALK THROUGH WASHINGTON SQUARE PARK.
LET ME SEE: WHOSE FACE AND FORM SHALL I MAGICALLY DON TONIGHT, FRESH FROM THE FLICKERING IMAGES ON "THE LATE LATE SHOW"?
BOGART?
JAMES DEAN?
PERCHANCE ELVIS?
MARILYN, EVEN?
ONE WAY

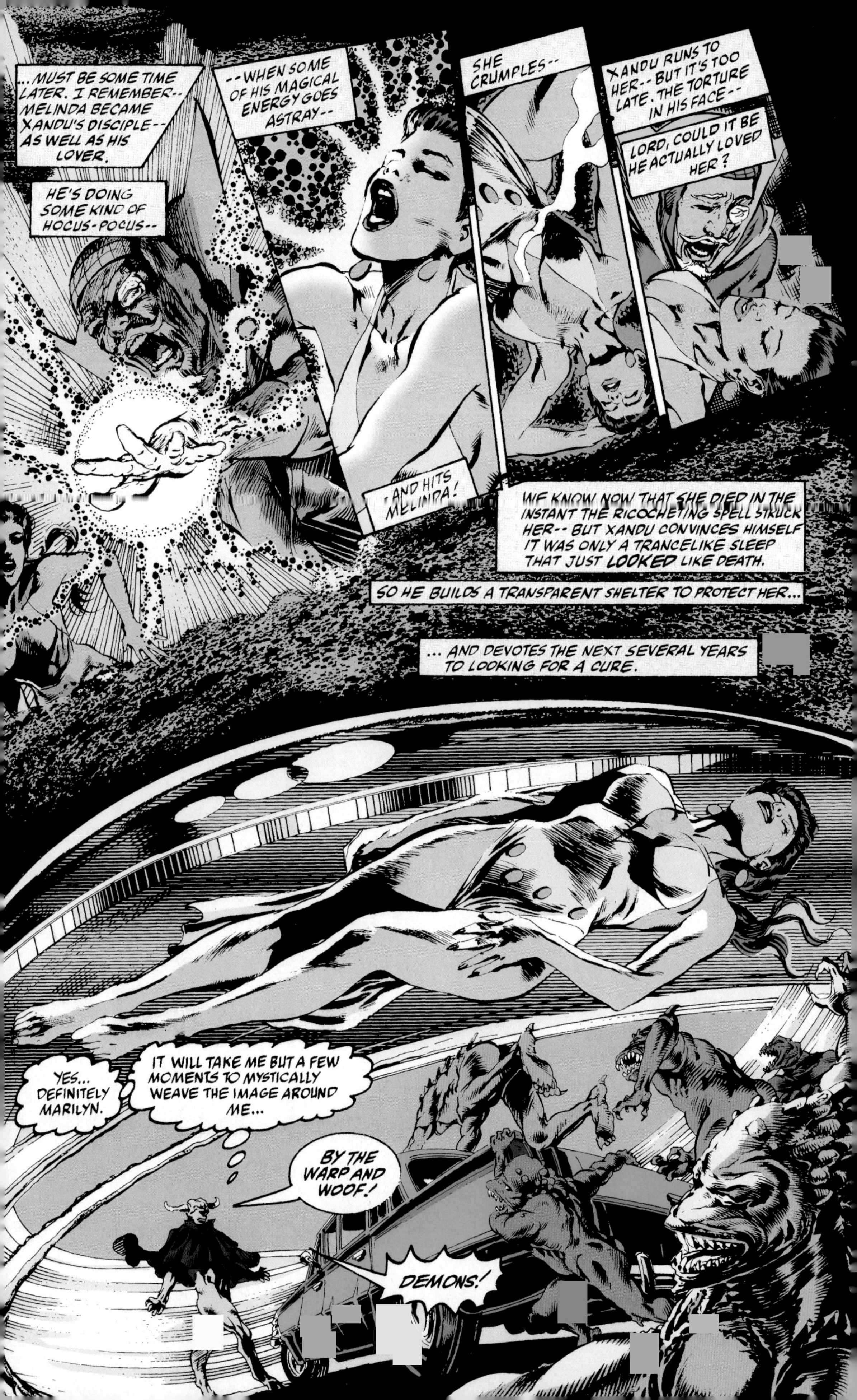
...MUST BE SOME TIME LATER. I REMEMBER-- MELINDA BECAME XANDU'S DISCIPLE-- AS WELL AS HIS LOVER.
HE'S DOING SOME KIND OF HOCUS-POCUS--
--WHEN SOME OF HIS MAGICAL ENERGY GOES ASTRAY--
--AND HITS MELINDA!
SHE CRUMPLES--
XANDU RUNS TO HER-- BUT IT'S TOO LATE. THE TORTURE IN HIS FACE--
LORD, COULD IT BE HE ACTUALLY LOVED HER?
WE KNOW NOW THAT SHE DIED IN THE INSTANT THE RICOCHETING SPELL STRUCK HER-- BUT XANDU CONVINCES HIMSELF IT WAS ONLY A TRANCELIKE SLEEP THAT JUST LOOKED LIKE DEATH.
SO HE BUILDS A TRANSPARENT SHELTER TO PROTECT HER...
... AND DEVOTES THE NEXT SEVERAL YEARS TO LOOKING FOR A CURE.
YES... DEFINITELY MARILYN.
IT WILL TAKE ME BUT A FEW MOMENTS TO MYSTICALLY WEAVE THE IMAGE AROUND ME...
BY THE WARP AND WOOF!
DEMONS!

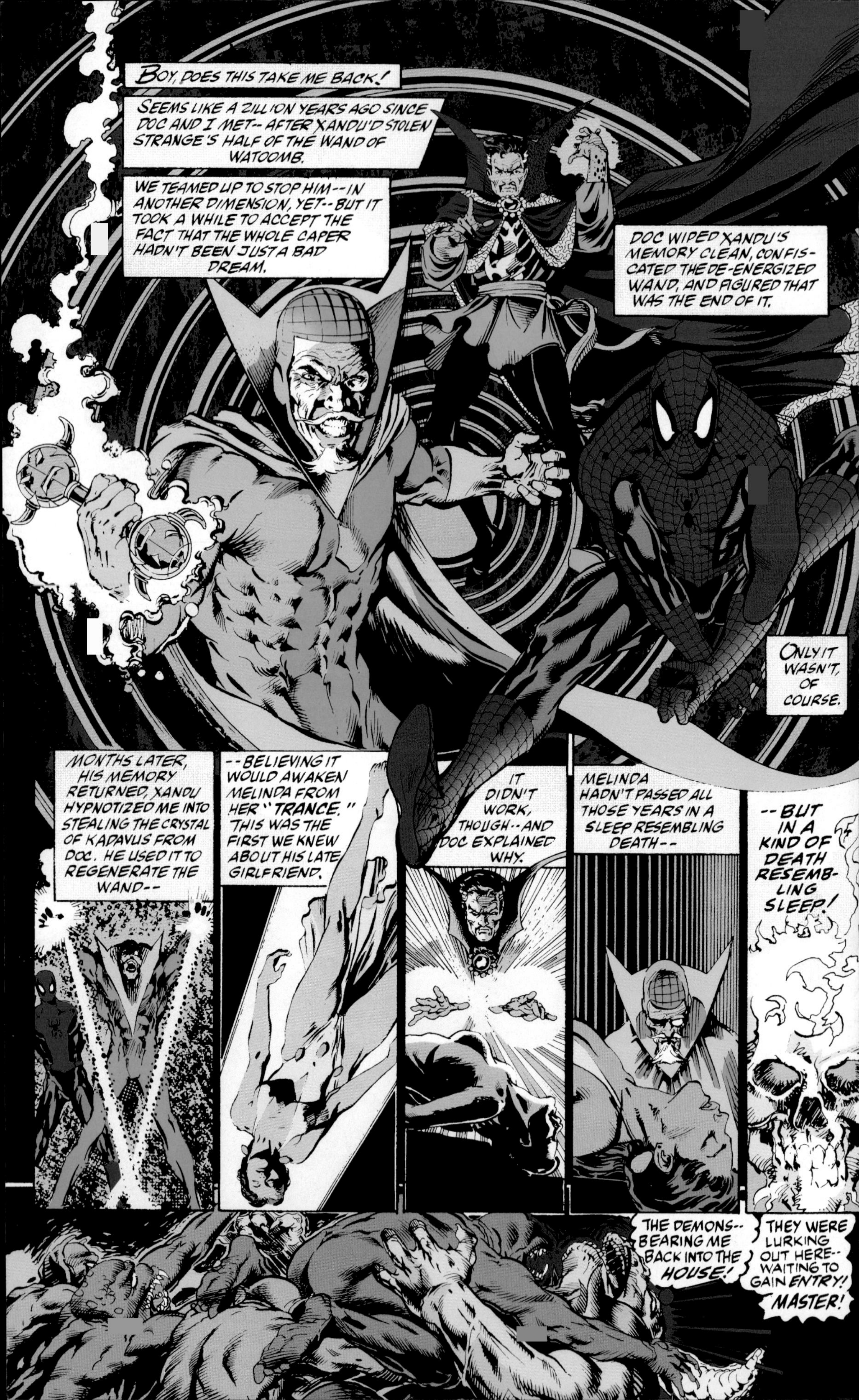
BOY, DOES THIS TAKE ME BACK!
SEEMS LIKE A ZILLION YEARS AGO SINCE DOC AND I MET-- AFTER XANDU'D STOLEN STRANGE'S HALF OF THE WAND OF WATOOMB.
WE TEAMED UP TO STOP HIM-- IN ANOTHER DIMENSION, YET-- BUT IT TOOK A WHILE TO ACCEPT THE FACT THAT THE WHOLE CAPER HADN'T BEEN JUST A BAD DREAM.
DOC WIPED XANDU'S MEMORY CLEAN, CONFISCATED THE DE-ENERGIZED WAND, AND FIGURED THAT WAS THE END OF IT.
ONLY IT WASN'T, OF COURSE.
MONTHS LATER, HIS MEMORY RETURNED, XANDU HYPNOTIZED ME INTO STEALING THE CRYSTAL OF KADAVUS FROM DOC. HE USED IT TO REGENERATE THE WAND--
--BELIEVING IT WOULD AWAKEN MELINDA FROM HER "TRANCE." THIS WAS THE FIRST WE KNEW ABOUT HIS LATE GIRLFRIEND.
IT DIDN'T WORK, THOUGH-- AND DOC EXPLAINED WHY.
MELINDA HADN'T PASSED ALL THOSE YEARS IN A SLEEP RESEMBLING DEATH--
--BUT IN A KIND OF DEATH RESEMBLING SLEEP!
THE DEMONS-- BEARING ME BACK INTO THE HOUSE!
THEY WERE LURKING OUT HERE-- WAITING TO GAIN ENTRY!
MASTER!

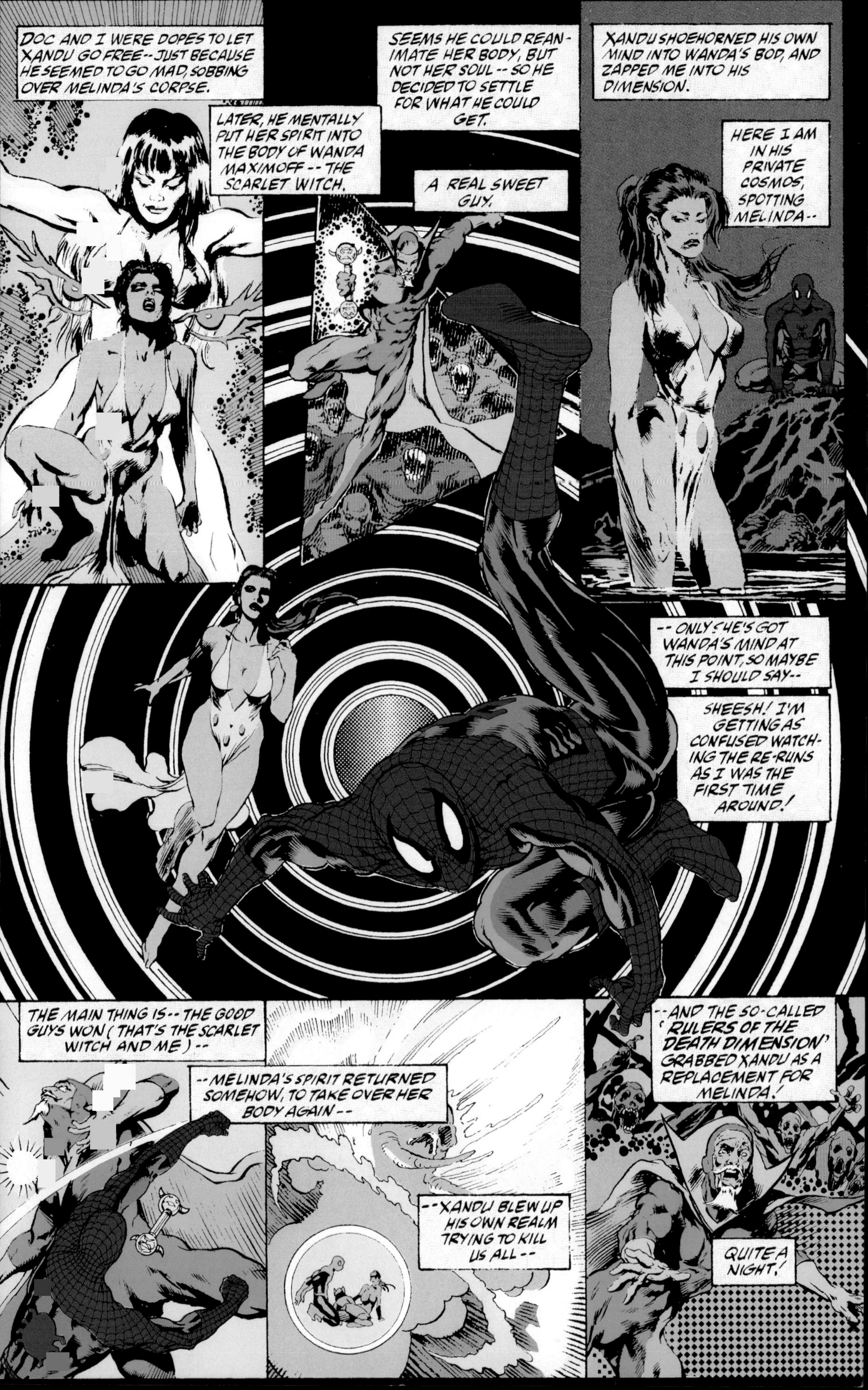
DOC AND I WERE DOPES TO LET XANDU GO FREE--JUST BECAUSE HE SEEMED TO GO MAD, SOBBING OVER MELINDA'S CORPSE.
LATER, HE MENTALLY PUT HER SPIRIT INTO THE BODY OF WANDA MAXIMOFF -- THE SCARLET WITCH.
SEEMS HE COULD REANIMATE HER BODY, BUT NOT HER SOUL -- SO HE DECIDED TO SETTLE FOR WHAT HE COULD GET.
A REAL SWEET GUY.
XANDU SHOEHORNED HIS OWN MIND INTO WANDA'S BOD, AND ZAPPED ME INTO HIS DIMENSION.
HERE I AM IN HIS PRIVATE COSMOS, SPOTTING MELINDA--
-- ONLY SHE'S GOT WANDA'S MIND AT THIS POINT, SO MAYBE I SHOULD SAY--
SHEESH! I'M GETTING AS CONFUSED WATCHING THE RE-RUNS AS I WAS THE FIRST TIME AROUND!
THE MAIN THING IS--THE GOOD GUYS WON (THAT'S THE SCARLET WITCH AND ME)--
--MELINDA'S SPIRIT RETURNED SOMEHOW, TO TAKE OVER HER BODY AGAIN--
--XANDU BLEW UP HIS OWN REALM TRYING TO KILL US ALL--
--AND THE SO-CALLED 'RULERS OF THE DEATH DIMENSION' GRABBED XANDU AS A REPLACEMENT FOR MELINDA!
QUITE A NIGHT!

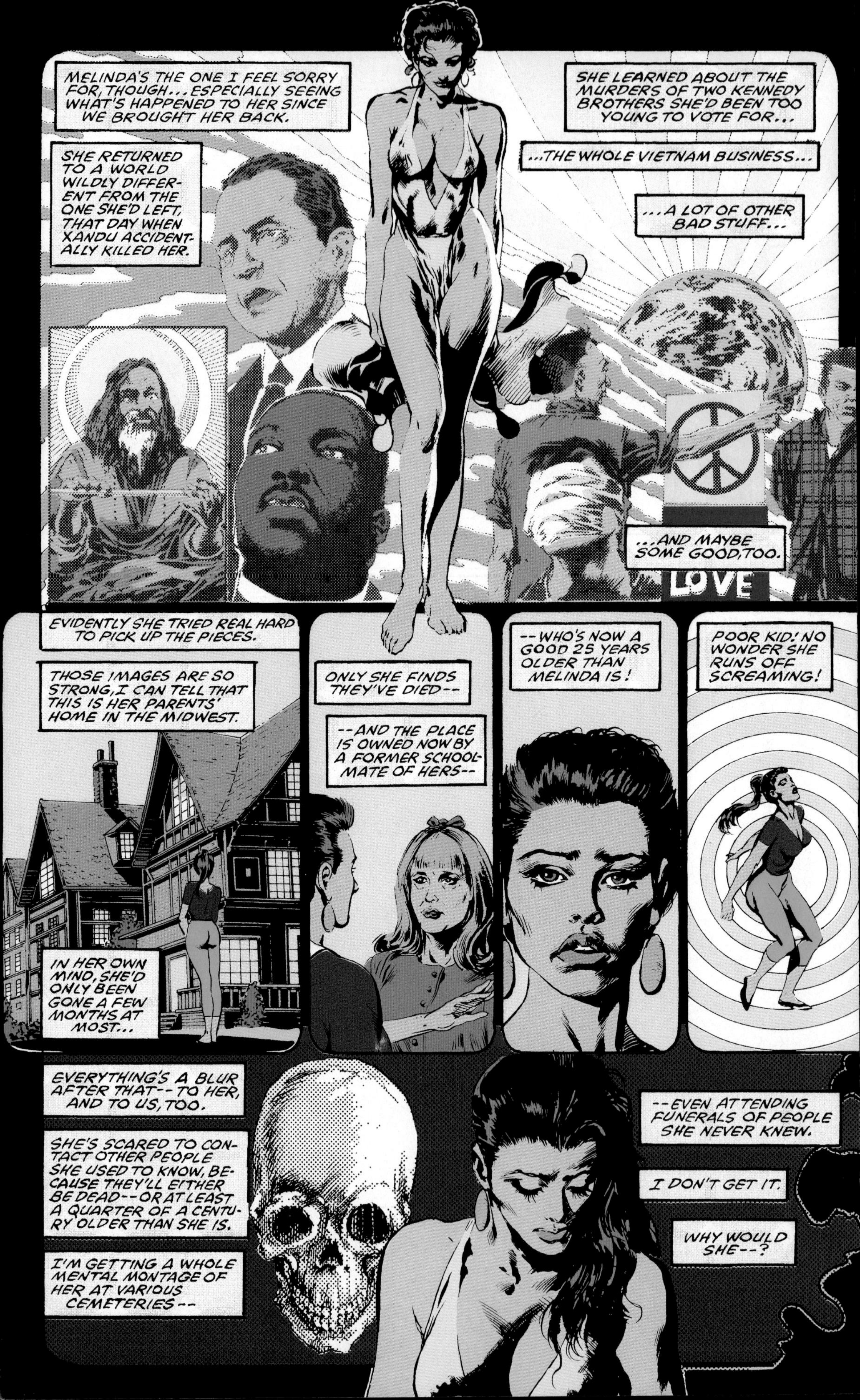
MELINDA'S THE ONE I FEEL SORRY FOR, THOUGH... ESPECIALLY SEEING WHAT'S HAPPENED TO HER SINCE WE BROUGHT HER BACK.
SHE RETURNED TO A WORLD WILDLY DIFFERENT FROM THE ONE SHE'D LEFT, THAT DAY WHEN XANDU ACCIDENTALLY KILLED HER.
SHE LEARNED ABOUT THE MURDERS OF TWO KENNEDY BROTHERS SHE'D BEEN TOO YOUNG TO VOTE FOR...
...THE WHOLE VIETNAM BUSINESS...
...A LOT OF OTHER BAD STUFF...
...AND MAYBE SOME GOOD, TOO.
LOVE
EVIDENTLY SHE TRIED REAL HARD TO PICK UP THE PIECES.
THOSE IMAGES ARE SO STRONG, I CAN TELL THAT THIS IS HER PARENTS' HOME IN THE MIDWEST.
IN HER OWN MIND, SHE'D ONLY BEEN GONE A FEW MONTHS AT MOST...
ONLY SHE FINDS THEY'VE DIED--
--AND THE PLACE IS OWNED NOW BY A FORMER SCHOOLMATE OF HERS--
--WHO'S NOW A GOOD 25 YEARS OLDER THAN MELINDA IS!
POOR KID! NO WONDER SHE RUNS OFF SCREAMING!
EVERYTHING'S A BLUR AFTER THAT--TO HER, AND TO US, TOO.
SHE'S SCARED TO CONTACT OTHER PEOPLE SHE USED TO KNOW, BECAUSE THEY'LL EITHER BE DEAD--OR AT LEAST A QUARTER OF A CENTURY OLDER THAN SHE IS.
I'M GETTING A WHOLE MENTAL MONTAGE OF HER AT VARIOUS CEMETERIES--
--EVEN ATTENDING FUNERALS OF PEOPLE SHE NEVER KNEW.
I DON'T GET IT.
WHY WOULD SHE--?

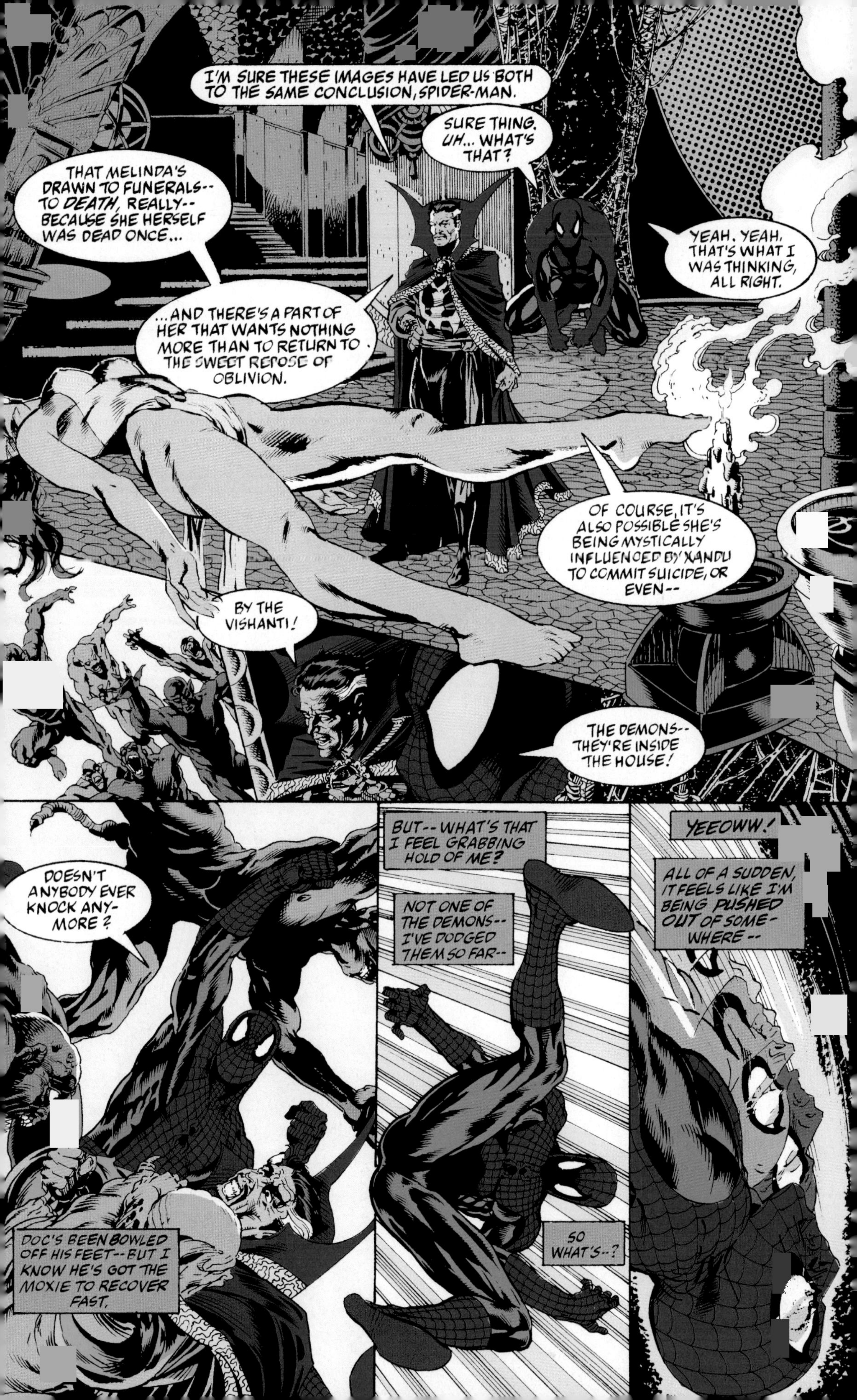

I'M SURE THESE IMAGES HAVE LED US BOTH TO THE SAME CONCLUSION, SPIDER-MAN.
SURE THING. UH... WHAT'S THAT?
THAT MELINDA'S DRAWN TO FUNERALS-- TO DEATH, REALLY-- BECAUSE SHE HERSELF WAS DEAD ONCE...
...AND THERE'S A PART OF HER THAT WANTS NOTHING MORE THAN TO RETURN TO THE SWEET REPOSE OF OBLIVION.
YEAH. YEAH, THAT'S WHAT I WAS THINKING, ALL RIGHT.
OF COURSE, IT'S ALSO POSSIBLE SHE'S BEING MYSTICALLY INFLUENCED BY XANDU TO COMMIT SUICIDE, OR EVEN--
BY THE VISHANTI!
THE DEMONS-- THEY'RE INSIDE THE HOUSE!
DOESN'T ANYBODY EVER KNOCK ANY-MORE?
DOC'S BEEN BOWLED OFF HIS FEET-- BUT I KNOW HE'S GOT THE MOXIE TO RECOVER FAST.
BUT-- WHAT'S THAT I FEEL GRABBING HOLD OF ME?
NOT ONE OF THE DEMONS-- I'VE DODGED THEM SO FAR--
SO WHAT'S--?
YEEOWW!
ALL OF A SUDDEN, IT FEELS LIKE I'M BEING PUSHED OUT OF SOME-WHERE--

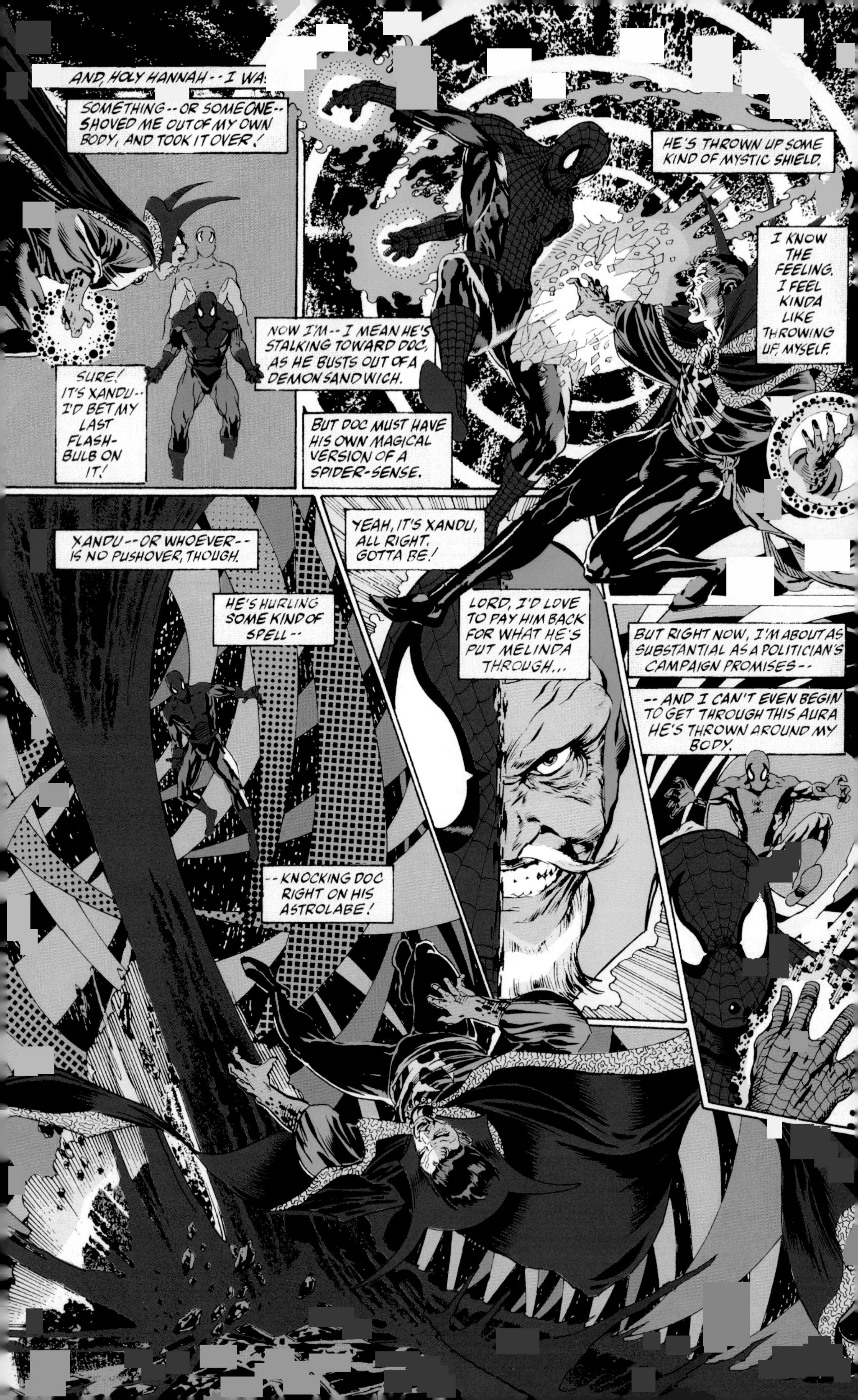
AND, HOLY HANNAH -- I WA
SOMETHING -- OR SOMEONE -- SHOVED ME OUT OF MY OWN BODY, AND TOOK IT OVER!
SURE! IT'S XANDU -- I'D BET MY LAST FLASH-BULB ON IT!
NOW I'M -- I MEAN HE'S STALKING TOWARD DOC, AS HE BUSTS OUT OF A DEMON SANDWICH.
BUT DOC MUST HAVE HIS OWN MAGICAL VERSION OF A SPIDER-SENSE.
HE'S THROWN UP SOME KIND OF MYSTIC SHIELD.
I KNOW THE FEELING. I FEEL KINDA LIKE THROWING UP, MYSELF.
XANDU -- OR WHOEVER -- IS NO PUSHOVER, THOUGH.
HE'S HURLING SOME KIND OF SPELL --
-- KNOCKING DOC RIGHT ON HIS ASTROLABE!
YEAH, IT'S XANDU, ALL RIGHT. GOTTA BE!
LORD, I'D LOVE TO PAY HIM BACK FOR WHAT HE'S PUT MELINDA THROUGH...
BUT RIGHT NOW, I'M ABOUT AS SUBSTANTIAL AS A POLITICIAN'S CAMPAIGN PROMISES --
-- AND I CAN'T EVEN BEGIN TO GET THROUGH THIS AURA HE'S THROWN AROUND MY BODY.

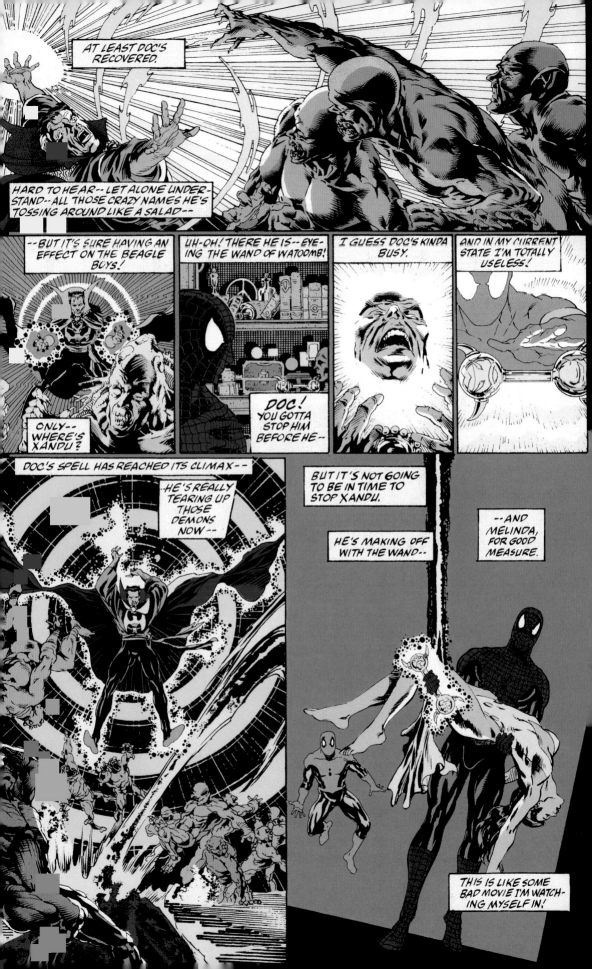

AT LEAST DOC'S RECOVERED.

HARD TO HEAR-- LET ALONE UNDERSTAND-- ALL THOSE CRAZY NAMES HE'S TOSSING AROUND LIKE A SALAD--

--BUT IT'S SURE HAVING AN EFFECT ON THE BEAGLE BOYS!

ONLY-- WHERE'S XANDU?

UH-OH! THERE HE IS-- EYEING THE WAND OF WATOOMB!

DOC! YOU GOTTA STOP HIM BEFORE HE--

I GUESS DOC'S KINDA BUSY.

AND IN MY CURRENT STATE I'M TOTALLY USELESS!

DOC'S SPELL HAS REACHED ITS CLIMAX--

--HE'S REALLY TEARING UP THOSE DEMONS NOW--

BUT IT'S NOT GOING TO BE IN TIME TO STOP XANDU.

HE'S MAKING OFF WITH THE WAND--

--AND MELINDA, FOR GOOD MEASURE.

THIS IS LIKE SOME BAD MOVIE I'M WATCHING MYSELF IN!

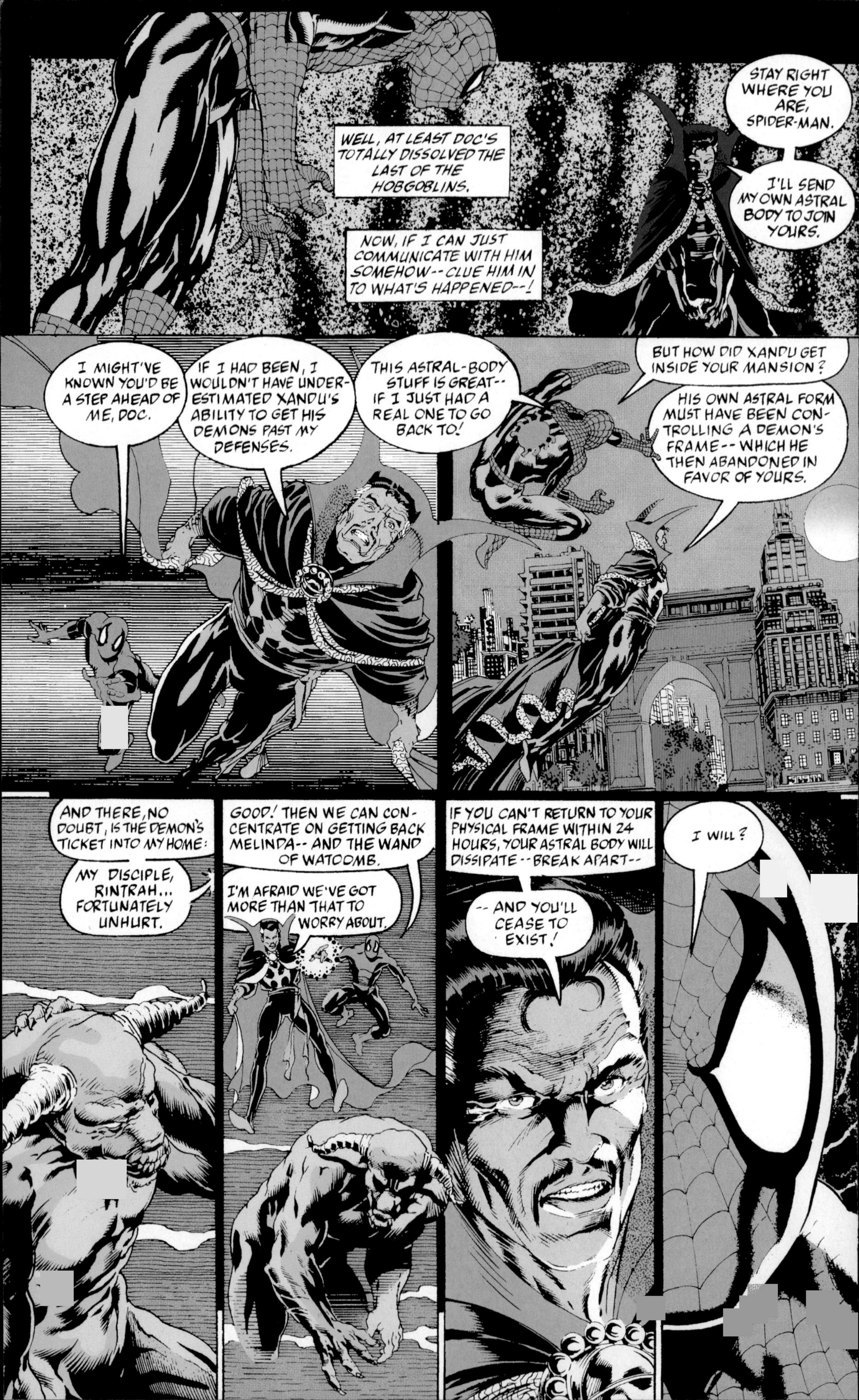
WELL, AT LEAST DOC'S TOTALLY DISSOLVED THE LAST OF THE HOBGOBLINS.
NOW, IF I CAN JUST COMMUNICATE WITH HIM SOMEHOW-- CLUE HIM IN TO WHAT'S HAPPENED--!
STAY RIGHT WHERE YOU ARE, SPIDER-MAN.
I'LL SEND MY OWN ASTRAL BODY TO JOIN YOURS.
I MIGHT'VE KNOWN YOU'D BE A STEP AHEAD OF ME, DOC.
IF I HAD BEEN, I WOULDN'T HAVE UNDER-ESTIMATED XANDU'S ABILITY TO GET HIS DEMONS PAST MY DEFENSES.
THIS ASTRAL-BODY STUFF IS GREAT-- IF I JUST HAD A REAL ONE TO GO BACK TO!
BUT HOW DID XANDU GET INSIDE YOUR MANSION?
HIS OWN ASTRAL FORM MUST HAVE BEEN CON-TROLLING A DEMON'S FRAME-- WHICH HE THEN ABANDONED IN FAVOR OF YOURS.
AND THERE, NO DOUBT, IS THE DEMON'S TICKET INTO MY HOME:
MY DISCIPLE, RINTRAH... FORTUNATELY UNHURT.
GOOD! THEN WE CAN CON-CENTRATE ON GETTING BACK MELINDA-- AND THE WAND OF WATOOMB.
I'M AFRAID WE'VE GOT MORE THAN THAT TO WORRY ABOUT.
IF YOU CAN'T RETURN TO YOUR PHYSICAL FRAME WITHIN 24 HOURS, YOUR ASTRAL BODY WILL DISSIPATE-- BREAK APART--
-- AND YOU'LL CEASE TO EXIST!
I WILL?

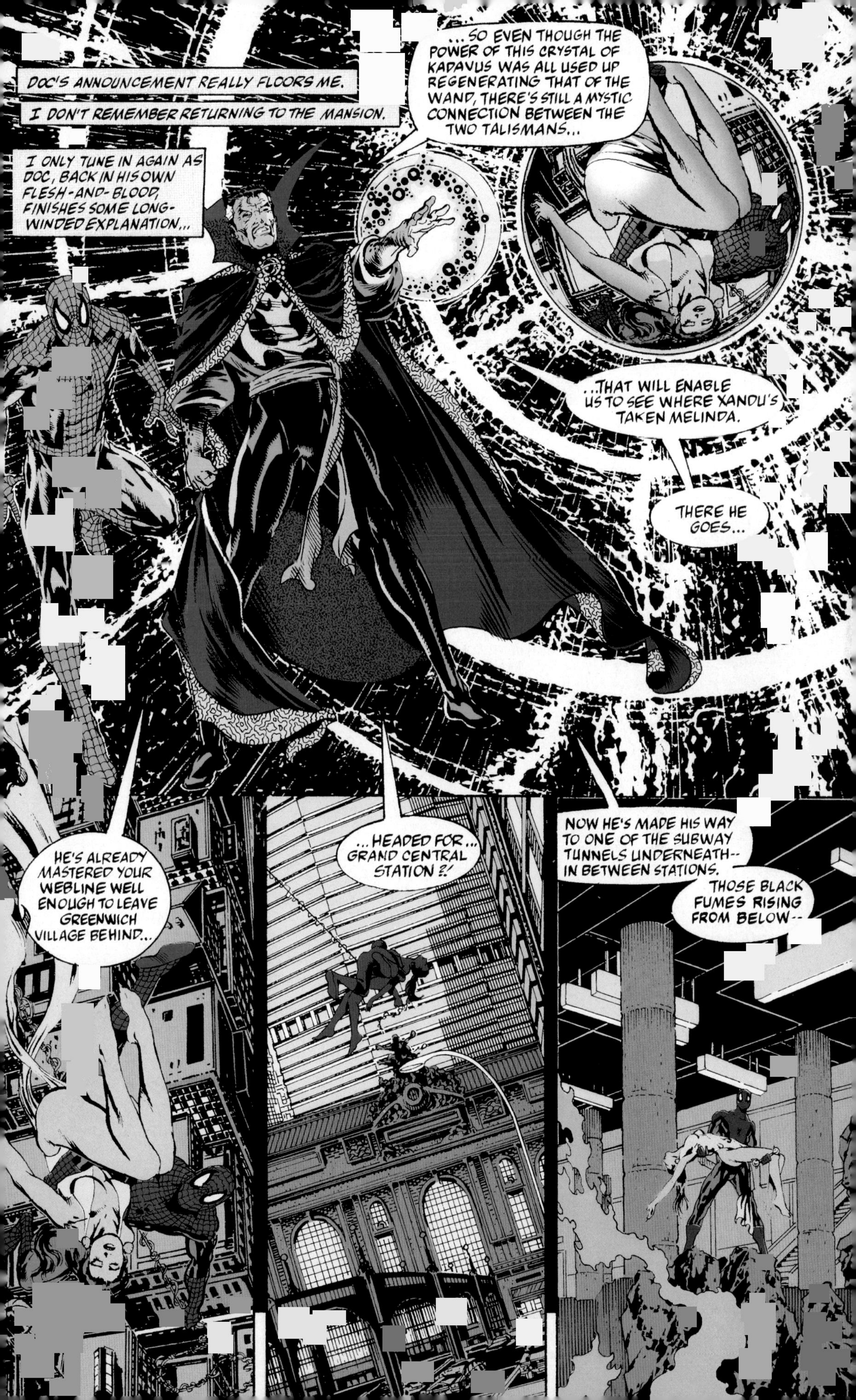
DOC'S ANNOUNCEMENT REALLY FLOORS ME.
I DON'T REMEMBER RETURNING TO THE MANSION.
I ONLY TUNE IN AGAIN AS DOC, BACK IN HIS OWN FLESH-AND-BLOOD, FINISHES SOME LONG-WINDED EXPLANATION...
...SO EVEN THOUGH THE POWER OF THIS CRYSTAL OF KADAVUS WAS ALL USED UP REGENERATING THAT OF THE WAND, THERE'S STILL A MYSTIC CONNECTION BETWEEN THE TWO TALISMANS...
...THAT WILL ENABLE US TO SEE WHERE XANDU'S TAKEN MELINDA.
THERE HE GOES...
HE'S ALREADY MASTERED YOUR WEBLINE WELL ENOUGH TO LEAVE GREENWICH VILLAGE BEHIND...
...HEADED FOR... GRAND CENTRAL STATION ?!
NOW HE'S MADE HIS WAY TO ONE OF THE SUBWAY TUNNELS UNDERNEATH-- IN BETWEEN STATIONS.
THOSE BLACK FUMES RISING FROM BELOW--

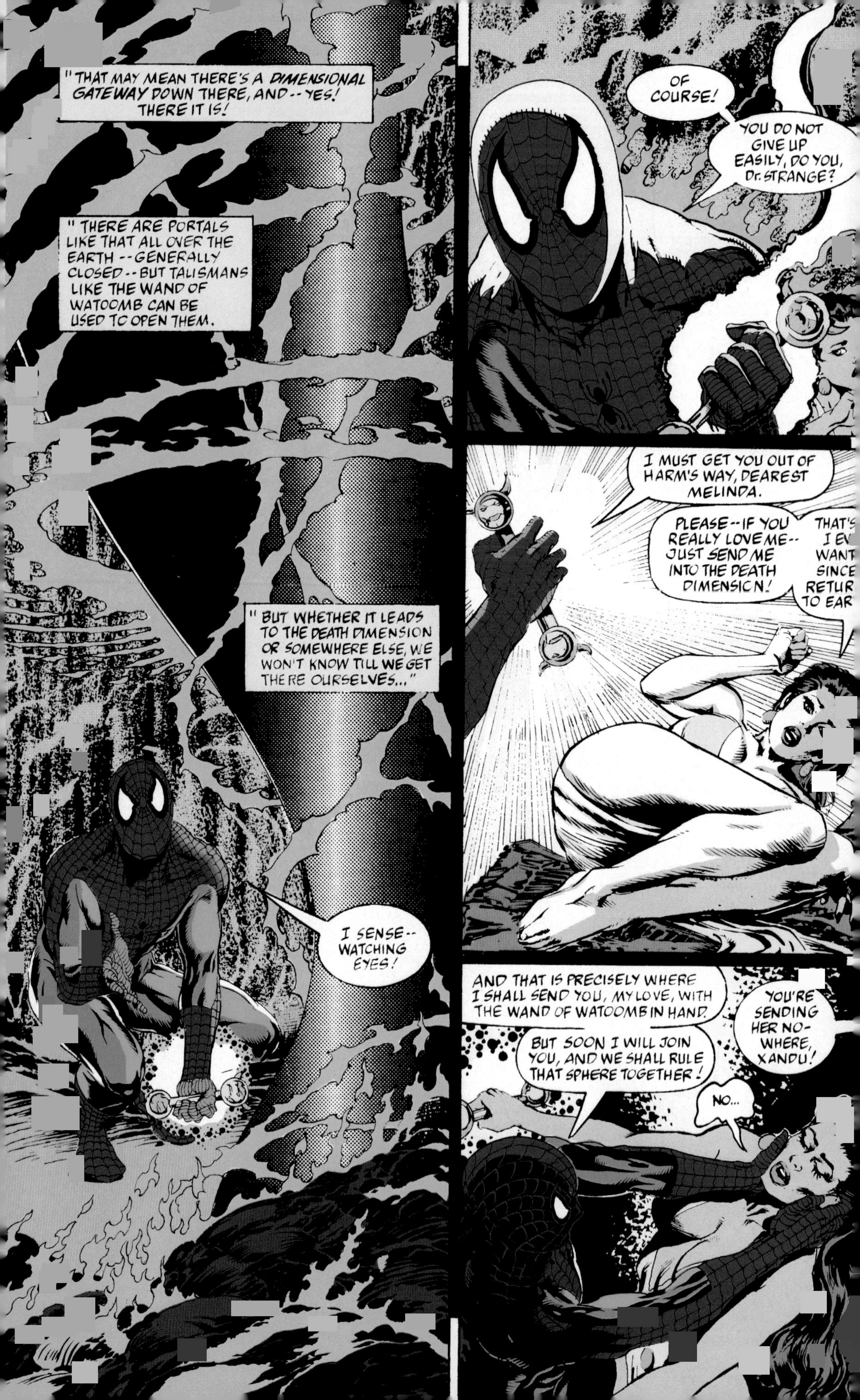
"THAT MAY MEAN THERE'S A DIMENSIONAL GATEWAY DOWN THERE, AND -- YES! THERE IT IS!
"THERE ARE PORTALS LIKE THAT ALL OVER THE EARTH -- GENERALLY CLOSED -- BUT TALISMANS LIKE THE WAND OF WATOOMB CAN BE USED TO OPEN THEM.
"BUT WHETHER IT LEADS TO THE DEATH DIMENSION OR SOMEWHERE ELSE, WE WON'T KNOW TILL WE GET THERE OURSELVES..."
I SENSE-- WATCHING EYES!
OF COURSE!
YOU DO NOT GIVE UP EASILY, DO YOU, Dr. STRANGE?
I MUST GET YOU OUT OF HARM'S WAY, DEAREST MELINDA.
PLEASE -- IF YOU REALLY LOVE ME -- JUST SEND ME INTO THE DEATH DIMENSION!
THAT'S I EV WANT SINCE RETUR TO EAR
AND THAT IS PRECISELY WHERE I SHALL SEND YOU, MY LOVE, WITH THE WAND OF WATOOMB IN HAND.
BUT SOON I WILL JOIN YOU, AND WE SHALL RULE THAT SPHERE TOGETHER!
YOU'RE SENDING HER NO-WHERE, XANDU!
NO...

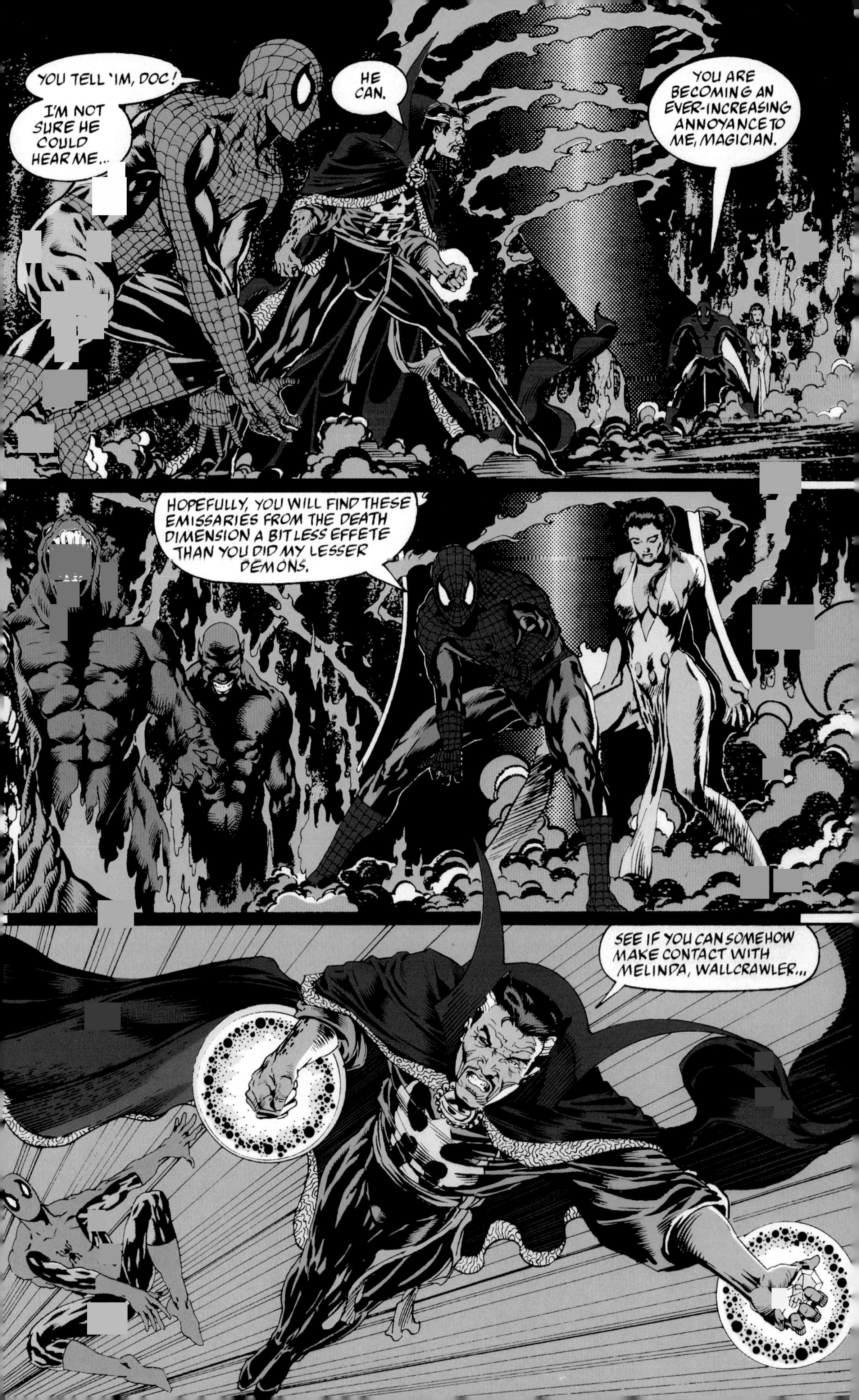
YOU TELL 'IM, DOC!
I'M NOT SURE HE COULD HEAR ME...
HE CAN.
YOU ARE BECOMING AN EVER-INCREASING ANNOYANCE TO ME, MAGICIAN.
HOPEFULLY, YOU WILL FIND THESE EMISSARIES FROM THE DEATH DIMENSION A BIT LESS EFFETE THAN YOU DID MY LESSER DEMONS.
SEE IF YOU CAN SOMEHOW MAKE CONTACT WITH MELINDA, WALLCRAWLER...

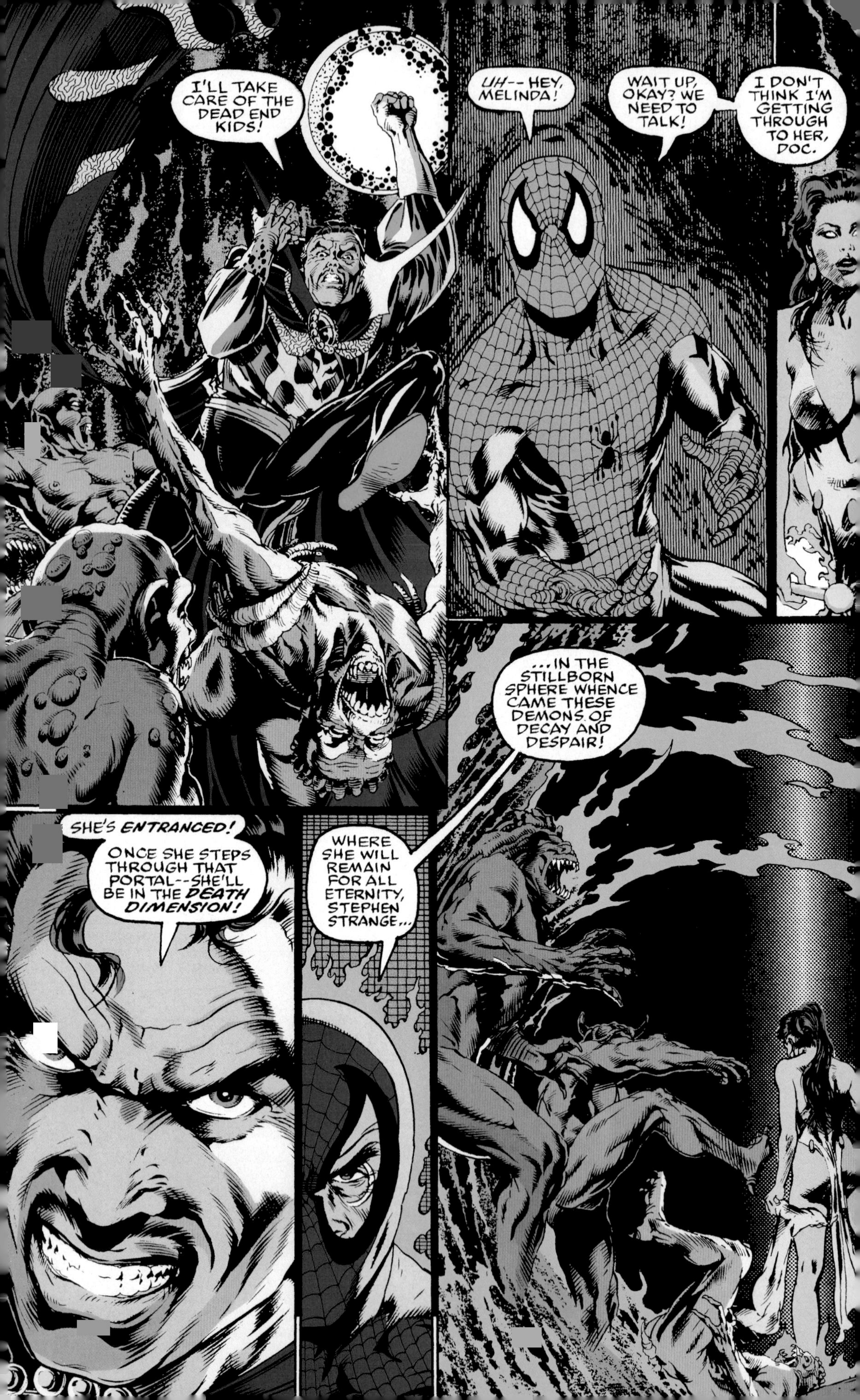
I'LL TAKE CARE OF THE DEAD END KIDS!
UH-- HEY, MELINDA!
WAIT UP, OKAY? WE NEED TO TALK!
I DON'T THINK I'M GETTING THROUGH TO HER, DOC.
SHE'S ENTRANCED!
ONCE SHE STEPS THROUGH THAT PORTAL--SHE'LL BE IN THE DEATH DIMENSION!
WHERE SHE WILL REMAIN FOR ALL ETERNITY, STEPHEN STRANGE...
...IN THE STILLBORN SPHERE WHENCE CAME THESE DEMONS OF DECAY AND DESPAIR!

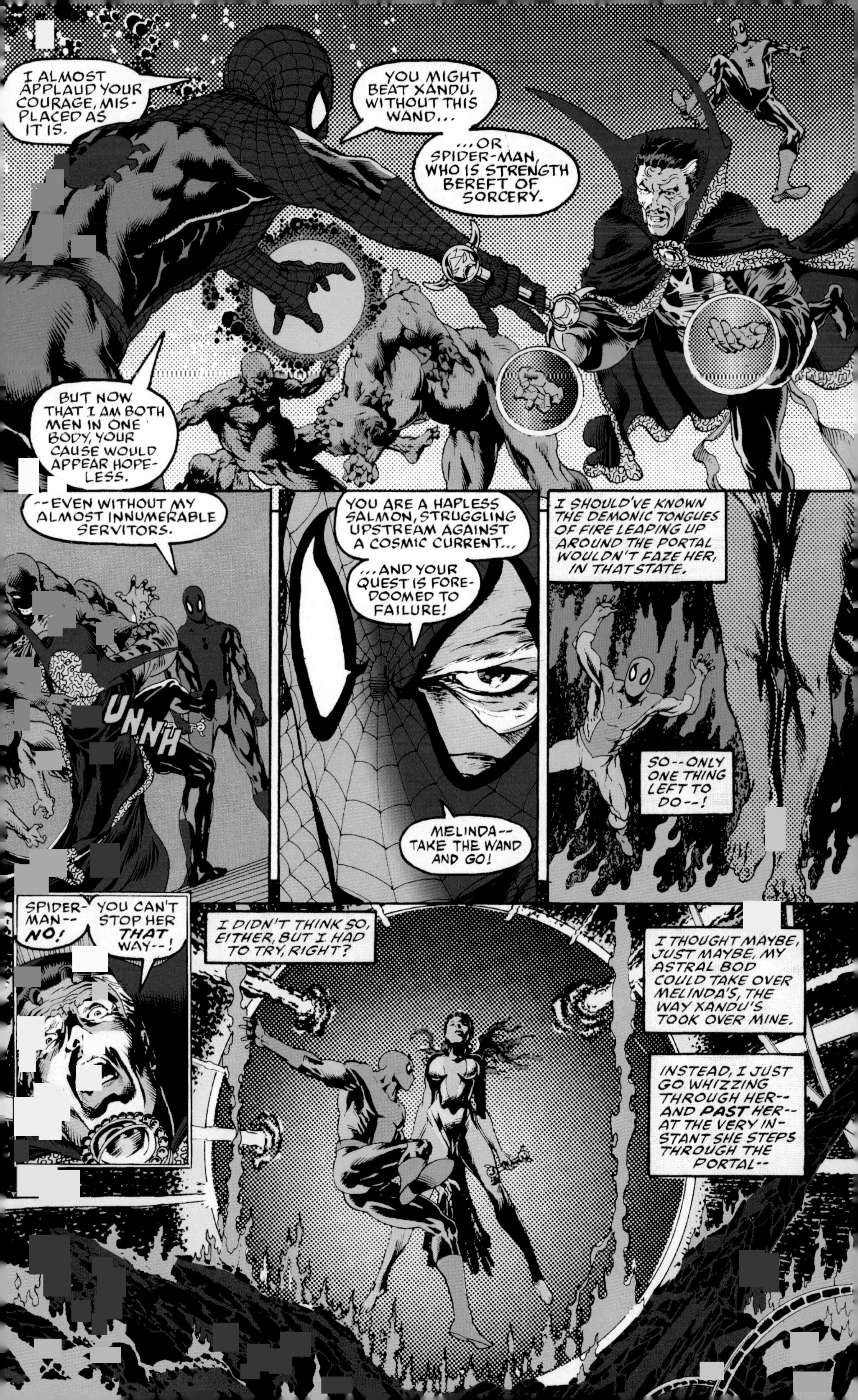

I ALMOST APPLAUD YOUR COURAGE, MISPLACED AS IT IS.
YOU MIGHT BEAT XANDU, WITHOUT THIS WAND...
...OR SPIDER-MAN, WHO IS STRENGTH BEREFT OF SORCERY.
BUT NOW THAT I AM BOTH MEN IN ONE BODY, YOUR CAUSE WOULD APPEAR HOPELESS.
--EVEN WITHOUT MY ALMOST INNUMERABLE SERVITORS.
UNNH
YOU ARE A HAPLESS SALMON, STRUGGLING UPSTREAM AGAINST A COSMIC CURRENT...
...AND YOUR QUEST IS FOREDOOMED TO FAILURE!
MELINDA-- TAKE THE WAND AND GO!
I SHOULD'VE KNOWN THE DEMONIC TONGUES OF FIRE LEAPING UP AROUND THE PORTAL WOULDN'T FAZE HER, IN THAT STATE.
SO--ONLY ONE THING LEFT TO DO--!
SPIDER-MAN-- NO!
YOU CAN'T STOP HER THAT WAY--!
I DIDN'T THINK SO, EITHER, BUT I HAD TO TRY, RIGHT?
I THOUGHT MAYBE, JUST MAYBE, MY ASTRAL BOD COULD TAKE OVER MELINDA'S, THE WAY XANDU'S TOOK OVER MINE.
INSTEAD, I JUST GO WHIZZING THROUGH HER-- AND PAST HER-- AT THE VERY INSTANT SHE STEPS THROUGH THE PORTAL--

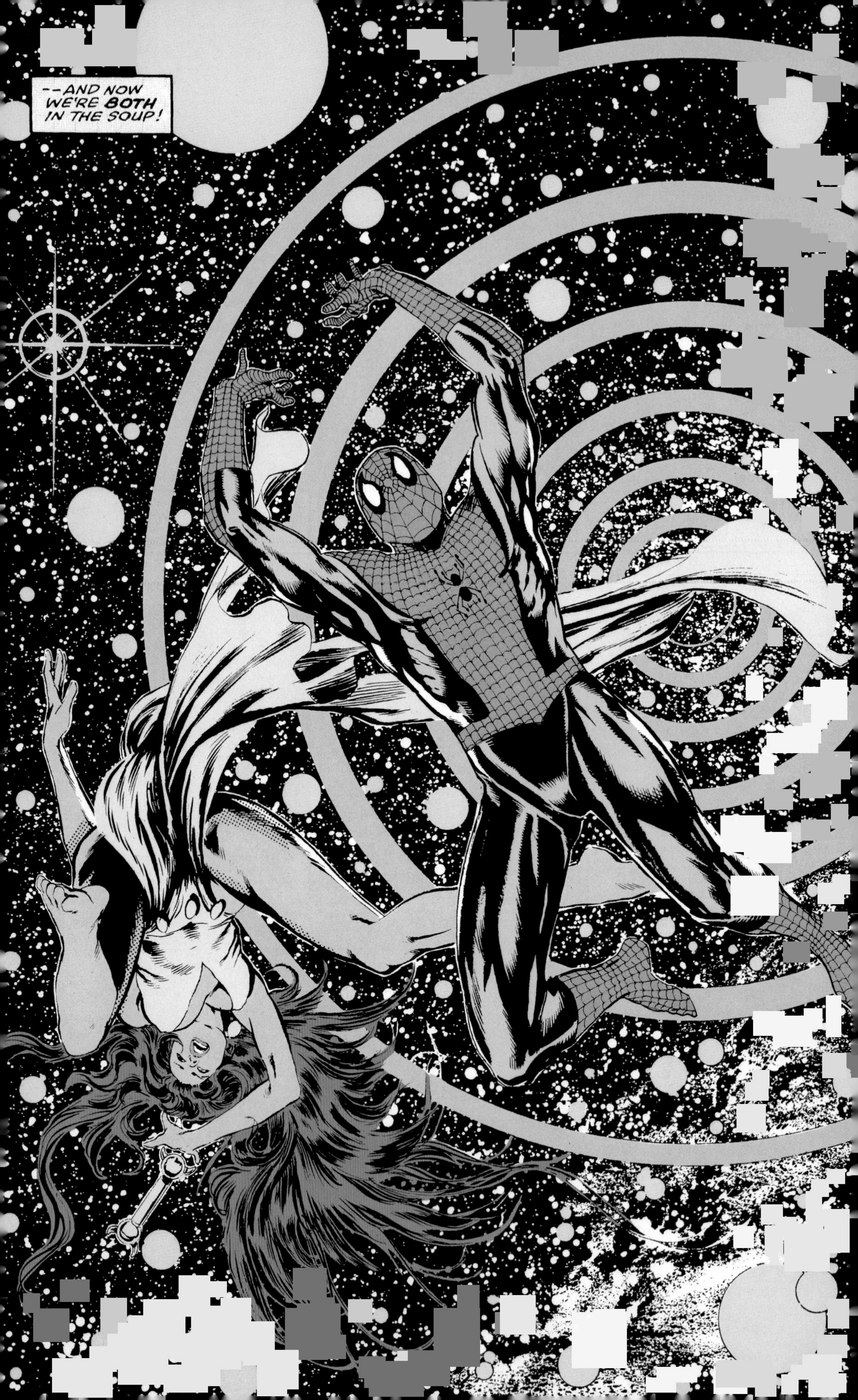
--AND NOW WE'RE BOTH IN THE SOUP!

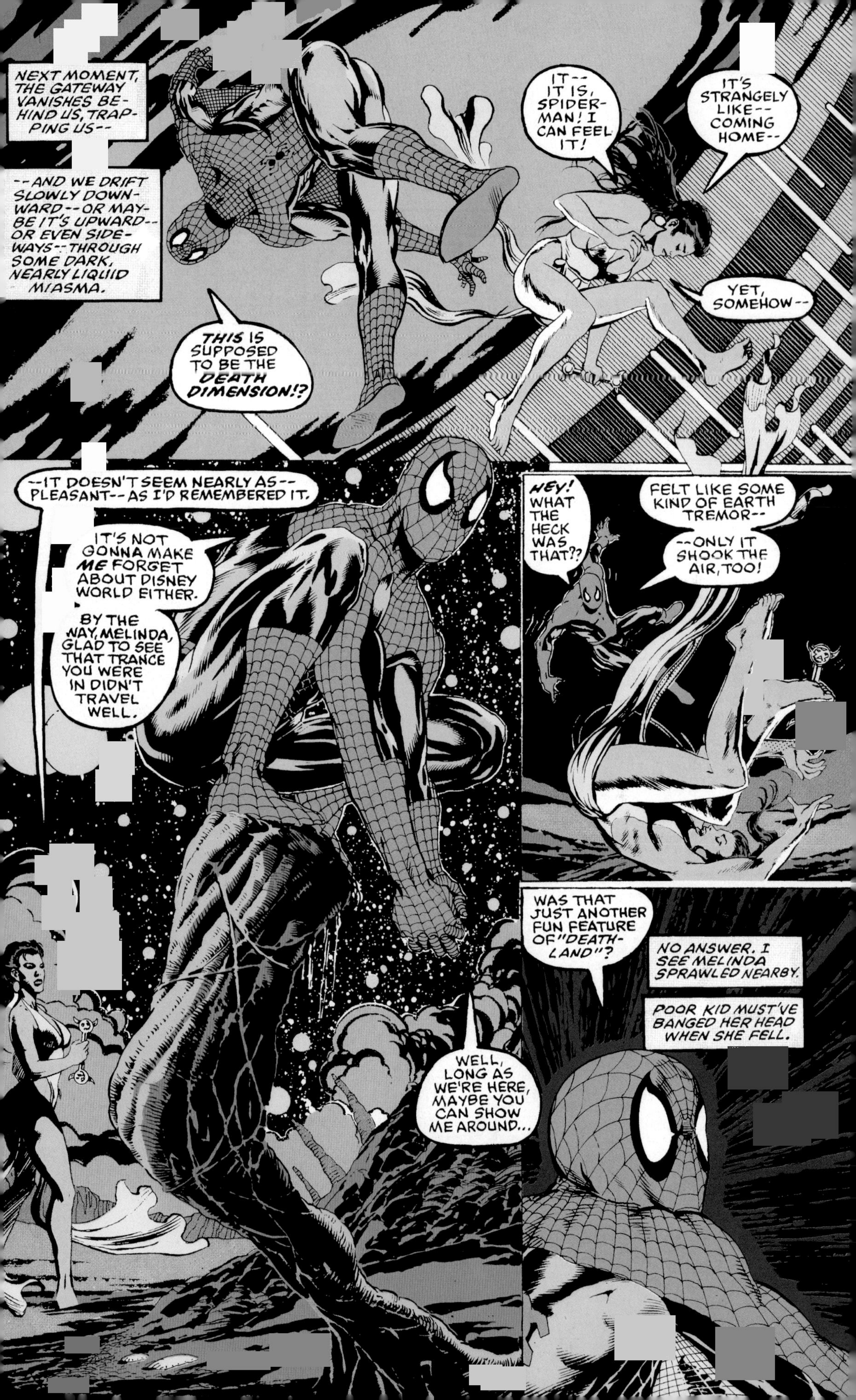
NEXT MOMENT, THE GATEWAY VANISHES BEHIND US, TRAPPING US--
--AND WE DRIFT SLOWLY DOWNWARD--OR MAYBE IT'S UPWARD--OR EVEN SIDEWAYS--THROUGH SOME DARK, NEARLY LIQUID MIASMA.
IT--IT IS, SPIDER-MAN! I CAN FEEL IT!
IT'S STRANGELY LIKE--COMING HOME--
YET, SOMEHOW--
THIS IS SUPPOSED TO BE THE DEATH DIMENSION!?
--IT DOESN'T SEEM NEARLY AS--PLEASANT--AS I'D REMEMBERED IT.
IT'S NOT GONNA MAKE ME FORGET ABOUT DISNEY WORLD EITHER.
BY THE WAY, MELINDA, GLAD TO SEE THAT TRANCE YOU WERE IN DIDN'T TRAVEL WELL.
HEY! WHAT THE HECK WAS THAT??
FELT LIKE SOME KIND OF EARTH TREMOR--
--ONLY IT SHOOK THE AIR, TOO!
WAS THAT JUST ANOTHER FUN FEATURE OF "DEATH-LAND"?
NO ANSWER. I SEE MELINDA SPRAWLED NEARBY.
POOR KID MUST'VE BANGED HER HEAD WHEN SHE FELL.
WELL, LONG AS WE'RE HERE, MAYBE YOU CAN SHOW ME AROUND...

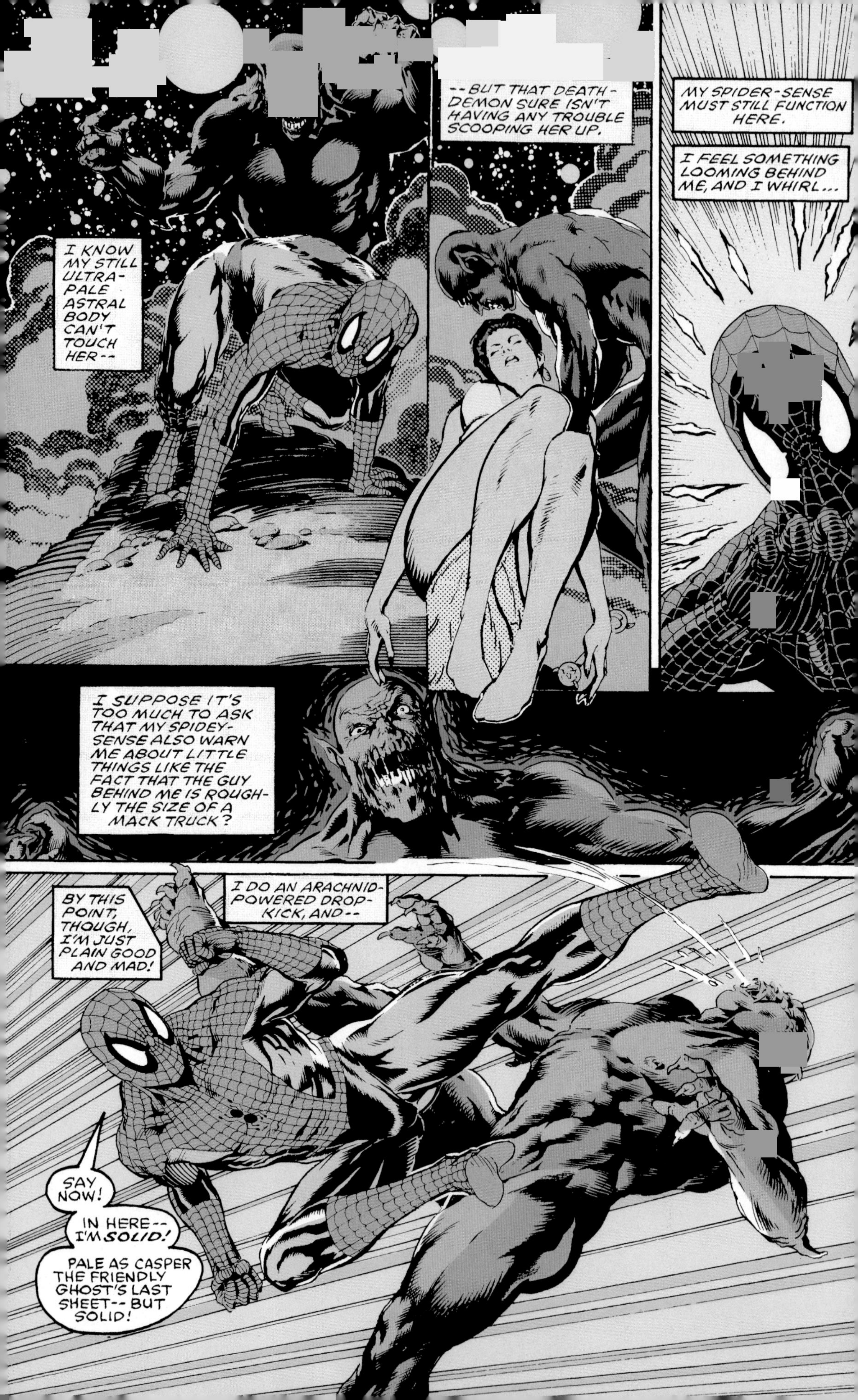

I KNOW MY STILL ULTRA-PALE ASTRAL BODY CAN'T TOUCH HER--
--BUT THAT DEATH-DEMON SURE ISN'T HAVING ANY TROUBLE SCOOPING HER UP.
MY SPIDER-SENSE MUST STILL FUNCTION HERE.
I FEEL SOMETHING LOOMING BEHIND ME, AND I WHIRL...
I SUPPOSE IT'S TOO MUCH TO ASK THAT MY SPIDEY-SENSE ALSO WARN ME ABOUT LITTLE THINGS LIKE THE FACT THAT THE GUY BEHIND ME IS ROUGHLY THE SIZE OF A MACK TRUCK?
BY THIS POINT, THOUGH, I'M JUST PLAIN GOOD AND MAD!
I DO AN ARACHNID-POWERED DROP-KICK, AND--
SAY NOW!
IN HERE-- I'M SOLID!
PALE AS CASPER THE FRIENDLY GHOST'S LAST SHEET-- BUT SOLID!

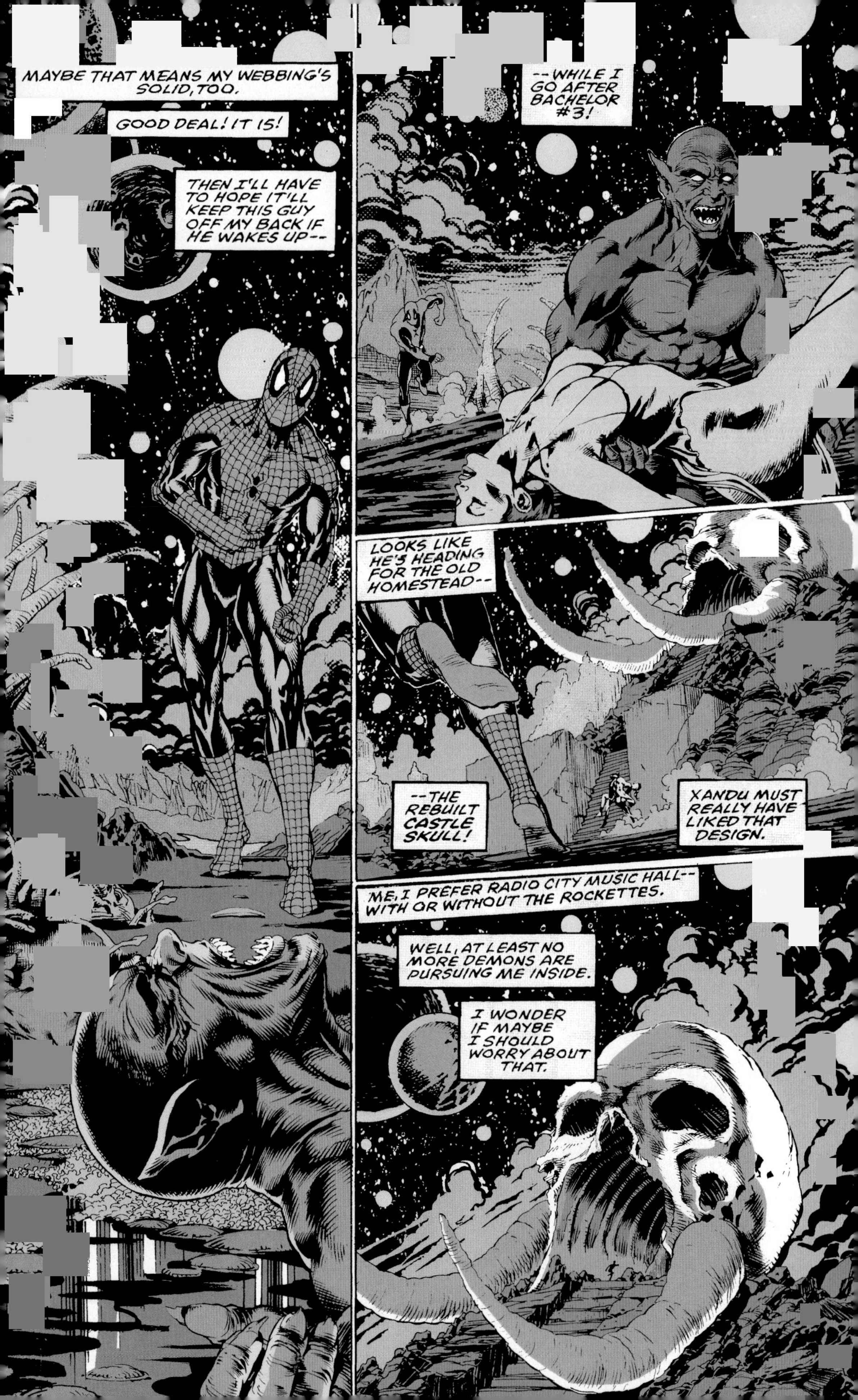
MAYBE THAT MEANS MY WEBBING'S SOLID, TOO.
GOOD DEAL! IT IS!
THEN I'LL HAVE TO HOPE IT'LL KEEP THIS GUY OFF MY BACK IF HE WAKES UP--
--WHILE I GO AFTER BACHELOR #3!
LOOKS LIKE HE'S HEADING FOR THE OLD HOMESTEAD--
--THE REBUILT CASTLE SKULL!
XANDU MUST REALLY HAVE LIKED THAT DESIGN.
ME, I PREFER RADIO CITY MUSIC HALL-- WITH OR WITHOUT THE ROCKETTES.
WELL, AT LEAST NO MORE DEMONS ARE PURSUING ME INSIDE.
I WONDER IF MAYBE I SHOULD WORRY ABOUT THAT.

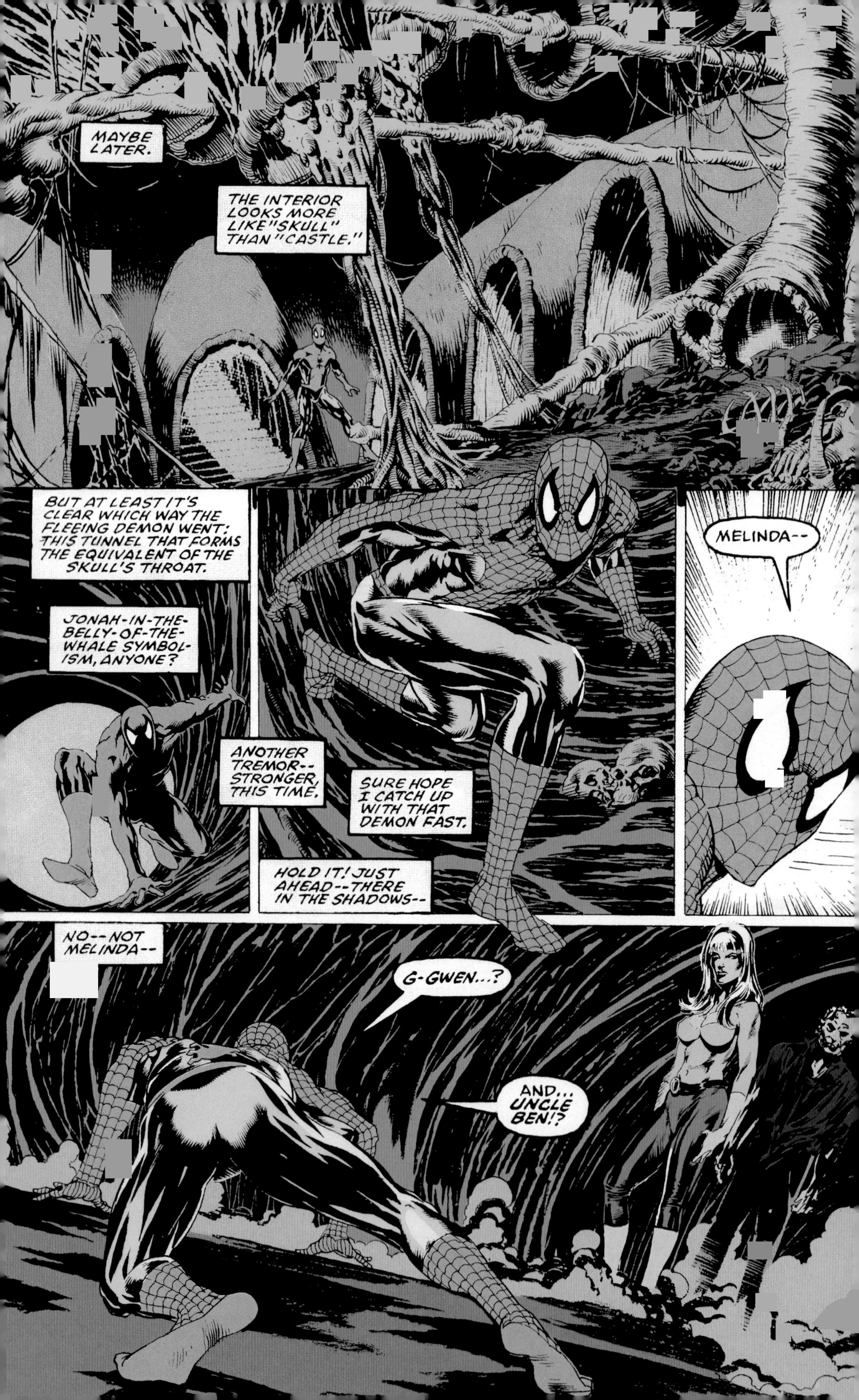
MAYBE LATER.
THE INTERIOR LOOKS MORE LIKE "SKULL" THAN "CASTLE."
BUT AT LEAST IT'S CLEAR WHICH WAY THE FLEEING DEMON WENT: THIS TUNNEL THAT FORMS THE EQUIVALENT OF THE SKULL'S THROAT.
JONAH-IN-THE-BELLY-OF-THE-WHALE SYMBOLISM, ANYONE?
ANOTHER TREMOR--STRONGER, THIS TIME.
SURE HOPE I CATCH UP WITH THAT DEMON FAST.
HOLD IT! JUST AHEAD--THERE IN THE SHADOWS--
MELINDA--
NO--NOT MELINDA--
G-GWEN...?
AND... UNCLE BEN!?

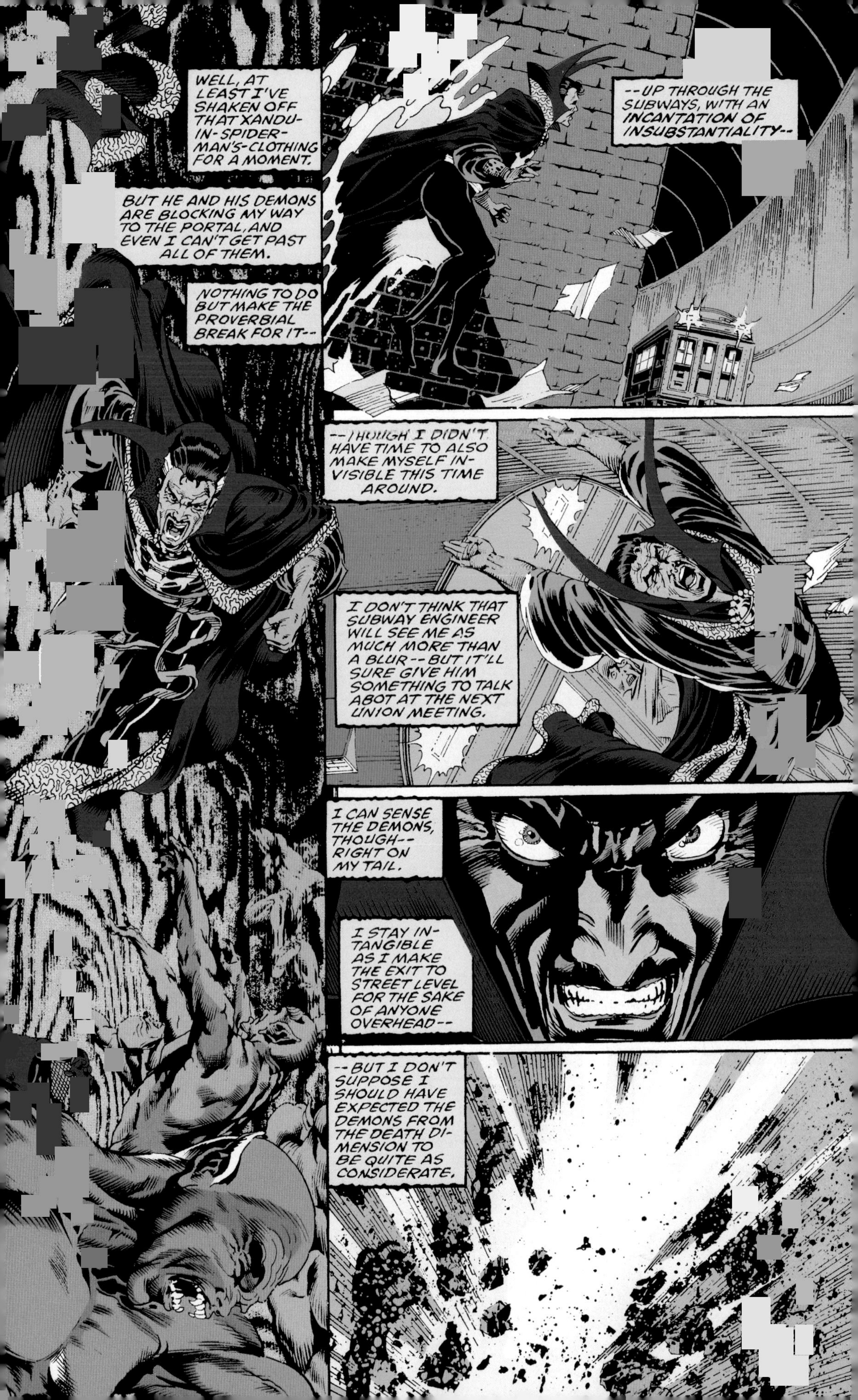
WELL, AT LEAST I'VE SHAKEN OFF THAT XANDU-IN-SPIDER-MAN'S-CLOTHING FOR A MOMENT.
BUT HE AND HIS DEMONS ARE BLOCKING MY WAY TO THE PORTAL, AND EVEN I CAN'T GET PAST ALL OF THEM.
NOTHING TO DO BUT MAKE THE PROVERBIAL BREAK FOR IT--
--UP THROUGH THE SUBWAYS, WITH AN INCANTATION OF INSUBSTANTIALITY--
--THOUGH I DIDN'T HAVE TIME TO ALSO MAKE MYSELF IN-VISIBLE THIS TIME AROUND.
I DON'T THINK THAT SUBWAY ENGINEER WILL SEE ME AS MUCH MORE THAN A BLUR--BUT IT'LL SURE GIVE HIM SOMETHING TO TALK ABOT AT THE NEXT UNION MEETING.
I CAN SENSE THE DEMONS, THOUGH--RIGHT ON MY TAIL.
I STAY IN-TANGIBLE AS I MAKE THE EXIT TO STREET LEVEL FOR THE SAKE OF ANYONE OVERHEAD--
--BUT I DON'T SUPPOSE I SHOULD HAVE EXPECTED THE DEMONS FROM THE DEATH DI-MENSION TO BE QUITE AS CONSIDERATE.

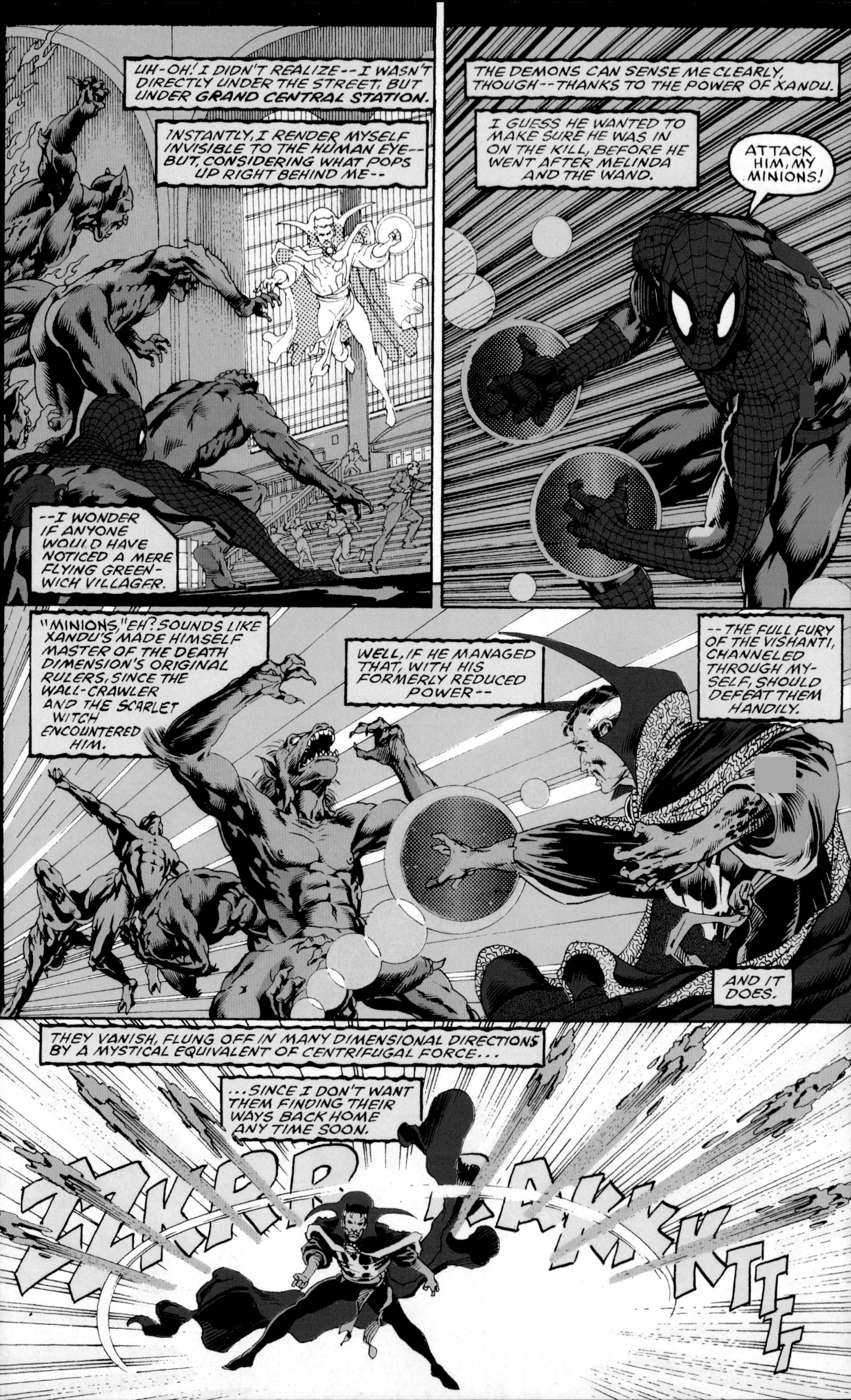
UH-OH! I DIDN'T REALIZE--I WASN'T DIRECTLY UNDER THE STREET, BUT UNDER GRAND CENTRAL STATION.
INSTANTLY, I RENDER MYSELF INVISIBLE TO THE HUMAN EYE--BUT, CONSIDERING WHAT POPS UP RIGHT BEHIND ME--
--I WONDER IF ANYONE WOULD HAVE NOTICED A MERE FLYING GREENWICH VILLAGER.
THE DEMONS CAN SENSE ME CLEARLY, THOUGH--THANKS TO THE POWER OF XANDU.
I GUESS HE WANTED TO MAKE SURE HE WAS IN ON THE KILL, BEFORE HE WENT AFTER MELINDA AND THE WAND.
ATTACK HIM, MY MINIONS!
"MINIONS," EH? SOUNDS LIKE XANDU'S MADE HIMSELF MASTER OF THE DEATH DIMENSION'S ORIGINAL RULERS, SINCE THE WALL-CRAWLER AND THE SCARLET WITCH ENCOUNTERED HIM.
WELL, IF HE MANAGED THAT, WITH HIS FORMERLY REDUCED POWER--
--THE FULL FURY OF THE VISHANTI, CHANNELED THROUGH MYSELF, SHOULD DEFEAT THEM HANDILY.
AND IT DOES.
THEY VANISH, FLUNG OFF IN MANY DIMENSIONAL DIRECTIONS BY A MYSTICAL EQUIVALENT OF CENTRIFUGAL FORCE...
...SINCE I DON'T WANT THEM FINDING THEIR WAYS BACK HOME ANY TIME SOON.

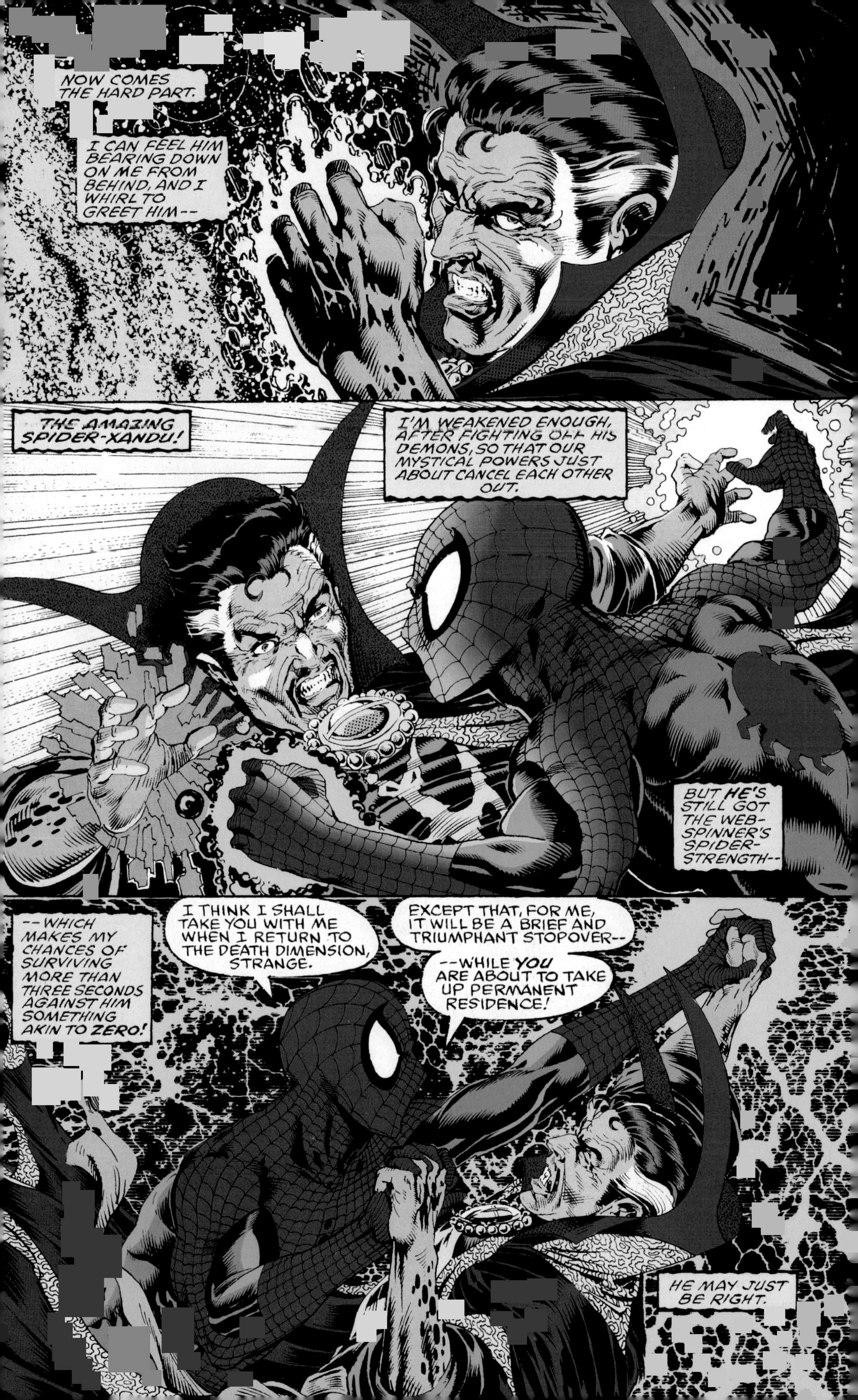
NOW COMES THE HARD PART.
I CAN FEEL HIM BEARING DOWN ON ME FROM BEHIND, AND I WHIRL TO GREET HIM--
THE AMAZING SPIDER-XANDU!
I'M WEAKENED ENOUGH, AFTER FIGHTING OFF HIS DEMONS, SO THAT OUR MYSTICAL POWERS JUST ABOUT CANCEL EACH OTHER OUT.
BUT HE'S STILL GOT THE WEB-SPINNER'S SPIDER-STRENGTH--
--WHICH MAKES MY CHANCES OF SURVIVING MORE THAN THREE SECONDS AGAINST HIM SOMETHING AKIN TO ZERO!
I THINK I SHALL TAKE YOU WITH ME WHEN I RETURN TO THE DEATH DIMENSION, STRANGE.
EXCEPT THAT, FOR ME, IT WILL BE A BRIEF AND TRIUMPHANT STOPOVER--
--WHILE YOU ARE ABOUT TO TAKE UP PERMANENT RESIDENCE!
HE MAY JUST BE RIGHT.

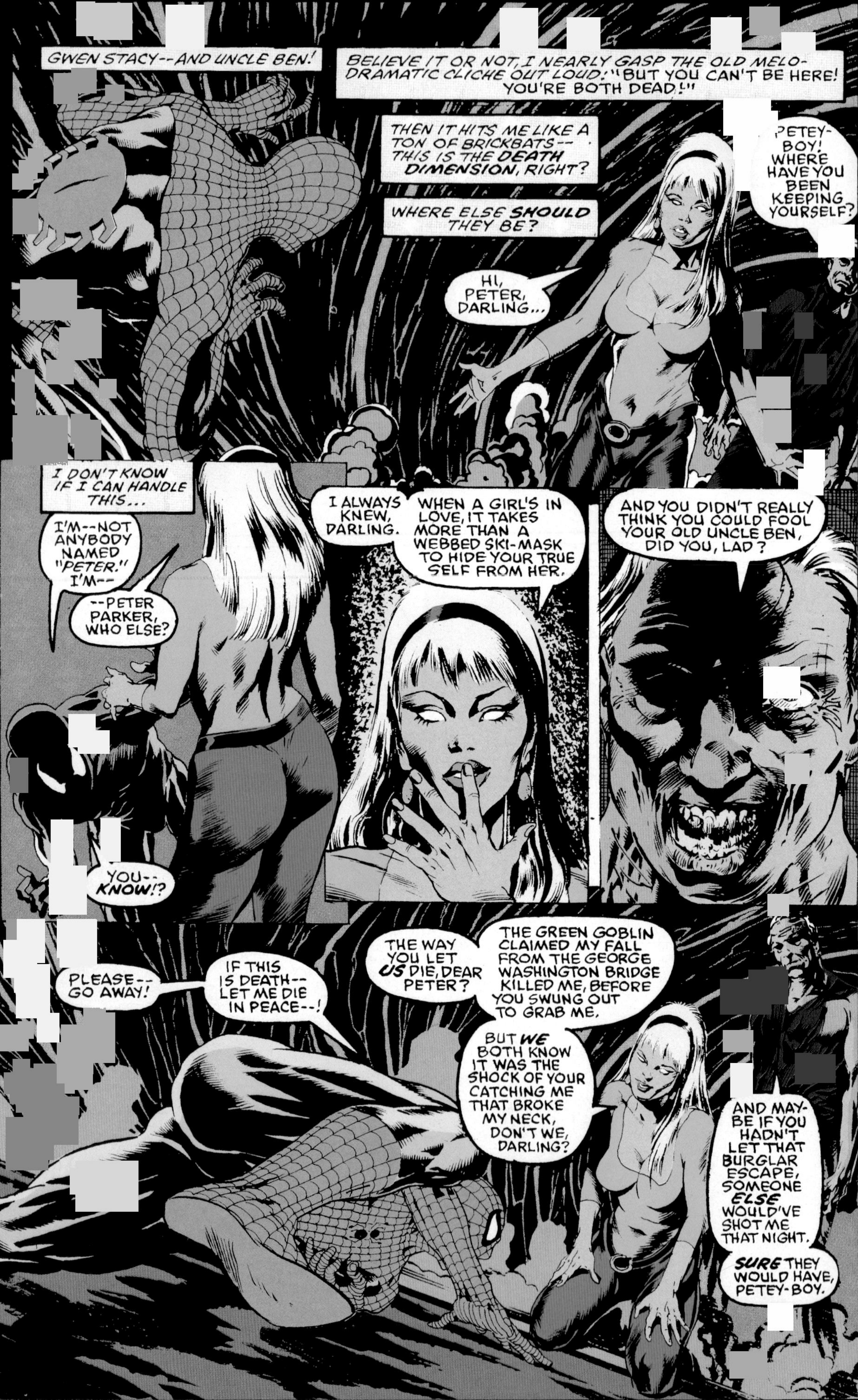
GWEN STACY--AND UNCLE BEN!
BELIEVE IT OR NOT, I NEARLY GASP THE OLD MELO-DRAMATIC CLICHE OUT LOUD: "BUT YOU CAN'T BE HERE! YOU'RE BOTH DEAD!"
THEN IT HITS ME LIKE A TON OF BRICKBATS-- THIS IS THE DEATH DIMENSION, RIGHT?
WHERE ELSE SHOULD THEY BE?
PETEY-BOY! WHERE HAVE YOU BEEN KEEPING YOURSELF?
HI, PETER, DARLING...
I DON'T KNOW IF I CAN HANDLE THIS...
I'M--NOT ANYBODY NAMED "PETER." I'M--
--PETER PARKER, WHO ELSE?
I ALWAYS KNEW, DARLING.
WHEN A GIRL'S IN LOVE, IT TAKES MORE THAN A WEBBED SKI-MASK TO HIDE YOUR TRUE SELF FROM HER.
AND YOU DIDN'T REALLY THINK YOU COULD FOOL YOUR OLD UNCLE BEN, DID YOU, LAD?
YOU--KNOW!?
PLEASE--GO AWAY!
IF THIS IS DEATH--LET ME DIE IN PEACE--!
THE WAY YOU LET US DIE, DEAR PETER?
THE GREEN GOBLIN CLAIMED MY FALL FROM THE GEORGE WASHINGTON BRIDGE KILLED ME, BEFORE YOU SWUNG OUT TO GRAB ME.
BUT WE BOTH KNOW IT WAS THE SHOCK OF YOUR CATCHING ME THAT BROKE MY NECK, DON'T WE, DARLING?
AND MAYBE IF YOU HADN'T LET THAT BURGLAR ESCAPE, SOMEONE ELSE WOULD'VE SHOT ME THAT NIGHT.
SURE THEY WOULD HAVE, PETEY-BOY.

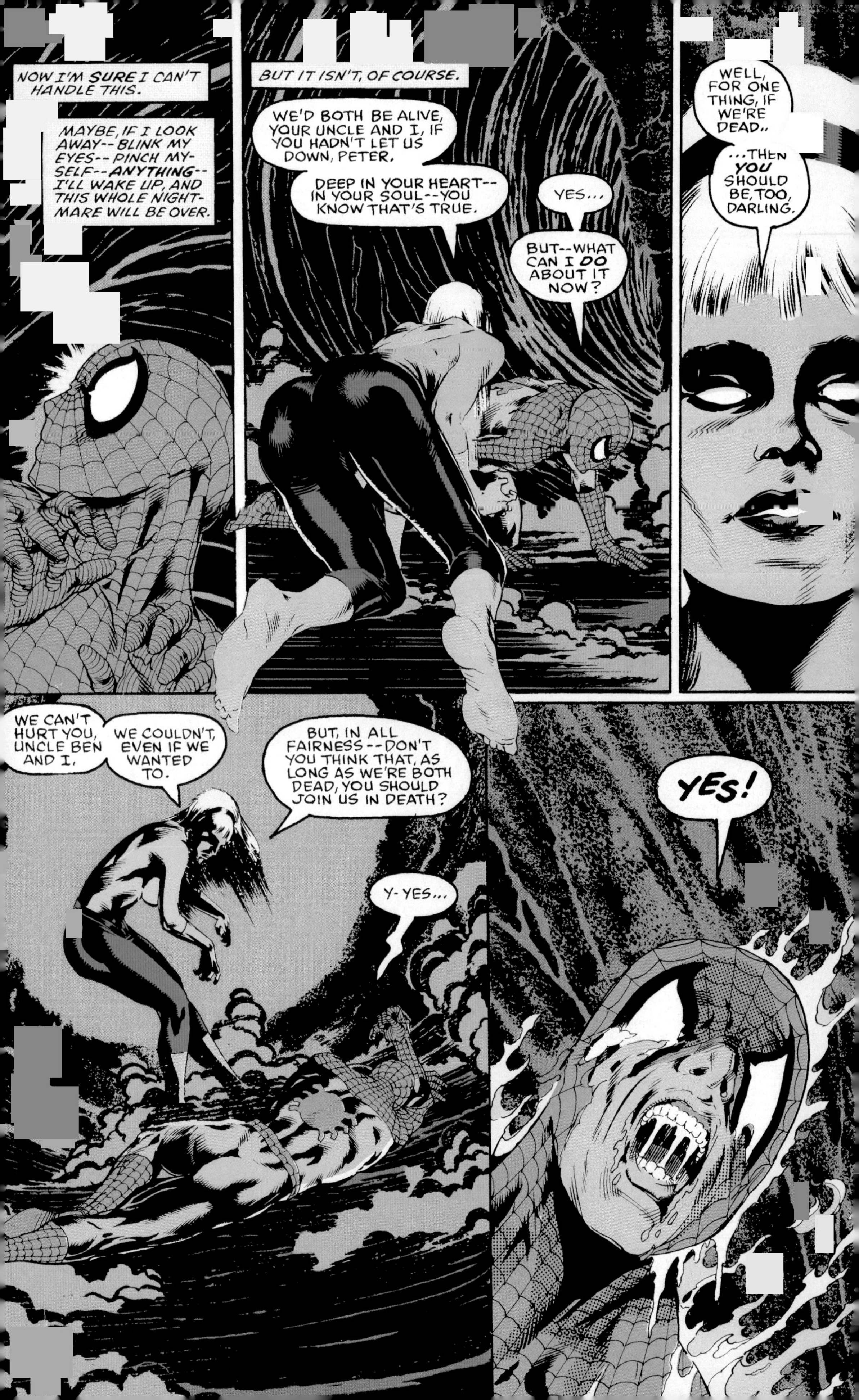
NOW I'M SURE I CAN'T HANDLE THIS.
MAYBE, IF I LOOK AWAY-- BLINK MY EYES-- PINCH MYSELF-- ANYTHING-- I'LL WAKE UP, AND THIS WHOLE NIGHTMARE WILL BE OVER.
BUT IT ISN'T, OF COURSE.
WE'D BOTH BE ALIVE, YOUR UNCLE AND I, IF YOU HADN'T LET US DOWN, PETER.
DEEP IN YOUR HEART-- IN YOUR SOUL--YOU KNOW THAT'S TRUE.
YES...
BUT--WHAT CAN I DO ABOUT IT NOW?
WELL, FOR ONE THING, IF WE'RE DEAD..
...THEN YOU SHOULD BE, TOO, DARLING.
WE CAN'T HURT YOU, UNCLE BEN AND I.
WE COULDN'T, EVEN IF WE WANTED TO.
BUT, IN ALL FAIRNESS --DON'T YOU THINK THAT, AS LONG AS WE'RE BOTH DEAD, YOU SHOULD JOIN US IN DEATH?
Y- YES...
YES!

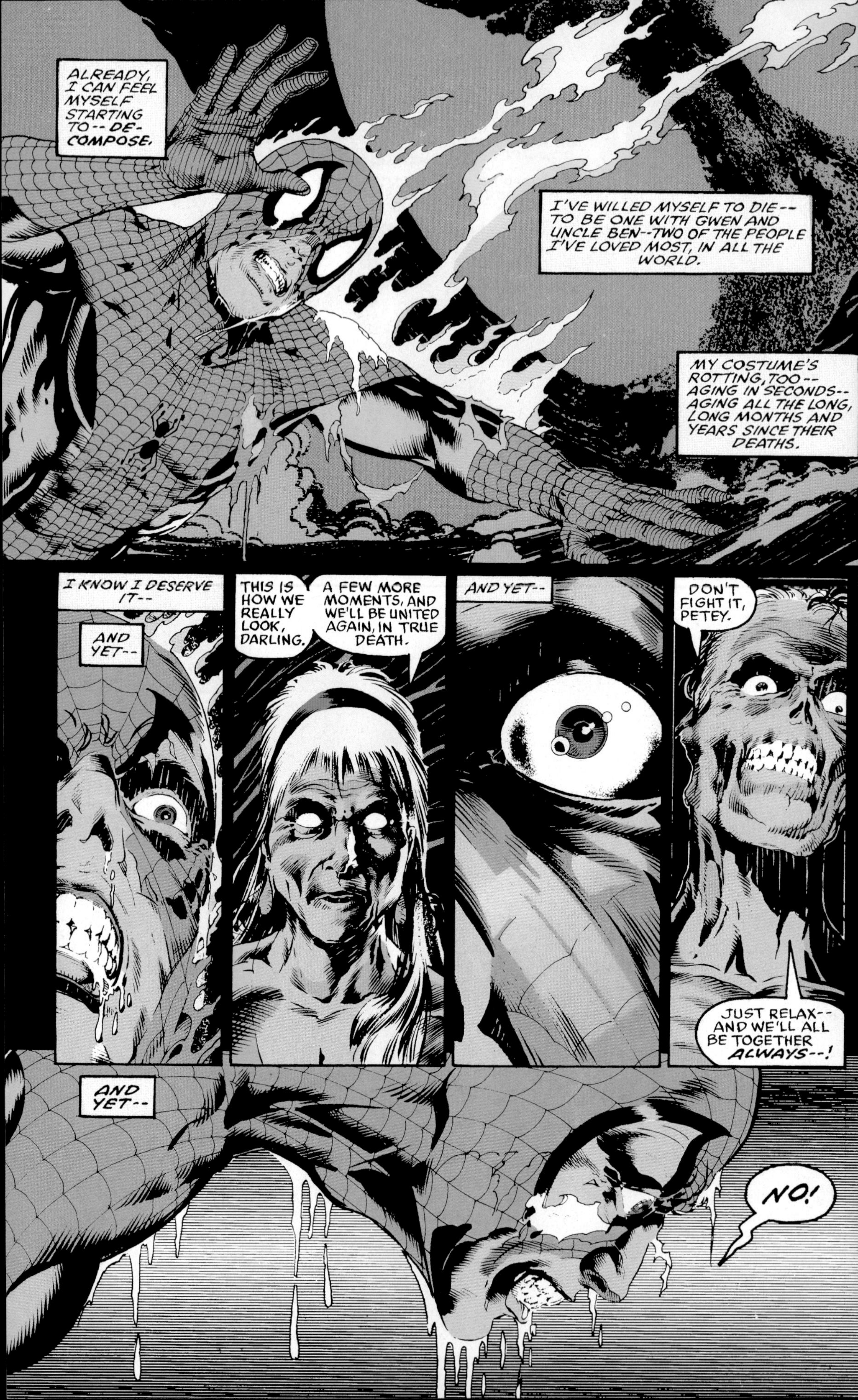

ALREADY, I CAN FEEL MYSELF STARTING TO--DE-COMPOSE.
I'VE WILLED MYSELF TO DIE--TO BE ONE WITH GWEN AND UNCLE BEN--TWO OF THE PEOPLE I'VE LOVED MOST, IN ALL THE WORLD.
MY COSTUME'S ROTTING, TOO--AGING IN SECONDS--AGING ALL THE LONG, LONG MONTHS AND YEARS SINCE THEIR DEATHS.
I KNOW I DESERVE IT--
AND YET--
THIS IS HOW WE REALLY LOOK, DARLING.
A FEW MORE MOMENTS, AND WE'LL BE UNITED AGAIN, IN TRUE DEATH.
AND YET--
DON'T FIGHT IT, PETEY.
JUST RELAX--AND WE'LL ALL BE TOGETHER ALWAYS--!
AND YET--
NO!

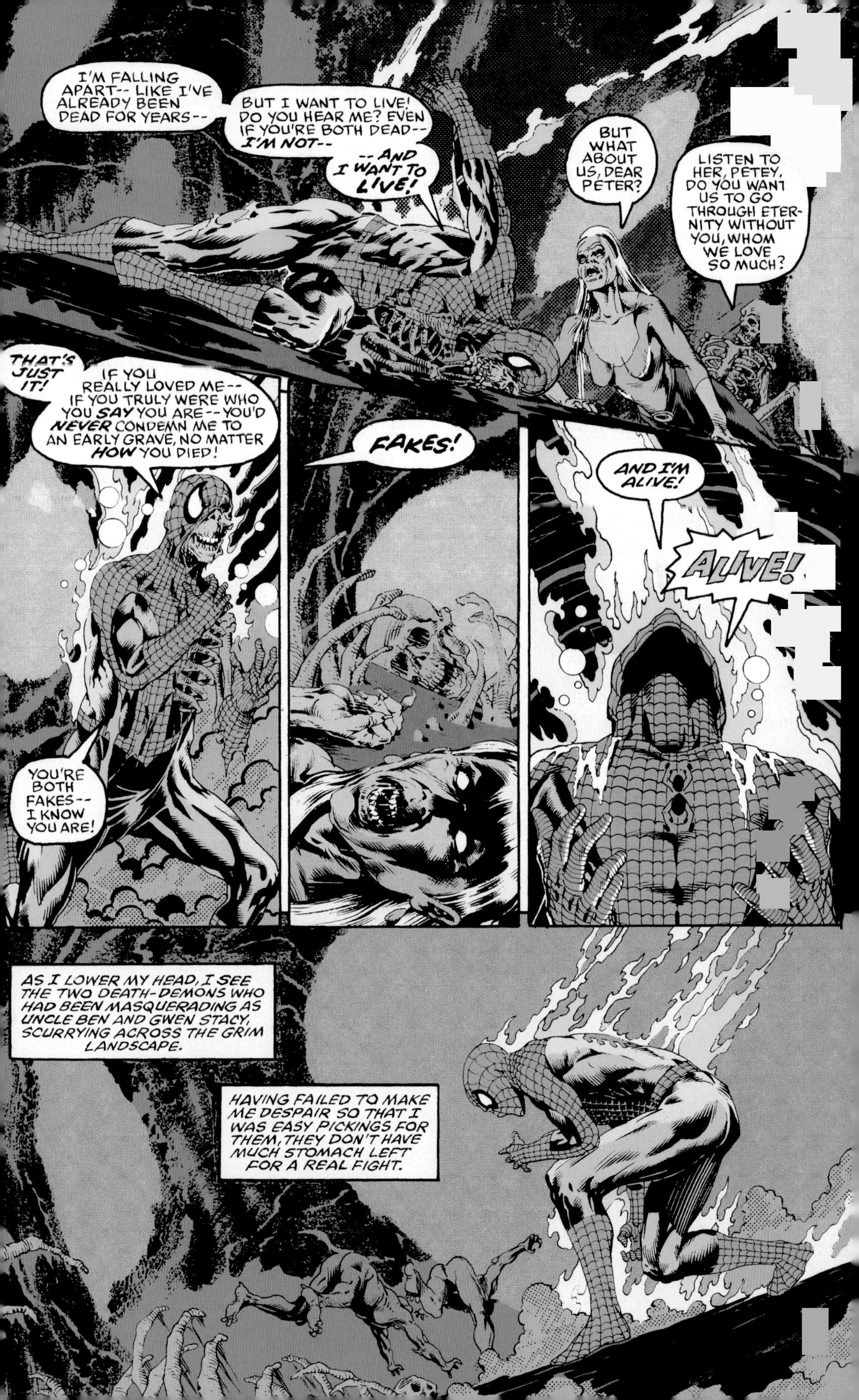
I'M FALLING APART-- LIKE I'VE ALREADY BEEN DEAD FOR YEARS--
BUT I WANT TO LIVE! DO YOU HEAR ME? EVEN IF YOU'RE BOTH DEAD-- I'M NOT--
-- AND I WANT TO LIVE!
BUT WHAT ABOUT US, DEAR PETER?
LISTEN TO HER, PETEY. DO YOU WANT US TO GO THROUGH ETERNITY WITHOUT YOU, WHOM WE LOVE SO MUCH?
THAT'S JUST IT!
IF YOU REALLY LOVED ME-- IF YOU TRULY WERE WHO YOU SAY YOU ARE-- YOU'D NEVER CONDEMN ME TO AN EARLY GRAVE, NO MATTER HOW YOU DIED!
YOU'RE BOTH FAKES-- I KNOW YOU ARE!
FAKES!
AND I'M ALIVE!
ALIVE!
AS I LOWER MY HEAD, I SEE THE TWO DEATH-DEMONS WHO HAD BEEN MASQUERADING AS UNCLE BEN AND GWEN STACY, SCURRYING ACROSS THE GRIM LANDSCAPE.
HAVING FAILED TO MAKE ME DESPAIR SO THAT I WAS EASY PICKINGS FOR THEM, THEY DON'T HAVE MUCH STOMACH LEFT FOR A REAL FIGHT.

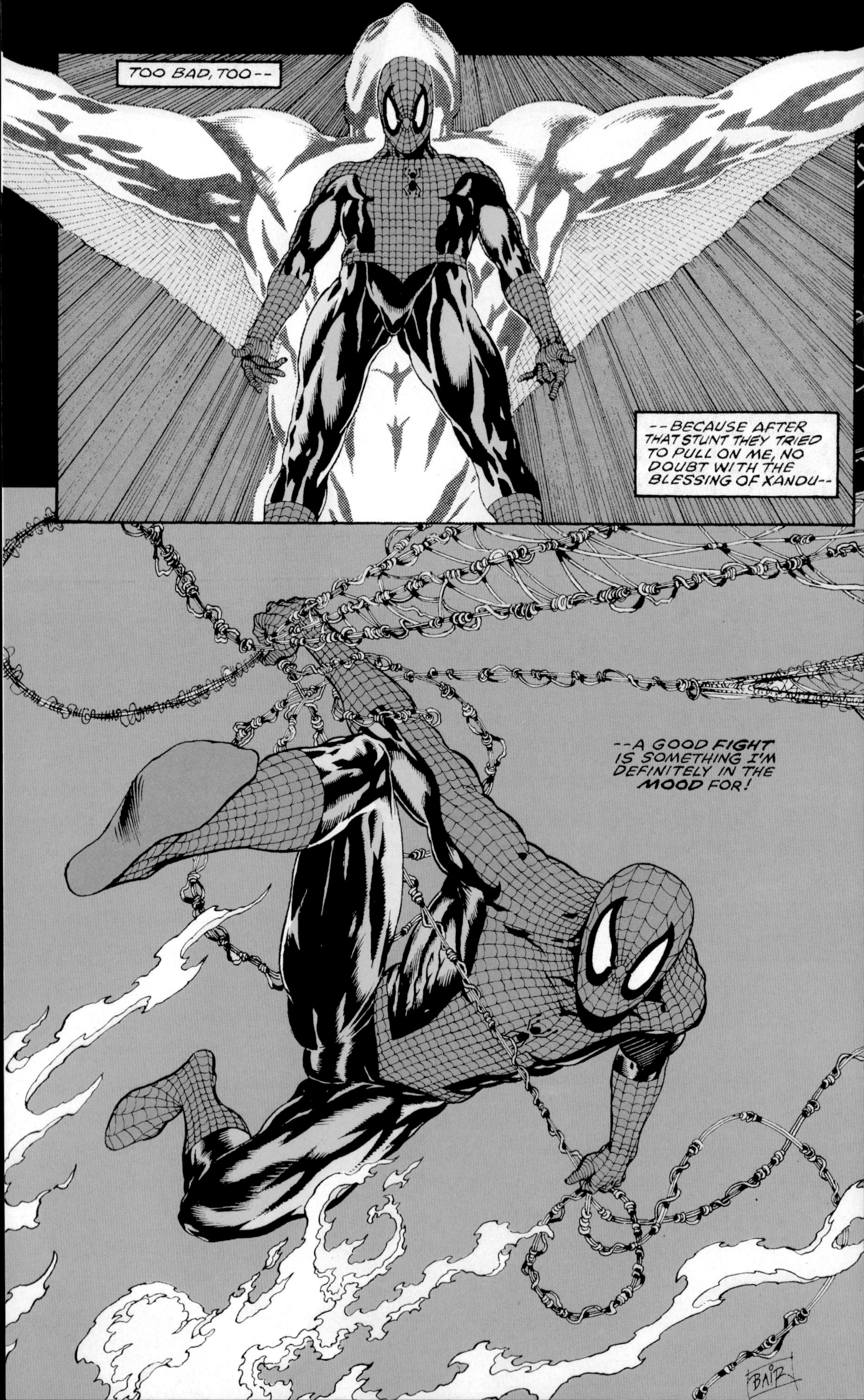
TOO BAD, TOO--
--BECAUSE AFTER THAT STUNT THEY TRIED TO PULL ON ME, NO DOUBT WITH THE BLESSING OF XANDU--
--A GOOD FIGHT IS SOMETHING I'M DEFINITELY IN THE MOOD FOR!
BAIR

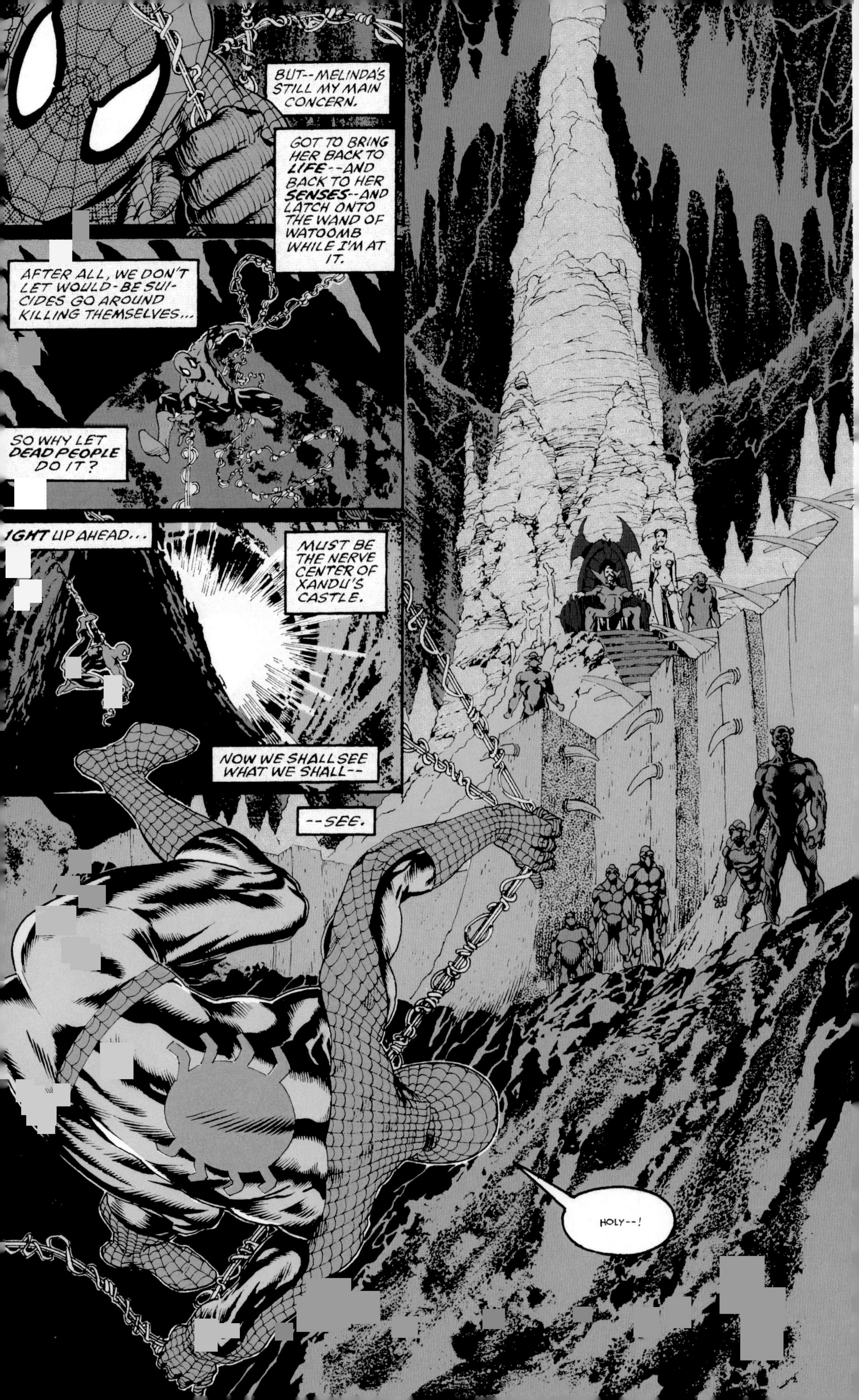
BUT--MELINDA'S STILL MY MAIN CONCERN.
GOT TO BRING HER BACK TO LIFE--AND BACK TO HER SENSES--AND LATCH ONTO THE WAND OF WATOOMB WHILE I'M AT IT.
AFTER ALL, WE DON'T LET WOULD-BE SUI-CIDES GO AROUND KILLING THEMSELVES...
SO WHY LET DEAD PEOPLE DO IT?
IGHT UP AHEAD...
MUST BE THE NERVE CENTER OF XANDU'S CASTLE.
NOW WE SHALL SEE WHAT WE SHALL--
--SEE.
HOLY--!

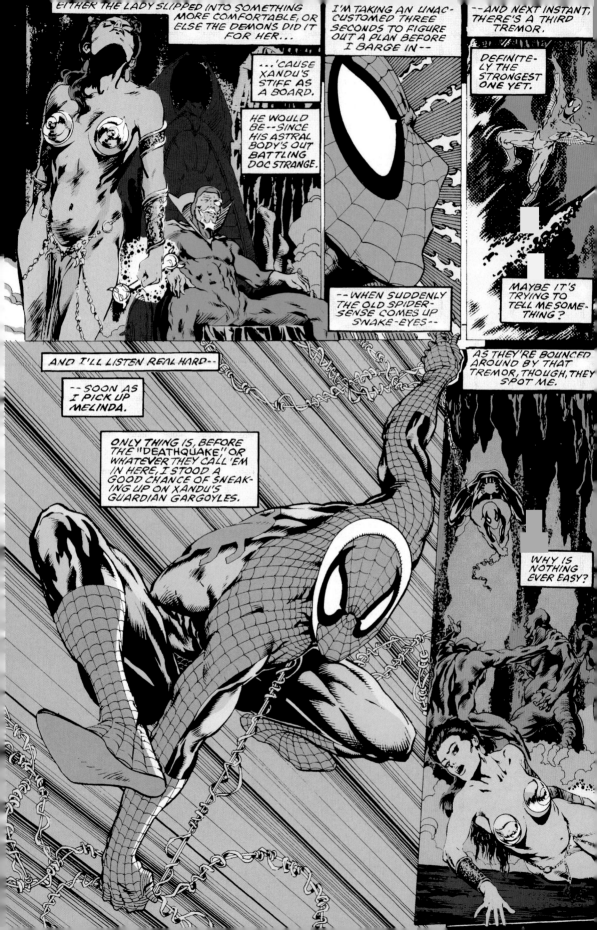

EITHER THE LADY SLIPPED INTO SOMETHING MORE COMFORTABLE, OR ELSE THE DEMONS DID IT FOR HER...

...'CAUSE XANDU'S STIFF AS A BOARD.

HE WOULD BE--SINCE HIS ASTRAL BODY'S OUT BATTLING DOC STRANGE.

I'M TAKING AN UNAC-CUSTOMED THREE SECONDS TO FIGURE OUT A PLAN BEFORE I BARGE IN--

--WHEN SUDDENLY THE OLD SPIDER-SENSE COMES UP SNAKE-EYES--

--AND NEXT INSTANT, THERE'S A THIRD TREMOR.

DEFINITE-LY THE STRONGEST ONE YET.

MAYBE IT'S TRYING TO TELL ME SOME-THING?

AND I'LL LISTEN REAL HARD--

--SOON AS I PICK UP MELINDA.

ONLY THING IS, BEFORE THE "DEATHQUAKE" OR WHATEVER THEY CALL 'EM IN HERE, I STOOD A GOOD CHANCE OF SNEAK-ING UP ON XANDU'S GUARDIAN GARGOYLES.

AS THEY'RE BOUNCED AROUND BY THAT TREMOR, THOUGH, THEY SPOT ME.

WHY IS NOTHING EVER EASY?

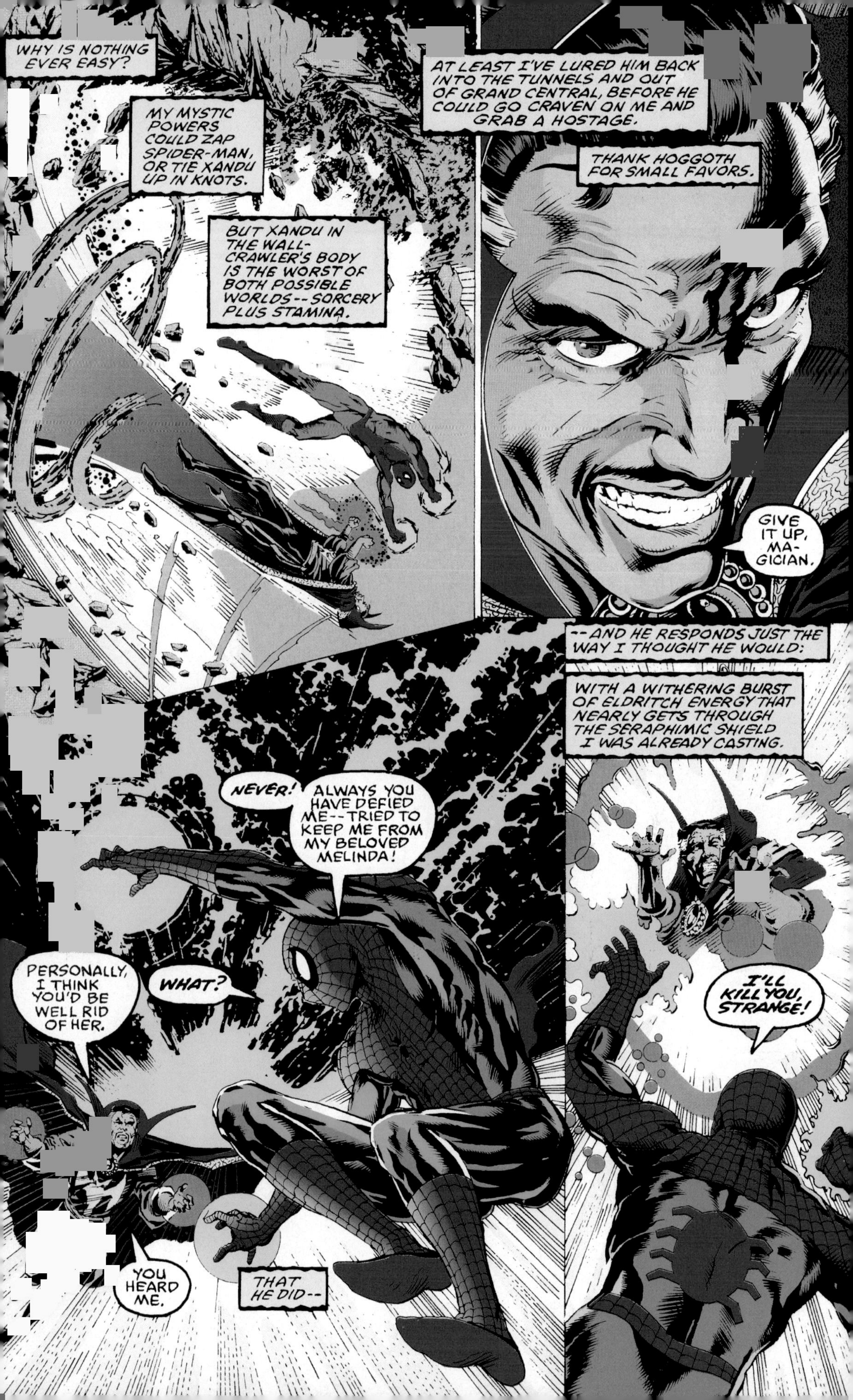
WHY IS NOTHING EVER EASY?
MY MYSTIC POWERS COULD ZAP SPIDER-MAN, OR TIE XANDU UP IN KNOTS.
BUT XANDU IN THE WALL-CRAWLER'S BODY IS THE WORST OF BOTH POSSIBLE WORLDS--SORCERY PLUS STAMINA.
AT LEAST I'VE LURED HIM BACK INTO THE TUNNELS AND OUT OF GRAND CENTRAL, BEFORE HE COULD GO CRAVEN ON ME AND GRAB A HOSTAGE.
THANK HOGGOTH FOR SMALL FAVORS.
GIVE IT UP, MA-GICIAN.
NEVER!
ALWAYS YOU HAVE DEFIED ME--TRIED TO KEEP ME FROM MY BELOVED MELINDA!
PERSONALLY, I THINK YOU'D BE WELL RID OF HER.
WHAT?
YOU HEARD ME.
THAT HE DID--
--AND HE RESPONDS JUST THE WAY I THOUGHT HE WOULD:
WITH A WITHERING BURST OF ELDRITCH ENERGY THAT NEARLY GETS THROUGH THE SERAPHIMIC SHIELD I WAS ALREADY CASTING.
I'LL KILL YOU, STRANGE!

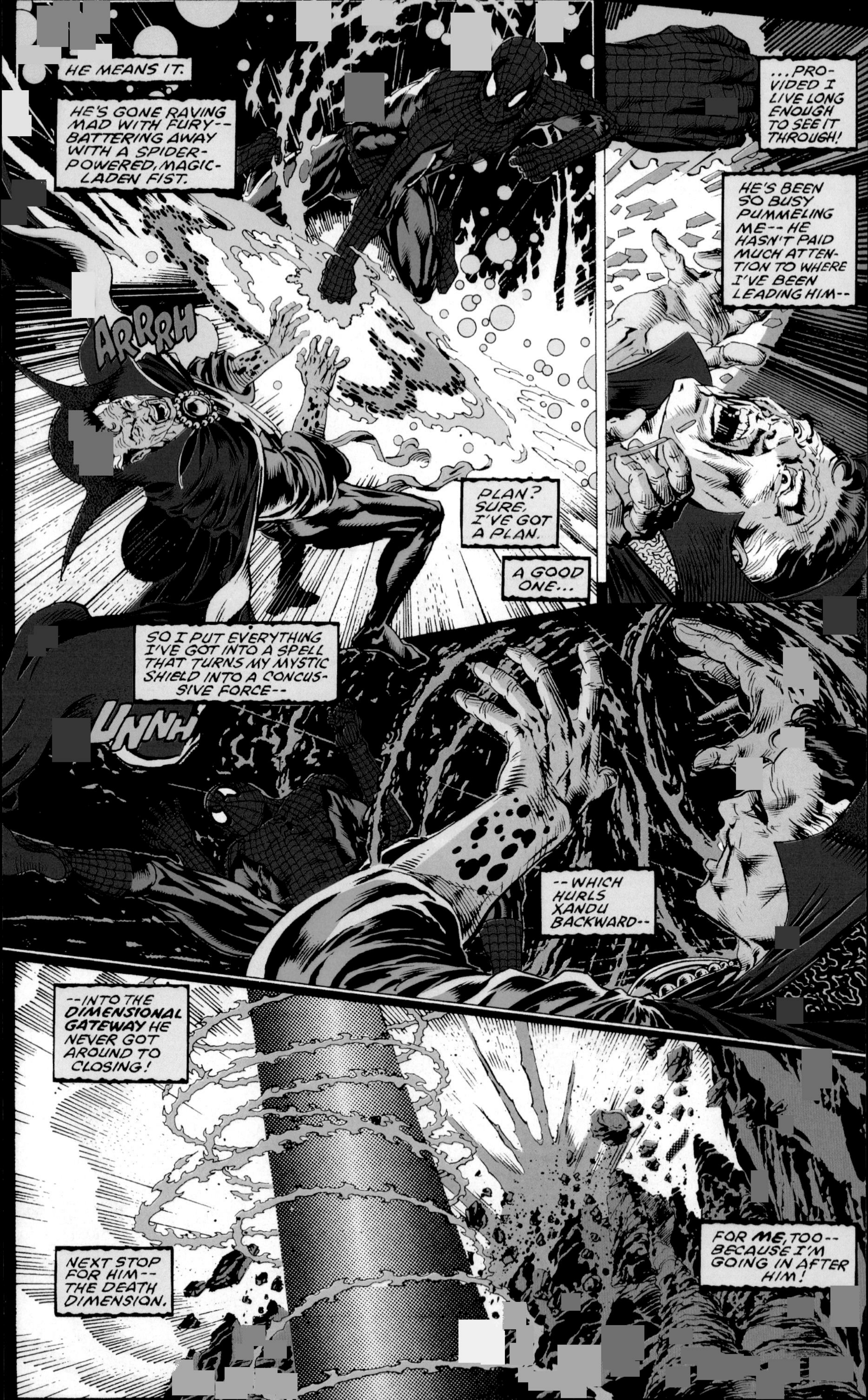

HE MEANS IT.
HE'S GONE RAVING MAD WITH FURY-- BATTERING AWAY WITH A SPIDER-POWERED, MAGIC-LADEN FIST.
ARRRH
PLAN? SURE, I'VE GOT A PLAN.
A GOOD ONE...
...PROVIDED I LIVE LONG ENOUGH TO SEE IT THROUGH!
HE'S BEEN SO BUSY PUMMELING ME-- HE HASN'T PAID MUCH ATTENTION TO WHERE I'VE BEEN LEADING HIM--
SO I PUT EVERYTHING I'VE GOT INTO A SPELL THAT TURNS MY MYSTIC SHIELD INTO A CONCUSSIVE FORCE--
UNNH
--WHICH HURLS XANDU BACKWARD--
--INTO THE DIMENSIONAL GATEWAY HE NEVER GOT AROUND TO CLOSING!
NEXT STOP FOR HIM-- THE DEATH DIMENSION.
FOR ME, TOO-- BECAUSE I'M GOING IN AFTER HIM!

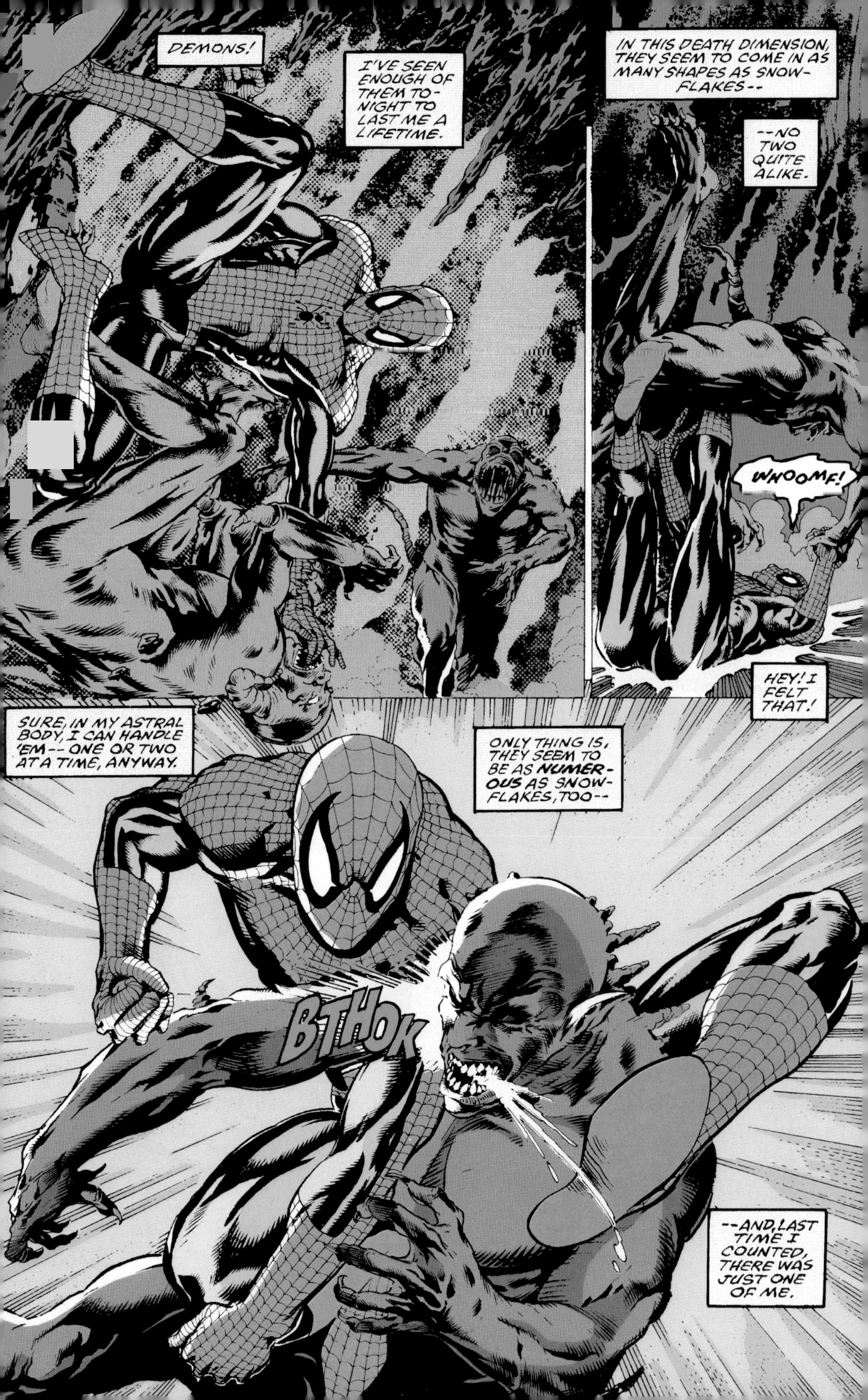

DEMONS!
I'VE SEEN ENOUGH OF THEM TO-NIGHT TO LAST ME A LIFETIME.
IN THIS DEATH DIMENSION, THEY SEEM TO COME IN AS MANY SHAPES AS SNOW-FLAKES--
--NO TWO QUITE ALIKE.
WHOOMF!
HEY! I FELT THAT!
SURE, IN MY ASTRAL BODY, I CAN HANDLE 'EM-- ONE OR TWO AT A TIME, ANYWAY.
ONLY THING IS, THEY SEEM TO BE AS NUMEROUS AS SNOW-FLAKES, TOO--
BTHOK
--AND, LAST TIME I COUNTED, THERE WAS JUST ONE OF ME.

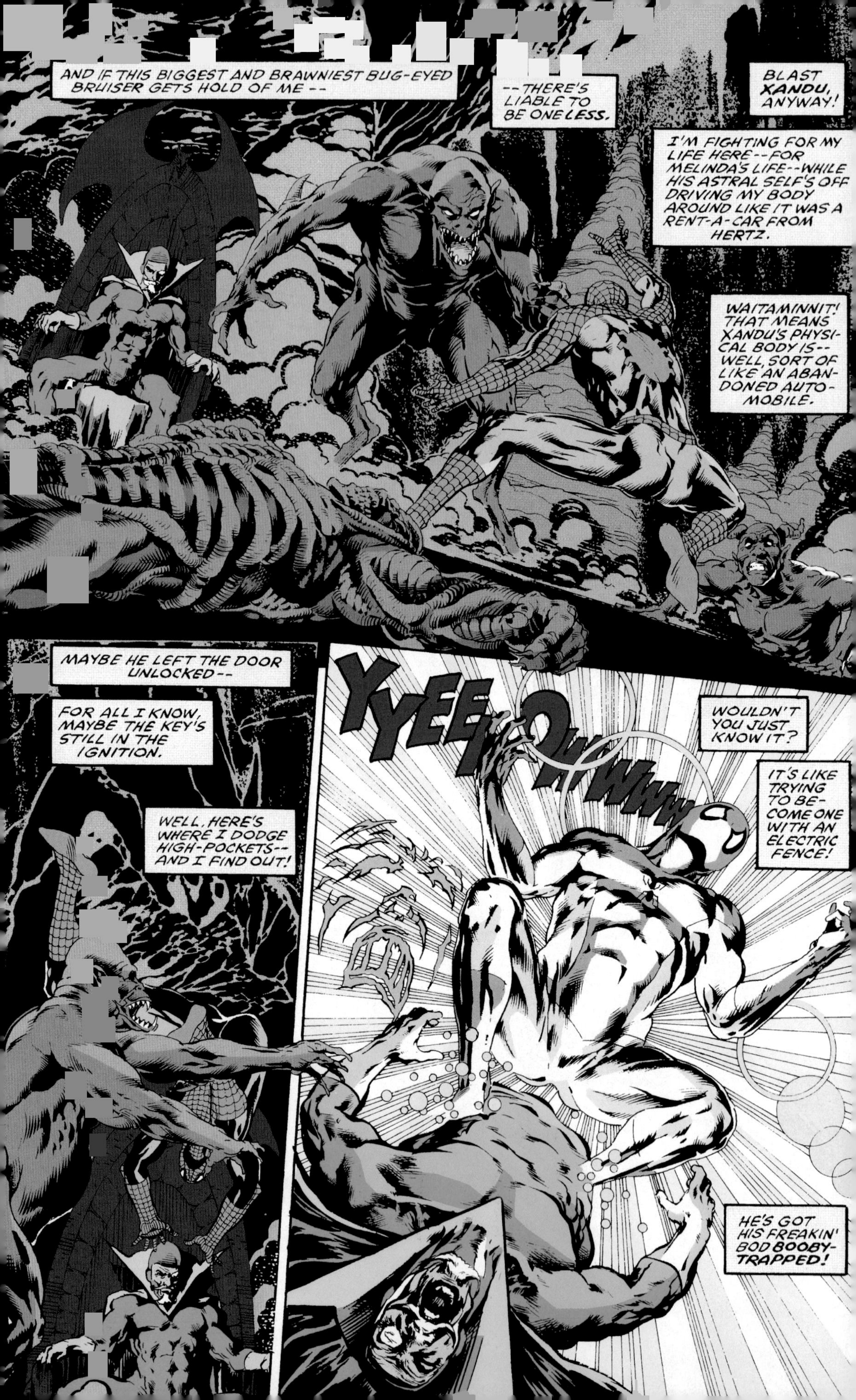
AND IF THIS BIGGEST AND BRAWNIEST BUG-EYED BRUISER GETS HOLD OF ME --
-- THERE'S LIABLE TO BE ONE LESS.
BLAST XANDU, ANYWAY!
I'M FIGHTING FOR MY LIFE HERE--FOR MELINDA'S LIFE--WHILE HIS ASTRAL SELF'S OFF DRIVING MY BODY AROUND LIKE IT WAS A RENT-A-CAR FROM HERTZ.
WAITAMINNIT! THAT MEANS XANDU'S PHYSICAL BODY IS-- WELL, SORT OF LIKE AN ABANDONED AUTOMOBILE.
MAYBE HE LEFT THE DOOR UNLOCKED--
FOR ALL I KNOW, MAYBE THE KEY'S STILL IN THE IGNITION.
WELL, HERE'S WHERE I DODGE HIGH-POCKETS-- AND I FIND OUT!
YYEEIIOWWWW
WOULDN'T YOU JUST KNOW IT?
IT'S LIKE TRYING TO BECOME ONE WITH AN ELECTRIC FENCE!
HE'S GOT HIS FREAKIN' BOD BOOBY-TRAPPED!

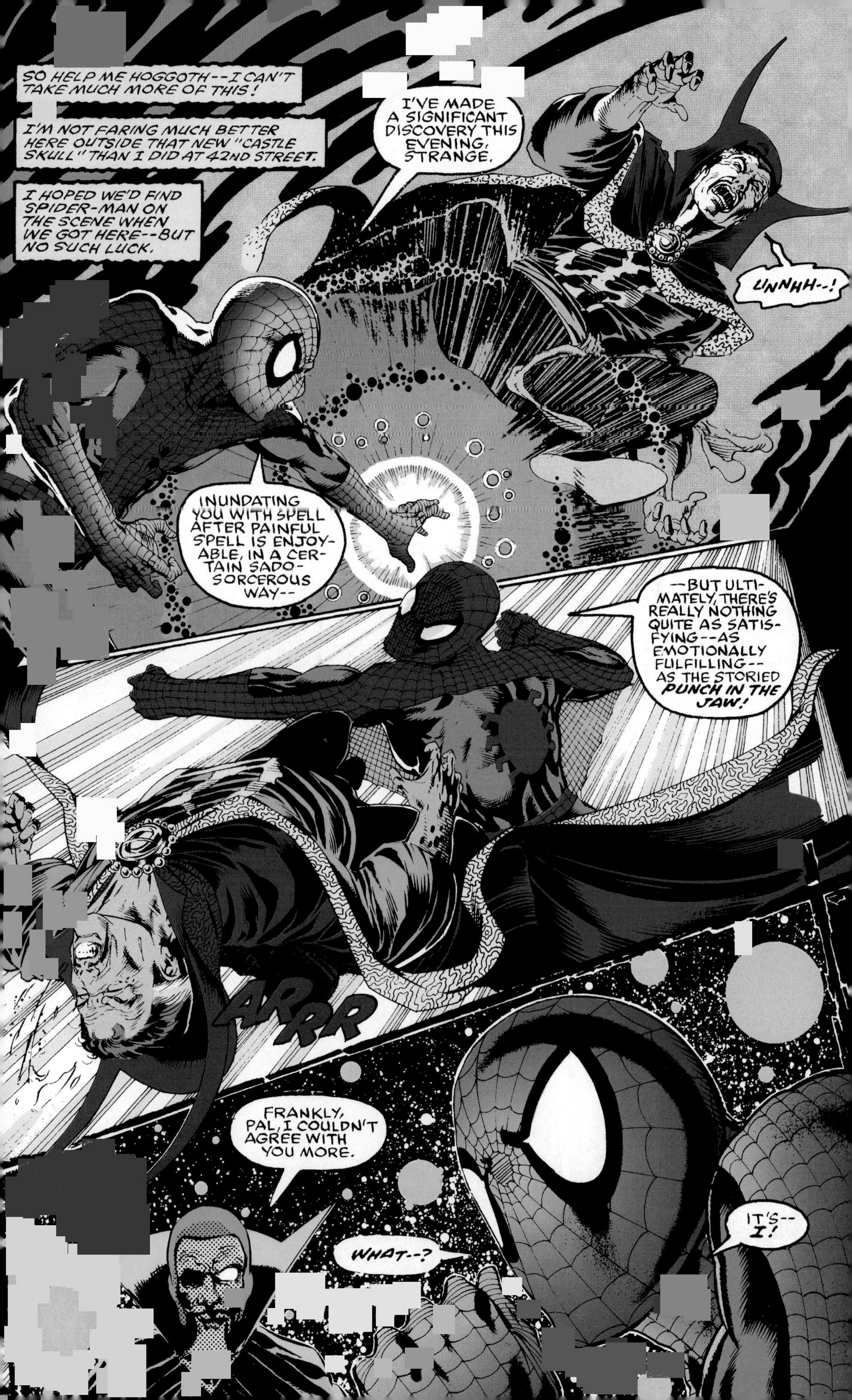

SO HELP ME HOGGOTH--I CAN'T TAKE MUCH MORE OF THIS!
I'M NOT FARING MUCH BETTER HERE OUTSIDE THAT NEW "CASTLE SKULL" THAN I DID AT 42ND STREET.
I HOPED WE'D FIND SPIDER-MAN ON THE SCENE WHEN WE GOT HERE--BUT NO SUCH LUCK.
I'VE MADE A SIGNIFICANT DISCOVERY THIS EVENING, STRANGE.
UNNHH--!
INUNDATING YOU WITH SPELL AFTER PAINFUL SPELL IS ENJOYABLE, IN A CERTAIN SADO-SORCEROUS WAY--
--BUT ULTIMATELY, THERE'S REALLY NOTHING QUITE AS SATISFYING--AS EMOTIONALLY FULFILLING--AS THE STORIED PUNCH IN THE JAW!
ARRR
FRANKLY, PAL, I COULDN'T AGREE WITH YOU MORE.
WHAT--?
IT'S-- I!

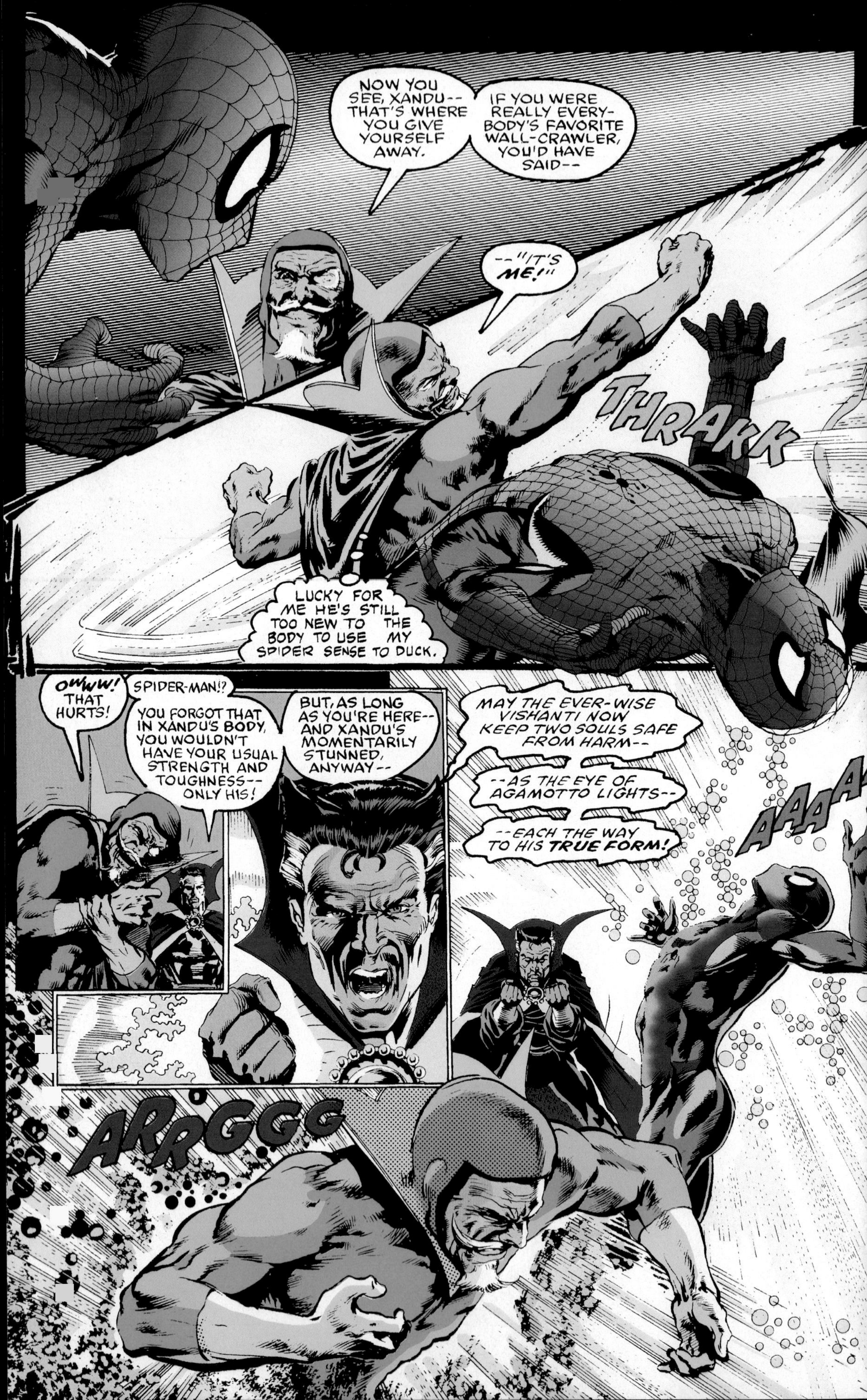
NOW YOU SEE, XANDU-- THAT'S WHERE YOU GIVE YOURSELF AWAY.
IF YOU WERE REALLY EVERY-BODY'S FAVORITE WALL-CRAWLER, YOU'D HAVE SAID--
--"IT'S ME!"
THRAKK
LUCKY FOR ME HE'S STILL TOO NEW TO THE BODY TO USE MY SPIDER SENSE TO DUCK.
OWWW! THAT HURTS!
SPIDER-MAN!?
YOU FORGOT THAT IN XANDU'S BODY, YOU WOULDN'T HAVE YOUR USUAL STRENGTH AND TOUGHNESS-- ONLY HIS!
BUT, AS LONG AS YOU'RE HERE-- AND XANDU'S MOMENTARILY STUNNED, ANYWAY--
MAY THE EVER-WISE VISHANTI NOW KEEP TWO SOULS SAFE FROM HARM--
--AS THE EYE OF AGAMOTTO LIGHTS--
--EACH THE WAY TO HIS TRUE FORM!
AAAA
ARRGGG

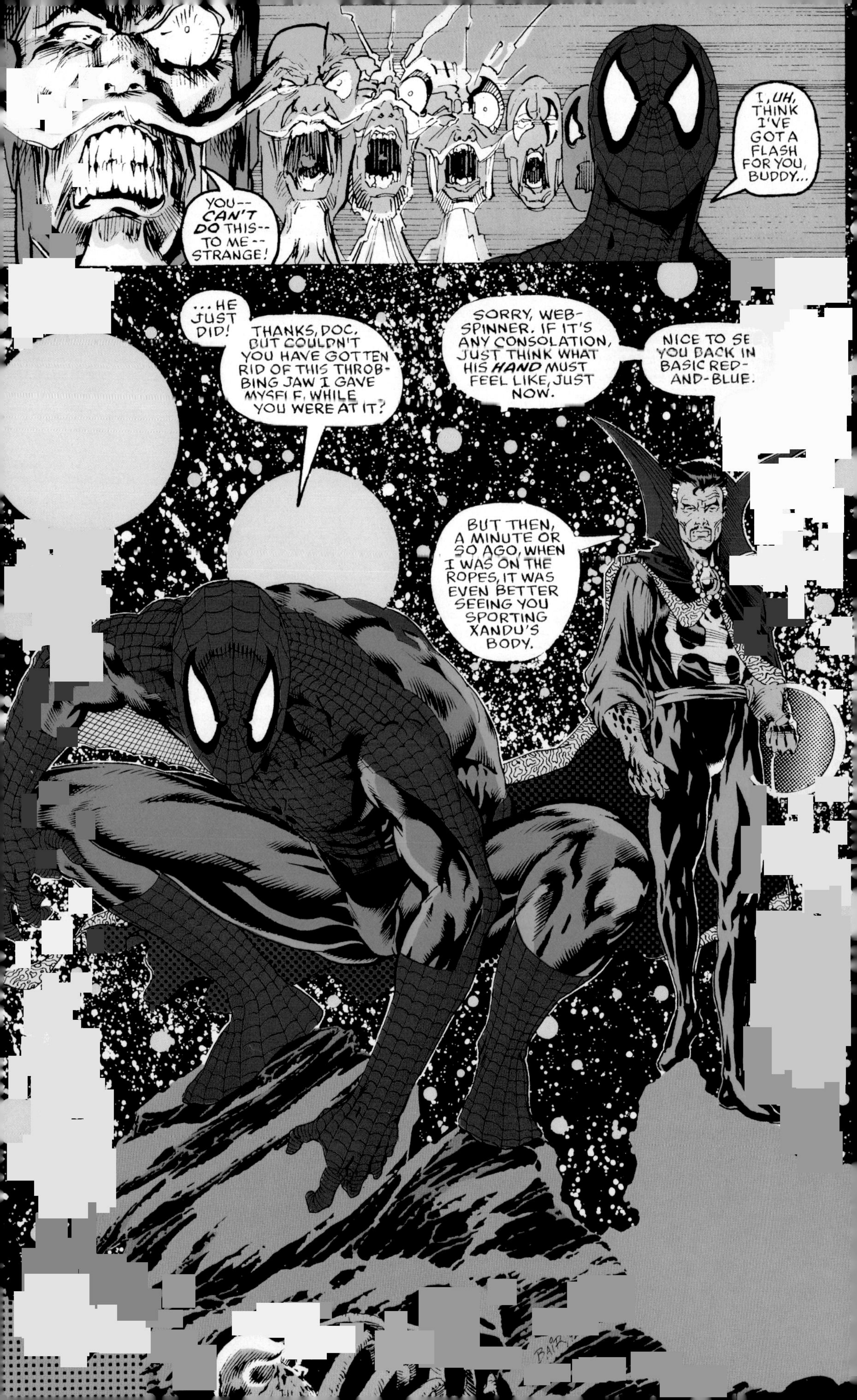
YOU-- CAN'T DO THIS-- TO ME-- STRANGE!
I, UH, THINK I'VE GOT A FLASH FOR YOU, BUDDY...
...HE JUST DID!
THANKS, DOC, BUT COULDN'T YOU HAVE GOTTEN RID OF THIS THROBBING JAW I GAVE MYSELF, WHILE YOU WERE AT IT?
SORRY, WEB-SPINNER. IF IT'S ANY CONSOLATION, JUST THINK WHAT HIS HAND MUST FEEL LIKE, JUST NOW.
NICE TO SE YOU BACK IN BASIC RED-AND-BLUE.
BUT THEN, A MINUTE OR SO AGO, WHEN I WAS ON THE ROPES, IT WAS EVEN BETTER SEEING YOU SPORTING XANDU'S BODY.

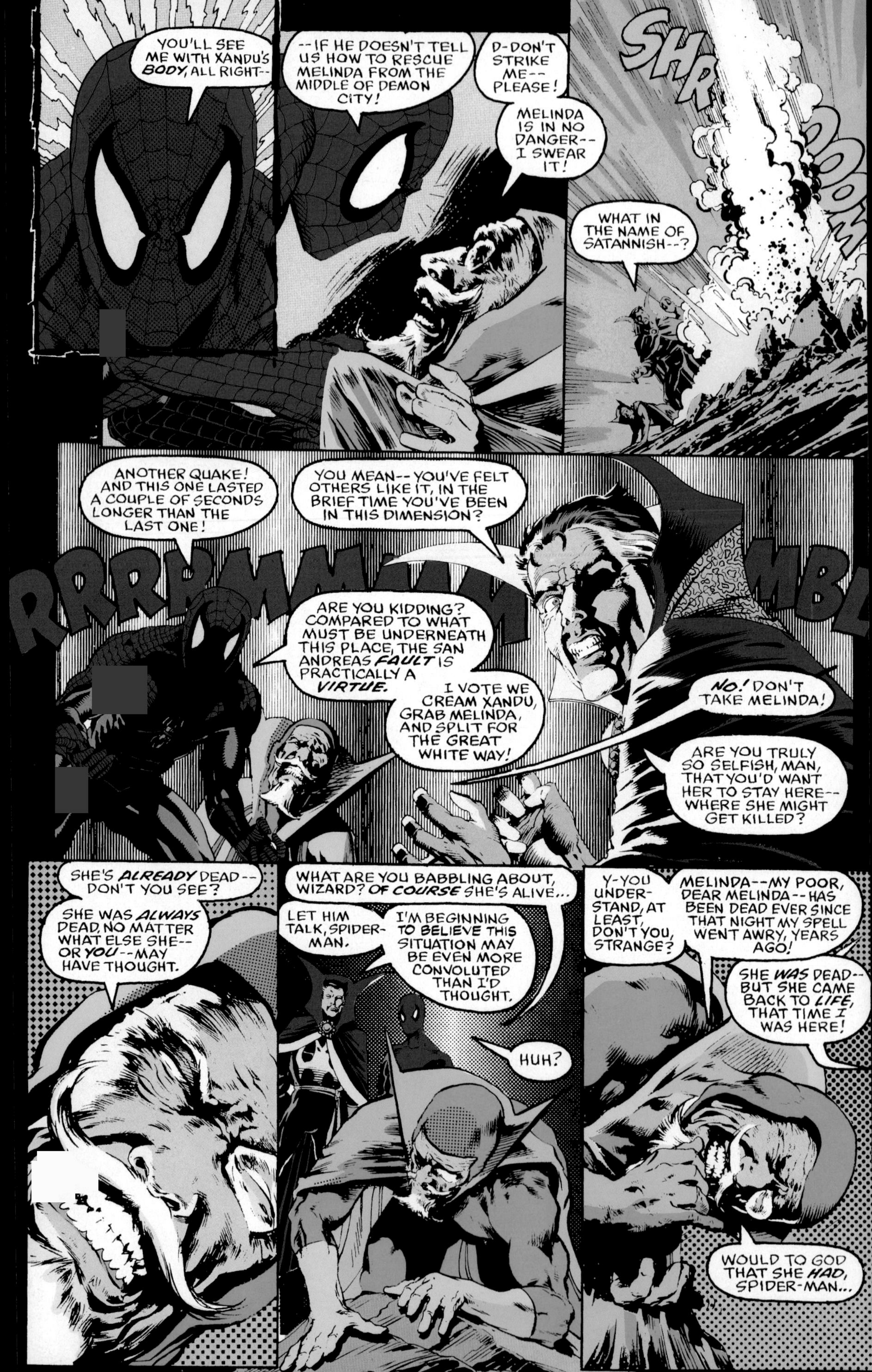

YOU'LL SEE ME WITH XANDU'S *BODY*, ALL RIGHT--
--IF HE DOESN'T TELL US HOW TO RESCUE MELINDA FROM THE MIDDLE OF DEMON CITY!
D-DON'T STRIKE ME-- PLEASE!
MELINDA IS IN NO DANGER-- I SWEAR IT!
SHR
WHAT IN THE NAME OF SATANNISH--?
ANOTHER QUAKE! AND THIS ONE LASTED A COUPLE OF SECONDS LONGER THAN THE LAST ONE!
YOU MEAN-- YOU'VE FELT OTHERS LIKE IT, IN THE BRIEF TIME YOU'VE BEEN IN THIS DIMENSION?
MBL
ARE YOU KIDDING? COMPARED TO WHAT MUST BE UNDERNEATH THIS PLACE, THE SAN ANDREAS *FAULT* IS PRACTICALLY A *VIRTUE*.
I VOTE WE CREAM XANDU, GRAB MELINDA, AND SPLIT FOR THE GREAT WHITE WAY!
NO! DON'T TAKE MELINDA!
ARE YOU TRULY SO SELFISH, MAN, THAT YOU'D WANT HER TO STAY HERE-- WHERE SHE MIGHT GET KILLED?
SHE'S *ALREADY* DEAD-- DON'T YOU SEE?
SHE WAS *ALWAYS* DEAD, NO MATTER WHAT ELSE SHE-- OR *YOU*--MAY HAVE THOUGHT.
WHAT ARE YOU BABBLING ABOUT, WIZARD? *OF COURSE* SHE'S ALIVE...
LET HIM TALK, SPIDER-MAN.
I'M BEGINNING TO BELIEVE THIS SITUATION MAY BE EVEN MORE CONVOLUTED THAN I'D THOUGHT.
HUH?
Y-YOU UNDERSTAND, AT LEAST, DON'T YOU, STRANGE?
MELINDA--MY POOR, DEAR MELINDA--HAS BEEN DEAD EVER SINCE THAT NIGHT MY SPELL WENT AWRY, YEARS AGO!
SHE *WAS* DEAD-- BUT SHE CAME BACK TO *LIFE*, THAT TIME *I* WAS HERE!
WOULD TO GOD THAT SHE *HAD*, SPIDER-MAN...

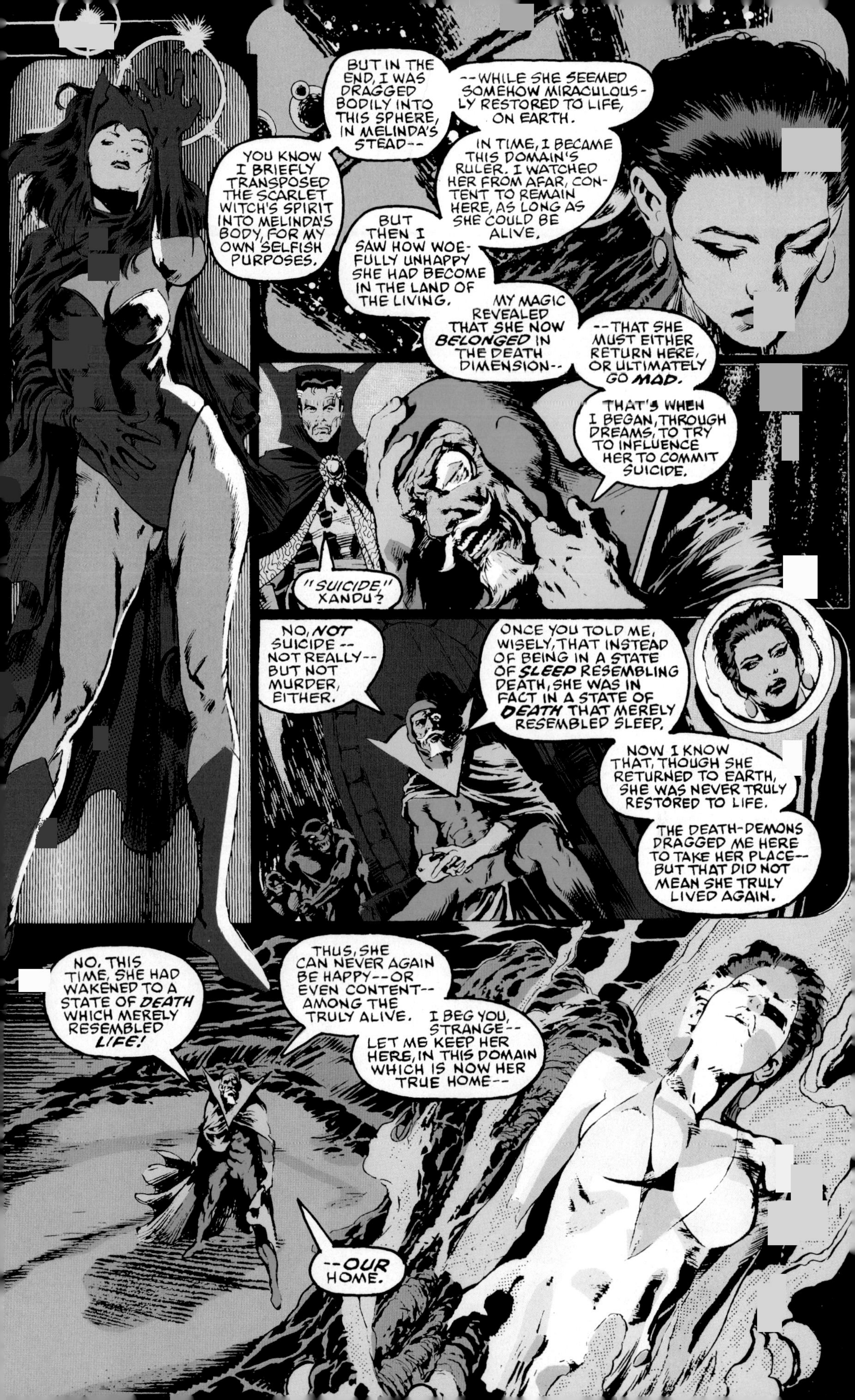
YOU KNOW I BRIEFLY TRANSPOSED THE SCARLET WITCH'S SPIRIT INTO MELINDA'S BODY, FOR MY OWN SELFISH PURPOSES.
BUT IN THE END, I WAS DRAGGED BODILY INTO THIS SPHERE, IN MELINDA'S STEAD--
--WHILE SHE SEEMED SOMEHOW MIRACULOUSLY RESTORED TO LIFE, ON EARTH.
IN TIME, I BECAME THIS DOMAIN'S RULER. I WATCHED HER FROM AFAR, CONTENT TO REMAIN HERE, AS LONG AS SHE COULD BE ALIVE.
BUT THEN I SAW HOW WOEFULLY UNHAPPY SHE HAD BECOME IN THE LAND OF THE LIVING.
MY MAGIC REVEALED THAT SHE NOW BELONGED IN THE DEATH DIMENSION--
--THAT SHE MUST EITHER RETURN HERE, OR ULTIMATELY GO MAD.
THAT'S WHEN I BEGAN, THROUGH DREAMS, TO TRY TO INFLUENCE HER TO COMMIT SUICIDE.
"SUICIDE," XANDU?
NO, NOT SUICIDE--NOT REALLY--BUT NOT MURDER, EITHER.
ONCE YOU TOLD ME, WISELY, THAT INSTEAD OF BEING IN A STATE OF SLEEP RESEMBLING DEATH, SHE WAS IN FACT IN A STATE OF DEATH THAT MERELY RESEMBLED SLEEP.
NOW I KNOW THAT, THOUGH SHE RETURNED TO EARTH, SHE WAS NEVER TRULY RESTORED TO LIFE.
THE DEATH-DEMONS DRAGGED ME HERE TO TAKE HER PLACE--BUT THAT DID NOT MEAN SHE TRULY LIVED AGAIN.
NO. THIS TIME, SHE HAD WAKENED TO A STATE OF DEATH WHICH MERELY RESEMBLED LIFE!
THUS, SHE CAN NEVER AGAIN BE HAPPY--OR EVEN CONTENT--AMONG THE TRULY ALIVE.
I BEG YOU, STRANGE--LET ME KEEP HER HERE, IN THIS DOMAIN WHICH IS NOW HER TRUE HOME--
--OUR HOME.

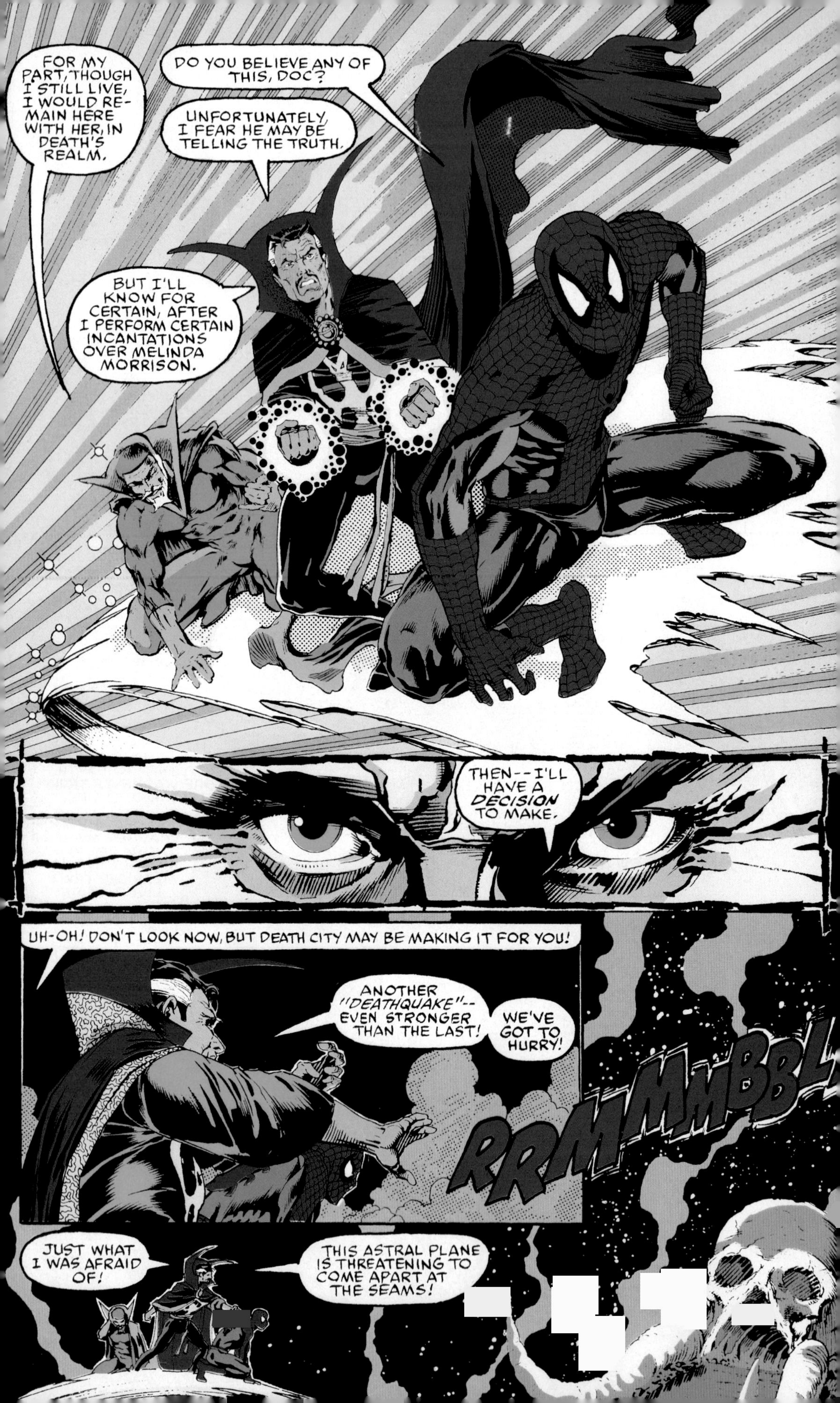
FOR MY PART, THOUGH I STILL LIVE, I WOULD RE-MAIN HERE WITH HER, IN DEATH'S REALM.
DO YOU BELIEVE ANY OF THIS, DOC?
UNFORTUNATELY, I FEAR HE MAY BE TELLING THE TRUTH.
BUT I'LL KNOW FOR CERTAIN, AFTER I PERFORM CERTAIN INCANTATIONS OVER MELINDA MORRISON.
THEN--I'LL HAVE A *DECISION* TO MAKE.
UH-OH! DON'T LOOK NOW, BUT DEATH CITY MAY BE MAKING IT FOR YOU!
ANOTHER "*DEATHQUAKE*"--EVEN STRONGER THAN THE LAST!
WE'VE GOT TO HURRY!
RRMMMMBBL
JUST WHAT I WAS AFRAID OF!
THIS ASTRAL PLANE IS THREATENING TO COME APART AT THE SEAMS!

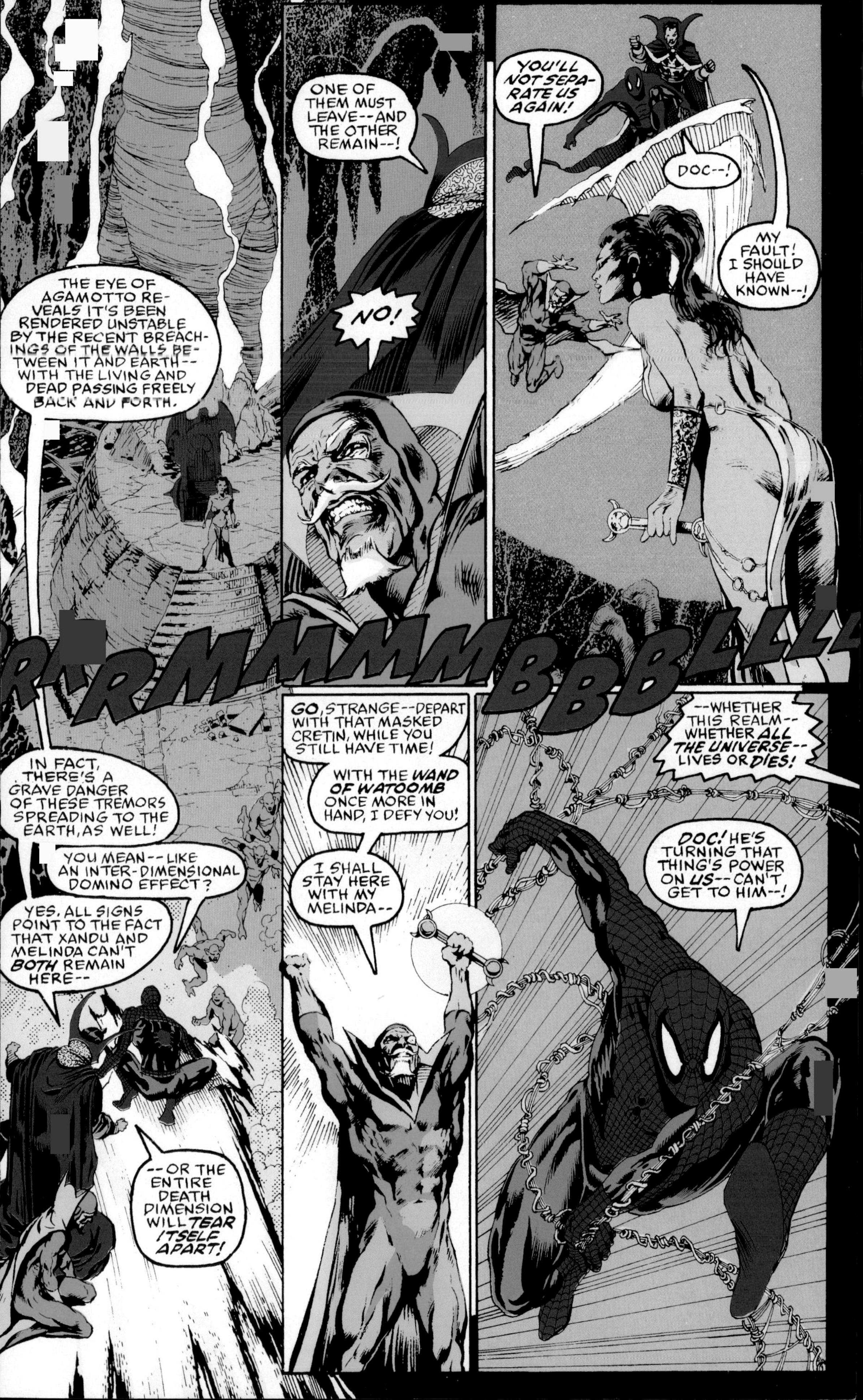

THE EYE OF AGAMOTTO REVEALS IT'S BEEN RENDERED UNSTABLE BY THE RECENT BREACHINGS OF THE WALLS BETWEEN IT AND EARTH-- WITH THE LIVING AND DEAD PASSING FREELY BACK AND FORTH.
ONE OF THEM MUST LEAVE--AND THE OTHER REMAIN--!
NO!
YOU'LL NOT SEPARATE US AGAIN!
DOC--!
MY FAULT! I SHOULD HAVE KNOWN--!
RRMMMMMBBBLLL
IN FACT, THERE'S A GRAVE DANGER OF THESE TREMORS SPREADING TO THE EARTH, AS WELL!
YOU MEAN-- LIKE AN INTER-DIMENSIONAL DOMINO EFFECT?
YES. ALL SIGNS POINT TO THE FACT THAT XANDU AND MELINDA CAN'T BOTH REMAIN HERE--
--OR THE ENTIRE DEATH DIMENSION WILL TEAR ITSELF APART!
GO, STRANGE--DEPART WITH THAT MASKED CRETIN, WHILE YOU STILL HAVE TIME!
WITH THE WAND OF WATOOMB ONCE MORE IN HAND, I DEFY YOU!
I SHALL STAY HERE WITH MY MELINDA--
--WHETHER THIS REALM-- WHETHER ALL THE UNIVERSE-- LIVES OR DIES!
DOC! HE'S TURNING THAT THING'S POWER ON US--CAN'T GET TO HIM--!

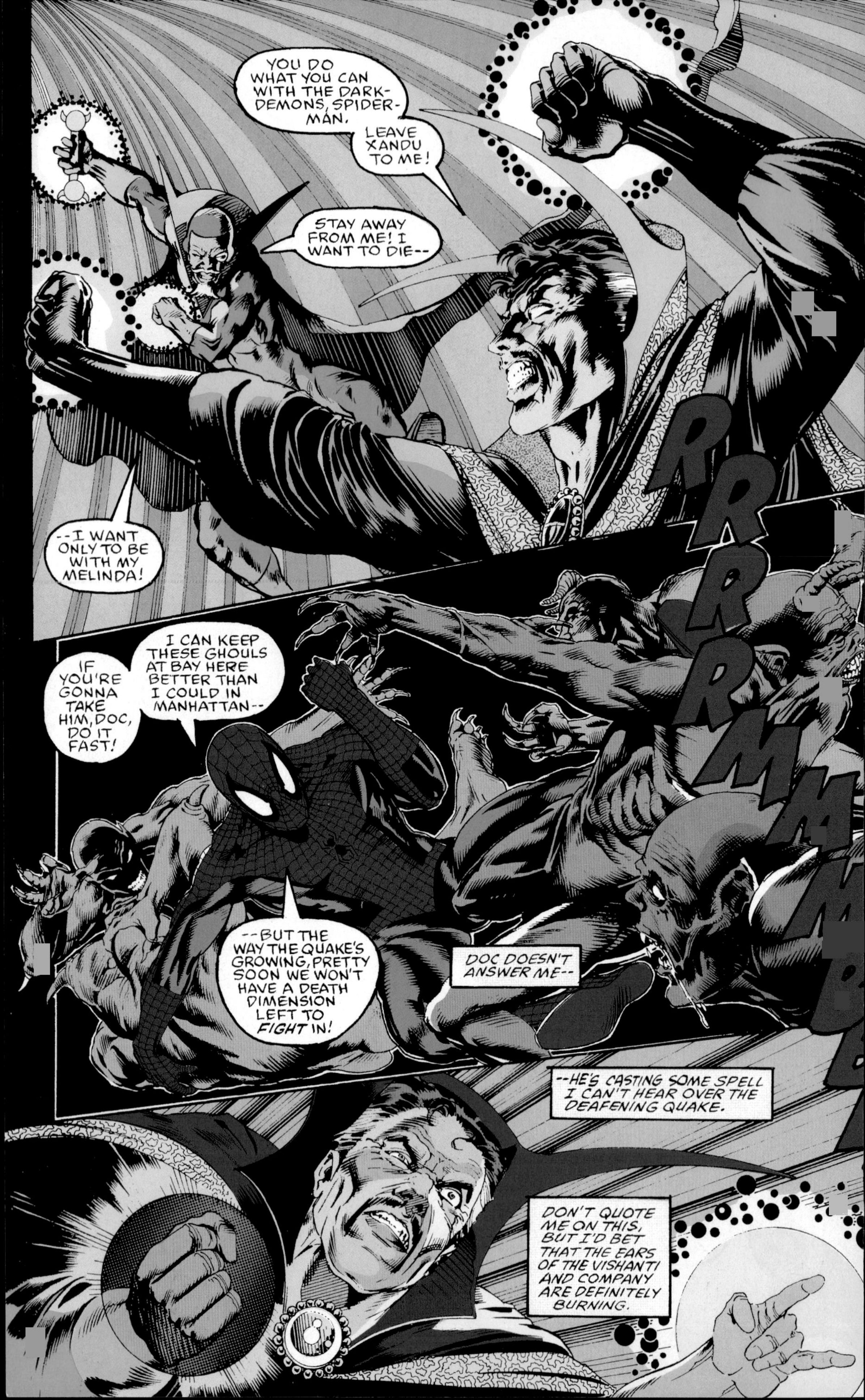
YOU DO WHAT YOU CAN WITH THE DARK-DEMONS, SPIDER-MAN.
LEAVE XANDU TO ME!
STAY AWAY FROM ME! I WANT TO DIE--
--I WANT ONLY TO BE WITH MY MELINDA!
RRRRRMMMMB
IF YOU'RE GONNA TAKE HIM, DOC, DO IT FAST!
I CAN KEEP THESE GHOULS AT BAY HERE BETTER THAN I COULD IN MANHATTAN--
--BUT THE WAY THE QUAKE'S GROWING, PRETTY SOON WE WON'T HAVE A DEATH DIMENSION LEFT TO FIGHT IN!
DOC DOESN'T ANSWER ME--
--HE'S CASTING SOME SPELL I CAN'T HEAR OVER THE DEAFENING QUAKE.
DON'T QUOTE ME ON THIS, BUT I'D BET THAT THE EARS OF THE VISHANTI AND COMPANY ARE DEFINITELY BURNING.

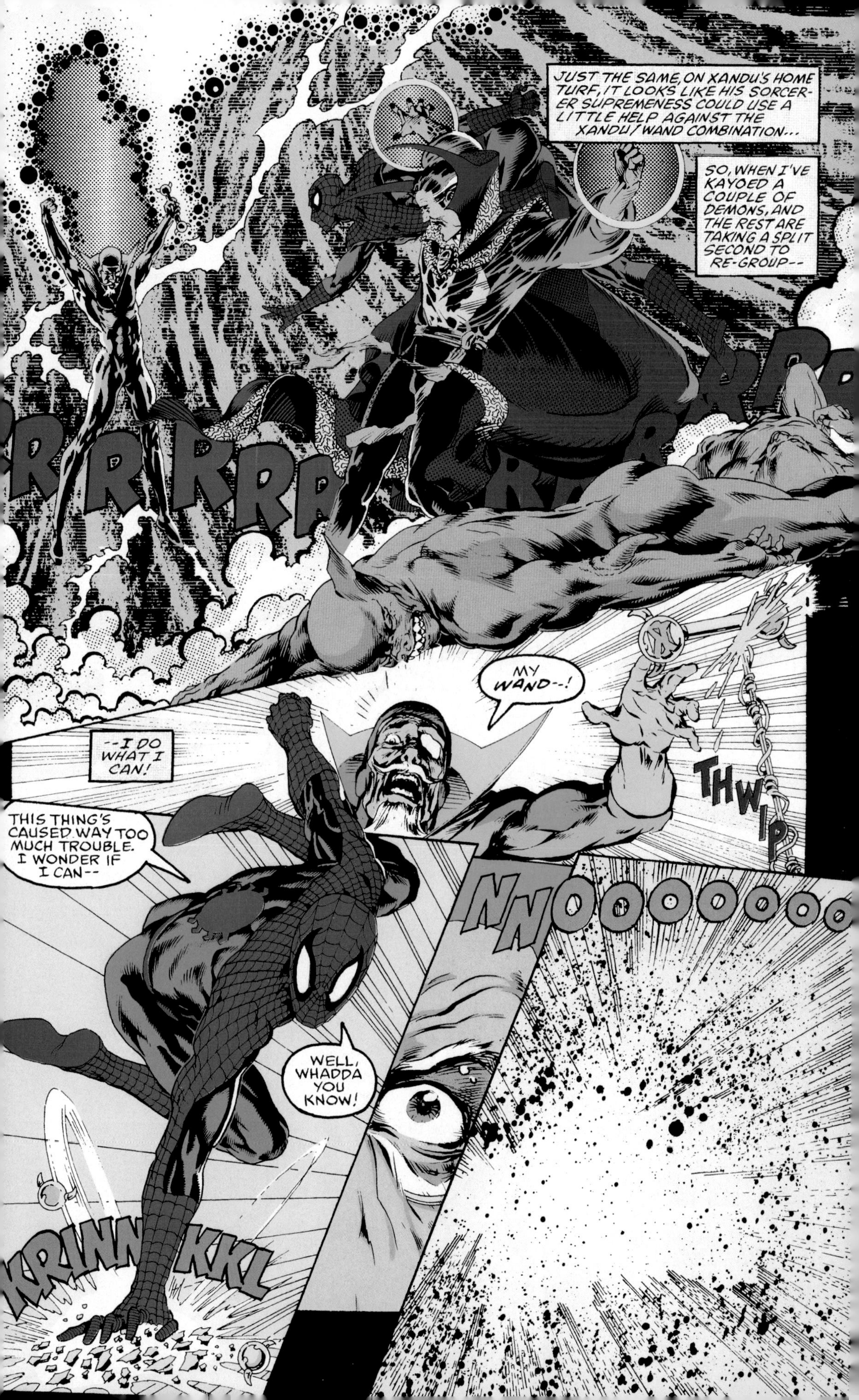
JUST THE SAME, ON XANDU'S HOME TURF, IT LOOKS LIKE HIS SORCERER SUPREMENESS COULD USE A LITTLE HELP AGAINST THE XANDU/WAND COMBINATION...
SO, WHEN I'VE KAYOED A COUPLE OF DEMONS, AND THE REST ARE TAKING A SPLIT SECOND TO RE-GROUP--
--I DO WHAT I CAN!
MY WAND--!
THWIP
THIS THING'S CAUSED WAY TOO MUCH TROUBLE. I WONDER IF I CAN--
NNOOOOOOOO
WELL, WHADDA YOU KNOW!
KRINNNKKL

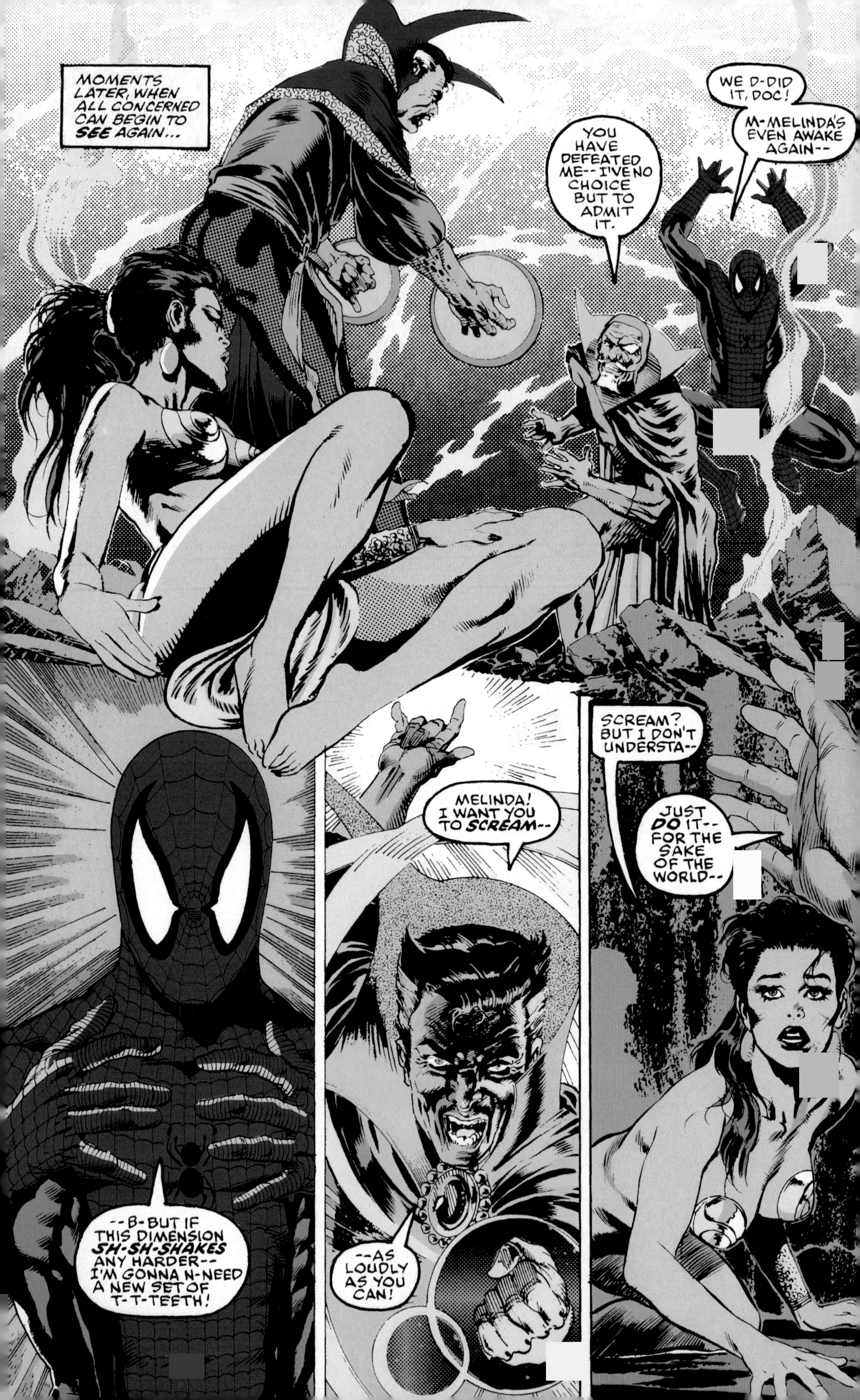
MOMENTS LATER, WHEN ALL CONCERNED CAN BEGIN TO SEE AGAIN...
YOU HAVE DEFEATED ME-- I'VE NO CHOICE BUT TO ADMIT IT.
WE D-DID IT, DOC!
M-MELINDA'S EVEN AWAKE AGAIN--
--B-BUT IF THIS DIMENSION SH-SH-SHAKES ANY HARDER-- I'M GONNA N-NEED A NEW SET OF T-T-TEETH!
MELINDA! I WANT YOU TO SCREAM--
--AS LOUDLY AS YOU CAN!
SCREAM? BUT I DON'T UNDERSTA--
JUST DO IT-- FOR THE SAKE OF THE WORLD--

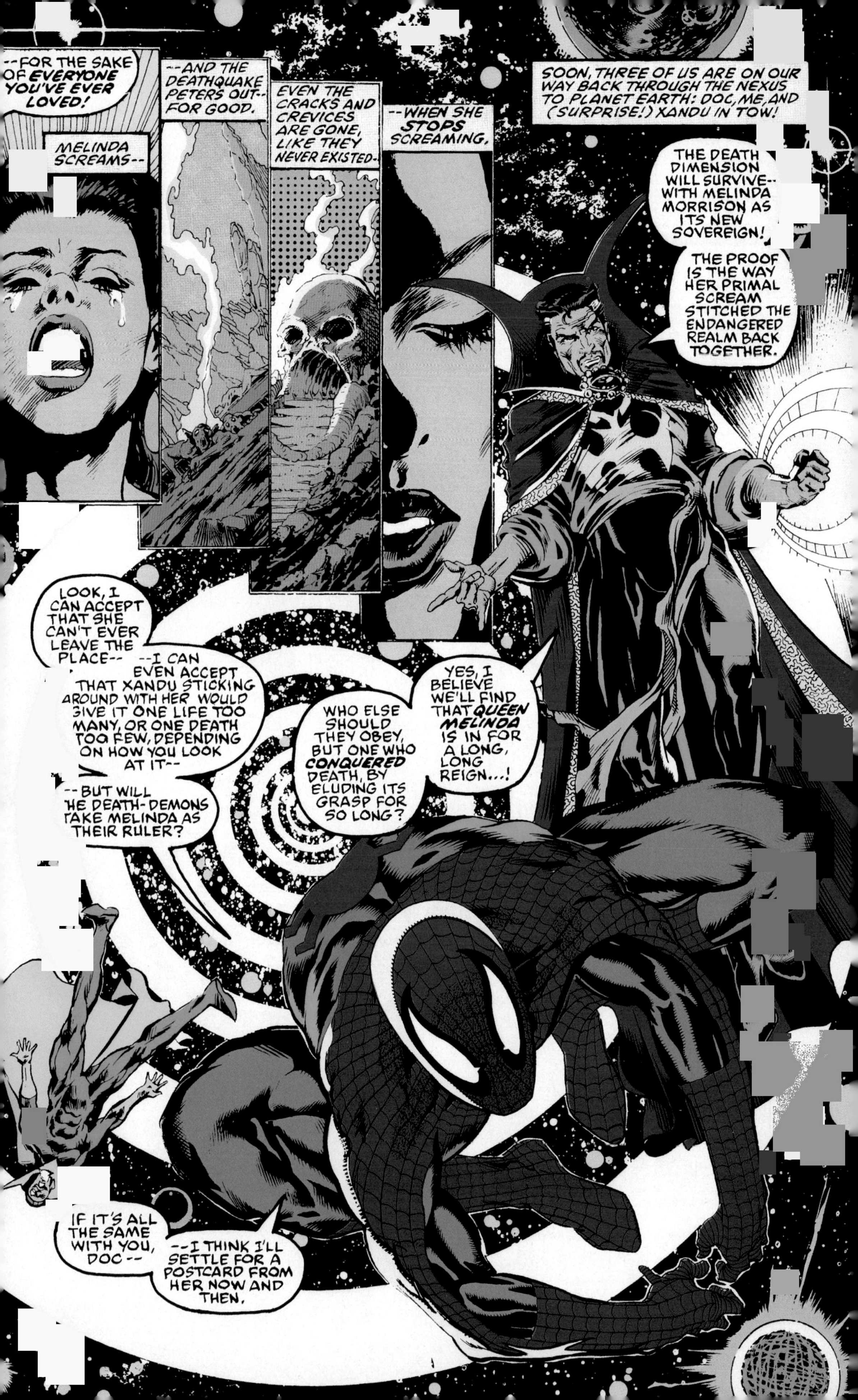
--FOR THE SAKE OF EVERYONE YOU'VE EVER LOVED!
MELINDA SCREAMS--
--AND THE DEATHQUAKE PETERS OUT-- FOR GOOD.
EVEN THE CRACKS AND CREVICES ARE GONE, LIKE THEY NEVER EXISTED--
--WHEN SHE STOPS SCREAMING.
SOON, THREE OF US ARE ON OUR WAY BACK THROUGH THE NEXUS TO PLANET EARTH: DOC, ME, AND (SURPRISE!) XANDU IN TOW!
THE DEATH DIMENSION WILL SURVIVE-- WITH MELINDA MORRISON AS ITS NEW SOVEREIGN!
THE PROOF IS THE WAY HER PRIMAL SCREAM STITCHED THE ENDANGERED REALM BACK TOGETHER.
LOOK, I CAN ACCEPT THAT SHE CAN'T EVER LEAVE THE PLACE--
--I CAN EVEN ACCEPT THAT XANDU STICKING AROUND WITH HER WOULD GIVE IT ONE LIFE TOO MANY, OR ONE DEATH TOO FEW, DEPENDING ON HOW YOU LOOK AT IT--
--BUT WILL THE DEATH-DEMONS TAKE MELINDA AS THEIR RULER?
WHO ELSE SHOULD THEY OBEY, BUT ONE WHO CONQUERED DEATH, BY ELUDING ITS GRASP FOR SO LONG?
YES, I BELIEVE WE'LL FIND THAT QUEEN MELINDA IS IN FOR A LONG, LONG REIGN...!
IF IT'S ALL THE SAME WITH YOU, DOC--
--I THINK I'LL SETTLE FOR A POSTCARD FROM HER NOW AND THEN.

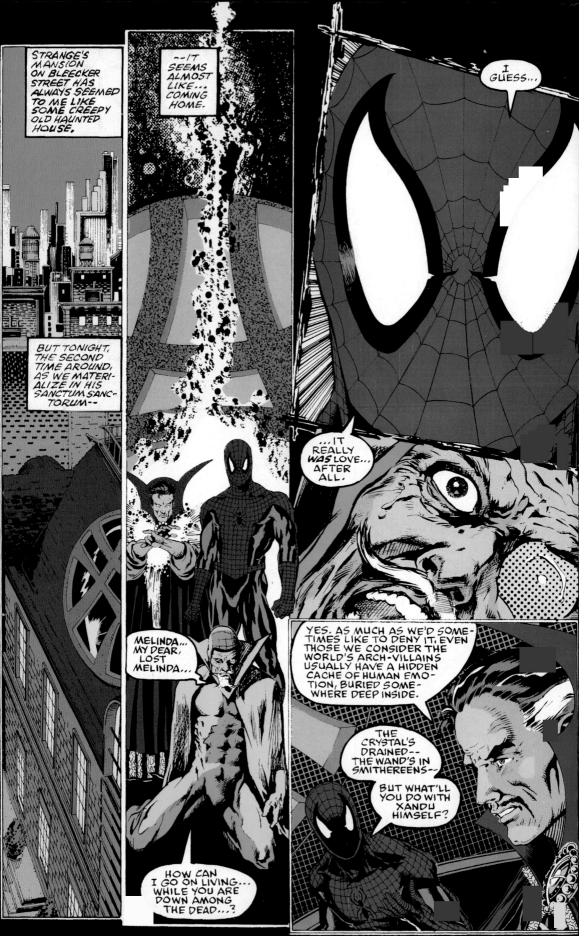

STRANGE'S MANSION ON BLEECKER STREET HAS ALWAYS SEEMED TO ME LIKE SOME CREEPY OLD HAUNTED HOUSE.

--IT SEEMS ALMOST LIKE... COMING HOME.

I GUESS...

BUT TONIGHT, THE SECOND TIME AROUND, AS WE MATERIALIZE IN HIS SANCTUM SANCTORUM--

...IT REALLY *WAS* LOVE... AFTER ALL.

MELINDA... MY DEAR, LOST MELINDA...

YES. AS MUCH AS WE'D SOMETIMES LIKE TO DENY IT, EVEN THOSE WE CONSIDER THE WORLD'S ARCH-VILLAINS USUALLY HAVE A HIDDEN CACHE OF HUMAN EMOTION, BURIED SOMEWHERE DEEP INSIDE.

THE CRYSTAL'S DRAINED-- THE WAND'S IN SMITHEREENS--

BUT WHAT'LL YOU DO WITH XANDU HIMSELF?

HOW CAN I GO ON LIVING... WHILE YOU ARE DOWN AMONG THE DEAD...?

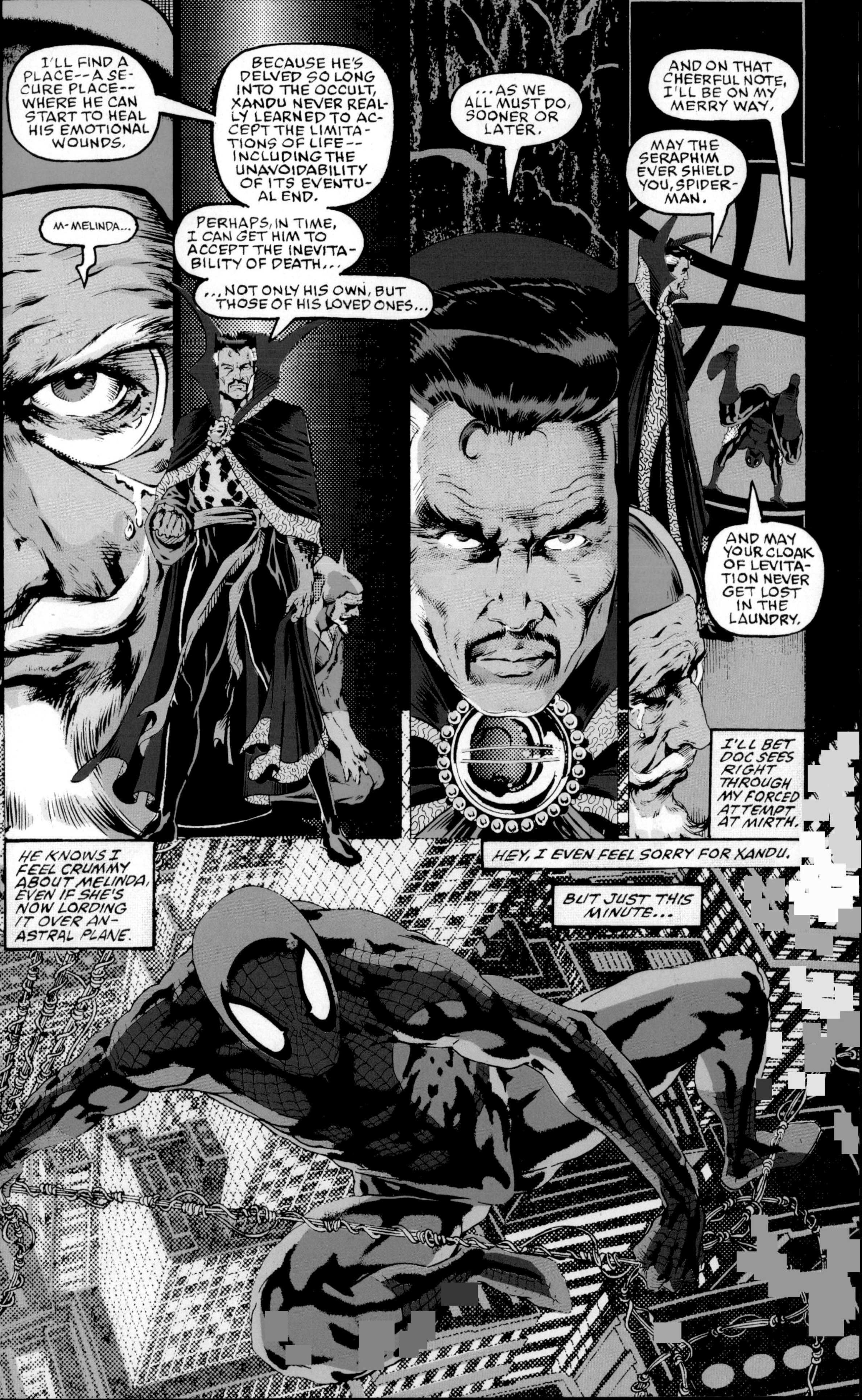

I'LL FIND A PLACE--A SECURE PLACE--WHERE HE CAN START TO HEAL HIS EMOTIONAL WOUNDS.
M-MELINDA...
BECAUSE HE'S DELVED SO LONG INTO THE OCCULT, XANDU NEVER REALLY LEARNED TO ACCEPT THE LIMITATIONS OF LIFE--INCLUDING THE UNAVOIDABILITY OF ITS EVENTUAL END.
PERHAPS, IN TIME, I CAN GET HIM TO ACCEPT THE INEVITABILITY OF DEATH...
...NOT ONLY HIS OWN, BUT THOSE OF HIS LOVED ONES...
...AS WE ALL MUST DO, SOONER OR LATER.
AND ON THAT CHEERFUL NOTE, I'LL BE ON MY MERRY WAY.
MAY THE SERAPHIM EVER SHIELD YOU, SPIDER-MAN.
AND MAY YOUR CLOAK OF LEVITATION NEVER GET LOST IN THE LAUNDRY.
I'LL BET DOC SEES RIGHT THROUGH MY FORCED ATTEMPT AT MIRTH.
HE KNOWS I FEEL CRUMMY ABOUT MELINDA, EVEN IF SHE'S NOW LORDING IT OVER AN ASTRAL PLANE.
HEY, I EVEN FEEL SORRY FOR XANDU.
BUT JUST THIS MINUTE...

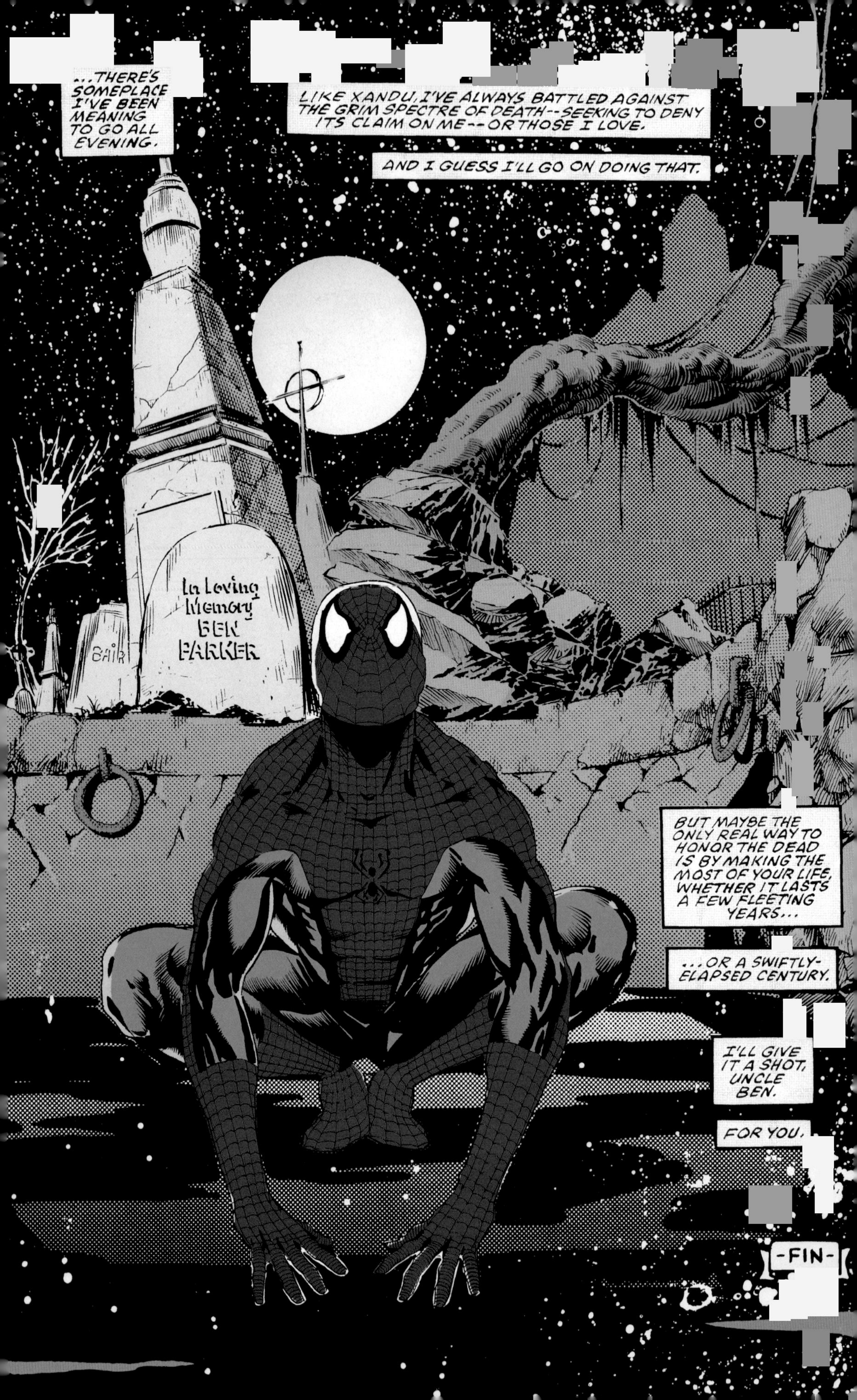

...THERE'S SOMEPLACE I'VE BEEN MEANING TO GO ALL EVENING.
LIKE XANDU, I'VE ALWAYS BATTLED AGAINST THE GRIM SPECTRE OF DEATH--SEEKING TO DENY ITS CLAIM ON ME--OR THOSE I LOVE.
AND I GUESS I'LL GO ON DOING THAT.
In Loving Memory BEN PARKER
BAIR
BUT MAYBE THE ONLY REAL WAY TO HONOR THE DEAD IS BY MAKING THE MOST OF YOUR LIFE, WHETHER IT LASTS A FEW FLEETING YEARS...
...OR A SWIFTLY-ELAPSED CENTURY.
I'LL GIVE IT A SHOT, UNCLE BEN.
FOR YOU.
-FIN-

DAWN GEIGER

designer

STEPHANIE FOGLE

manufacturing coordinator

DAN CUDDY

assistant editor

ROB TOKAR

editor

DANNY FINGEROTH

group editor

TOM DeFALCO

editor in chief

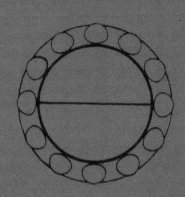

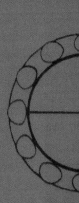

SPIDER-MAN AND DR. STRANGE HAVE TEAMED UP ON SEVERAL OTHER OCCASIONS. IN *MARVEL TEAM-UP #48-49*, SPIDER-MAN AND IRON MAN HELPED POLICE CAPTAIN JEAN DeWOLFF INVESTIGATE BOMBINGS COMMITTED BY THE WRAITH, A MENTAL-POWERED VILLAIN. LATER, JEAN'S FATHER PHILLIP SHOWED HER A NOTE CLAIMING THE WRAITH WAS HER BROTHER BRIAN — A FORMER POLICEMAN BELIEVED KILLED YEARS BEFORE. WONDERING IF THE WRAITH WAS A GHOST, SPIDER-MAN SOUGHT OUT DR. STRANGE...

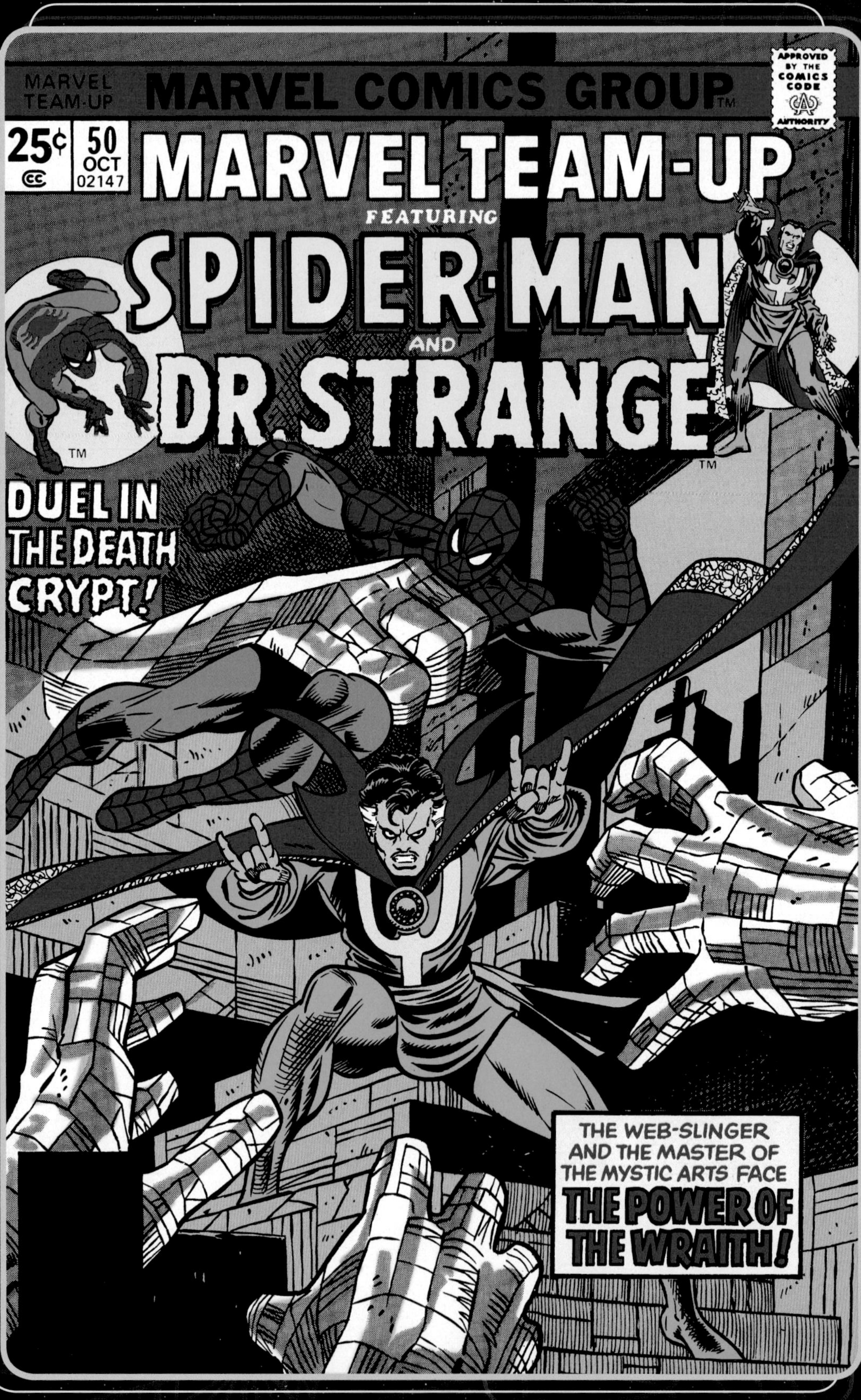

MARVEL TEAM-UP
MARVEL COMICS GROUP
APPROVED BY THE COMICS CODE AUTHORITY
25¢
50 OCT 02147
MARVEL TEAM-UP
FEATURING
SPIDER-MAN
AND
DR. STRANGE
DUEL IN THE DEATH CRYPT!
THE WEB-SLINGER AND THE MASTER OF THE MYSTIC ARTS FACE
THE POWER OF THE WRAITH!

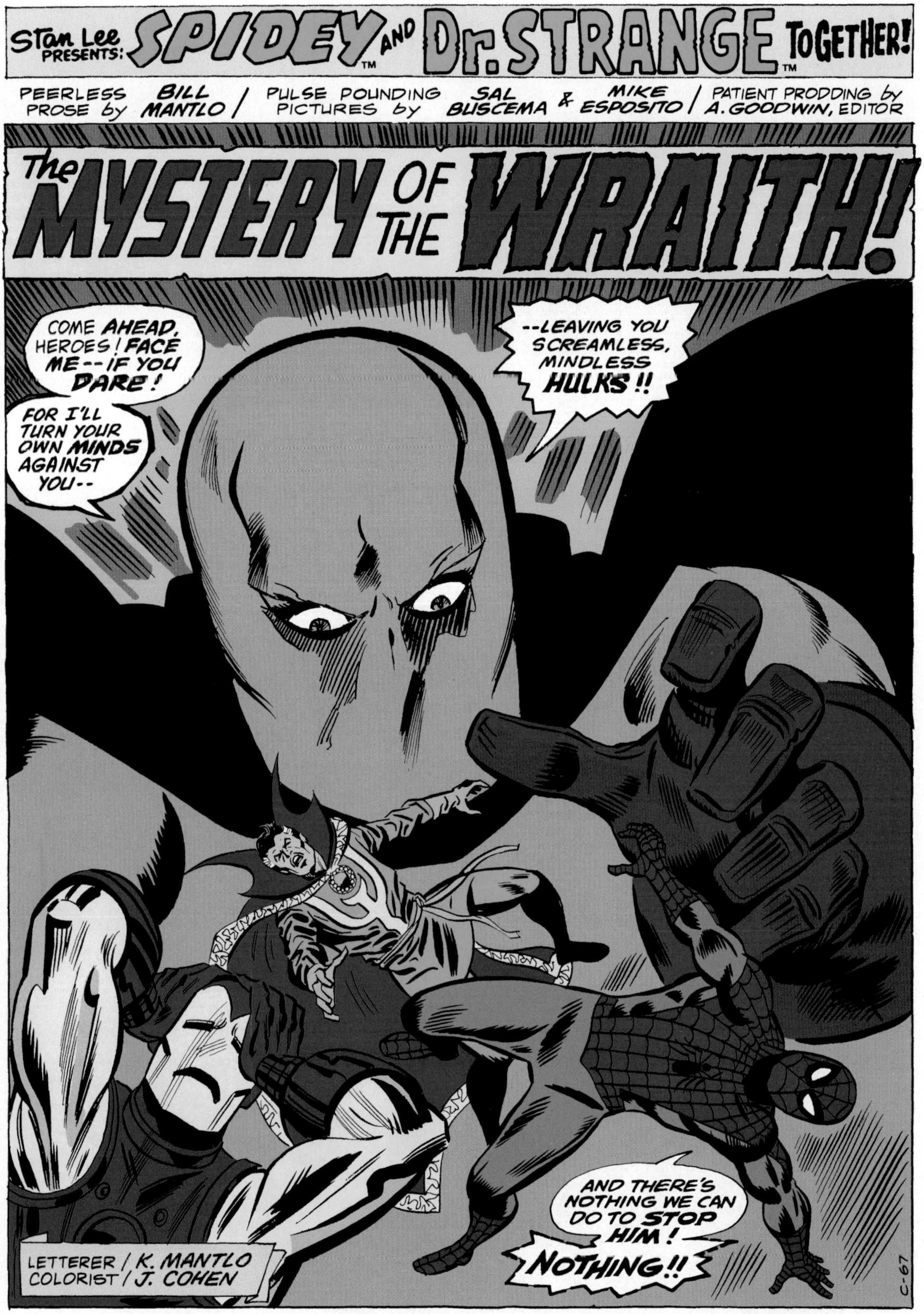
Stan Lee PRESENTS: SPIDEY™ AND Dr. STRANGE™ TOGETHER!
PEERLESS PROSE by BILL MANTLO / PULSE POUNDING PICTURES by SAL BUSCEMA & MIKE ESPOSITO / PATIENT PRODDING by A. GOODWIN, EDITOR
The MYSTERY OF THE WRAITH!
COME AHEAD, HEROES! FACE ME--IF YOU DARE!
FOR I'LL TURN YOUR OWN MINDS AGAINST YOU--
--LEAVING YOU SCREAMLESS, MINDLESS HULKS!!
AND THERE'S NOTHING WE CAN DO TO STOP HIM!
NOTHING!!
LETTERER / K. MANTLO
COLORIST / J. COHEN
C-67

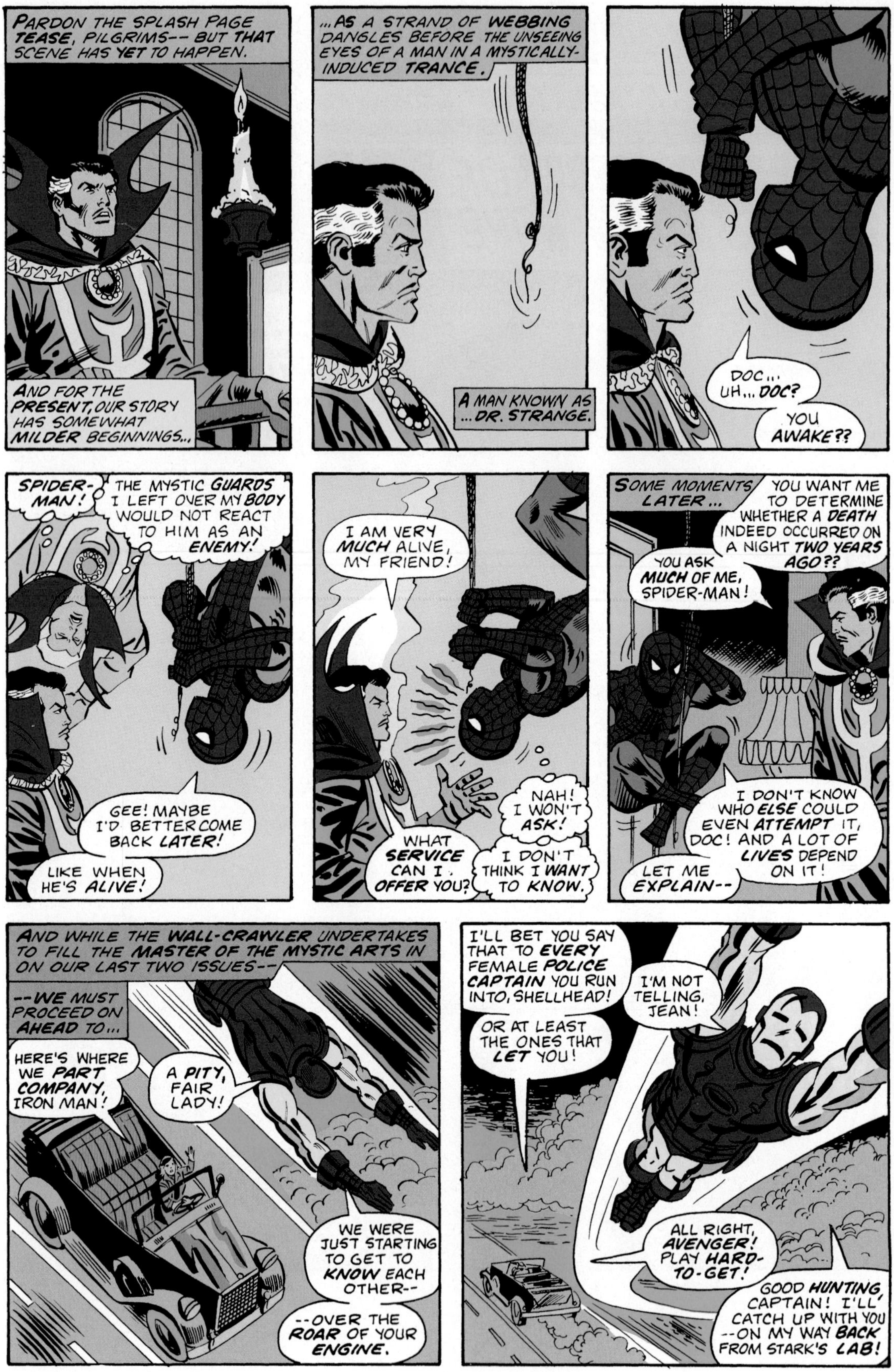
PARDON THE SPLASH PAGE TEASE, PILGRIMS-- BUT THAT SCENE HAS YET TO HAPPEN.
AND FOR THE PRESENT, OUR STORY HAS SOMEWHAT MILDER BEGINNINGS...
...AS A STRAND OF WEBBING DANGLES BEFORE THE UNSEEING EYES OF A MAN IN A MYSTICALLY-INDUCED TRANCE.
A MAN KNOWN AS ...DR. STRANGE.
DOC... UH... DOC?
YOU AWAKE??
SPIDER-MAN!
THE MYSTIC GUARDS I LEFT OVER MY BODY WOULD NOT REACT TO HIM AS AN ENEMY!
GEE! MAYBE I'D BETTER COME BACK LATER!
LIKE WHEN HE'S ALIVE!
I AM VERY MUCH ALIVE, MY FRIEND!
NAH! I WON'T ASK!
WHAT SERVICE CAN I OFFER YOU?
I DON'T THINK I WANT TO KNOW.
SOME MOMENTS LATER...
YOU WANT ME TO DETERMINE WHETHER A DEATH INDEED OCCURRED ON A NIGHT TWO YEARS AGO??
YOU ASK MUCH OF ME, SPIDER-MAN!
I DON'T KNOW WHO ELSE COULD EVEN ATTEMPT IT, DOC! AND A LOT OF LIVES DEPEND ON IT!
LET ME EXPLAIN--
AND WHILE THE WALL-CRAWLER UNDERTAKES TO FILL THE MASTER OF THE MYSTIC ARTS IN ON OUR LAST TWO ISSUES--
--WE MUST PROCEED ON AHEAD TO...
HERE'S WHERE WE PART COMPANY, IRON MAN!
A PITY, FAIR LADY!
WE WERE JUST STARTING TO GET TO KNOW EACH OTHER--
--OVER THE ROAR OF YOUR ENGINE.
I'LL BET YOU SAY THAT TO EVERY FEMALE POLICE CAPTAIN YOU RUN INTO, SHELLHEAD!
OR AT LEAST THE ONES THAT LET YOU!
I'M NOT TELLING, JEAN!
ALL RIGHT, AVENGER! PLAY HARD-TO-GET!
GOOD HUNTING, CAPTAIN! I'LL CATCH UP WITH YOU --ON MY WAY BACK FROM STARK'S LAB!

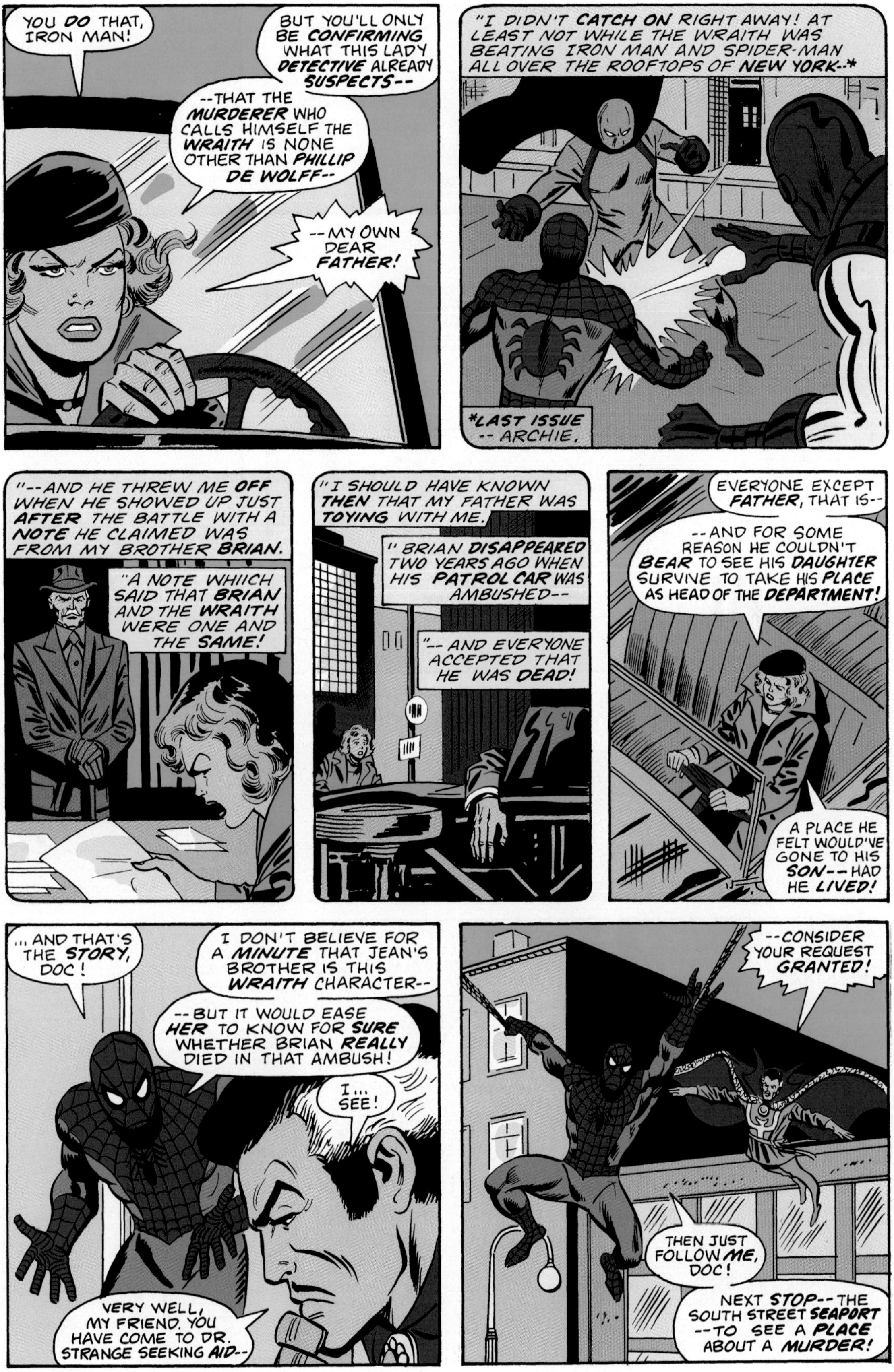

YOU DO THAT, IRON MAN!
BUT YOU'LL ONLY BE CONFIRMING WHAT THIS LADY DETECTIVE ALREADY SUSPECTS--
--THAT THE MURDERER WHO CALLS HIMSELF THE WRAITH IS NONE OTHER THAN PHILLIP DE WOLFF--
--MY OWN DEAR FATHER!
"I DIDN'T CATCH ON RIGHT AWAY! AT LEAST NOT WHILE THE WRAITH WAS BEATING IRON MAN AND SPIDER-MAN ALL OVER THE ROOFTOPS OF NEW YORK-*
*LAST ISSUE -- ARCHIE.
"--AND HE THREW ME OFF WHEN HE SHOWED UP JUST AFTER THE BATTLE WITH A NOTE HE CLAIMED WAS FROM MY BROTHER BRIAN.
"A NOTE WHIICH SAID THAT BRIAN AND THE WRAITH WERE ONE AND THE SAME!
"I SHOULD HAVE KNOWN THEN THAT MY FATHER WAS TOYING WITH ME.
"BRIAN DISAPPEARED TWO YEARS AGO WHEN HIS PATROL CAR WAS AMBUSHED--
"--AND EVERYONE ACCEPTED THAT HE WAS DEAD!
EVERYONE EXCEPT FATHER, THAT IS--
--AND FOR SOME REASON HE COULDN'T BEAR TO SEE HIS DAUGHTER SURVIVE TO TAKE HIS PLACE AS HEAD OF THE DEPARTMENT!
A PLACE HE FELT WOULD'VE GONE TO HIS SON--HAD HE LIVED!
...AND THAT'S THE STORY, DOC!
I DON'T BELIEVE FOR A MINUTE THAT JEAN'S BROTHER IS THIS WRAITH CHARACTER--
--BUT IT WOULD EASE HER TO KNOW FOR SURE WHETHER BRIAN REALLY DIED IN THAT AMBUSH!
I... SEE!
VERY WELL, MY FRIEND. YOU HAVE COME TO DR. STRANGE SEEKING AID--
--CONSIDER YOUR REQUEST GRANTED!
THEN JUST FOLLOW ME, DOC!
NEXT STOP--THE SOUTH STREET SEAPORT --TO SEE A PLACE ABOUT A MURDER!

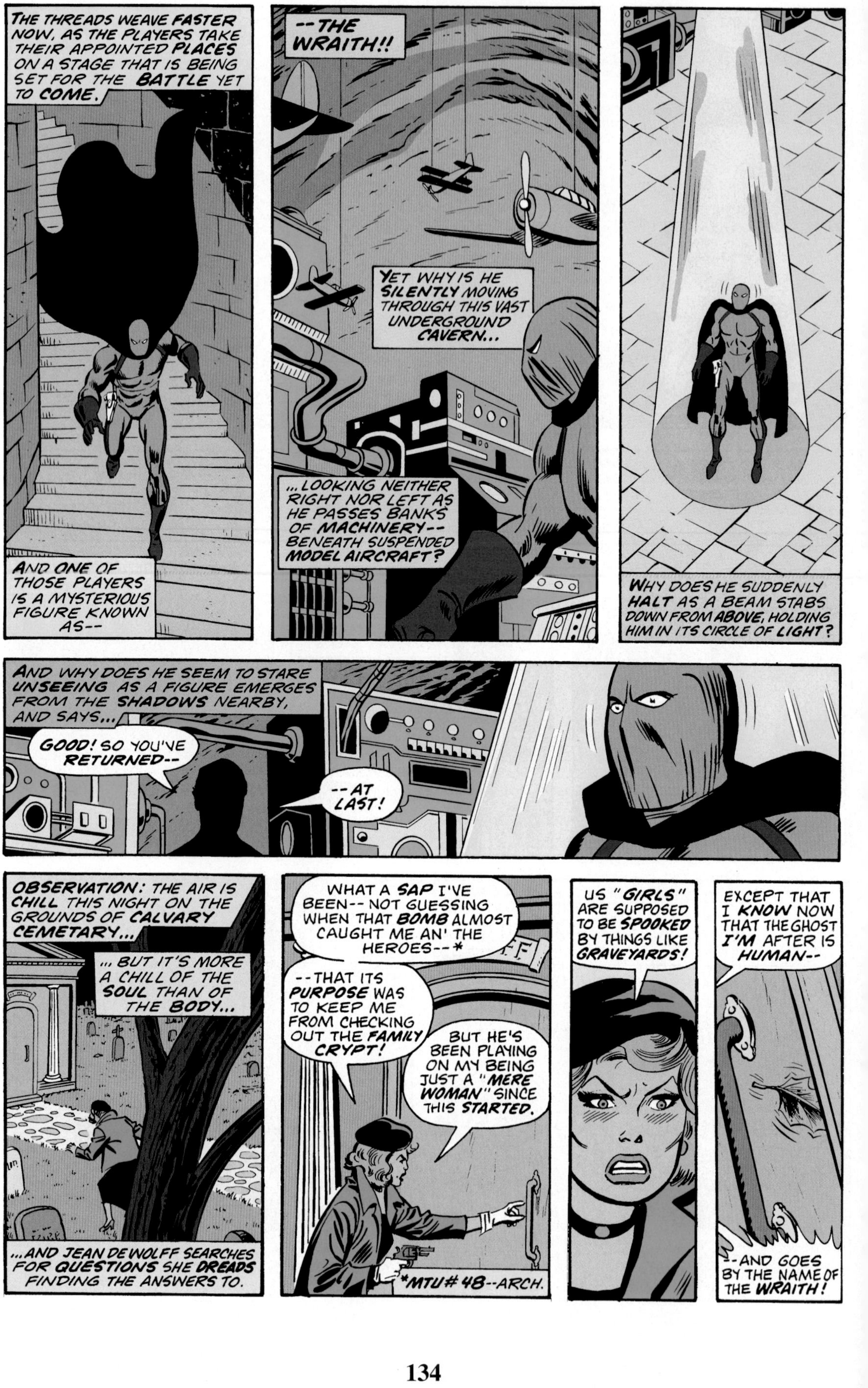
THE THREADS WEAVE FASTER NOW, AS THE PLAYERS TAKE THEIR APPOINTED PLACES ON A STAGE THAT IS BEING SET FOR THE BATTLE YET TO COME.
AND ONE OF THOSE PLAYERS IS A MYSTERIOUS FIGURE KNOWN AS--
--THE WRAITH!!
YET WHY IS HE SILENTLY MOVING THROUGH THIS VAST UNDERGROUND CAVERN...
...LOOKING NEITHER RIGHT NOR LEFT AS HE PASSES BANKS OF MACHINERY-- BENEATH SUSPENDED MODEL AIRCRAFT?
WHY DOES HE SUDDENLY HALT AS A BEAM STABS DOWN FROM ABOVE, HOLDING HIM IN ITS CIRCLE OF LIGHT?
AND WHY DOES HE SEEM TO STARE UNSEEING AS A FIGURE EMERGES FROM THE SHADOWS NEARBY, AND SAYS...
GOOD! SO YOU'VE RETURNED--
--AT LAST!
OBSERVATION: THE AIR IS CHILL THIS NIGHT ON THE GROUNDS OF CALVARY CEMETARY...
...BUT IT'S MORE A CHILL OF THE SOUL THAN OF THE BODY...
...AND JEAN DEWOLFF SEARCHES FOR QUESTIONS SHE DREADS FINDING THE ANSWERS TO.
WHAT A SAP I'VE BEEN-- NOT GUESSING WHEN THAT BOMB ALMOST CAUGHT ME AN' THE HEROES--*
--THAT ITS PURPOSE WAS TO KEEP ME FROM CHECKING OUT THE FAMILY CRYPT!
BUT HE'S BEEN PLAYING ON MY BEING JUST A "MERE WOMAN" SINCE THIS STARTED.
*MTU #48--ARCH.
US "GIRLS" ARE SUPPOSED TO BE SPOOKED BY THINGS LIKE GRAVEYARDS!
EXCEPT THAT I KNOW NOW THAT THE GHOST I'M AFTER IS HUMAN--
--AND GOES BY THE NAME OF THE WRAITH!

THIS IS THE **PLACE**, DOC--

--ACCORDING TO A LADY WHO'D **KNOW**!

YES. I SENSED CERTAIN...**EMANATIONS** ...AS WE DREW **NEAR**!

THERE IS A **MYSTERY** HERE!

YOU DON'T WASTE ANY **TIME**, DO YOU?

NOT IF IT MAY BE **HELPED**, SPIDER-MAN! AH--

--MY **AMULET** CONJURES FORTH **SPECTERS** OF THE **PAST**--

--AND COMMANDS THEM TO **RE-ENACT** THE EVENTS WHOSE **NATURE** WE SEEK TO **LEARN**!

"**THERE**! THAT MUST BE JEAN'S BROTHER-- **BRIAN**! HE'S JUST BEEN SHOT!"

"THESE IMAGES ARE BUT **REMEMBRANCES** OF THINGS PAST, MY **FRIEND**!"

"OKAY--BUT WHO'S THAT **SHOOTING** THE GUY WHO **PLUGGED** BRIAN?"

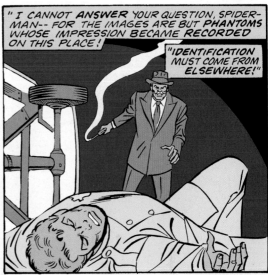

"I CANNOT **ANSWER** YOUR QUESTION, SPIDER-MAN-- FOR THE IMAGES ARE BUT **PHANTOMS** WHOSE IMPRESSION BECAME **RECORDED** ON THIS PLACE!"

"**IDENTIFICATION** MUST COME FROM **ELSEWHERE**!"

NOW THE TABLEAU DRAWS TO A **CLOSE**-- AS BRIAN IS CARRIED **OFF** BY **ANOTHER**!

YET WHETHER THE BOY **LIVED**-- OR **DIED**-- THE **GENII** LOCATED IN THIS SPOT CANNOT--

--OR **WILL NOT** SAY!

DOESN'T **MATTER**, DOC! I'VE **GOT** MY **ANSWER**!

OUR "MYSTERY" PHANTOM'S **NAME** IS PHILLIP DE WOLFF--

--AND I HAVE A **HUNCH** THAT WHEN WE FIND **HIM**--

--WE'LL FIND THE **WRAITH**!

WANT TO COME ALONG FOR THE **RIDE**, DOC?

YES, MY FRIEND! I **DO**!

135

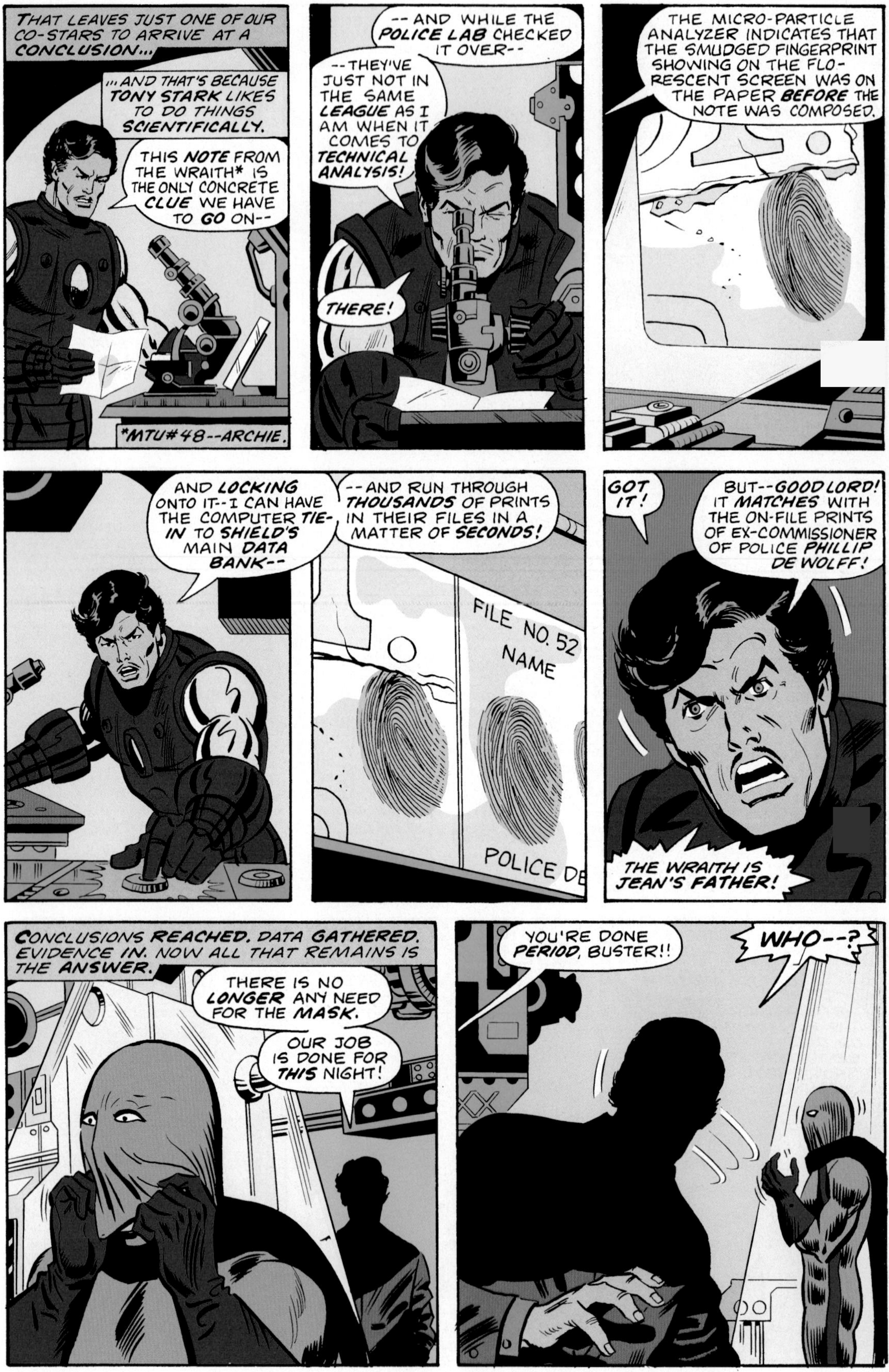
THAT LEAVES JUST ONE OF OUR CO-STARS TO ARRIVE AT A CONCLUSION...
...AND THAT'S BECAUSE TONY STARK LIKES TO DO THINGS SCIENTIFICALLY.
THIS NOTE FROM THE WRAITH* IS THE ONLY CONCRETE CLUE WE HAVE TO GO ON--
*MTU#48--ARCHIE.
--AND WHILE THE POLICE LAB CHECKED IT OVER--
--THEY'VE JUST NOT IN THE SAME LEAGUE AS I AM WHEN IT COMES TO TECHNICAL ANALYSIS!
THERE!
THE MICRO-PARTICLE ANALYZER INDICATES THAT THE SMUDGED FINGERPRINT SHOWING ON THE FLO-RESCENT SCREEN WAS ON THE PAPER BEFORE THE NOTE WAS COMPOSED.
AND LOCKING ONTO IT--I CAN HAVE THE COMPUTER TIE-IN TO SHIELD'S MAIN DATA BANK--
--AND RUN THROUGH THOUSANDS OF PRINTS IN THEIR FILES IN A MATTER OF SECONDS!
FILE NO. 52
NAME
POLICE DE
GOT IT!
BUT--GOOD LORD! IT MATCHES WITH THE ON-FILE PRINTS OF EX-COMMISSIONER OF POLICE PHILLIP DE WOLFF!
THE WRAITH IS JEAN'S FATHER!
CONCLUSIONS REACHED. DATA GATHERED. EVIDENCE IN. NOW ALL THAT REMAINS IS THE ANSWER.
THERE IS NO LONGER ANY NEED FOR THE MASK.
OUR JOB IS DONE FOR THIS NIGHT!
YOU'RE DONE PERIOD, BUSTER!!
WHO--?

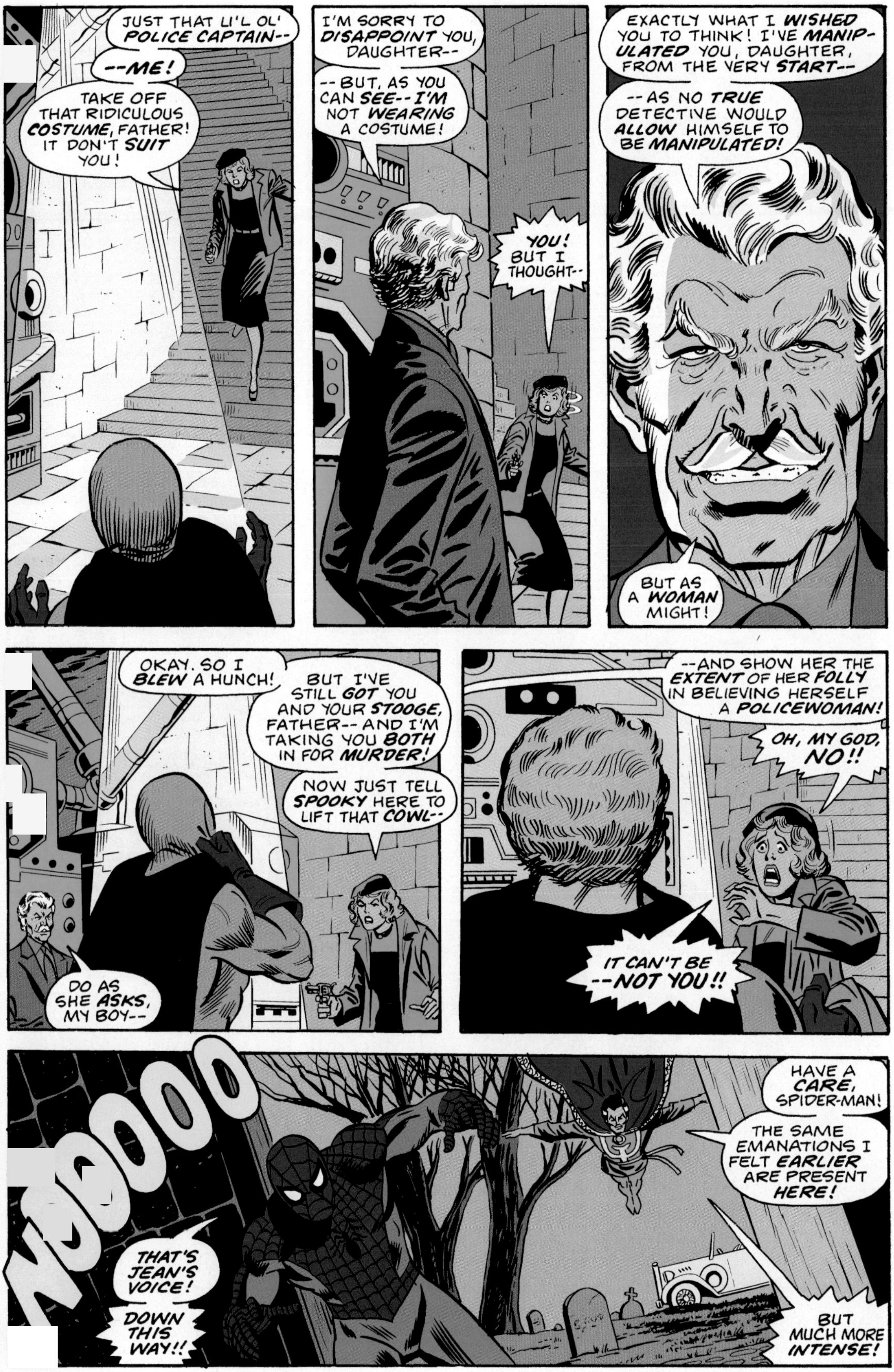
JUST THAT LI'L OL' POLICE CAPTAIN--
--ME!
TAKE OFF THAT RIDICULOUS COSTUME, FATHER! IT DON'T SUIT YOU!
I'M SORRY TO DISAPPOINT YOU, DAUGHTER--
--BUT, AS YOU CAN SEE--I'M NOT WEARING A COSTUME!
YOU! BUT I THOUGHT--
EXACTLY WHAT I WISHED YOU TO THINK! I'VE MANIPULATED YOU, DAUGHTER, FROM THE VERY START--
--AS NO TRUE DETECTIVE WOULD ALLOW HIMSELF TO BE MANIPULATED!
BUT AS A WOMAN MIGHT!
OKAY. SO I BLEW A HUNCH!
BUT I'VE STILL GOT YOU AND YOUR STOOGE, FATHER--AND I'M TAKING YOU BOTH IN FOR MURDER!
NOW JUST TELL SPOOKY HERE TO LIFT THAT COWL--
DO AS SHE ASKS, MY BOY--
--AND SHOW HER THE EXTENT OF HER FOLLY IN BELIEVING HERSELF A POLICEWOMAN!
OH, MY GOD, NO!!
IT CAN'T BE --NOT YOU!!
NOOOOO
THAT'S JEAN'S VOICE!
DOWN THIS WAY!!
HAVE A CARE, SPIDER-MAN!
THE SAME EMANATIONS I FELT EARLIER ARE PRESENT HERE!
BUT MUCH MORE INTENSE!

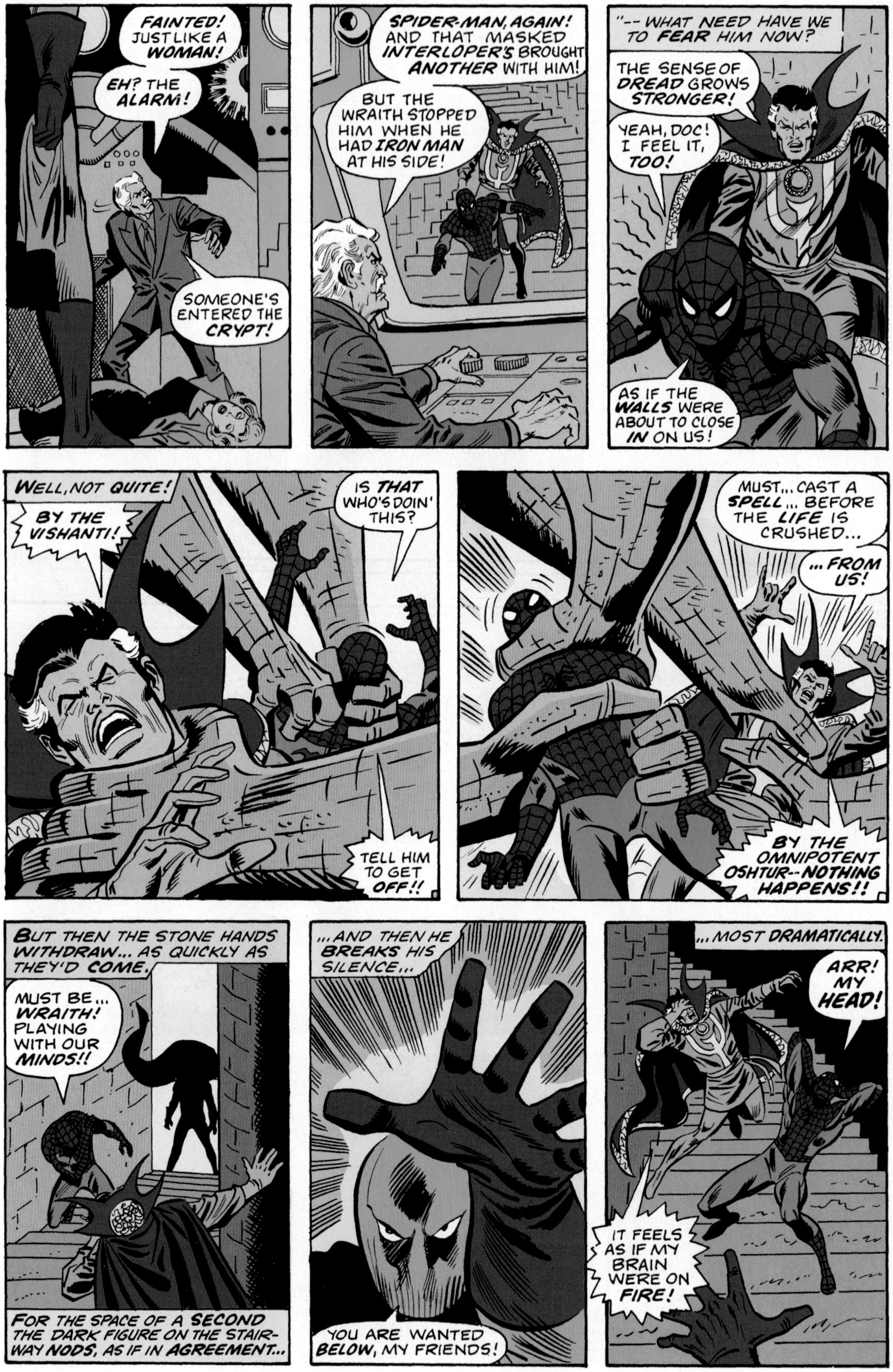
FAINTED! JUST LIKE A WOMAN!
EH? THE ALARM!
SOMEONE'S ENTERED THE CRYPT!
SPIDER-MAN, AGAIN! AND THAT MASKED INTERLOPER'S BROUGHT ANOTHER WITH HIM!
BUT THE WRAITH STOPPED HIM WHEN HE HAD IRON MAN AT HIS SIDE!
"-- WHAT NEED HAVE WE TO FEAR HIM NOW?
THE SENSE OF DREAD GROWS STRONGER!
YEAH, DOC! I FEEL IT, TOO!
AS IF THE WALLS WERE ABOUT TO CLOSE IN ON US!
WELL, NOT QUITE!
BY THE VISHANTI!
IS THAT WHO'S DOIN' THIS?
TELL HIM TO GET OFF!!
MUST... CAST A SPELL... BEFORE THE LIFE IS CRUSHED...
...FROM US!
BY THE OMNIPOTENT OSHTUR-- NOTHING HAPPENS!!
BUT THEN THE STONE HANDS WITHDRAW... AS QUICKLY AS THEY'D COME.
MUST BE... WRAITH! PLAYING WITH OUR MINDS!!
FOR THE SPACE OF A SECOND THE DARK FIGURE ON THE STAIRWAY NODS, AS IF IN AGREEMENT...
...AND THEN HE BREAKS HIS SILENCE...
YOU ARE WANTED BELOW, MY FRIENDS!
...MOST DRAMATICALLY.
ARR! MY HEAD!
IT FEELS AS IF MY BRAIN WERE ON FIRE!

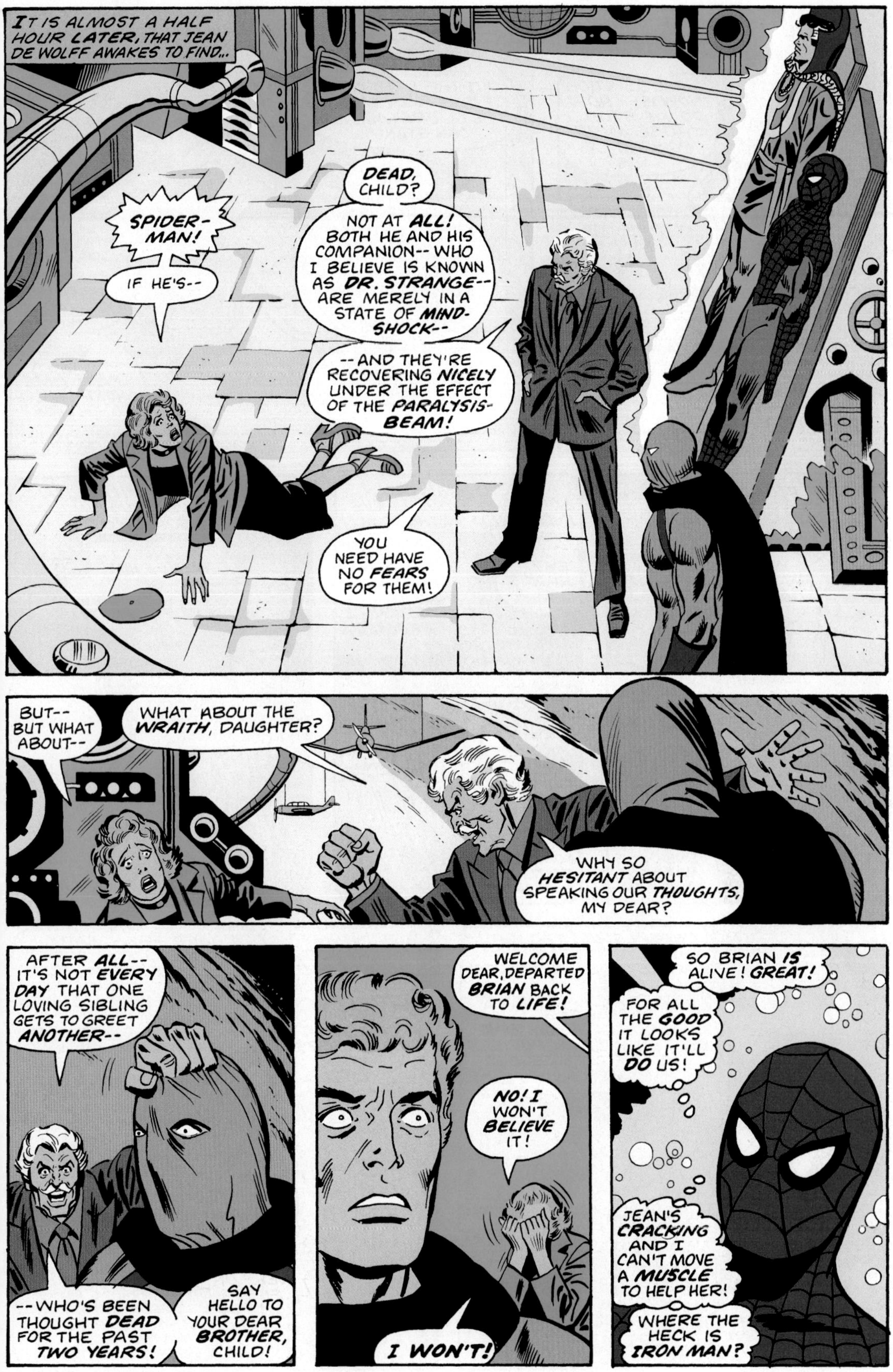

IT IS ALMOST A HALF HOUR LATER, THAT JEAN DE WOLFF AWAKES TO FIND...
SPIDER-MAN!
IF HE'S--
DEAD, CHILD?
NOT AT ALL! BOTH HE AND HIS COMPANION-- WHO I BELIEVE IS KNOWN AS DR. STRANGE-- ARE MERELY IN A STATE OF MIND-SHOCK--
--AND THEY'RE RECOVERING NICELY UNDER THE EFFECT OF THE PARALYSIS-BEAM!
YOU NEED HAVE NO FEARS FOR THEM!
BUT-- BUT WHAT ABOUT--
WHAT ABOUT THE WRAITH, DAUGHTER?
WHY SO HESITANT ABOUT SPEAKING OUR THOUGHTS, MY DEAR?
AFTER ALL-- IT'S NOT EVERY DAY THAT ONE LOVING SIBLING GETS TO GREET ANOTHER--
--WHO'S BEEN THOUGHT DEAD FOR THE PAST TWO YEARS!
SAY HELLO TO YOUR DEAR BROTHER, CHILD!
WELCOME DEAR, DEPARTED BRIAN BACK TO LIFE!
NO! I WON'T BELIEVE IT!
I WON'T!
SO BRIAN IS ALIVE! GREAT!
FOR ALL THE GOOD IT LOOKS LIKE IT'LL DO US!
JEAN'S CRACKING AND I CAN'T MOVE A MUSCLE TO HELP HER!
WHERE THE HECK IS IRON MAN?

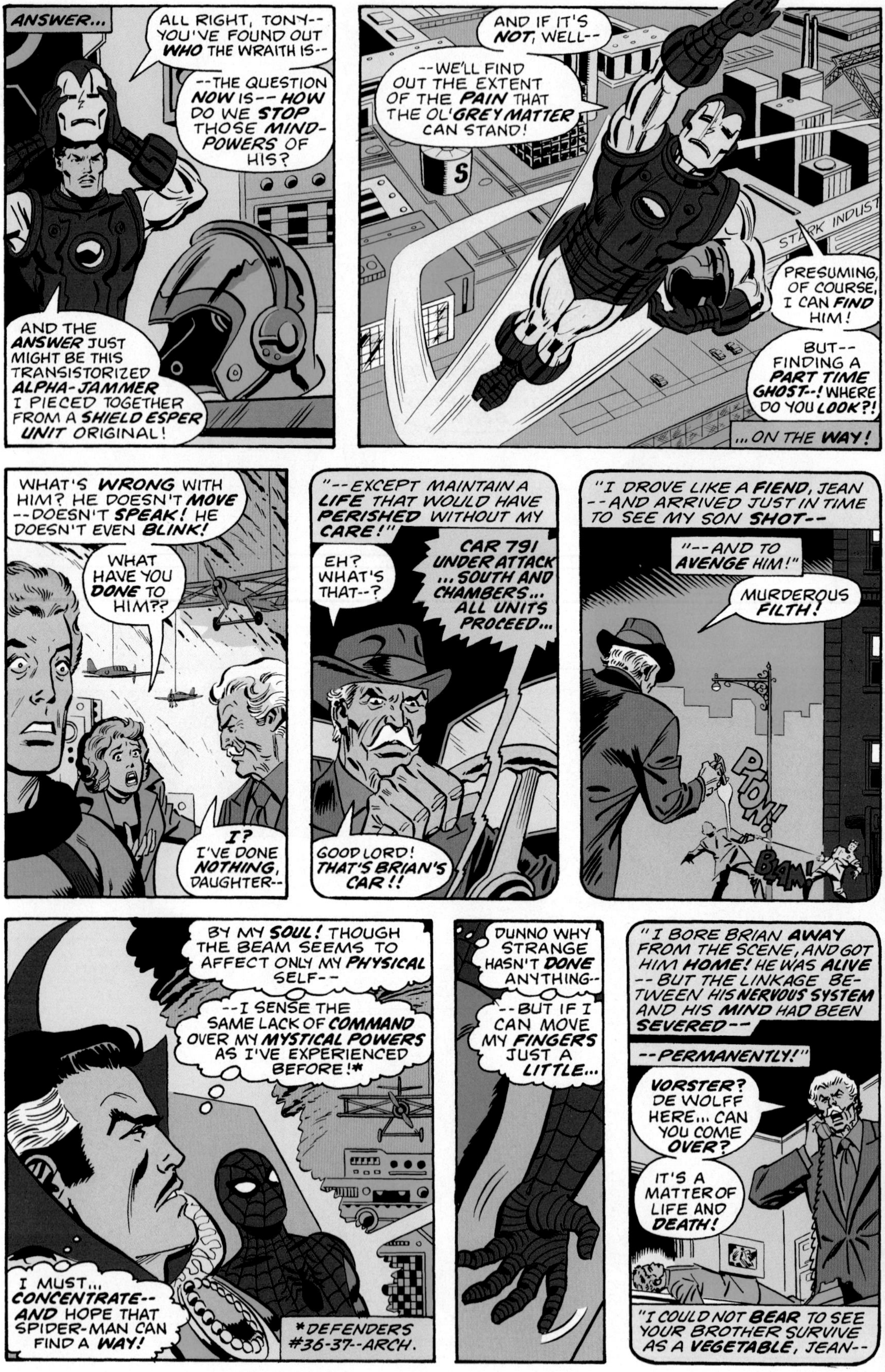
ANSWER...
ALL RIGHT, TONY-- YOU'VE FOUND OUT WHO THE WRAITH IS--
--THE QUESTION NOW IS-- HOW DO WE STOP THOSE MIND-POWERS OF HIS?
AND THE ANSWER JUST MIGHT BE THIS TRANSISTORIZED ALPHA-JAMMER I PIECED TOGETHER FROM A SHIELD ESPER UNIT ORIGINAL!
AND IF IT'S NOT, WELL--
--WE'LL FIND OUT THE EXTENT OF THE PAIN THAT THE OL' GREY MATTER CAN STAND!
STARK INDUST
PRESUMING, OF COURSE, I CAN FIND HIM!
BUT-- FINDING A PART TIME GHOST--! WHERE DO YOU LOOK?!
...ON THE WAY!
WHAT'S WRONG WITH HIM? HE DOESN'T MOVE --DOESN'T SPEAK! HE DOESN'T EVEN BLINK!
WHAT HAVE YOU DONE TO HIM??
I? I'VE DONE NOTHING, DAUGHTER--
"--EXCEPT MAINTAIN A LIFE THAT WOULD HAVE PERISHED WITHOUT MY CARE!"
EH? WHAT'S THAT--?
CAR 791 UNDER ATTACK ...SOUTH AND CHAMBERS... ALL UNITS PROCEED...
GOOD LORD! THAT'S BRIAN'S CAR!!
"I DROVE LIKE A FIEND, JEAN --AND ARRIVED JUST IN TIME TO SEE MY SON SHOT--
"--AND TO AVENGE HIM!"
MURDEROUS FILTH!
PTOW!
BLAM!
BY MY SOUL! THOUGH THE BEAM SEEMS TO AFFECT ONLY MY PHYSICAL SELF--
--I SENSE THE SAME LACK OF COMMAND OVER MY MYSTICAL POWERS AS I'VE EXPERIENCED BEFORE!*
I MUST... CONCENTRATE-- AND HOPE THAT SPIDER-MAN CAN FIND A WAY!
*DEFENDERS #36-37--ARCH.
DUNNO WHY STRANGE HASN'T DONE ANYTHING--
--BUT IF I CAN MOVE MY FINGERS JUST A LITTLE...
"I BORE BRIAN AWAY FROM THE SCENE, AND GOT HIM HOME! HE WAS ALIVE --BUT THE LINKAGE BETWEEN HIS NERVOUS SYSTEM AND HIS MIND HAD BEEN SEVERED--
--PERMANENTLY!"
VORSTER? DE WOLFF HERE... CAN YOU COME OVER?
IT'S A MATTER OF LIFE AND DEATH!
"I COULD NOT BEAR TO SEE YOUR BROTHER SURVIVE AS A VEGETABLE, JEAN--

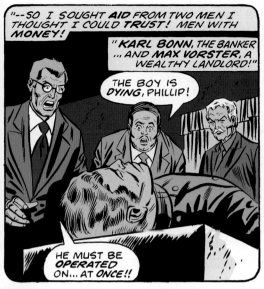

"--SO I SOUGHT **AID** FROM TWO MEN I THOUGHT I COULD **TRUST**! MEN WITH MONEY!"

"KARL BONN, THE BANKER ...AND MAX VORSTER, A WEALTHY LANDLORD!"

THE BOY IS **DYING**, PHILLIP!

HE MUST BE **OPERATED** ON... AT **ONCE**!!

FEELS LIKE... AN **ELEPHANT** ...IS SITTING ON MY **HAND**...

...BUT ONLY A LITTLE ...**MORE**!

NO! HE ISN'T **DYING!**

AND NO ONE MUST **KNOW** THAT HE'S **HERE!** THAT HE'S **ALIVE!!**

BUT--BUT **WHY**, PHILLIP?

SLAM!

DID IT!

THWIP!

BECAUSE MY SON MUST BE **RESTORED** TO LIFE--AND **MORE** THAN LIFE--IN **SECRET!**

HE MUST **RETURN** TO SEARCH OUT THOSE WHO WOULD **PREY** ON THE INNOCENT --THE **LAW-ABIDING** --AND **DESTROY** THEM!

HE WILL BE A **WRAITH**-- DEALING **JUSTICE** FROM BEYOND THE **GRAVE!**

"BONN AND VORSTER AGREED TO **HELP** ME--OR SO I THOUGHT!"

"ONLY LATER DID I LEARN THE **PRICE** THEY WOULD ASK OF ME."

OH, **GREAT!** I KILL MYSELF TO REACH MY **WEB-SHOOTER**--

--AND THEN HIT THE **WRONG** BUTTON!

WHIR-R-R

THWAP!

SPIDER-MAN HAS **FAILED!**

NOW I MUST **SUCCEED**--

--OR **LOSE ALL!**

FOR IF WE ARE **DISCOVERED** WITH MY POWERS REFUSING TO **RESPOND**--DE WOLFF WILL HAVE HIS SON **FINISH** US!

SO-- WHILE MY ABILITY TO CAST **SPELLS** HAS FAILED ME--

--THE POWER TO COMPEL MY ENCHANTED **CLOAK** OF LEVITATION HAS NOT!

AND MAY IT BE **ENOUGH** TO KEEP THE BEAM WHICH **BINDS** ME FROM HOLDING ME **FURTHER!**

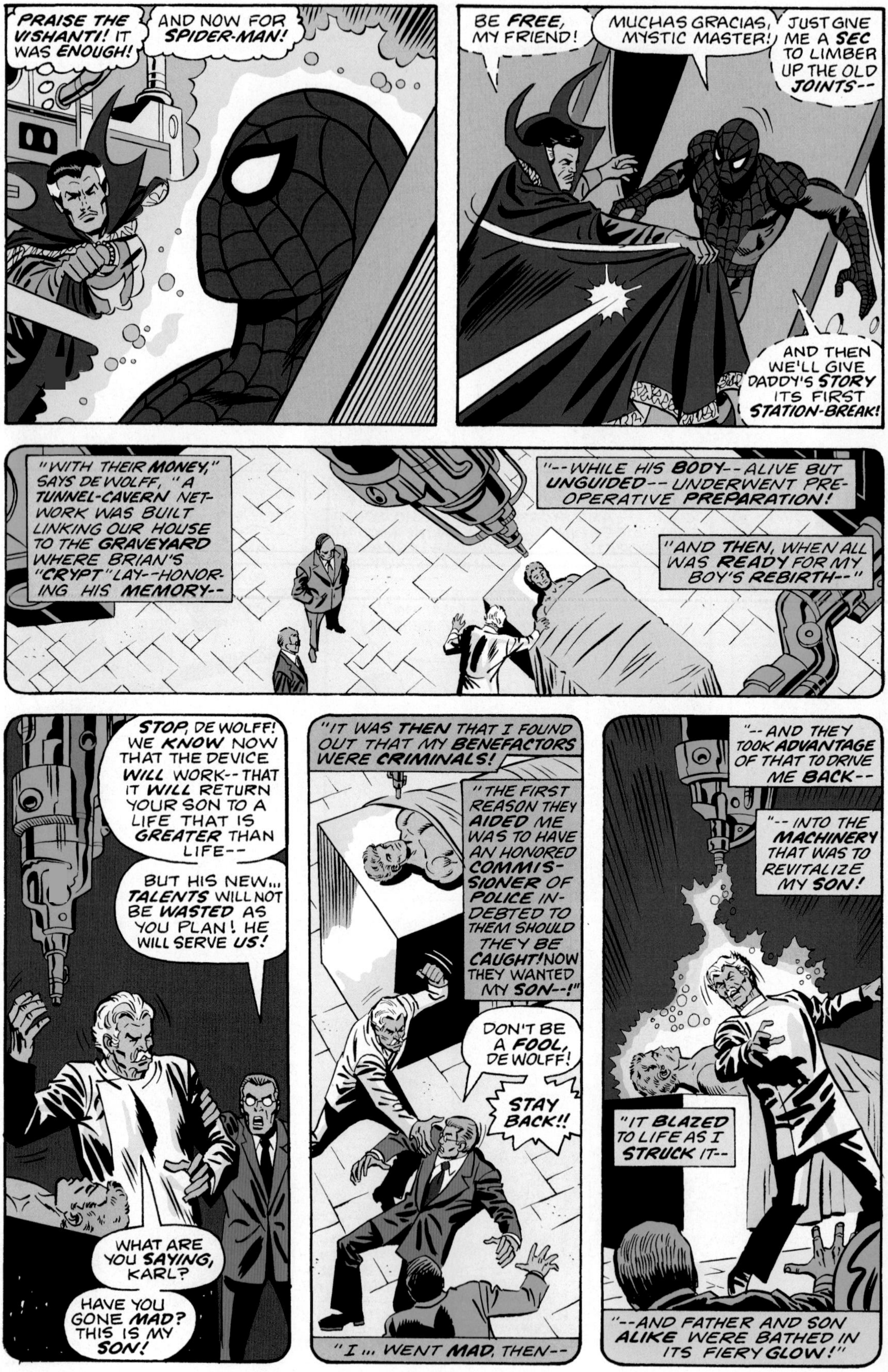
PRAISE THE VISHANTI! IT WAS ENOUGH!
AND NOW FOR SPIDER-MAN!
BE FREE, MY FRIEND!
MUCHAS GRACIAS, MYSTIC MASTER!
JUST GIVE ME A SEC TO LIMBER UP THE OLD JOINTS--
AND THEN WE'LL GIVE DADDY'S STORY ITS FIRST STATION-BREAK!
"WITH THEIR MONEY," SAYS DE WOLFF, "A TUNNEL-CAVERN NET-WORK WAS BUILT LINKING OUR HOUSE TO THE GRAVEYARD WHERE BRIAN'S "CRYPT" LAY--HONORING HIS MEMORY--
"--WHILE HIS BODY--ALIVE BUT UNGUIDED--UNDERWENT PRE-OPERATIVE PREPARATION!
"AND THEN, WHEN ALL WAS READY FOR MY BOY'S REBIRTH--"
STOP, DE WOLFF! WE KNOW NOW THAT THE DEVICE WILL WORK--THAT IT WILL RETURN YOUR SON TO A LIFE THAT IS GREATER THAN LIFE--
BUT HIS NEW... TALENTS WILL NOT BE WASTED AS YOU PLAN! HE WILL SERVE US!
WHAT ARE YOU SAYING, KARL?
HAVE YOU GONE MAD? THIS IS MY SON!
"IT WAS THEN THAT I FOUND OUT THAT MY BENEFACTORS WERE CRIMINALS!
"THE FIRST REASON THEY AIDED ME WAS TO HAVE AN HONORED COMMIS-SIONER OF POLICE IN-DEBTED TO THEM SHOULD THEY BE CAUGHT! NOW THEY WANTED MY SON--!"
DON'T BE A FOOL, DE WOLFF!
STAY BACK!!
"I... WENT MAD, THEN--
"--AND THEY TOOK ADVANTAGE OF THAT TO DRIVE ME BACK--
"--INTO THE MACHINERY THAT WAS TO REVITALIZE MY SON!
"IT BLAZED TO LIFE AS I STRUCK IT--
"--AND FATHER AND SON ALIKE WERE BATHED IN ITS FIERY GLOW!"

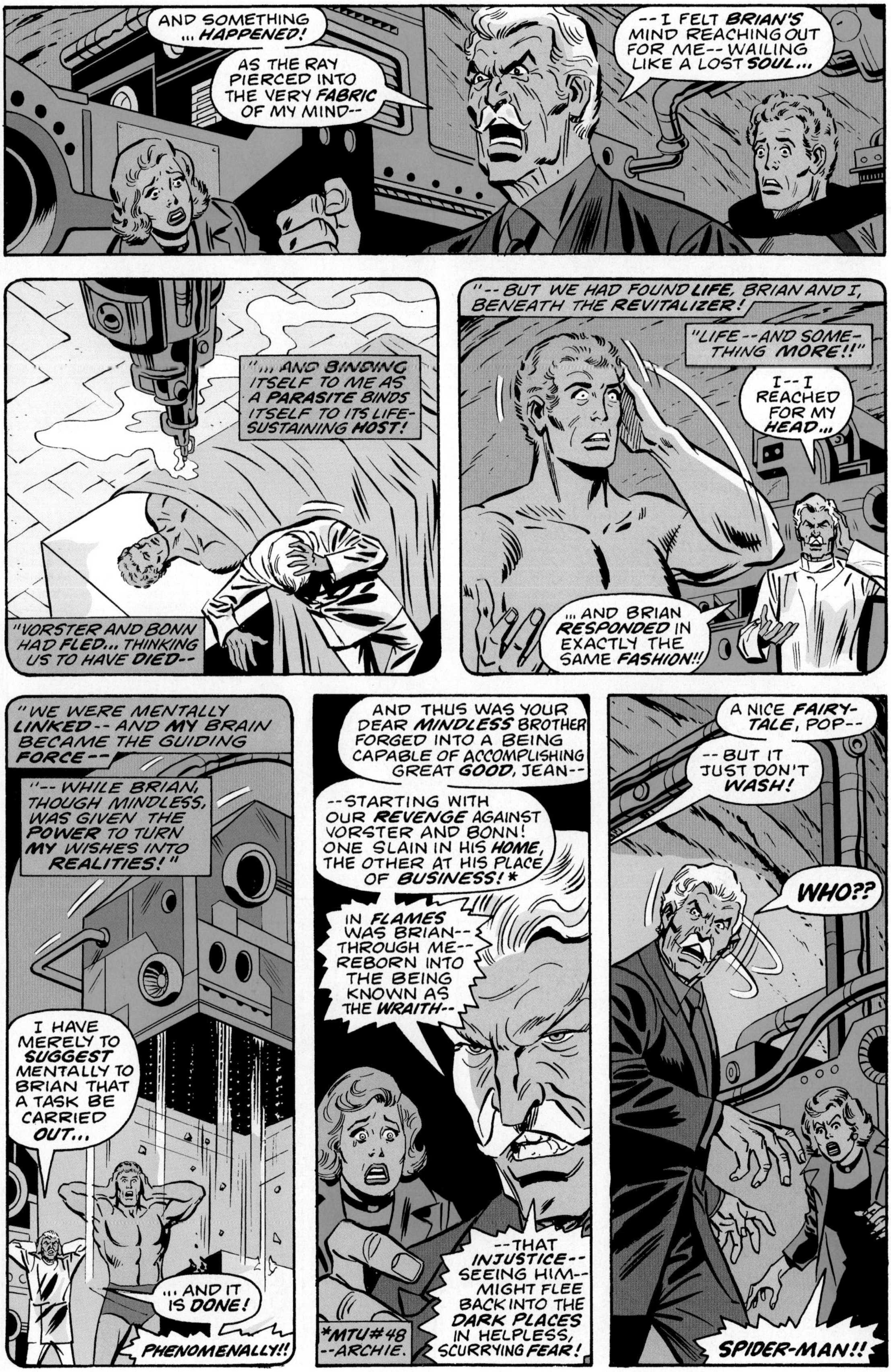
AND SOMETHING ...HAPPENED!
AS THE RAY PIERCED INTO THE VERY FABRIC OF MY MIND--
--I FELT BRIAN'S MIND REACHING OUT FOR ME--WAILING LIKE A LOST SOUL...
"...AND BINDING ITSELF TO ME AS A PARASITE BINDS ITSELF TO ITS LIFE-SUSTAINING HOST!
"VORSTER AND BONN HAD FLED... THINKING US TO HAVE DIED--
"--BUT WE HAD FOUND LIFE, BRIAN AND I, BENEATH THE REVITALIZER!
"LIFE--AND SOMETHING MORE!!"
I--I REACHED FOR MY HEAD...
...AND BRIAN RESPONDED IN EXACTLY THE SAME FASHION!!
"WE WERE MENTALLY LINKED--AND MY BRAIN BECAME THE GUIDING FORCE--
"--WHILE BRIAN, THOUGH MINDLESS, WAS GIVEN THE POWER TO TURN MY WISHES INTO REALITIES!"
I HAVE MERELY TO SUGGEST MENTALLY TO BRIAN THAT A TASK BE CARRIED OUT...
...AND IT IS DONE!
PHENOMENALLY!!
AND THUS WAS YOUR DEAR MINDLESS BROTHER FORGED INTO A BEING CAPABLE OF ACCOMPLISHING GREAT GOOD, JEAN--
--STARTING WITH OUR REVENGE AGAINST VORSTER AND BONN! ONE SLAIN IN HIS HOME, THE OTHER AT HIS PLACE OF BUSINESS!*
IN FLAMES WAS BRIAN--THROUGH ME--REBORN INTO THE BEING KNOWN AS THE WRAITH--
--THAT INJUSTICE--SEEING HIM--MIGHT FLEE BACK INTO THE DARK PLACES IN HELPLESS, SCURRYING FEAR!
*MTU #48 --ARCHIE.
A NICE FAIRY-TALE, POP--
--BUT IT JUST DON'T WASH!
WHO??
SPIDER-MAN!!

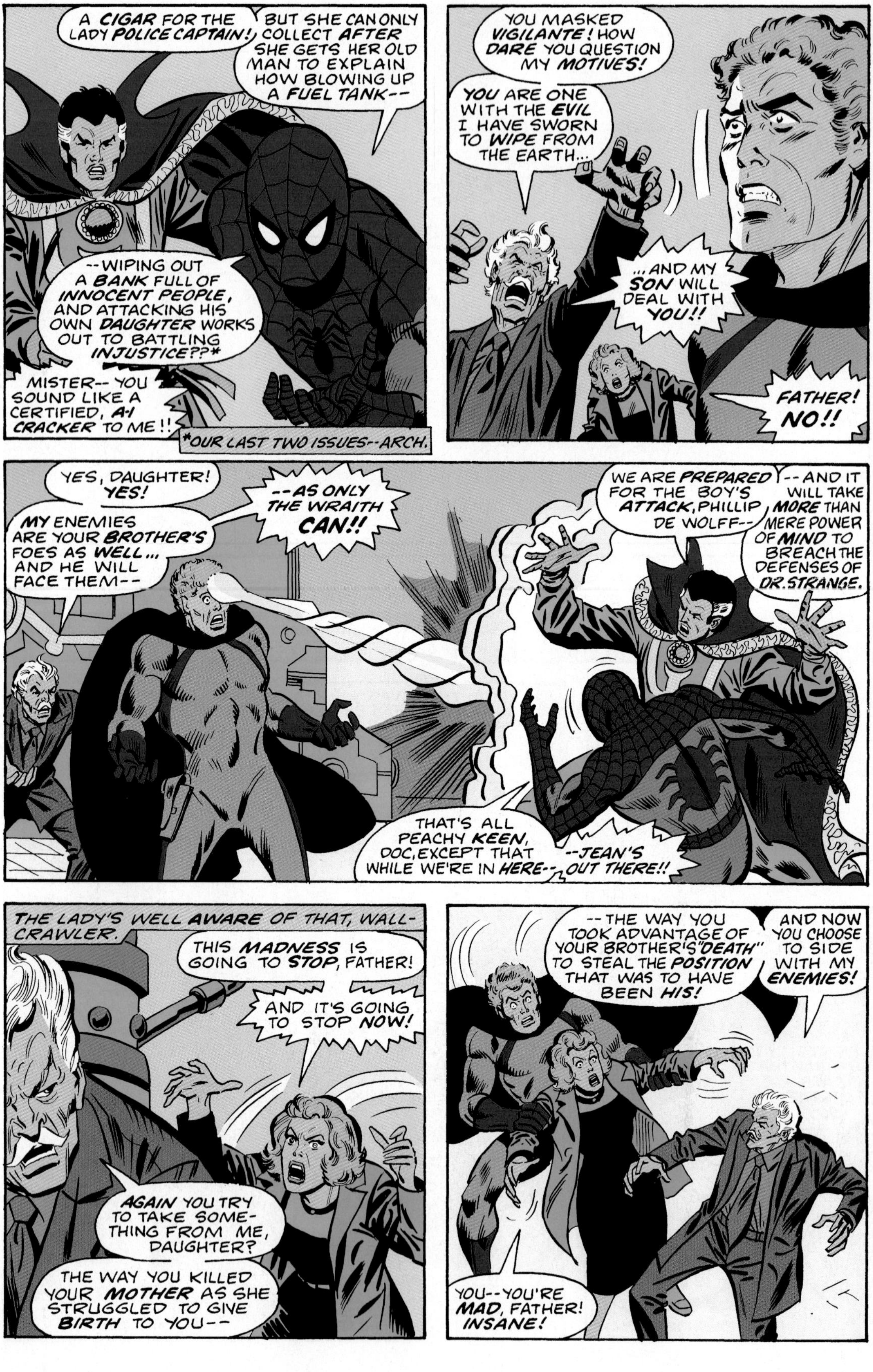
A CIGAR FOR THE LADY POLICE CAPTAIN!
BUT SHE CAN ONLY COLLECT AFTER SHE GETS HER OLD MAN TO EXPLAIN HOW BLOWING UP A FUEL TANK--
--WIPING OUT A BANK FULL OF INNOCENT PEOPLE, AND ATTACKING HIS OWN DAUGHTER WORKS OUT TO BATTLING INJUSTICE??*
MISTER-- YOU SOUND LIKE A CERTIFIED, A-1 CRACKER TO ME!!
*OUR LAST TWO ISSUES--ARCH.
YOU MASKED VIGILANTE! HOW DARE YOU QUESTION MY MOTIVES!
YOU ARE ONE WITH THE EVIL I HAVE SWORN TO WIPE FROM THE EARTH...
...AND MY SON WILL DEAL WITH YOU!!
FATHER! NO!!
YES, DAUGHTER! YES!
MY ENEMIES ARE YOUR BROTHER'S FOES AS WELL... AND HE WILL FACE THEM--
--AS ONLY THE WRAITH CAN!!
WE ARE PREPARED FOR THE BOY'S ATTACK, PHILLIP DE WOLFF--
--AND IT WILL TAKE MORE THAN MERE POWER OF MIND TO BREACH THE DEFENSES OF DR. STRANGE.
THAT'S ALL PEACHY KEEN, DOC, EXCEPT THAT WHILE WE'RE IN HERE--
--JEAN'S OUT THERE!!
THE LADY'S WELL AWARE OF THAT, WALL-CRAWLER.
THIS MADNESS IS GOING TO STOP, FATHER!
AND IT'S GOING TO STOP NOW!
AGAIN YOU TRY TO TAKE SOMETHING FROM ME, DAUGHTER?
THE WAY YOU KILLED YOUR MOTHER AS SHE STRUGGLED TO GIVE BIRTH TO YOU--
--THE WAY YOU TOOK ADVANTAGE OF YOUR BROTHER'S "DEATH" TO STEAL THE POSITION THAT WAS TO HAVE BEEN HIS!
AND NOW YOU CHOOSE TO SIDE WITH MY ENEMIES!
YOU--YOU'RE MAD, FATHER! INSANE!

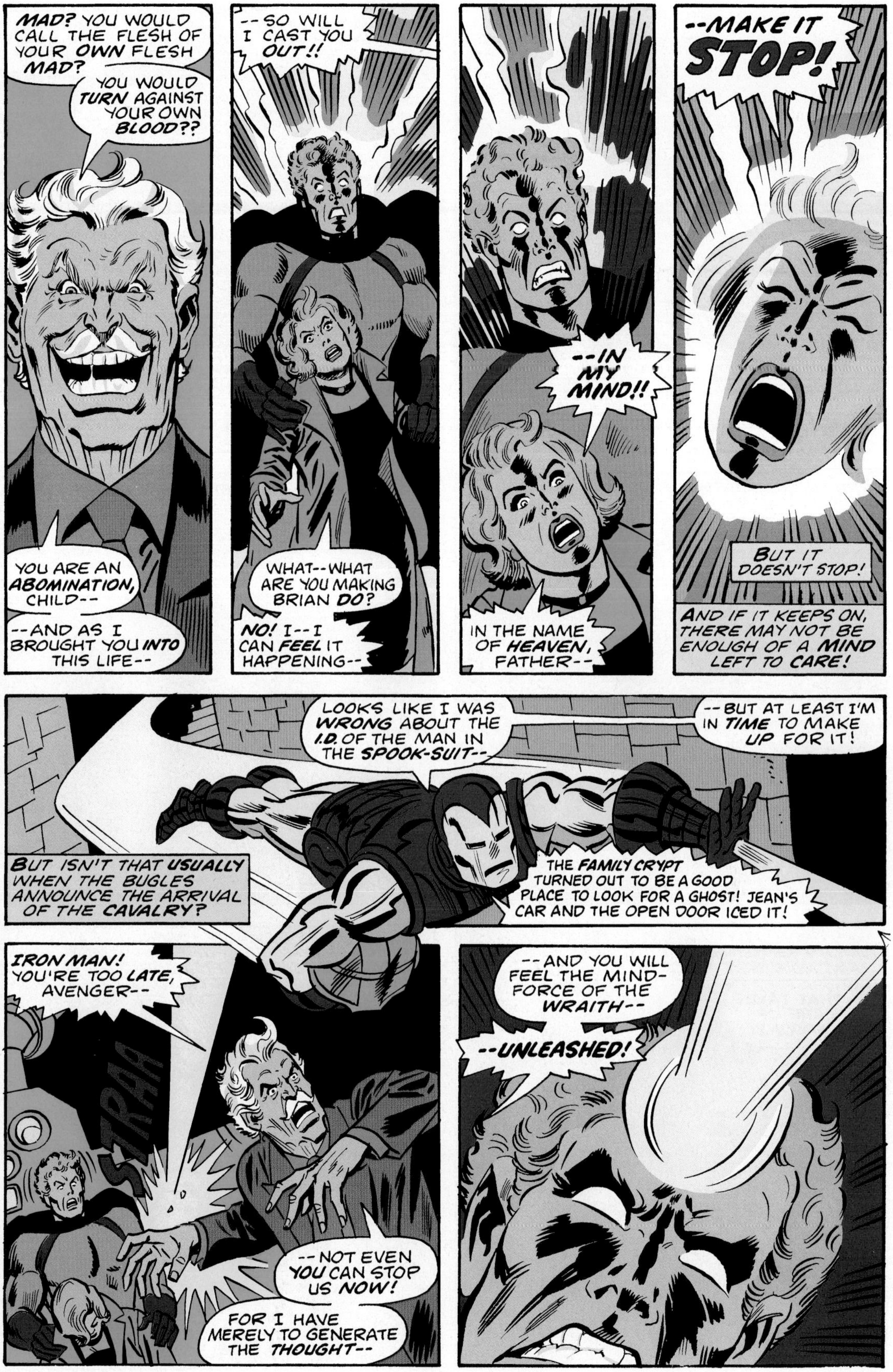

MAD? YOU WOULD CALL THE FLESH OF YOUR OWN FLESH MAD?
YOU WOULD TURN AGAINST YOUR OWN BLOOD??
YOU ARE AN ABOMINATION, CHILD--
--AND AS I BROUGHT YOU INTO THIS LIFE--
--SO WILL I CAST YOU OUT!!
WHAT--WHAT ARE YOU MAKING BRIAN DO?
NO! I--I CAN FEEL IT HAPPENING--
--IN MY MIND!!
IN THE NAME OF HEAVEN, FATHER--
--MAKE IT STOP!
BUT IT DOESN'T STOP!
AND IF IT KEEPS ON, THERE MAY NOT BE ENOUGH OF A MIND LEFT TO CARE!
LOOKS LIKE I WAS WRONG ABOUT THE I.D. OF THE MAN IN THE SPOOK-SUIT--
--BUT AT LEAST I'M IN TIME TO MAKE UP FOR IT!
BUT ISN'T THAT USUALLY WHEN THE BUGLES ANNOUNCE THE ARRIVAL OF THE CAVALRY?
THE FAMILY CRYPT TURNED OUT TO BE A GOOD PLACE TO LOOK FOR A GHOST! JEAN'S CAR AND THE OPEN DOOR ICED IT!
IRON MAN! YOU'RE TOO LATE, AVENGER--
TRAK
--NOT EVEN YOU CAN STOP US NOW!
FOR I HAVE MERELY TO GENERATE THE THOUGHT--
--AND YOU WILL FEEL THE MIND-FORCE OF THE WRAITH--
--UNLEASHED!

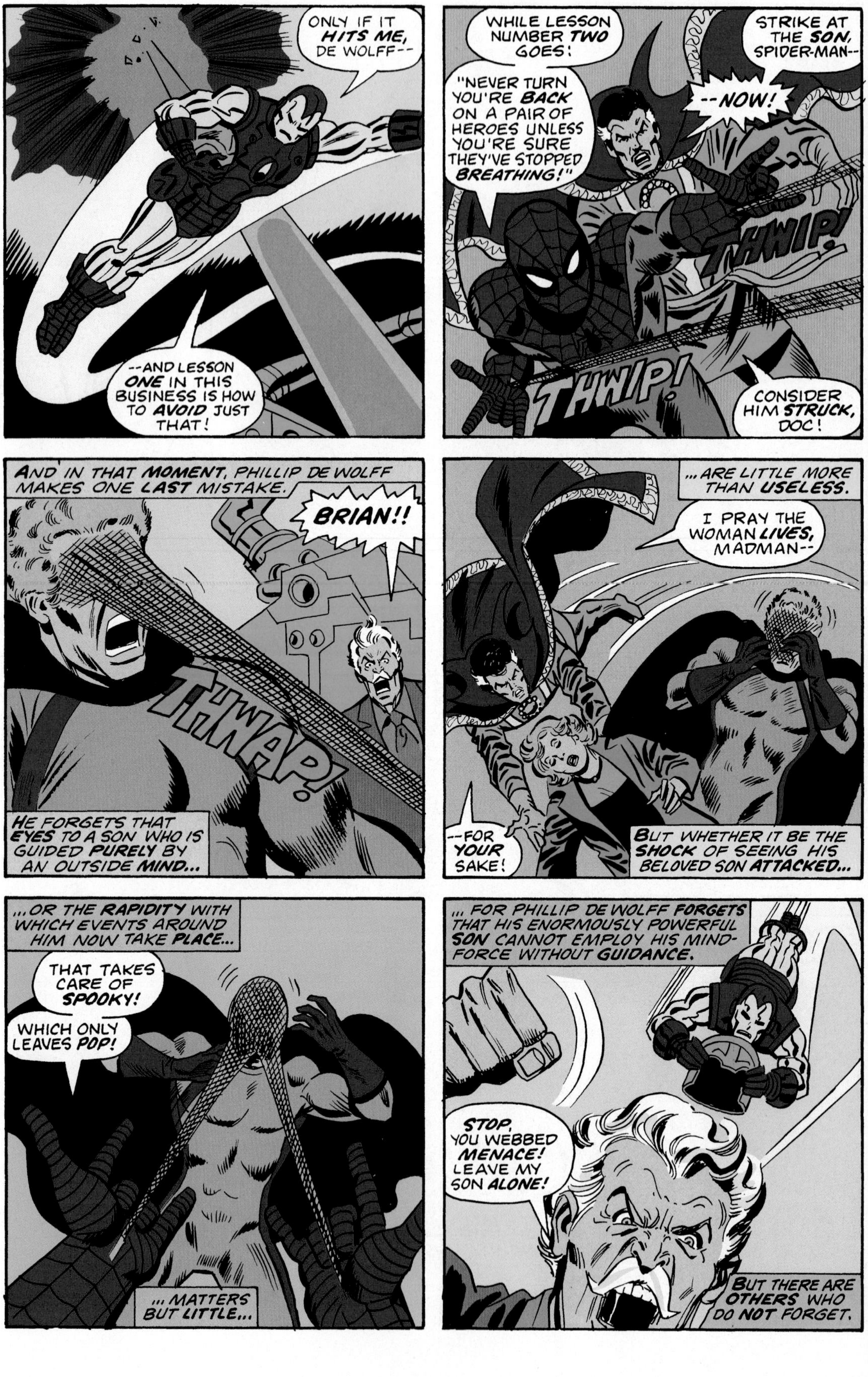
ONLY IF IT HITS ME, DE WOLFF--
--AND LESSON ONE IN THIS BUSINESS IS HOW TO AVOID JUST THAT!
WHILE LESSON NUMBER TWO GOES:
"NEVER TURN YOU'RE BACK ON A PAIR OF HEROES UNLESS YOU'RE SURE THEY'VE STOPPED BREATHING!"
STRIKE AT THE SON, SPIDER-MAN--
--NOW!
THWIP!
THWIP!
CONSIDER HIM STRUCK, DOC!
AND IN THAT MOMENT, PHILLIP DE WOLFF MAKES ONE LAST MISTAKE.
BRIAN!!
THWAP!
HE FORGETS THAT EYES TO A SON WHO IS GUIDED PURELY BY AN OUTSIDE MIND...
...ARE LITTLE MORE THAN USELESS.
I PRAY THE WOMAN LIVES, MADMAN--
--FOR YOUR SAKE!
BUT WHETHER IT BE THE SHOCK OF SEEING HIS BELOVED SON ATTACKED...
...OR THE RAPIDITY WITH WHICH EVENTS AROUND HIM NOW TAKE PLACE...
THAT TAKES CARE OF SPOOKY!
WHICH ONLY LEAVES POP!
...MATTERS BUT LITTLE...
...FOR PHILLIP DE WOLFF FORGETS THAT HIS ENORMOUSLY POWERFUL SON CANNOT EMPLOY HIS MIND-FORCE WITHOUT GUIDANCE.
STOP, YOU WEBBED MENACE! LEAVE MY SON ALONE!
BUT THERE ARE OTHERS WHO DO NOT FORGET.

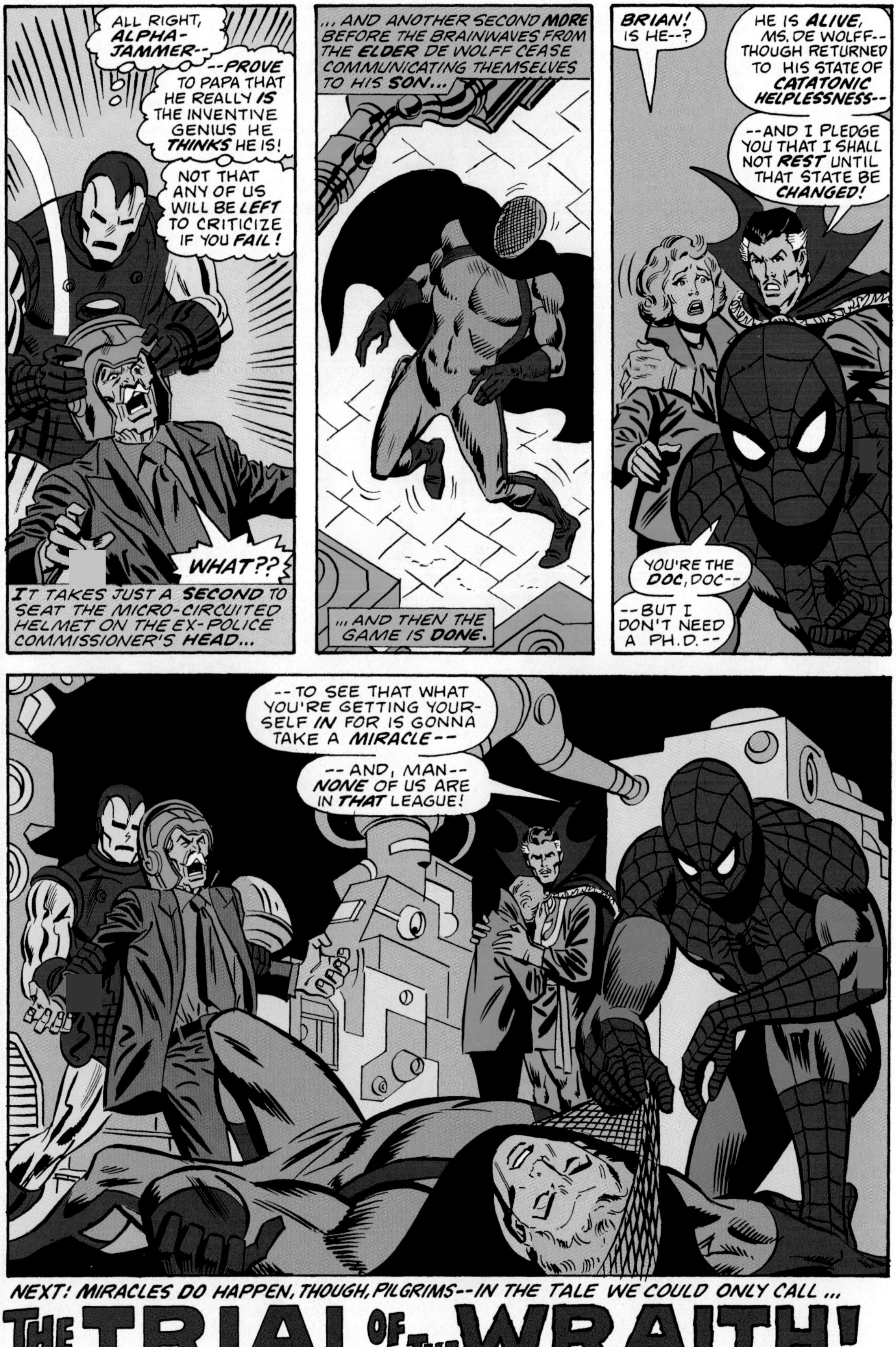

ALL RIGHT, ALPHA-JAMMER--
--PROVE TO PAPA THAT HE REALLY IS THE INVENTIVE GENIUS HE THINKS HE IS!
NOT THAT ANY OF US WILL BE LEFT TO CRITICIZE IF YOU FAIL!
WHAT??
IT TAKES JUST A SECOND TO SEAT THE MICRO-CIRCUITED HELMET ON THE EX-POLICE COMMISSIONER'S HEAD...
...AND ANOTHER SECOND MORE BEFORE THE BRAINWAVES FROM THE ELDER DE WOLFF CEASE COMMUNICATING THEMSELVES TO HIS SON...
...AND THEN THE GAME IS DONE.
BRIAN! IS HE--?
HE IS ALIVE, MS. DE WOLFF--THOUGH RETURNED TO HIS STATE OF CATATONIC HELPLESSNESS--
--AND I PLEDGE YOU THAT I SHALL NOT REST UNTIL THAT STATE BE CHANGED!
YOU'RE THE DOC, DOC--
--BUT I DON'T NEED A PH.D.--
--TO SEE THAT WHAT YOU'RE GETTING YOURSELF IN FOR IS GONNA TAKE A MIRACLE--
--AND, MAN--NONE OF US ARE IN THAT LEAGUE!
NEXT: MIRACLES DO HAPPEN, THOUGH, PILGRIMS--IN THE TALE WE COULD ONLY CALL ...
THE TRIAL OF THE WRAITH!

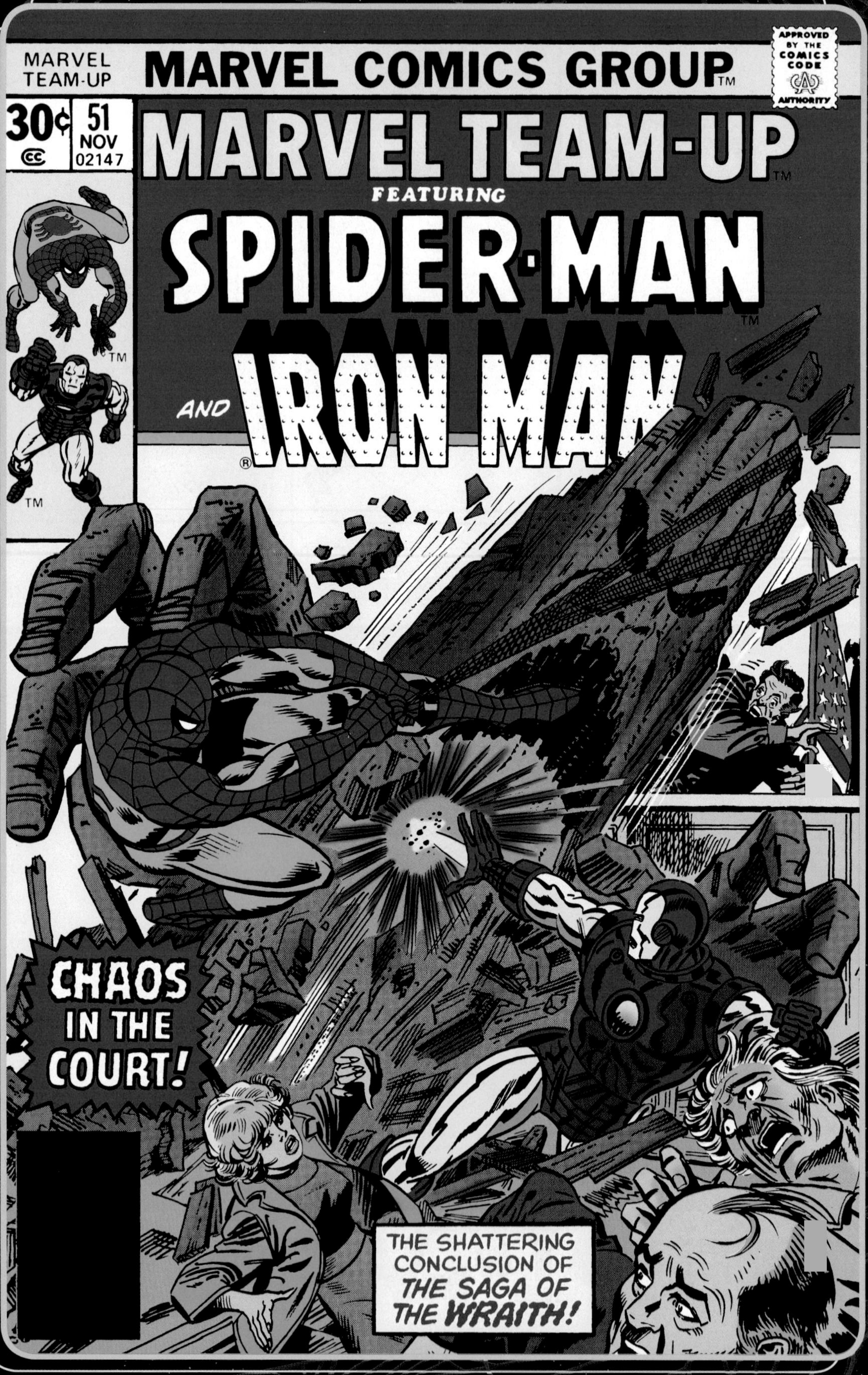
MARVEL TEAM-UP
MARVEL COMICS GROUP
APPROVED BY THE COMICS CODE AUTHORITY
30¢
51 NOV 02147
MARVEL TEAM-UP
FEATURING
SPIDER-MAN
AND
IRON MAN
CHAOS IN THE COURT!
THE SHATTERING CONCLUSION OF THE SAGA OF THE WRAITH!

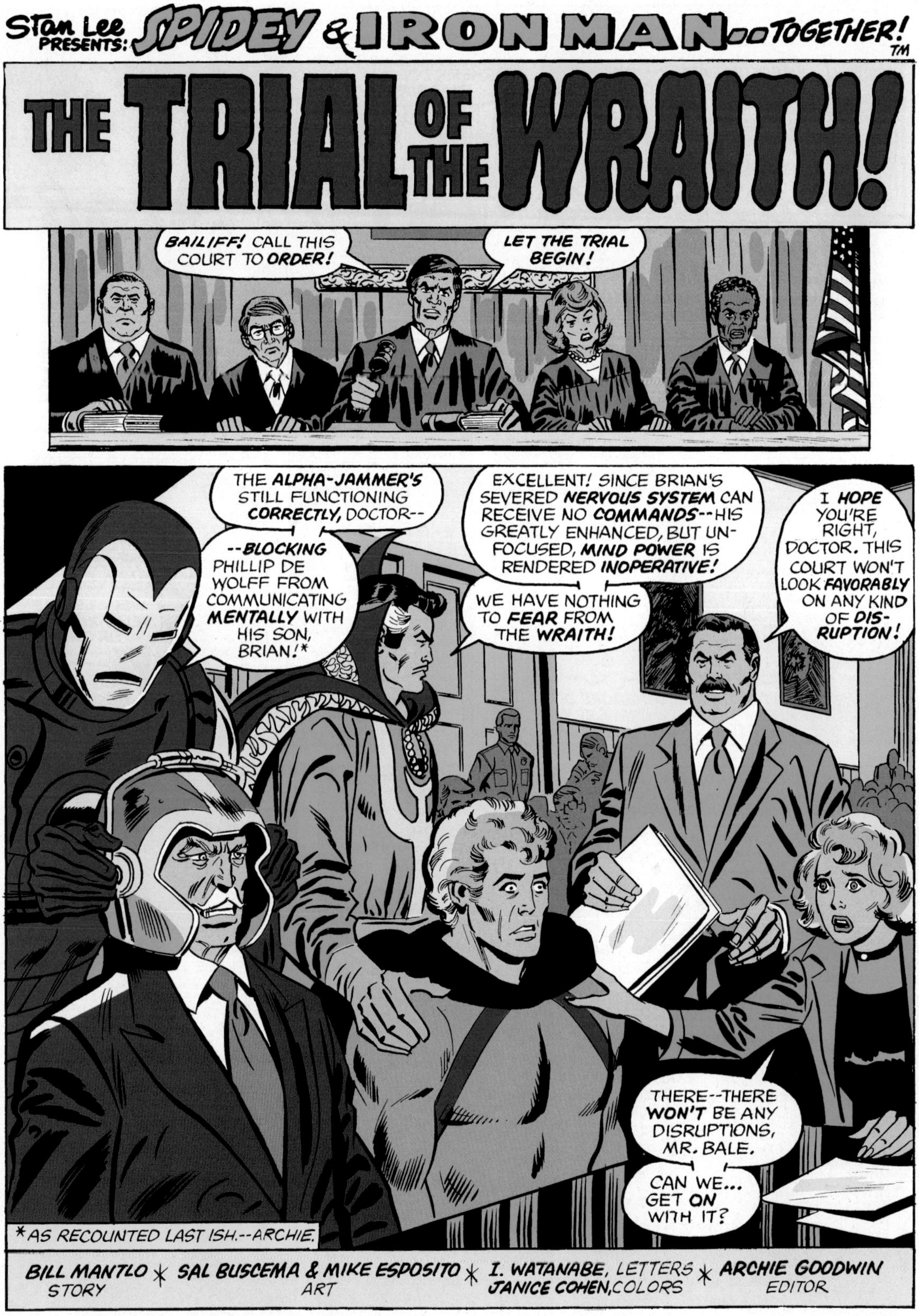
STAN LEE PRESENTS: SPIDEY & IRON MAN--TOGETHER!
THE TRIAL OF THE WRAITH!
BAILIFF! CALL THIS COURT TO ORDER!
LET THE TRIAL BEGIN!
THE ALPHA-JAMMER'S STILL FUNCTIONING CORRECTLY, DOCTOR--
--BLOCKING PHILLIP DE WOLFF FROM COMMUNICATING MENTALLY WITH HIS SON, BRIAN!*
EXCELLENT! SINCE BRIAN'S SEVERED NERVOUS SYSTEM CAN RECEIVE NO COMMANDS--HIS GREATLY ENHANCED, BUT UN-FOCUSED, MIND POWER IS RENDERED INOPERATIVE!
WE HAVE NOTHING TO FEAR FROM THE WRAITH!
I HOPE YOU'RE RIGHT, DOCTOR. THIS COURT WON'T LOOK FAVORABLY ON ANY KIND OF DIS-RUPTION!
THERE--THERE WON'T BE ANY DISRUPTIONS, MR. BALE.
CAN WE... GET ON WITH IT?
*AS RECOUNTED LAST ISH.--ARCHIE.
BILL MANTLO STORY * SAL BUSCEMA & MIKE ESPOSITO ART * I. WATANABE, LETTERS JANICE COHEN, COLORS * ARCHIE GOODWIN EDITOR

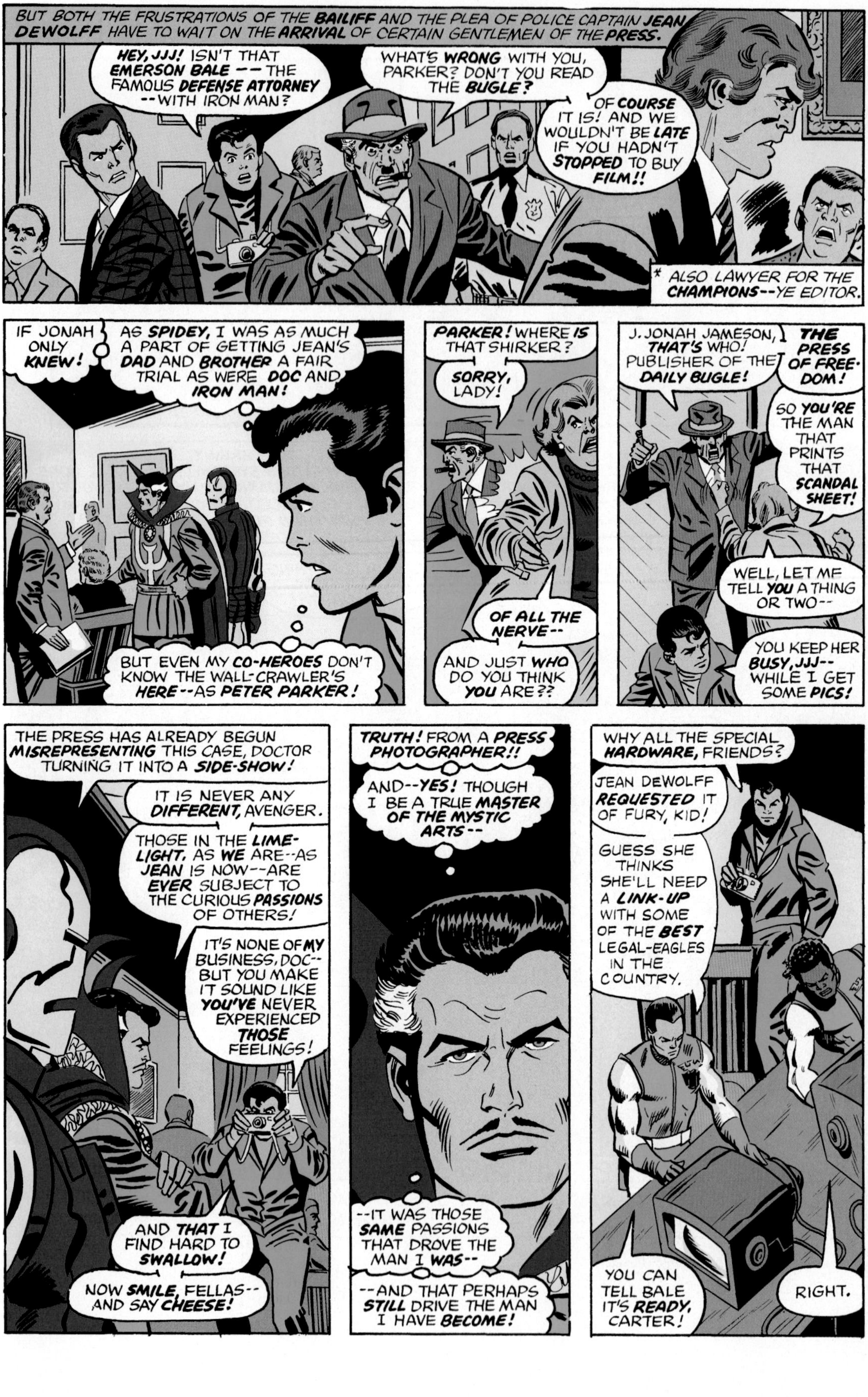

BUT BOTH THE FRUSTRATIONS OF THE BAILIFF AND THE PLEA OF POLICE CAPTAIN JEAN DEWOLFF HAVE TO WAIT ON THE ARRIVAL OF CERTAIN GENTLEMEN OF THE PRESS.
HEY, JJJ! ISN'T THAT EMERSON BALE -- THE FAMOUS DEFENSE ATTORNEY --WITH IRON MAN?
WHAT'S WRONG WITH YOU, PARKER? DON'T YOU READ THE BUGLE?
OF COURSE IT IS! AND WE WOULDN'T BE LATE IF YOU HADN'T STOPPED TO BUY FILM!!
* ALSO LAWYER FOR THE CHAMPIONS--YE EDITOR.
IF JONAH ONLY KNEW!
AS SPIDEY, I WAS AS MUCH A PART OF GETTING JEAN'S DAD AND BROTHER A FAIR TRIAL AS WERE DOC AND IRON MAN!
BUT EVEN MY CO-HEROES DON'T KNOW THE WALL-CRAWLER'S HERE--AS PETER PARKER!
PARKER! WHERE IS THAT SHIRKER?
SORRY, LADY!
OF ALL THE NERVE--
AND JUST WHO DO YOU THINK YOU ARE??
J. JONAH JAMESON, THAT'S WHO! PUBLISHER OF THE DAILY BUGLE!
THE PRESS OF FREE-DOM!
SO YOU'RE THE MAN THAT PRINTS THAT SCANDAL SHEET!
WELL, LET ME TELL YOU A THING OR TWO--
YOU KEEP HER BUSY, JJJ-- WHILE I GET SOME PICS!
THE PRESS HAS ALREADY BEGUN MISREPRESENTING THIS CASE, DOCTOR TURNING IT INTO A SIDE-SHOW!
IT IS NEVER ANY DIFFERENT, AVENGER.
THOSE IN THE LIME-LIGHT, AS WE ARE--AS JEAN IS NOW--ARE EVER SUBJECT TO THE CURIOUS PASSIONS OF OTHERS!
IT'S NONE OF MY BUSINESS, DOC-- BUT YOU MAKE IT SOUND LIKE YOU'VE NEVER EXPERIENCED THOSE FEELINGS!
AND THAT I FIND HARD TO SWALLOW!
NOW SMILE, FELLAS-- AND SAY CHEESE!
TRUTH! FROM A PRESS PHOTOGRAPHER!!
AND--YES! THOUGH I BE A TRUE MASTER OF THE MYSTIC ARTS--
--IT WAS THOSE SAME PASSIONS THAT DROVE THE MAN I WAS--
--AND THAT PERHAPS STILL DRIVE THE MAN I HAVE BECOME!
WHY ALL THE SPECIAL HARDWARE, FRIENDS?
JEAN DEWOLFF REQUESTED IT OF FURY, KID!
GUESS SHE THINKS SHE'LL NEED A LINK-UP WITH SOME OF THE BEST LEGAL-EAGLES IN THE COUNTRY.
YOU CAN TELL BALE IT'S READY, CARTER!
RIGHT.

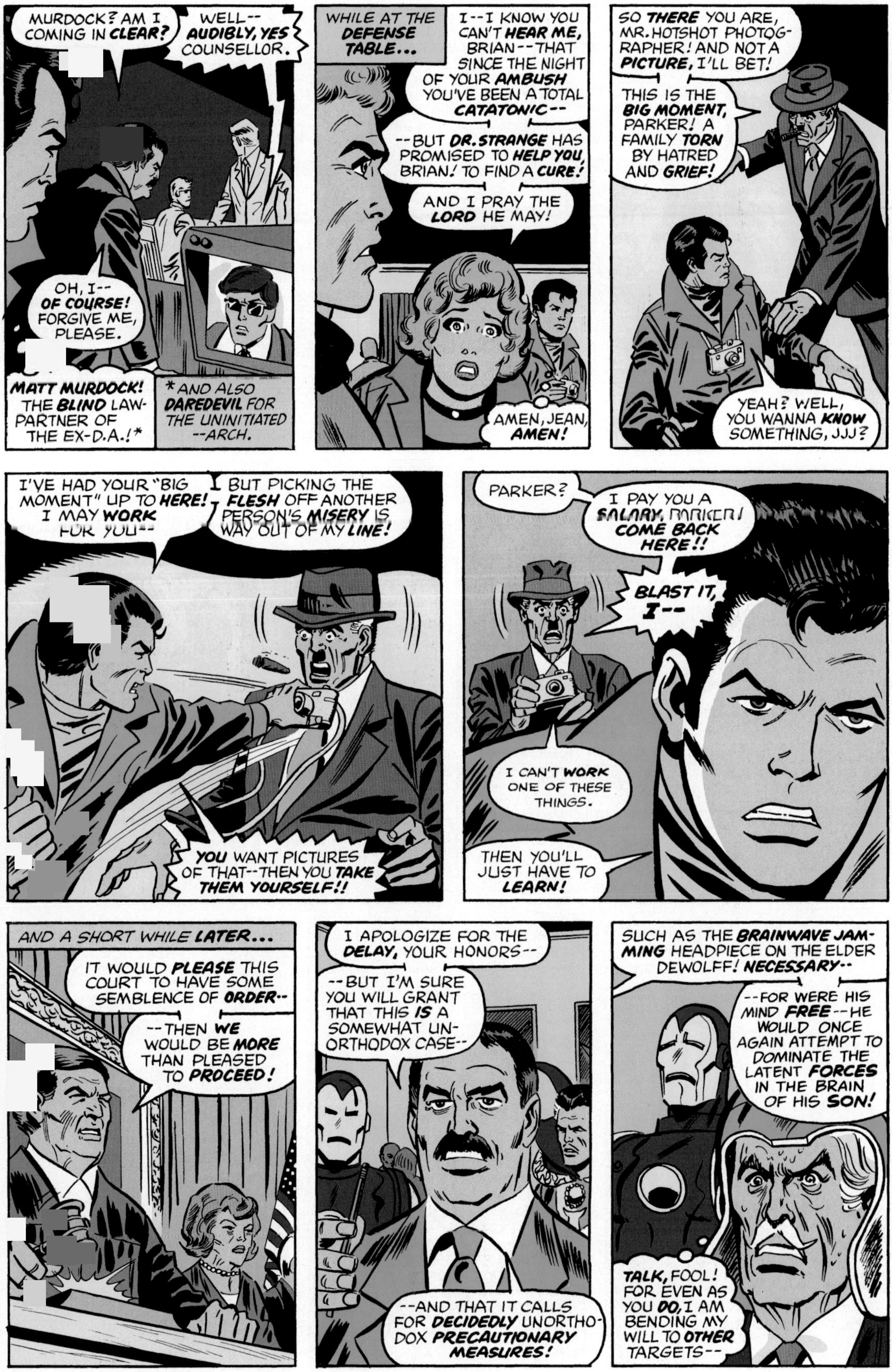
MURDOCK? AM I COMING IN CLEAR?
WELL-- AUDIBLY, YES COUNSELLOR.
OH, I-- OF COURSE! FORGIVE ME, PLEASE.
MATT MURDOCK! THE BLIND LAW-PARTNER OF THE EX-D.A.!*
*AND ALSO DAREDEVIL FOR THE UNINITIATED --ARCH.
WHILE AT THE DEFENSE TABLE...
I--I KNOW YOU CAN'T HEAR ME, BRIAN--THAT SINCE THE NIGHT OF YOUR AMBUSH YOU'VE BEEN A TOTAL CATATONIC--
--BUT DR. STRANGE HAS PROMISED TO HELP YOU, BRIAN! TO FIND A CURE!
AND I PRAY THE LORD HE MAY!
AMEN, JEAN, AMEN!
SO THERE YOU ARE, MR. HOTSHOT PHOTOG-RAPHER! AND NOT A PICTURE, I'LL BET!
THIS IS THE BIG MOMENT, PARKER! A FAMILY TORN BY HATRED AND GRIEF!
YEAH? WELL, YOU WANNA KNOW SOMETHING, JJJ?
I'VE HAD YOUR "BIG MOMENT" UP TO HERE! I MAY WORK FOR YOU--
BUT PICKING THE FLESH OFF ANOTHER PERSON'S MISERY IS WAY OUT OF MY LINE!
YOU WANT PICTURES OF THAT--THEN YOU TAKE THEM YOURSELF!!
PARKER?
I PAY YOU A SALARY, PARKER! COME BACK HERE!!
BLAST IT, I--
I CAN'T WORK ONE OF THESE THINGS.
THEN YOU'LL JUST HAVE TO LEARN!
AND A SHORT WHILE LATER...
IT WOULD PLEASE THIS COURT TO HAVE SOME SEMBLENCE OF ORDER--
--THEN WE WOULD BE MORE THAN PLEASED TO PROCEED!
I APOLOGIZE FOR THE DELAY, YOUR HONORS--
--BUT I'M SURE YOU WILL GRANT THAT THIS IS A SOMEWHAT UN-ORTHODOX CASE--
--AND THAT IT CALLS FOR DECIDEDLY UNORTHO-DOX PRECAUTIONARY MEASURES!
SUCH AS THE BRAINWAVE JAM-MING HEADPIECE ON THE ELDER DEWOLFF! NECESSARY--
--FOR WERE HIS MIND FREE--HE WOULD ONCE AGAIN ATTEMPT TO DOMINATE THE LATENT FORCES IN THE BRAIN OF HIS SON!
TALK, FOOL! FOR EVEN AS YOU DO, I AM BENDING MY WILL TO OTHER TARGETS--

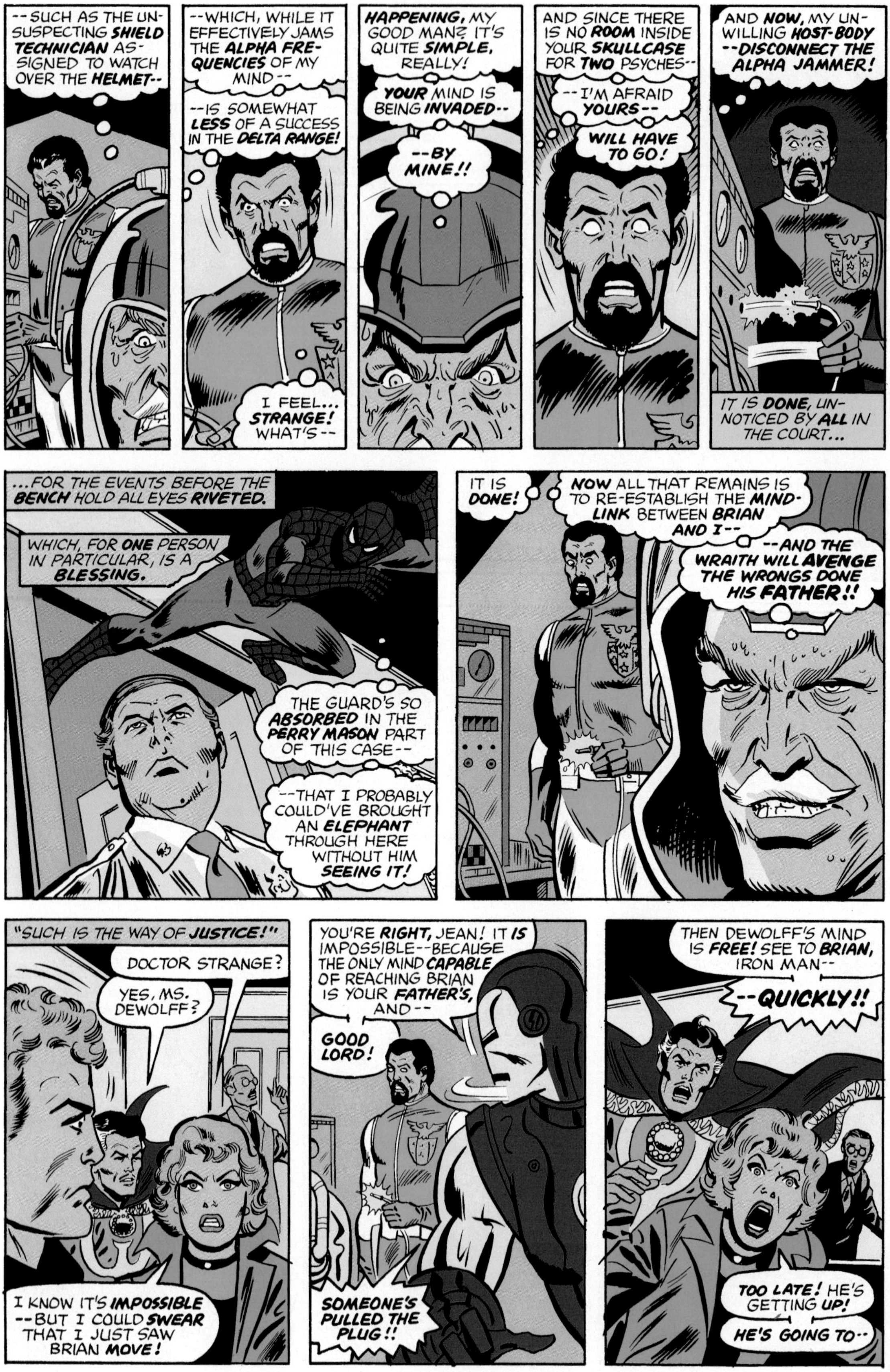
--SUCH AS THE UN-SUSPECTING SHIELD TECHNICIAN AS-SIGNED TO WATCH OVER THE HELMET--
--WHICH, WHILE IT EFFECTIVELY JAMS THE ALPHA FRE-QUENCIES OF MY MIND--
--IS SOMEWHAT LESS OF A SUCCESS IN THE DELTA RANGE!
I FEEL... STRANGE! WHAT'S--
HAPPENING, MY GOOD MAN? IT'S QUITE SIMPLE, REALLY!
YOUR MIND IS BEING INVADED--
--BY MINE!!
AND SINCE THERE IS NO ROOM INSIDE YOUR SKULLCASE FOR TWO PSYCHES--
--I'M AFRAID YOURS--
WILL HAVE TO GO!
AND NOW, MY UN-WILLING HOST-BODY --DISCONNECT THE ALPHA JAMMER!
IT IS DONE, UN-NOTICED BY ALL IN THE COURT...
...FOR THE EVENTS BEFORE THE BENCH HOLD ALL EYES RIVETED.
WHICH, FOR ONE PERSON IN PARTICULAR, IS A BLESSING.
THE GUARD'S SO ABSORBED IN THE PERRY MASON PART OF THIS CASE--
--THAT I PROBABLY COULD'VE BROUGHT AN ELEPHANT THROUGH HERE WITHOUT HIM SEEING IT!
IT IS DONE!
NOW ALL THAT REMAINS IS TO RE-ESTABLISH THE MIND-LINK BETWEEN BRIAN AND I--
--AND THE WRAITH WILL AVENGE THE WRONGS DONE HIS FATHER!!
"SUCH IS THE WAY OF JUSTICE!"
DOCTOR STRANGE?
YES, MS. DEWOLFF?
I KNOW IT'S IMPOSSIBLE --BUT I COULD SWEAR THAT I JUST SAW BRIAN MOVE!
YOU'RE RIGHT, JEAN! IT IS IMPOSSIBLE--BECAUSE THE ONLY MIND CAPABLE OF REACHING BRIAN IS YOUR FATHER'S, AND--
GOOD LORD!
SOMEONE'S PULLED THE PLUG!!
THEN DEWOLFF'S MIND IS FREE! SEE TO BRIAN, IRON MAN--
--QUICKLY!!
TOO LATE! HE'S GETTING UP!
HE'S GOING TO--

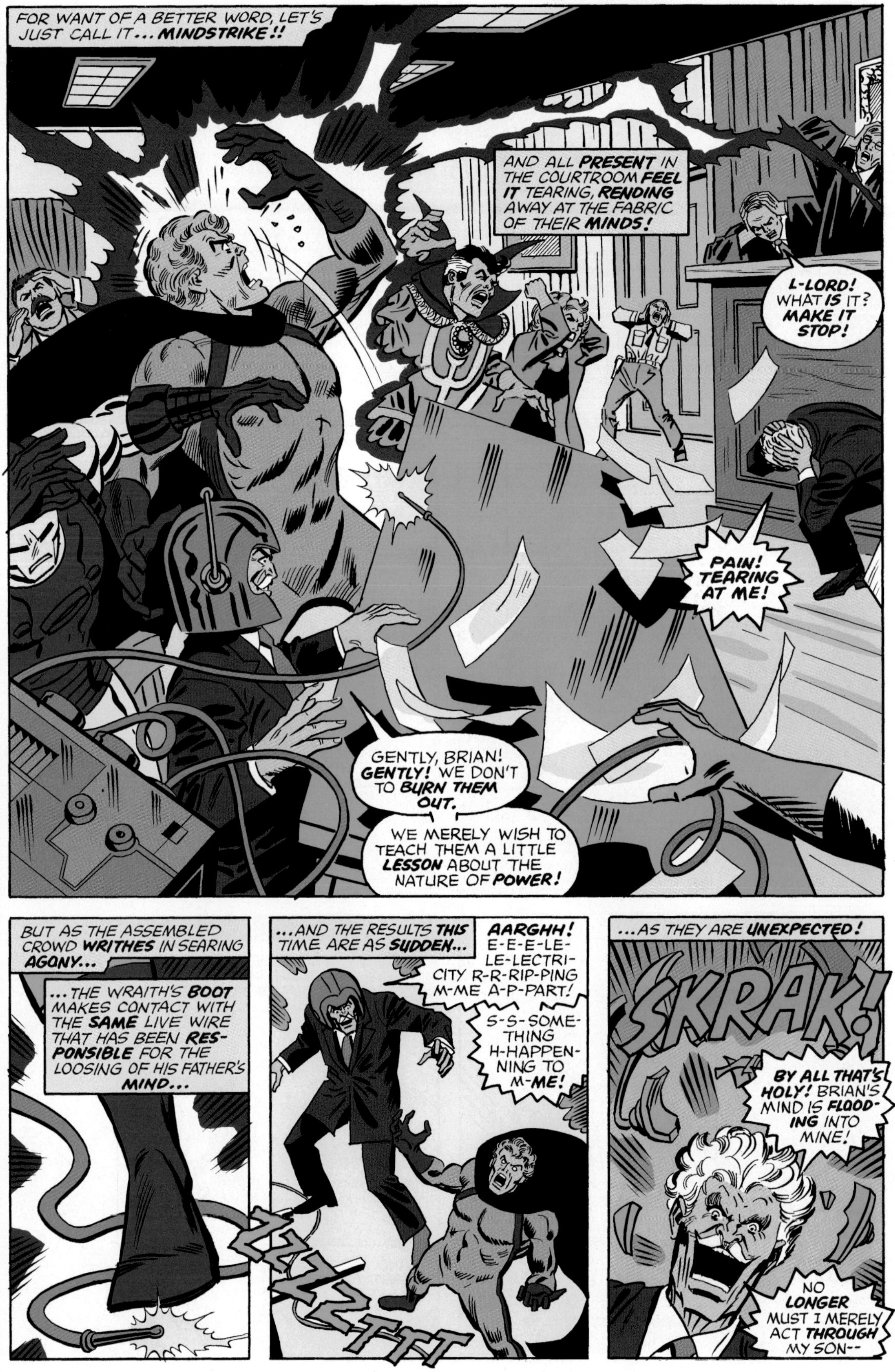
FOR WANT OF A BETTER WORD, LET'S JUST CALL IT... MINDSTRIKE!!
AND ALL PRESENT IN THE COURTROOM FEEL IT TEARING, RENDING AWAY AT THE FABRIC OF THEIR MINDS!
L-LORD! WHAT IS IT? MAKE IT STOP!
PAIN! TEARING AT ME!
GENTLY, BRIAN! GENTLY! WE DON'T TO BURN THEM OUT.
WE MERELY WISH TO TEACH THEM A LITTLE LESSON ABOUT THE NATURE OF POWER!
BUT AS THE ASSEMBLED CROWD WRITHES IN SEARING AGONY...
...THE WRAITH'S BOOT MAKES CONTACT WITH THE SAME LIVE WIRE THAT HAS BEEN RESPONSIBLE FOR THE LOOSING OF HIS FATHER'S MIND...
...AND THE RESULTS THIS TIME ARE AS SUDDEN...
AARGHH! E-E-E-LE-LE-LECTRI-CITY R-R-RIP-PING M-ME A-P-PART!
S-S-SOME-THING H-HAPPEN-NING TO M-ME!
ZZZZTTT
...AS THEY ARE UNEXPECTED!
SKRAK!
BY ALL THAT'S HOLY! BRIAN'S MIND IS FLOODING INTO MINE!
NO LONGER MUST I MERELY ACT THROUGH MY SON--

--FOR NOW WE **SHARE** THE **POWER**! WE ARE **EQUALS**!

WE ARE **ONE**, BOTH IN OUR **THIRST** FOR VENGEANCE--

--AND IN THE ABILITY TO **ACHIEVE** IT!!

*UNDOUBTEDLY THERE ARE NO CON-GRATULATORY **CHEERS** FORTHCOMING FROM THE AGONIZED ONLOOKERS.*

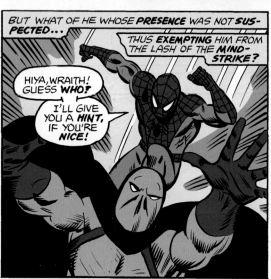

*BUT WHAT OF HE WHOSE **PRESENCE** WAS NOT **SUS-PECTED**...*

*THUS **EXEMPTING** HIM FROM THE LASH OF THE **MIND-STRIKE**?*

HIYA, WRAITH! GUESS **WHO**?

I'LL GIVE YOU A **HINT**, IF YOU'RE **NICE**!

WHAT'S RED, BLUE, AND **WEBBED**, CLIMBS UP **WALLS**--

--AND PACKS ONE HECKUVA **WALLOP**?

GIVE UP?

OKAY, SPOIL-SPORT! IT'S THAT L'IL OL **WEB-SLINGER** ...**ME!!**

YEEOWW!

JUST MY **LUCK** TO PICK A **SORE LOSER**!

ALL HE HAS TO DO IS **THINK** ABOUT IT--

--AND I GET TOSSED THROUGH THE **AIR** LIKE A RUNAWAY **FRISBEE**!

AND IF I DON'T WANT TO LAND ON MY EVER-LOVIN' **HEAD**--

I THINK IT'S TIME I EXECUTED SOME **FANCY FLIPPING**--

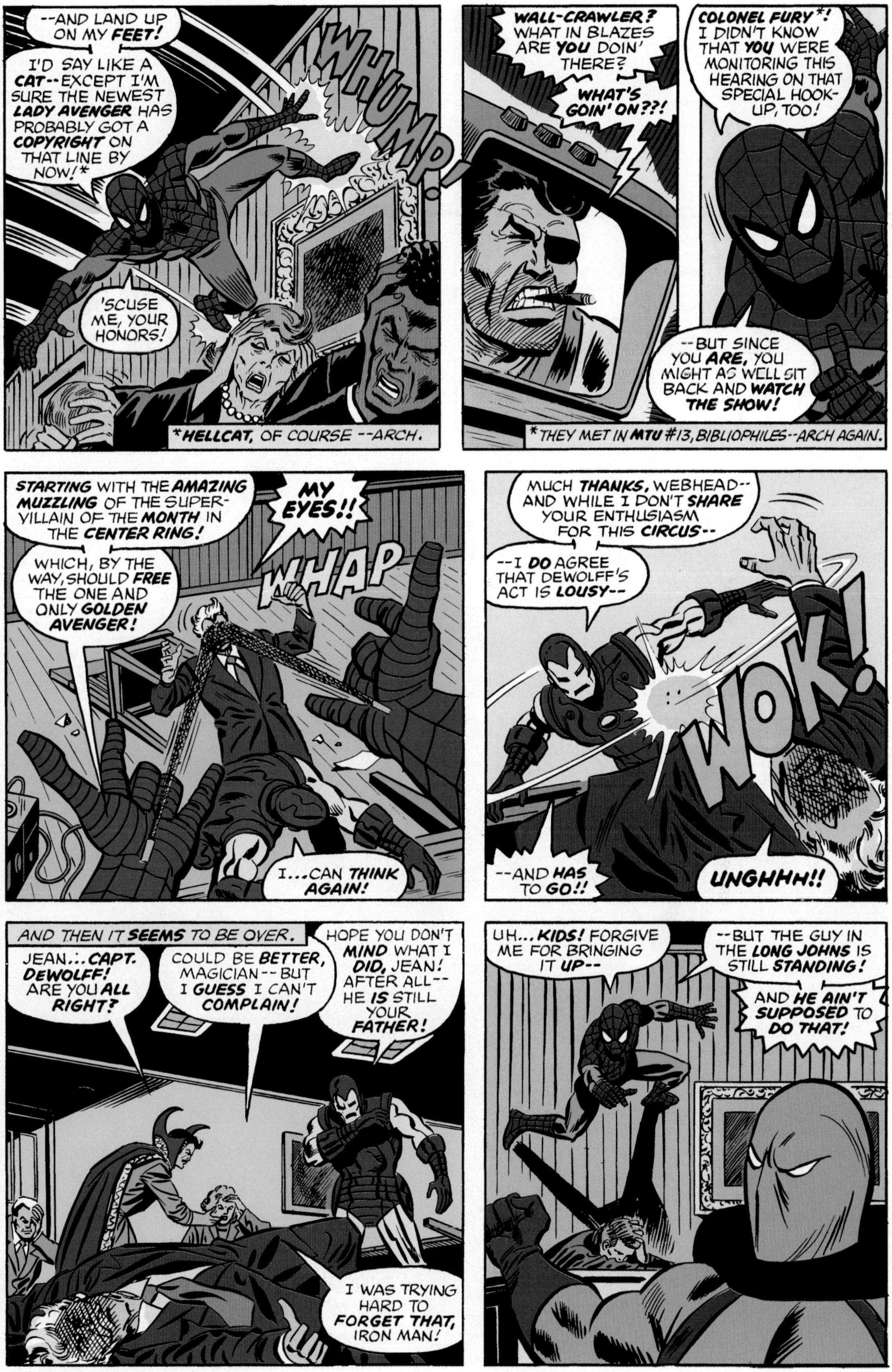
--AND LAND UP ON MY FEET!
I'D SAY LIKE A CAT--EXCEPT I'M SURE THE NEWEST LADY AVENGER HAS PROBABLY GOT A COPYRIGHT ON THAT LINE BY NOW!*
WHUMP!
'SCUSE ME, YOUR HONORS!
*HELLCAT, OF COURSE --ARCH.
WALL-CRAWLER? WHAT IN BLAZES ARE YOU DOIN' THERE?
WHAT'S GOIN' ON??!
COLONEL FURY*! I DIDN'T KNOW THAT YOU WERE MONITORING THIS HEARING ON THAT SPECIAL HOOK-UP, TOO!
--BUT SINCE YOU ARE, YOU MIGHT AS WELL SIT BACK AND WATCH THE SHOW!
*THEY MET IN MTU #13, BIBLIOPHILES--ARCH AGAIN.
STARTING WITH THE AMAZING MUZZLING OF THE SUPER-VILLAIN OF THE MONTH IN THE CENTER RING!
WHICH, BY THE WAY, SHOULD FREE THE ONE AND ONLY GOLDEN AVENGER!
MY EYES!!
WHAP
I...CAN THINK AGAIN!
MUCH THANKS, WEBHEAD--AND WHILE I DON'T SHARE YOUR ENTHUSIASM FOR THIS CIRCUS--
--I DO AGREE THAT DEWOLFF'S ACT IS LOUSY--
WOK!
--AND HAS TO GO!!
UNGHHH!!
AND THEN IT SEEMS TO BE OVER.
JEAN...CAPT. DEWOLFF! ARE YOU ALL RIGHT?
COULD BE BETTER, MAGICIAN--BUT I GUESS I CAN'T COMPLAIN!
HOPE YOU DON'T MIND WHAT I DID, JEAN! AFTER ALL--HE IS STILL YOUR FATHER!
I WAS TRYING HARD TO FORGET THAT, IRON MAN!
UH...KIDS! FORGIVE ME FOR BRINGING IT UP--
--BUT THE GUY IN THE LONG JOHNS IS STILL STANDING!
AND HE AIN'T SUPPOSED TO DO THAT!

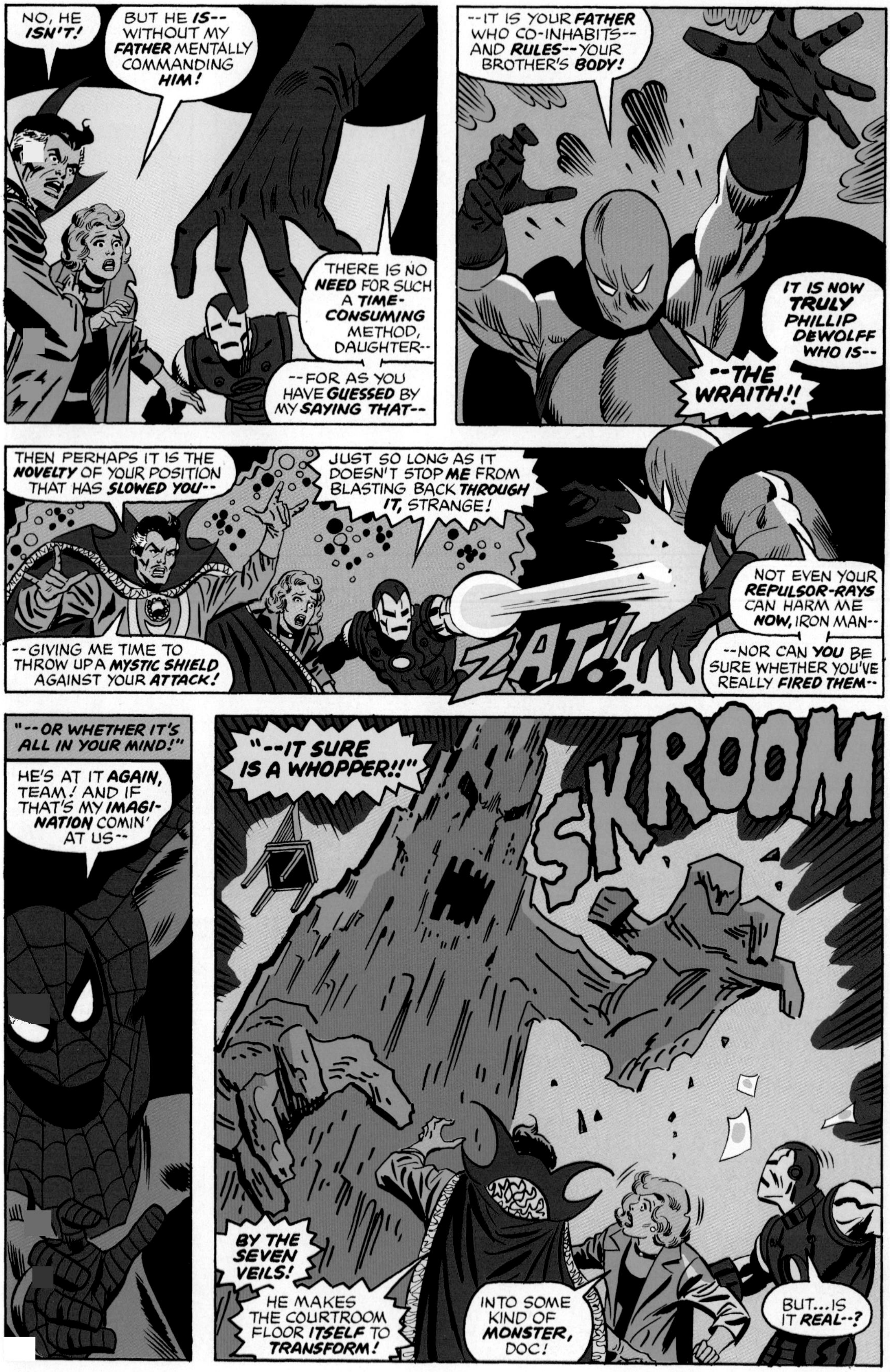

NO, HE ISN'T!
BUT HE IS-- WITHOUT MY FATHER MENTALLY COMMANDING HIM!
THERE IS NO NEED FOR SUCH A TIME-CONSUMING METHOD, DAUGHTER--
--FOR AS YOU HAVE GUESSED BY MY SAYING THAT--
--IT IS YOUR FATHER WHO CO-INHABITS-- AND RULES-- YOUR BROTHER'S BODY!
IT IS NOW TRULY PHILLIP DEWOLFF WHO IS--
--THE WRAITH!!
THEN PERHAPS IT IS THE NOVELTY OF YOUR POSITION THAT HAS SLOWED YOU--
--GIVING ME TIME TO THROW UP A MYSTIC SHIELD AGAINST YOUR ATTACK!
JUST SO LONG AS IT DOESN'T STOP ME FROM BLASTING BACK THROUGH IT, STRANGE!
ZAT!
NOT EVEN YOUR REPULSOR-RAYS CAN HARM ME NOW, IRON MAN--
--NOR CAN YOU BE SURE WHETHER YOU'VE REALLY FIRED THEM--
"--OR WHETHER IT'S ALL IN YOUR MIND!"
HE'S AT IT AGAIN, TEAM! AND IF THAT'S MY IMAGI-NATION COMIN' AT US--
"--IT SURE IS A WHOPPER!!"
SKROOM
BY THE SEVEN VEILS!
HE MAKES THE COURTROOM FLOOR ITSELF TO TRANSFORM!
INTO SOME KIND OF MONSTER, DOC!
BUT... IS IT REAL--?

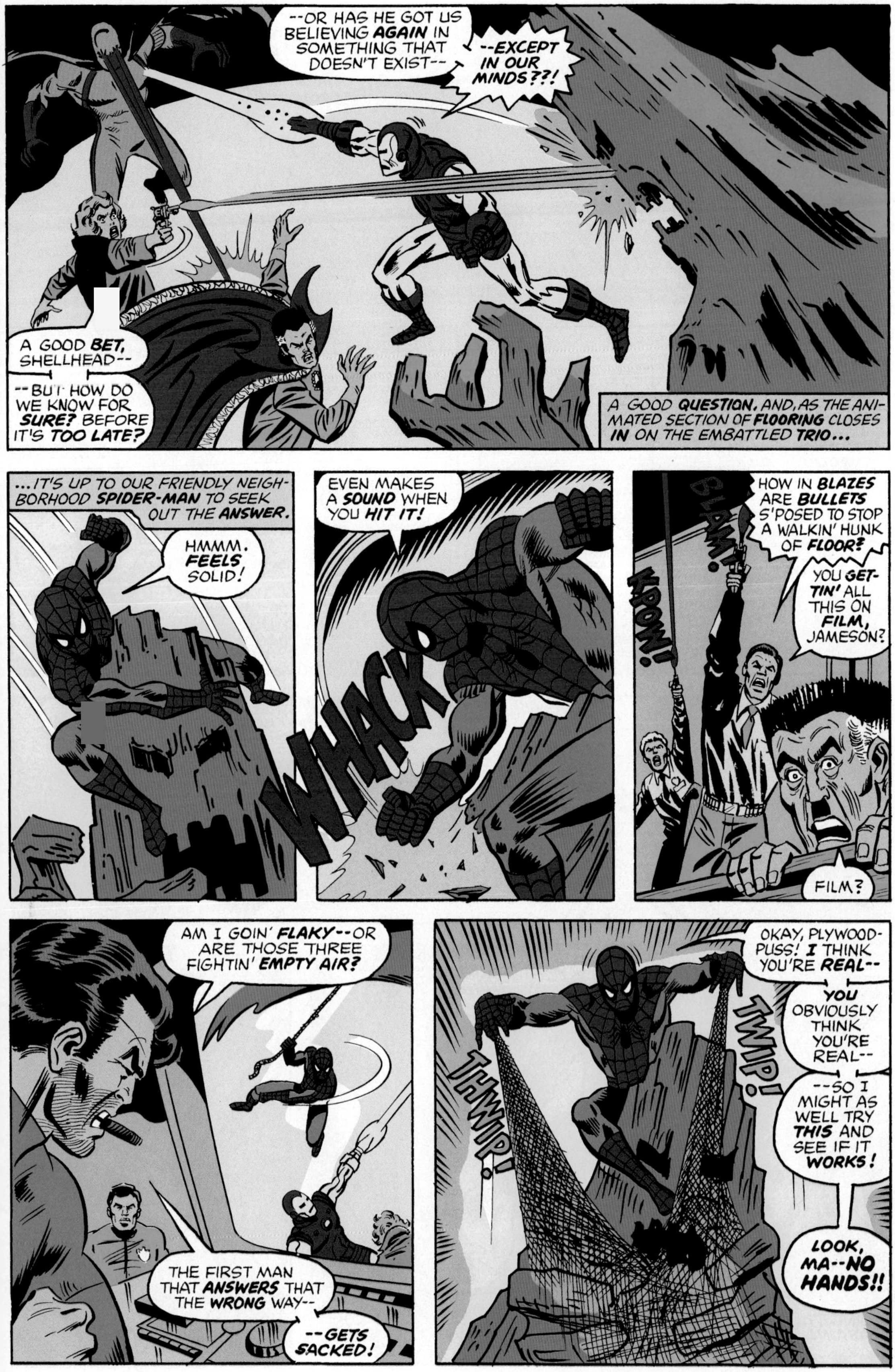
--OR HAS HE GOT US BELIEVING AGAIN IN SOMETHING THAT DOESN'T EXIST--
--EXCEPT IN OUR MINDS??!
A GOOD BET, SHELLHEAD--
--BUT HOW DO WE KNOW FOR SURE? BEFORE IT'S TOO LATE?
A GOOD QUESTION. AND, AS THE ANIMATED SECTION OF FLOORING CLOSES IN ON THE EMBATTLED TRIO...
...IT'S UP TO OUR FRIENDLY NEIGHBORHOOD SPIDER-MAN TO SEEK OUT THE ANSWER.
HMMM. FEELS SOLID!
EVEN MAKES A SOUND WHEN YOU HIT IT!
WHACK
BLAM!
KPOW!
HOW IN BLAZES ARE BULLETS S'POSED TO STOP A WALKIN' HUNK OF FLOOR?
YOU GETTIN' ALL THIS ON FILM, JAMESON?
FILM?
AM I GOIN' FLAKY--OR ARE THOSE THREE FIGHTIN' EMPTY AIR?
THE FIRST MAN THAT ANSWERS THAT THE WRONG WAY--
--GETS SACKED!
OKAY, PLYWOOD-PUSS! I THINK YOU'RE REAL--
YOU OBVIOUSLY THINK YOU'RE REAL--
--SO I MIGHT AS WELL TRY THIS AND SEE IF IT WORKS!
THWIP!
TWIP!
LOOK, MA--NO HANDS!!

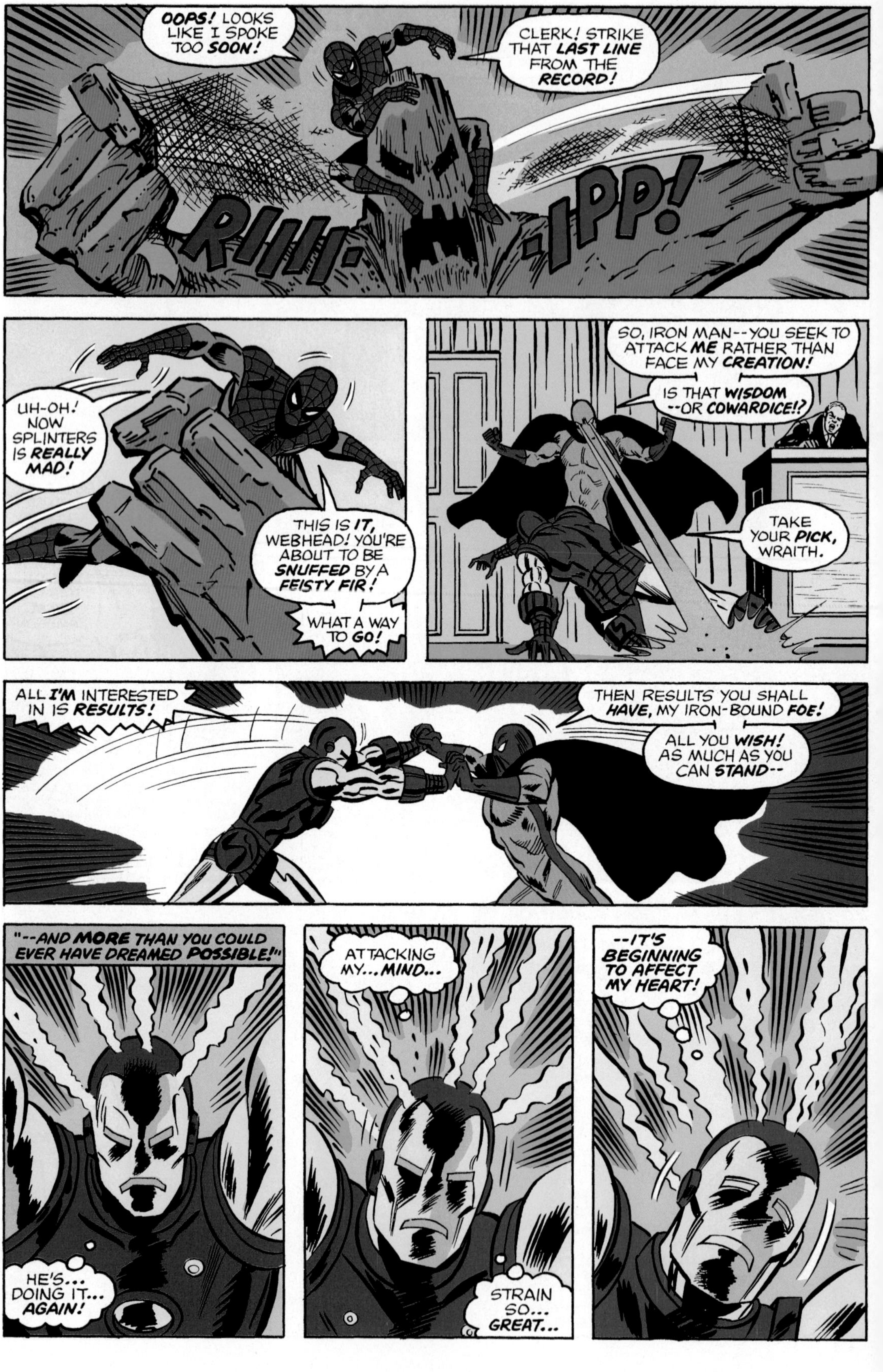
OOPS! LOOKS LIKE I SPOKE TOO SOON!
CLERK! STRIKE THAT LAST LINE FROM THE RECORD!
RIIII--IPP!
UH-OH! NOW SPLINTERS IS REALLY MAD!
THIS IS IT, WEBHEAD! YOU'RE ABOUT TO BE SNUFFED BY A FEISTY FIR!
WHAT A WAY TO GO!
SO, IRON MAN--YOU SEEK TO ATTACK ME RATHER THAN FACE MY CREATION!
IS THAT WISDOM --OR COWARDICE!?
TAKE YOUR PICK, WRAITH.
ALL I'M INTERESTED IN IS RESULTS!
THEN RESULTS YOU SHALL HAVE, MY IRON-BOUND FOE!
ALL YOU WISH! AS MUCH AS YOU CAN STAND--
"--AND MORE THAN YOU COULD EVER HAVE DREAMED POSSIBLE!"
HE'S... DOING IT... AGAIN!
ATTACKING MY... MIND...
STRAIN SO... GREAT...
--IT'S BEGINNING TO AFFECT MY HEART!

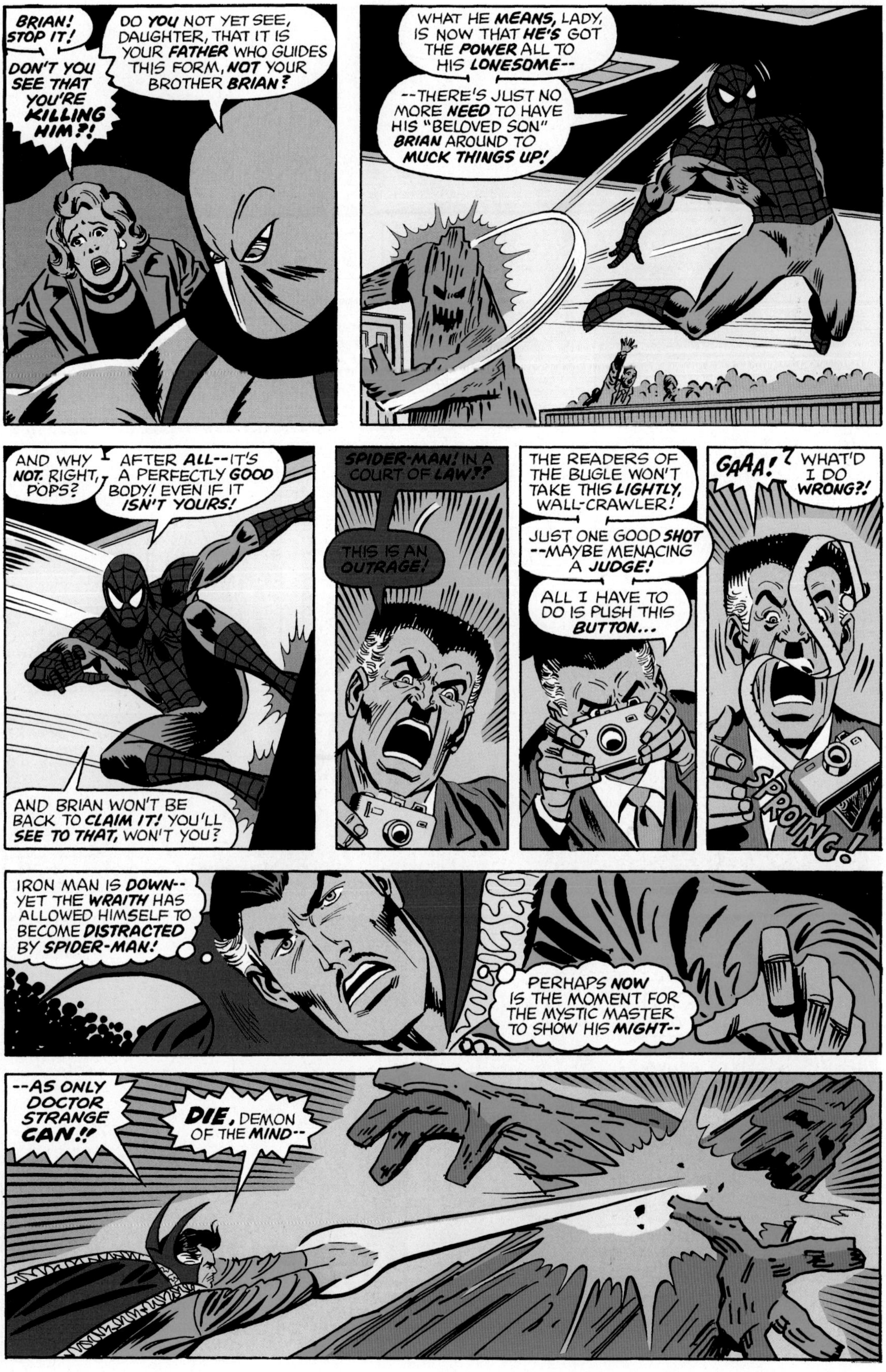
BRIAN! STOP IT!
DON'T YOU SEE THAT YOU'RE KILLING HIM?!
DO YOU NOT YET SEE, DAUGHTER, THAT IT IS YOUR FATHER WHO GUIDES THIS FORM, NOT YOUR BROTHER BRIAN?
WHAT HE MEANS, LADY, IS NOW THAT HE'S GOT THE POWER ALL TO HIS LONESOME--
--THERE'S JUST NO MORE NEED TO HAVE HIS "BELOVED SON" BRIAN AROUND TO MUCK THINGS UP!
AND WHY NOT, RIGHT, POPS?
AFTER ALL--IT'S A PERFECTLY GOOD BODY! EVEN IF IT ISN'T YOURS!
AND BRIAN WON'T BE BACK TO CLAIM IT! YOU'LL SEE TO THAT, WON'T YOU?
SPIDER-MAN! IN A COURT OF LAW?!
THIS IS AN OUTRAGE!
THE READERS OF THE BUGLE WON'T TAKE THIS LIGHTLY, WALL-CRAWLER!
JUST ONE GOOD SHOT --MAYBE MENACING A JUDGE!
ALL I HAVE TO DO IS PUSH THIS BUTTON...
GAAA!
WHAT'D I DO WRONG?!
SPROING!
IRON MAN IS DOWN--YET THE WRAITH HAS ALLOWED HIMSELF TO BECOME DISTRACTED BY SPIDER-MAN!
PERHAPS NOW IS THE MOMENT FOR THE MYSTIC MASTER TO SHOW HIS MIGHT--
--AS ONLY DOCTOR STRANGE CAN!!
DIE, DEMON OF THE MIND--

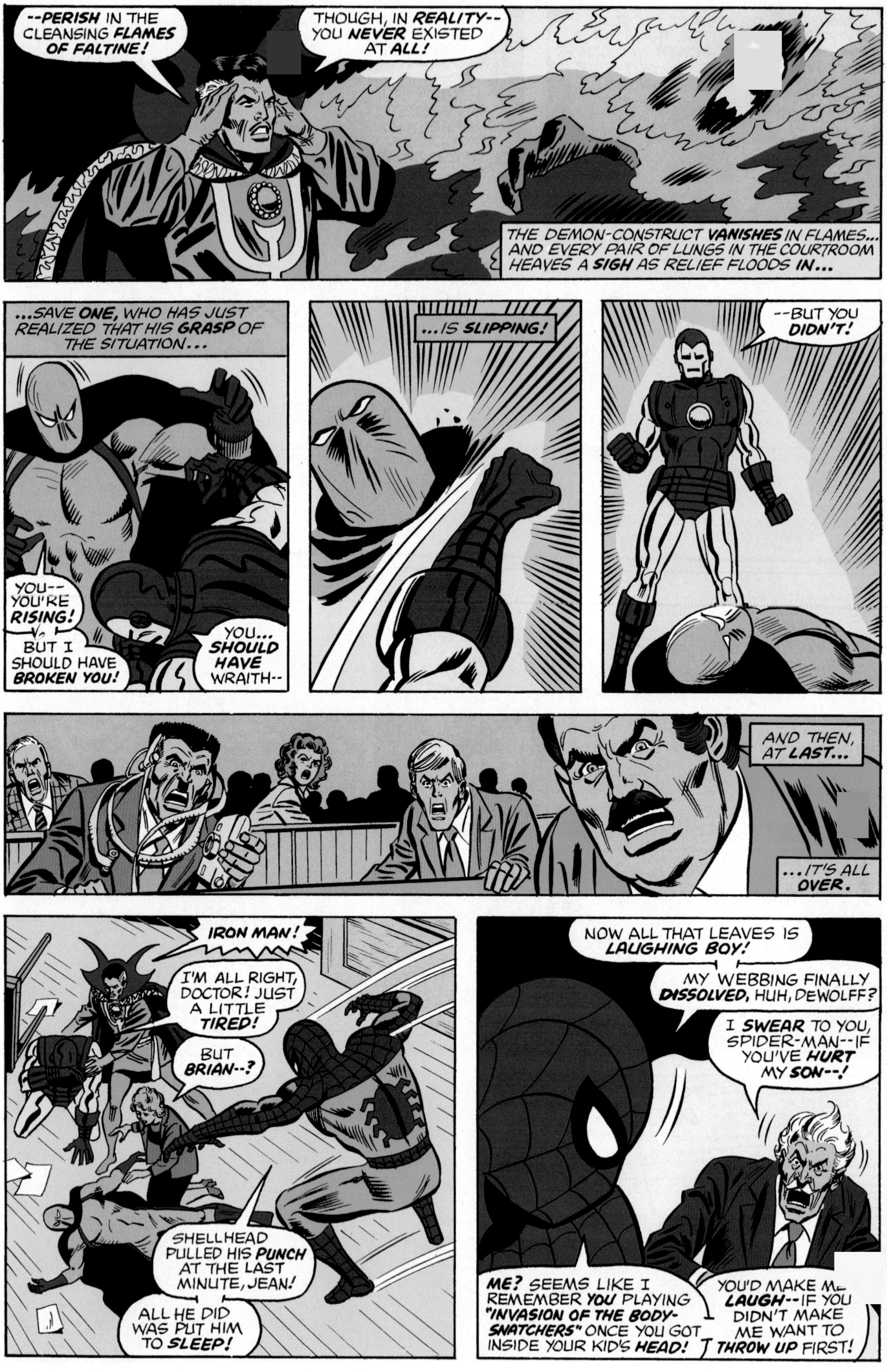
--PERISH IN THE CLEANSING FLAMES OF FALTINE!
THOUGH, IN REALITY-- YOU NEVER EXISTED AT ALL!
THE DEMON-CONSTRUCT VANISHES IN FLAMES... AND EVERY PAIR OF LUNGS IN THE COURTROOM HEAVES A SIGH AS RELIEF FLOODS IN...
...SAVE ONE, WHO HAS JUST REALIZED THAT HIS GRASP OF THE SITUATION...
YOU-- YOU'RE RISING!
BUT I SHOULD HAVE BROKEN YOU!
YOU... SHOULD HAVE WRAITH--
...IS SLIPPING!
--BUT YOU DIDN'T!
AND THEN, AT LAST...
...IT'S ALL OVER.
IRON MAN!
I'M ALL RIGHT, DOCTOR! JUST A LITTLE TIRED!
BUT BRIAN--?
SHELLHEAD PULLED HIS PUNCH AT THE LAST MINUTE, JEAN!
ALL HE DID WAS PUT HIM TO SLEEP!
NOW ALL THAT LEAVES IS LAUGHING BOY!
MY WEBBING FINALLY DISSOLVED, HUH, DEWOLFF?
I SWEAR TO YOU, SPIDER-MAN--IF YOU'VE HURT MY SON--!
ME? SEEMS LIKE I REMEMBER YOU PLAYING "INVASION OF THE BODY-SNATCHERS" ONCE YOU GOT INSIDE YOUR KID'S HEAD!
YOU'D MAKE M LAUGH--IF YOU DIDN'T MAKE ME WANT TO THROW UP FIRST!

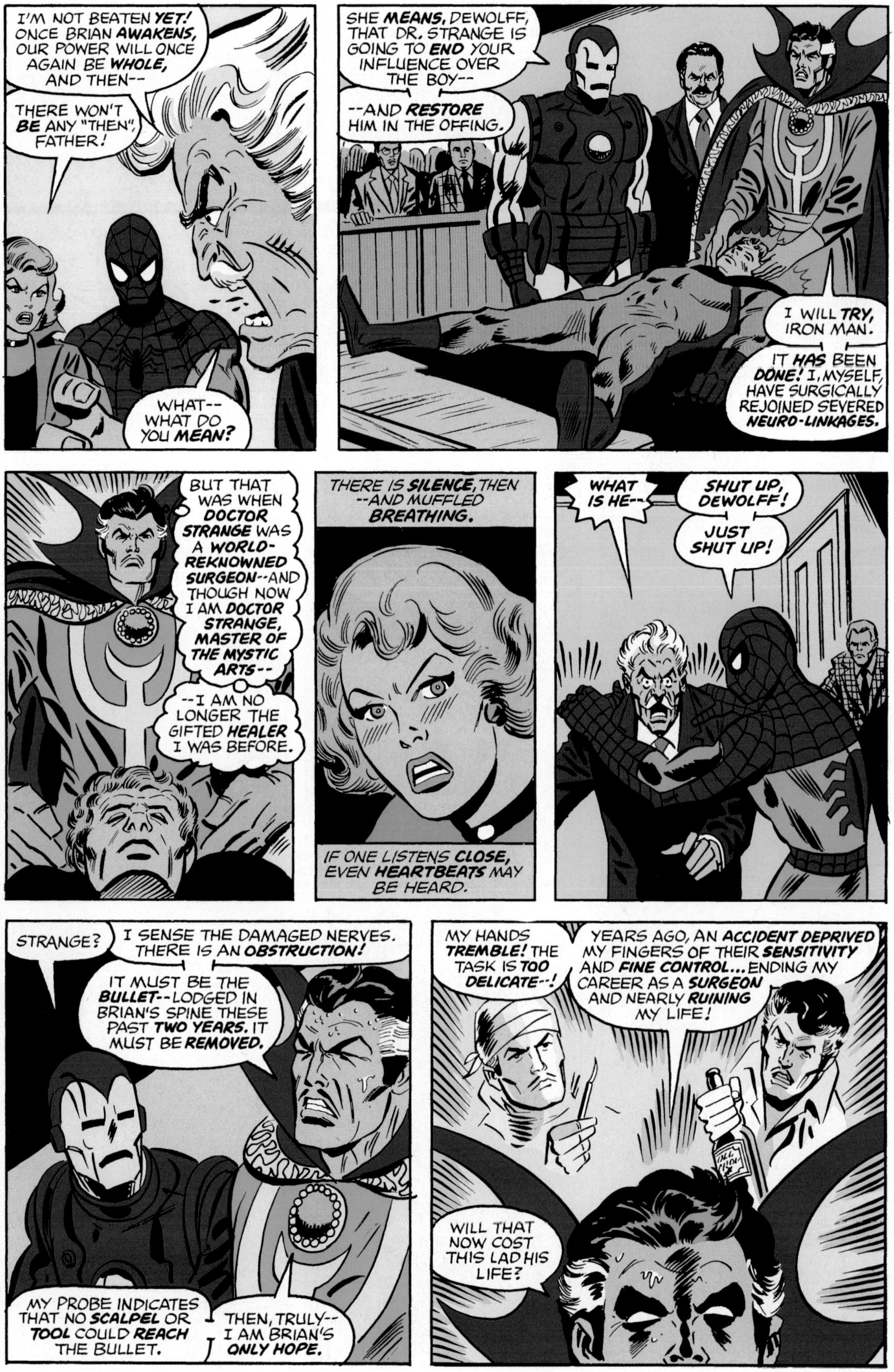
I'M NOT BEATEN YET! ONCE BRIAN AWAKENS, OUR POWER WILL ONCE AGAIN BE WHOLE, AND THEN--
THERE WON'T BE ANY "THEN", FATHER!
WHAT-- WHAT DO YOU MEAN?
SHE MEANS, DEWOLFF, THAT DR. STRANGE IS GOING TO END YOUR INFLUENCE OVER THE BOY--
--AND RESTORE HIM IN THE OFFING.
I WILL TRY, IRON MAN.
IT HAS BEEN DONE! I, MYSELF, HAVE SURGICALLY REJOINED SEVERED NEURO-LINKAGES.
BUT THAT WAS WHEN DOCTOR STRANGE WAS A WORLD-REKNOWNED SURGEON--AND THOUGH NOW I AM DOCTOR STRANGE, MASTER OF THE MYSTIC ARTS--
--I AM NO LONGER THE GIFTED HEALER I WAS BEFORE.
THERE IS SILENCE, THEN --AND MUFFLED BREATHING.
IF ONE LISTENS CLOSE, EVEN HEARTBEATS MAY BE HEARD.
WHAT IS HE--
SHUT UP, DEWOLFF!
JUST SHUT UP!
STRANGE?
I SENSE THE DAMAGED NERVES. THERE IS AN OBSTRUCTION!
IT MUST BE THE BULLET--LODGED IN BRIAN'S SPINE THESE PAST TWO YEARS. IT MUST BE REMOVED.
MY PROBE INDICATES THAT NO SCALPEL OR TOOL COULD REACH THE BULLET.
THEN, TRULY-- I AM BRIAN'S ONLY HOPE.
MY HANDS TREMBLE! THE TASK IS TOO DELICATE--!
YEARS AGO, AN ACCIDENT DEPRIVED MY FINGERS OF THEIR SENSITIVITY AND FINE CONTROL... ENDING MY CAREER AS A SURGEON AND NEARLY RUINING MY LIFE!
WILL THAT NOW COST THIS LAD HIS LIFE?

I HAVE RENDERED MY HAND *IMMATERIAL!* FOR ONE BRIEF *SECOND*--AS I TOUCH THE BULLET THAT ENDANGERS BRIAN'S *LIFE*--AND RENDER IT IMMATERIAL AS WELL--

--MY HAND WILL BECOME PARTIALLY *TANGIBLE* ONCE MORE!

IF I SHOULD QUIVER --EVEN SLIGHTLY--AT THAT CRUCIAL POINT--!

NOW.

BRIAN DEWOLFF *SCREAMS.*

AN *EERIE, BANSHEE* WAIL OF THE *MINDLESS.*

IN THE NAME OF *HEAVEN,* STRANGE!

I FAILED! MY HAND-- I--

BUT, WAIT! THERE IS *ANOTHER* FORCE AT WORK HERE--

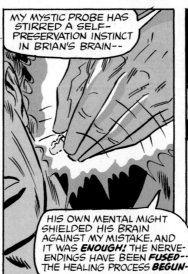

MY MYSTIC PROBE HAS STIRRED A SELF-PRESERVATION INSTINCT IN BRIAN'S BRAIN--

HIS OWN MENTAL MIGHT SHIELDED HIS BRAIN AGAINST MY MISTAKE. AND IT WAS *ENOUGH!* THE NERVE-ENDINGS HAVE BEEN *FUSED*-- THE HEALING PROCESS *BEGUN*--

--AND THE *OBSTRUCTION*--

--IS *REMOVED!*

WH-WHERE *AM I? SIS?* IS...THAT *YOU?*

WELL I'LL BE...

BRIAN!

OH, BRIAN!

TAKE A LONG, *HARD* LOOK, DEWOLFF! AT ALL YOU TRIED TO *DESTROY!*

YOU *BLEW IT,* MADMAN --AND I HOPE IT MAKES YOU *CHOKE!*

A--HEMMM!

THIS *IS* STILL A COURTROOM, AND WHILE THE BENCH WILL *CONCEDE* THAT THERE ARE UNUSUAL CIRCUMSTANCES SURROUNDING THIS CASE--

--WE FEEL WE MUST *RESUME* BEFORE *JUSTICE* IS THROWN OUT WITH THE *BATHWATER!*

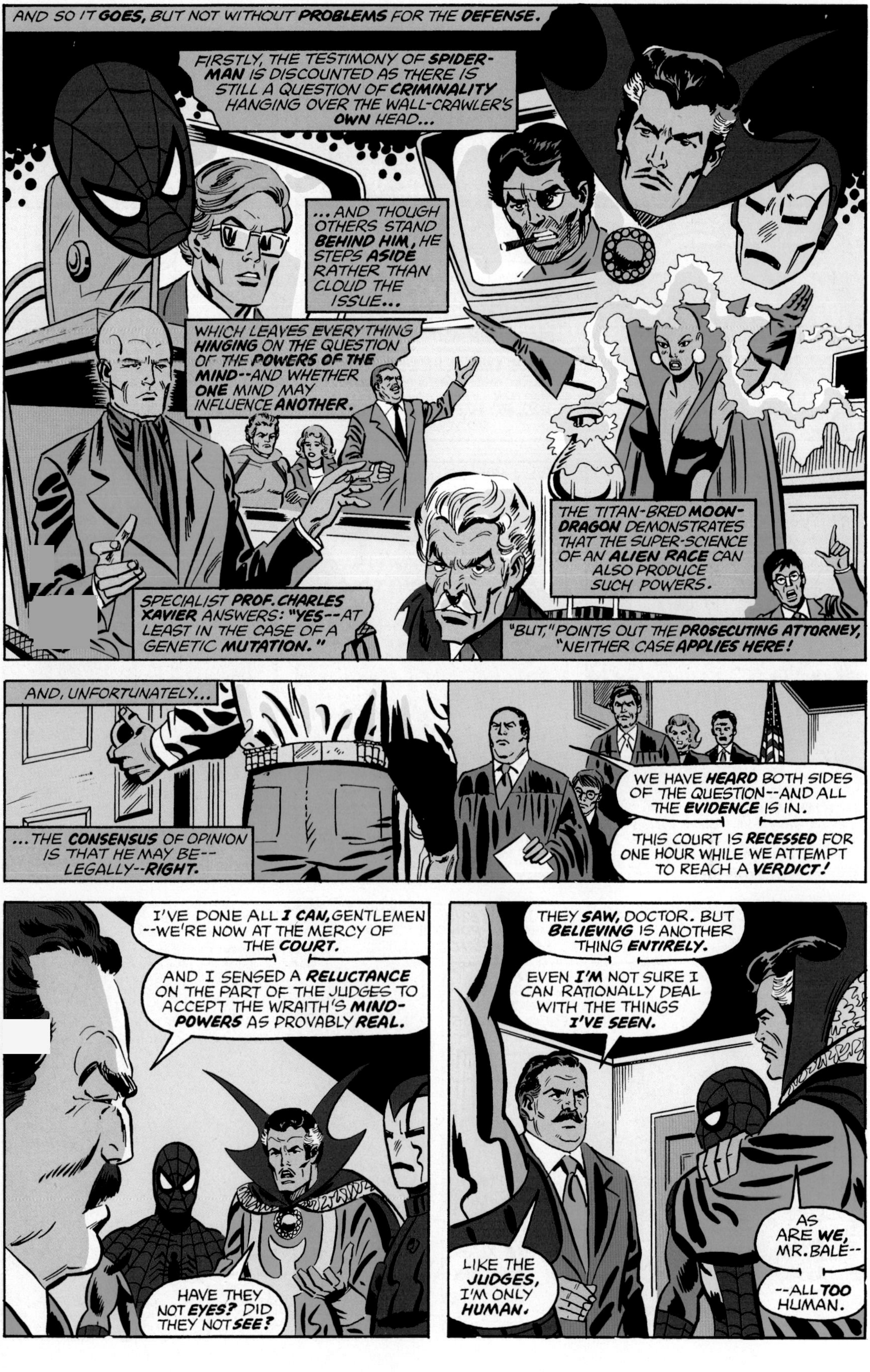
AND SO IT GOES, BUT NOT WITHOUT PROBLEMS FOR THE DEFENSE.
FIRSTLY, THE TESTIMONY OF SPIDER-MAN IS DISCOUNTED AS THERE IS STILL A QUESTION OF CRIMINALITY HANGING OVER THE WALL-CRAWLER'S OWN HEAD...
...AND THOUGH OTHERS STAND BEHIND HIM, HE STEPS ASIDE RATHER THAN CLOUD THE ISSUE...
WHICH LEAVES EVERYTHING HINGING ON THE QUESTION OF THE POWERS OF THE MIND--AND WHETHER ONE MIND MAY INFLUENCE ANOTHER.
SPECIALIST PROF. CHARLES XAVIER ANSWERS: "YES--AT LEAST IN THE CASE OF A GENETIC MUTATION."
THE TITAN-BRED MOONDRAGON DEMONSTRATES THAT THE SUPER-SCIENCE OF AN ALIEN RACE CAN ALSO PRODUCE SUCH POWERS.
"BUT," POINTS OUT THE PROSECUTING ATTORNEY, "NEITHER CASE APPLIES HERE!
AND, UNFORTUNATELY...
...THE CONSENSUS OF OPINION IS THAT HE MAY BE--LEGALLY--RIGHT.
WE HAVE HEARD BOTH SIDES OF THE QUESTION--AND ALL THE EVIDENCE IS IN.
THIS COURT IS RECESSED FOR ONE HOUR WHILE WE ATTEMPT TO REACH A VERDICT!
I'VE DONE ALL I CAN, GENTLEMEN--WE'RE NOW AT THE MERCY OF THE COURT.
AND I SENSED A RELUCTANCE ON THE PART OF THE JUDGES TO ACCEPT THE WRAITH'S MIND-POWERS AS PROVABLY REAL.
HAVE THEY NOT EYES? DID THEY NOT SEE?
THEY SAW, DOCTOR. BUT BELIEVING IS ANOTHER THING ENTIRELY.
EVEN I'M NOT SURE I CAN RATIONALLY DEAL WITH THE THINGS I'VE SEEN.
LIKE THE JUDGES, I'M ONLY HUMAN.
AS ARE WE, MR. BALE--
--ALL TOO HUMAN.

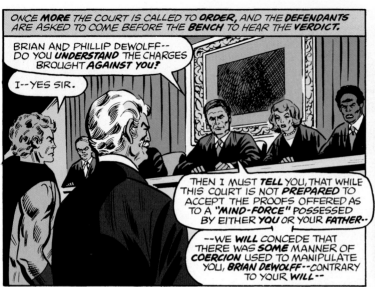

ONCE **MORE** THE COURT IS CALLED TO **ORDER**, AND THE **DEFENDANTS** ARE ASKED TO COME BEFORE THE **BENCH** TO HEAR THE **VERDICT**.

BRIAN AND PHILLIP DEWOLFF-- DO YOU **UNDERSTAND** THE CHARGES BROUGHT **AGAINST YOU**?

I--YES SIR.

THEN I MUST **TELL** YOU, THAT WHILE THIS COURT IS NOT **PREPARED** TO ACCEPT THE PROOFS OFFERED AS TO A "**MIND-FORCE**" POSSESSED BY EITHER **YOU** OR YOUR **FATHER**--

--WE **WILL** CONCEDE THAT THERE WAS **SOME** MANNER OF **COERCION** USED TO MANIPULATE YOU, **BRIAN DEWOLFF**--CONTRARY TO YOUR **WILL**--

--AND THAT SAID MANIPULATION WAS CARRIED OUT BY THE FATHER --**PHILLIP DEWOLFF**--AND THAT IT **DOES** CONSTITUTE A VIOLATION OF **ONE MAN'S RIGHTS** BY ANOTHER.

IN BRIEF-- THE COURT FINDS BRIAN DEWOLFF **INNOCENT** OF ANY CRIMES--

--AND PHILLIP DEWOLF...**GUILTY AS CHARGED**!

NO! THAT'S **IMPOSSIBLE**!

I CAN'T BE GUILTY OF **WISHING** SOMEONE DEAD! **BRIAN** KILLED PEOPLE--**HE** SENT THOSE **BOMBS**!*

*MTU 48-50--ARCH.

EVEN **NOW** YOU'D THROW BRIAN TO THE **DOGS** TO SAVE **YOURSELF**-- WOULDN'T YOU, FATHER?

YOU'RE ALL **AGAINST** ME! IT'S THE **WRAITH** WHO'S A **KILLER**-- NOT ME!!

YET IT WAS **YOU** WHO **CREATED** THE WRAITH! I-- I'M **SORRY** FOR YOU, FATHER.

THAT'S ONLY PART **ONE**, JEAN. YOUR DAD'S NIGHTMARE IS JUST BEGINNING.

BUT **OUR** TASK IS DONE. THE **TRULY INNOCENT** ONE HAS BEEN **SPARED**.

JEAN **TOLD** ME WHAT HAPPENED, DOCTOR.

I CAN'T THANK **ALL** OF YOU **ENOUGH**!

PERHAPS YOU **CAN**, BRIAN DEWOLFF!

HUH? WHAT DO YOU--?

HE MEANS THAT BRIAN STILL POSSESSES THE **MIND-POWERS** THAT MADE HIM THE **WRAITH**!

YOU'RE BOTH **LAW-OFFICERS**! IF SUCH A POWER IS **THERE** TO BE USED--THEN IT SEEMS IT **SHOULD** BE USED--

--AND MAYBE THE **WRAITH** SHOULD **LIVE AGAIN**--

--AS A FORCE FOR **GOOD**!

THINK **WELL** ON IT!

AND THEN THE GOLDEN AVENGER AND THE MYSTIC MASTER ARE **GONE**...

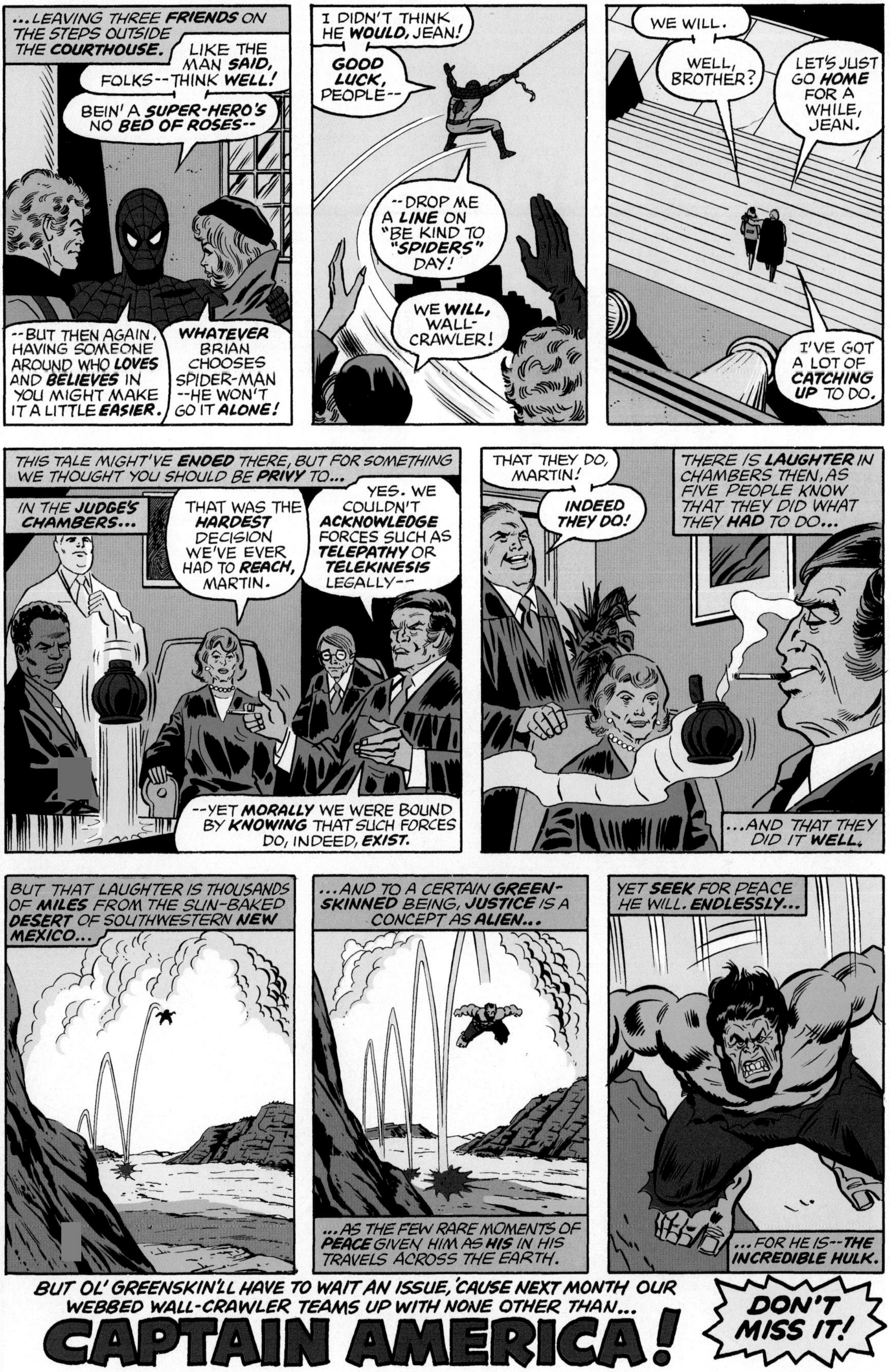
...LEAVING THREE FRIENDS ON THE STEPS OUTSIDE THE COURTHOUSE.
LIKE THE MAN SAID, FOLKS--THINK WELL!
BEIN' A SUPER-HERO'S NO BED OF ROSES--
--BUT THEN AGAIN, HAVING SOMEONE AROUND WHO LOVES AND BELIEVES IN YOU MIGHT MAKE IT A LITTLE EASIER.
WHATEVER BRIAN CHOOSES SPIDER-MAN --HE WON'T GO IT ALONE!
I DIDN'T THINK HE WOULD, JEAN!
GOOD LUCK, PEOPLE--
--DROP ME A LINE ON "BE KIND TO "SPIDERS" DAY!
WE WILL, WALL-CRAWLER!
WE WILL.
WELL, BROTHER?
LET'S JUST GO HOME FOR A WHILE, JEAN.
I'VE GOT A LOT OF CATCHING UP TO DO.
THIS TALE MIGHT'VE ENDED THERE, BUT FOR SOMETHING WE THOUGHT YOU SHOULD BE PRIVY TO...
IN THE JUDGE'S CHAMBERS...
THAT WAS THE HARDEST DECISION WE'VE EVER HAD TO REACH, MARTIN.
YES. WE COULDN'T ACKNOWLEDGE FORCES SUCH AS TELEPATHY OR TELEKINESIS LEGALLY--
--YET MORALLY WE WERE BOUND BY KNOWING THAT SUCH FORCES DO, INDEED, EXIST.
THAT THEY DO, MARTIN!
INDEED THEY DO!
THERE IS LAUGHTER IN CHAMBERS THEN, AS FIVE PEOPLE KNOW THAT THEY DID WHAT THEY HAD TO DO...
...AND THAT THEY DID IT WELL.
BUT THAT LAUGHTER IS THOUSANDS OF MILES FROM THE SUN-BAKED DESERT OF SOUTHWESTERN NEW MEXICO...
...AND TO A CERTAIN GREEN-SKINNED BEING, JUSTICE IS A CONCEPT AS ALIEN...
...AS THE FEW RARE MOMENTS OF PEACE GIVEN HIM AS HIS IN HIS TRAVELS ACROSS THE EARTH.
YET SEEK FOR PEACE HE WILL. ENDLESSLY...
...FOR HE IS--THE INCREDIBLE HULK.
BUT OL' GREENSKIN'LL HAVE TO WAIT AN ISSUE, 'CAUSE NEXT MONTH OUR WEBBED WALL-CRAWLER TEAMS UP WITH NONE OTHER THAN...
CAPTAIN AMERICA!
DON'T MISS IT!

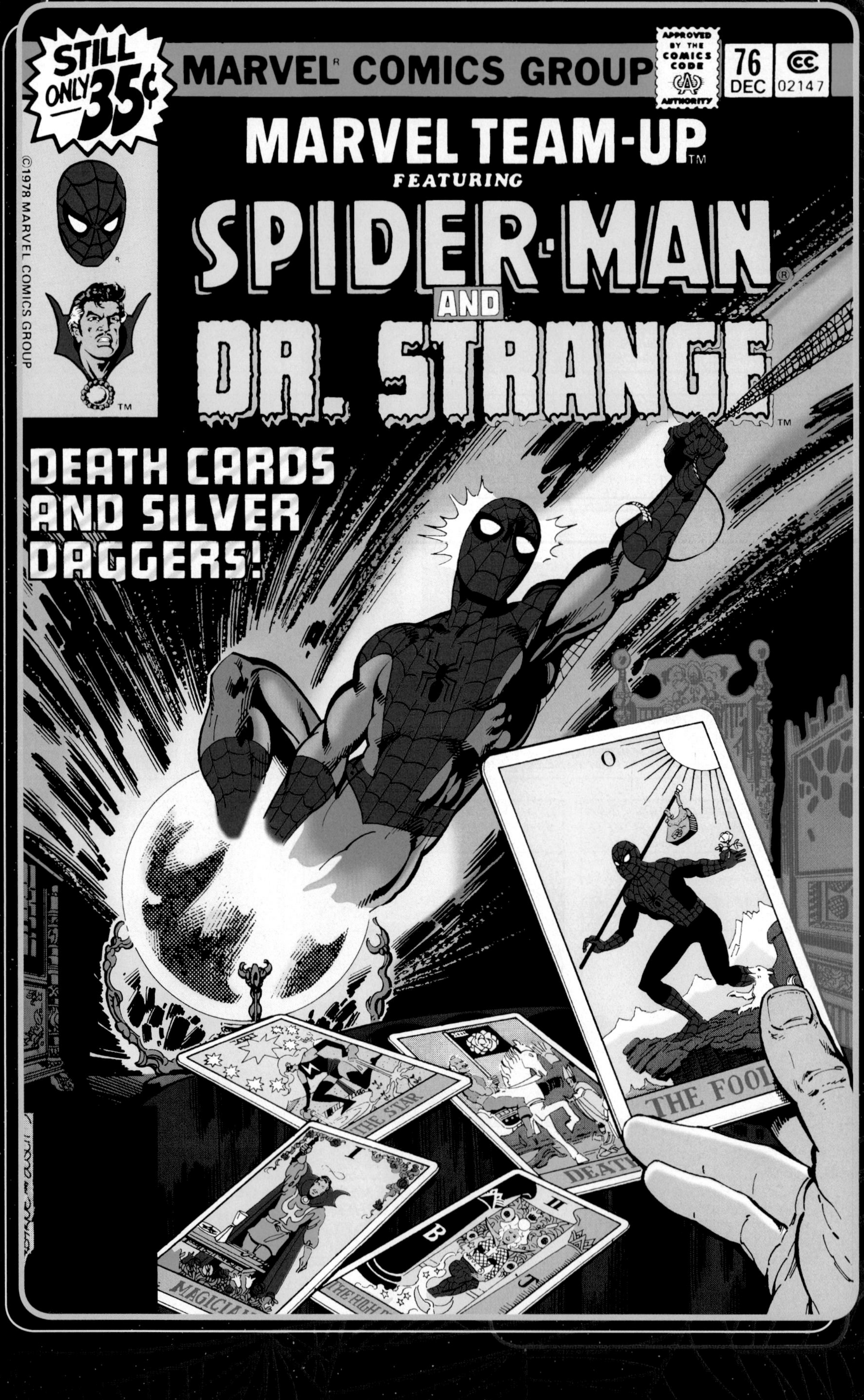
STILL ONLY 35¢
MARVEL COMICS GROUP
APPROVED BY THE COMICS CODE AUTHORITY
76 DEC
CC 02147
MARVEL TEAM-UP
FEATURING
SPIDER-MAN
AND
DR. STRANGE
©1978 MARVEL COMICS GROUP
DEATH CARDS AND SILVER DAGGERS!
THE FOOL
THE STAR

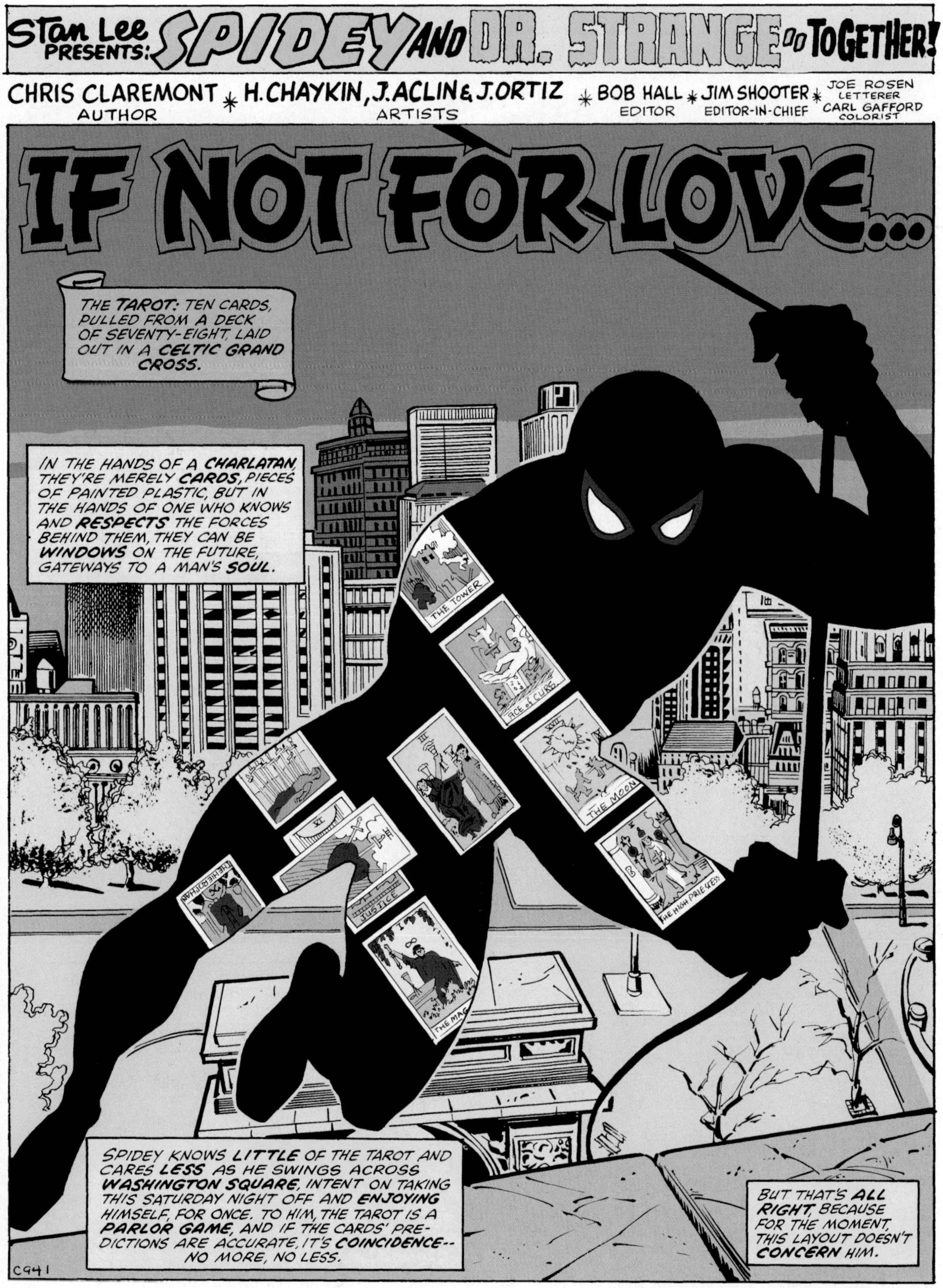
STAN LEE PRESENTS: SPIDEY AND DR. STRANGE TOGETHER!
CHRIS CLAREMONT AUTHOR * H. CHAYKIN, J. ACLIN & J. ORTIZ ARTISTS * BOB HALL EDITOR * JIM SHOOTER EDITOR-IN-CHIEF * JOE ROSEN LETTERER CARL GAFFORD COLORIST
IF NOT FOR LOVE...
THE TAROT: TEN CARDS, PULLED FROM A DECK OF SEVENTY-EIGHT, LAID OUT IN A CELTIC GRAND CROSS.
IN THE HANDS OF A CHARLATAN, THEY'RE MERELY CARDS, PIECES OF PAINTED PLASTIC, BUT IN THE HANDS OF ONE WHO KNOWS AND RESPECTS THE FORCES BEHIND THEM, THEY CAN BE WINDOWS ON THE FUTURE, GATEWAYS TO A MAN'S SOUL.
THE TOWER
ACE OF CUPS
THE MOON
JUSTICE
THE HIGH PRIESTESS
SPIDEY KNOWS LITTLE OF THE TAROT AND CARES LESS AS HE SWINGS ACROSS WASHINGTON SQUARE, INTENT ON TAKING THIS SATURDAY NIGHT OFF AND ENJOYING HIMSELF, FOR ONCE. TO HIM, THE TAROT IS A PARLOR GAME, AND IF THE CARDS' PREDICTIONS ARE ACCURATE, IT'S COINCIDENCE-- NO MORE, NO LESS.
BUT THAT'S ALL RIGHT, BECAUSE FOR THE MOMENT, THIS LAYOUT DOESN'T CONCERN HIM.
C941

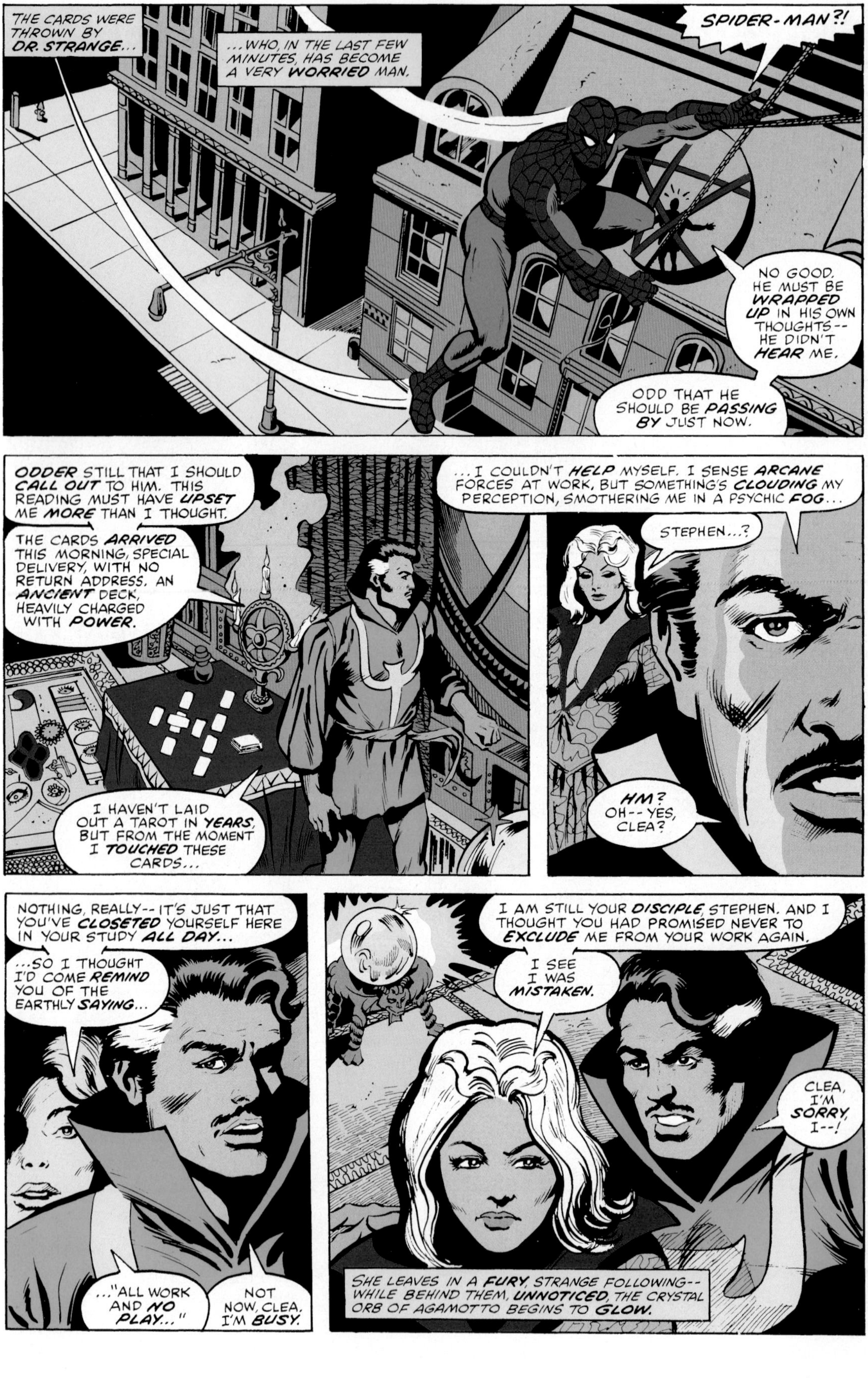
THE CARDS WERE THROWN BY DR. STRANGE...
...WHO, IN THE LAST FEW MINUTES, HAS BECOME A VERY WORRIED MAN.
SPIDER-MAN?!
NO GOOD. HE MUST BE WRAPPED UP IN HIS OWN THOUGHTS-- HE DIDN'T HEAR ME.
ODD THAT HE SHOULD BE PASSING BY JUST NOW.
ODDER STILL THAT I SHOULD CALL OUT TO HIM. THIS READING MUST HAVE UPSET ME MORE THAN I THOUGHT.
THE CARDS ARRIVED THIS MORNING, SPECIAL DELIVERY, WITH NO RETURN ADDRESS. AN ANCIENT DECK, HEAVILY CHARGED WITH POWER.
I HAVEN'T LAID OUT A TAROT IN YEARS, BUT FROM THE MOMENT I TOUCHED THESE CARDS...
...I COULDN'T HELP MYSELF. I SENSE ARCANE FORCES AT WORK, BUT SOMETHING'S CLOUDING MY PERCEPTION, SMOTHERING ME IN A PSYCHIC FOG...
STEPHEN...?
HM? OH-- YES, CLEA?
NOTHING, REALLY-- IT'S JUST THAT YOU'VE CLOSETED YOURSELF HERE IN YOUR STUDY ALL DAY...
...SO I THOUGHT I'D COME REMIND YOU OF THE EARTHLY SAYING...
..."ALL WORK AND NO PLAY..."
NOT NOW, CLEA. I'M BUSY.
I AM STILL YOUR DISCIPLE, STEPHEN. AND I THOUGHT YOU HAD PROMISED NEVER TO EXCLUDE ME FROM YOUR WORK AGAIN.
I SEE I WAS MISTAKEN.
CLEA, I'M SORRY, I--!
SHE LEAVES IN A FURY, STRANGE FOLLOWING-- WHILE BEHIND THEM, UNNOTICED, THE CRYSTAL ORB OF AGAMOTTO BEGINS TO GLOW.

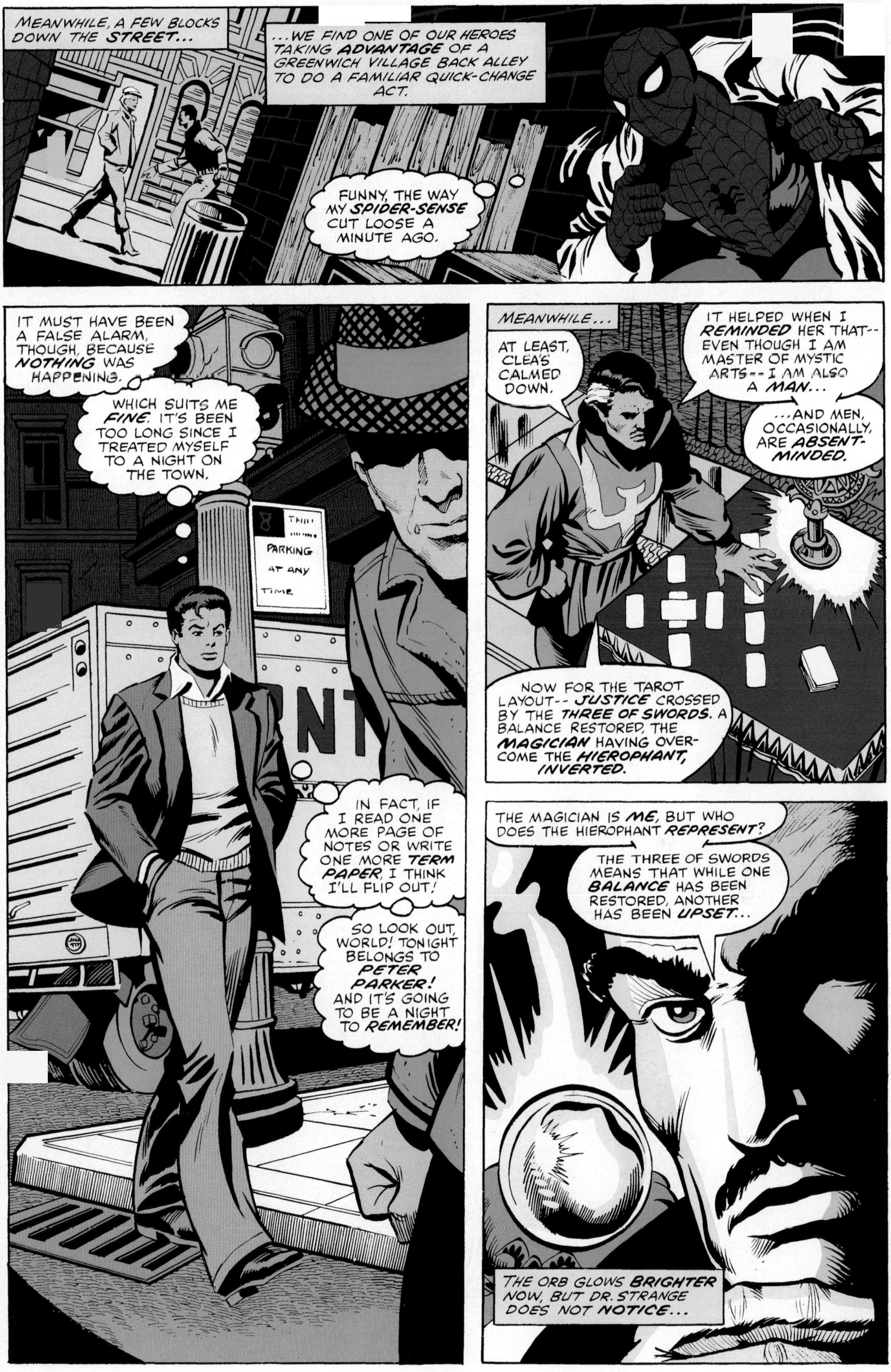
MEANWHILE, A FEW BLOCKS DOWN THE STREET...
...WE FIND ONE OF OUR HEROES TAKING ADVANTAGE OF A GREENWICH VILLAGE BACK ALLEY TO DO A FAMILIAR QUICK-CHANGE ACT.
FUNNY, THE WAY MY SPIDER-SENSE CUT LOOSE A MINUTE AGO.
IT MUST HAVE BEEN A FALSE ALARM, THOUGH, BECAUSE NOTHING WAS HAPPENING.
WHICH SUITS ME FINE. IT'S BEEN TOO LONG SINCE I TREATED MYSELF TO A NIGHT ON THE TOWN.
PARKING AT ANY TIME
IN FACT, IF I READ ONE MORE PAGE OF NOTES OR WRITE ONE MORE TERM PAPER, I THINK I'LL FLIP OUT!
SO LOOK OUT, WORLD! TONIGHT BELONGS TO PETER PARKER! AND IT'S GOING TO BE A NIGHT TO REMEMBER!
MEANWHILE...
AT LEAST, CLEA'S CALMED DOWN.
IT HELPED WHEN I REMINDED HER THAT-- EVEN THOUGH I AM MASTER OF MYSTIC ARTS-- I AM ALSO A MAN...
...AND MEN, OCCASIONALLY, ARE ABSENT-MINDED.
NOW FOR THE TAROT LAYOUT-- JUSTICE CROSSED BY THE THREE OF SWORDS. A BALANCE RESTORED, THE MAGICIAN HAVING OVERCOME THE HIEROPHANT, INVERTED.
THE MAGICIAN IS ME, BUT WHO DOES THE HIEROPHANT REPRESENT?
THE THREE OF SWORDS MEANS THAT WHILE ONE BALANCE HAS BEEN RESTORED, ANOTHER HAS BEEN UPSET...
THE ORB GLOWS BRIGHTER NOW, BUT DR. STRANGE DOES NOT NOTICE...

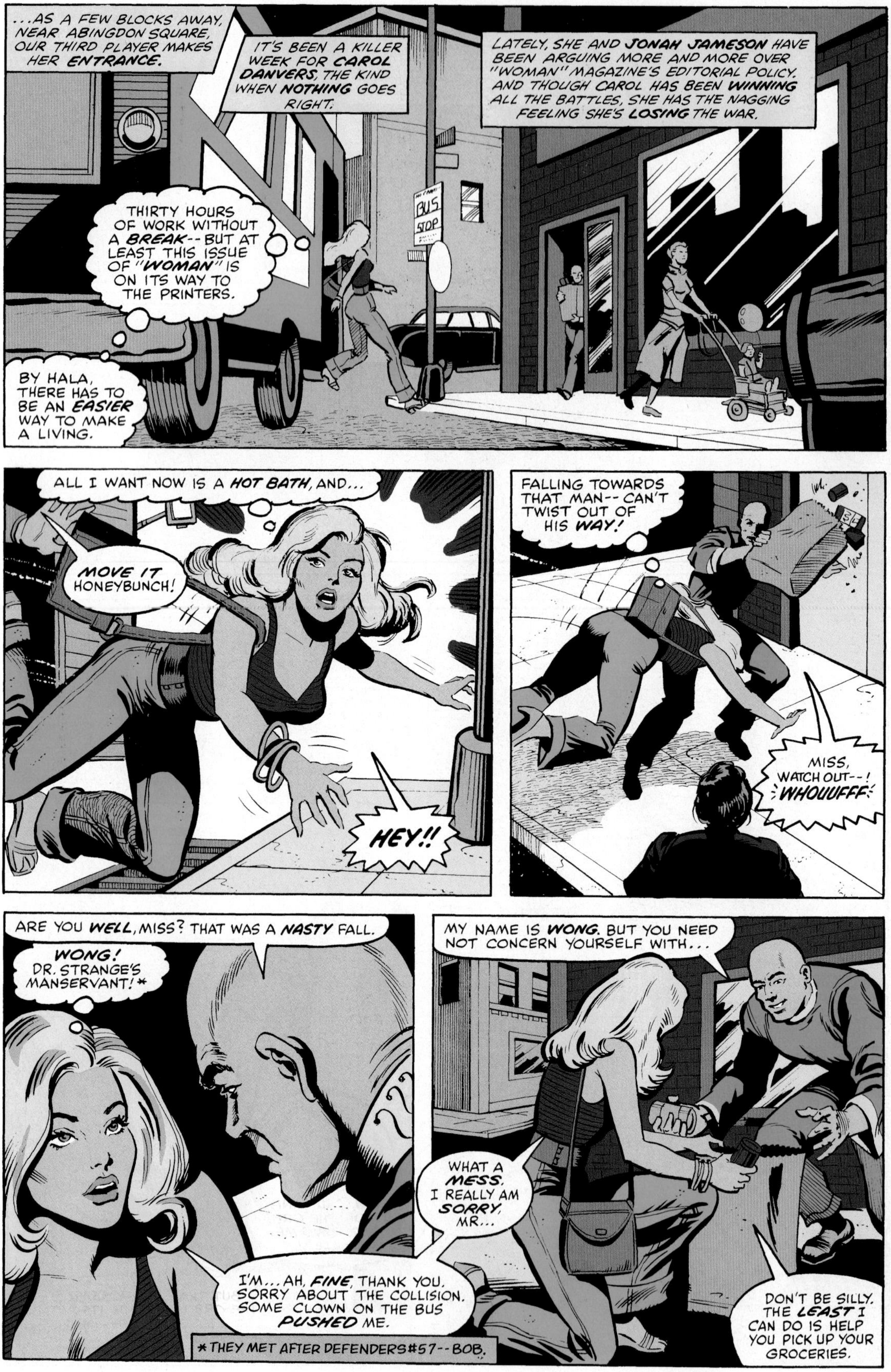
...AS A FEW BLOCKS AWAY, NEAR ABINGDON SQUARE, OUR THIRD PLAYER MAKES HER ENTRANCE.
IT'S BEEN A KILLER WEEK FOR CAROL DANVERS, THE KIND WHEN NOTHING GOES RIGHT.
LATELY, SHE AND JONAH JAMESON HAVE BEEN ARGUING MORE AND MORE OVER "WOMAN" MAGAZINE'S EDITORIAL POLICY. AND THOUGH CAROL HAS BEEN WINNING ALL THE BATTLES, SHE HAS THE NAGGING FEELING SHE'S LOSING THE WAR.
THIRTY HOURS OF WORK WITHOUT A BREAK-- BUT AT LEAST THIS ISSUE OF "WOMAN" IS ON ITS WAY TO THE PRINTERS.
BY HALA, THERE HAS TO BE AN EASIER WAY TO MAKE A LIVING.
BUS STOP
ALL I WANT NOW IS A HOT BATH, AND...
MOVE IT HONEYBUNCH!
HEY!!
FALLING TOWARDS THAT MAN-- CAN'T TWIST OUT OF HIS WAY!
MISS, WATCH OUT--! WHOUUFFF!
ARE YOU WELL, MISS? THAT WAS A NASTY FALL.
WONG! DR. STRANGE'S MANSERVANT! *
I'M... AH, FINE, THANK YOU. SORRY ABOUT THE COLLISION. SOME CLOWN ON THE BUS PUSHED ME.
* THEY MET AFTER DEFENDERS #57--BOB.
MY NAME IS WONG. BUT YOU NEED NOT CONCERN YOURSELF WITH...
WHAT A MESS. I REALLY AM SORRY, MR...
DON'T BE SILLY. THE LEAST I CAN DO IS HELP YOU PICK UP YOUR GROCERIES.

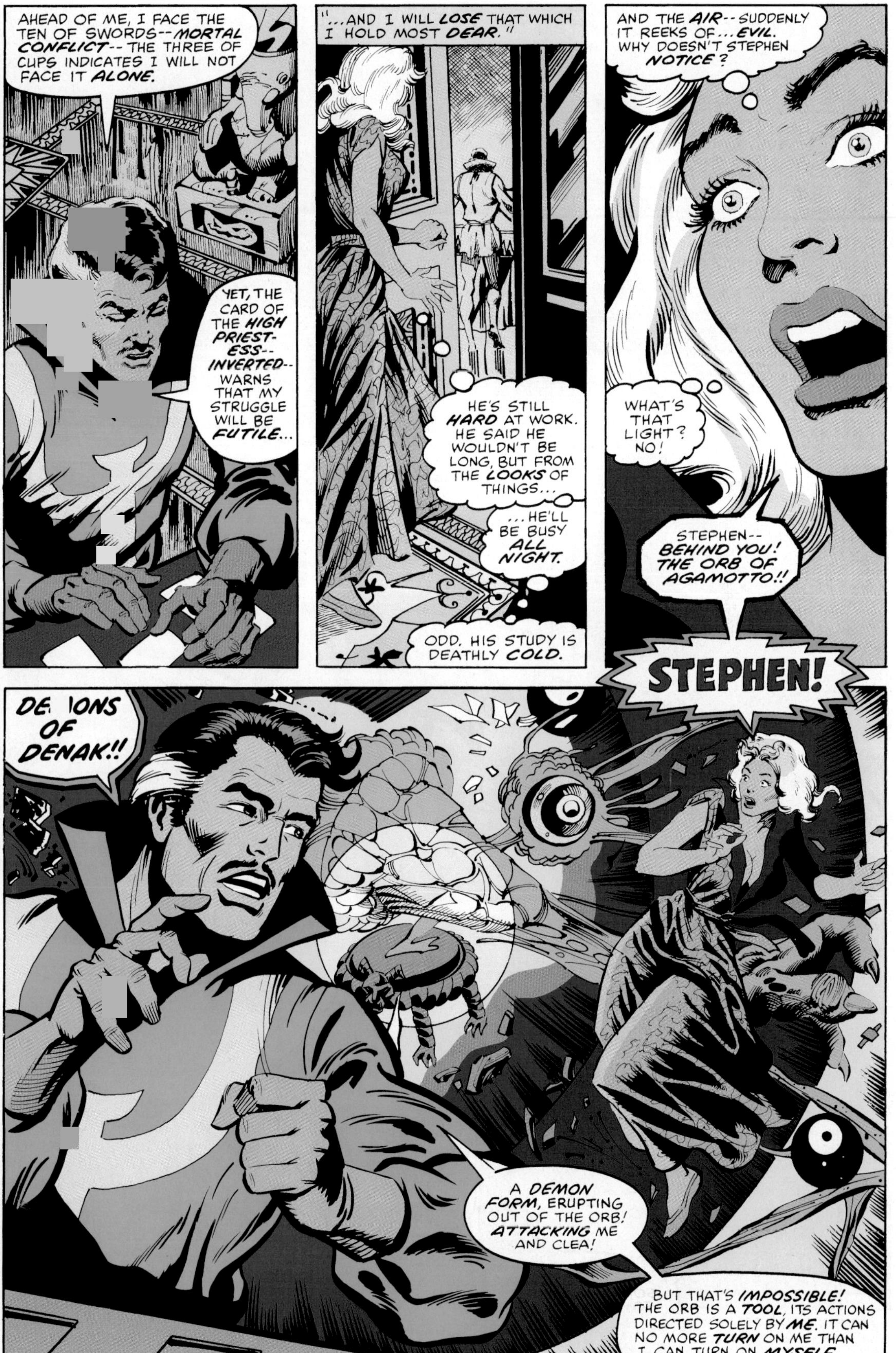

AHEAD OF ME, I FACE THE TEN OF SWORDS--MORTAL CONFLICT-- THE THREE OF CUPS INDICATES I WILL NOT FACE IT ALONE.
YET, THE CARD OF THE HIGH PRIEST-ESS--INVERTED--WARNS THAT MY STRUGGLE WILL BE FUTILE...
"...AND I WILL LOSE THAT WHICH I HOLD MOST DEAR."
HE'S STILL HARD AT WORK. HE SAID HE WOULDN'T BE LONG, BUT FROM THE LOOKS OF THINGS...
...HE'LL BE BUSY ALL NIGHT.
ODD. HIS STUDY IS DEATHLY COLD.
AND THE AIR-- SUDDENLY IT REEKS OF... EVIL. WHY DOESN'T STEPHEN NOTICE?
WHAT'S THAT LIGHT? NO!
STEPHEN-- BEHIND YOU! THE ORB OF AGAMOTTO!!
STEPHEN!
DE IONS OF DENAK!!
A DEMON FORM, ERUPTING OUT OF THE ORB! ATTACKING ME AND CLEA!
BUT THAT'S IMPOSSIBLE! THE ORB IS A TOOL, ITS ACTIONS DIRECTED SOLELY BY ME. IT CAN NO MORE TURN ON ME THAN I CAN TURN ON MYSELF.

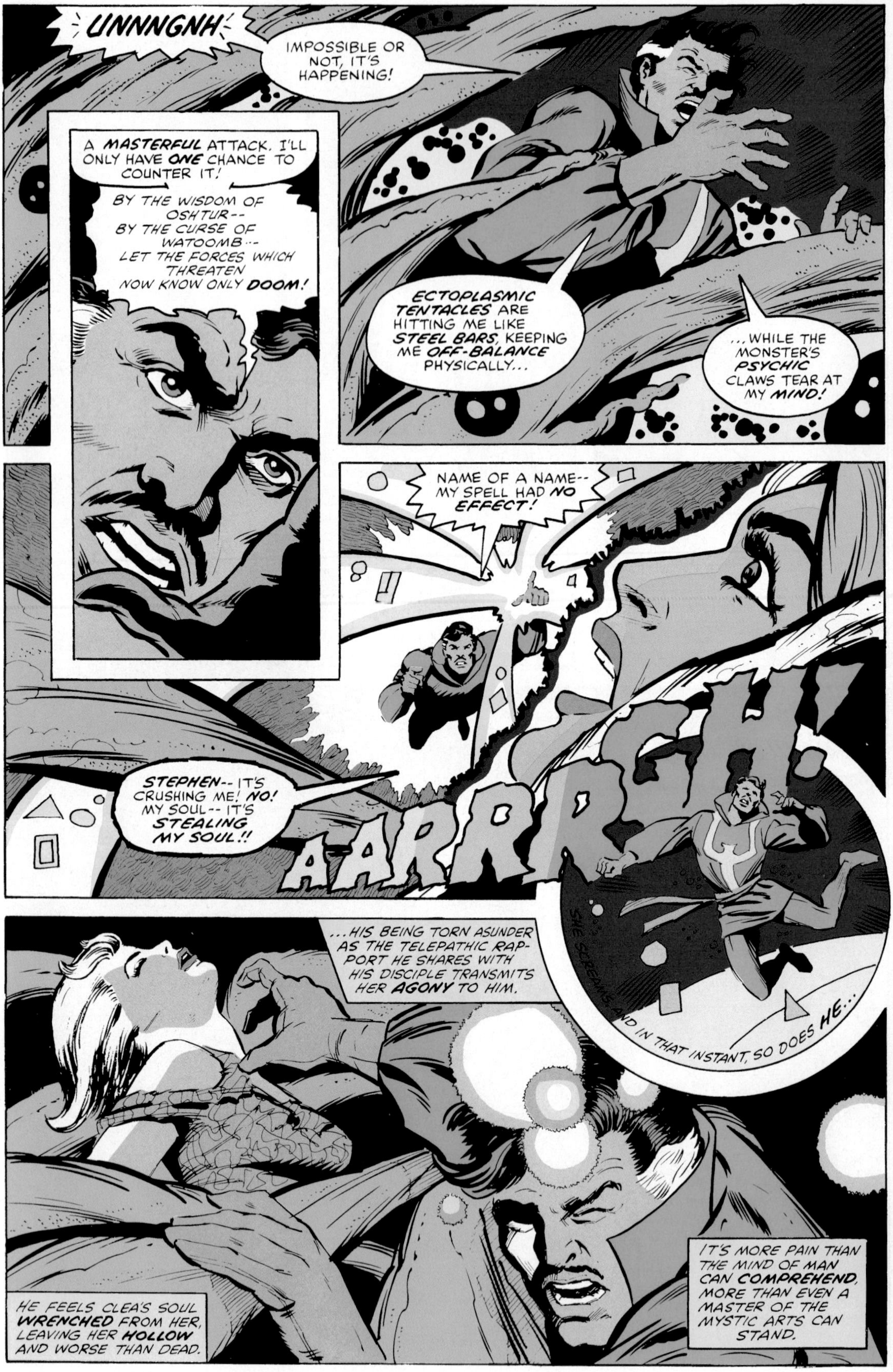
UNNNGNH
IMPOSSIBLE OR NOT, IT'S HAPPENING!
A MASTERFUL ATTACK. I'LL ONLY HAVE ONE CHANCE TO COUNTER IT!
BY THE WISDOM OF OSHTUR-- BY THE CURSE OF WATOOMB-- LET THE FORCES WHICH THREATEN NOW KNOW ONLY DOOM!
ECTOPLASMIC TENTACLES ARE HITTING ME LIKE STEEL BARS, KEEPING ME OFF-BALANCE PHYSICALLY...
...WHILE THE MONSTER'S PSYCHIC CLAWS TEAR AT MY MIND!
NAME OF A NAME-- MY SPELL HAD NO EFFECT!
STEPHEN-- IT'S CRUSHING ME! NO! MY SOUL-- IT'S STEALING MY SOUL!!
AARRRGH!
SHE SCREAMS AND IN THAT INSTANT, SO DOES HE...
...HIS BEING TORN ASUNDER AS THE TELEPATHIC RAPPORT HE SHARES WITH HIS DISCIPLE TRANSMITS HER AGONY TO HIM.
HE FEELS CLEA'S SOUL WRENCHED FROM HER, LEAVING HER HOLLOW AND WORSE THAN DEAD.
IT'S MORE PAIN THAN THE MIND OF MAN CAN COMPREHEND, MORE THAN EVEN A MASTER OF THE MYSTIC ARTS CAN STAND.

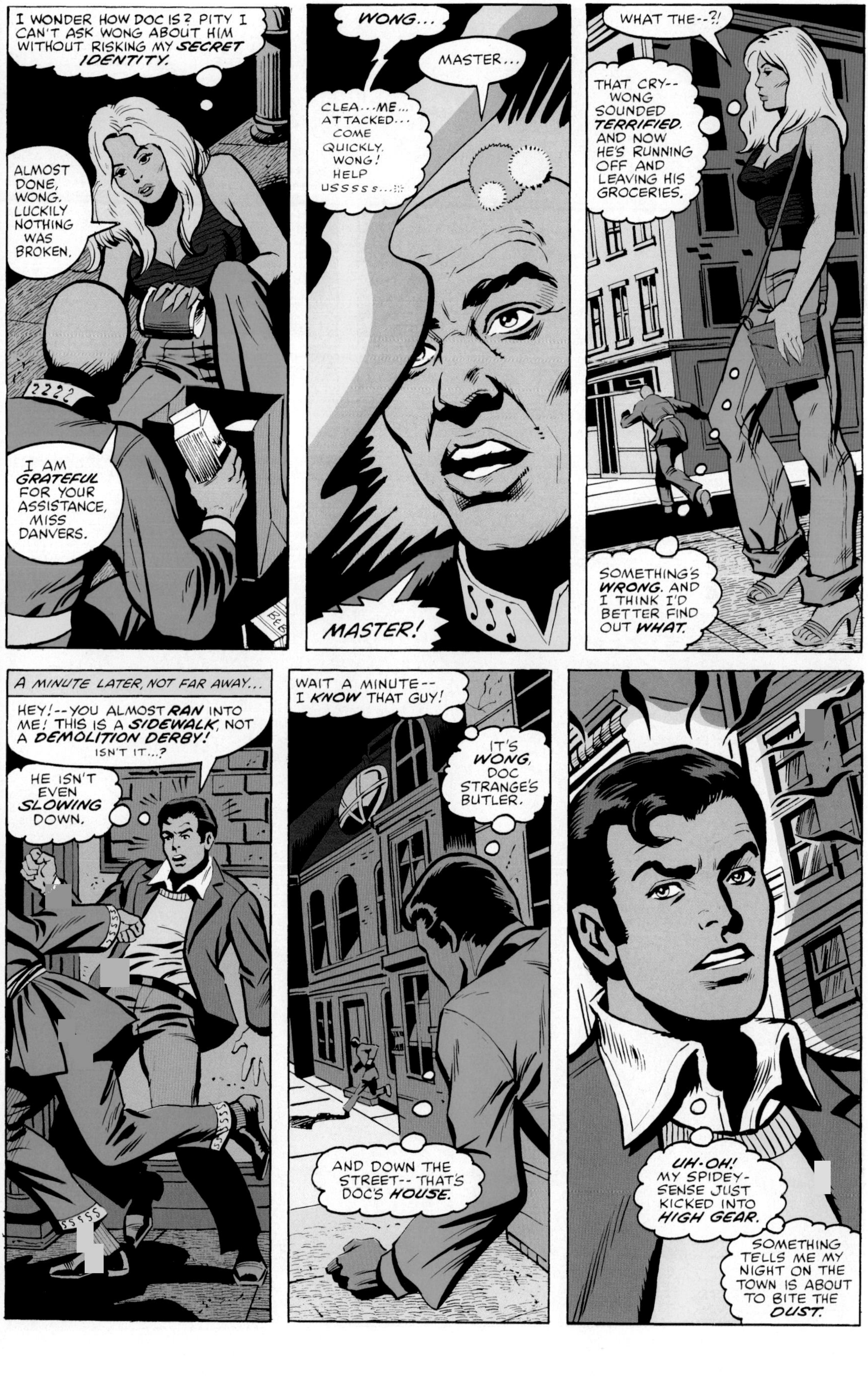
I WONDER HOW DOC IS? PITY I CAN'T ASK WONG ABOUT HIM WITHOUT RISKING MY SECRET IDENTITY.
ALMOST DONE, WONG. LUCKILY NOTHING WAS BROKEN.
I AM GRATEFUL FOR YOUR ASSISTANCE, MISS DANVERS.
WONG...
MASTER...
CLEA...ME... ATTACKED... COME QUICKLY. WONG! HELP USSSSS...
MASTER!
WHAT THE--?!
THAT CRY--WONG SOUNDED TERRIFIED. AND NOW HE'S RUNNING OFF AND LEAVING HIS GROCERIES.
SOMETHING'S WRONG. AND I THINK I'D BETTER FIND OUT WHAT.
A MINUTE LATER, NOT FAR AWAY...
HEY!--YOU ALMOST RAN INTO ME! THIS IS A SIDEWALK, NOT A DEMOLITION DERBY! ISN'T IT...?
HE ISN'T EVEN SLOWING DOWN.
WAIT A MINUTE-- I KNOW THAT GUY!
IT'S WONG, DOC STRANGE'S BUTLER.
AND DOWN THE STREET-- THAT'S DOC'S HOUSE.
UH-OH! MY SPIDEY-SENSE JUST KICKED INTO HIGH GEAR.
SOMETHING TELLS ME MY NIGHT ON THE TOWN IS ABOUT TO BITE THE DUST.

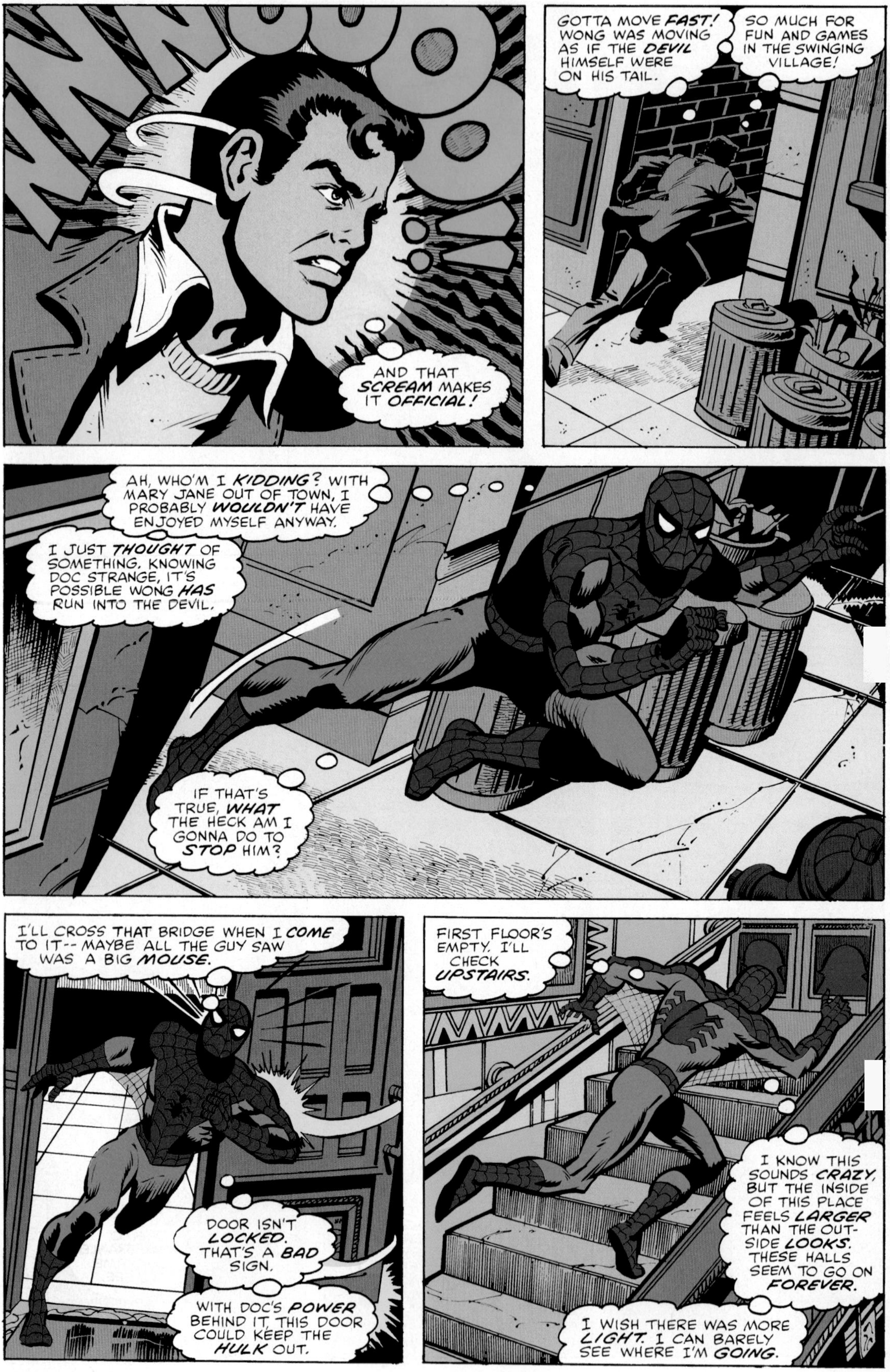
NNNOOOOOO!!
AND THAT SCREAM MAKES IT OFFICIAL!
GOTTA MOVE FAST! WONG WAS MOVING AS IF THE DEVIL HIMSELF WERE ON HIS TAIL.
SO MUCH FOR FUN AND GAMES IN THE SWINGING VILLAGE!
AH, WHO'M I KIDDING? WITH MARY JANE OUT OF TOWN, I PROBABLY WOULDN'T HAVE ENJOYED MYSELF ANYWAY.
I JUST THOUGHT OF SOMETHING. KNOWING DOC STRANGE, IT'S POSSIBLE WONG HAS RUN INTO THE DEVIL.
IF THAT'S TRUE, WHAT THE HECK AM I GONNA DO TO STOP HIM?
I'LL CROSS THAT BRIDGE WHEN I COME TO IT-- MAYBE ALL THE GUY SAW WAS A BIG MOUSE.
DOOR ISN'T LOCKED. THAT'S A BAD SIGN.
WITH DOC'S POWER BEHIND IT, THIS DOOR COULD KEEP THE HULK OUT.
FIRST FLOOR'S EMPTY. I'LL CHECK UPSTAIRS.
I KNOW THIS SOUNDS CRAZY, BUT THE INSIDE OF THIS PLACE FEELS LARGER THAN THE OUT-SIDE LOOKS. THESE HALLS SEEM TO GO ON FOREVER.
I WISH THERE WAS MORE LIGHT. I CAN BARELY SEE WHERE I'M GOING.

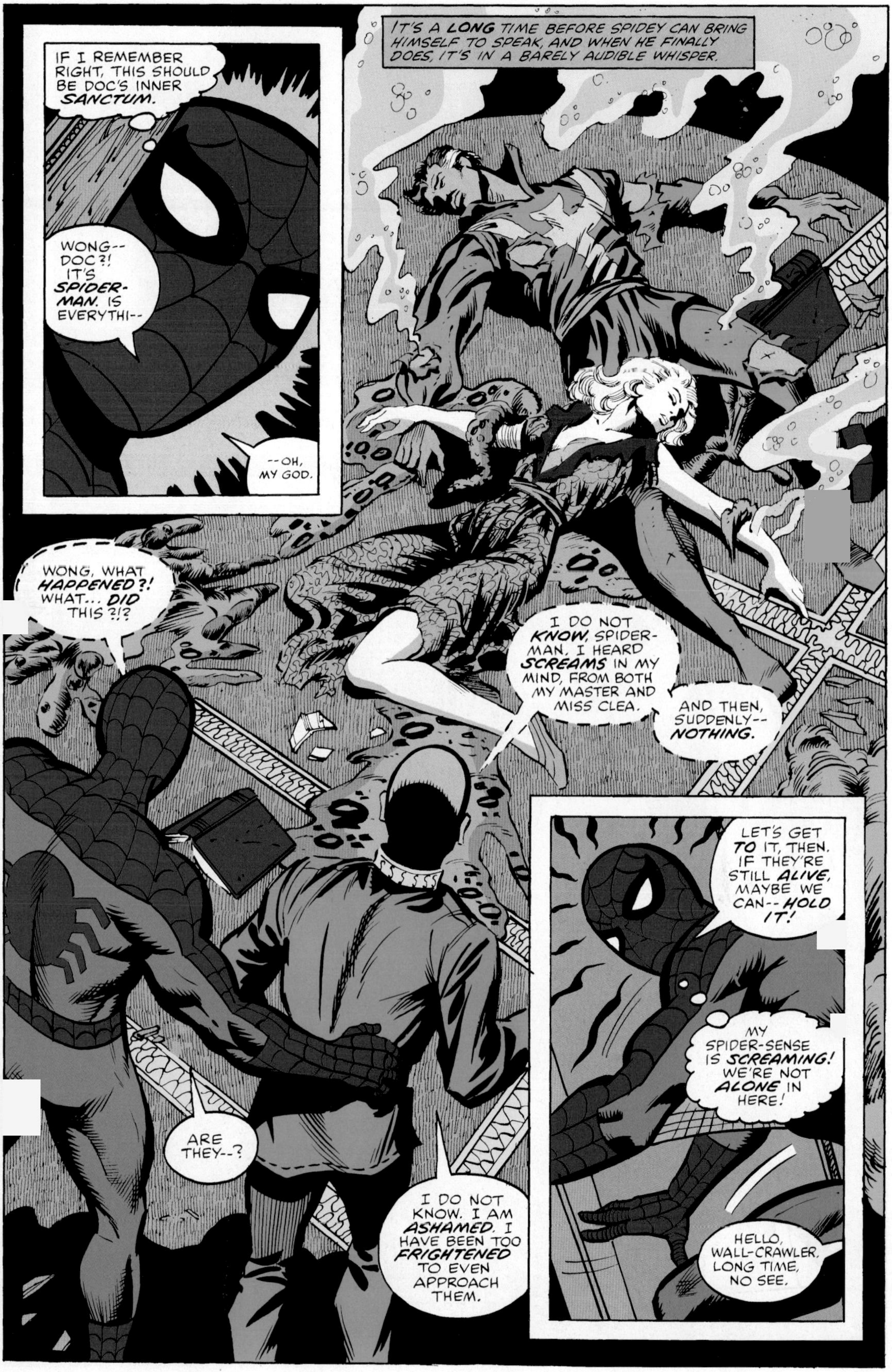
IF I REMEMBER RIGHT, THIS SHOULD BE DOC'S INNER SANCTUM.
WONG-- DOC?! IT'S SPIDER-MAN. IS EVERYTHI--
--OH, MY GOD.
IT'S A LONG TIME BEFORE SPIDEY CAN BRING HIMSELF TO SPEAK, AND WHEN HE FINALLY DOES, IT'S IN A BARELY AUDIBLE WHISPER.
WONG, WHAT HAPPENED?! WHAT... DID THIS?!?
I DO NOT KNOW, SPIDER-MAN. I HEARD SCREAMS IN MY MIND, FROM BOTH MY MASTER AND MISS CLEA.
AND THEN, SUDDENLY-- NOTHING.
ARE THEY--?
I DO NOT KNOW. I AM ASHAMED. I HAVE BEEN TOO FRIGHTENED TO EVEN APPROACH THEM.
LET'S GET TO IT, THEN. IF THEY'RE STILL ALIVE, MAYBE WE CAN-- HOLD IT!
MY SPIDER-SENSE IS SCREAMING! WE'RE NOT ALONE IN HERE!
HELLO, WALL-CRAWLER. LONG TIME, NO SEE.

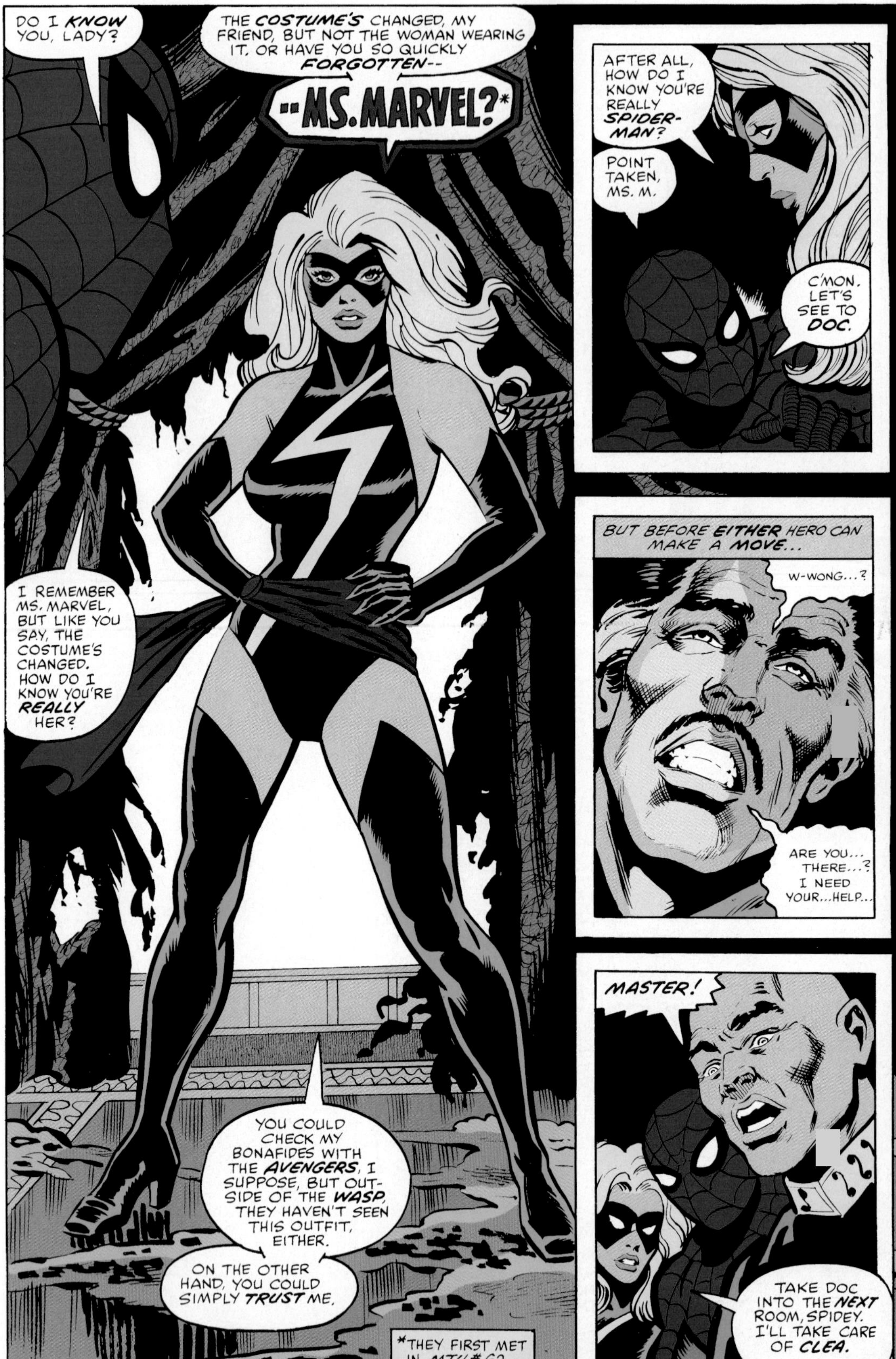
DO I KNOW YOU, LADY?
THE COSTUME'S CHANGED, MY FRIEND, BUT NOT THE WOMAN WEARING IT. OR HAVE YOU SO QUICKLY FORGOTTEN--
--MS. MARVEL?*
I REMEMBER MS. MARVEL, BUT LIKE YOU SAY, THE COSTUME'S CHANGED. HOW DO I KNOW YOU'RE REALLY HER?
YOU COULD CHECK MY BONAFIDES WITH THE AVENGERS, I SUPPOSE, BUT OUTSIDE OF THE WASP, THEY HAVEN'T SEEN THIS OUTFIT, EITHER.
ON THE OTHER HAND, YOU COULD SIMPLY TRUST ME.
*THEY FIRST MET IN MTU #62 --BOB.
AFTER ALL, HOW DO I KNOW YOU'RE REALLY SPIDER-MAN?
POINT TAKEN, MS. M.
C'MON. LET'S SEE TO DOC.
BUT BEFORE EITHER HERO CAN MAKE A MOVE...
W-WONG...?
ARE YOU... THERE...? I NEED YOUR...HELP...
MASTER!
TAKE DOC INTO THE NEXT ROOM, SPIDEY. I'LL TAKE CARE OF CLEA.

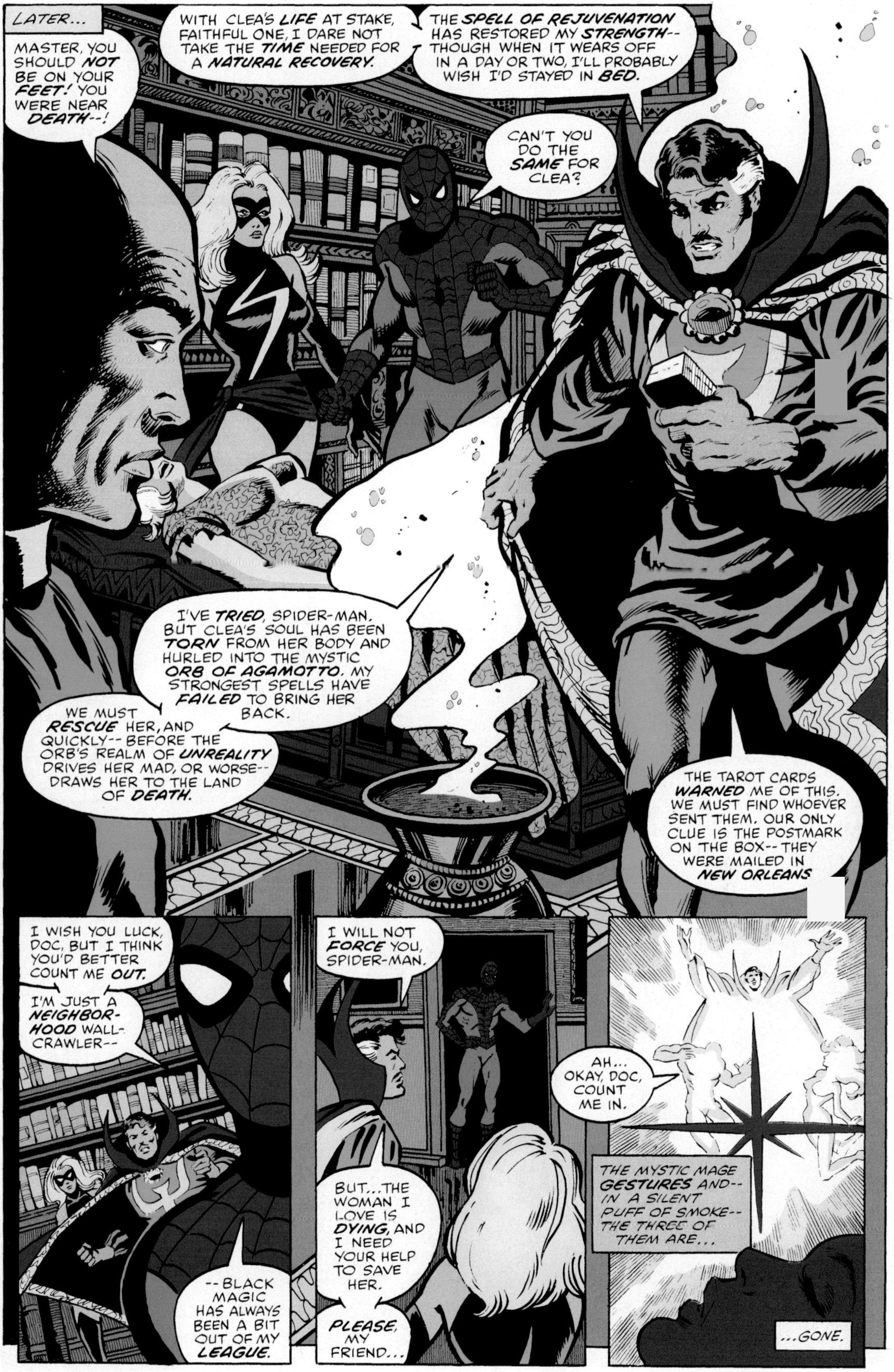
LATER...
MASTER, YOU SHOULD NOT BE ON YOUR FEET! YOU WERE NEAR DEATH--!
WITH CLEA'S LIFE AT STAKE, FAITHFUL ONE, I DARE NOT TAKE THE TIME NEEDED FOR A NATURAL RECOVERY.
THE SPELL OF REJUVENATION HAS RESTORED MY STRENGTH-- THOUGH WHEN IT WEARS OFF IN A DAY OR TWO, I'LL PROBABLY WISH I'D STAYED IN BED.
CAN'T YOU DO THE SAME FOR CLEA?
I'VE TRIED, SPIDER-MAN, BUT CLEA'S SOUL HAS BEEN TORN FROM HER BODY AND HURLED INTO THE MYSTIC ORB OF AGAMOTTO. MY STRONGEST SPELLS HAVE FAILED TO BRING HER BACK.
WE MUST RESCUE HER, AND QUICKLY-- BEFORE THE ORB'S REALM OF UNREALITY DRIVES HER MAD, OR WORSE-- DRAWS HER TO THE LAND OF DEATH.
THE TAROT CARDS WARNED ME OF THIS. WE MUST FIND WHOEVER SENT THEM. OUR ONLY CLUE IS THE POSTMARK ON THE BOX--THEY WERE MAILED IN NEW ORLEANS
I WISH YOU LUCK, DOC, BUT I THINK YOU'D BETTER COUNT ME OUT.
I'M JUST A NEIGHBOR-HOOD WALL-CRAWLER--
--BLACK MAGIC HAS ALWAYS BEEN A BIT OUT OF MY LEAGUE.
I WILL NOT FORCE YOU, SPIDER-MAN.
BUT...THE WOMAN I LOVE IS DYING, AND I NEED YOUR HELP TO SAVE HER.
PLEASE, MY FRIEND...
AH... OKAY, DOC, COUNT ME IN.
THE MYSTIC MAGE GESTURES AND-- IN A SILENT PUFF OF SMOKE-- THE THREE OF THEM ARE...
...GONE.

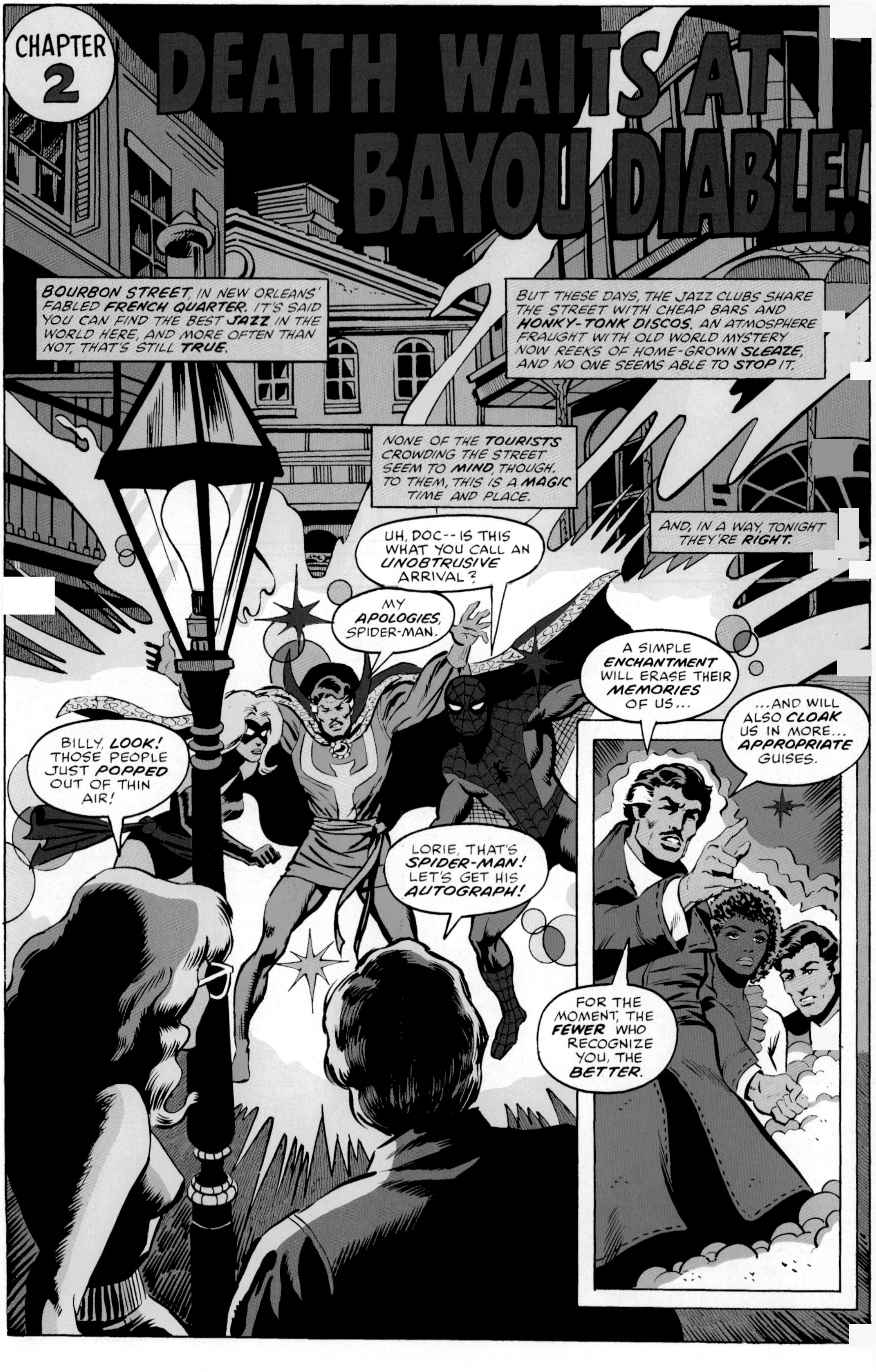
CHAPTER 2
DEATH WAITS AT BAYOU DIABLE!
BOURBON STREET, IN NEW ORLEANS' FABLED FRENCH QUARTER. IT'S SAID YOU CAN FIND THE BEST JAZZ IN THE WORLD HERE, AND MORE OFTEN THAN NOT, THAT'S STILL TRUE.
BUT THESE DAYS, THE JAZZ CLUBS SHARE THE STREET WITH CHEAP BARS AND HONKY-TONK DISCOS. AN ATMOSPHERE FRAUGHT WITH OLD WORLD MYSTERY NOW REEKS OF HOME-GROWN SLEAZE, AND NO ONE SEEMS ABLE TO STOP IT.
NONE OF THE TOURISTS CROWDING THE STREET SEEM TO MIND, THOUGH. TO THEM, THIS IS A MAGIC TIME AND PLACE.
AND, IN A WAY, TONIGHT THEY'RE RIGHT.
UH, DOC-- IS THIS WHAT YOU CALL AN UNOBTRUSIVE ARRIVAL?
MY APOLOGIES, SPIDER-MAN.
BILLY, LOOK! THOSE PEOPLE JUST POPPED OUT OF THIN AIR!
LORIE, THAT'S SPIDER-MAN! LET'S GET HIS AUTOGRAPH!
A SIMPLE ENCHANTMENT WILL ERASE THEIR MEMORIES OF US...
...AND WILL ALSO CLOAK US IN MORE... APPROPRIATE GUISES.
FOR THE MOMENT, THE FEWER WHO RECOGNIZE YOU, THE BETTER.

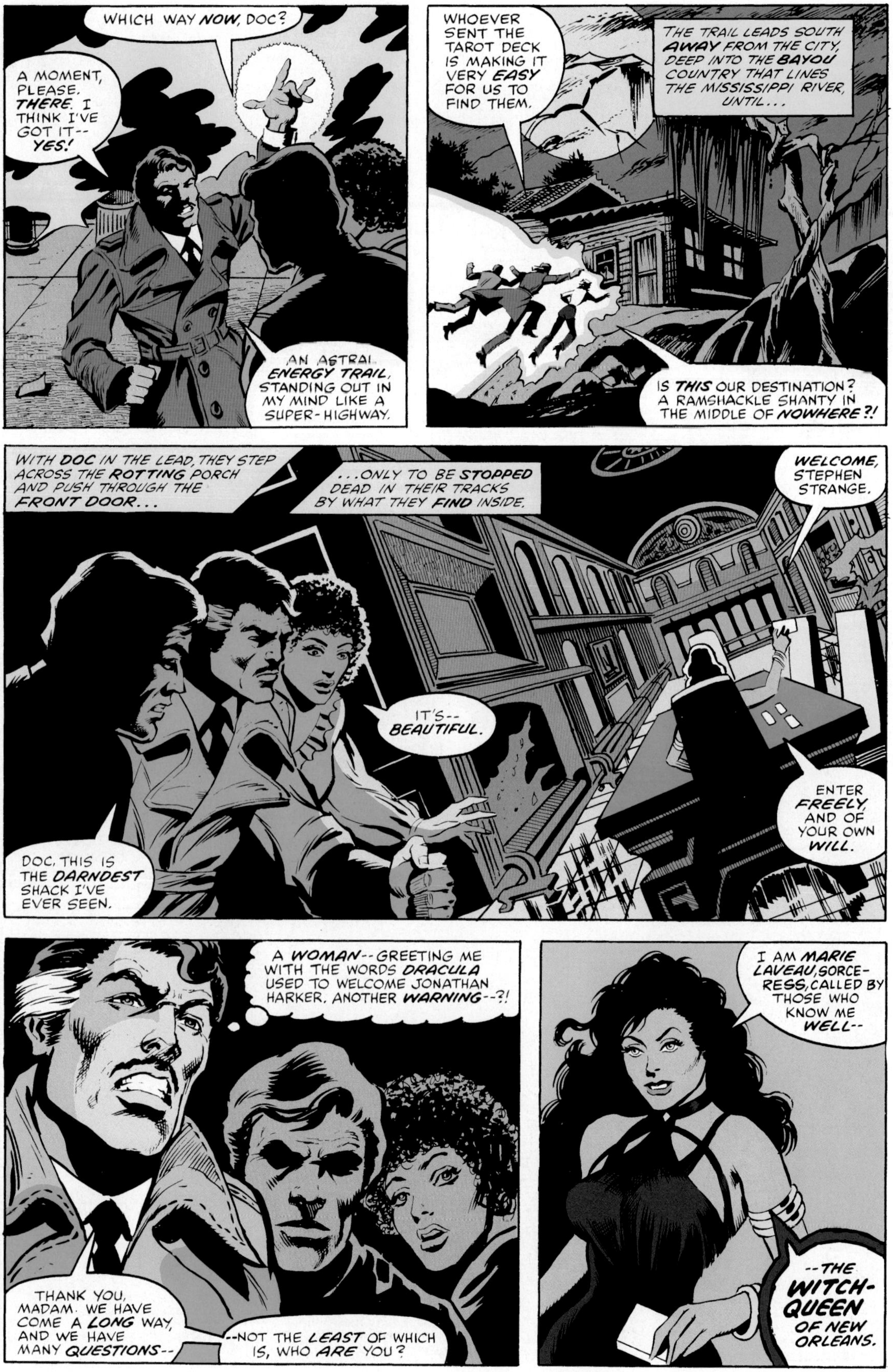
WHICH WAY NOW, DOC?
A MOMENT, PLEASE. THERE. I THINK I'VE GOT IT-- YES!
AN ASTRAL ENERGY TRAIL, STANDING OUT IN MY MIND LIKE A SUPER-HIGHWAY.
WHOEVER SENT THE TAROT DECK IS MAKING IT VERY EASY FOR US TO FIND THEM.
THE TRAIL LEADS SOUTH AWAY FROM THE CITY, DEEP INTO THE BAYOU COUNTRY THAT LINES THE MISSISSIPPI RIVER, UNTIL...
IS THIS OUR DESTINATION? A RAMSHACKLE SHANTY IN THE MIDDLE OF NOWHERE?!
WITH DOC IN THE LEAD, THEY STEP ACROSS THE ROTTING PORCH AND PUSH THROUGH THE FRONT DOOR...
...ONLY TO BE STOPPED DEAD IN THEIR TRACKS BY WHAT THEY FIND INSIDE.
WELCOME, STEPHEN STRANGE.
IT'S-- BEAUTIFUL.
ENTER FREELY, AND OF YOUR OWN WILL.
DOC, THIS IS THE DARNDEST SHACK I'VE EVER SEEN.
A WOMAN--GREETING ME WITH THE WORDS DRACULA USED TO WELCOME JONATHAN HARKER. ANOTHER WARNING--?!
THANK YOU, MADAM. WE HAVE COME A LONG WAY, AND WE HAVE MANY QUESTIONS--
--NOT THE LEAST OF WHICH IS, WHO ARE YOU?
I AM MARIE LAVEAU, SORCERESS, CALLED BY THOSE WHO KNOW ME WELL--
--THE WITCH-QUEEN OF NEW ORLEANS.

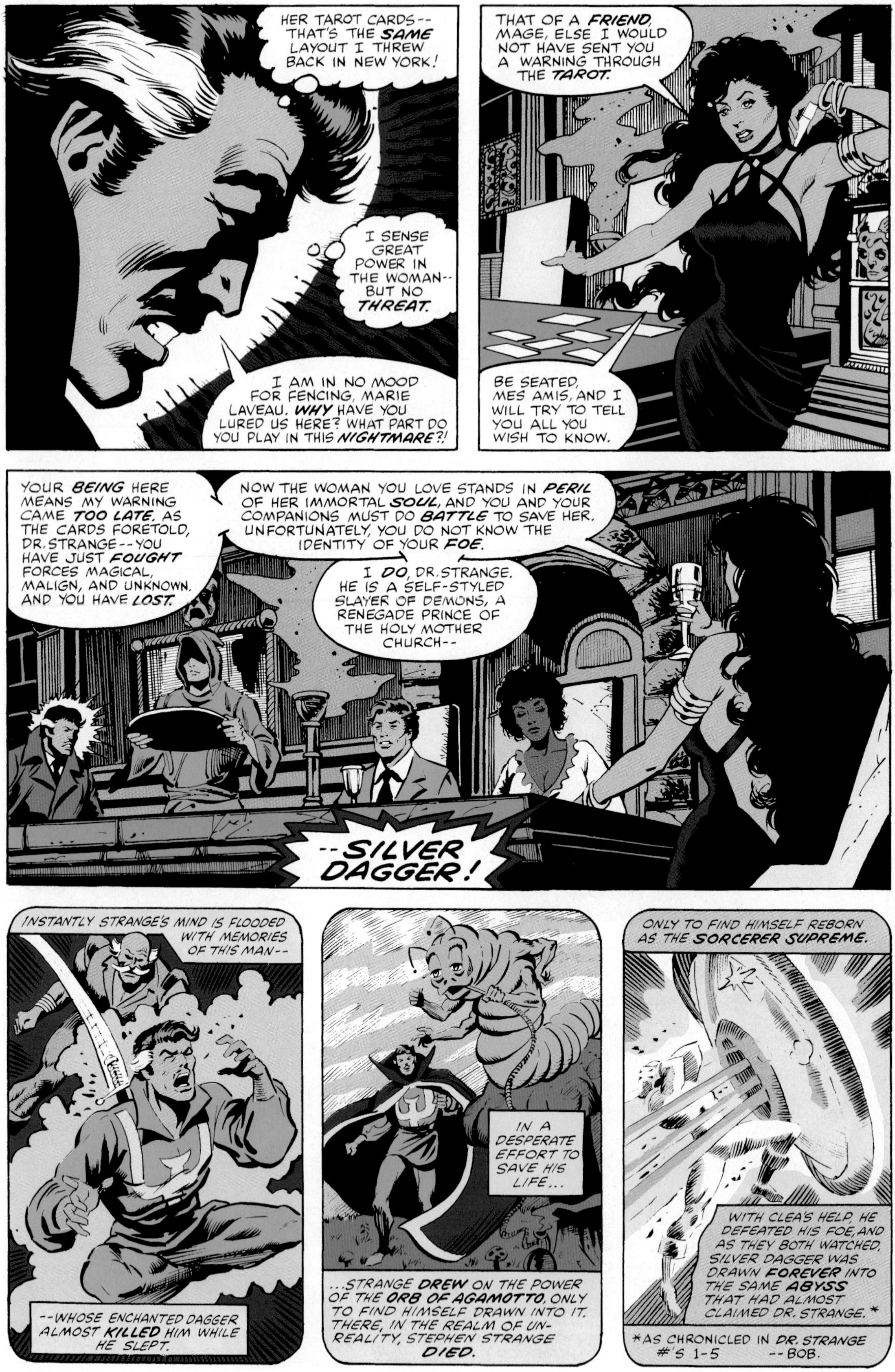
HER TAROT CARDS-- THAT'S THE SAME LAYOUT I THREW BACK IN NEW YORK!
I SENSE GREAT POWER IN THE WOMAN-- BUT NO THREAT.
I AM IN NO MOOD FOR FENCING, MARIE LAVEAU. WHY HAVE YOU LURED US HERE? WHAT PART DO YOU PLAY IN THIS NIGHTMARE?!
THAT OF A FRIEND, MAGE, ELSE I WOULD NOT HAVE SENT YOU A WARNING THROUGH THE TAROT.
BE SEATED, MES AMIS, AND I WILL TRY TO TELL YOU ALL YOU WISH TO KNOW.
YOUR BEING HERE MEANS MY WARNING CAME TOO LATE. AS THE CARDS FORETOLD, DR. STRANGE--YOU HAVE JUST FOUGHT FORCES MAGICAL, MALIGN, AND UNKNOWN. AND YOU HAVE LOST.
NOW THE WOMAN YOU LOVE STANDS IN PERIL OF HER IMMORTAL SOUL, AND YOU AND YOUR COMPANIONS MUST DO BATTLE TO SAVE HER. UNFORTUNATELY, YOU DO NOT KNOW THE IDENTITY OF YOUR FOE.
I DO, DR. STRANGE. HE IS A SELF-STYLED SLAYER OF DEMONS, A RENEGADE PRINCE OF THE HOLY MOTHER CHURCH--
--SILVER DAGGER!
INSTANTLY STRANGE'S MIND IS FLOODED WITH MEMORIES OF THIS MAN--
--WHOSE ENCHANTED DAGGER ALMOST KILLED HIM WHILE HE SLEPT.
IN A DESPERATE EFFORT TO SAVE HIS LIFE...
...STRANGE DREW ON THE POWER OF THE ORB OF AGAMOTTO, ONLY TO FIND HIMSELF DRAWN INTO IT. THERE, IN THE REALM OF UN-REALITY, STEPHEN STRANGE DIED.
ONLY TO FIND HIMSELF REBORN AS THE SORCERER SUPREME.
WITH CLEA'S HELP, HE DEFEATED HIS FOE, AND AS THEY BOTH WATCHED, SILVER DAGGER WAS DRAWN FOREVER INTO THE SAME ABYSS THAT HAD ALMOST CLAIMED DR. STRANGE.*
*AS CHRONICLED IN DR. STRANGE #'S 1-5 --BOB.

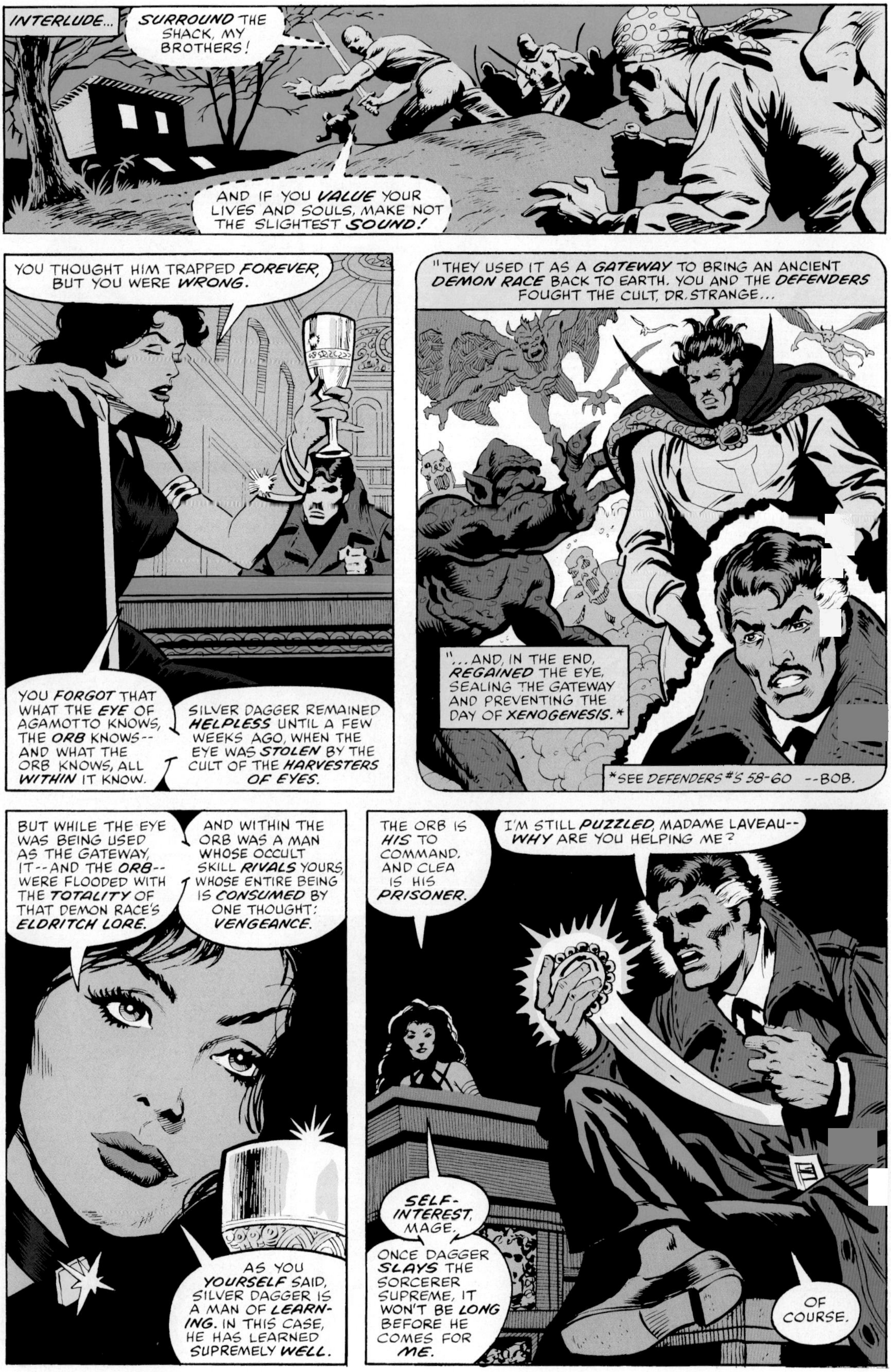
INTERLUDE...
SURROUND THE SHACK, MY BROTHERS!
AND IF YOU VALUE YOUR LIVES AND SOULS, MAKE NOT THE SLIGHTEST SOUND!
YOU THOUGHT HIM TRAPPED FOREVER, BUT YOU WERE WRONG.
YOU FORGOT THAT WHAT THE EYE OF AGAMOTTO KNOWS, THE ORB KNOWS-- AND WHAT THE ORB KNOWS, ALL WITHIN IT KNOW.
SILVER DAGGER REMAINED HELPLESS UNTIL A FEW WEEKS AGO, WHEN THE EYE WAS STOLEN BY THE CULT OF THE HARVESTERS OF EYES.
"THEY USED IT AS A GATEWAY TO BRING AN ANCIENT DEMON RACE BACK TO EARTH. YOU AND THE DEFENDERS FOUGHT THE CULT, DR. STRANGE...
"...AND, IN THE END, REGAINED THE EYE, SEALING THE GATEWAY AND PREVENTING THE DAY OF XENOGENESIS.*
*SEE DEFENDERS #'S 58-60 --BOB.
BUT WHILE THE EYE WAS BEING USED AS THE GATEWAY, IT--AND THE ORB-- WERE FLOODED WITH THE TOTALITY OF THAT DEMON RACE'S ELDRITCH LORE.
AND WITHIN THE ORB WAS A MAN WHOSE OCCULT SKILL RIVALS YOURS, WHOSE ENTIRE BEING IS CONSUMED BY ONE THOUGHT: VENGEANCE.
AS YOU YOURSELF SAID, SILVER DAGGER IS A MAN OF LEARNING. IN THIS CASE, HE HAS LEARNED SUPREMELY WELL.
THE ORB IS HIS TO COMMAND, AND CLEA IS HIS PRISONER.
I'M STILL PUZZLED, MADAME LAVEAU-- WHY ARE YOU HELPING ME?
SELF-INTEREST, MAGE.
ONCE DAGGER SLAYS THE SORCERER SUPREME, IT WON'T BE LONG BEFORE HE COMES FOR ME.
OF COURSE.

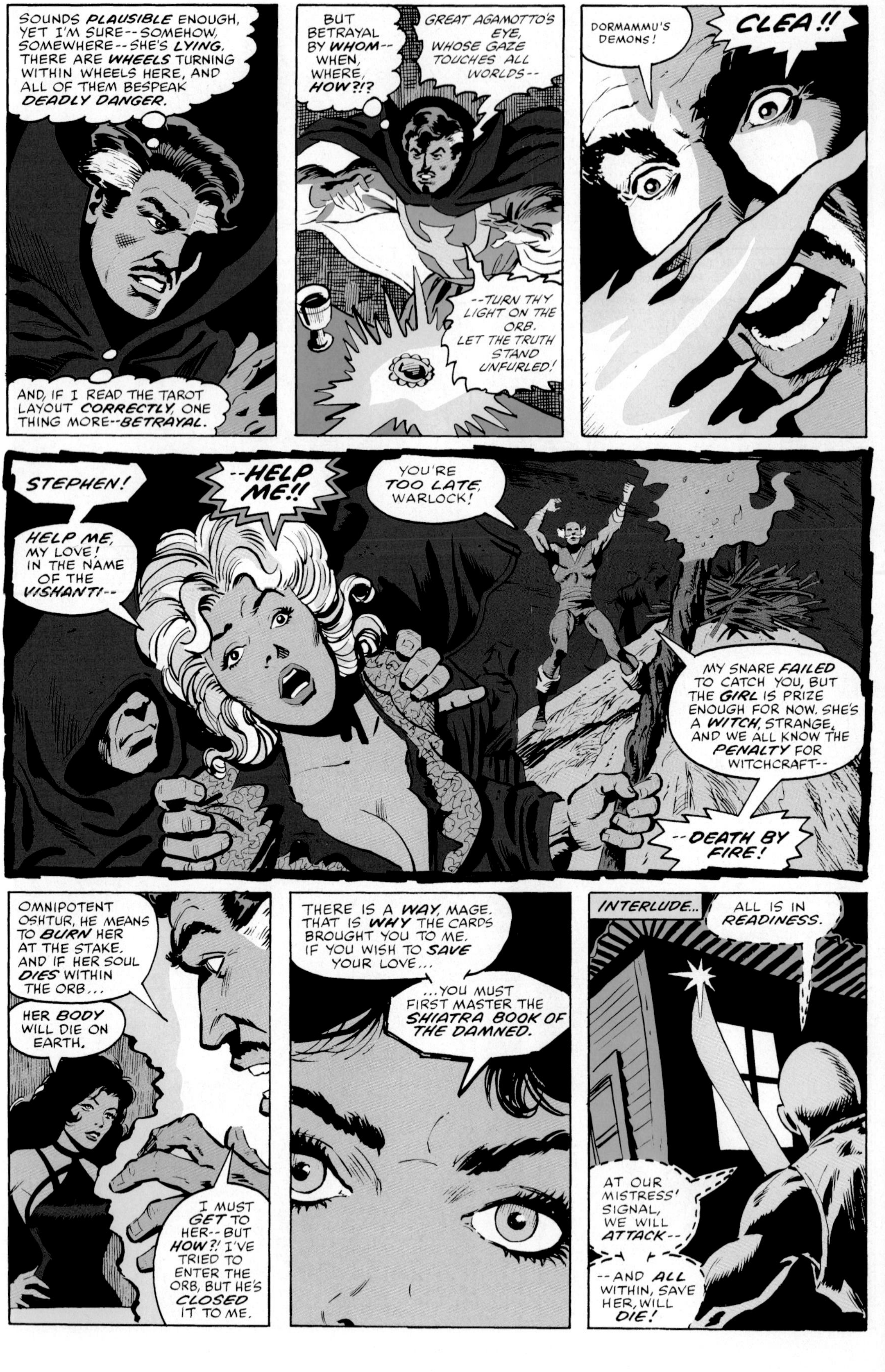

SOUNDS PLAUSIBLE ENOUGH, YET I'M SURE--SOMEHOW, SOMEWHERE--SHE'S LYING. THERE ARE WHEELS TURNING WITHIN WHEELS HERE, AND ALL OF THEM BESPEAK DEADLY DANGER.
AND, IF I READ THE TAROT LAYOUT CORRECTLY, ONE THING MORE--BETRAYAL.
BUT BETRAYAL BY WHOM--WHEN, WHERE, HOW?!?
GREAT AGAMOTTO'S EYE, WHOSE GAZE TOUCHES ALL WORLDS--
--TURN THY LIGHT ON THE ORB. LET THE TRUTH STAND UNFURLED!
DORMAMMU'S DEMONS!
CLEA!!
STEPHEN!
HELP ME, MY LOVE! IN THE NAME OF THE VISHANTI--
--HELP ME!!
YOU'RE TOO LATE, WARLOCK!
MY SNARE FAILED TO CATCH YOU, BUT THE GIRL IS PRIZE ENOUGH FOR NOW. SHE'S A WITCH, STRANGE, AND WE ALL KNOW THE PENALTY FOR WITCHCRAFT--
--DEATH BY FIRE!
OMNIPOTENT OSHTUR, HE MEANS TO BURN HER AT THE STAKE. AND IF HER SOUL DIES WITHIN THE ORB...
HER BODY WILL DIE ON EARTH.
I MUST GET TO HER--BUT HOW?! I'VE TRIED TO ENTER THE ORB, BUT HE'S CLOSED IT TO ME.
THERE IS A WAY, MAGE. THAT IS WHY THE CARDS BROUGHT YOU TO ME. IF YOU WISH TO SAVE YOUR LOVE...
...YOU MUST FIRST MASTER THE SHIATRA BOOK OF THE DAMNED.
INTERLUDE...
ALL IS IN READINESS.
AT OUR MISTRESS' SIGNAL, WE WILL ATTACK--
--AND ALL WITHIN, SAVE HER, WILL DIE!

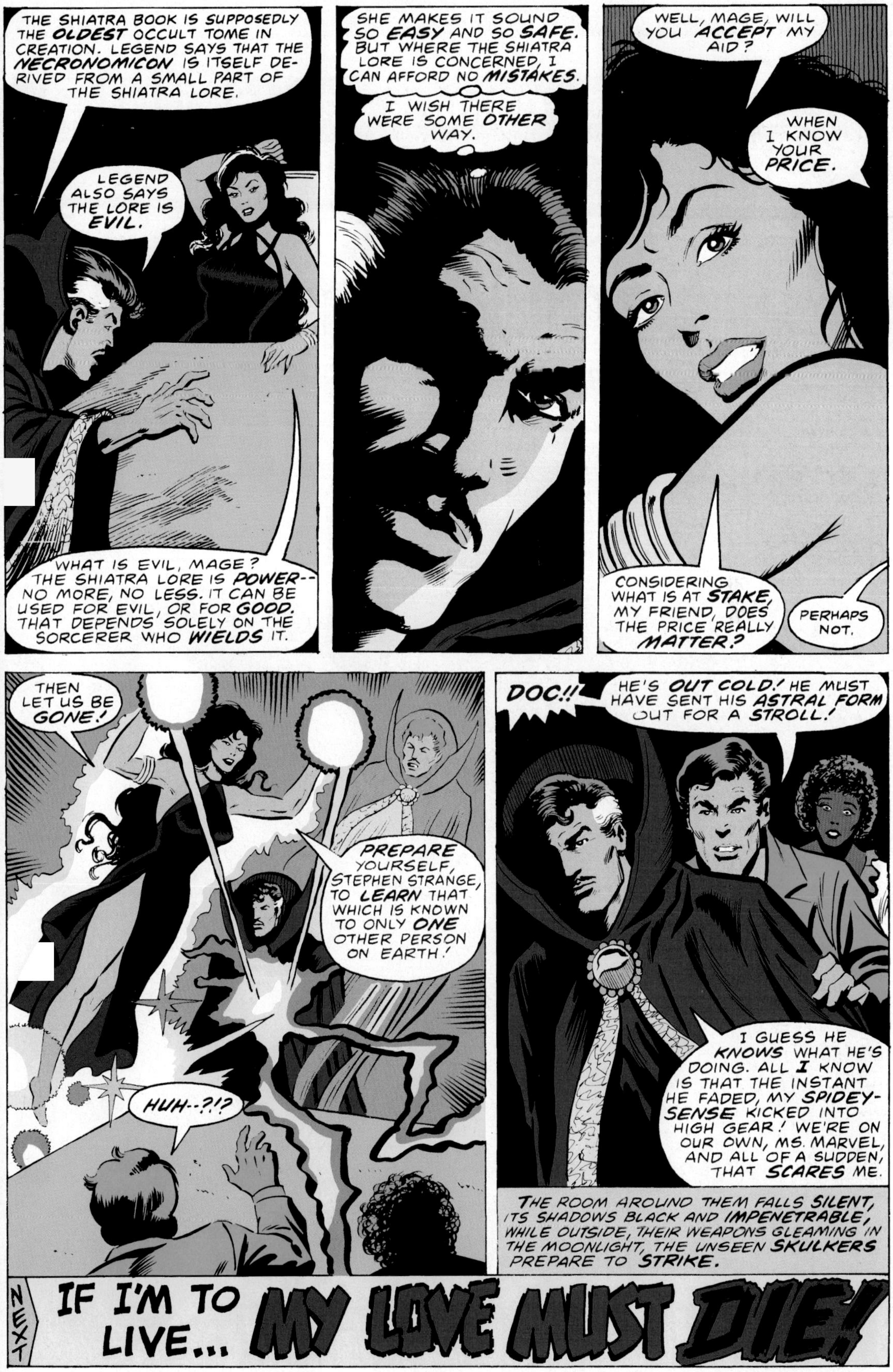

THE SHIATRA BOOK IS SUPPOSEDLY THE OLDEST OCCULT TOME IN CREATION. LEGEND SAYS THAT THE NECRONOMICON IS ITSELF DERIVED FROM A SMALL PART OF THE SHIATRA LORE.
LEGEND ALSO SAYS THE LORE IS EVIL.
WHAT IS EVIL, MAGE? THE SHIATRA LORE IS POWER-- NO MORE, NO LESS. IT CAN BE USED FOR EVIL, OR FOR GOOD. THAT DEPENDS SOLELY ON THE SORCERER WHO WIELDS IT.
SHE MAKES IT SOUND SO EASY AND SO SAFE. BUT WHERE THE SHIATRA LORE IS CONCERNED, I CAN AFFORD NO MISTAKES.
I WISH THERE WERE SOME OTHER WAY.
WELL, MAGE, WILL YOU ACCEPT MY AID?
WHEN I KNOW YOUR PRICE.
CONSIDERING WHAT IS AT STAKE, MY FRIEND, DOES THE PRICE REALLY MATTER?
PERHAPS NOT.
THEN LET US BE GONE!
PREPARE YOURSELF, STEPHEN STRANGE, TO LEARN THAT WHICH IS KNOWN TO ONLY ONE OTHER PERSON ON EARTH!
HUH--?!?
DOC!!
HE'S OUT COLD! HE MUST HAVE SENT HIS ASTRAL FORM OUT FOR A STROLL!
I GUESS HE KNOWS WHAT HE'S DOING. ALL I KNOW IS THAT THE INSTANT HE FADED, MY SPIDEY-SENSE KICKED INTO HIGH GEAR! WE'RE ON OUR OWN, MS. MARVEL, AND ALL OF A SUDDEN, THAT SCARES ME.
THE ROOM AROUND THEM FALLS SILENT, ITS SHADOWS BLACK AND IMPENETRABLE, WHILE OUTSIDE, THEIR WEAPONS GLEAMING IN THE MOONLIGHT, THE UNSEEN SKULKERS PREPARE TO STRIKE.
NEXT
IF I'M TO LIVE... MY LOVE MUST DIE!

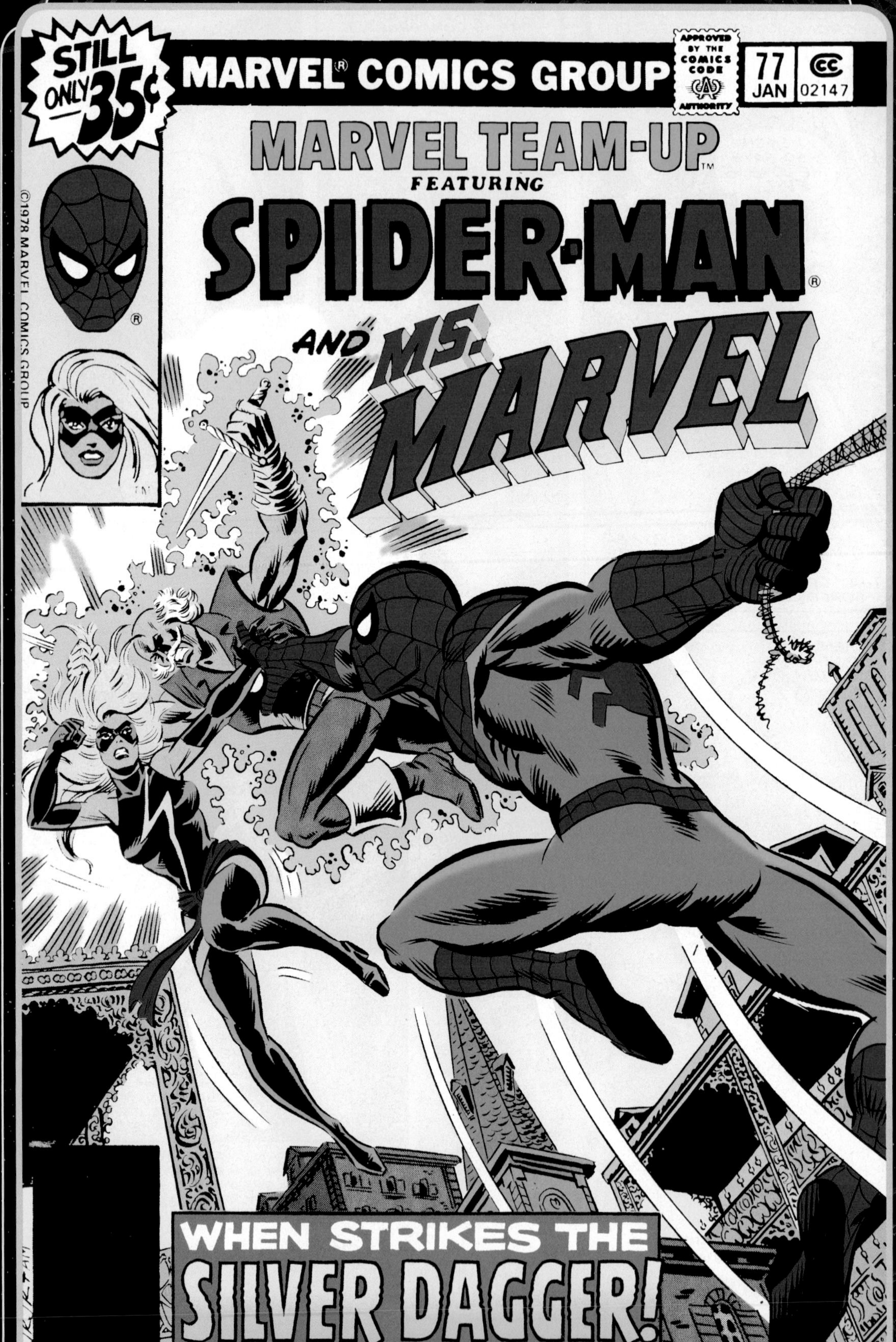
STILL ONLY 35¢
MARVEL® COMICS GROUP
APPROVED BY THE COMICS CODE AUTHORITY
77 JAN
CC 02147
MARVEL TEAM-UP™
FEATURING
SPIDER-MAN®
AND MS. MARVEL
©1978 MARVEL COMICS GROUP
WHEN STRIKES THE
SILVER DAGGER!

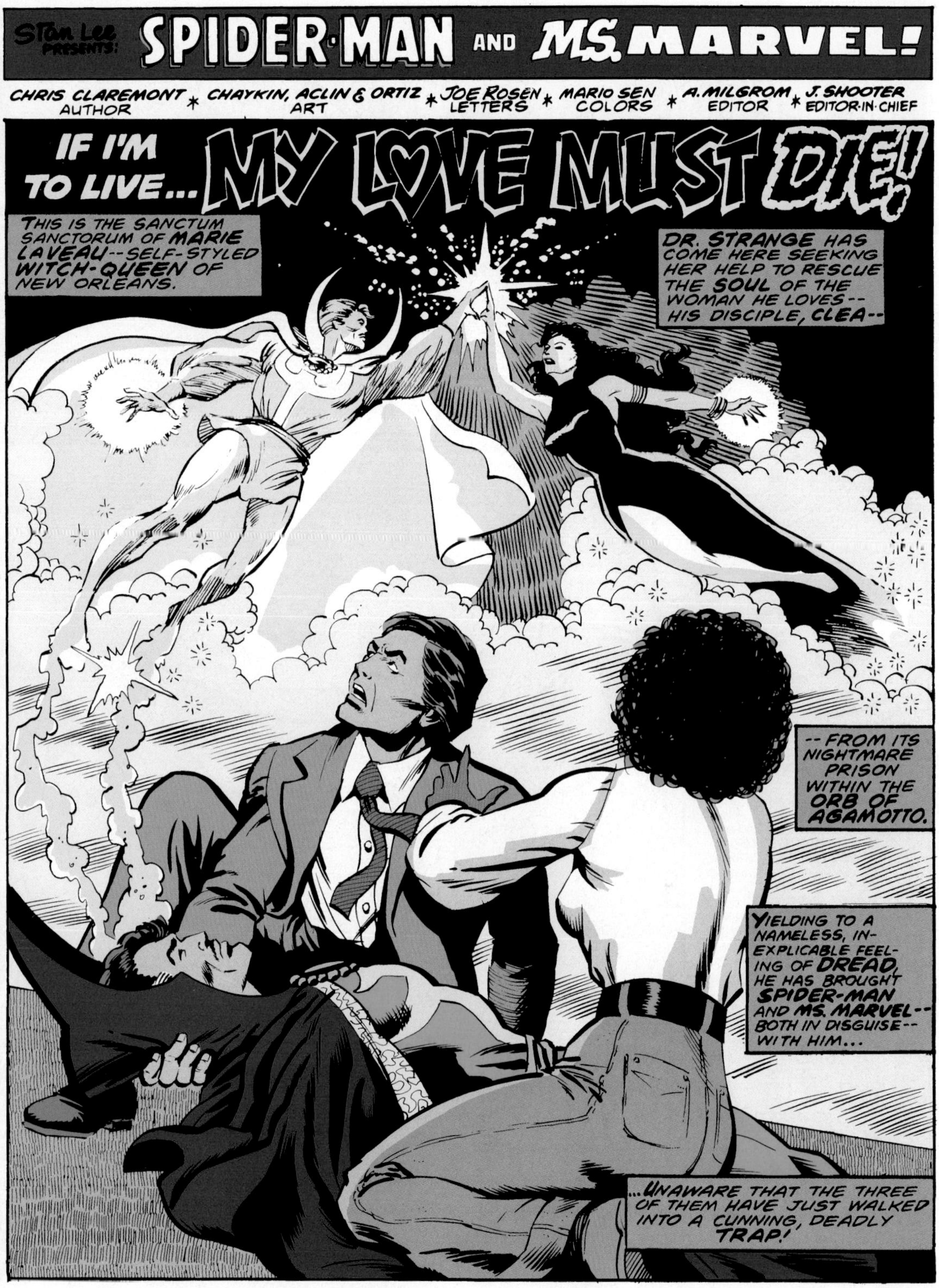

Stan Lee presents: SPIDER-MAN AND MS. MARVEL!
CHRIS CLAREMONT AUTHOR * CHAYKIN, ACLIN & ORTIZ ART * JOE ROSEN LETTERS * MARIO SEN COLORS * A. MILGROM EDITOR * J. SHOOTER EDITOR-IN-CHIEF
IF I'M TO LIVE... MY LOVE MUST DIE!
THIS IS THE SANCTUM SANCTORUM OF MARIE LAVEAU--SELF-STYLED WITCH-QUEEN OF NEW ORLEANS.
DR. STRANGE HAS COME HERE SEEKING HER HELP TO RESCUE THE SOUL OF THE WOMAN HE LOVES--HIS DISCIPLE, CLEA--
--FROM ITS NIGHTMARE PRISON WITHIN THE ORB OF AGAMOTTO.
YIELDING TO A NAMELESS, INEXPLICABLE FEELING OF DREAD, HE HAS BROUGHT SPIDER-MAN AND MS. MARVEL--BOTH IN DISGUISE--WITH HIM...
...UNAWARE THAT THE THREE OF THEM HAVE JUST WALKED INTO A CUNNING, DEADLY TRAP!

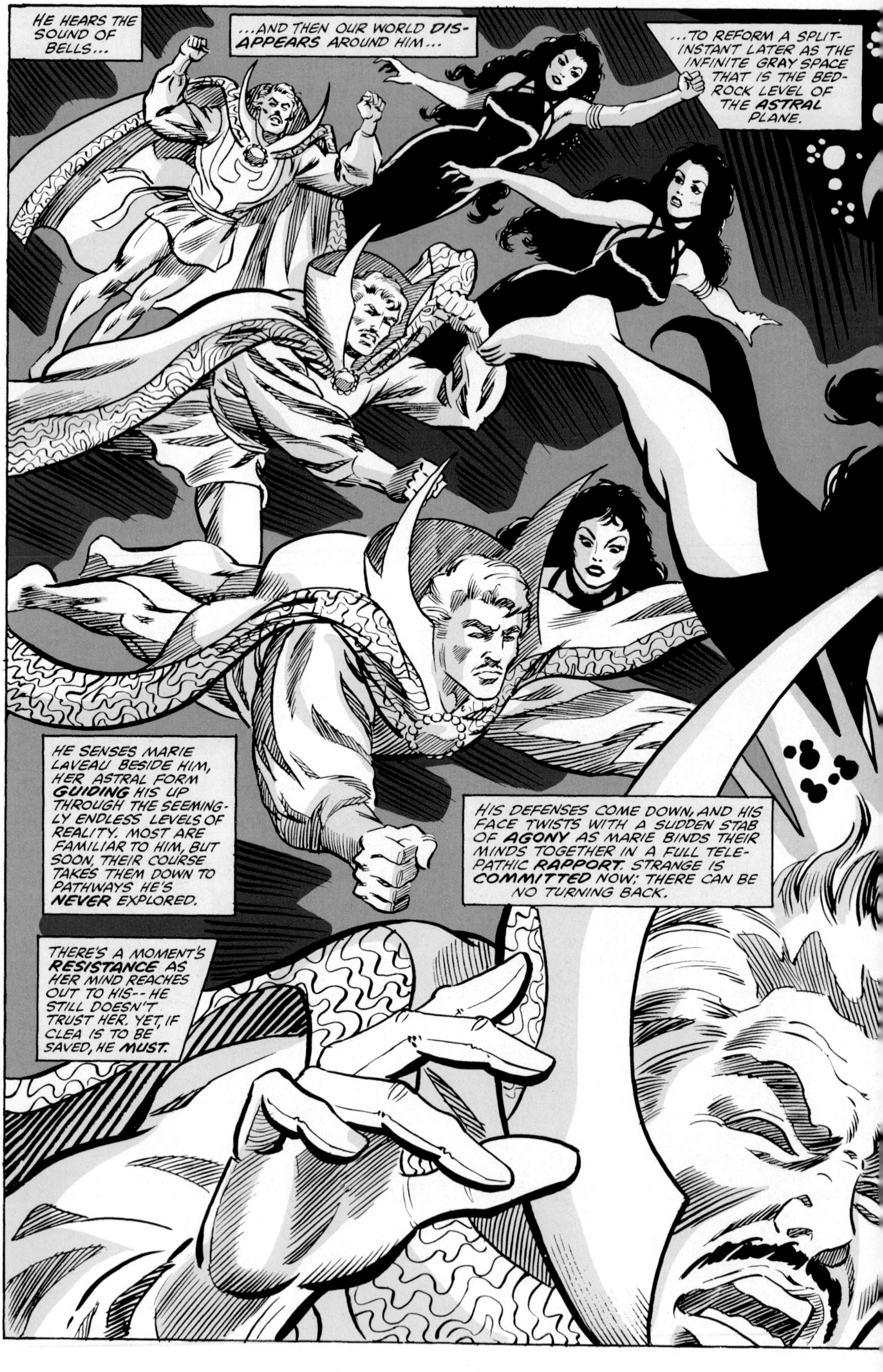
HE HEARS THE SOUND OF BELLS...
...AND THEN OUR WORLD DIS-APPEARS AROUND HIM...
...TO REFORM A SPLIT-INSTANT LATER AS THE INFINITE GRAY SPACE THAT IS THE BED-ROCK LEVEL OF THE ASTRAL PLANE.
HE SENSES MARIE LAVEAU BESIDE HIM, HER ASTRAL FORM GUIDING HIS UP THROUGH THE SEEMING-LY ENDLESS LEVELS OF REALITY. MOST ARE FAMILIAR TO HIM, BUT SOON, THEIR COURSE TAKES THEM DOWN TO PATHWAYS HE'S NEVER EXPLORED.
HIS DEFENSES COME DOWN, AND HIS FACE TWISTS WITH A SUDDEN STAB OF AGONY AS MARIE BINDS THEIR MINDS TOGETHER IN A FULL TELE-PATHIC RAPPORT. STRANGE IS COMMITTED NOW; THERE CAN BE NO TURNING BACK.
THERE'S A MOMENT'S RESISTANCE AS HER MIND REACHES OUT TO HIS-- HE STILL DOESN'T TRUST HER. YET, IF CLEA IS TO BE SAVED, HE MUST.

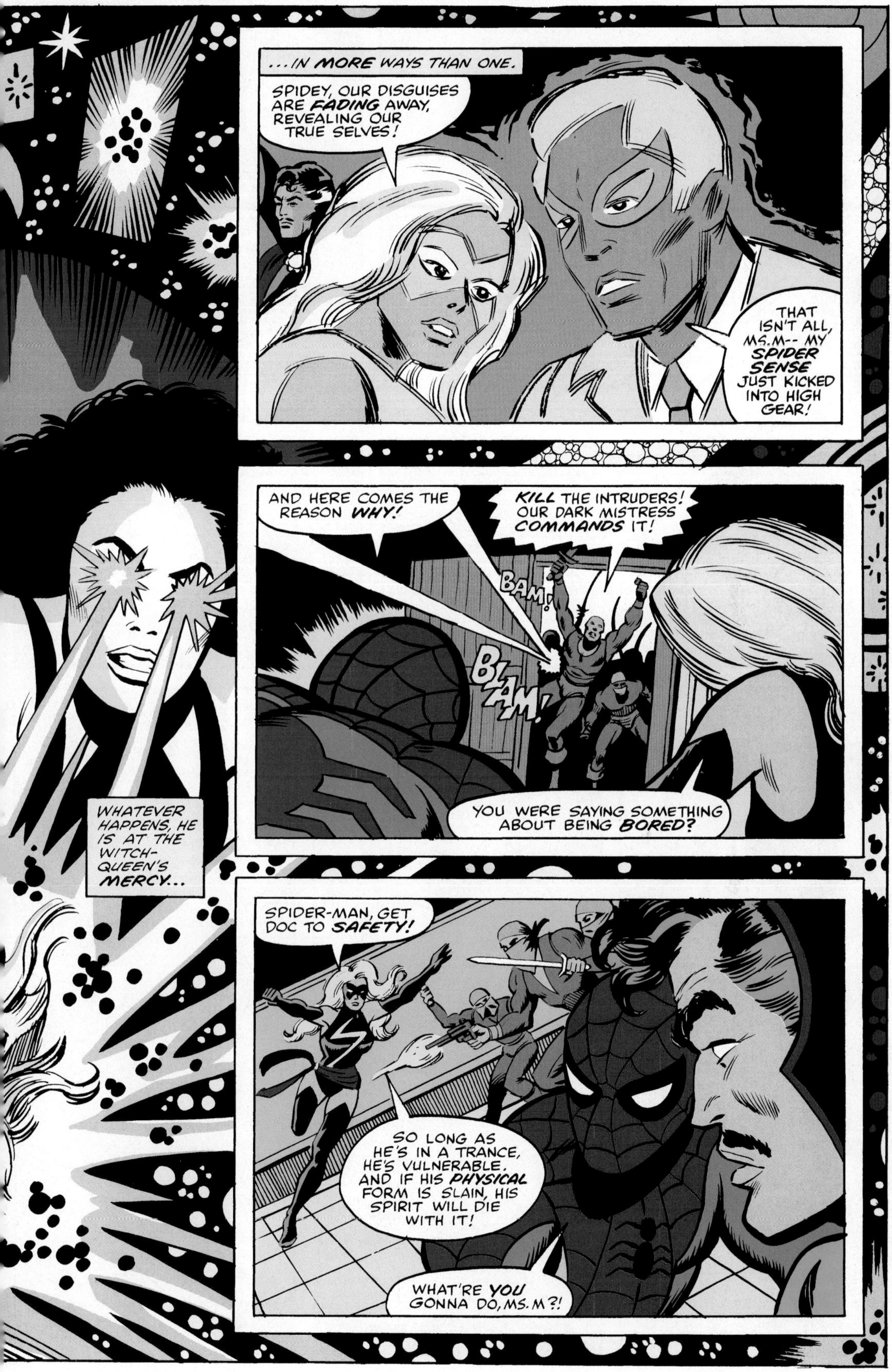
...IN MORE WAYS THAN ONE.
SPIDEY, OUR DISGUISES ARE FADING AWAY, REVEALING OUR TRUE SELVES!
THAT ISN'T ALL, MS.M-- MY SPIDER SENSE JUST KICKED INTO HIGH GEAR!
AND HERE COMES THE REASON WHY!
KILL THE INTRUDERS! OUR DARK MISTRESS COMMANDS IT!
BAM!
BLAM!
YOU WERE SAYING SOMETHING ABOUT BEING BORED?
WHATEVER HAPPENS, HE IS AT THE WITCH-QUEEN'S MERCY...
SPIDER-MAN, GET DOC TO SAFETY!
SO LONG AS HE'S IN A TRANCE, HE'S VULNERABLE. AND IF HIS PHYSICAL FORM IS SLAIN, HIS SPIRIT WILL DIE WITH IT!
WHAT'RE YOU GONNA DO, MS. M?!

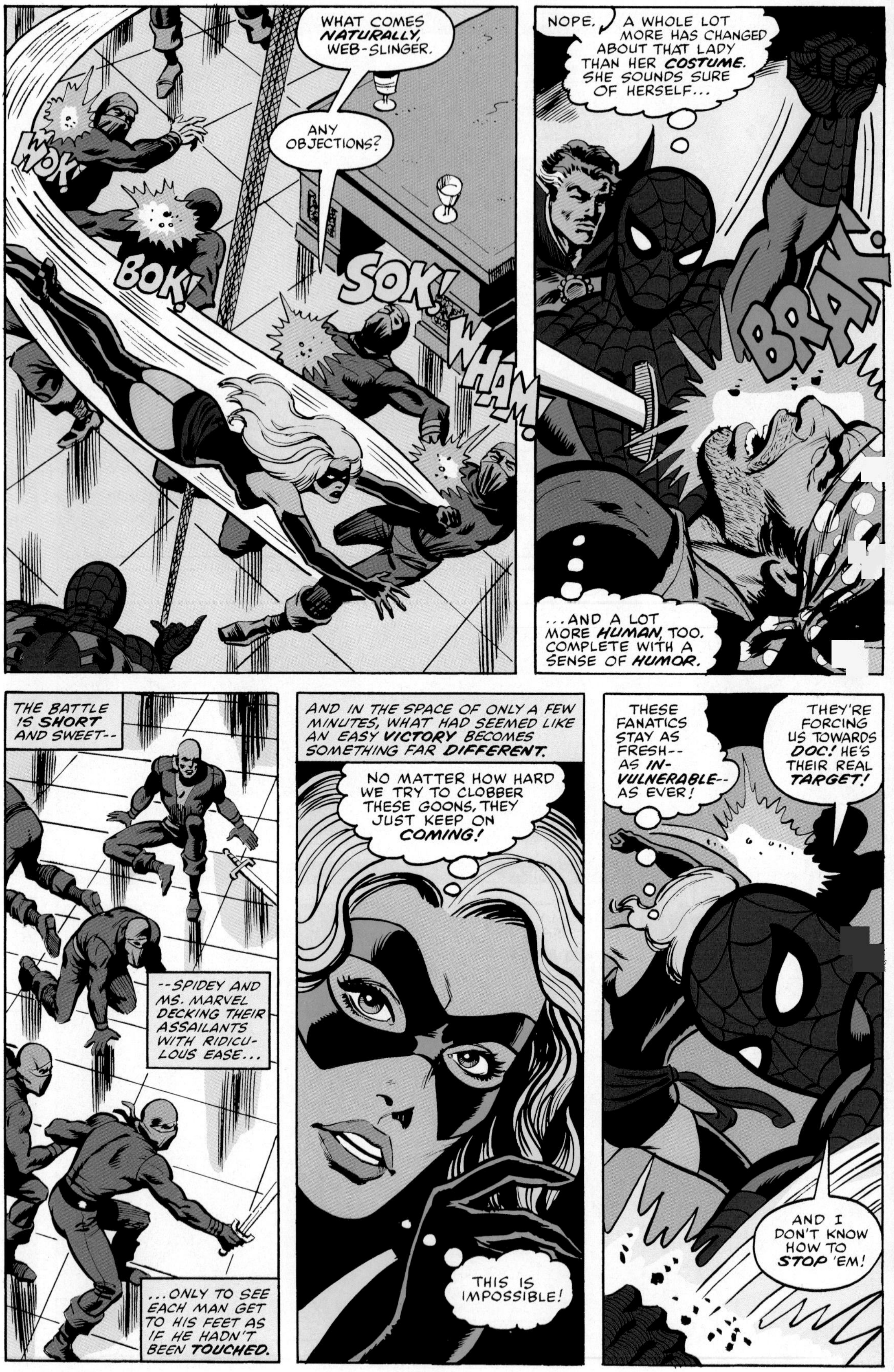
WOK!
BOK!
WHAT COMES NATURALLY, WEB-SLINGER.
ANY OBJECTIONS?
SOK!
WHAM!
NOPE.
A WHOLE LOT MORE HAS CHANGED ABOUT THAT LADY THAN HER COSTUME. SHE SOUNDS SURE OF HERSELF...
BRAK!
...AND A LOT MORE HUMAN, TOO. COMPLETE WITH A SENSE OF HUMOR.
THE BATTLE IS SHORT AND SWEET--
--SPIDEY AND MS. MARVEL DECKING THEIR ASSAILANTS WITH RIDICULOUS EASE...
...ONLY TO SEE EACH MAN GET TO HIS FEET AS IF HE HADN'T BEEN TOUCHED.
AND IN THE SPACE OF ONLY A FEW MINUTES, WHAT HAD SEEMED LIKE AN EASY VICTORY BECOMES SOMETHING FAR DIFFERENT.
NO MATTER HOW HARD WE TRY TO CLOBBER THESE GOONS, THEY JUST KEEP ON COMING!
THIS IS IMPOSSIBLE!
THESE FANATICS STAY AS FRESH-- AS INVULNERABLE-- AS EVER!
THEY'RE FORCING US TOWARDS DOC! HE'S THEIR REAL TARGET!
AND I DON'T KNOW HOW TO STOP 'EM!

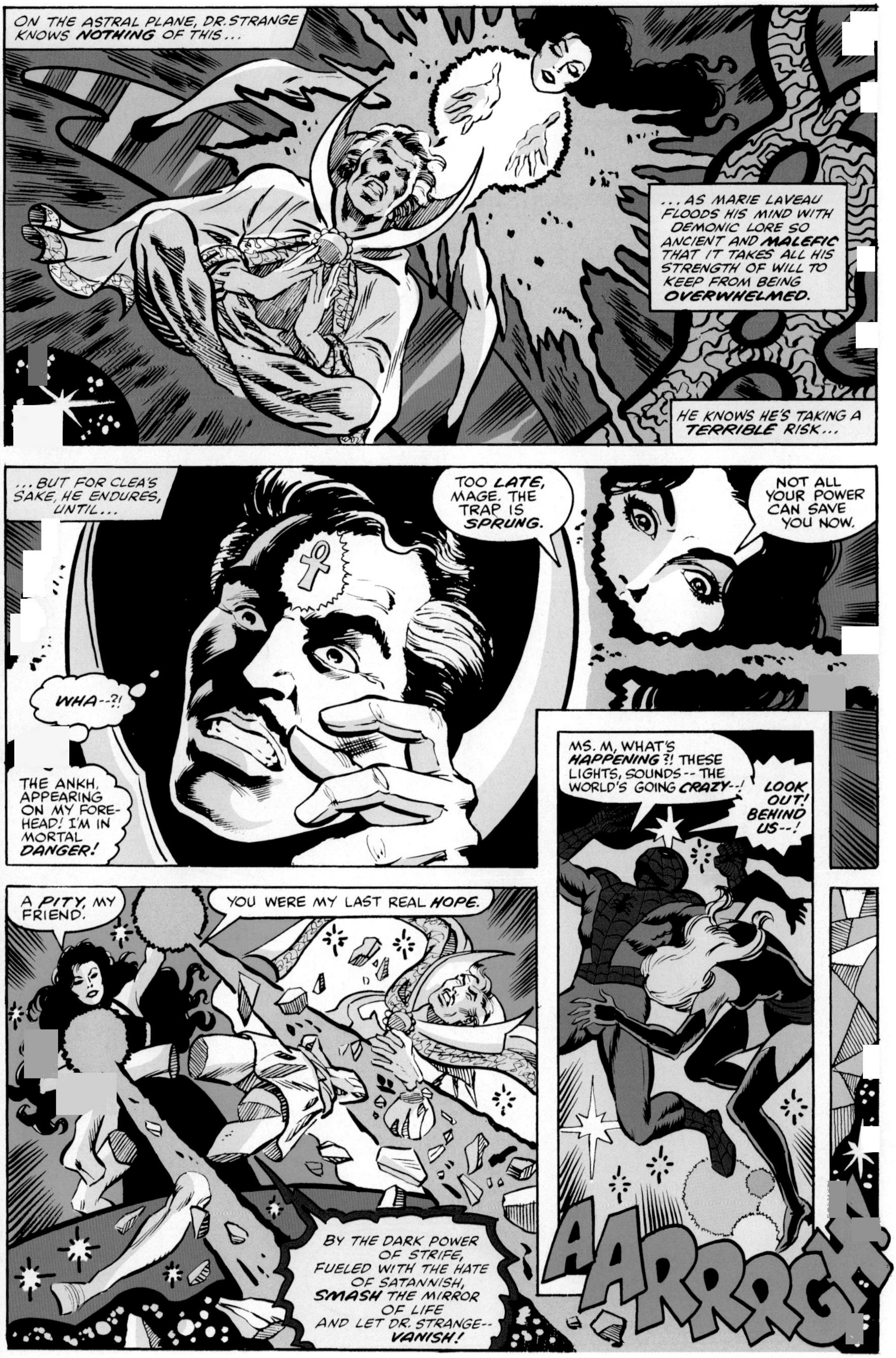

ON THE ASTRAL PLANE, DR. STRANGE KNOWS NOTHING OF THIS...
...AS MARIE LAVEAU FLOODS HIS MIND WITH DEMONIC LORE SO ANCIENT AND MALEFIC THAT IT TAKES ALL HIS STRENGTH OF WILL TO KEEP FROM BEING OVERWHELMED.
HE KNOWS HE'S TAKING A TERRIBLE RISK...
...BUT FOR CLEA'S SAKE, HE ENDURES, UNTIL...
TOO LATE, MAGE. THE TRAP IS SPRUNG.
NOT ALL YOUR POWER CAN SAVE YOU NOW.
WHA--?!
THE ANKH, APPEARING ON MY FOREHEAD! I'M IN MORTAL DANGER!
MS. M, WHAT'S HAPPENING?! THESE LIGHTS, SOUNDS-- THE WORLD'S GOING CRAZY--!
LOOK OUT! BEHIND US--!
A PITY, MY FRIEND.
YOU WERE MY LAST REAL HOPE.
BY THE DARK POWER OF STRIFE, FUELED WITH THE HATE OF SATANNISH, SMASH THE MIRROR OF LIFE AND LET DR. STRANGE-- VANISH!
AARRRGH

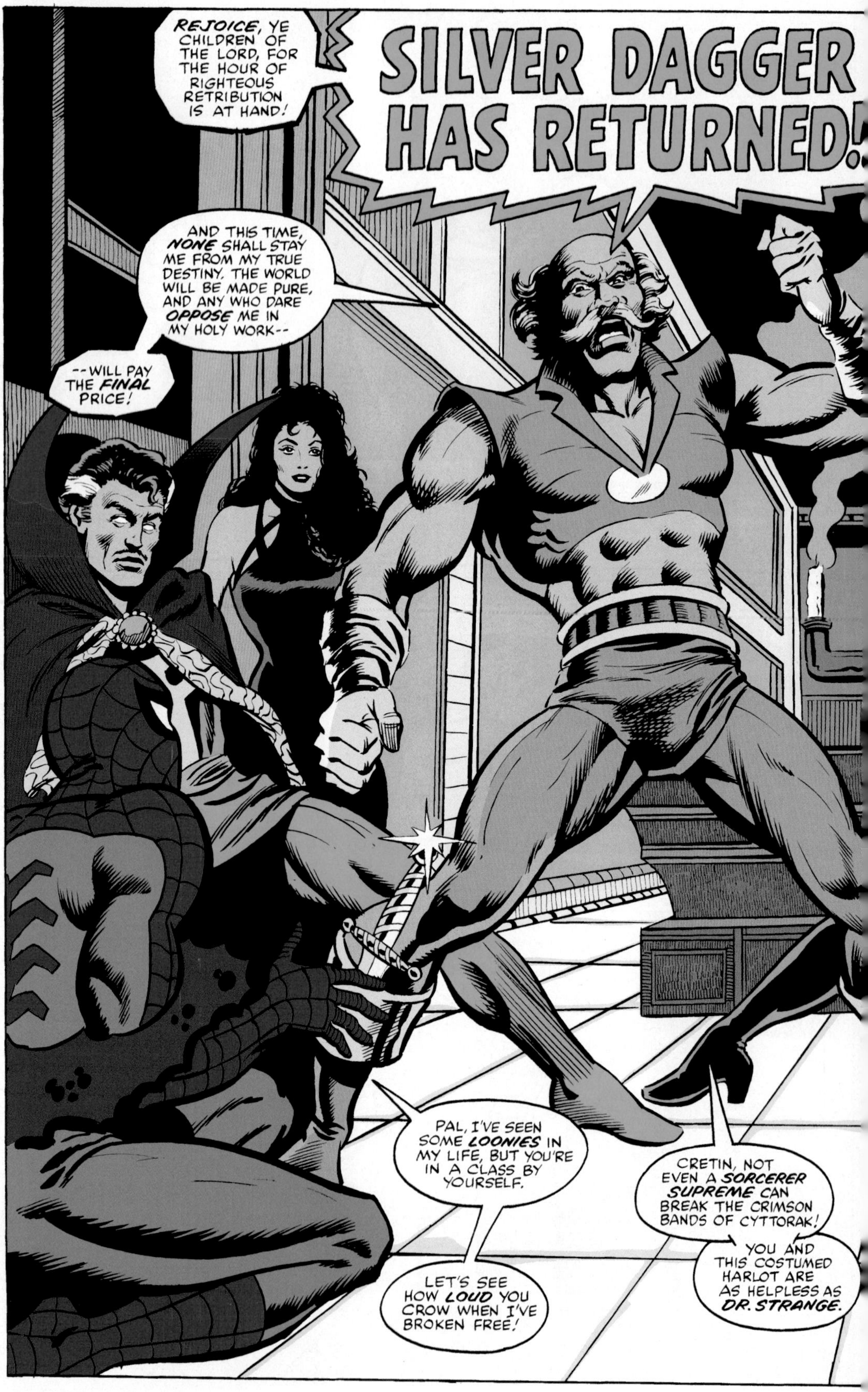
REJOICE, YE CHILDREN OF THE LORD, FOR THE HOUR OF RIGHTEOUS RETRIBUTION IS AT HAND!
SILVER DAGGER HAS RETURNED!
AND THIS TIME, NONE SHALL STAY ME FROM MY TRUE DESTINY. THE WORLD WILL BE MADE PURE, AND ANY WHO DARE OPPOSE ME IN MY HOLY WORK--
--WILL PAY THE FINAL PRICE!
PAL, I'VE SEEN SOME LOONIES IN MY LIFE, BUT YOU'RE IN A CLASS BY YOURSELF.
LET'S SEE HOW LOUD YOU CROW WHEN I'VE BROKEN FREE!
CRETIN, NOT EVEN A SORCERER SUPREME CAN BREAK THE CRIMSON BANDS OF CYTTORAK!
YOU AND THIS COSTUMED HARLOT ARE AS HELPLESS AS DR. STRANGE.

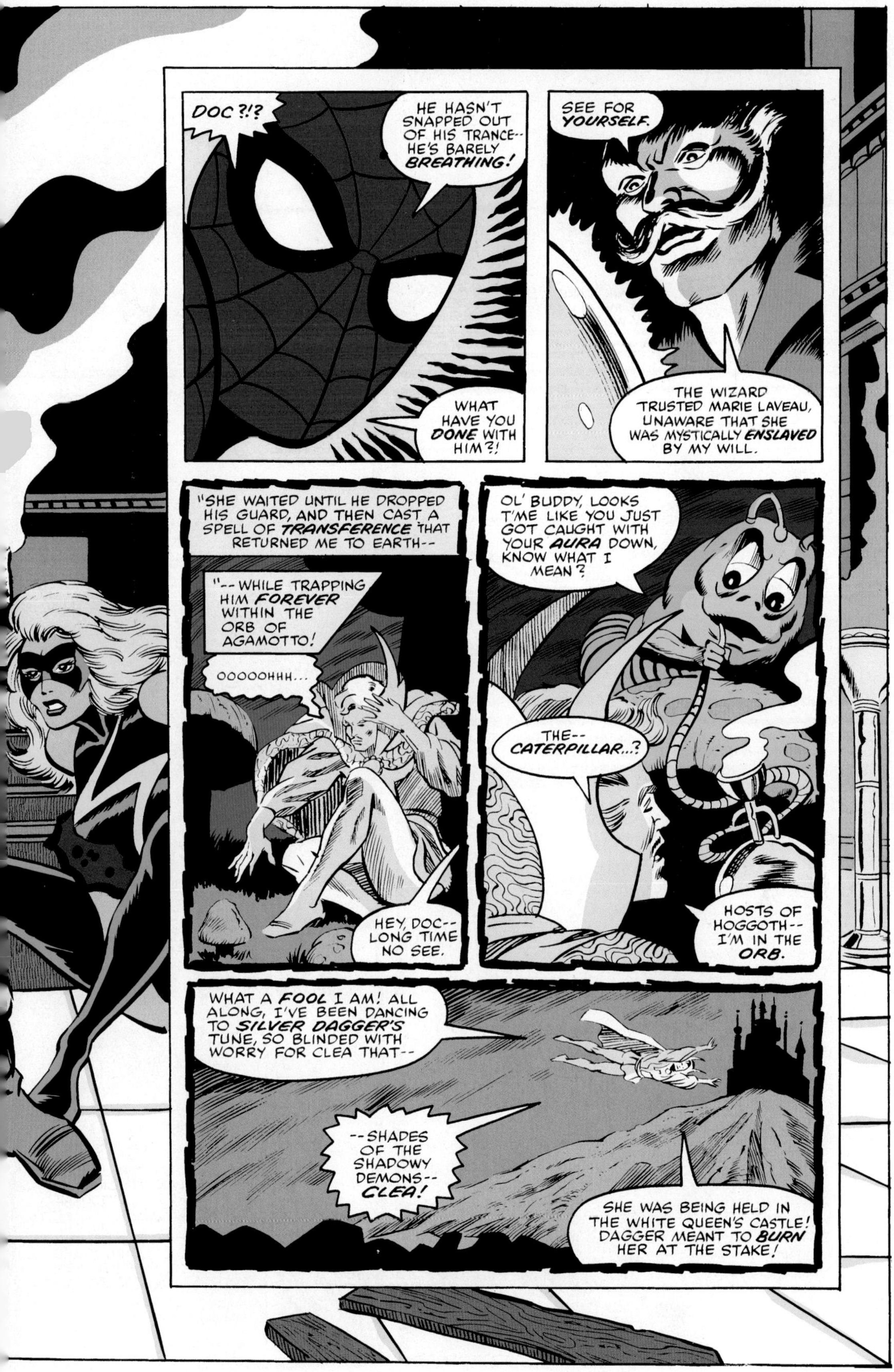
DOC?!?
HE HASN'T SNAPPED OUT OF HIS TRANCE-- HE'S BARELY BREATHING!
WHAT HAVE YOU DONE WITH HIM?!
SEE FOR YOURSELF.
THE WIZARD TRUSTED MARIE LAVEAU, UNAWARE THAT SHE WAS MYSTICALLY ENSLAVED BY MY WILL.
"SHE WAITED UNTIL HE DROPPED HIS GUARD, AND THEN CAST A SPELL OF TRANSFERENCE THAT RETURNED ME TO EARTH--
"--WHILE TRAPPING HIM FOREVER WITHIN THE ORB OF AGAMOTTO!
OOOOOHHH...
HEY, DOC-- LONG TIME NO SEE.
OL' BUDDY, LOOKS T'ME LIKE YOU JUST GOT CAUGHT WITH YOUR AURA DOWN, KNOW WHAT I MEAN?
THE-- CATERPILLAR...?
HOSTS OF HOGGOTH-- I'M IN THE ORB.
WHAT A FOOL I AM! ALL ALONG, I'VE BEEN DANCING TO SILVER DAGGER'S TUNE, SO BLINDED WITH WORRY FOR CLEA THAT--
--SHADES OF THE SHADOWY DEMONS-- CLEA!
SHE WAS BEING HELD IN THE WHITE QUEEN'S CASTLE! DAGGER MEANT TO BURN HER AT THE STAKE!

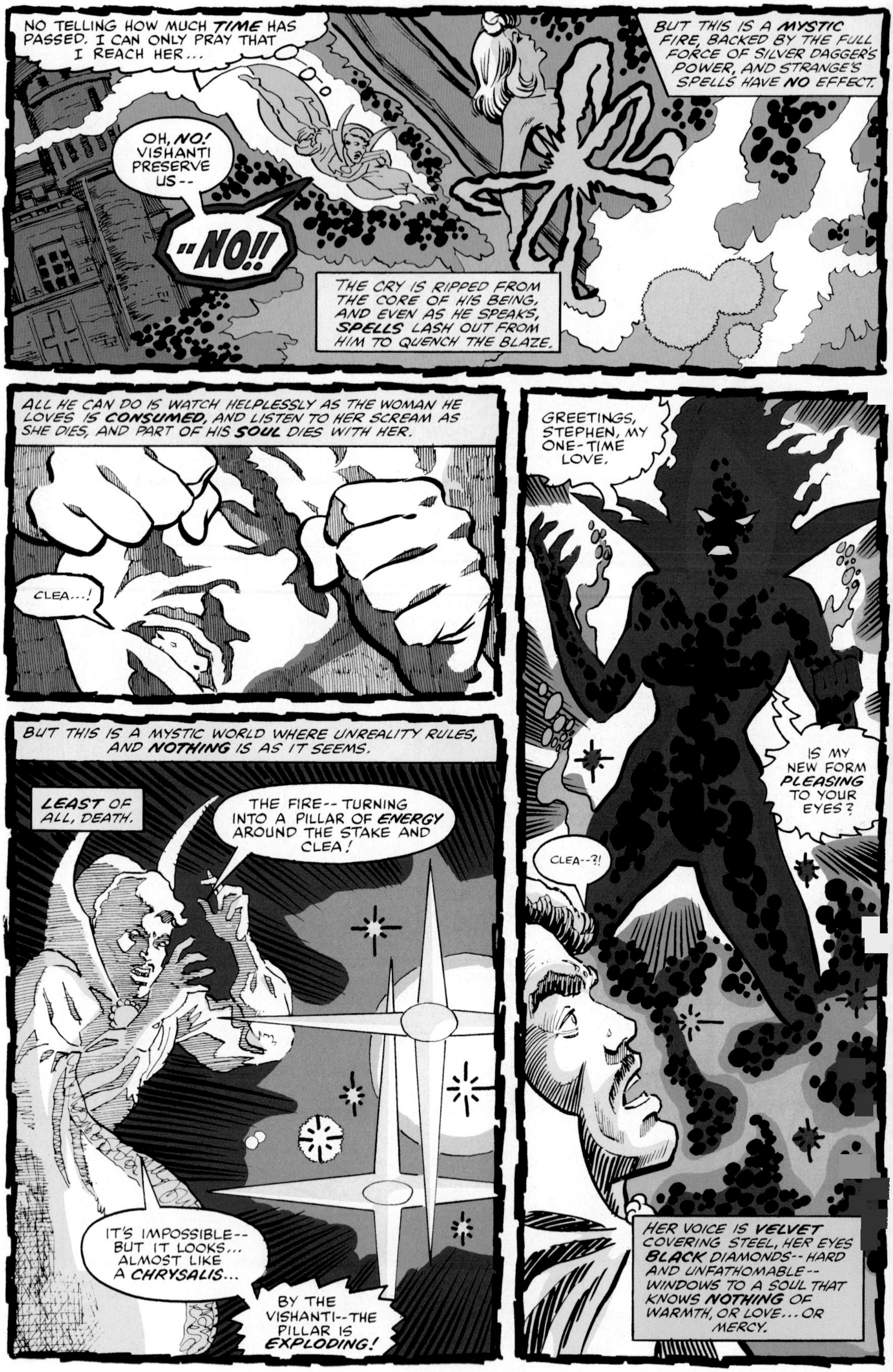
NO TELLING HOW MUCH TIME HAS PASSED. I CAN ONLY PRAY THAT I REACH HER...
BUT THIS IS A MYSTIC FIRE, BACKED BY THE FULL FORCE OF SILVER DAGGER'S POWER, AND STRANGE'S SPELLS HAVE NO EFFECT.
OH, NO! VISHANTI PRESERVE US--
--NO!!
THE CRY IS RIPPED FROM THE CORE OF HIS BEING, AND EVEN AS HE SPEAKS, SPELLS LASH OUT FROM HIM TO QUENCH THE BLAZE.
ALL HE CAN DO IS WATCH HELPLESSLY AS THE WOMAN HE LOVES IS CONSUMED, AND LISTEN TO HER SCREAM AS SHE DIES, AND PART OF HIS SOUL DIES WITH HER.
CLEA...!
BUT THIS IS A MYSTIC WORLD WHERE UNREALITY RULES, AND NOTHING IS AS IT SEEMS.
LEAST OF ALL, DEATH.
THE FIRE-- TURNING INTO A PILLAR OF ENERGY AROUND THE STAKE AND CLEA!
IT'S IMPOSSIBLE-- BUT IT LOOKS... ALMOST LIKE A CHRYSALIS...
BY THE VISHANTI--THE PILLAR IS EXPLODING!
GREETINGS, STEPHEN, MY ONE-TIME LOVE.
IS MY NEW FORM PLEASING TO YOUR EYES?
CLEA--?!
HER VOICE IS VELVET COVERING STEEL, HER EYES BLACK DIAMONDS-- HARD AND UNFATHOMABLE-- WINDOWS TO A SOUL THAT KNOWS NOTHING OF WARMTH, OR LOVE... OR MERCY.

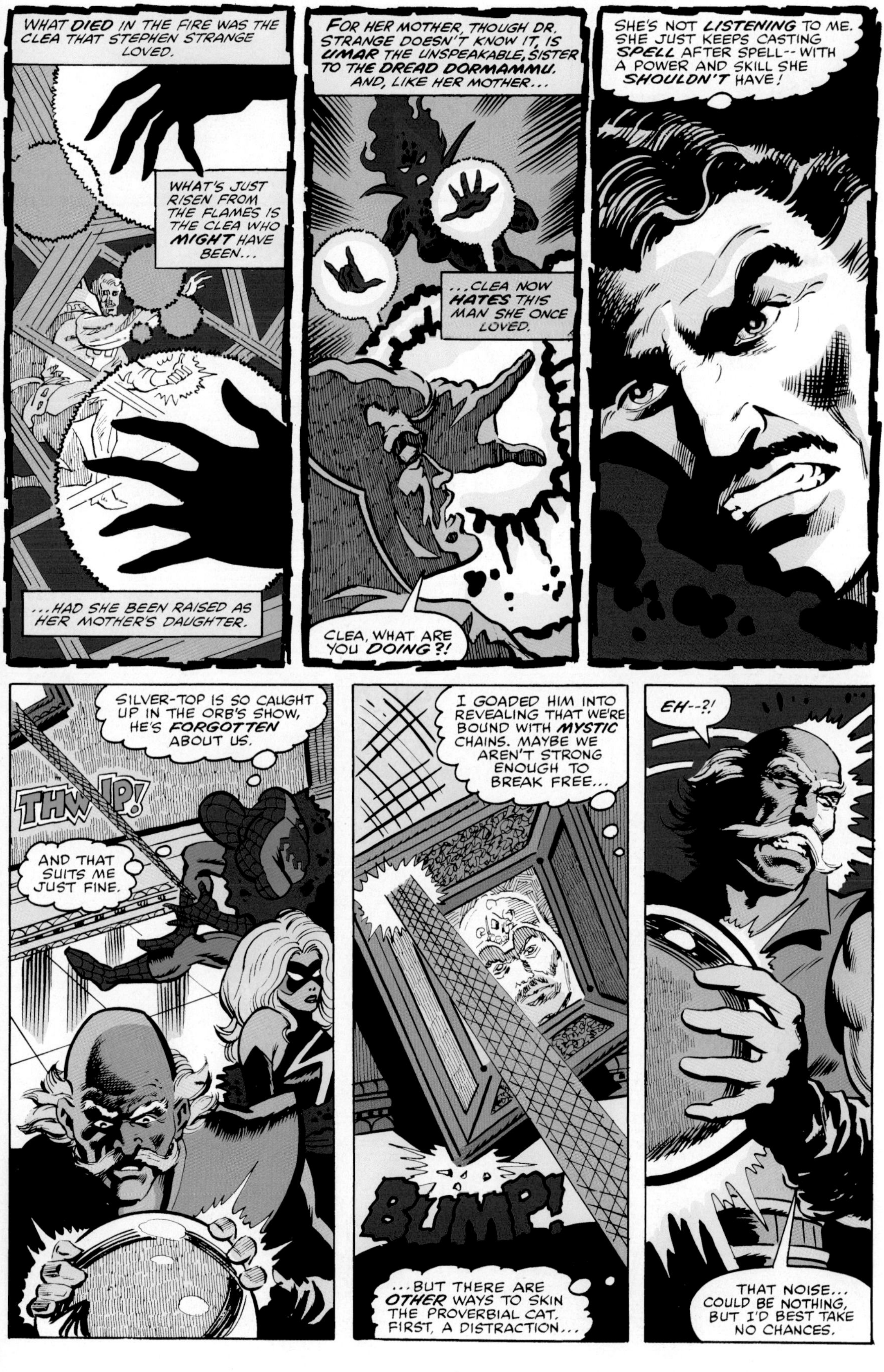
WHAT DIED IN THE FIRE WAS THE CLEA THAT STEPHEN STRANGE LOVED.
WHAT'S JUST RISEN FROM THE FLAMES IS THE CLEA WHO MIGHT HAVE BEEN...
...HAD SHE BEEN RAISED AS HER MOTHER'S DAUGHTER.
FOR HER MOTHER, THOUGH DR. STRANGE DOESN'T KNOW IT, IS UMAR THE UNSPEAKABLE, SISTER TO THE DREAD DORMAMMU. AND, LIKE HER MOTHER...
...CLEA NOW HATES THIS MAN SHE ONCE LOVED.
CLEA, WHAT ARE YOU DOING?!
SHE'S NOT LISTENING TO ME. SHE JUST KEEPS CASTING SPELL AFTER SPELL-- WITH A POWER AND SKILL SHE SHOULDN'T HAVE!
SILVER-TOP IS SO CAUGHT UP IN THE ORB'S SHOW, HE'S FORGOTTEN ABOUT US.
THWIP!
AND THAT SUITS ME JUST FINE.
I GOADED HIM INTO REVEALING THAT WE'RE BOUND WITH MYSTIC CHAINS. MAYBE WE AREN'T STRONG ENOUGH TO BREAK FREE...
BUMP!
...BUT THERE ARE OTHER WAYS TO SKIN THE PROVERBIAL CAT. FIRST, A DISTRACTION...
EH--?!
THAT NOISE... COULD BE NOTHING, BUT I'D BEST TAKE NO CHANCES.

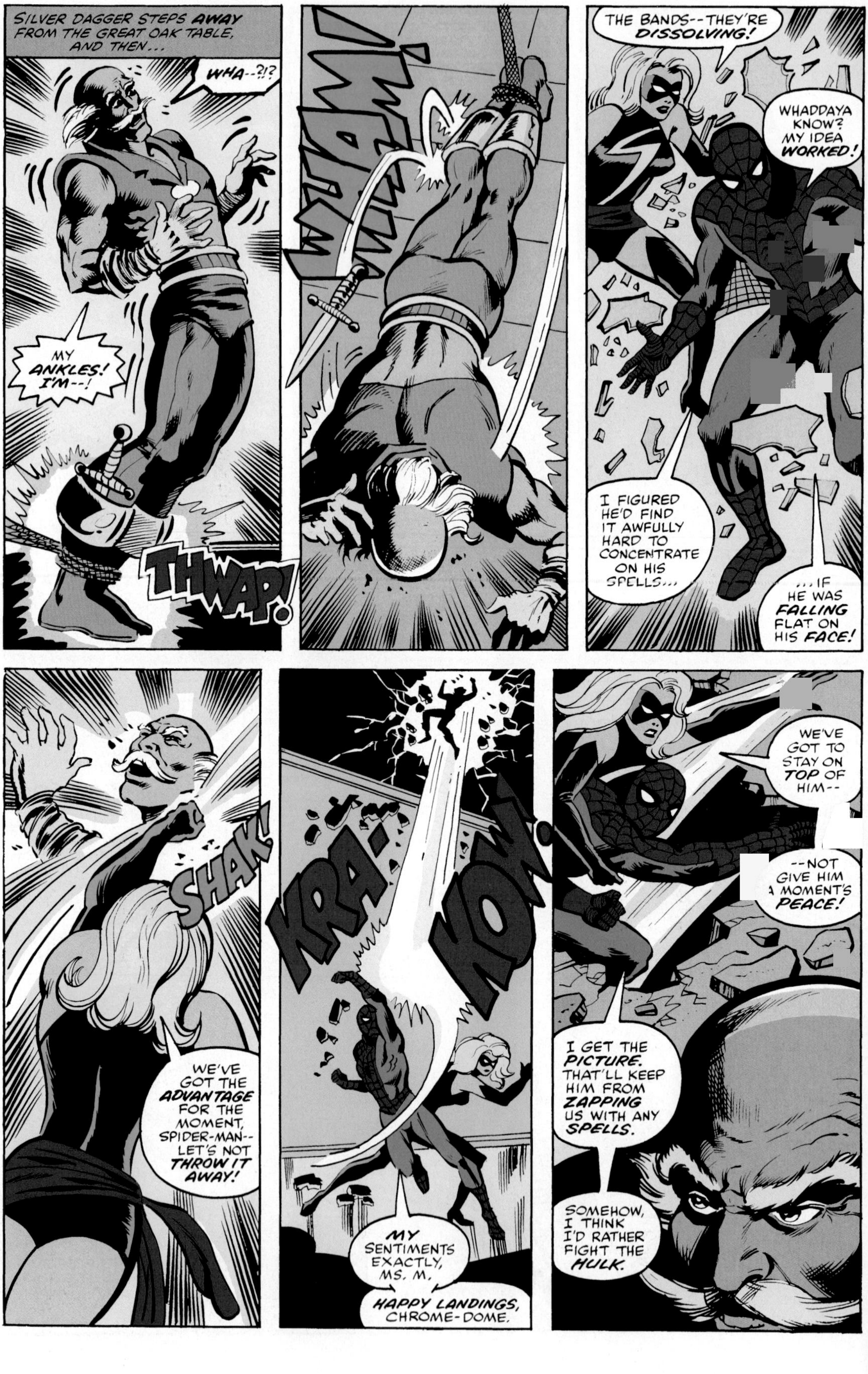
SILVER DAGGER STEPS AWAY FROM THE GREAT OAK TABLE, AND THEN...
WHA--?!?
MY ANKLES! I'M--!
THWAP!
WHAM!
THE BANDS--THEY'RE DISSOLVING!
WHADDAYA KNOW? MY IDEA WORKED!
I FIGURED HE'D FIND IT AWFULLY HARD TO CONCENTRATE ON HIS SPELLS...
...IF HE WAS FALLING FLAT ON HIS FACE!
SHAK!
WE'VE GOT THE ADVANTAGE FOR THE MOMENT, SPIDER-MAN-- LET'S NOT THROW IT AWAY!
KRA-KOW!
MY SENTIMENTS EXACTLY, MS. M.
HAPPY LANDINGS, CHROME-DOME.
WE'VE GOT TO STAY ON TOP OF HIM--
--NOT GIVE HIM A MOMENT'S PEACE!
I GET THE PICTURE. THAT'LL KEEP HIM FROM ZAPPING US WITH ANY SPELLS.
SOMEHOW, I THINK I'D RATHER FIGHT THE HULK.

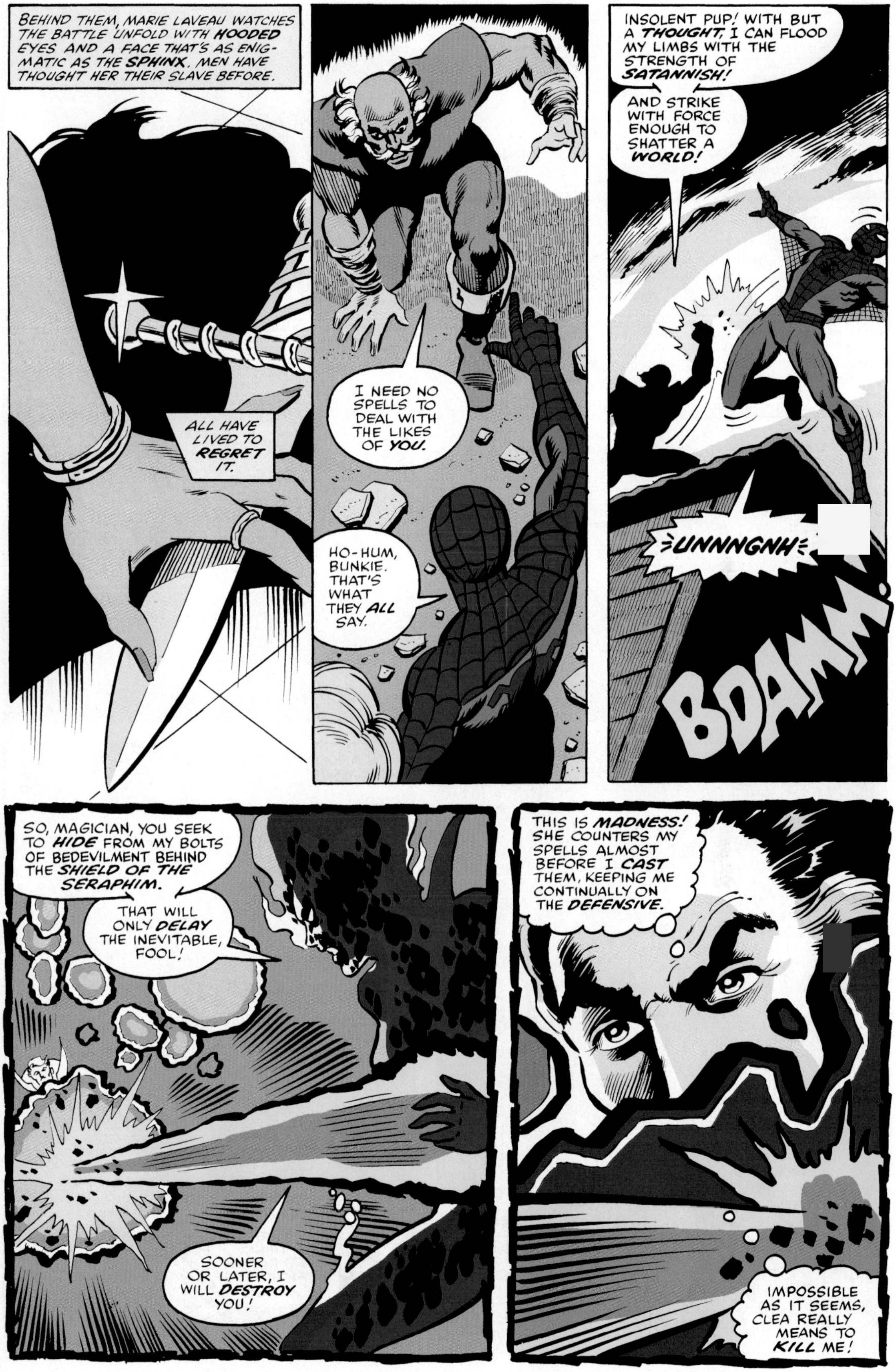
BEHIND THEM, MARIE LAVEAU WATCHES THE BATTLE UNFOLD WITH HOODED EYES AND A FACE THAT'S AS ENIGMATIC AS THE SPHINX. MEN HAVE THOUGHT HER THEIR SLAVE BEFORE.
ALL HAVE LIVED TO REGRET IT.
I NEED NO SPELLS TO DEAL WITH THE LIKES OF YOU.
HO-HUM, BUNKIE. THAT'S WHAT THEY ALL SAY.
INSOLENT PUP! WITH BUT A THOUGHT, I CAN FLOOD MY LIMBS WITH THE STRENGTH OF SATANNISH!
AND STRIKE WITH FORCE ENOUGH TO SHATTER A WORLD!
UNNNGNH
BDAMM!
SO, MAGICIAN, YOU SEEK TO HIDE FROM MY BOLTS OF BEDEVILMENT BEHIND THE SHIELD OF THE SERAPHIM.
THAT WILL ONLY DELAY THE INEVITABLE, FOOL!
SOONER OR LATER, I WILL DESTROY YOU!
THIS IS MADNESS! SHE COUNTERS MY SPELLS ALMOST BEFORE I CAST THEM, KEEPING ME CONTINUALLY ON THE DEFENSIVE.
IMPOSSIBLE AS IT SEEMS, CLEA REALLY MEANS TO KILL ME!

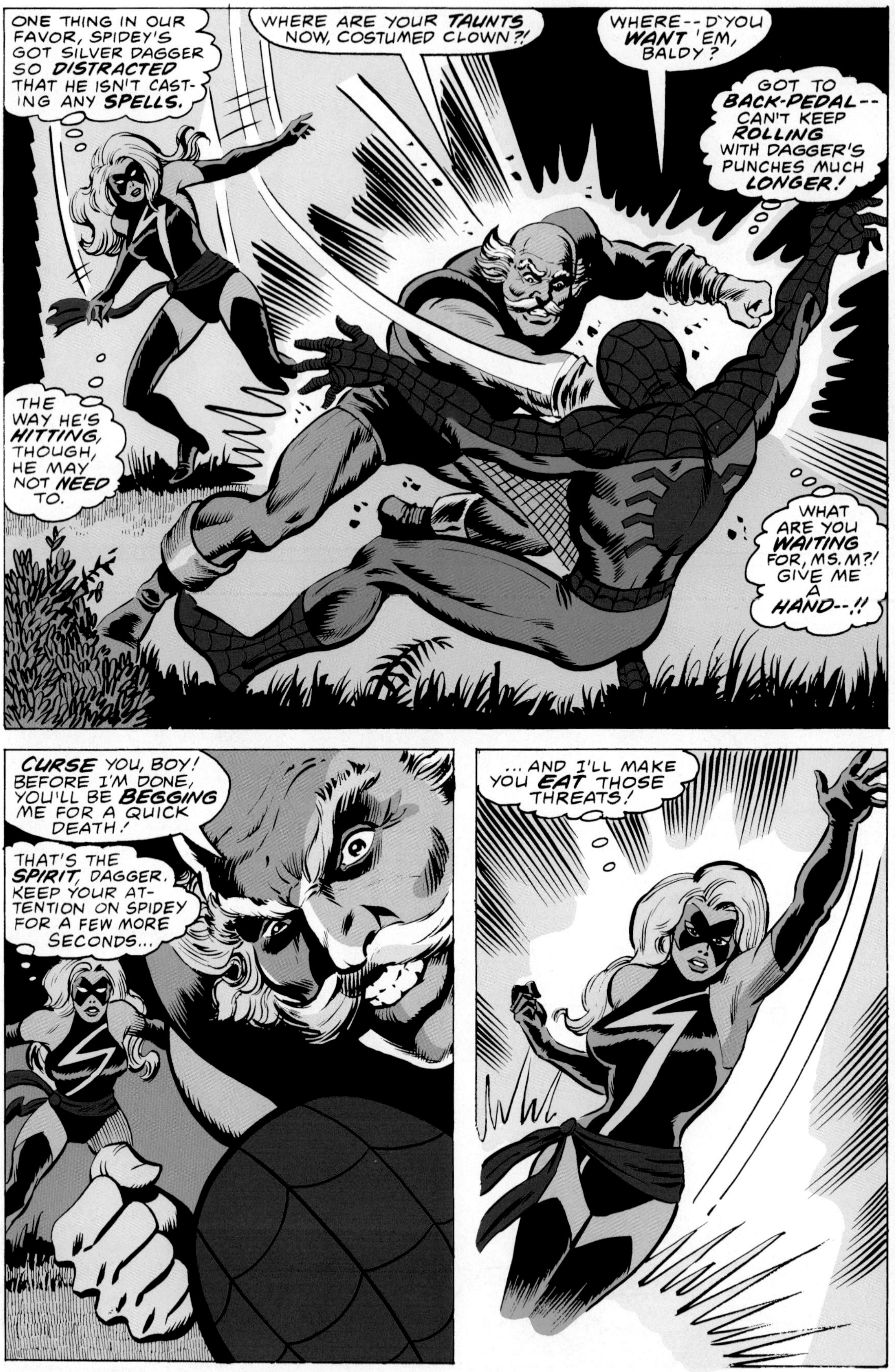
ONE THING IN OUR FAVOR, SPIDEY'S GOT SILVER DAGGER SO DISTRACTED THAT HE ISN'T CAST-ING ANY SPELLS.
WHERE ARE YOUR TAUNTS NOW, COSTUMED CLOWN?!
WHERE--D'YOU WANT 'EM, BALDY?
GOT TO BACK-PEDAL--CAN'T KEEP ROLLING WITH DAGGER'S PUNCHES MUCH LONGER!
THE WAY HE'S HITTING, THOUGH, HE MAY NOT NEED TO.
WHAT ARE YOU WAITING FOR, MS. M?! GIVE ME A HAND--!!
CURSE YOU, BOY! BEFORE I'M DONE, YOU'LL BE BEGGING ME FOR A QUICK DEATH!
THAT'S THE SPIRIT, DAGGER. KEEP YOUR AT-TENTION ON SPIDEY FOR A FEW MORE SECONDS...
...AND I'LL MAKE YOU EAT THOSE THREATS!

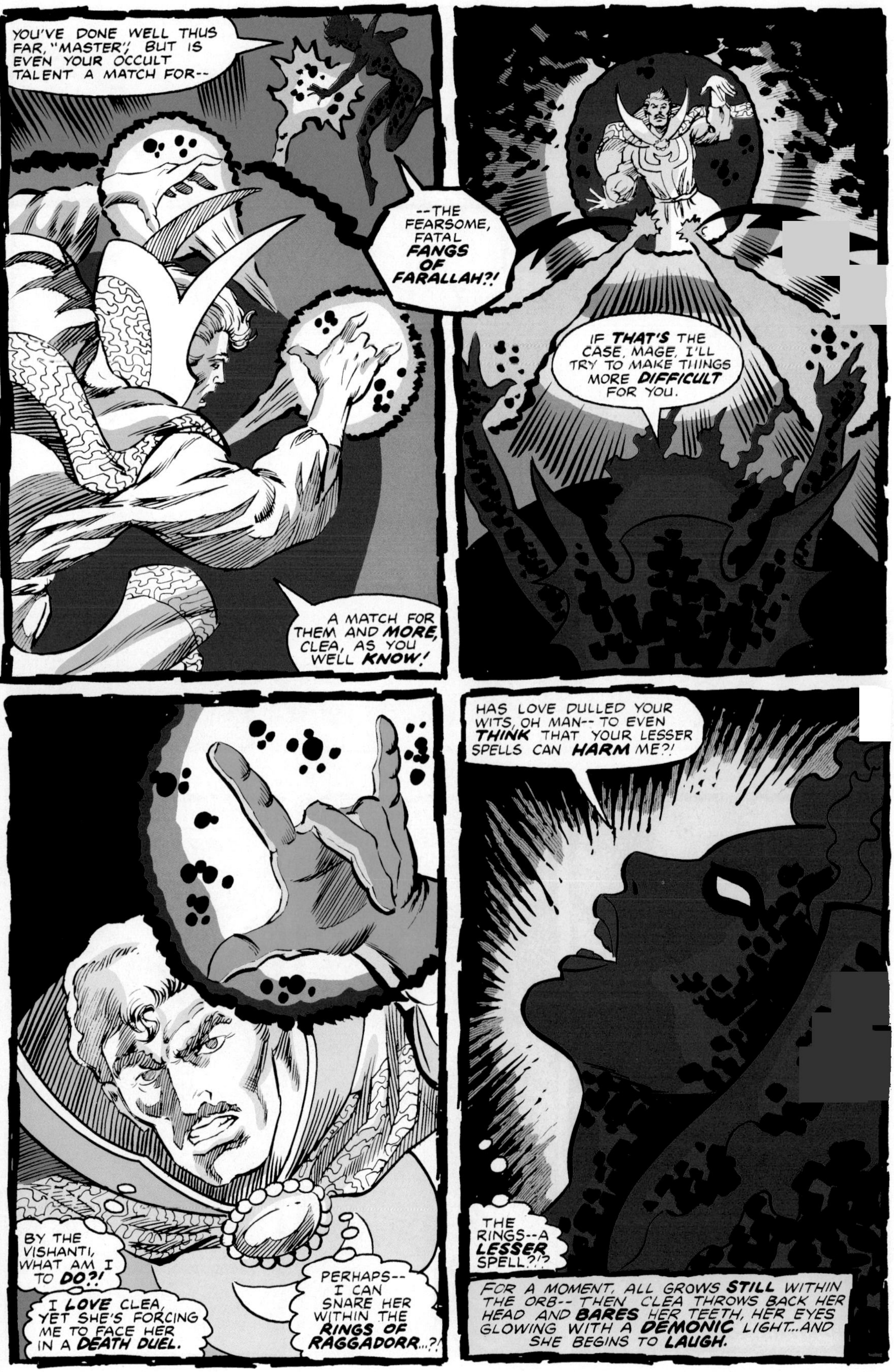
YOU'VE DONE WELL THUS FAR, "MASTER", BUT IS EVEN YOUR OCCULT TALENT A MATCH FOR--
--THE FEARSOME, FATAL FANGS OF FARALLAH?!
A MATCH FOR THEM AND MORE, CLEA, AS YOU WELL KNOW!
IF THAT'S THE CASE, MAGE, I'LL TRY TO MAKE THINGS MORE DIFFICULT FOR YOU.
BY THE VISHANTI, WHAT AM I TO DO?!
I LOVE CLEA, YET SHE'S FORCING ME TO FACE HER IN A DEATH DUEL.
PERHAPS-- I CAN SNARE HER WITHIN THE RINGS OF RAGGADORR...?!
HAS LOVE DULLED YOUR WITS, OH MAN-- TO EVEN THINK THAT YOUR LESSER SPELLS CAN HARM ME?!
THE RINGS--A LESSER SPELL?!?
FOR A MOMENT, ALL GROWS STILL WITHIN THE ORB-- THEN CLEA THROWS BACK HER HEAD AND BARES HER TEETH, HER EYES GLOWING WITH A DEMONIC LIGHT...AND SHE BEGINS TO LAUGH.

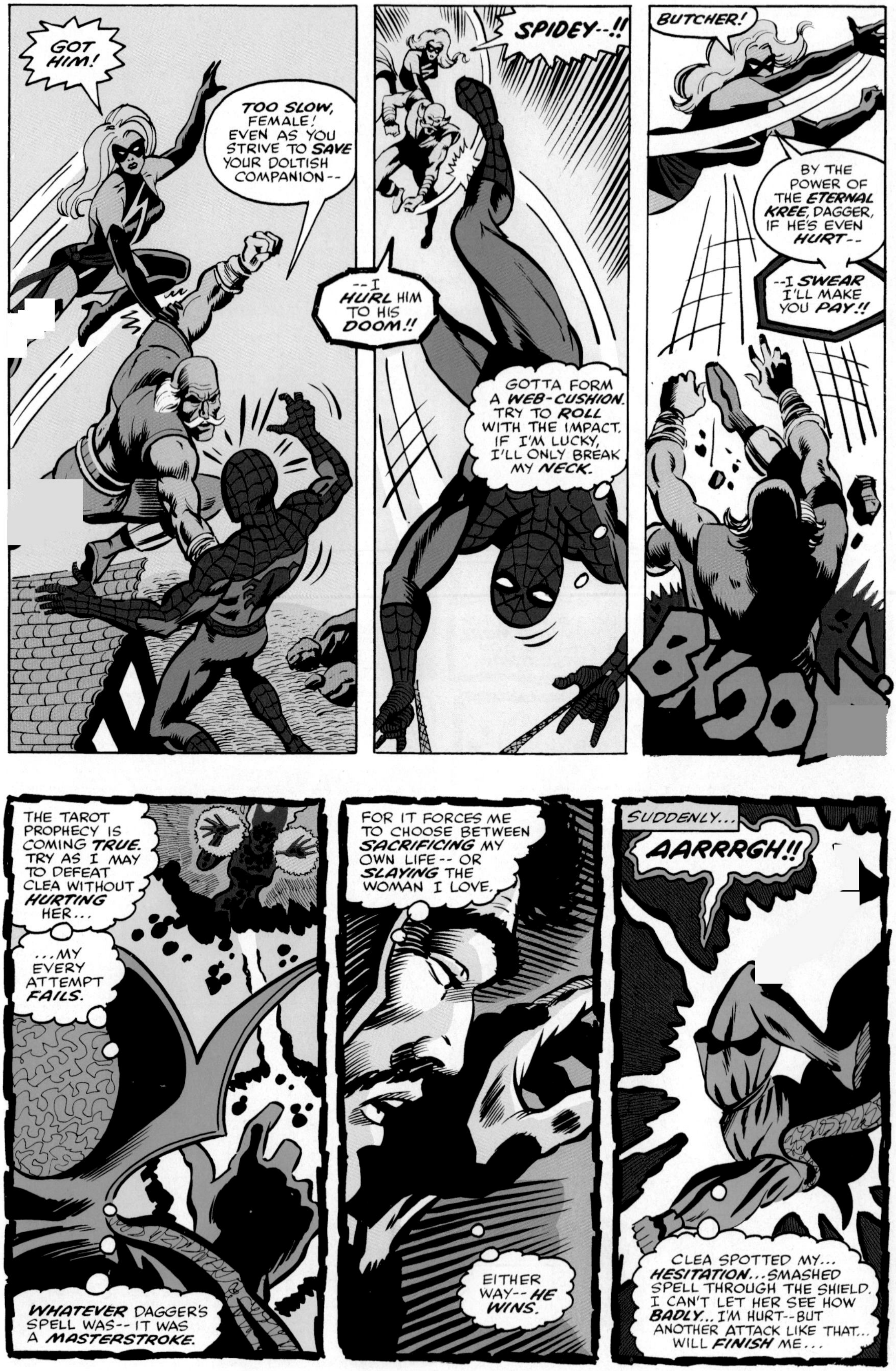
GOT HIM!
TOO SLOW, FEMALE! EVEN AS YOU STRIVE TO SAVE YOUR DOLTISH COMPANION--
--I HURL HIM TO HIS DOOM!!
SPIDEY--!!
GOTTA FORM A WEB-CUSHION. TRY TO ROLL WITH THE IMPACT. IF I'M LUCKY, I'LL ONLY BREAK MY NECK.
BUTCHER!
BY THE POWER OF THE ETERNAL KREE, DAGGER, IF HE'S EVEN HURT--
--I SWEAR I'LL MAKE YOU PAY!!
THE TAROT PROPHECY IS COMING TRUE. TRY AS I MAY TO DEFEAT CLEA WITHOUT HURTING HER...
...MY EVERY ATTEMPT FAILS.
WHATEVER DAGGER'S SPELL WAS-- IT WAS A MASTERSTROKE.
FOR IT FORCES ME TO CHOOSE BETWEEN SACRIFICING MY OWN LIFE-- OR SLAYING THE WOMAN I LOVE.
EITHER WAY-- HE WINS.
SUDDENLY...
AARRRGH!!
CLEA SPOTTED MY... HESITATION...SMASHED SPELL THROUGH THE SHIELD. I CAN'T LET HER SEE HOW BADLY... I'M HURT--BUT ANOTHER ATTACK LIKE THAT... WILL FINISH ME...

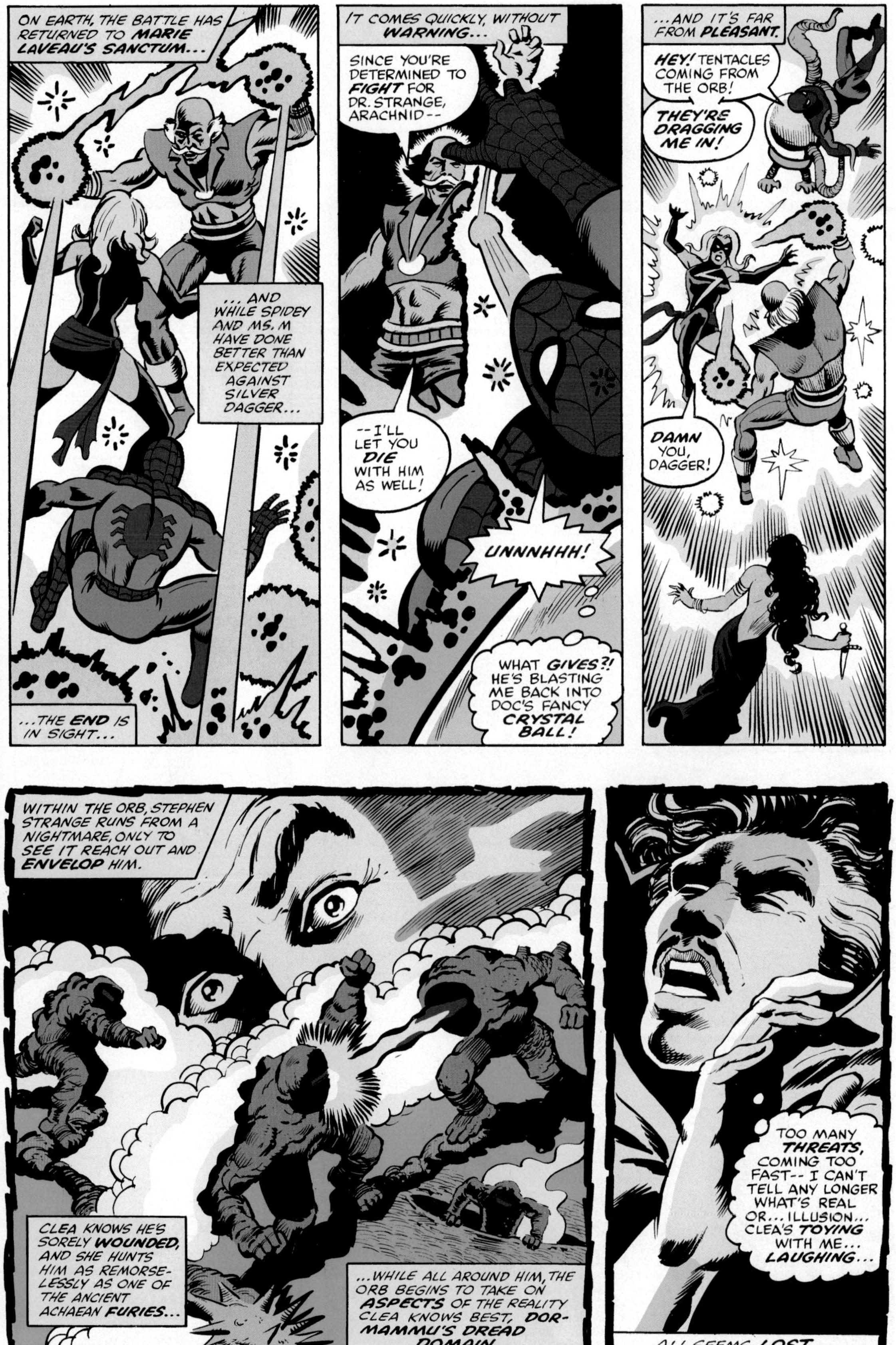
ON EARTH, THE BATTLE HAS RETURNED TO MARIE LAVEAU'S SANCTUM...
...AND WHILE SPIDEY AND MS. M HAVE DONE BETTER THAN EXPECTED AGAINST SILVER DAGGER...
...THE END IS IN SIGHT...
IT COMES QUICKLY, WITHOUT WARNING...
SINCE YOU'RE DETERMINED TO FIGHT FOR DR. STRANGE, ARACHNID--
--I'LL LET YOU DIE WITH HIM AS WELL!
UNNNHHH!
WHAT GIVES?! HE'S BLASTING ME BACK INTO DOC'S FANCY CRYSTAL BALL!
...AND IT'S FAR FROM PLEASANT.
HEY! TENTACLES COMING FROM THE ORB!
THEY'RE DRAGGING ME IN!
DAMN YOU, DAGGER!
WITHIN THE ORB, STEPHEN STRANGE RUNS FROM A NIGHTMARE, ONLY TO SEE IT REACH OUT AND ENVELOP HIM.
CLEA KNOWS HE'S SORELY WOUNDED, AND SHE HUNTS HIM AS REMORSELESSLY AS ONE OF THE ANCIENT ACHAEAN FURIES...
...WHILE ALL AROUND HIM, THE ORB BEGINS TO TAKE ON ASPECTS OF THE REALITY CLEA KNOWS BEST, DORMAMMU'S DREAD DOMAIN.
TOO MANY THREATS, COMING TOO FAST-- I CAN'T TELL ANY LONGER WHAT'S REAL OR... ILLUSION... CLEA'S TOYING WITH ME... LAUGHING...
ALL SEEMS LOST...

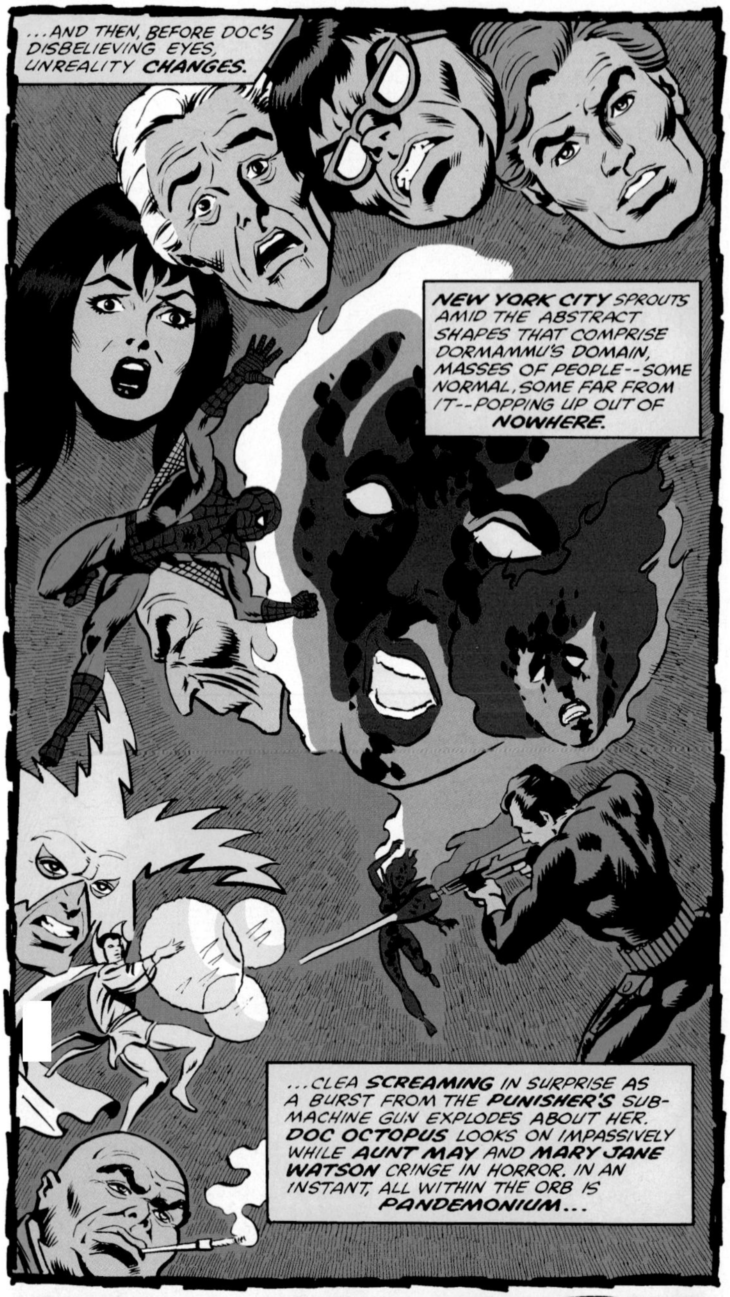

...AND THEN, BEFORE DOC'S DISBELIEVING EYES, UNREALITY CHANGES.
NEW YORK CITY SPROUTS AMID THE ABSTRACT SHAPES THAT COMPRISE DORMAMMU'S DOMAIN, MASSES OF PEOPLE--SOME NORMAL, SOME FAR FROM IT--POPPING UP OUT OF NOWHERE.
...CLEA SCREAMING IN SURPRISE AS A BURST FROM THE PUNISHER'S SUB-MACHINE GUN EXPLODES ABOUT HER. DOC OCTOPUS LOOKS ON IMPASSIVELY WHILE AUNT MAY AND MARY JANE WATSON CRINGE IN HORROR. IN AN INSTANT, ALL WITHIN THE ORB IS PANDEMONIUM...

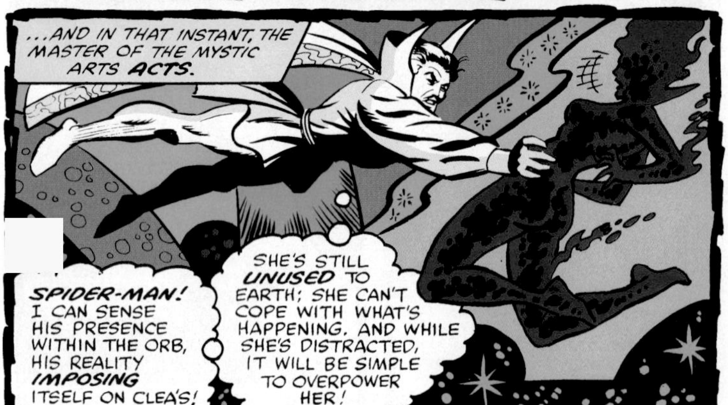

...AND IN THAT INSTANT, THE MASTER OF THE MYSTIC ARTS ACTS.
SPIDER-MAN! I CAN SENSE HIS PRESENCE WITHIN THE ORB, HIS REALITY IMPOSING ITSELF ON CLEA'S!
SHE'S STILL UNUSED TO EARTH; SHE CAN'T COPE WITH WHAT'S HAPPENING, AND WHILE SHE'S DISTRACTED, IT WILL BE SIMPLE TO OVERPOWER HER!

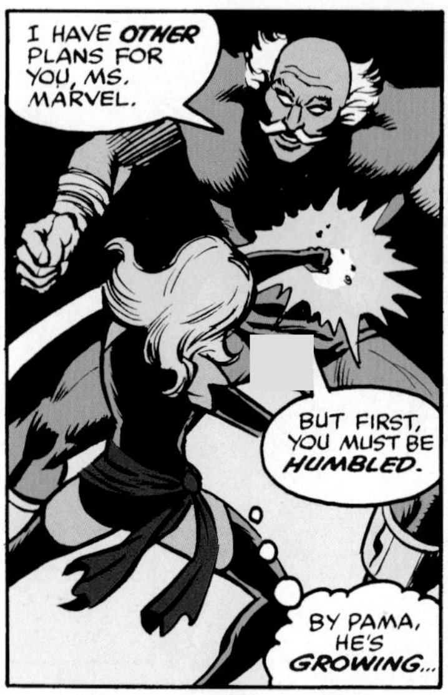

I HAVE OTHER PLANS FOR YOU, MS. MARVEL.
BUT FIRST, YOU MUST BE HUMBLED.
BY PAMA, HE'S GROWING...

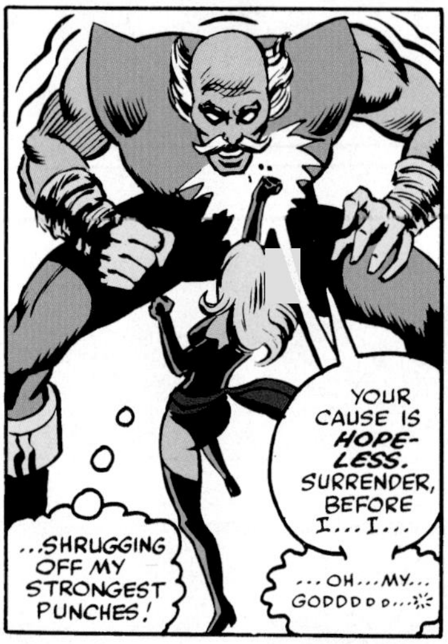

YOUR CAUSE IS HOPE-LESS. SURRENDER, BEFORE I... I...
...SHRUGGING OFF MY STRONGEST PUNCHES!
...OH...MY... GODDDDD...

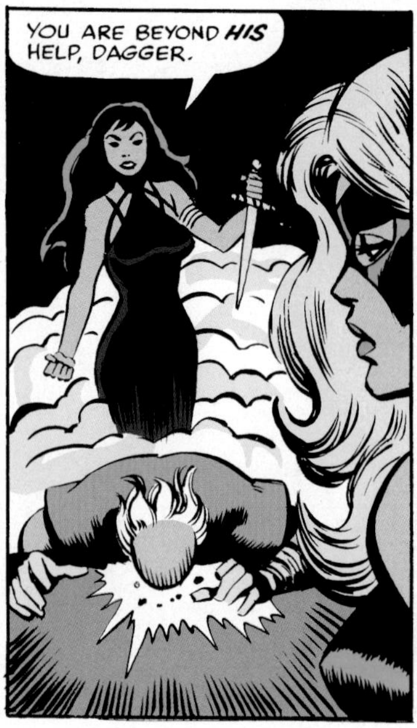

YOU ARE BEYOND HIS HELP, DAGGER.

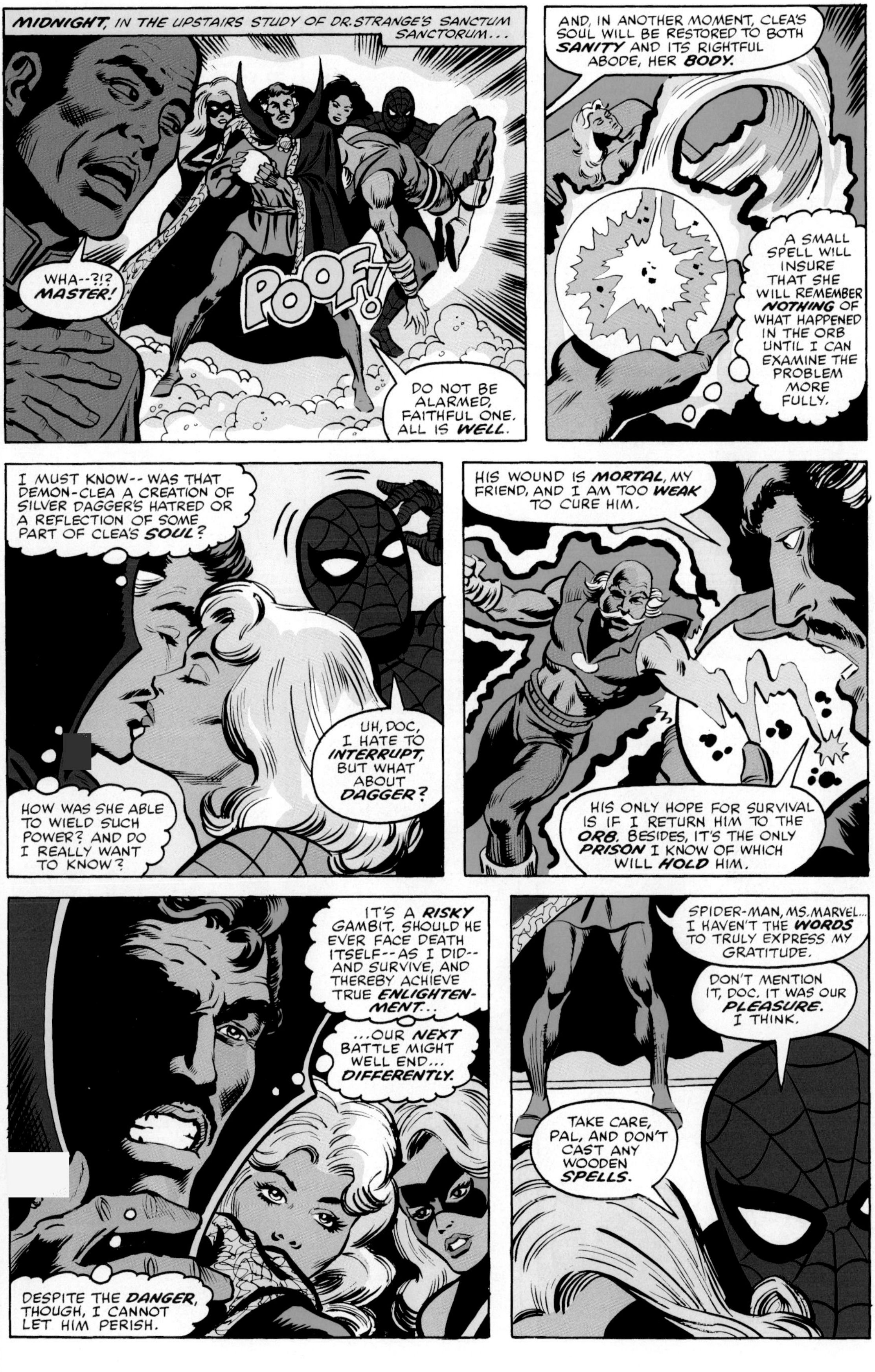
MIDNIGHT, IN THE UPSTAIRS STUDY OF DR. STRANGE'S SANCTUM SANCTORUM...
WHA--?!? MASTER!
POOF!
DO NOT BE ALARMED, FAITHFUL ONE. ALL IS WELL.
AND, IN ANOTHER MOMENT, CLEA'S SOUL WILL BE RESTORED TO BOTH SANITY AND ITS RIGHTFUL ABODE, HER BODY.
A SMALL SPELL WILL INSURE THAT SHE WILL REMEMBER NOTHING OF WHAT HAPPENED IN THE ORB UNTIL I CAN EXAMINE THE PROBLEM MORE FULLY.
I MUST KNOW-- WAS THAT DEMON-CLEA A CREATION OF SILVER DAGGER'S HATRED OR A REFLECTION OF SOME PART OF CLEA'S SOUL?
UH, DOC, I HATE TO INTERRUPT, BUT WHAT ABOUT DAGGER?
HOW WAS SHE ABLE TO WIELD SUCH POWER? AND DO I REALLY WANT TO KNOW?
HIS WOUND IS MORTAL, MY FRIEND, AND I AM TOO WEAK TO CURE HIM.
HIS ONLY HOPE FOR SURVIVAL IS IF I RETURN HIM TO THE ORB. BESIDES, IT'S THE ONLY PRISON I KNOW OF WHICH WILL HOLD HIM.
IT'S A RISKY GAMBIT. SHOULD HE EVER FACE DEATH ITSELF--AS I DID--AND SURVIVE, AND THEREBY ACHIEVE TRUE ENLIGHTEN-MENT...
...OUR NEXT BATTLE MIGHT WELL END... DIFFERENTLY.
DESPITE THE DANGER, THOUGH, I CANNOT LET HIM PERISH.
SPIDER-MAN, MS. MARVEL... I HAVEN'T THE WORDS TO TRULY EXPRESS MY GRATITUDE.
DON'T MENTION IT, DOC. IT WAS OUR PLEASURE. I THINK.
TAKE CARE, PAL, AND DON'T CAST ANY WOODEN SPELLS.

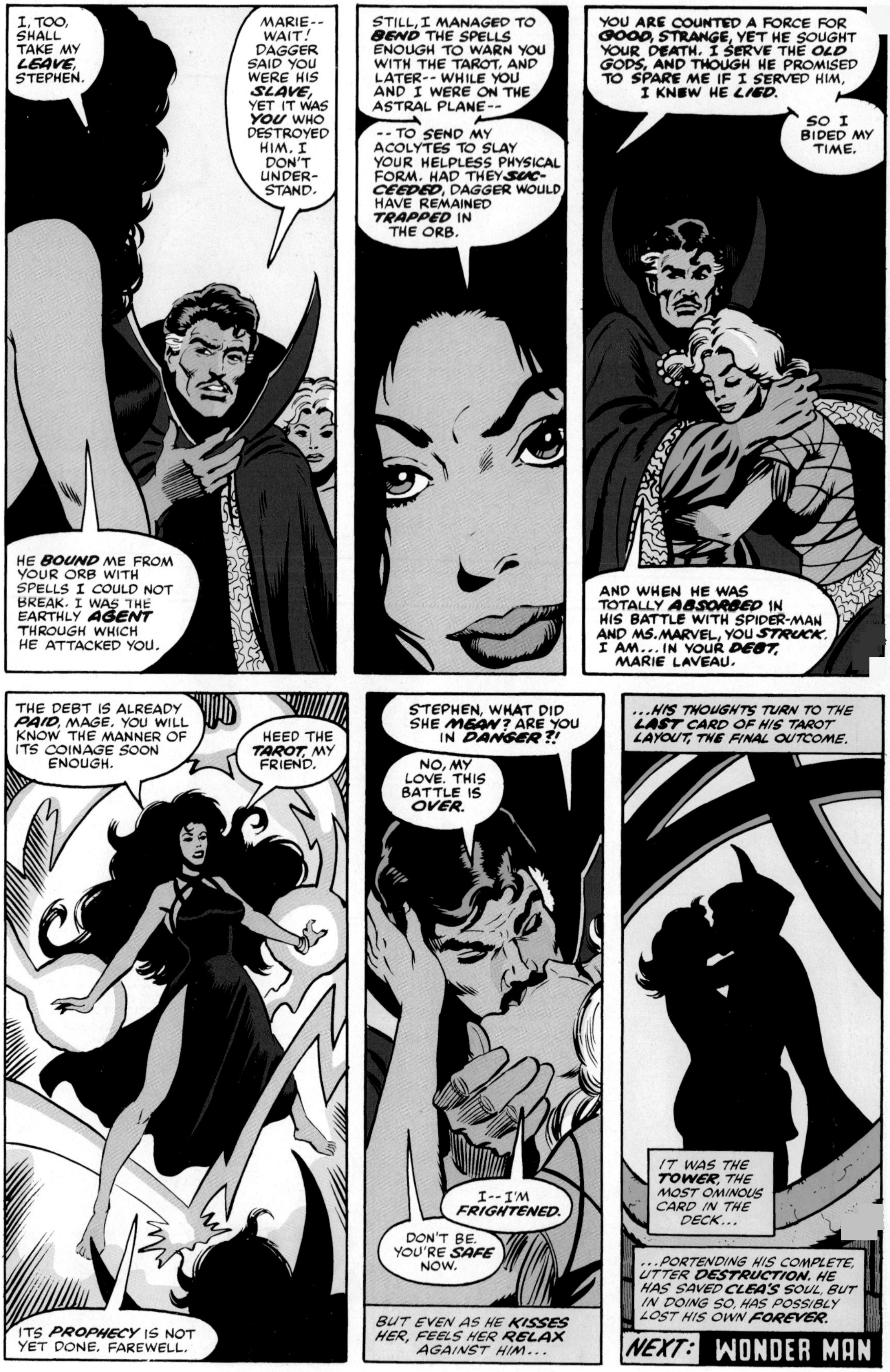
I, TOO, SHALL TAKE MY LEAVE, STEPHEN.
MARIE-- WAIT! DAGGER SAID YOU WERE HIS SLAVE, YET IT WAS YOU WHO DESTROYED HIM. I DON'T UNDER-STAND.
HE BOUND ME FROM YOUR ORB WITH SPELLS I COULD NOT BREAK. I WAS THE EARTHLY AGENT THROUGH WHICH HE ATTACKED YOU.
STILL, I MANAGED TO BEND THE SPELLS ENOUGH TO WARN YOU WITH THE TAROT, AND LATER-- WHILE YOU AND I WERE ON THE ASTRAL PLANE--
-- TO SEND MY ACOLYTES TO SLAY YOUR HELPLESS PHYSICAL FORM. HAD THEY SUC-CEEDED, DAGGER WOULD HAVE REMAINED TRAPPED IN THE ORB.
YOU ARE COUNTED A FORCE FOR GOOD, STRANGE, YET HE SOUGHT YOUR DEATH. I SERVE THE OLD GODS, AND THOUGH HE PROMISED TO SPARE ME IF I SERVED HIM, I KNEW HE LIED.
SO I BIDED MY TIME.
AND WHEN HE WAS TOTALLY ABSORBED IN HIS BATTLE WITH SPIDER-MAN AND MS. MARVEL, YOU STRUCK. I AM... IN YOUR DEBT, MARIE LAVEAU.
THE DEBT IS ALREADY PAID, MAGE. YOU WILL KNOW THE MANNER OF ITS COINAGE SOON ENOUGH.
HEED THE TAROT, MY FRIEND.
ITS PROPHECY IS NOT YET DONE. FAREWELL.
STEPHEN, WHAT DID SHE MEAN? ARE YOU IN DANGER?!
NO, MY LOVE. THIS BATTLE IS OVER.
I--I'M FRIGHTENED.
DON'T BE. YOU'RE SAFE NOW.
BUT EVEN AS HE KISSES HER, FEELS HER RELAX AGAINST HIM...
...HIS THOUGHTS TURN TO THE LAST CARD OF HIS TAROT LAYOUT, THE FINAL OUTCOME.
IT WAS THE TOWER, THE MOST OMINOUS CARD IN THE DECK...
...PORTENDING HIS COMPLETE, UTTER DESTRUCTION. HE HAS SAVED CLEA'S SOUL, BUT IN DOING SO, HAS POSSIBLY LOST HIS OWN FOREVER.
NEXT: WONDER MAN

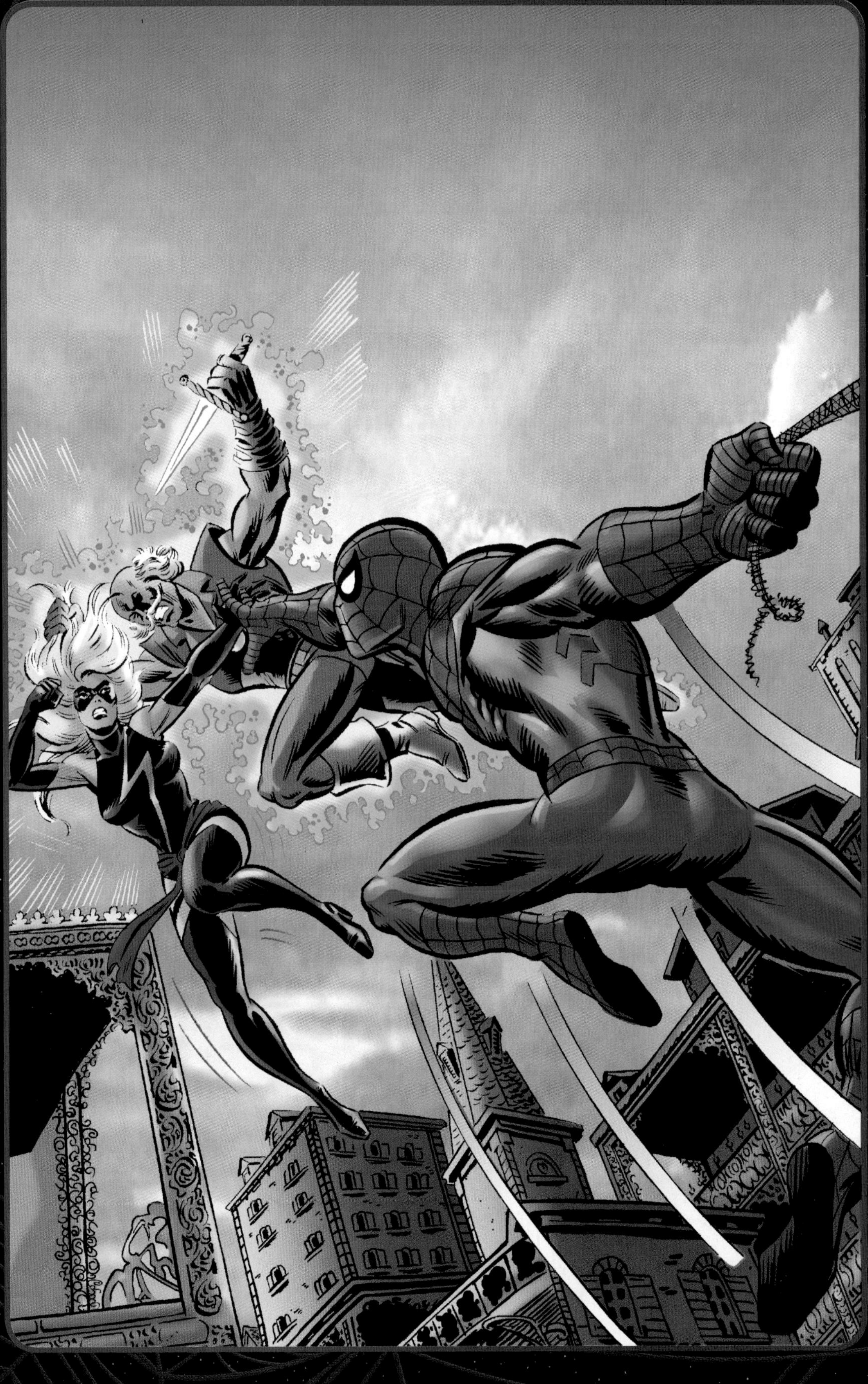

ESSENTIAL MARVEL TEAM-UP VOL. 4 TPB
COVER ART BY JOHN ROMITA JR., AL MILGROM & TOM SMITH

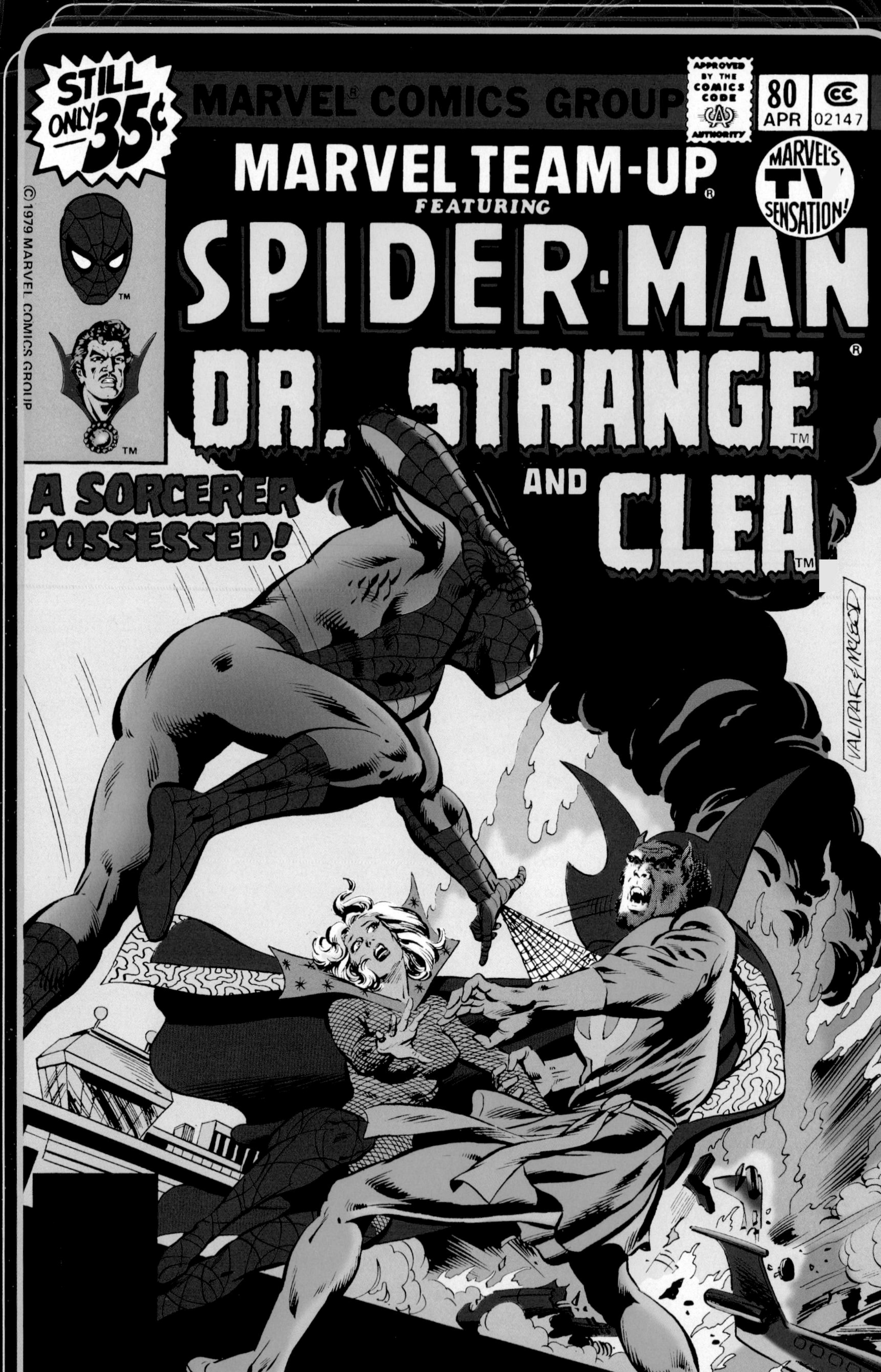
STILL ONLY 35¢
MARVEL® COMICS GROUP
APPROVED BY THE COMICS CODE AUTHORITY
80 APR
CC 02147
MARVEL TEAM-UP®
FEATURING
SPIDER-MAN®
MARVEL'S TV SENSATION!
DR. STRANGE™
AND CLEA™
A SORCERER POSSESSED!
© 1979 MARVEL COMICS GROUP

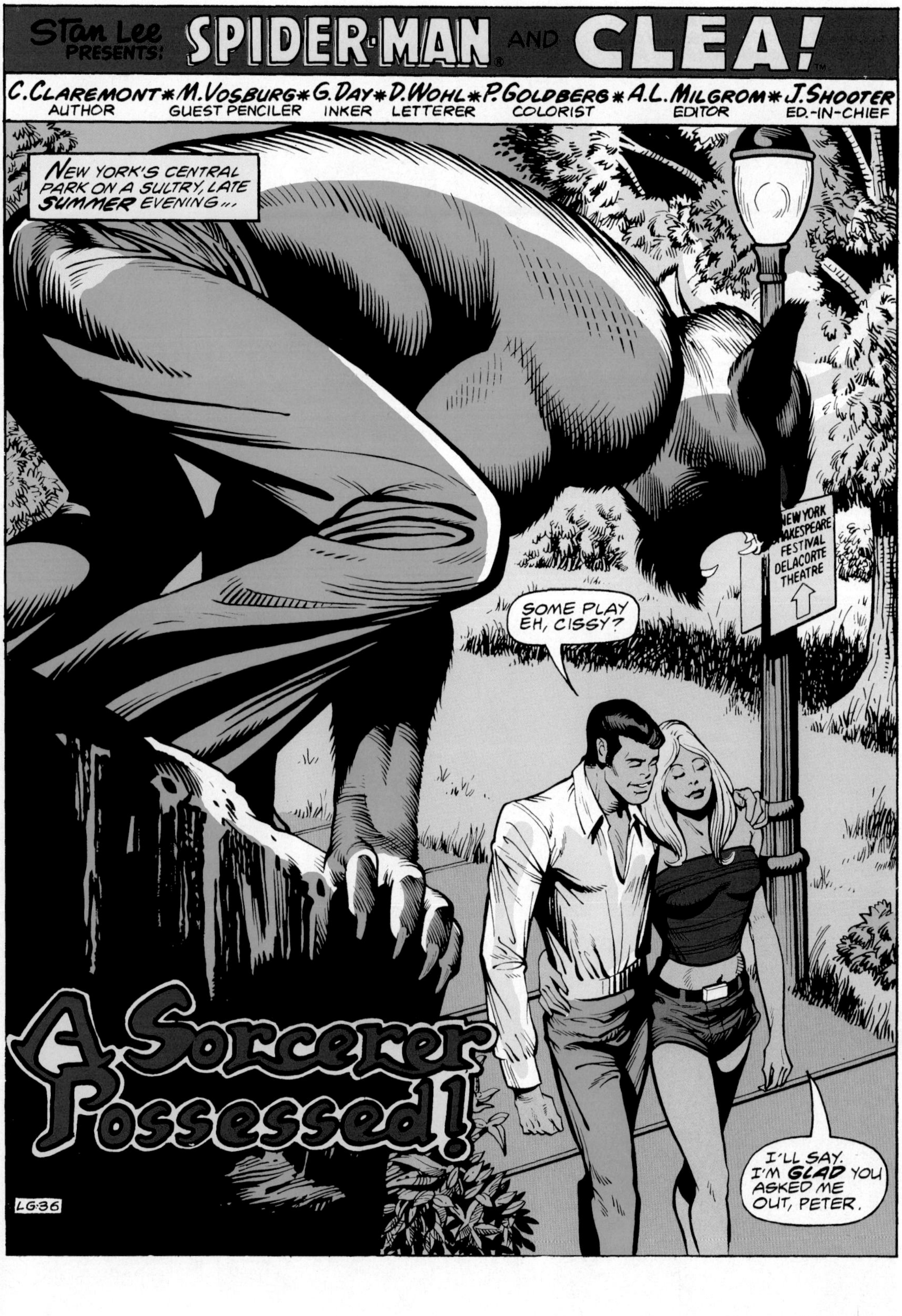

Stan Lee PRESENTS: SPIDER-MAN AND CLEA!
C. CLAREMONT * M. VOSBURG * G. DAY * D. WOHL * P. GOLDBERG * A.L. MILGROM * J. SHOOTER
AUTHOR GUEST PENCILER INKER LETTERER COLORIST EDITOR ED.-IN-CHIEF
NEW YORK'S CENTRAL PARK ON A SULTRY, LATE SUMMER EVENING...
NEW YORK SHAKESPEARE FESTIVAL DELACORTE THEATRE
SOME PLAY EH, CISSY?
A Sorcerer Possessed!
I'LL SAY. I'M GLAD YOU ASKED ME OUT, PETER.
LG:36

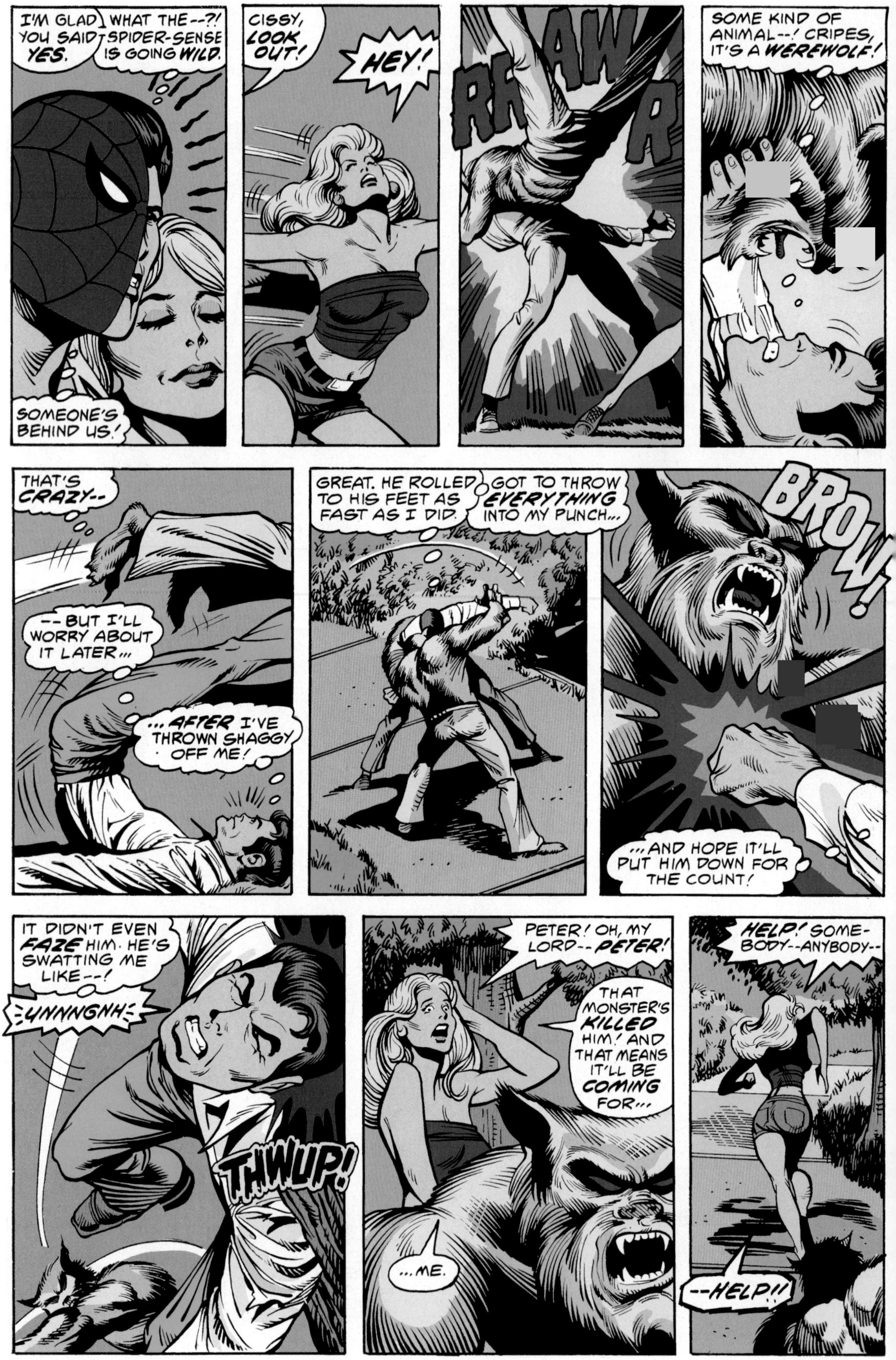

I'M GLAD YOU SAID YES.
WHAT THE--?! SPIDER-SENSE IS GOING WILD.
SOMEONE'S BEHIND US!
CISSY, LOOK OUT!
HEY!
RRAWR
SOME KIND OF ANIMAL--! CRIPES, IT'S A WEREWOLF!
THAT'S CRAZY--
--BUT I'LL WORRY ABOUT IT LATER...
...AFTER I'VE THROWN SHAGGY OFF ME!
GREAT. HE ROLLED TO HIS FEET AS FAST AS I DID.
GOT TO THROW EVERYTHING INTO MY PUNCH...
BROW!
...AND HOPE IT'LL PUT HIM DOWN FOR THE COUNT!
IT DIDN'T EVEN FAZE HIM. HE'S SWATTING ME LIKE--!
UNNNGNH
THWUP!
PETER! OH, MY LORD--PETER!
THAT MONSTER'S KILLED HIM! AND THAT MEANS IT'LL BE COMING FOR...
...ME.
HELP! SOME-BODY--ANYBODY--
--HELP!!

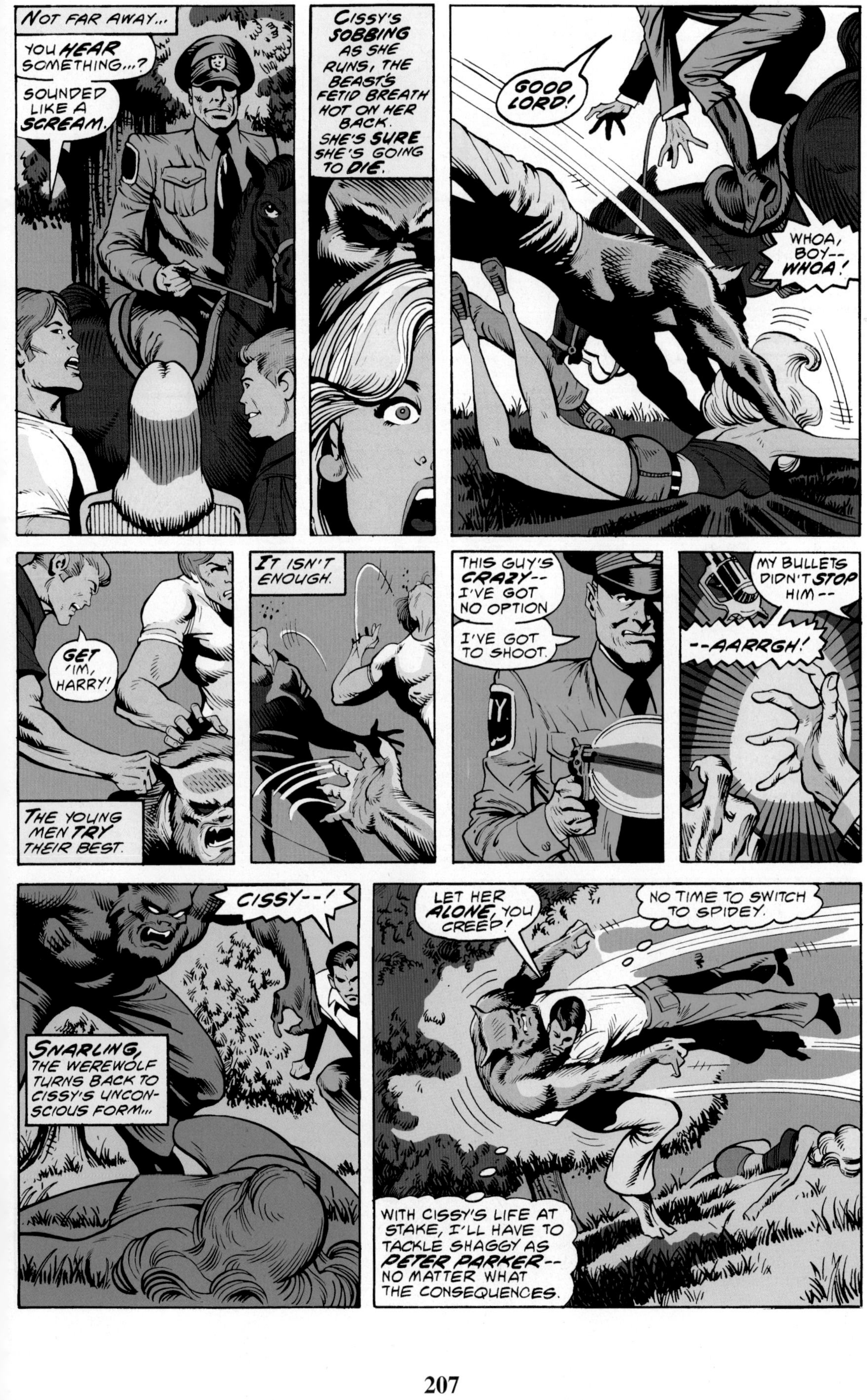
NOT FAR AWAY...
YOU HEAR SOMETHING...?
SOUNDED LIKE A SCREAM.
CISSY'S SOBBING AS SHE RUNS, THE BEAST'S FETID BREATH HOT ON HER BACK. SHE'S SURE SHE'S GOING TO DIE.
GOOD LORD!
WHOA, BOY-- WHOA!
GET 'IM, HARRY!
THE YOUNG MEN TRY THEIR BEST.
IT ISN'T ENOUGH.
THIS GUY'S CRAZY-- I'VE GOT NO OPTION
I'VE GOT TO SHOOT.
MY BULLETS DIDN'T STOP HIM --
--AARRGH!
CISSY--!
SNARLING, THE WEREWOLF TURNS BACK TO CISSY'S UNCONSCIOUS FORM...
LET HER ALONE, YOU CREEP!
NO TIME TO SWITCH TO SPIDEY.
WITH CISSY'S LIFE AT STAKE, I'LL HAVE TO TACKLE SHAGGY AS PETER PARKER-- NO MATTER WHAT THE CONSEQUENCES.

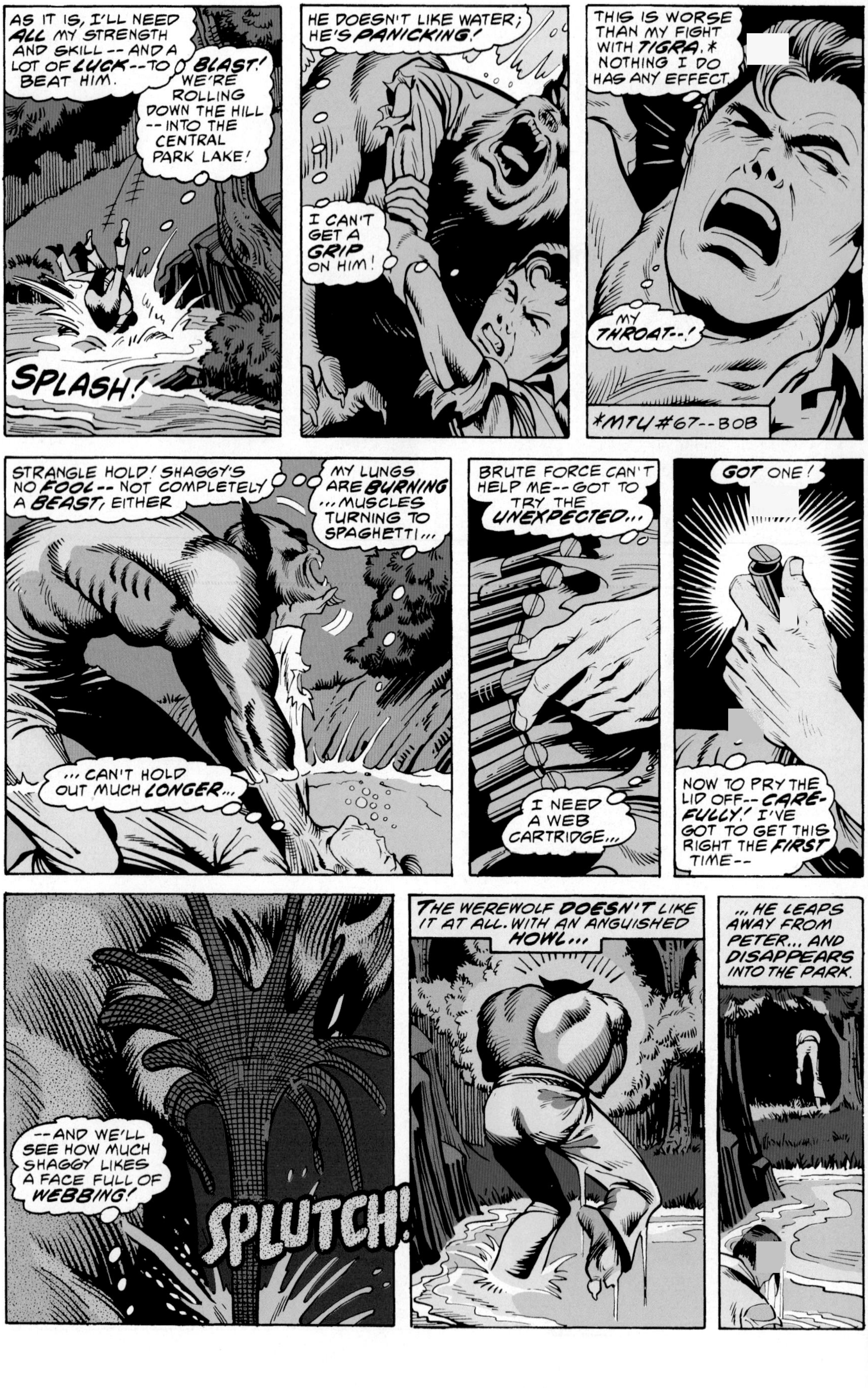
AS IT IS, I'LL NEED ALL MY STRENGTH AND SKILL -- AND A LOT OF LUCK -- TO BEAT HIM.
BLAST! WE'RE ROLLING DOWN THE HILL -- INTO THE CENTRAL PARK LAKE!
SPLASH!
HE DOESN'T LIKE WATER; HE'S PANICKING!
I CAN'T GET A GRIP ON HIM!
THIS IS WORSE THAN MY FIGHT WITH TIGRA.* NOTHING I DO HAS ANY EFFECT.
MY THROAT--!
*MTU #67--BOB
STRANGLE HOLD! SHAGGY'S NO FOOL -- NOT COMPLETELY A BEAST, EITHER
MY LUNGS ARE BURNING ...MUSCLES TURNING TO SPAGHETTI...
...CAN'T HOLD OUT MUCH LONGER...
BRUTE FORCE CAN'T HELP ME -- GOT TO TRY THE UNEXPECTED...
I NEED A WEB CARTRIDGE...
GOT ONE!
NOW TO PRY THE LID OFF -- CARE-FULLY! I'VE GOT TO GET THIS RIGHT THE FIRST TIME--
--AND WE'LL SEE HOW MUCH SHAGGY LIKES A FACE FULL OF WEBBING!
SPLUTCH!
THE WEREWOLF DOESN'T LIKE IT AT ALL. WITH AN ANGUISHED HOWL...
...HE LEAPS AWAY FROM PETER... AND DISAPPEARS INTO THE PARK.

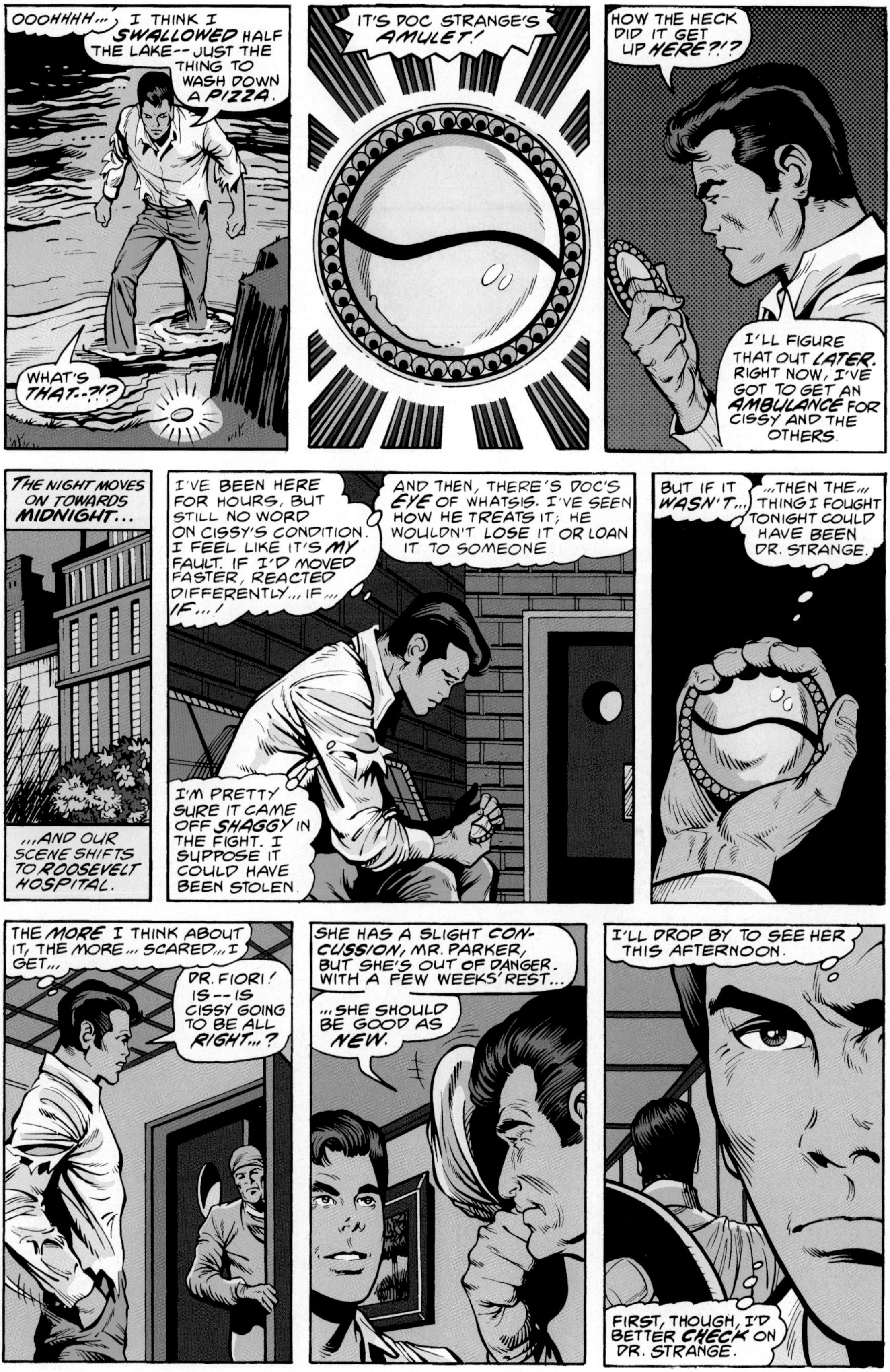
OOOHHHH..., I THINK I SWALLOWED HALF THE LAKE--JUST THE THING TO WASH DOWN A PIZZA.
WHAT'S THAT--?!?
IT'S DOC STRANGE'S AMULET!
HOW THE HECK DID IT GET UP HERE?!?
I'LL FIGURE THAT OUT LATER. RIGHT NOW, I'VE GOT TO GET AN AMBULANCE FOR CISSY AND THE OTHERS.
THE NIGHT MOVES ON TOWARDS MIDNIGHT...
...AND OUR SCENE SHIFTS TO ROOSEVELT HOSPITAL.
I'VE BEEN HERE FOR HOURS, BUT STILL NO WORD ON CISSY'S CONDITION. I FEEL LIKE IT'S MY FAULT. IF I'D MOVED FASTER, REACTED DIFFERENTLY..., IF..., IF...!
AND THEN, THERE'S DOC'S EYE OF WHATSIS. I'VE SEEN HOW HE TREATS IT; HE WOULDN'T LOSE IT OR LOAN IT TO SOMEONE.
I'M PRETTY SURE IT CAME OFF SHAGGY IN THE FIGHT. I SUPPOSE IT COULD HAVE BEEN STOLEN.
BUT IF IT WASN'T...
...THEN THE... THING I FOUGHT TONIGHT COULD HAVE BEEN DR. STRANGE.
THE MORE I THINK ABOUT IT, THE MORE... SCARED... I GET...
DR. FIORI! IS--IS CISSY GOING TO BE ALL RIGHT...?
SHE HAS A SLIGHT CONCUSSION, MR. PARKER, BUT SHE'S OUT OF DANGER. WITH A FEW WEEKS' REST...
...SHE SHOULD BE GOOD AS NEW.
I'LL DROP BY TO SEE HER THIS AFTERNOON.
FIRST, THOUGH, I'D BETTER CHECK ON DR. STRANGE.

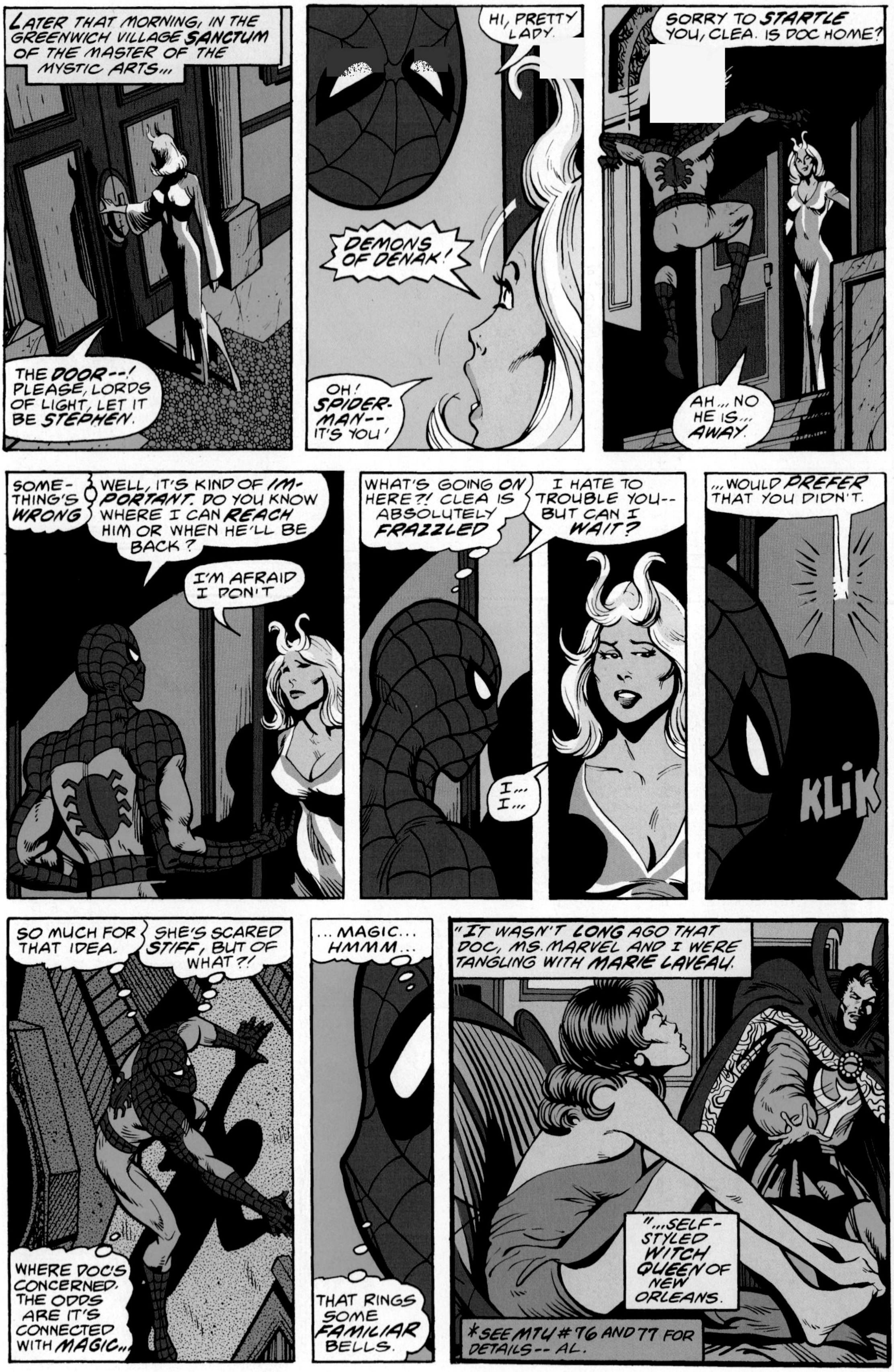
LATER THAT MORNING, IN THE GREENWICH VILLAGE SANCTUM OF THE MASTER OF THE MYSTIC ARTS...
THE DOOR--! PLEASE, LORDS OF LIGHT, LET IT BE STEPHEN.
HI, PRETTY LADY.
DEMONS OF DENAK!
OH! SPIDER-MAN-- IT'S YOU!
SORRY TO STARTLE YOU, CLEA. IS DOC HOME?
AH... NO HE IS... AWAY.
SOME-THING'S WRONG
WELL, IT'S KIND OF IM-PORTANT. DO YOU KNOW WHERE I CAN REACH HIM OR WHEN HE'LL BE BACK?
I'M AFRAID I DON'T
WHAT'S GOING ON HERE?! CLEA IS ABSOLUTELY FRAZZLED
I HATE TO TROUBLE YOU-- BUT CAN I WAIT?
I... I...
...WOULD PREFER THAT YOU DIDN'T.
KLIK
SO MUCH FOR THAT IDEA.
SHE'S SCARED STIFF, BUT OF WHAT?!
WHERE DOC'S CONCERNED, THE ODDS ARE IT'S CONNECTED WITH MAGIC...
...MAGIC... HMMM...
THAT RINGS SOME FAMILIAR BELLS.
"IT WASN'T LONG AGO THAT DOC, MS. MARVEL AND I WERE TANGLING WITH MARIE LAVEAU.
"...SELF-STYLED WITCH QUEEN OF NEW ORLEANS.
*SEE MTU #76 AND 77 FOR DETAILS-- AL.

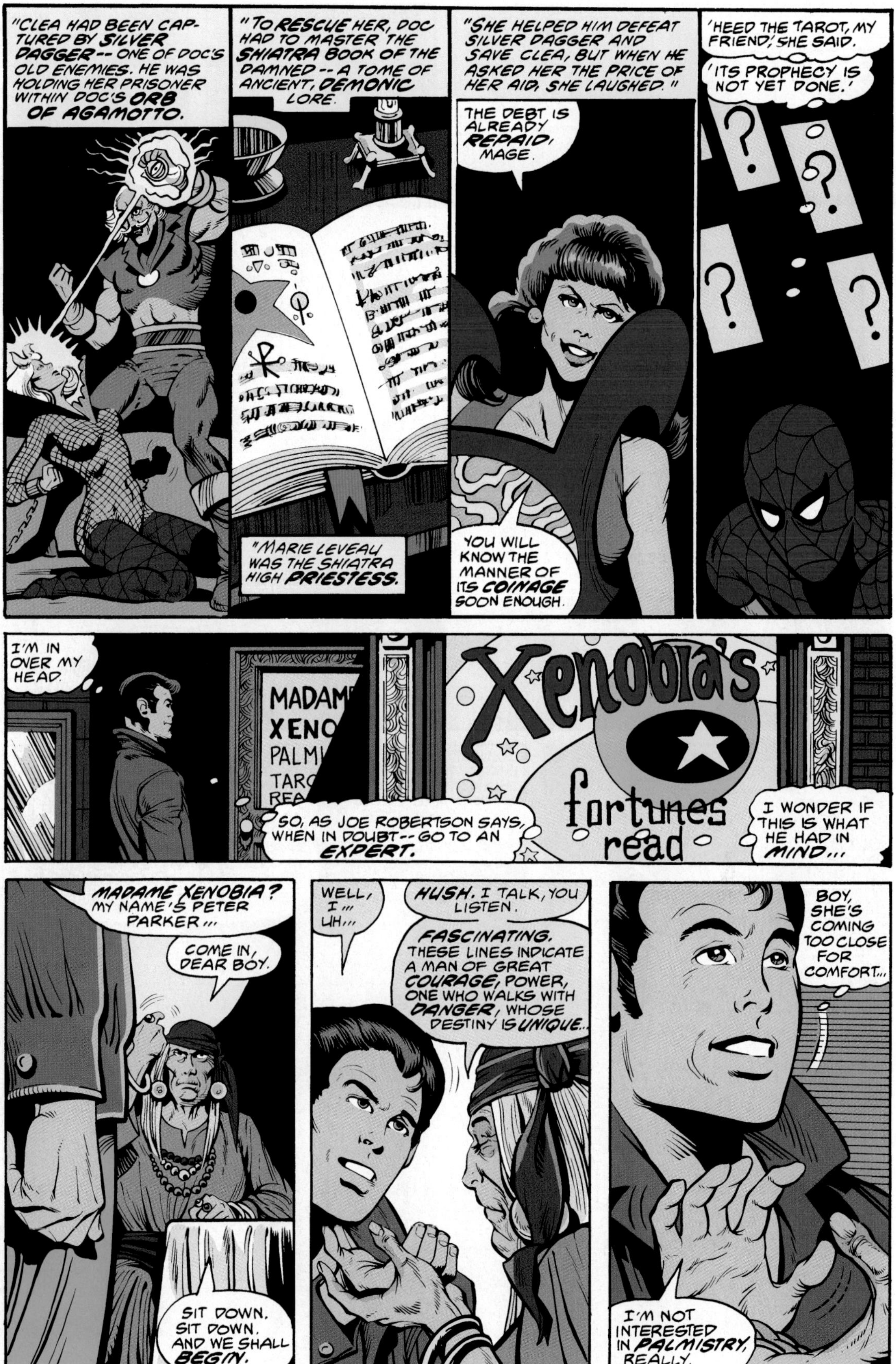
"CLEA HAD BEEN CAPTURED BY SILVER DAGGER-- ONE OF DOC'S OLD ENEMIES. HE WAS HOLDING HER PRISONER WITHIN DOC'S ORB OF AGAMOTTO.
"TO RESCUE HER, DOC HAD TO MASTER THE SHIATRA BOOK OF THE DAMNED -- A TOME OF ANCIENT, DEMONIC LORE.
"MARIE LEVEAU WAS THE SHIATRA HIGH PRIESTESS.
"SHE HELPED HIM DEFEAT SILVER DAGGER AND SAVE CLEA, BUT WHEN HE ASKED HER THE PRICE OF HER AID, SHE LAUGHED."
THE DEBT IS ALREADY REPAID, MAGE.
YOU WILL KNOW THE MANNER OF ITS COINAGE SOON ENOUGH.
'HEED THE TAROT, MY FRIEND,' SHE SAID.
'ITS PROPHECY IS NOT YET DONE.'
I'M IN OVER MY HEAD.
MADAM XENO PALM TARO REA
SO, AS JOE ROBERTSON SAYS, WHEN IN DOUBT-- GO TO AN EXPERT.
Xenobia's fortunes read
I WONDER IF THIS IS WHAT HE HAD IN MIND...
MADAME XENOBIA? MY NAME'S PETER PARKER...
COME IN, DEAR BOY.
SIT DOWN. SIT DOWN. AND WE SHALL BEGIN.
WELL, I... UH...
HUSH. I TALK, YOU LISTEN.
FASCINATING. THESE LINES INDICATE A MAN OF GREAT COURAGE, POWER, ONE WHO WALKS WITH DANGER, WHOSE DESTINY IS UNIQUE...
BOY, SHE'S COMING TOO CLOSE FOR COMFORT...
I'M NOT INTERESTED IN PALMISTRY, REALLY.

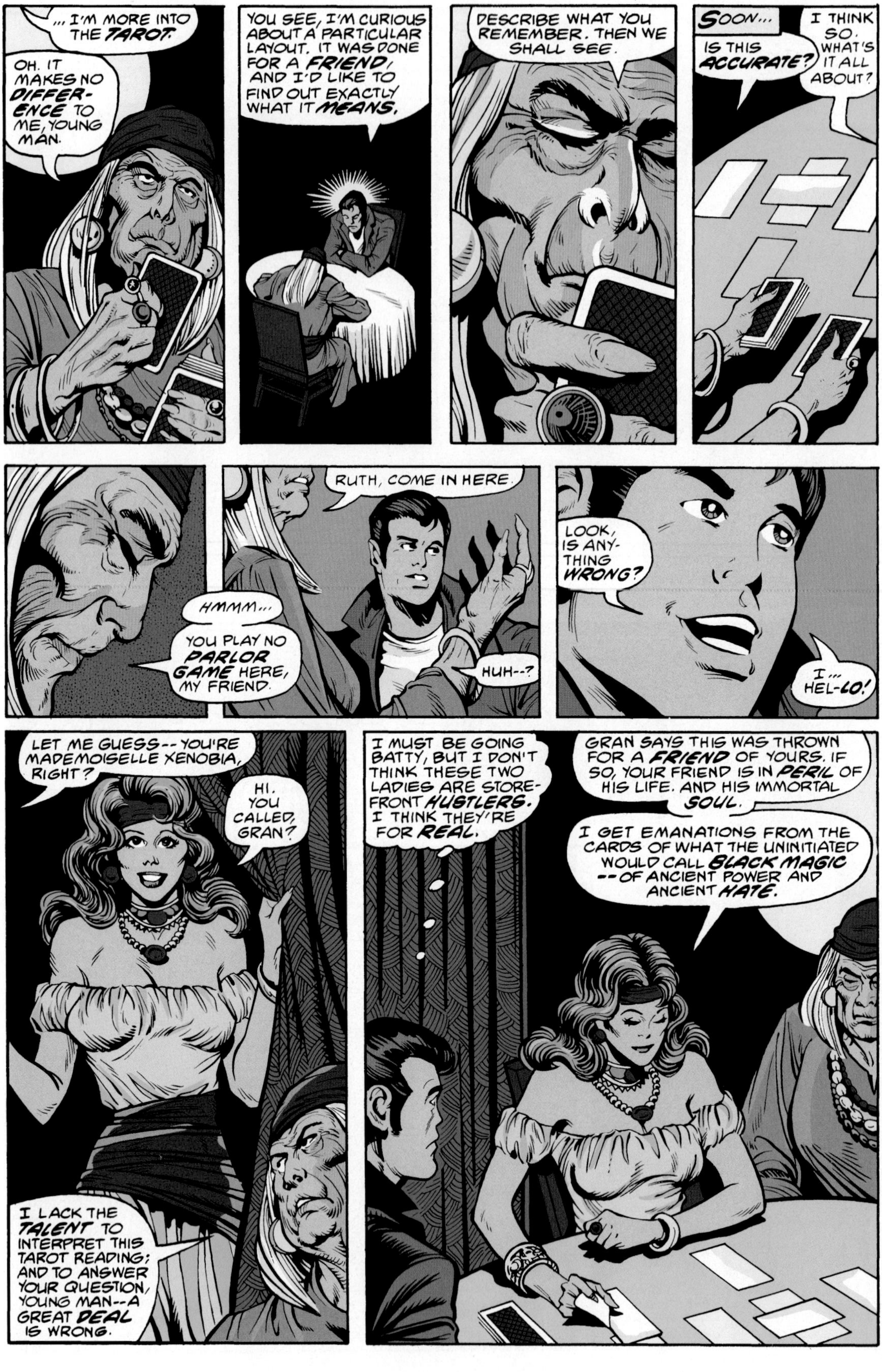

...I'M MORE INTO THE TAROT.
OH. IT MAKES NO DIFFERENCE TO ME, YOUNG MAN.
YOU SEE, I'M CURIOUS ABOUT A PARTICULAR LAYOUT. IT WAS DONE FOR A FRIEND, AND I'D LIKE TO FIND OUT EXACTLY WHAT IT MEANS.
DESCRIBE WHAT YOU REMEMBER. THEN WE SHALL SEE.
SOON...
IS THIS ACCURATE?
I THINK SO. WHAT'S IT ALL ABOUT?
HMMM...
YOU PLAY NO PARLOR GAME HERE, MY FRIEND.
RUTH, COME IN HERE.
HUH--?
LOOK, IS ANYTHING WRONG?
I... HEL-LO!
LET ME GUESS--YOU'RE MADEMOISELLE XENOBIA, RIGHT?
HI. YOU CALLED, GRAN?
I LACK THE TALENT TO INTERPRET THIS TAROT READING; AND TO ANSWER YOUR QUESTION, YOUNG MAN--A GREAT DEAL IS WRONG.
I MUST BE GOING BATTY, BUT I DON'T THINK THESE TWO LADIES ARE STOREFRONT HUSTLERS. I THINK THEY'RE FOR REAL.
GRAN SAYS THIS WAS THROWN FOR A FRIEND OF YOURS. IF SO, YOUR FRIEND IS IN PERIL OF HIS LIFE. AND HIS IMMORTAL SOUL.
I GET EMANATIONS FROM THE CARDS OF WHAT THE UNINITIATED WOULD CALL BLACK MAGIC--OF ANCIENT POWER AND ANCIENT HATE.

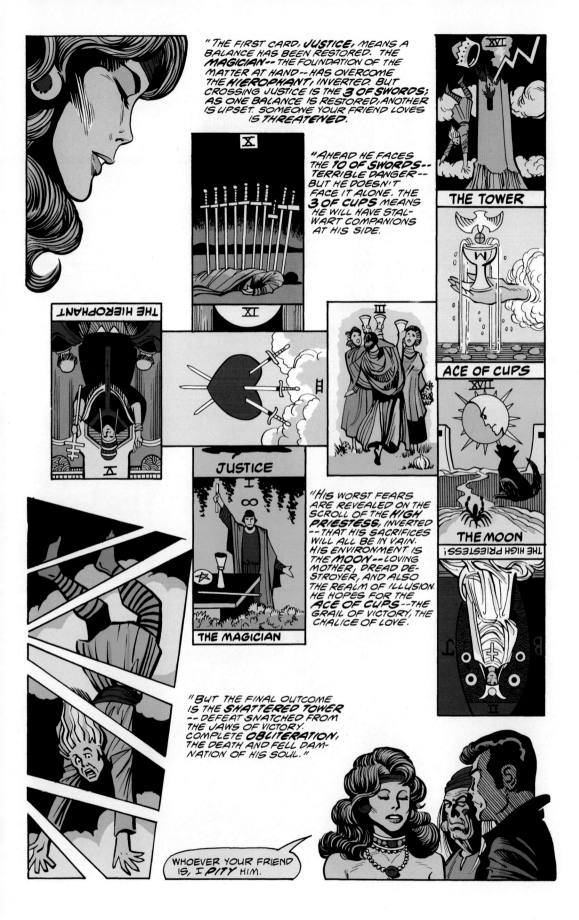

"THE FIRST CARD, *JUSTICE*, MEANS A BALANCE HAS BEEN RESTORED. THE *MAGICIAN* -- THE FOUNDATION OF THE MATTER AT HAND -- HAS OVERCOME THE *HIEROPHANT*, INVERTED. BUT CROSSING JUSTICE IS THE *3 OF SWORDS*; AS ONE BALANCE IS RESTORED, ANOTHER IS UPSET. SOMEONE YOUR FRIEND LOVES IS *THREATENED*.

"AHEAD HE FACES THE *10 OF SWORDS* -- TERRIBLE DANGER -- BUT HE DOESN'T FACE IT ALONE. THE *3 OF CUPS* MEANS HE WILL HAVE STAL-WART COMPANIONS AT HIS SIDE.

THE TOWER

THE HIEROPHANT

ACE OF CUPS

JUSTICE

"HIS WORST FEARS ARE REVEALED ON THE SCROLL OF THE *HIGH PRIESTESS*, INVERTED -- THAT HIS SACRIFICES WILL ALL BE IN VAIN. HIS ENVIRONMENT IS THE *MOON* -- LOVING MOTHER, DREAD DE-STROYER, AND ALSO THE REALM OF ILLUSION. HE HOPES FOR THE *ACE OF CUPS* -- THE GRAIL OF VICTORY, THE CHALICE OF LOVE.

THE MAGICIAN

THE MOON

THE HIGH PRIESTESS!

"BUT THE FINAL OUTCOME IS THE *SHATTERED TOWER* -- DEFEAT SNATCHED FROM THE JAWS OF VICTORY. COMPLETE *OBLITERATION*, THE DEATH AND FELL DAM-NATION OF HIS SOUL."

WHOEVER YOUR FRIEND IS, I *PITY* HIM.

IT ALL MAKES SENSE. THE HIEROPHANT IS *SILVER DAGGER*, THE STALWART FRIENDS, ME AND *MS. MARVEL.*

THE CARDS SAID WE'D WIN, AND BY WINNING DOC WOULD LOSE *EVERYTHING*-- AND THAT'S WHAT HAPPENED. SOME- HOW, I'LL BET MARIE LAVEAU *ZAPPED* DOC DURING THE FIGHT...

SPEAK OF THE DEVIL-- BY DAYLIGHT, HE LOOKS *FINE.*

I SUPPOSE I COULD BE *WRONG.*

I'LL JUST HAVE TO WAIT AND SEE-- *HOLD IT!*

SPIDEY- SENSE STARTED *TINGLING* THE INSTANT DOC ENTERED HIS HOUSE

AND INSIDE...

...I TOLD YOU TO *LEAVE* ME ALONE!

STEPHEN, YOU'RE *HURTING* ME. LISTEN TO YOUR- SELF, MY LOVE; YOU'RE NOT WELL

SILENCE!

SLAP!

THAT TEARS IT!

IF THAT'S REALLY DOC--

--HE'S OFF HIS *ROCKER!*

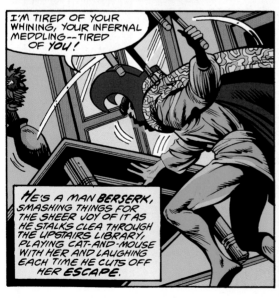

I'M TIRED OF YOUR WHINING, YOUR INFERNAL MEDDLING--TIRED OF *YOU!*

HE'S A MAN *BERSERK*, SMASHING THINGS FOR THE SHEER JOY OF IT AS HE STALKS CLEA THROUGH THE UPSTAIRS LIBRARY, PLAYING CAT-AND-MOUSE WITH HER AND LAUGHING EACH TIME HE CUTS OFF HER *ESCAPE.*

SLOWLY, SURELY, HE BACKS HER TOWARDS A CORNER, AND WHEN-- IN DESPERATION SHE FLINGS A CHAIR AT HIM...

...HE CASUALLY THROWS IT OUT THE WINDOW.

214

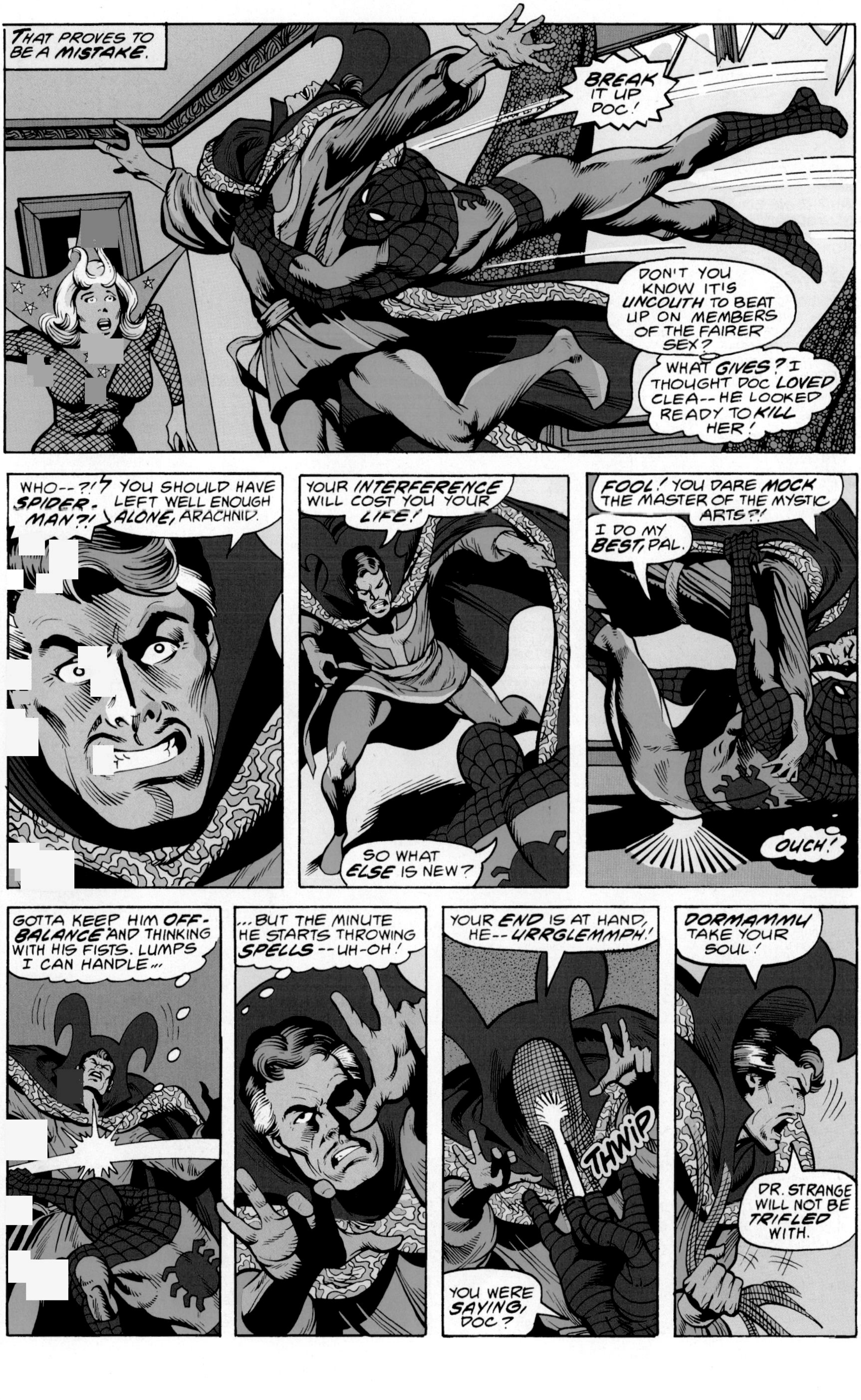

THAT PROVES TO BE A MISTAKE.
BREAK IT UP DOC!
DON'T YOU KNOW IT'S UNCOUTH TO BEAT UP ON MEMBERS OF THE FAIRER SEX?
WHAT GIVES? I THOUGHT DOC LOVED CLEA--HE LOOKED READY TO KILL HER!
WHO--?! SPIDER-MAN?!
YOU SHOULD HAVE LEFT WELL ENOUGH ALONE, ARACHNID.
YOUR INTERFERENCE WILL COST YOU YOUR LIFE!
SO WHAT ELSE IS NEW?
FOOL! YOU DARE MOCK THE MASTER OF THE MYSTIC ARTS?!
I DO MY BEST, PAL.
OUCH!
GOTTA KEEP HIM OFF-BALANCE AND THINKING WITH HIS FISTS. LUMPS I CAN HANDLE...
...BUT THE MINUTE HE STARTS THROWING SPELLS--UH-OH!
YOUR END IS AT HAND, HE--URRGLEMMPH!
THWIP
YOU WERE SAYING, DOC?
DORMAMMU TAKE YOUR SOUL!
DR. STRANGE WILL NOT BE TRIFLED WITH.

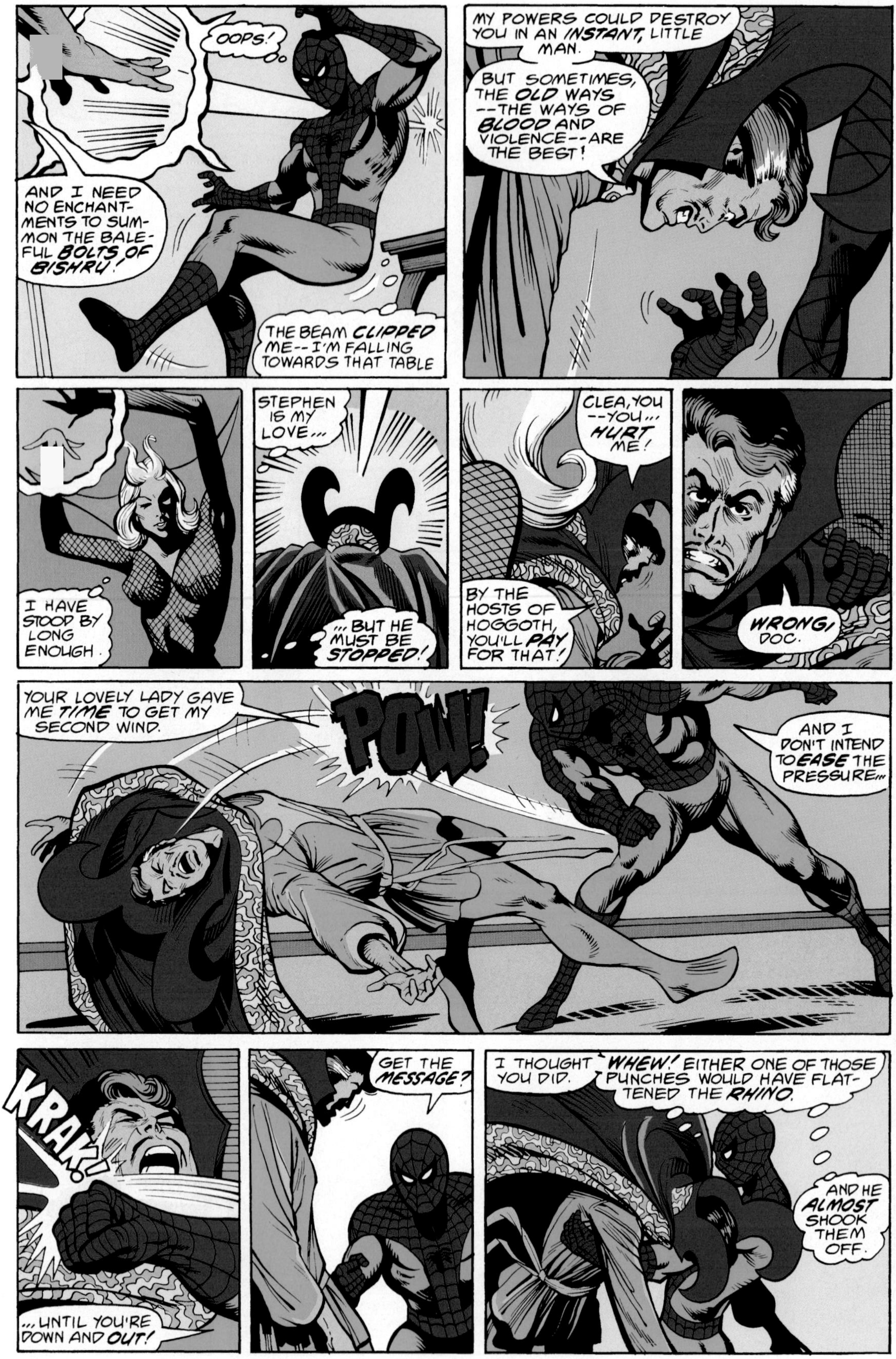
OOPS!
AND I NEED NO ENCHANTMENTS TO SUMMON THE BALEFUL BOLTS OF BISHRU!
THE BEAM CLIPPED ME-- I'M FALLING TOWARDS THAT TABLE
MY POWERS COULD DESTROY YOU IN AN INSTANT, LITTLE MAN.
BUT SOMETIMES, THE OLD WAYS --THE WAYS OF BLOOD AND VIOLENCE--ARE THE BEST!
I HAVE STOOD BY LONG ENOUGH.
STEPHEN IS MY LOVE...
...BUT HE MUST BE STOPPED!
CLEA, YOU --YOU... HURT ME!
BY THE HOSTS OF HOGGOTH, YOU'LL PAY FOR THAT!
WRONG, DOC.
YOUR LOVELY LADY GAVE ME TIME TO GET MY SECOND WIND.
POW!
AND I DON'T INTEND TO EASE THE PRESSURE...
KRAK!
...UNTIL YOU'RE DOWN AND OUT!
GET THE MESSAGE?
I THOUGHT YOU DID.
WHEW! EITHER ONE OF THOSE PUNCHES WOULD HAVE FLATTENED THE RHINO.
AND HE ALMOST SHOOK THEM OFF.

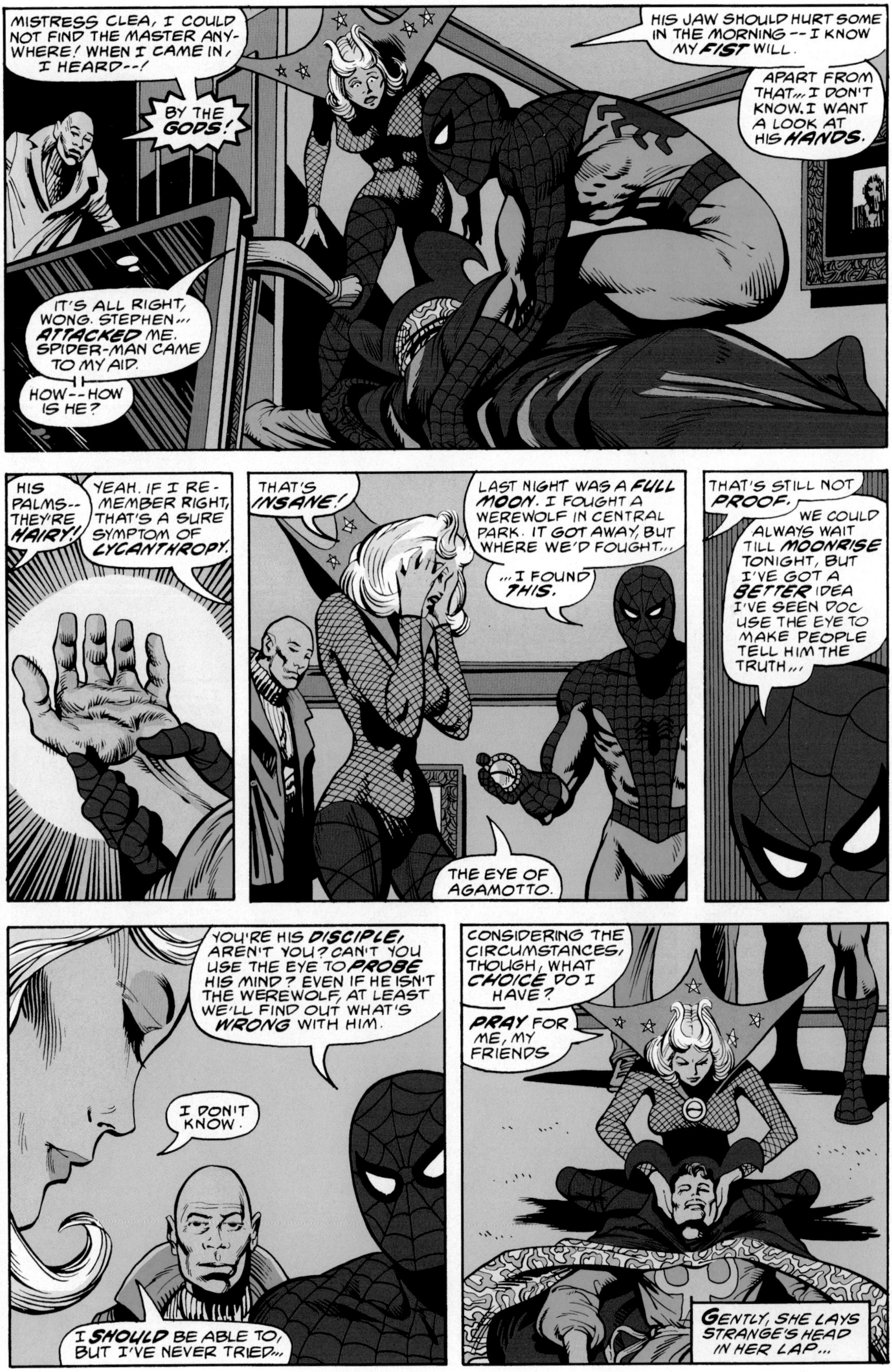
MISTRESS CLEA, I COULD NOT FIND THE MASTER ANYWHERE! WHEN I CAME IN, I HEARD--!
BY THE GODS!
HIS JAW SHOULD HURT SOME IN THE MORNING -- I KNOW MY FIST WILL.
APART FROM THAT... I DON'T KNOW. I WANT A LOOK AT HIS HANDS.
IT'S ALL RIGHT, WONG. STEPHEN... ATTACKED ME. SPIDER-MAN CAME TO MY AID.
HOW--HOW IS HE?
HIS PALMS-- THEY'RE HAIRY!
YEAH. IF I REMEMBER RIGHT, THAT'S A SURE SYMPTOM OF LYCANTHROPY.
THAT'S INSANE!
LAST NIGHT WAS A FULL MOON. I FOUGHT A WEREWOLF IN CENTRAL PARK. IT GOT AWAY, BUT WHERE WE'D FOUGHT...
...I FOUND THIS.
THE EYE OF AGAMOTTO.
THAT'S STILL NOT PROOF.
WE COULD ALWAYS WAIT TILL MOONRISE TONIGHT, BUT I'VE GOT A BETTER IDEA I'VE SEEN DOC USE THE EYE TO MAKE PEOPLE TELL HIM THE TRUTH...
YOU'RE HIS DISCIPLE, AREN'T YOU? CAN'T YOU USE THE EYE TO PROBE HIS MIND? EVEN IF HE ISN'T THE WEREWOLF, AT LEAST WE'LL FIND OUT WHAT'S WRONG WITH HIM.
I DON'T KNOW.
I SHOULD BE ABLE TO, BUT I'VE NEVER TRIED...
CONSIDERING THE CIRCUMSTANCES, THOUGH, WHAT CHOICE DO I HAVE?
PRAY FOR ME, MY FRIENDS
GENTLY, SHE LAYS STRANGE'S HEAD IN HER LAP...

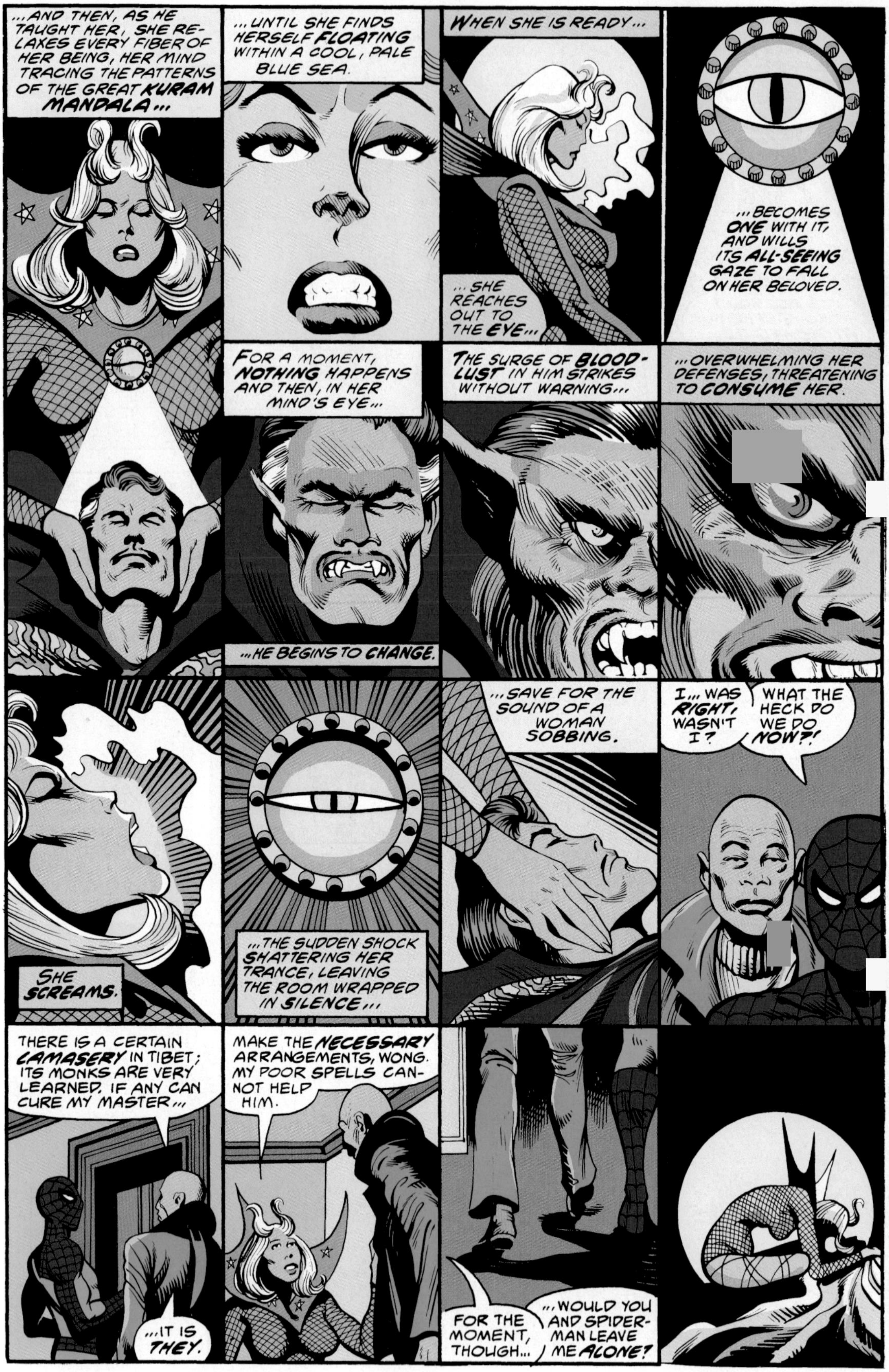
...AND THEN, AS HE TAUGHT HER, SHE RELAXES EVERY FIBER OF HER BEING, HER MIND TRACING THE PATTERNS OF THE GREAT KURAM MANDALA...
...UNTIL SHE FINDS HERSELF FLOATING WITHIN A COOL, PALE BLUE SEA.
WHEN SHE IS READY...
...SHE REACHES OUT TO THE EYE...
...BECOMES ONE WITH IT, AND WILLS ITS ALL-SEEING GAZE TO FALL ON HER BELOVED.
FOR A MOMENT, NOTHING HAPPENS AND THEN, IN HER MIND'S EYE...
...HE BEGINS TO CHANGE.
THE SURGE OF BLOOD-LUST IN HIM STRIKES WITHOUT WARNING...
...OVERWHELMING HER DEFENSES, THREATENING TO CONSUME HER.
SHE SCREAMS.
...THE SUDDEN SHOCK SHATTERING HER TRANCE, LEAVING THE ROOM WRAPPED IN SILENCE...
...SAVE FOR THE SOUND OF A WOMAN SOBBING.
I... WAS RIGHT, WASN'T I?
WHAT THE HECK DO WE DO NOW?!
THERE IS A CERTAIN LAMASERY IN TIBET; ITS MONKS ARE VERY LEARNED. IF ANY CAN CURE MY MASTER...
...IT IS THEY.
MAKE THE NECESSARY ARRANGEMENTS, WONG. MY POOR SPELLS CANNOT HELP HIM.
FOR THE MOMENT, THOUGH...
...WOULD YOU AND SPIDER-MAN LEAVE ME ALONE?

IT TAKES THE BETTER PART OF THE DAY TO SET-UP THE FLIGHT, AND IT'S EARLY *EVENING* BY THE TIME A SLEEK ROLLS-ROYCE LIMOUSINE MAKES ITS WAY ACROSS KENNEDY INTER-NATIONAL AIRPORT...

...TO PULL UP BESIDE A RENTED *707.*

I CAN MANAGE FROM HERE, SPIDER-MAN. THERE IS NO NEED FOR YOU TO ACCOMPANY ME FURTHER.

HE'S MY *FRIEND,* WONG. I OWE IT TO HIM TO SEE THIS THROUGH.

I AM *GLAD.* THE CREW IS ABOARD AND READY. WITH LUCK, WE SHOULD BE AIRBORNE WITHIN THE HOUR.

I HOPE WE *HAVE* AN HOUR. THE FULL MOON WILL BE UP SOON.

A LOT OF *CLOUDS* TONIGHT. I WONDER IF THEY'LL BLOCK WHATEVER LUNAR RAYS TRIGGER DOC'S *CHANGE.*

ALL IN ALL, I THINK I'D RATHER NOT FIND OUT.

WITH PRAC-TICED *PRE-CISION* THE PILOT JOCKEYS THE BIG JET-LINER TOWARDS THE *RUNWAY...*

ONCE WE'RE IN THE AIR...

...WE'LL BE ABLE TO STAY *AHEAD* OF THE MOON ALL THE WAY.

GLAD TO *HEAR* IT.

HOW ABOUT HELPING ME *SHUT* ALL THE WINDOW SHADES...

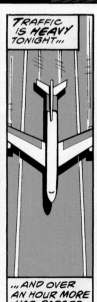

TRAFFIC IS *HEAVY* TONIGHT...

...AND OVER AN HOUR MORE HAS PASSED WHEN THE JET IS FINALLY CLEARED FOR TAKE-OFF.

AS IT *ACCELERATES* DOWN THE RUNWAY...

...THE CLOUD COVER SUDDENLY *BREAKS...*

...*MOONLIGHT* PAINTING THE AIRPORT GLEAMING *SILVER.*

THE *707* IS ALMOST OFF THE GROUND...

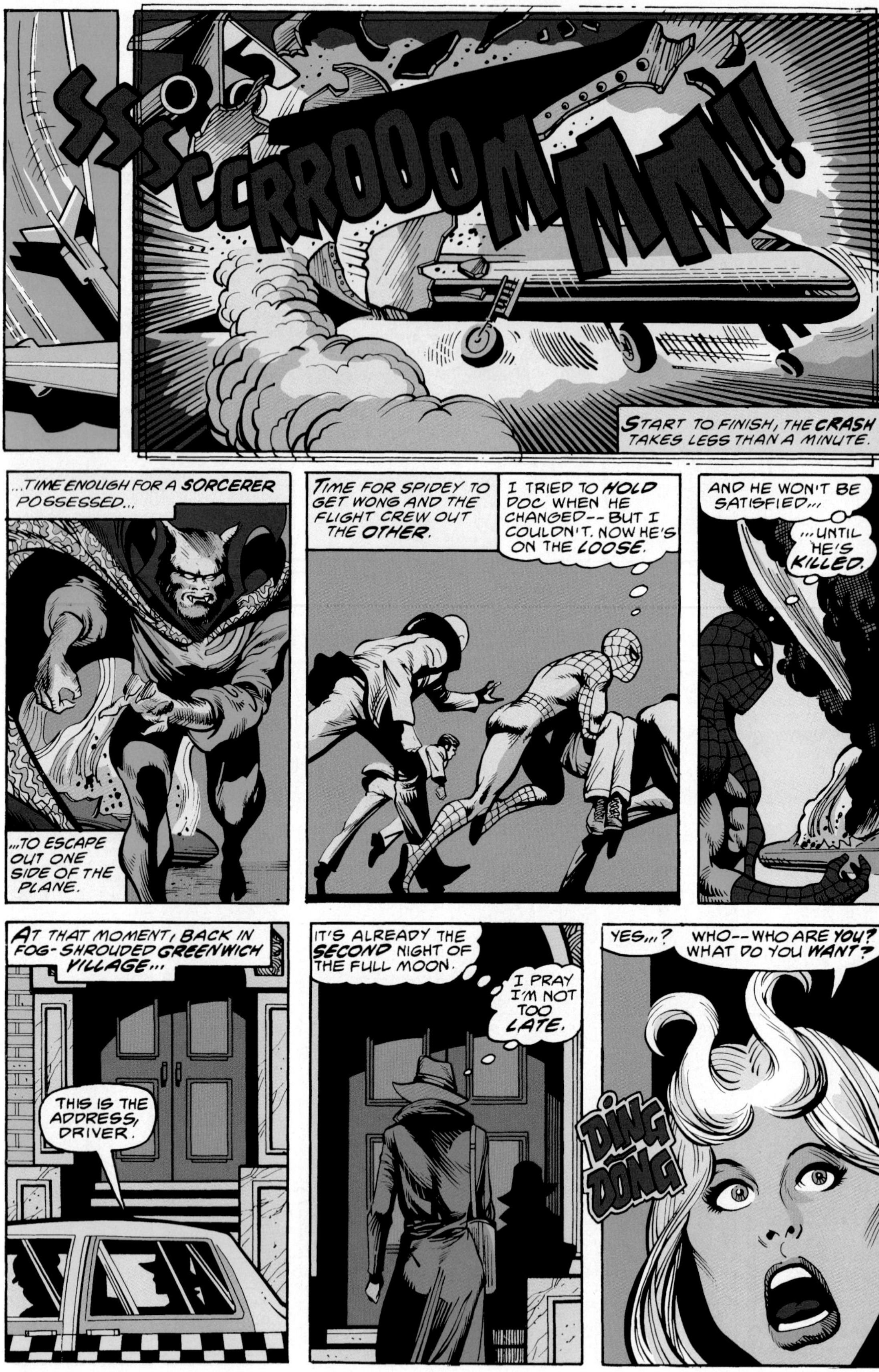
SSSCCRROOOOMMM!!
START TO FINISH, THE CRASH TAKES LESS THAN A MINUTE.
...TIME ENOUGH FOR A SORCERER POSSESSED...
...TO ESCAPE OUT ONE SIDE OF THE PLANE.
TIME FOR SPIDEY TO GET WONG AND THE FLIGHT CREW OUT THE OTHER.
I TRIED TO HOLD DOC WHEN HE CHANGED-- BUT I COULDN'T. NOW HE'S ON THE LOOSE.
AND HE WON'T BE SATISFIED...
...UNTIL HE'S KILLED.
AT THAT MOMENT, BACK IN FOG-SHROUDED GREENWICH VILLAGE...
THIS IS THE ADDRESS, DRIVER.
IT'S ALREADY THE SECOND NIGHT OF THE FULL MOON.
I PRAY I'M NOT TOO LATE.
DING DONG
YES...?
WHO--WHO ARE YOU? WHAT DO YOU WANT?

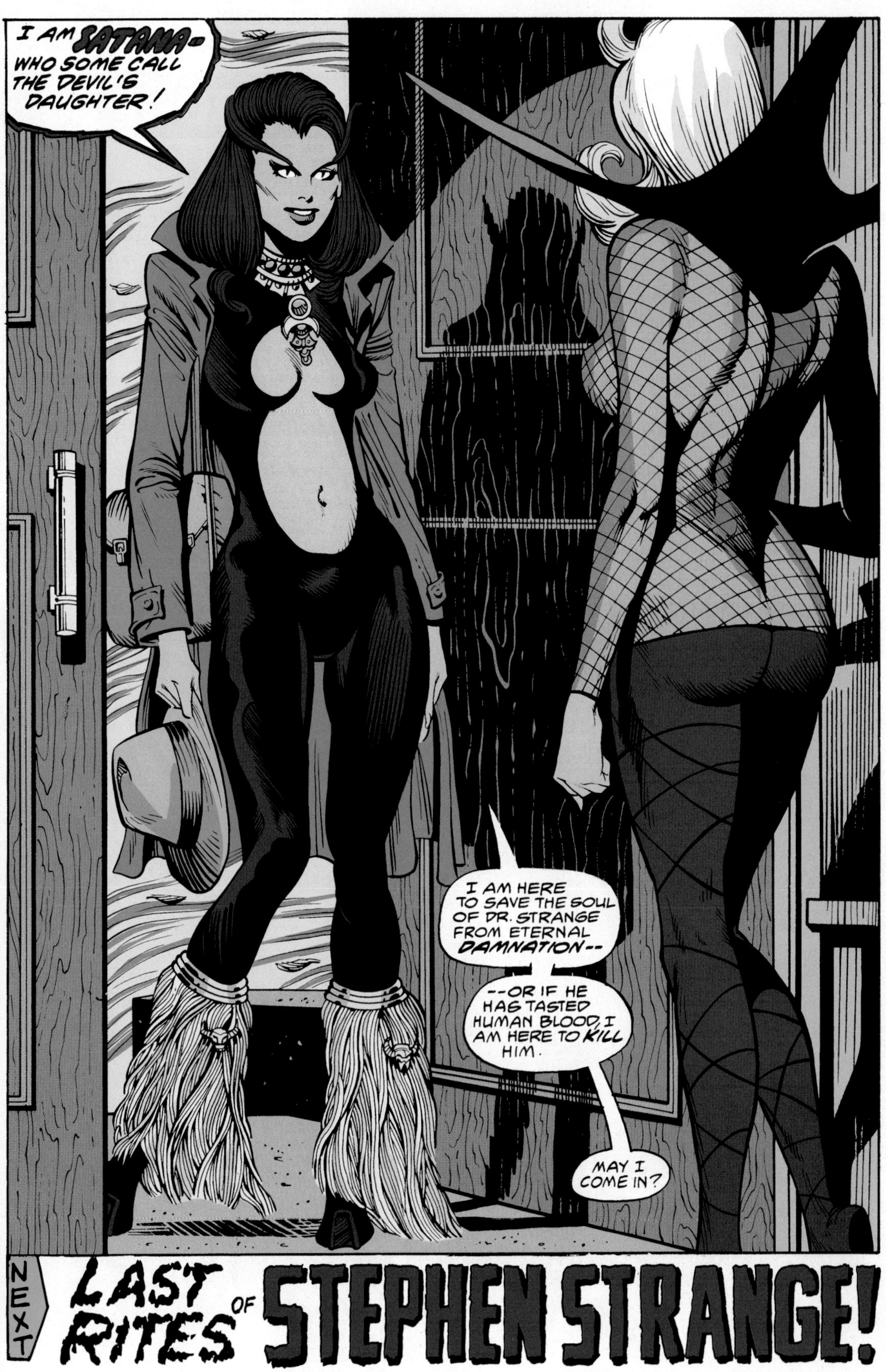
I AM SATANA--WHO SOME CALL THE DEVIL'S DAUGHTER!
I AM HERE TO SAVE THE SOUL OF DR. STRANGE FROM ETERNAL DAMNATION--
--OR IF HE HAS TASTED HUMAN BLOOD, I AM HERE TO KILL HIM.
MAY I COME IN?
NEXT
LAST RITES OF STEPHEN STRANGE!

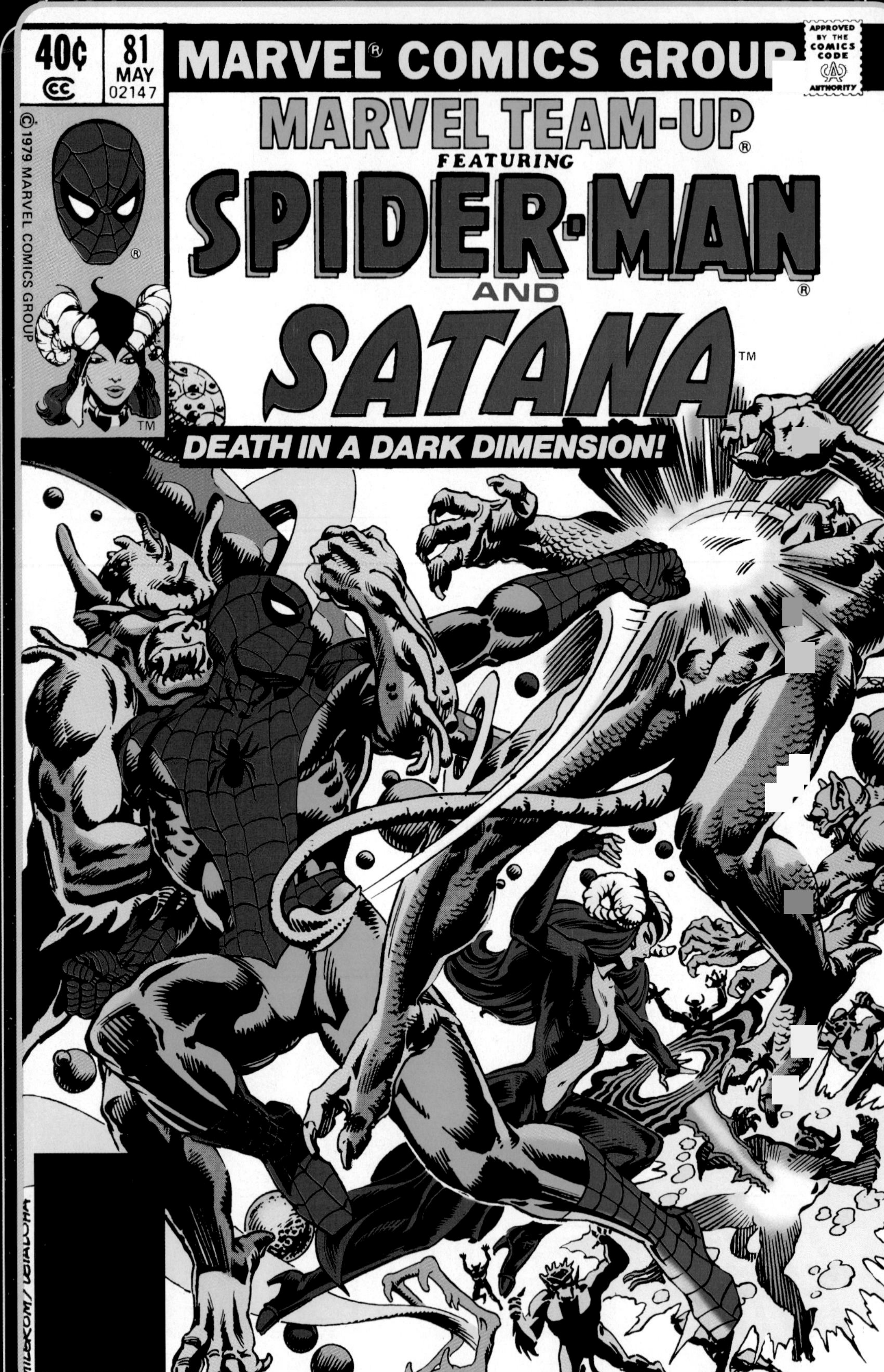
40¢
81
MAY
02147
MARVEL® COMICS GROUP
APPROVED BY THE COMICS CODE AUTHORITY
© 1979 MARVEL COMICS GROUP
MARVEL TEAM-UP®
FEATURING
SPIDER-MAN®
AND
SATANA™
DEATH IN A DARK DIMENSION!

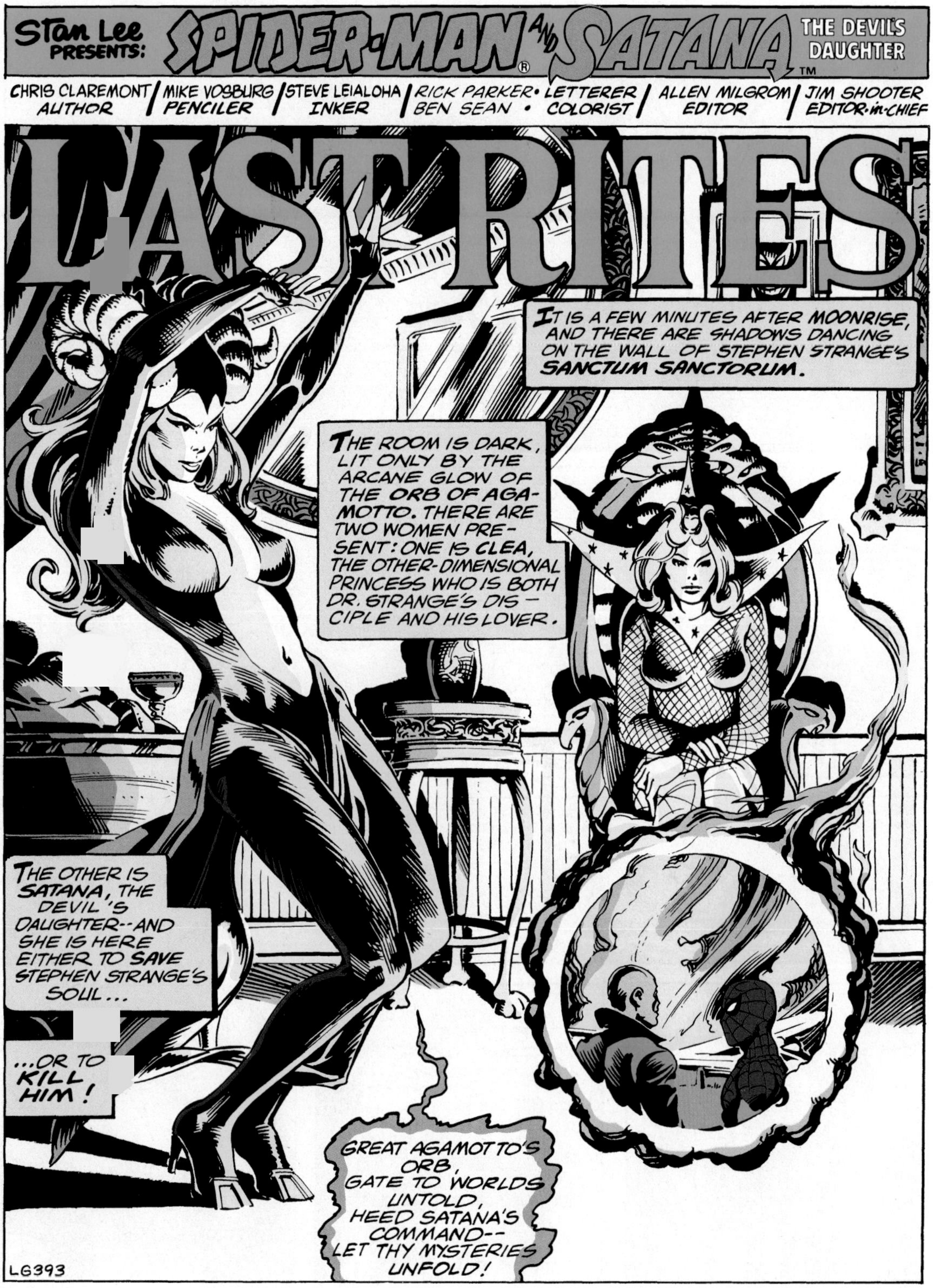
Stan Lee PRESENTS:
SPIDER-MAN® AND SATANA THE DEVIL'S DAUGHTER™
CHRIS CLAREMONT AUTHOR / MIKE VOSBURG PENCILER / STEVE LEIALOHA INKER / RICK PARKER • LETTERER / BEN SEAN • COLORIST / ALLEN MILGROM EDITOR / JIM SHOOTER EDITOR-in-CHIEF
LAST RITES
IT IS A FEW MINUTES AFTER MOONRISE, AND THERE ARE SHADOWS DANCING ON THE WALL OF STEPHEN STRANGE'S SANCTUM SANCTORUM.
THE ROOM IS DARK, LIT ONLY BY THE ARCANE GLOW OF THE ORB OF AGAMOTTO. THERE ARE TWO WOMEN PRESENT: ONE IS CLEA, THE OTHER-DIMENSIONAL PRINCESS WHO IS BOTH DR. STRANGE'S DISCIPLE AND HIS LOVER.
THE OTHER IS SATANA, THE DEVIL'S DAUGHTER--AND SHE IS HERE EITHER TO SAVE STEPHEN STRANGE'S SOUL...
...OR TO KILL HIM!
GREAT AGAMOTTO'S ORB, GATE TO WORLDS UNTOLD, HEED SATANA'S COMMAND-- LET THY MYSTERIES UNFOLD!
LG393

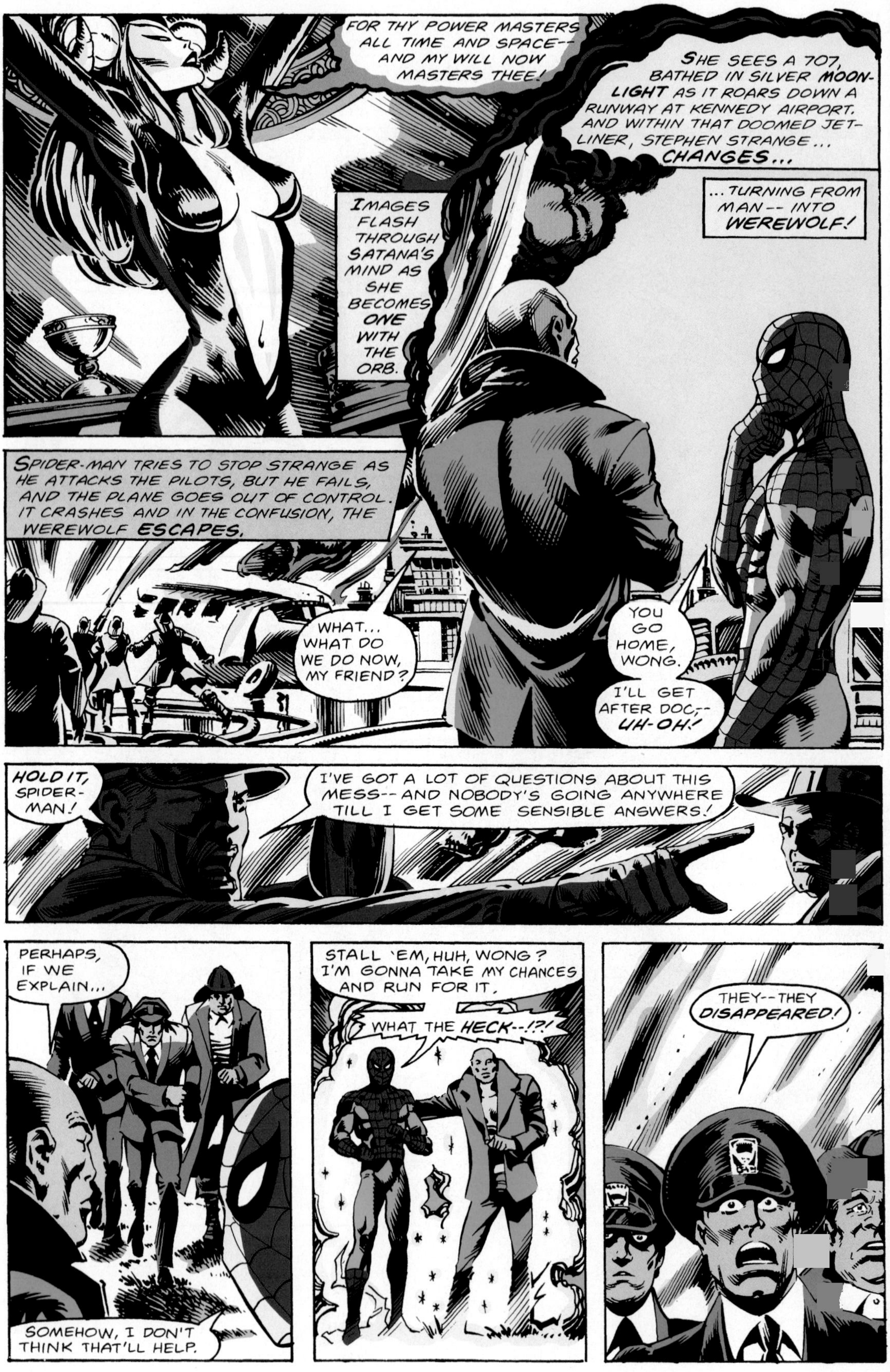
FOR THY POWER MASTERS ALL TIME AND SPACE-- AND MY WILL NOW MASTERS THEE!
SHE SEES A 707, BATHED IN SILVER MOON-LIGHT AS IT ROARS DOWN A RUNWAY AT KENNEDY AIRPORT. AND WITHIN THAT DOOMED JET-LINER, STEPHEN STRANGE ... CHANGES...
...TURNING FROM MAN-- INTO WEREWOLF!
IMAGES FLASH THROUGH SATANA'S MIND AS SHE BECOMES ONE WITH THE ORB.
SPIDER-MAN TRIES TO STOP STRANGE AS HE ATTACKS THE PILOTS, BUT HE FAILS, AND THE PLANE GOES OUT OF CONTROL. IT CRASHES AND IN THE CONFUSION, THE WEREWOLF ESCAPES.
WHAT... WHAT DO WE DO NOW, MY FRIEND?
YOU GO HOME, WONG.
I'LL GET AFTER DOC,-- UH-OH!
HOLD IT, SPIDER-MAN!
I'VE GOT A LOT OF QUESTIONS ABOUT THIS MESS-- AND NOBODY'S GOING ANYWHERE TILL I GET SOME SENSIBLE ANSWERS!
PERHAPS, IF WE EXPLAIN...
SOMEHOW, I DON'T THINK THAT'LL HELP.
STALL 'EM, HUH, WONG? I'M GONNA TAKE MY CHANCES AND RUN FOR IT.
WHAT THE HECK--!?!
THEY--THEY DISAPPEARED!

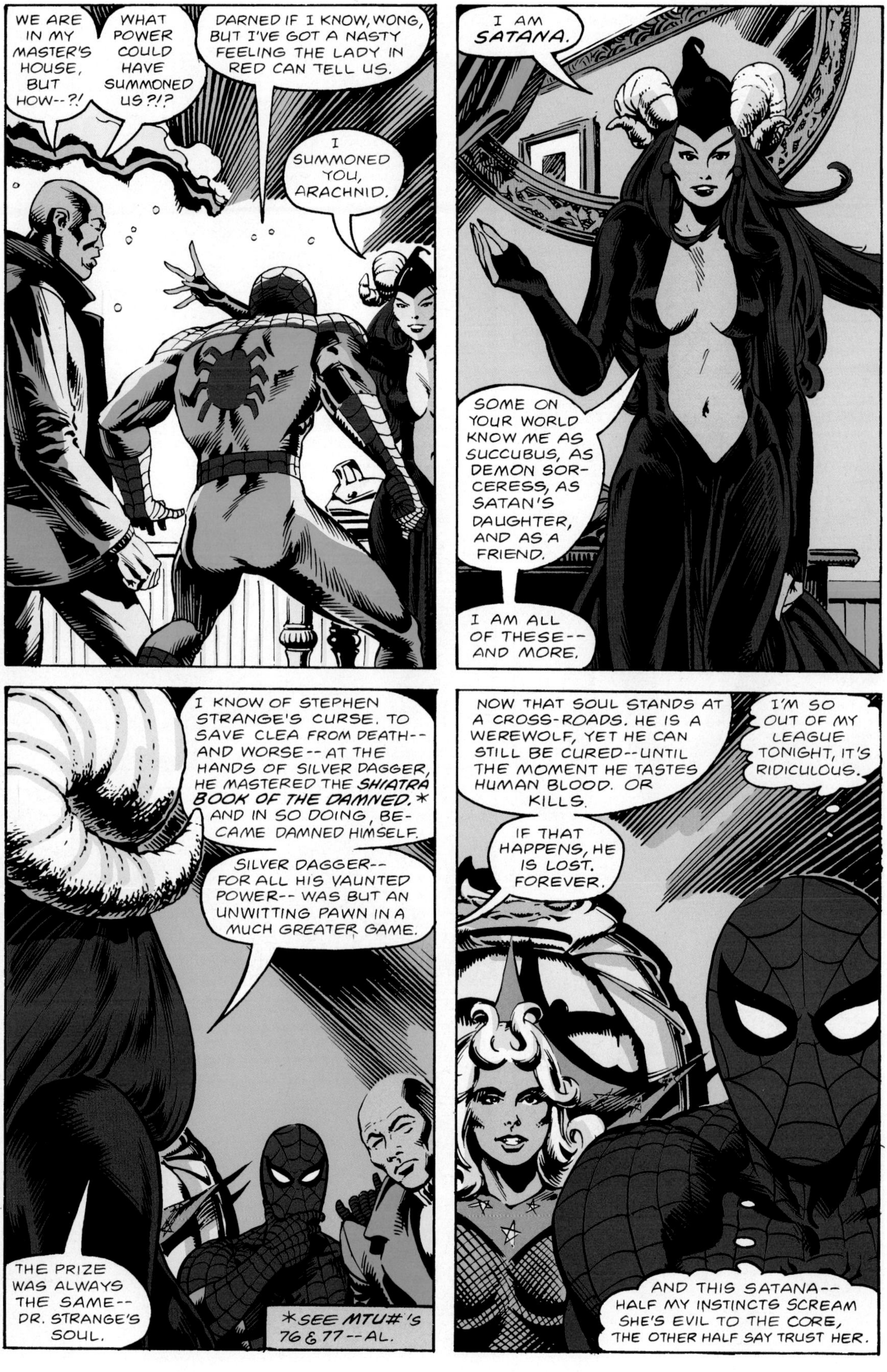

WE ARE IN MY MASTER'S HOUSE, BUT HOW--?!
WHAT POWER COULD HAVE SUMMONED US?!?
DARNED IF I KNOW, WONG, BUT I'VE GOT A NASTY FEELING THE LADY IN RED CAN TELL US.
I SUMMONED YOU, ARACHNID.
I AM SATANA.
SOME ON YOUR WORLD KNOW ME AS SUCCUBUS, AS DEMON SORCERESS, AS SATAN'S DAUGHTER, AND AS A FRIEND.
I AM ALL OF THESE-- AND MORE.
I KNOW OF STEPHEN STRANGE'S CURSE. TO SAVE CLEA FROM DEATH-- AND WORSE-- AT THE HANDS OF SILVER DAGGER, HE MASTERED THE SHIATRA BOOK OF THE DAMNED.* AND IN SO DOING, BECAME DAMNED HIMSELF.
SILVER DAGGER-- FOR ALL HIS VAUNTED POWER-- WAS BUT AN UNWITTING PAWN IN A MUCH GREATER GAME.
THE PRIZE WAS ALWAYS THE SAME-- DR. STRANGE'S SOUL.
*SEE MTU#'S 76 & 77 --AL.
NOW THAT SOUL STANDS AT A CROSS-ROADS. HE IS A WEREWOLF, YET HE CAN STILL BE CURED--UNTIL THE MOMENT HE TASTES HUMAN BLOOD. OR KILLS.
IF THAT HAPPENS, HE IS LOST. FOREVER.
I'M SO OUT OF MY LEAGUE TONIGHT, IT'S RIDICULOUS.
AND THIS SATANA-- HALF MY INSTINCTS SCREAM SHE'S EVIL TO THE CORE, THE OTHER HALF SAY TRUST HER.

I'VE HEARD STEPHEN SPEAK OF YOU, SATANA. YOU WERE CONSECRATED TO EVIL FROM THE MOMENT OF YOUR CONCEPTION. DR. STRANGE IS A FORCE FOR GOOD. WHY HELP HIM?

PERHAPS BECAUSE... IT AMUSES ME?

OR BECAUSE I AM PART HUMAN, AND IT IS HUMAN NATURE TO CHANGE, TO GROW, TO REBEL.

I BOW TO NEITHER HEAVEN NOR HELL, CLEA. IN THAT, I AM MUCH LIKE MY SATANIC SIRE.

I WOULD RATHER LIVE ON EARTH-- AND BE FREE, WHATEVER THE COST-- THAN SERVE IN HELL.

THE ANCIENT ONE CANNOT HELP. MARIE LEVEAU WILL NOT.

ONLY I CAN SAVE HIM.

FEW SORCERERS HAVE THE POWER, OR LEARNING, TO EXCORCISE THE DEMON WITHIN STEPHEN STRANGE.

AND IF I AM TOO LATE-- OR IF MY SPELLS SHOULD FAIL--

--I WILL SHOOT HIM THROUGH THE HEART WITH A SILVER BULLET.

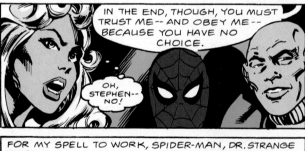

IN THE END, THOUGH, YOU MUST TRUST ME-- AND OBEY ME-- BECAUSE YOU HAVE NO CHOICE.

OH, STEPHEN-- NO!

FOR MY SPELL TO WORK, SPIDER-MAN, DR. STRANGE MUST BE HELD WITHIN A MYSTIC PENTAGRAM. I CANNOT AFFORD THE POWER NEEDED TO OVERCOME HIS NATURAL MYSTIC DEFENSES AND BRING HIM HERE.

I GET IT. THAT'S MY JOB. LUCKY ME. I'LL DO MY BEST, LUCKILY, I TAGGED HIM WITH A SPIDEY-TRACER-- JUST IN CASE-- BEFORE WE LEFT FOR THE AIRPORT.

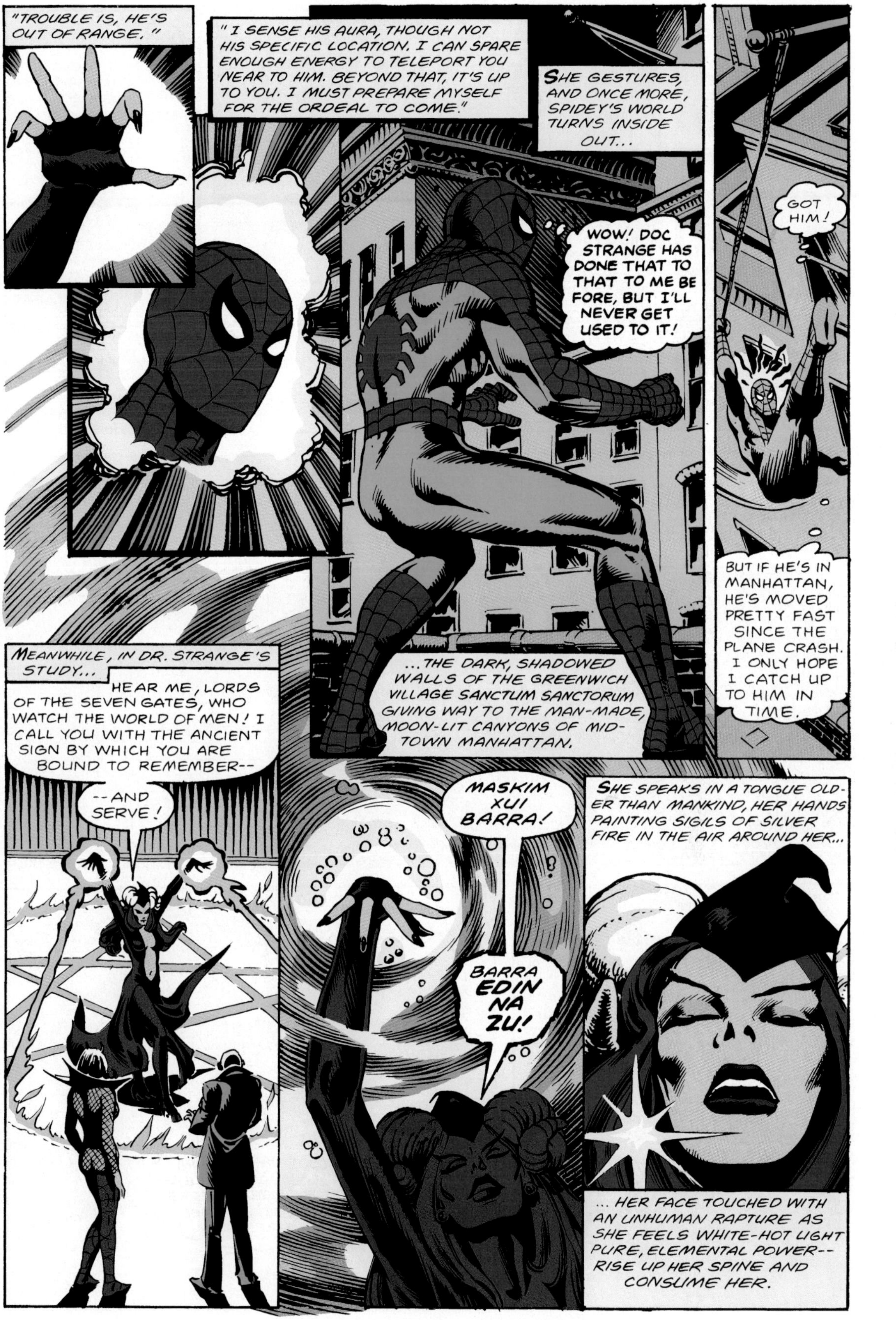
"TROUBLE IS, HE'S OUT OF RANGE."
"I SENSE HIS AURA, THOUGH NOT HIS SPECIFIC LOCATION. I CAN SPARE ENOUGH ENERGY TO TELEPORT YOU NEAR TO HIM. BEYOND THAT, IT'S UP TO YOU. I MUST PREPARE MYSELF FOR THE ORDEAL TO COME."
SHE GESTURES, AND ONCE MORE, SPIDEY'S WORLD TURNS INSIDE OUT...
WOW! DOC STRANGE HAS DONE THAT TO THAT TO ME BE FORE, BUT I'LL NEVER GET USED TO IT!
...THE DARK, SHADOWED WALLS OF THE GREENWICH VILLAGE SANCTUM SANCTORUM GIVING WAY TO THE MAN-MADE, MOON-LIT CANYONS OF MID-TOWN MANHATTAN.
GOT HIM!
BUT IF HE'S IN MANHATTAN, HE'S MOVED PRETTY FAST SINCE THE PLANE CRASH. I ONLY HOPE I CATCH UP TO HIM IN TIME.
MEANWHILE, IN DR. STRANGE'S STUDY...
HEAR ME, LORDS OF THE SEVEN GATES, WHO WATCH THE WORLD OF MEN! I CALL YOU WITH THE ANCIENT SIGN BY WHICH YOU ARE BOUND TO REMEMBER--
--AND SERVE!
MASKIM XUI BARRA!
BARRA EDIN NA ZU!
SHE SPEAKS IN A TONGUE OLDER THAN MANKIND, HER HANDS PAINTING SIGILS OF SILVER FIRE IN THE AIR AROUND HER...
... HER FACE TOUCHED WITH AN UNHUMAN RAPTURE AS SHE FEELS WHITE-HOT LIGHT PURE, ELEMENTAL POWER-- RISE UP HER SPINE AND CONSUME HER.

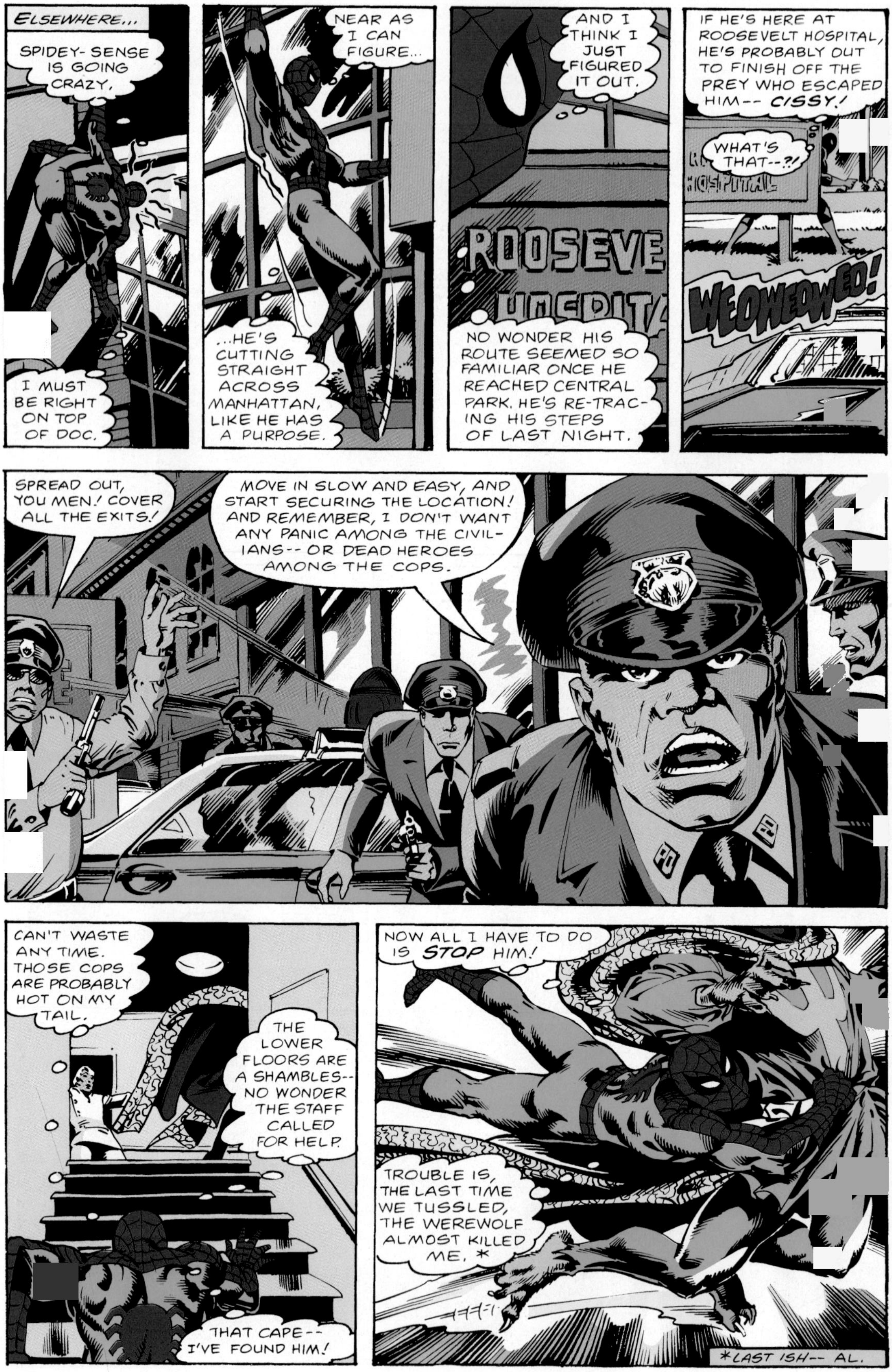
ELSEWHERE...
SPIDEY-SENSE IS GOING CRAZY.
I MUST BE RIGHT ON TOP OF DOC.
NEAR AS I CAN FIGURE...
...HE'S CUTTING STRAIGHT ACROSS MANHATTAN, LIKE HE HAS A PURPOSE.
AND I THINK I JUST FIGURED IT OUT.
ROOSEVE
NO WONDER HIS ROUTE SEEMED SO FAMILIAR ONCE HE REACHED CENTRAL PARK. HE'S RE-TRACING HIS STEPS OF LAST NIGHT.
IF HE'S HERE AT ROOSEVELT HOSPITAL, HE'S PROBABLY OUT TO FINISH OFF THE PREY WHO ESCAPED HIM-- CISSY!
WHAT'S THAT--?!
HOSPITAL
WEOWEOWEO!
SPREAD OUT, YOU MEN! COVER ALL THE EXITS!
MOVE IN SLOW AND EASY, AND START SECURING THE LOCATION! AND REMEMBER, I DON'T WANT ANY PANIC AMONG THE CIVILIANS-- OR DEAD HEROES AMONG THE COPS.
CAN'T WASTE ANY TIME. THOSE COPS ARE PROBABLY HOT ON MY TAIL.
THE LOWER FLOORS ARE A SHAMBLES-- NO WONDER THE STAFF CALLED FOR HELP.
THAT CAPE-- I'VE FOUND HIM!
NOW ALL I HAVE TO DO IS STOP HIM!
TROUBLE IS, THE LAST TIME WE TUSSLED, THE WEREWOLF ALMOST KILLED ME. *
*LAST ISH-- AL.

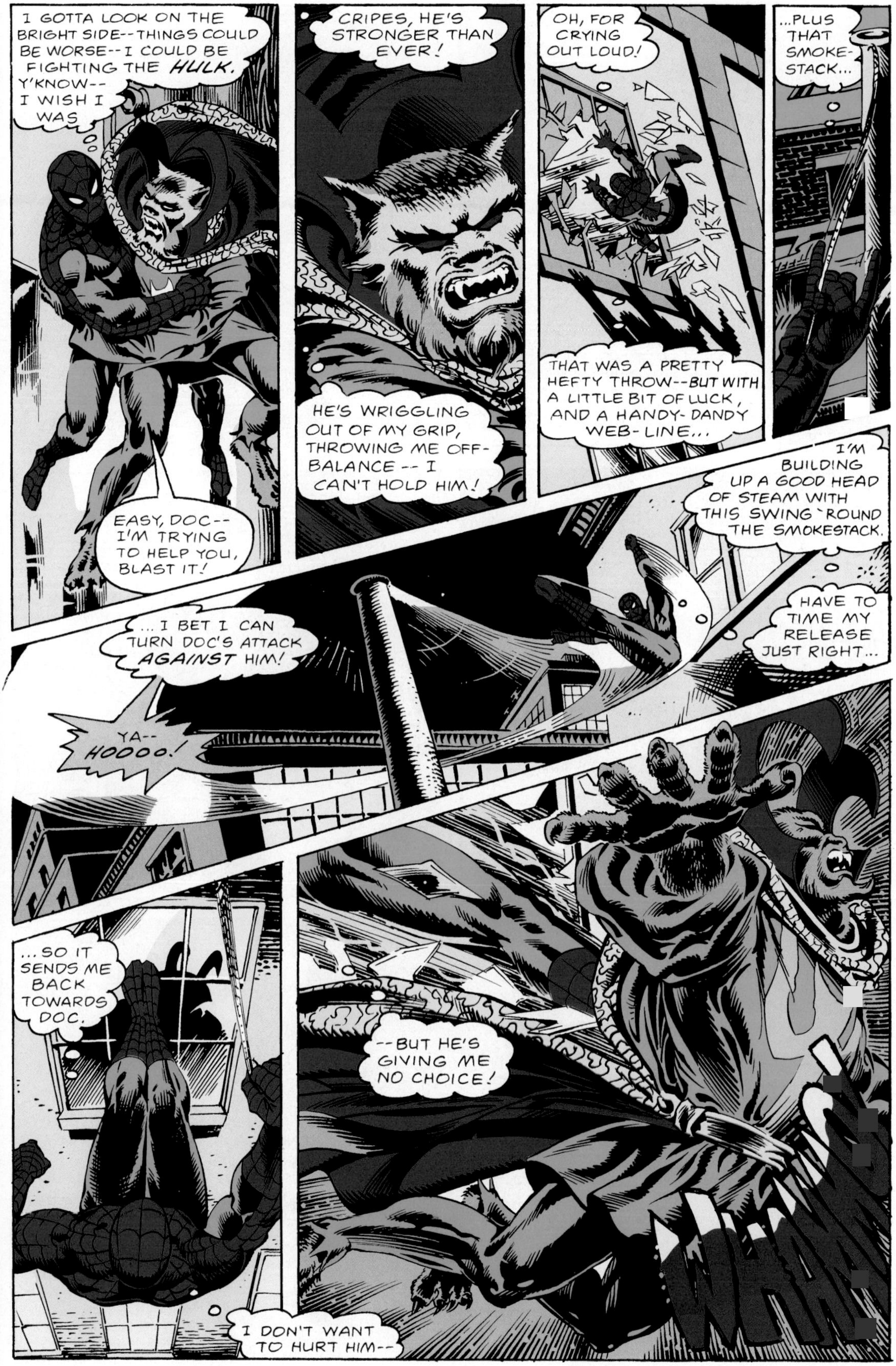
I GOTTA LOOK ON THE BRIGHT SIDE--THINGS COULD BE WORSE--I COULD BE FIGHTING THE HULK.
Y'KNOW-- I WISH I WAS
EASY, DOC-- I'M TRYING TO HELP YOU, BLAST IT!
CRIPES, HE'S STRONGER THAN EVER!
HE'S WRIGGLING OUT OF MY GRIP, THROWING ME OFF-BALANCE -- I CAN'T HOLD HIM!
OH, FOR CRYING OUT LOUD!
THAT WAS A PRETTY HEFTY THROW--BUT WITH A LITTLE BIT OF LUCK, AND A HANDY-DANDY WEB-LINE...
...PLUS THAT SMOKE-STACK...
...I BET I CAN TURN DOC'S ATTACK AGAINST HIM!
I'M BUILDING UP A GOOD HEAD OF STEAM WITH THIS SWING 'ROUND THE SMOKESTACK.
HAVE TO TIME MY RELEASE JUST RIGHT...
YA--HOOOO!
...SO IT SENDS ME BACK TOWARDS DOC.
I DON'T WANT TO HURT HIM--
--BUT HE'S GIVING ME NO CHOICE!

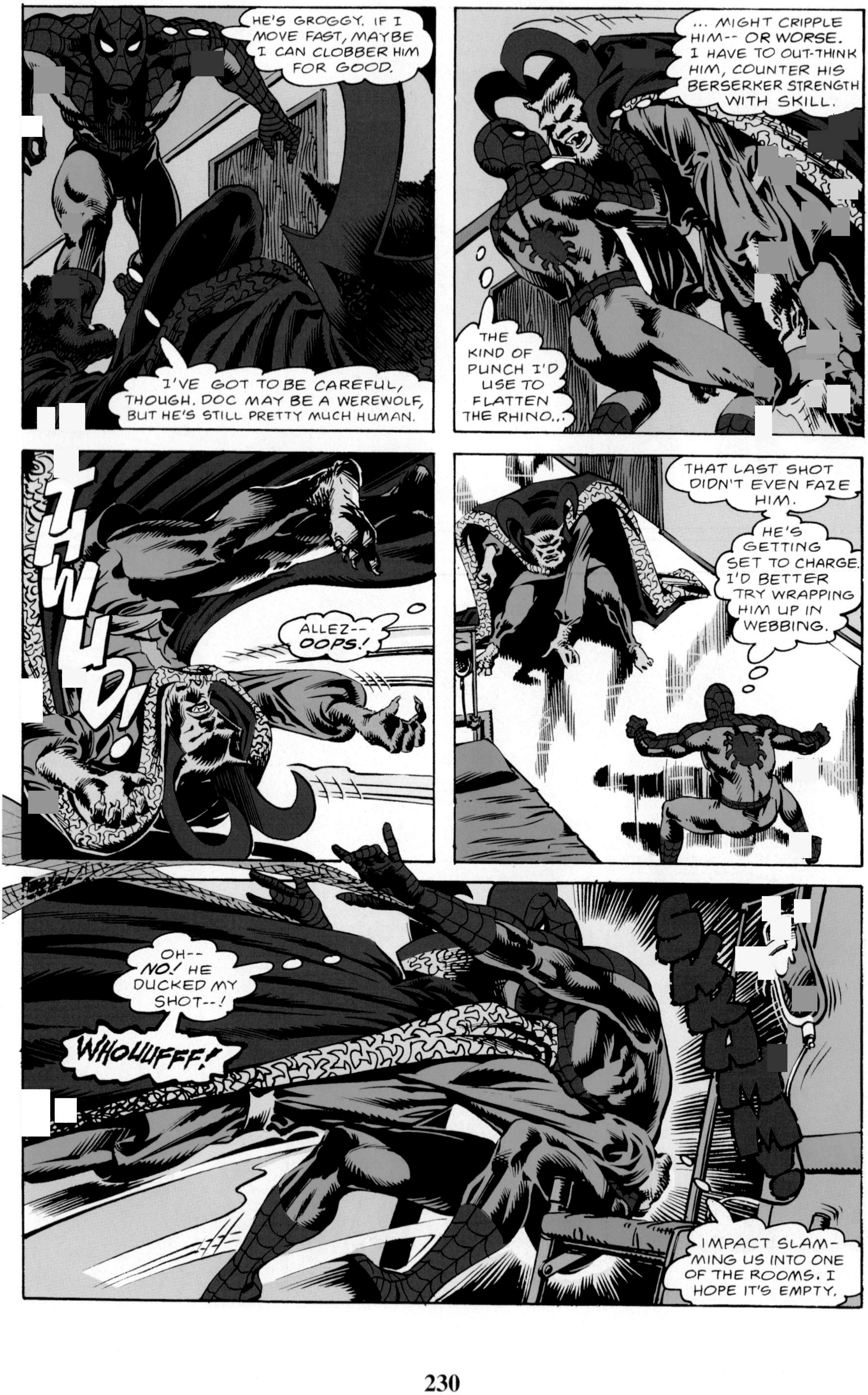
HE'S GROGGY. IF I MOVE FAST, MAYBE I CAN CLOBBER HIM FOR GOOD.
I'VE GOT TO BE CAREFUL, THOUGH. DOC MAY BE A WEREWOLF, BUT HE'S STILL PRETTY MUCH HUMAN.
... MIGHT CRIPPLE HIM-- OR WORSE. I HAVE TO OUT-THINK HIM, COUNTER HIS BERSERKER STRENGTH WITH SKILL.
THE KIND OF PUNCH I'D USE TO FLATTEN THE RHINO...
THWUD!
ALLEZ-- OOPS!
THAT LAST SHOT DIDN'T EVEN FAZE HIM.
HE'S GETTING SET TO CHARGE. I'D BETTER TRY WRAPPING HIM UP IN WEBBING.
OH-- NO! HE DUCKED MY SHOT--!
WHOUUFFF!
IMPACT SLAMMING US INTO ONE OF THE ROOMS. I HOPE IT'S EMPTY.

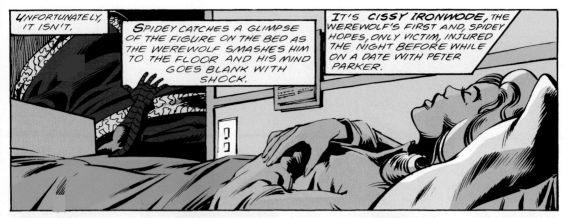

UNFORTUNATELY, IT ISN'T.

SPIDEY CATCHES A GLIMPSE OF THE FIGURE ON THE BED AS THE WEREWOLF SMASHES HIM TO THE FLOOR AND HIS MIND GOES BLANK WITH SHOCK.

IT'S *CISSY IRONWODE*, THE WEREWOLF'S FIRST AND, SPIDEY HOPES, ONLY VICTIM, INJURED THE NIGHT BEFORE WHILE ON A DATE WITH PETER PARKER.

LUCK'S RUNNING... TRUE TO FORM.

SHAGGY... KNOCKED... WIND OUT OF ME.

CAN'T CATCH... BREATH.

PETER...?!

GROWLS -- OH LORD, THE MONSTER'S KILLED PETER!

NOW-- NOW IT'LL COME FOR ME!

CISSY-- SHE'S DREAMING OF LAST NIGHT, WHEN DOC ALMOST... KILLED HER.

HE'S GOT THE LEVERAGE-- MY ARMS FEEL-- ABOUT TO BREAK. BUT I CAN'T GIVE IN! TOO MUCH... DEPENDING ON ME-- MY LIFE-- CISSY'S-- DOC'S SOUL.

I OWE DOC STRANGE TOO MUCH TO FAIL HIM--

--AND I WON'T!

BROW

OOPS! THAT SWIPE CAME A LITTLE TOO CLOSE FOR COMFORT.

BUT IT MISSED. THAT'S ALL THAT COUNTS.

NOW, SHAGGY, IT'S *MY* TURN!

I'VE GOT TO IMMOBILIZE DOC WITH A HALF-NELSON...

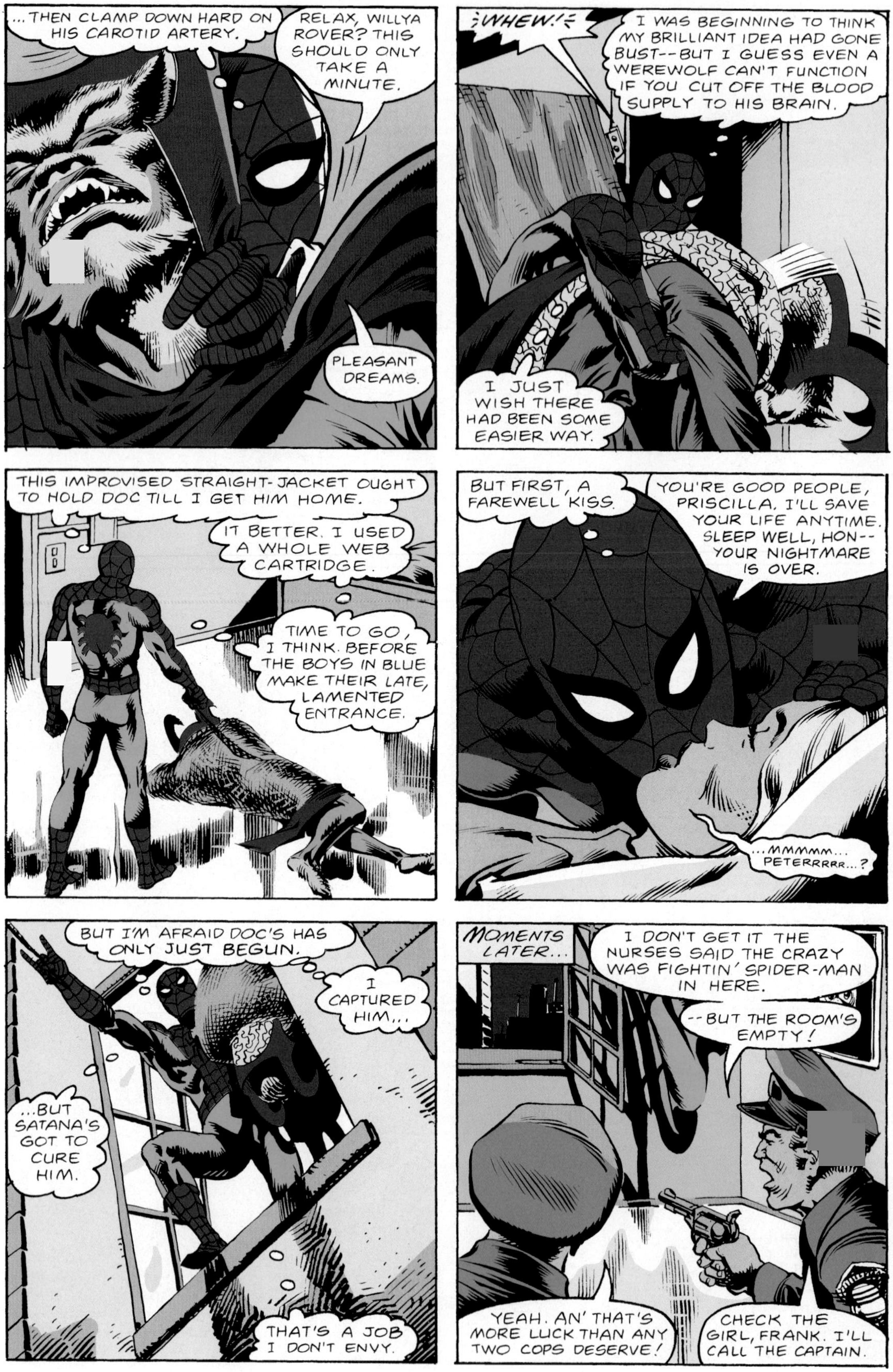
...THEN CLAMP DOWN HARD ON HIS CAROTID ARTERY.
RELAX, WILLYA ROVER? THIS SHOULD ONLY TAKE A MINUTE.
PLEASANT DREAMS.
WHEW!
I WAS BEGINNING TO THINK MY BRILLIANT IDEA HAD GONE BUST--BUT I GUESS EVEN A WEREWOLF CAN'T FUNCTION IF YOU CUT OFF THE BLOOD SUPPLY TO HIS BRAIN.
I JUST WISH THERE HAD BEEN SOME EASIER WAY.
THIS IMPROVISED STRAIGHT-JACKET OUGHT TO HOLD DOC TILL I GET HIM HOME.
IT BETTER. I USED A WHOLE WEB CARTRIDGE.
TIME TO GO, I THINK. BEFORE THE BOYS IN BLUE MAKE THEIR LATE, LAMENTED ENTRANCE.
BUT FIRST, A FAREWELL KISS.
YOU'RE GOOD PEOPLE, PRISCILLA. I'LL SAVE YOUR LIFE ANYTIME. SLEEP WELL, HON--YOUR NIGHTMARE IS OVER.
...MMMMM... PETERRRRR...?
BUT I'M AFRAID DOC'S HAS ONLY JUST BEGUN.
I CAPTURED HIM...
...BUT SATANA'S GOT TO CURE HIM.
THAT'S A JOB I DON'T ENVY.
MOMENTS LATER...
I DON'T GET IT THE NURSES SAID THE CRAZY WAS FIGHTIN' SPIDER-MAN IN HERE.
--BUT THE ROOM'S EMPTY!
YEAH. AN' THAT'S MORE LUCK THAN ANY TWO COPS DESERVE!
CHECK THE GIRL, FRANK. I'LL CALL THE CAPTAIN.

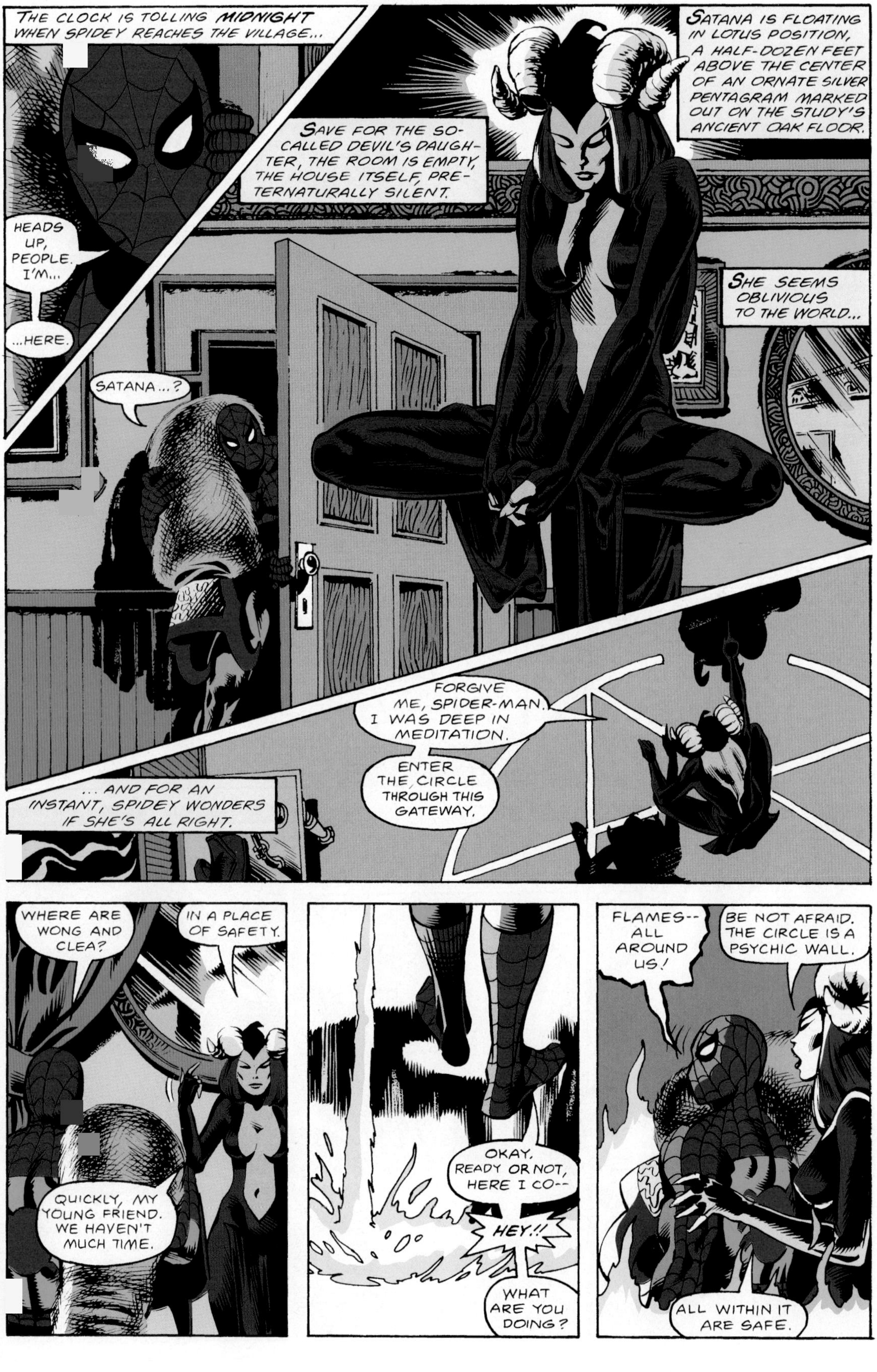
THE CLOCK IS TOLLING MIDNIGHT WHEN SPIDEY REACHES THE VILLAGE...
HEADS UP, PEOPLE. I'M...
...HERE.
SAVE FOR THE SO-CALLED DEVIL'S DAUGHTER, THE ROOM IS EMPTY, THE HOUSE ITSELF, PRETERNATURALLY SILENT.
SATANA IS FLOATING IN LOTUS POSITION, A HALF-DOZEN FEET ABOVE THE CENTER OF AN ORNATE SILVER PENTAGRAM MARKED OUT ON THE STUDY'S ANCIENT OAK FLOOR.
SATANA...?
SHE SEEMS OBLIVIOUS TO THE WORLD...
... AND FOR AN INSTANT, SPIDEY WONDERS IF SHE'S ALL RIGHT.
FORGIVE ME, SPIDER-MAN. I WAS DEEP IN MEDITATION.
ENTER THE CIRCLE THROUGH THIS GATEWAY.
WHERE ARE WONG AND CLEA?
IN A PLACE OF SAFETY.
QUICKLY, MY YOUNG FRIEND. WE HAVEN'T MUCH TIME.
OKAY. READY OR NOT, HERE I CO--
HEY!!
WHAT ARE YOU DOING?
FLAMES-- ALL AROUND US!
BE NOT AFRAID. THE CIRCLE IS A PSYCHIC WALL.
ALL WITHIN IT ARE SAFE.

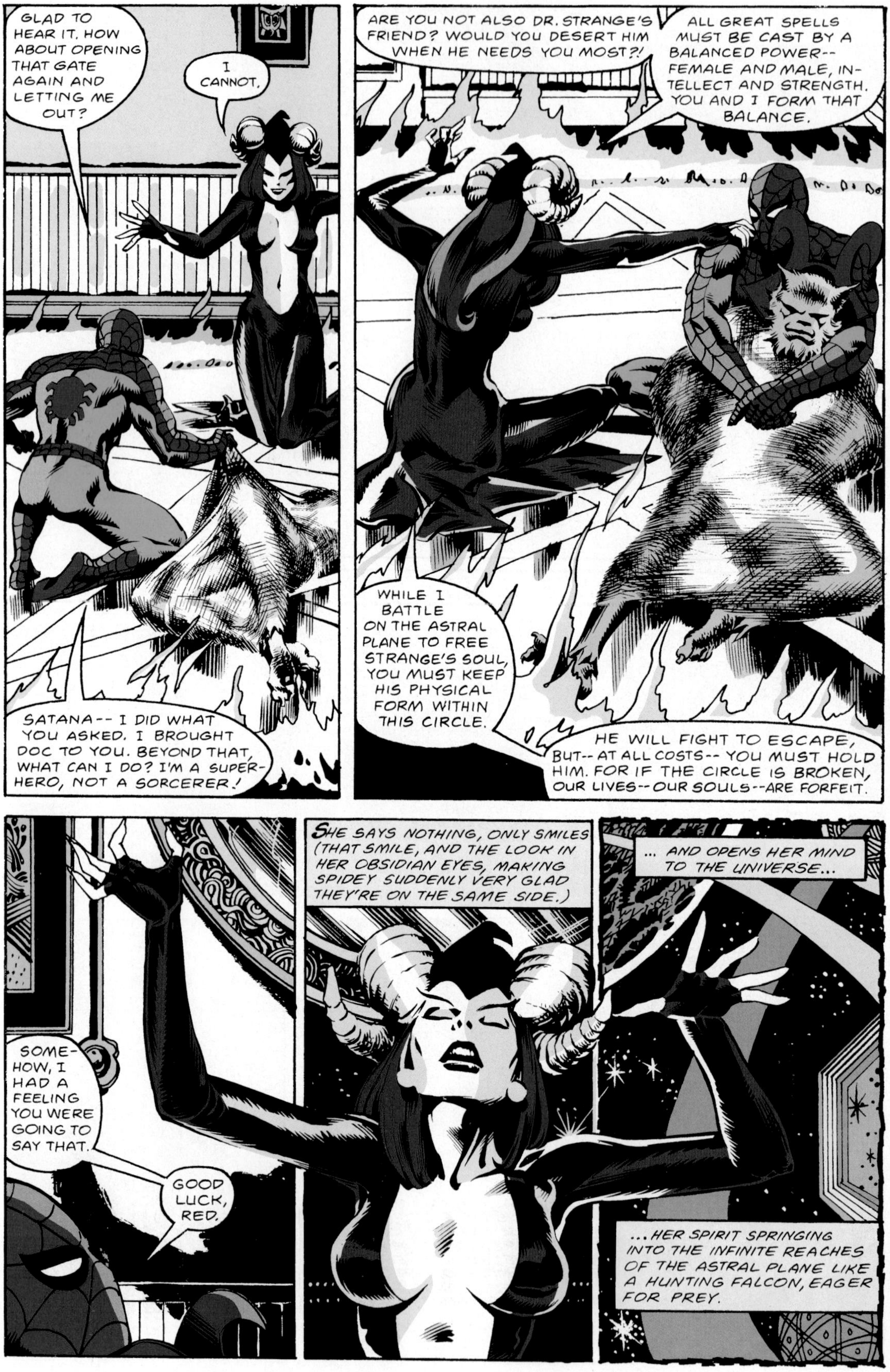
GLAD TO HEAR IT. HOW ABOUT OPENING THAT GATE AGAIN AND LETTING ME OUT?
I CANNOT.
SATANA-- I DID WHAT YOU ASKED. I BROUGHT DOC TO YOU. BEYOND THAT, WHAT CAN I DO? I'M A SUPER-HERO, NOT A SORCERER!
ARE YOU NOT ALSO DR. STRANGE'S FRIEND? WOULD YOU DESERT HIM WHEN HE NEEDS YOU MOST?!
ALL GREAT SPELLS MUST BE CAST BY A BALANCED POWER-- FEMALE AND MALE, INTELLECT AND STRENGTH. YOU AND I FORM THAT BALANCE.
WHILE I BATTLE ON THE ASTRAL PLANE TO FREE STRANGE'S SOUL, YOU MUST KEEP HIS PHYSICAL FORM WITHIN THIS CIRCLE.
HE WILL FIGHT TO ESCAPE, BUT-- AT ALL COSTS-- YOU MUST HOLD HIM. FOR IF THE CIRCLE IS BROKEN, OUR LIVES--OUR SOULS--ARE FORFEIT.
SHE SAYS NOTHING, ONLY SMILES (THAT SMILE, AND THE LOOK IN HER OBSIDIAN EYES, MAKING SPIDEY SUDDENLY VERY GLAD THEY'RE ON THE SAME SIDE.)
SOME-HOW, I HAD A FEELING YOU WERE GOING TO SAY THAT.
GOOD LUCK, RED.
... AND OPENS HER MIND TO THE UNIVERSE...
...HER SPIRIT SPRINGING INTO THE INFINITE REACHES OF THE ASTRAL PLANE LIKE A HUNTING FALCON, EAGER FOR PREY.

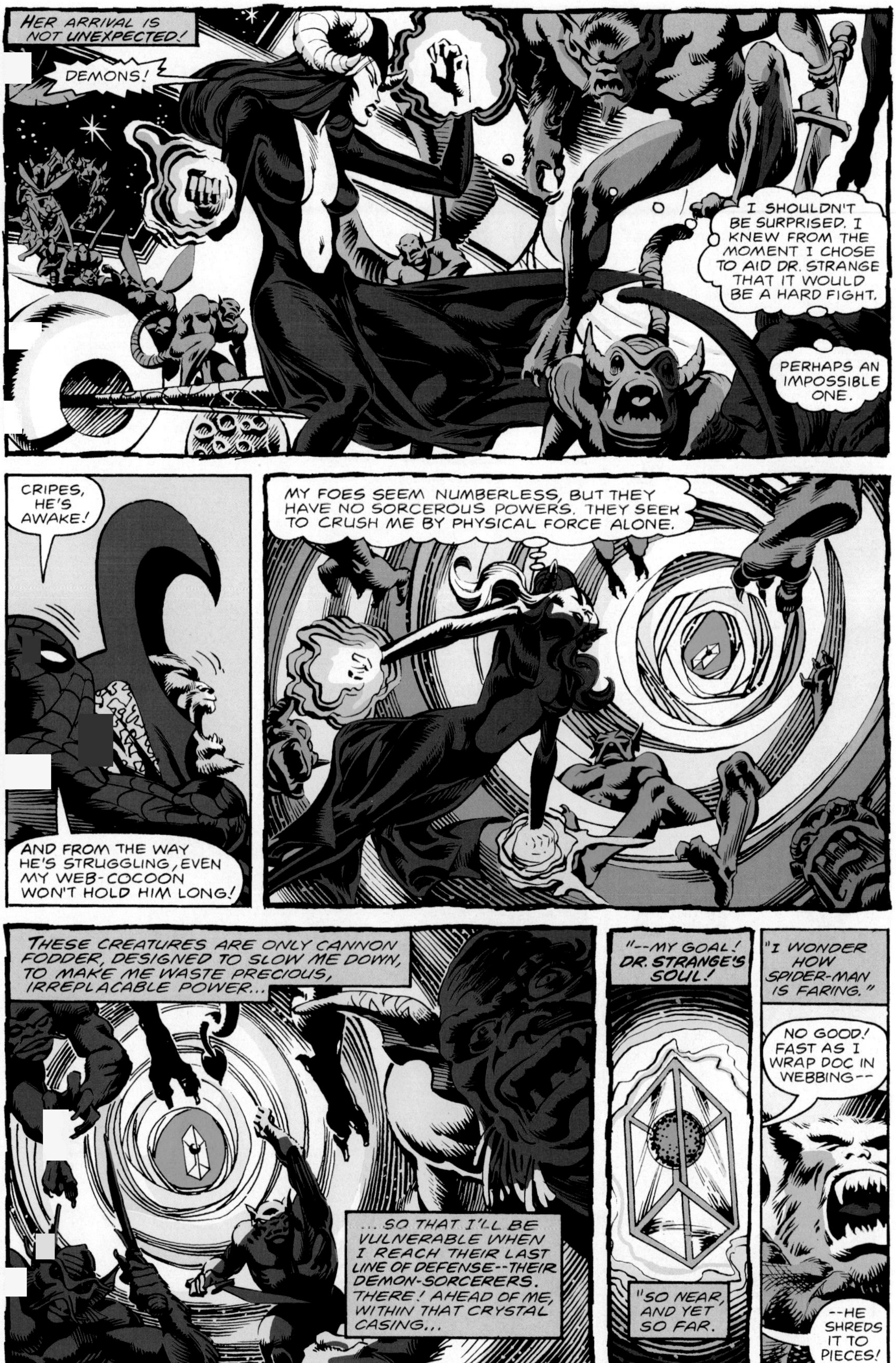

HER ARRIVAL IS NOT UNEXPECTED!
DEMONS!
I SHOULDN'T BE SURPRISED. I KNEW FROM THE MOMENT I CHOSE TO AID DR. STRANGE THAT IT WOULD BE A HARD FIGHT.
PERHAPS AN IMPOSSIBLE ONE.
CRIPES, HE'S AWAKE!
AND FROM THE WAY HE'S STRUGGLING, EVEN MY WEB-COCOON WON'T HOLD HIM LONG!
MY FOES SEEM NUMBERLESS, BUT THEY HAVE NO SORCEROUS POWERS. THEY SEEK TO CRUSH ME BY PHYSICAL FORCE ALONE.
THESE CREATURES ARE ONLY CANNON FODDER, DESIGNED TO SLOW ME DOWN, TO MAKE ME WASTE PRECIOUS, IRREPLACABLE POWER...
...SO THAT I'LL BE VULNERABLE WHEN I REACH THEIR LAST LINE OF DEFENSE--THEIR DEMON-SORCERERS. THERE! AHEAD OF ME, WITHIN THAT CRYSTAL CASING...
"--MY GOAL! DR. STRANGE'S SOUL!
"SO NEAR, AND YET SO FAR.
"I WONDER HOW SPIDER-MAN IS FARING."
NO GOOD! FAST AS I WRAP DOC IN WEBBING--
--HE SHREDS IT TO PIECES!

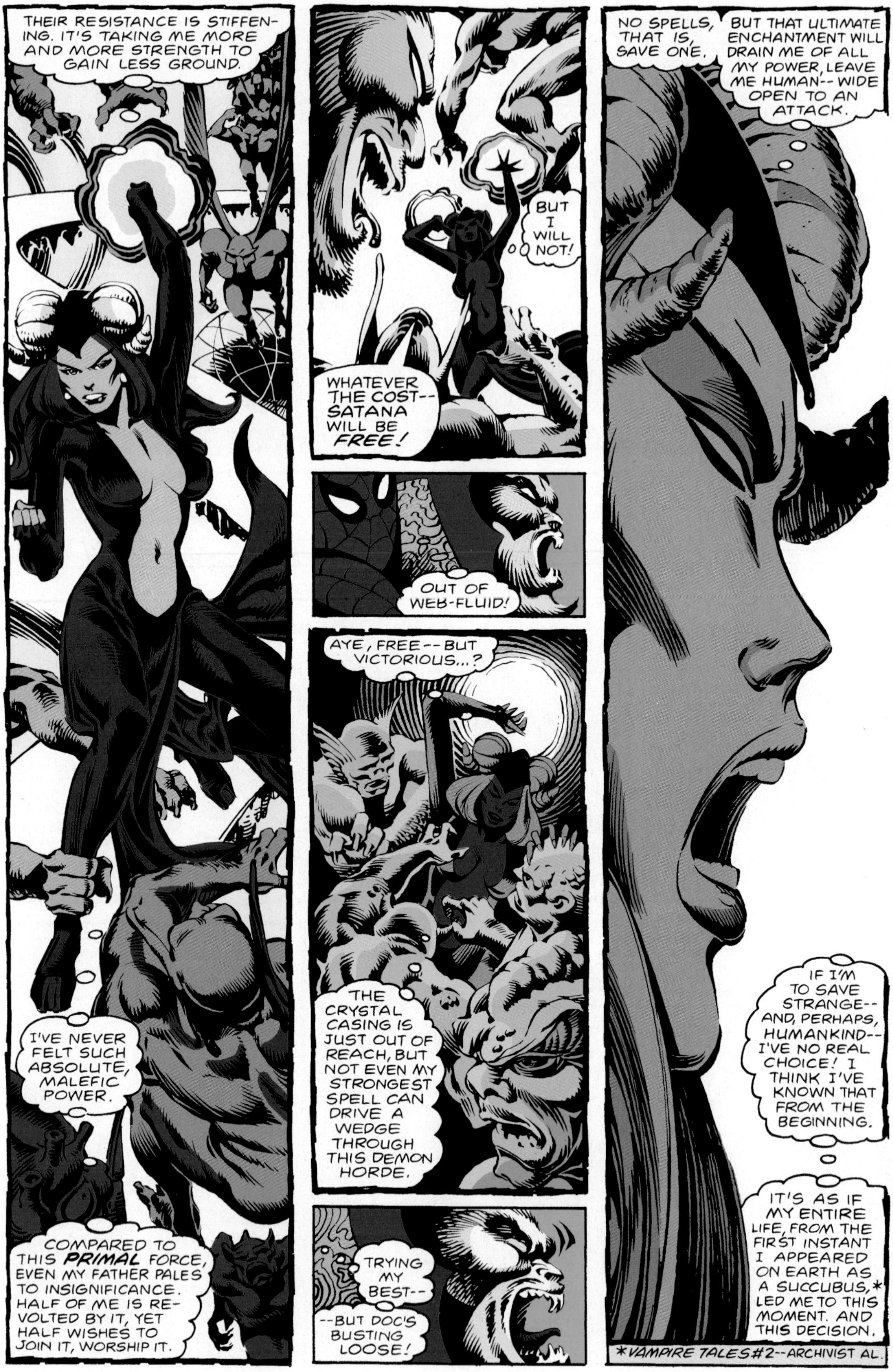
THEIR RESISTANCE IS STIFFENING. IT'S TAKING ME MORE AND MORE STRENGTH TO GAIN LESS GROUND.
I'VE NEVER FELT SUCH ABSOLUTE, MALEFIC POWER.
COMPARED TO THIS PRIMAL FORCE, EVEN MY FATHER PALES TO INSIGNIFICANCE. HALF OF ME IS REVOLTED BY IT, YET HALF WISHES TO JOIN IT, WORSHIP IT.
BUT I WILL NOT!
WHATEVER THE COST-- SATANA WILL BE FREE!
OUT OF WEB-FLUID!
AYE, FREE--BUT VICTORIOUS...?
THE CRYSTAL CASING IS JUST OUT OF REACH, BUT NOT EVEN MY STRONGEST SPELL CAN DRIVE A WEDGE THROUGH THIS DEMON HORDE.
TRYING MY BEST--
--BUT DOC'S BUSTING LOOSE!
NO SPELLS, THAT IS, SAVE ONE.
BUT THAT ULTIMATE ENCHANTMENT WILL DRAIN ME OF ALL MY POWER, LEAVE ME HUMAN--WIDE OPEN TO AN ATTACK.
IF I'M TO SAVE STRANGE-- AND, PERHAPS, HUMANKIND-- I'VE NO REAL CHOICE! I THINK I'VE KNOWN THAT FROM THE BEGINNING.
IT'S AS IF MY ENTIRE LIFE, FROM THE FIRST INSTANT I APPEARED ON EARTH AS A SUCCUBUS,* LED ME TO THIS MOMENT. AND THIS DECISION.
*VAMPIRE TALES #2--ARCHIVIST AL.

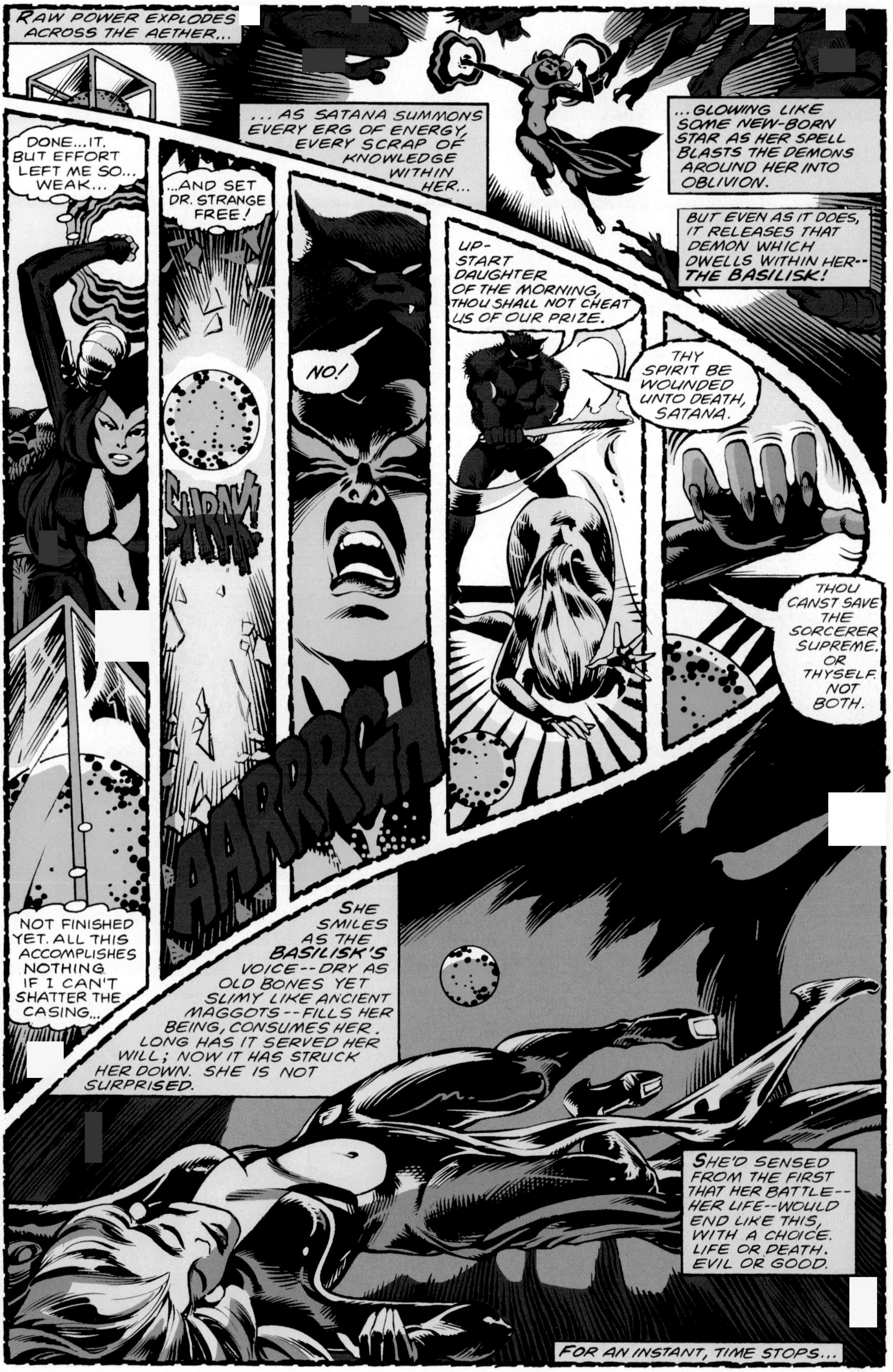

RAW POWER EXPLODES ACROSS THE AETHER...
...AS SATANA SUMMONS EVERY ERG OF ENERGY, EVERY SCRAP OF KNOWLEDGE WITHIN HER...
...GLOWING LIKE SOME NEW-BORN STAR AS HER SPELL BLASTS THE DEMONS AROUND HER INTO OBLIVION.
BUT EVEN AS IT DOES, IT RELEASES THAT DEMON WHICH DWELLS WITHIN HER-- THE BASILISK!
DONE...IT. BUT EFFORT LEFT ME SO... WEAK...
...AND SET DR. STRANGE FREE!
SHRAK!
NO!
AARRRGH
UP-START DAUGHTER OF THE MORNING, THOU SHALL NOT CHEAT US OF OUR PRIZE.
THY SPIRIT BE WOUNDED UNTO DEATH, SATANA.
THOU CANST SAVE THE SORCERER SUPREME. OR THYSELF. NOT BOTH.
NOT FINISHED YET. ALL THIS ACCOMPLISHES NOTHING IF I CAN'T SHATTER THE CASING...
SHE SMILES AS THE BASILISK'S VOICE--DRY AS OLD BONES YET SLIMY LIKE ANCIENT MAGGOTS--FILLS HER BEING, CONSUMES HER. LONG HAS IT SERVED HER WILL; NOW IT HAS STRUCK HER DOWN. SHE IS NOT SURPRISED.
SHE'D SENSED FROM THE FIRST THAT HER BATTLE-- HER LIFE--WOULD END LIKE THIS, WITH A CHOICE. LIFE OR DEATH. EVIL OR GOOD.
FOR AN INSTANT, TIME STOPS...

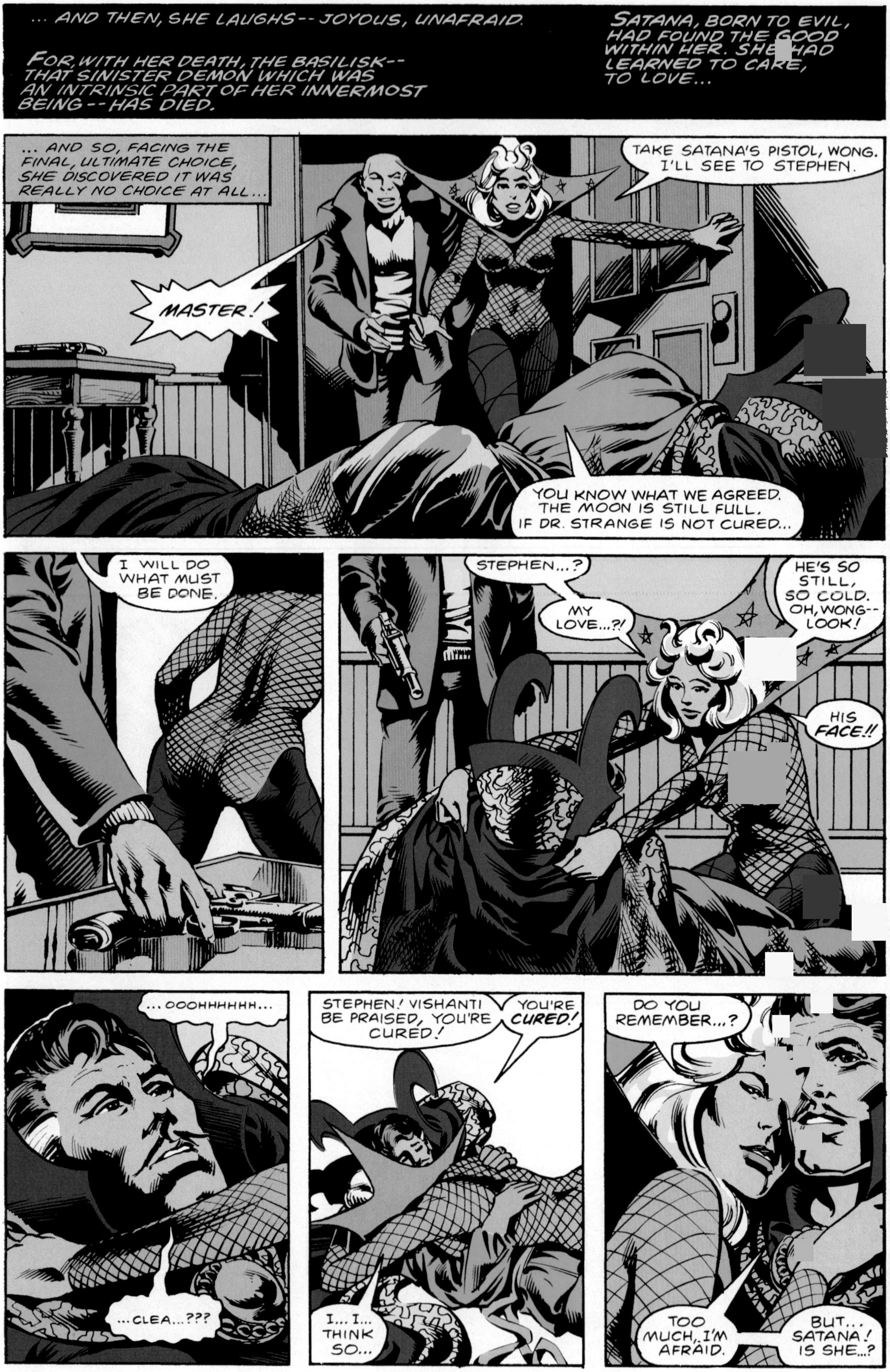
... AND THEN, SHE LAUGHS -- JOYOUS, UNAFRAID.
FOR, WITH HER DEATH, THE BASILISK-- THAT SINISTER DEMON WHICH WAS AN INTRINSIC PART OF HER INNERMOST BEING -- HAS DIED.
SATANA, BORN TO EVIL, HAD FOUND THE GOOD WITHIN HER. SHE HAD LEARNED TO CARE, TO LOVE...
... AND SO, FACING THE FINAL, ULTIMATE CHOICE, SHE DISCOVERED IT WAS REALLY NO CHOICE AT ALL...
MASTER!
TAKE SATANA'S PISTOL, WONG. I'LL SEE TO STEPHEN.
YOU KNOW WHAT WE AGREED. THE MOON IS STILL FULL. IF DR. STRANGE IS NOT CURED...
I WILL DO WHAT MUST BE DONE.
STEPHEN...?
MY LOVE...?!
HE'S SO STILL, SO COLD. OH, WONG-- LOOK!
HIS FACE!!
... OOOHHHHHH...
... CLEA...???
STEPHEN! VISHANTI BE PRAISED, YOU'RE CURED!
YOU'RE CURED!
I... I... THINK SO...
DO YOU REMEMBER...?
BUT... SATANA! IS SHE...?
TOO MUCH, I'M AFRAID.

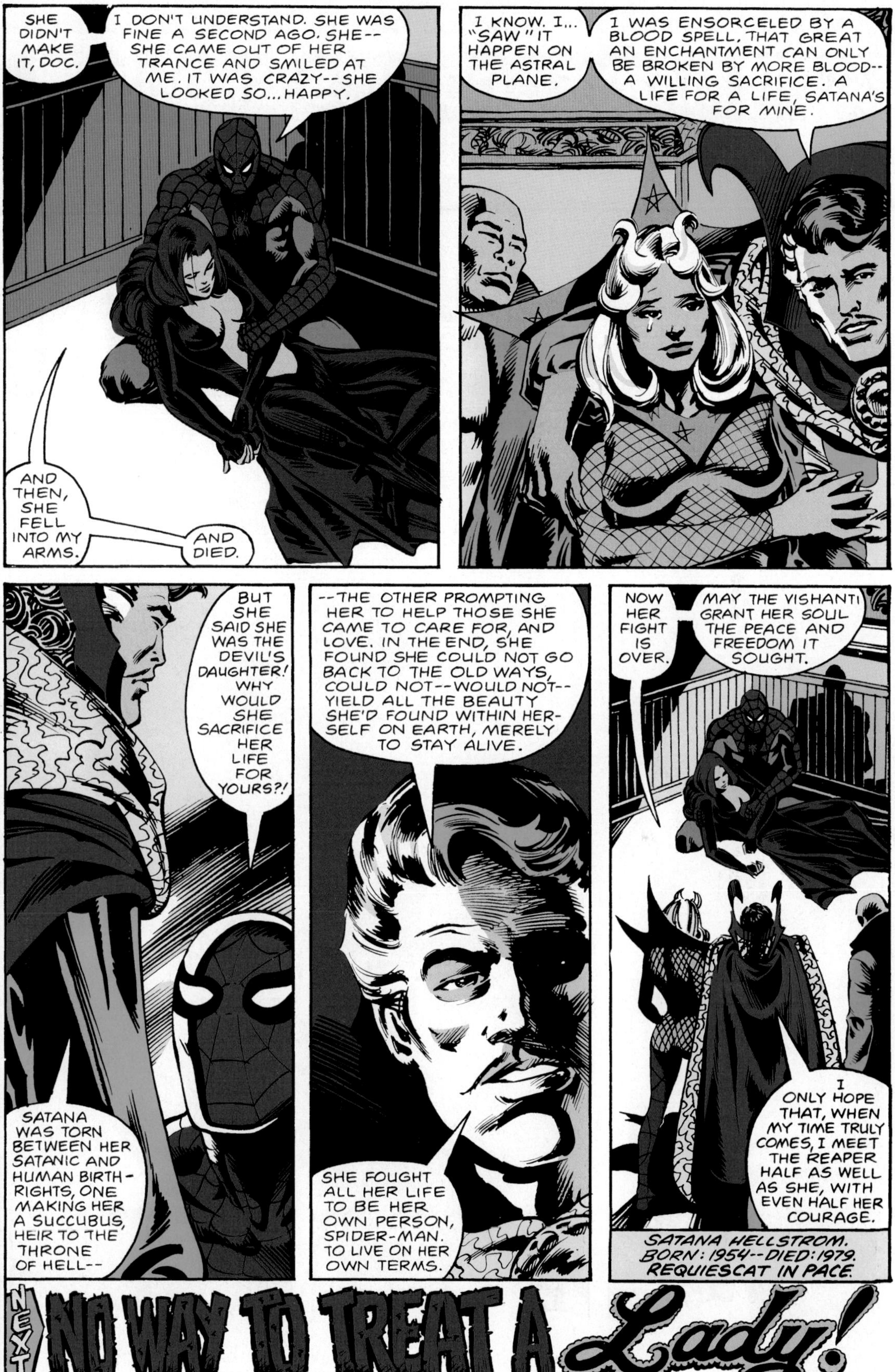
SHE DIDN'T MAKE IT, DOC.
I DON'T UNDERSTAND. SHE WAS FINE A SECOND AGO. SHE-- SHE CAME OUT OF HER TRANCE AND SMILED AT ME. IT WAS CRAZY--SHE LOOKED SO... HAPPY.
AND THEN, SHE FELL INTO MY ARMS.
AND DIED.
I KNOW. I... "SAW" IT HAPPEN ON THE ASTRAL PLANE.
I WAS ENSORCELED BY A BLOOD SPELL. THAT GREAT AN ENCHANTMENT CAN ONLY BE BROKEN BY MORE BLOOD-- A WILLING SACRIFICE. A LIFE FOR A LIFE, SATANA'S FOR MINE.
BUT SHE SAID SHE WAS THE DEVIL'S DAUGHTER! WHY WOULD SHE SACRIFICE HER LIFE FOR YOURS?!
SATANA WAS TORN BETWEEN HER SATANIC AND HUMAN BIRTH-RIGHTS, ONE MAKING HER A SUCCUBUS, HEIR TO THE THRONE OF HELL--
--THE OTHER PROMPTING HER TO HELP THOSE SHE CAME TO CARE FOR, AND LOVE. IN THE END, SHE FOUND SHE COULD NOT GO BACK TO THE OLD WAYS, COULD NOT--WOULD NOT-- YIELD ALL THE BEAUTY SHE'D FOUND WITHIN HER-SELF ON EARTH, MERELY TO STAY ALIVE.
SHE FOUGHT ALL HER LIFE TO BE HER OWN PERSON, SPIDER-MAN. TO LIVE ON HER OWN TERMS.
NOW HER FIGHT IS OVER.
MAY THE VISHANTI GRANT HER SOUL THE PEACE AND FREEDOM IT SOUGHT.
I ONLY HOPE THAT, WHEN MY TIME TRULY COMES, I MEET THE REAPER HALF AS WELL AS SHE, WITH EVEN HALF HER COURAGE.
SATANA HELLSTROM. BORN: 1954--DIED: 1979. REQUIESCAT IN PACE.
NEXT
NO WAY TO TREAT A Lady!

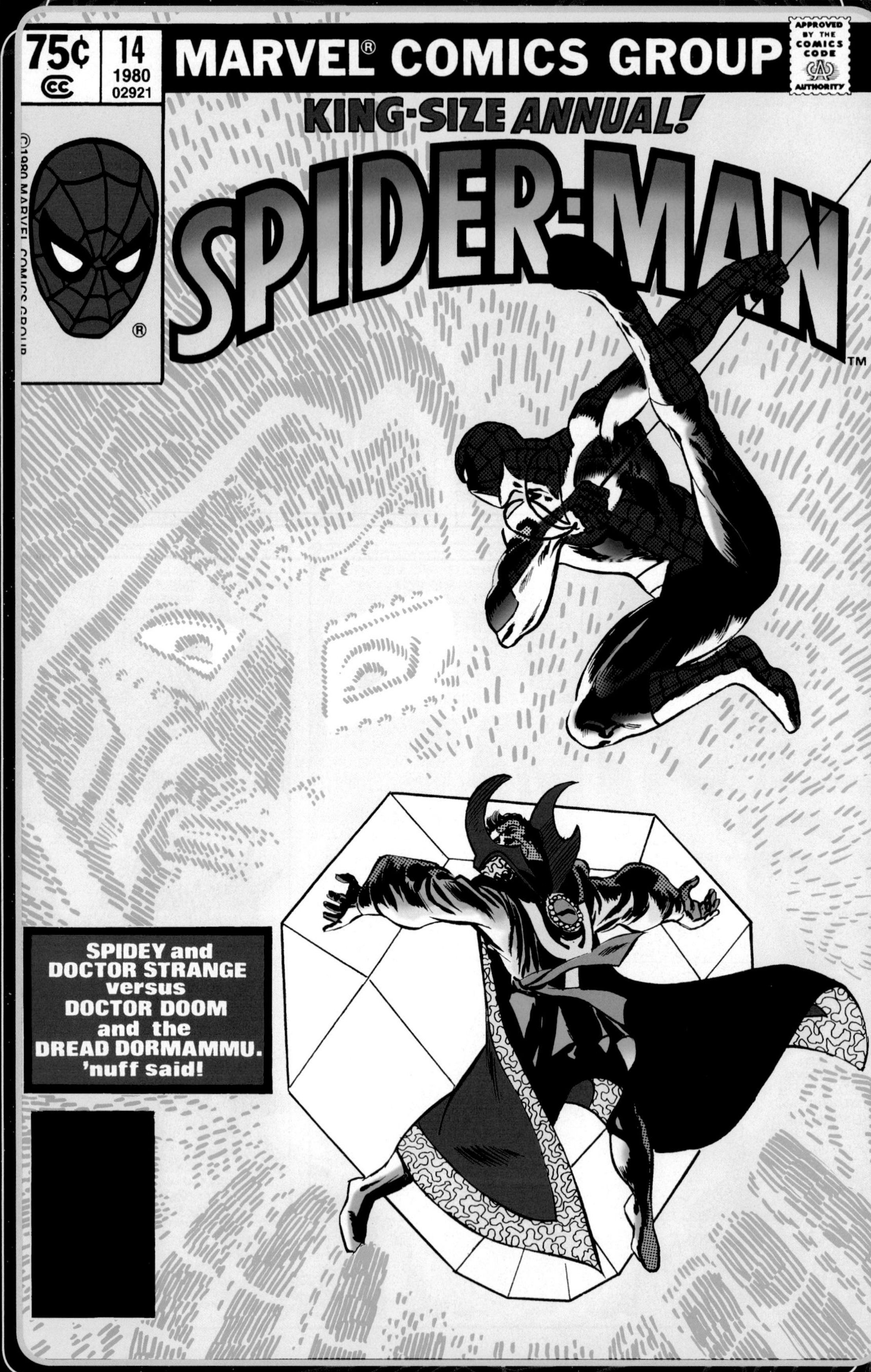
75¢
14
1980
02921
MARVEL® COMICS GROUP
APPROVED BY THE COMICS CODE AUTHORITY
KING-SIZE ANNUAL!
SPIDER-MAN™
©1980 MARVEL COMICS GROUP
SPIDEY and DOCTOR STRANGE versus DOCTOR DOOM and the DREAD DORMAMMU. 'nuff said!

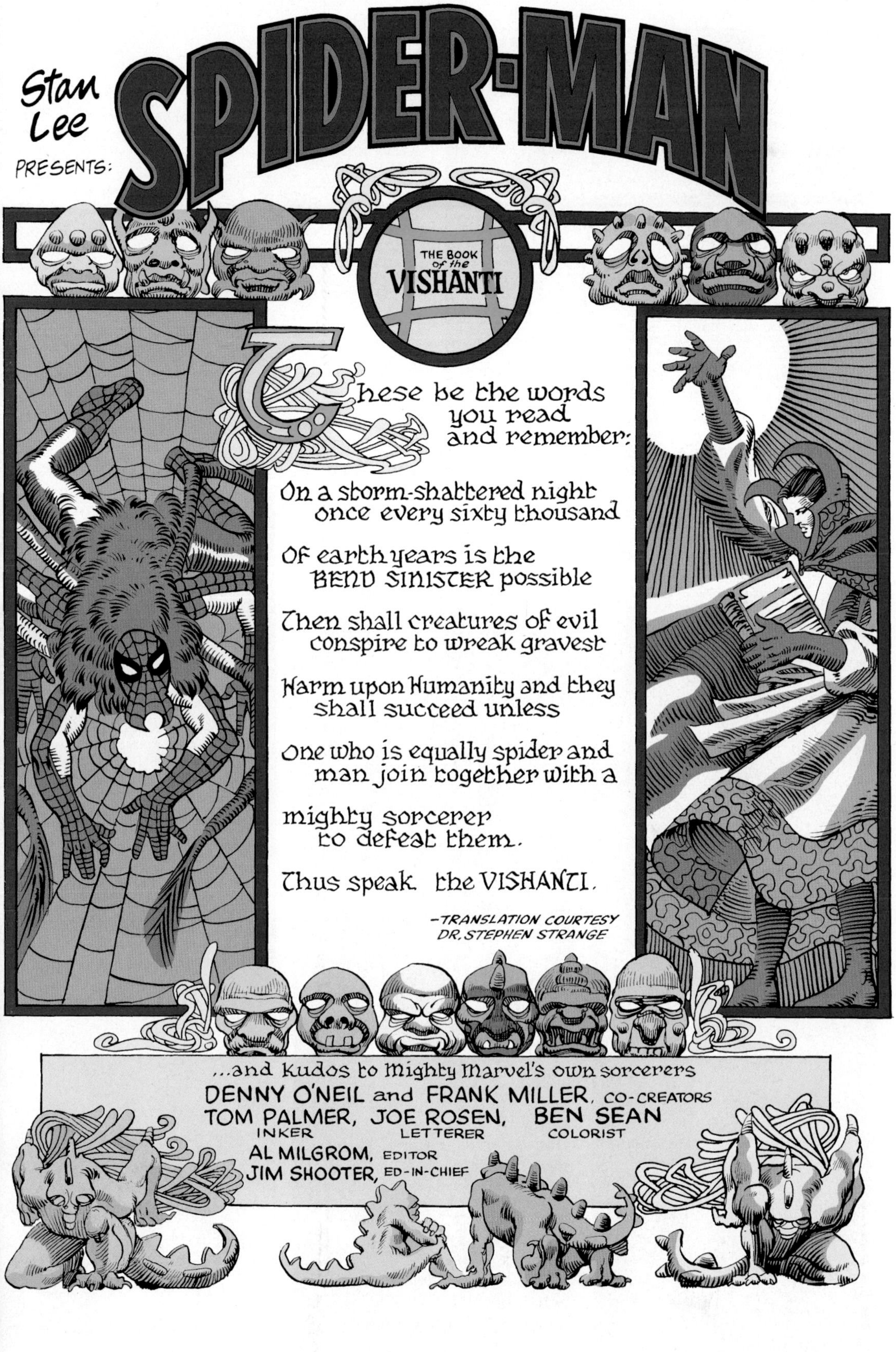
Stan Lee
PRESENTS:
SPIDER-MAN
THE BOOK of the VISHANTI
These be the words you read and remember:
On a storm-shattered night once every sixty thousand
Of earth years is the BEND SINISTER possible
Then shall creatures of evil conspire to wreak gravest
Harm upon Humanity and they shall succeed unless
One who is equally spider and man join together with a
mighty sorcerer to defeat them.
Thus speak the VISHANTI.
—TRANSLATION COURTESY DR. STEPHEN STRANGE
...and kudos to mighty Marvel's own sorcerers
DENNY O'NEIL and FRANK MILLER, CO-CREATORS
TOM PALMER, INKER
JOE ROSEN, LETTERER
BEN SEAN COLORIST
AL MILGROM, EDITOR
JIM SHOOTER, ED-IN-CHIEF

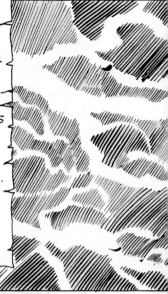

And it shall be that these dire and eldritch events begin in the Kingdom of Latveria on a night when lightning seams the sky and thunder rocks the very foundations of the Castle of Doctor Doom.

YOU CHITTERING IDIOTS DO NOT *UNDERSTAND*, DO YOU? WHAT THE MASTER AND I HAVE *ACCOMPLISHED--*?

THE INTERFACE BETWEEN *MAGIC* AND *SCIENCE* HAS BEEN *BREECHED--*

--AND WE ARE ABLE TO *HARNESS* AND *COMBINE* THE POWERS OF *EACH!*

HURRY UP, HURRY UP... SUMMON THE MASTER AND FINISH THOSE CONNECTIONS AND GET ME SOME COOKIES.

YOU *DARE?!*

YOU DARE CONTEMPLATE *FOOD* WHILE DOING THE BIDDING OF *DOCTOR DOOM?!*

MASTER! F-FORGIVE ME! I MEANT NO HARM!

B-BUT MY REPORT IS READY-- WE HAVE *SUCCEEDED!*

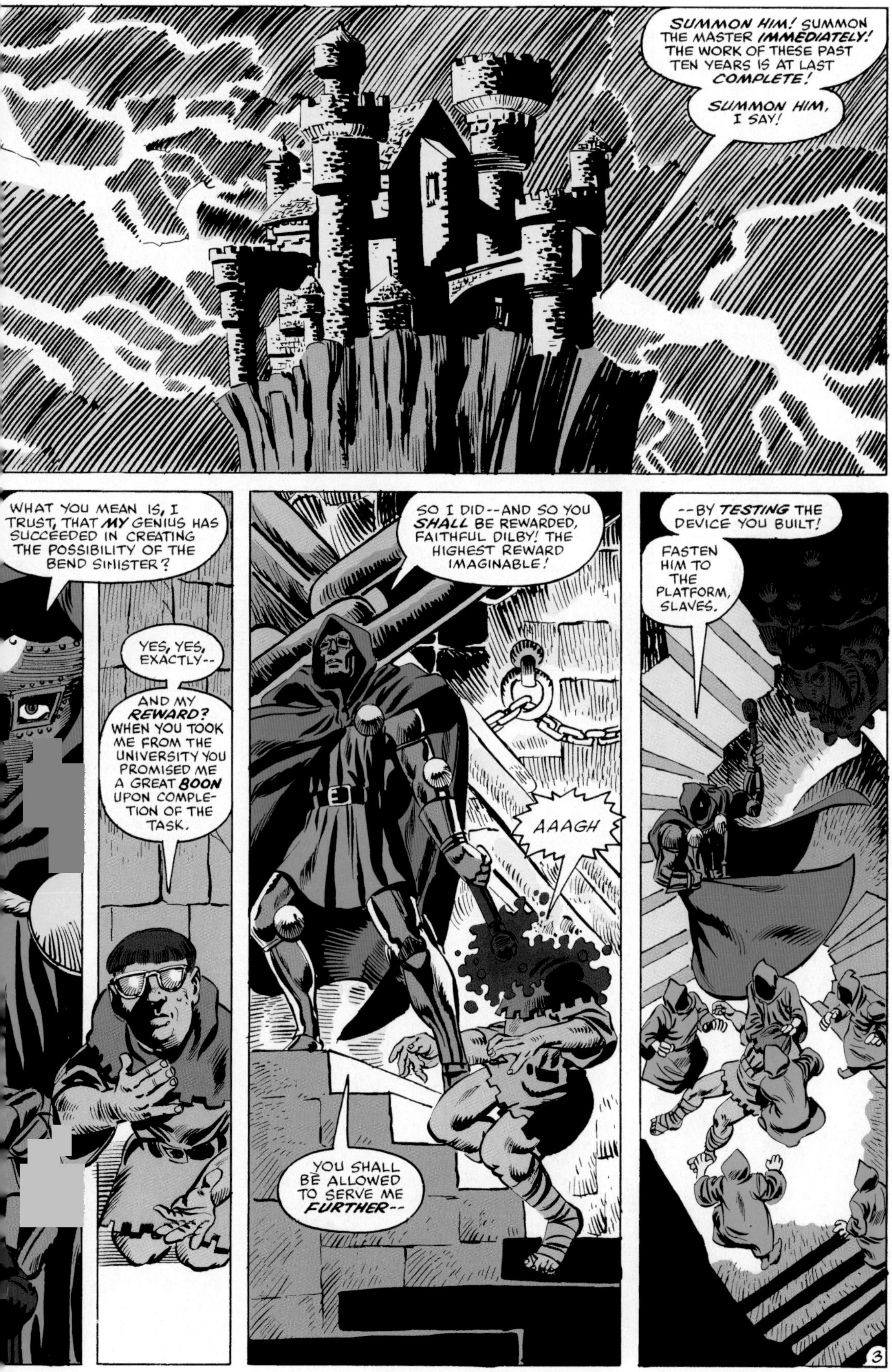
SUMMON HIM! SUMMON THE MASTER IMMEDIATELY! THE WORK OF THESE PAST TEN YEARS IS AT LAST COMPLETE!
SUMMON HIM, I SAY!
WHAT YOU MEAN IS, I TRUST, THAT MY GENIUS HAS SUCCEEDED IN CREATING THE POSSIBILITY OF THE BEND SINISTER?
YES, YES, EXACTLY--
AND MY REWARD? WHEN YOU TOOK ME FROM THE UNIVERSITY YOU PROMISED ME A GREAT BOON UPON COMPLETION OF THE TASK.
SO I DID--AND SO YOU SHALL BE REWARDED, FAITHFUL DILBY! THE HIGHEST REWARD IMAGINABLE!
YOU SHALL BE ALLOWED TO SERVE ME FURTHER--
AAAGH
--BY TESTING THE DEVICE YOU BUILT!
FASTEN HIM TO THE PLATFORM, SLAVES.
3

CONSIDER YOURSELF *PRIVILEGED*-- FOR YOU ARE ABOUT TO VISIT A PLANE OF EXISTENCE NO *MORTAL* HAS EVER SEEN... THE DIMENSION OF THE *DREAD DORMAMMU!*

I ALMOST *ENVY* YOU!

I WOULD GLADLY PERMIT YOU TO TAKE MY *PLACE*--

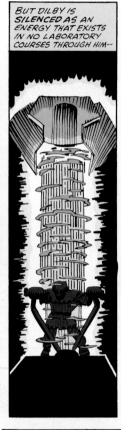

BUT DILBY IS *SILENCED* AS AN ENERGY THAT EXISTS IN NO LABORATORY COURSES THROUGH HIM--

--SUFFUSES HIM--

--CONSUMES HIM...

I WONDER IF HE WILL LIVE?

NO MATTER... IF HE DOES NOT, I WILL FIND *ANOTHER* LACKEY.

BEYOND MATTER AND ENERGY--

--BEYOND TRUTH AND ILLUSION AND *DREAMING*--

--HE SHRINKS AND FALLS AND PERHAPS, FOR A FLEETING INSTANT BECOMES *INFINITE*--

--BUT HE IS AWARE OF *NONE* OF THIS. HE KNOWS ONLY A *TERROR* MIXED WITH SOMETHING ANOTHER MIGHT RECOGNIZE AS *ECSTASY*, AS HE DWINDLES TO A NAMELESS BEYOND...

4

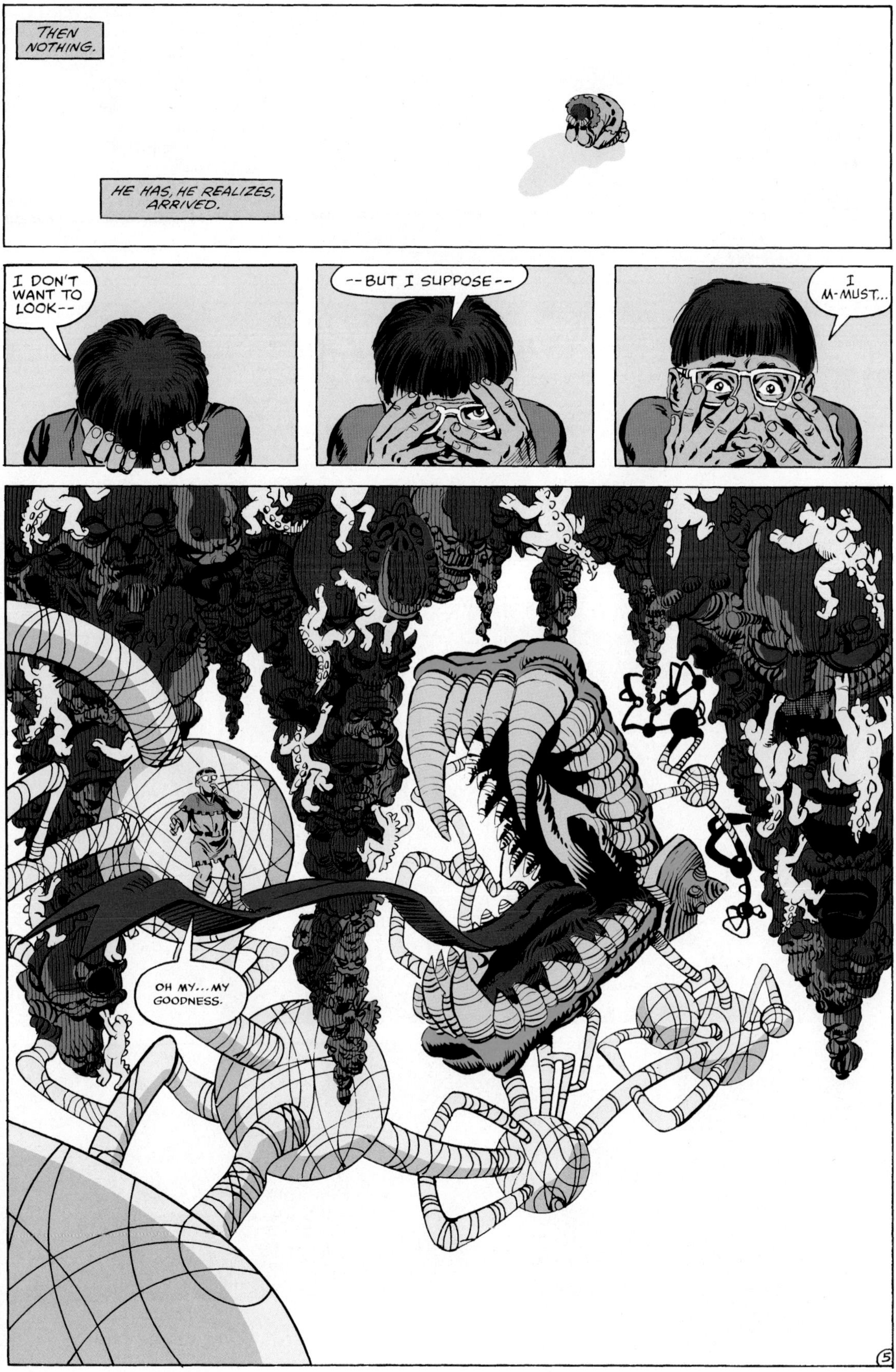
THEN NOTHING.
HE HAS, HE REALIZES, ARRIVED.
I DON'T WANT TO LOOK--
--BUT I SUPPOSE--
I M-MUST...
OH MY...MY GOODNESS.
5

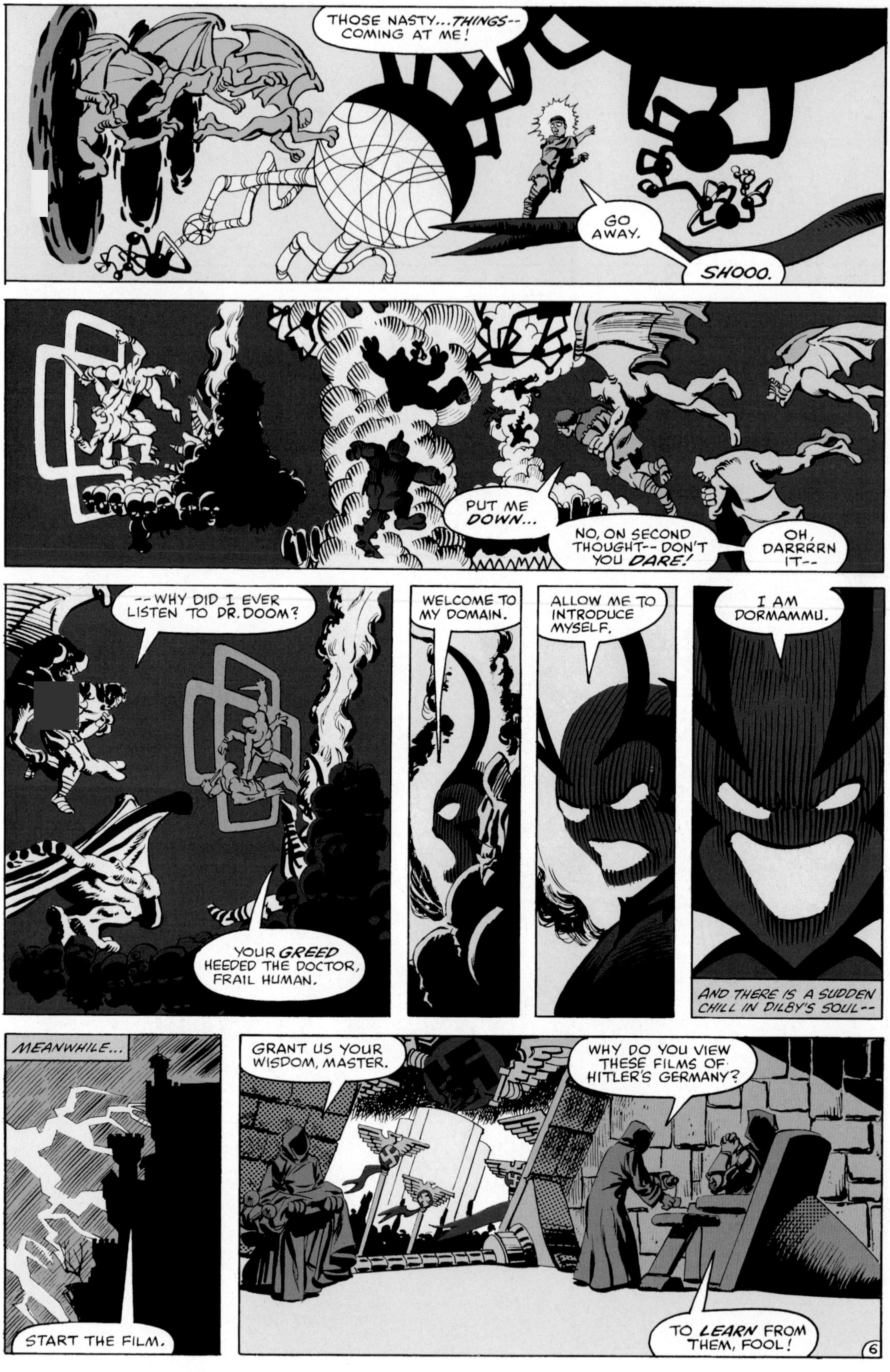
THOSE NASTY... THINGS-- COMING AT ME!
GO AWAY.
SHOOO.
PUT ME DOWN...
NO, ON SECOND THOUGHT-- DON'T YOU DARE!
OH, DARRRRN IT--
--WHY DID I EVER LISTEN TO DR. DOOM?
YOUR GREED HEEDED THE DOCTOR, FRAIL HUMAN.
WELCOME TO MY DOMAIN.
ALLOW ME TO INTRODUCE MYSELF.
I AM DORMAMMU.
AND THERE IS A SUDDEN CHILL IN DILBY'S SOUL--
MEANWHILE...
START THE FILM.
GRANT US YOUR WISDOM, MASTER.
WHY DO YOU VIEW THESE FILMS OF HITLER'S GERMANY?
TO LEARN FROM THEM, FOOL!
6

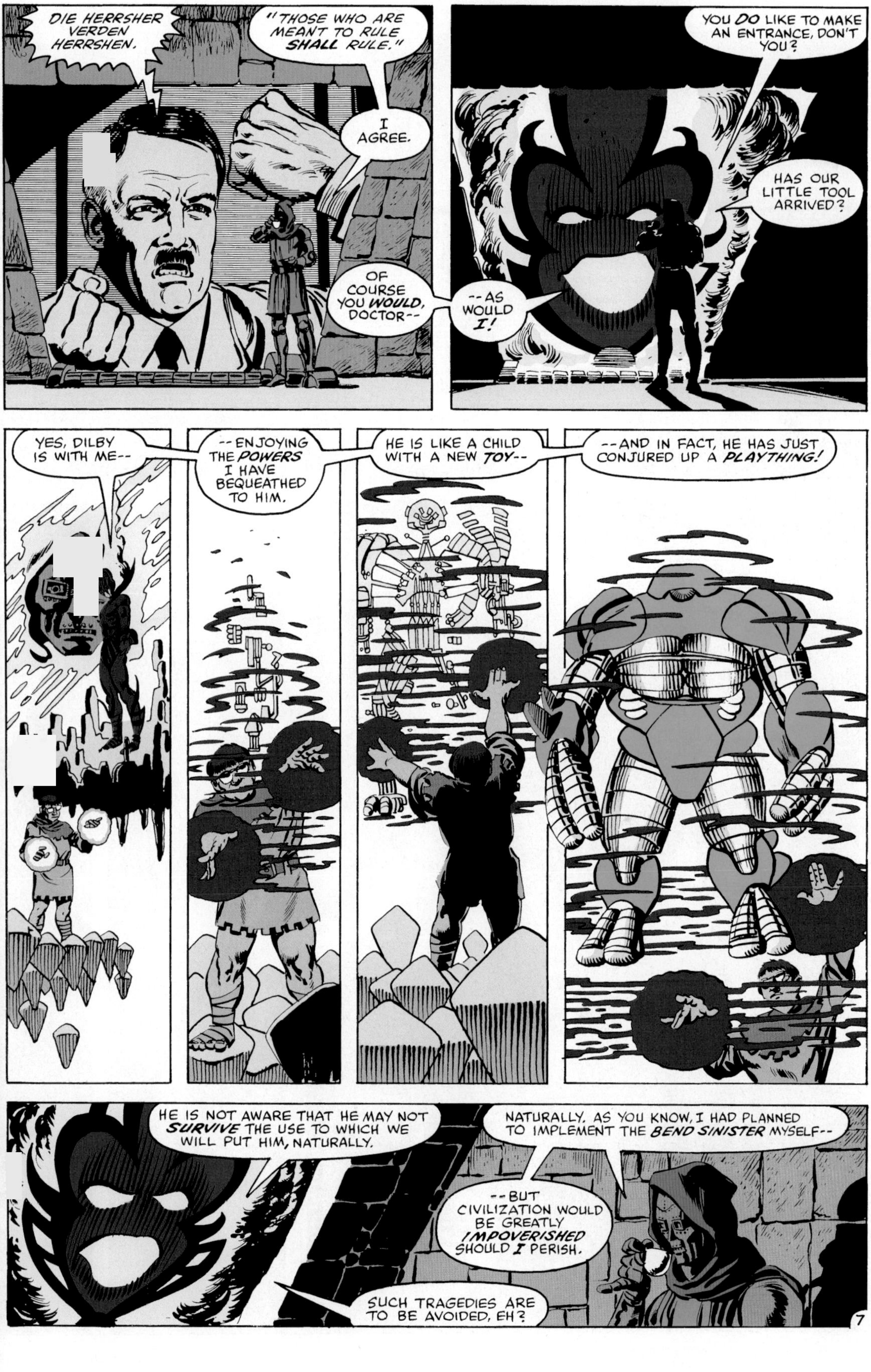
DIE HERRSHER VERDEN HERRSHEN.
"THOSE WHO ARE MEANT TO RULE SHALL RULE."
I AGREE.
YOU DO LIKE TO MAKE AN ENTRANCE, DON'T YOU?
HAS OUR LITTLE TOOL ARRIVED?
OF COURSE YOU WOULD, DOCTOR--
--AS WOULD I!
YES, DILBY IS WITH ME--
--ENJOYING THE POWERS I HAVE BEQUEATHED TO HIM.
HE IS LIKE A CHILD WITH A NEW TOY--
--AND IN FACT, HE HAS JUST CONJURED UP A PLAYTHING!
HE IS NOT AWARE THAT HE MAY NOT SURVIVE THE USE TO WHICH WE WILL PUT HIM, NATURALLY.
NATURALLY. AS YOU KNOW, I HAD PLANNED TO IMPLEMENT THE BEND SINISTER MYSELF--
--BUT CIVILIZATION WOULD BE GREATLY IMPOVERISHED SHOULD I PERISH.
SUCH TRAGEDIES ARE TO BE AVOIDED, EH?
7

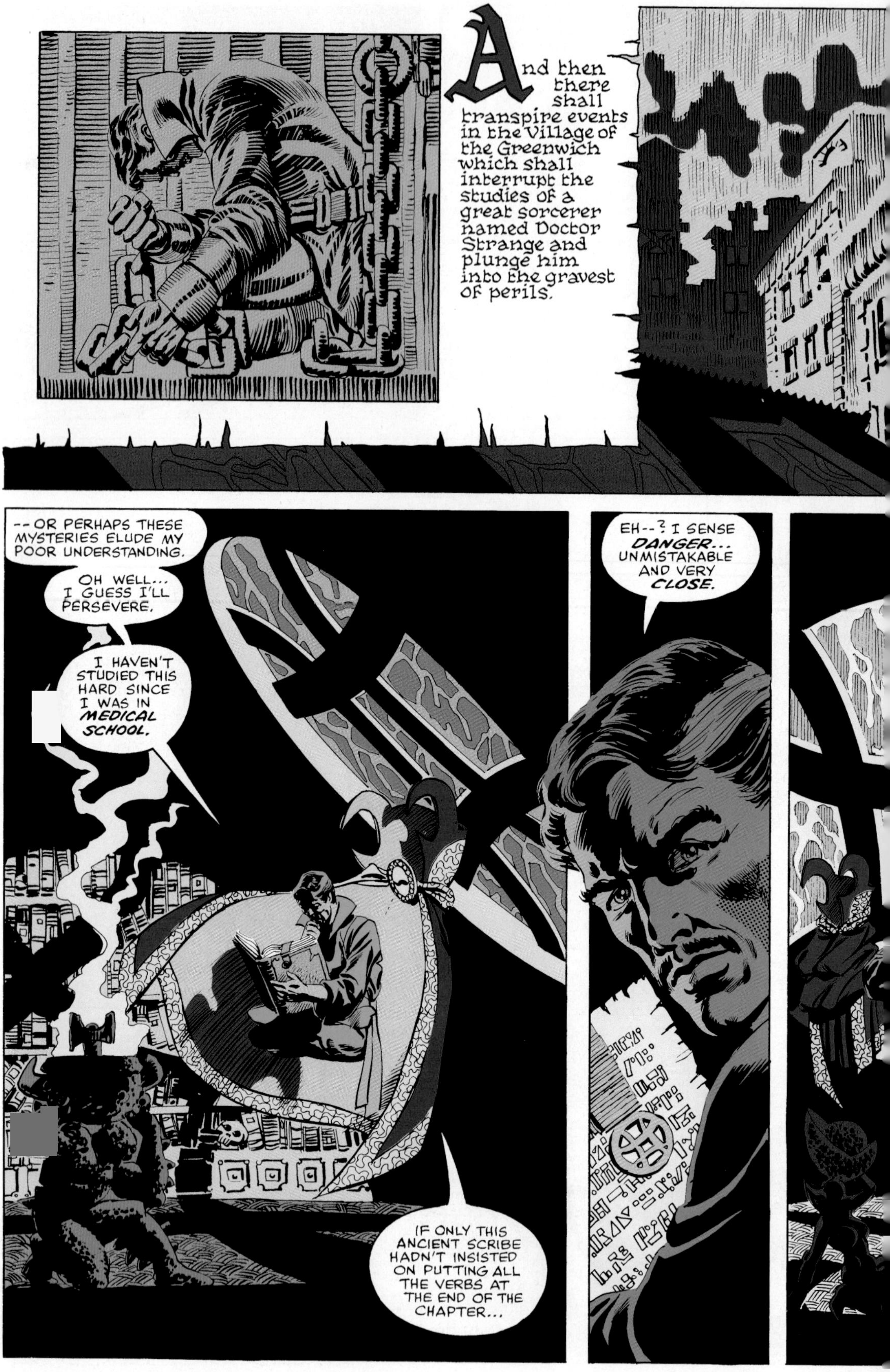
And then there shall transpire events in the Village of the Greenwich which shall interrupt the studies of a great sorcerer named Doctor Strange and plunge him into the gravest of perils.
--OR PERHAPS THESE MYSTERIES ELUDE MY POOR UNDERSTANDING.
OH WELL... I GUESS I'LL PERSEVERE.
I HAVEN'T STUDIED THIS HARD SINCE I WAS IN MEDICAL SCHOOL.
IF ONLY THIS ANCIENT SCRIBE HADN'T INSISTED ON PUTTING ALL THE VERBS AT THE END OF THE CHAPTER...
EH--? I SENSE DANGER... UNMISTAKABLE AND VERY CLOSE.

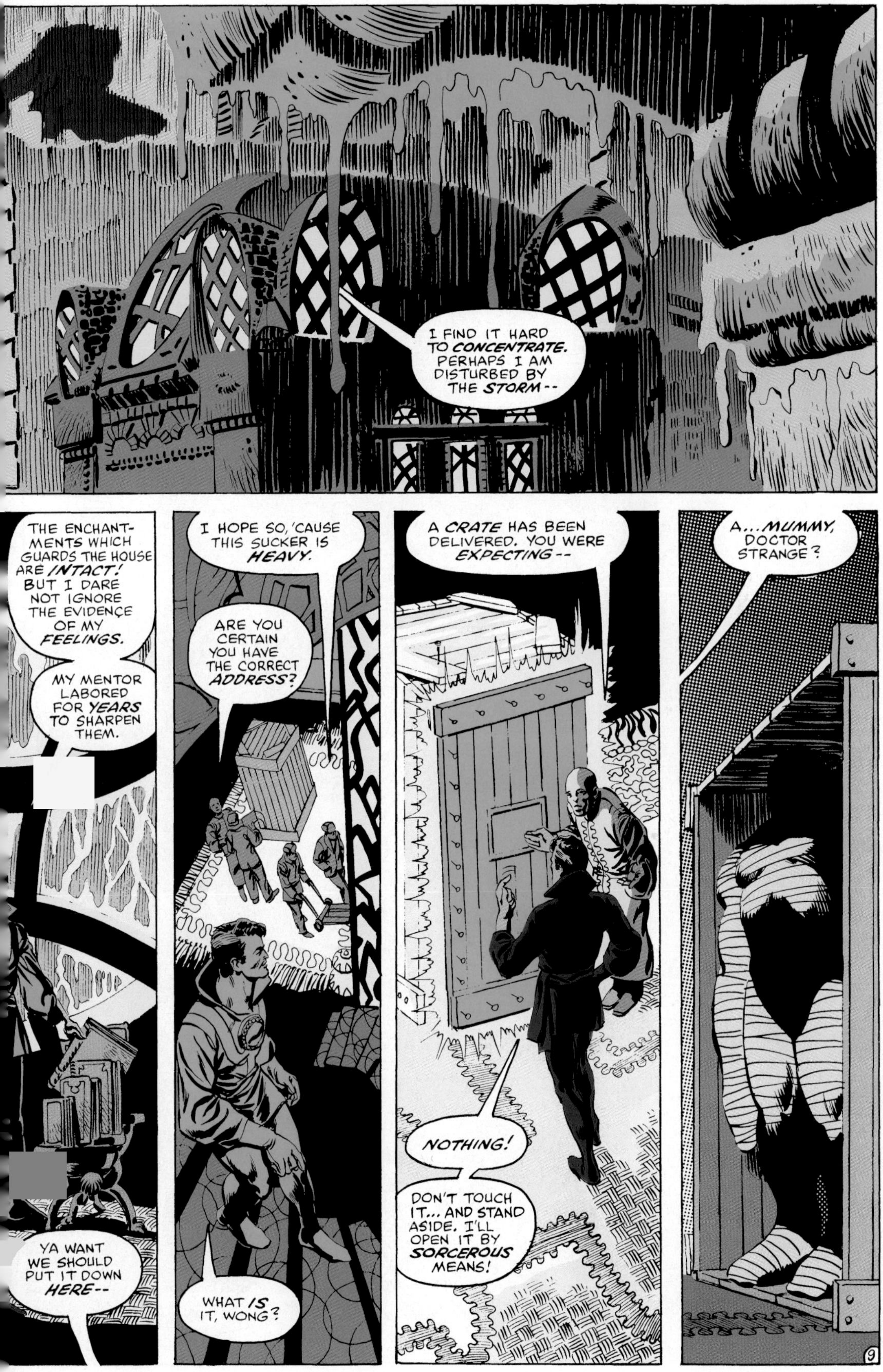
I FIND IT HARD TO CONCENTRATE. PERHAPS I AM DISTURBED BY THE STORM--
THE ENCHANTMENTS WHICH GUARDS THE HOUSE ARE INTACT! BUT I DARE NOT IGNORE THE EVIDENCE OF MY FEELINGS.
MY MENTOR LABORED FOR YEARS TO SHARPEN THEM.
YA WANT WE SHOULD PUT IT DOWN HERE--
I HOPE SO, 'CAUSE THIS SUCKER IS HEAVY.
ARE YOU CERTAIN YOU HAVE THE CORRECT ADDRESS?
WHAT IS IT, WONG?
A CRATE HAS BEEN DELIVERED. YOU WERE EXPECTING--
NOTHING!
DON'T TOUCH IT... AND STAND ASIDE. I'LL OPEN IT BY SORCEROUS MEANS!
A...MUMMY, DOCTOR STRANGE?
9

I THINK *NOT!* PERHAPS THE EYE OF AGAMOTTO WILL REVEAL ITS *TRUE* NATURE.

LET THE ENCHANTED RAYS ISSUE FORTH AND PENETRATE WHERE MORTAL VISION CANNOT--

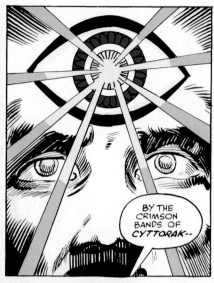

BY THE CRIMSON BANDS OF *CYTTORAK*--

WONG...GET *BACK*--

Sha-RAAAAKKK

UNNHH! THE FORCE OF THAT BLACK-LIGHT BLAST WAS LESSENED BY THE BEAM FROM MY AMULET--

--BUT I CAN'T TAKE *ANOTHER!*

GOT TO *COUNTER-ATTACK...* AND TRY TO FIGURE OUT WHAT I'M *FIGHTING*--

--AND *WHY!*

10

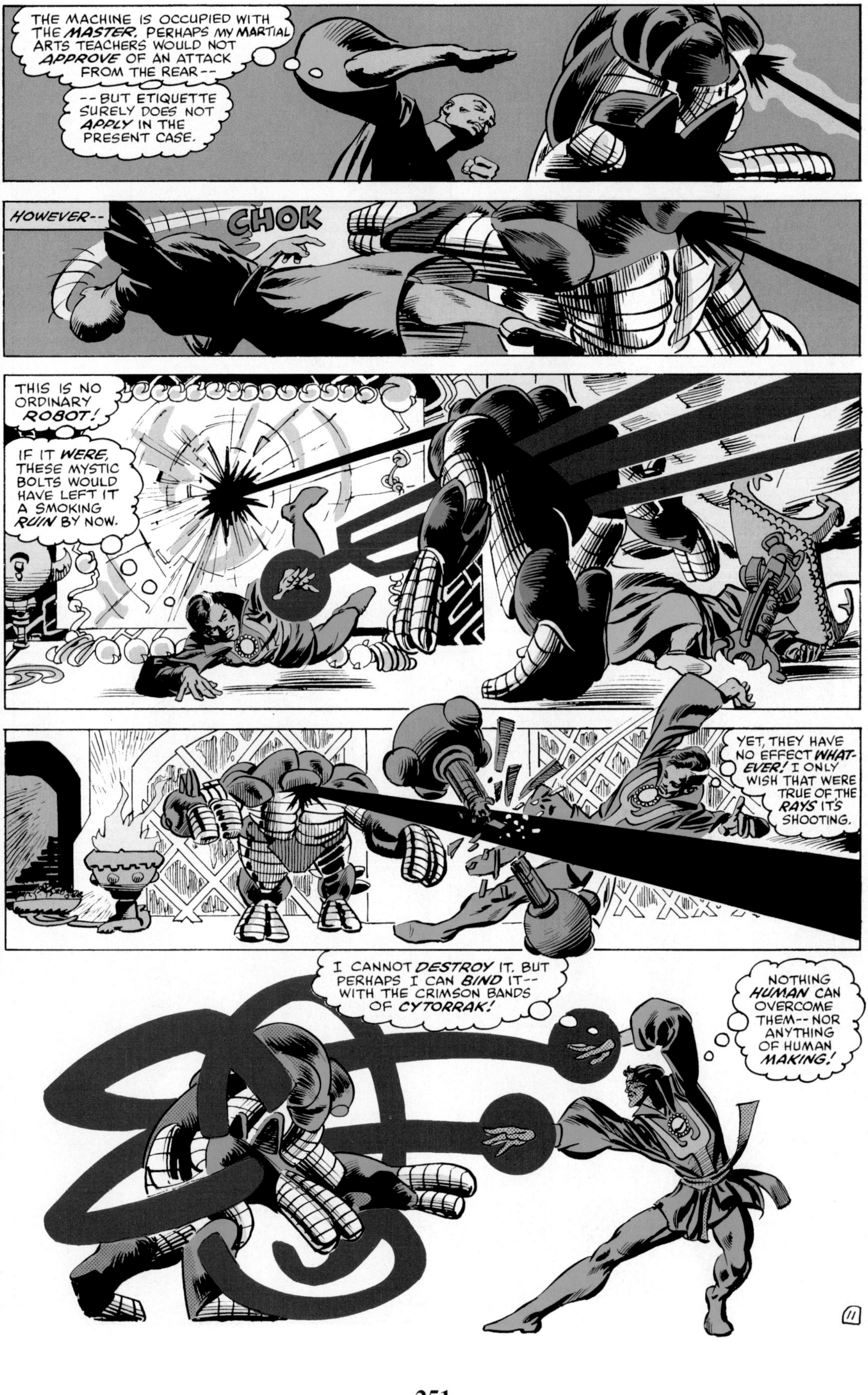
THE MACHINE IS OCCUPIED WITH THE MASTER. PERHAPS MY MARTIAL ARTS TEACHERS WOULD NOT APPROVE OF AN ATTACK FROM THE REAR--
--BUT ETIQUETTE SURELY DOES NOT APPLY IN THE PRESENT CASE.
HOWEVER--
CHOK
THIS IS NO ORDINARY ROBOT!
IF IT WERE, THESE MYSTIC BOLTS WOULD HAVE LEFT IT A SMOKING RUIN BY NOW.
YET, THEY HAVE NO EFFECT WHAT-EVER! I ONLY WISH THAT WERE TRUE OF THE RAYS IT'S SHOOTING.
I CANNOT DESTROY IT. BUT PERHAPS I CAN BIND IT-- WITH THE CRIMSON BANDS OF CYTORRAK!
NOTHING HUMAN CAN OVERCOME THEM--NOR ANYTHING OF HUMAN MAKING!
11

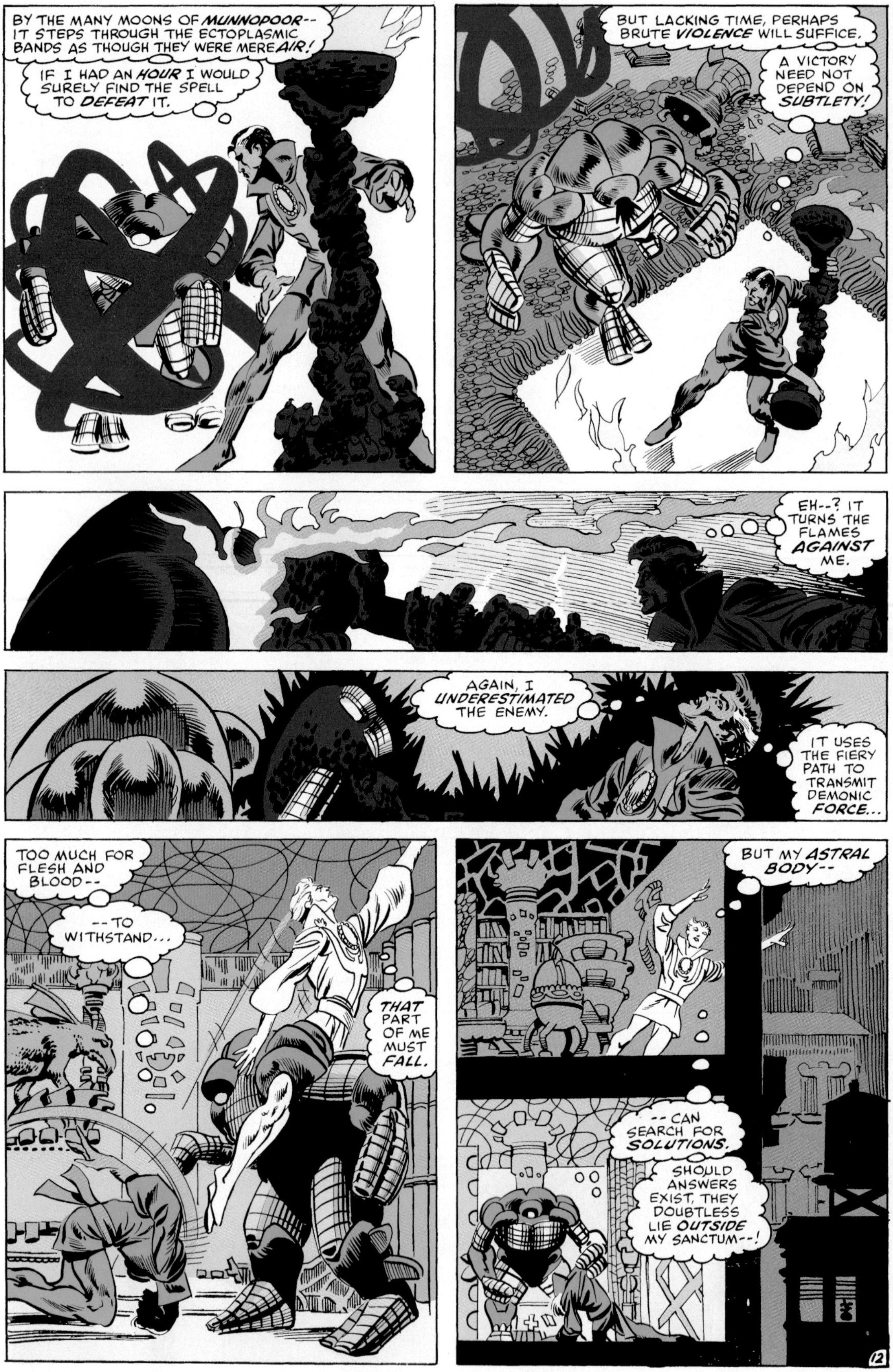
BY THE MANY MOONS OF MUNNOPOOR-- IT STEPS THROUGH THE ECTOPLASMIC BANDS AS THOUGH THEY WERE MERE AIR!
IF I HAD AN HOUR I WOULD SURELY FIND THE SPELL TO DEFEAT IT.
BUT LACKING TIME, PERHAPS BRUTE VIOLENCE WILL SUFFICE.
A VICTORY NEED NOT DEPEND ON SUBTLETY!
EH--? IT TURNS THE FLAMES AGAINST ME.
AGAIN, I UNDERESTIMATED THE ENEMY.
IT USES THE FIERY PATH TO TRANSMIT DEMONIC FORCE...
TOO MUCH FOR FLESH AND BLOOD--
--TO WITHSTAND...
THAT PART OF ME MUST FALL.
BUT MY ASTRAL BODY--
--CAN SEARCH FOR SOLUTIONS.
SHOULD ANSWERS EXIST, THEY DOUBTLESS LIE OUTSIDE MY SANCTUM--!
12

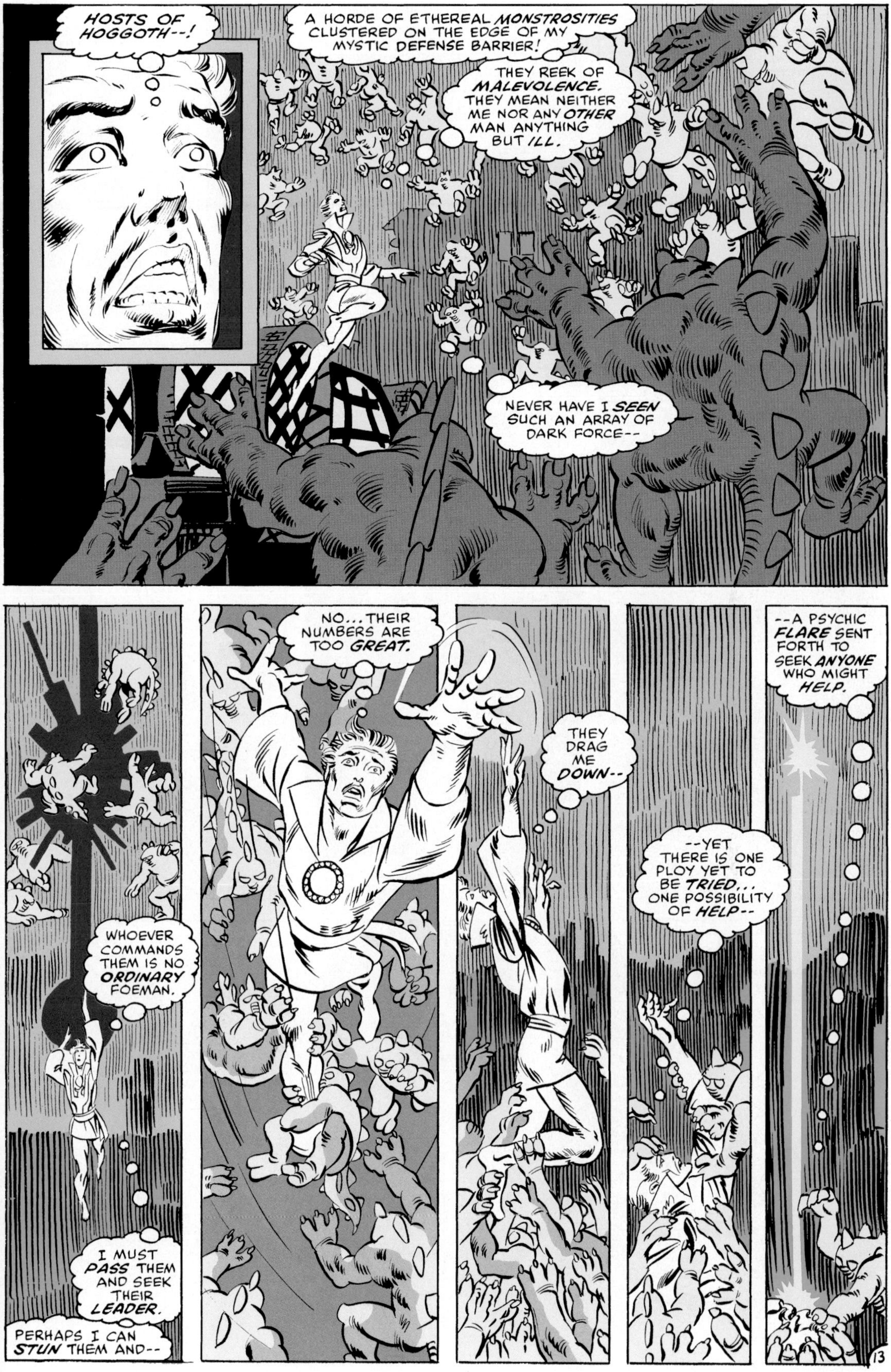
HOSTS OF HOGGOTH--!
A HORDE OF ETHEREAL MONSTROSITIES CLUSTERED ON THE EDGE OF MY MYSTIC DEFENSE BARRIER!
THEY REEK OF MALEVOLENCE. THEY MEAN NEITHER ME NOR ANY OTHER MAN ANYTHING BUT ILL.
NEVER HAVE I SEEN SUCH AN ARRAY OF DARK FORCE--
WHOEVER COMMANDS THEM IS NO ORDINARY FOEMAN.
I MUST PASS THEM AND SEEK THEIR LEADER.
PERHAPS I CAN STUN THEM AND--
NO... THEIR NUMBERS ARE TOO GREAT.
THEY DRAG ME DOWN--
--YET THERE IS ONE PLOY YET TO BE TRIED... ONE POSSIBILITY OF HELP--
--A PSYCHIC FLARE SENT FORTH TO SEEK ANYONE WHO MIGHT HELP.
13

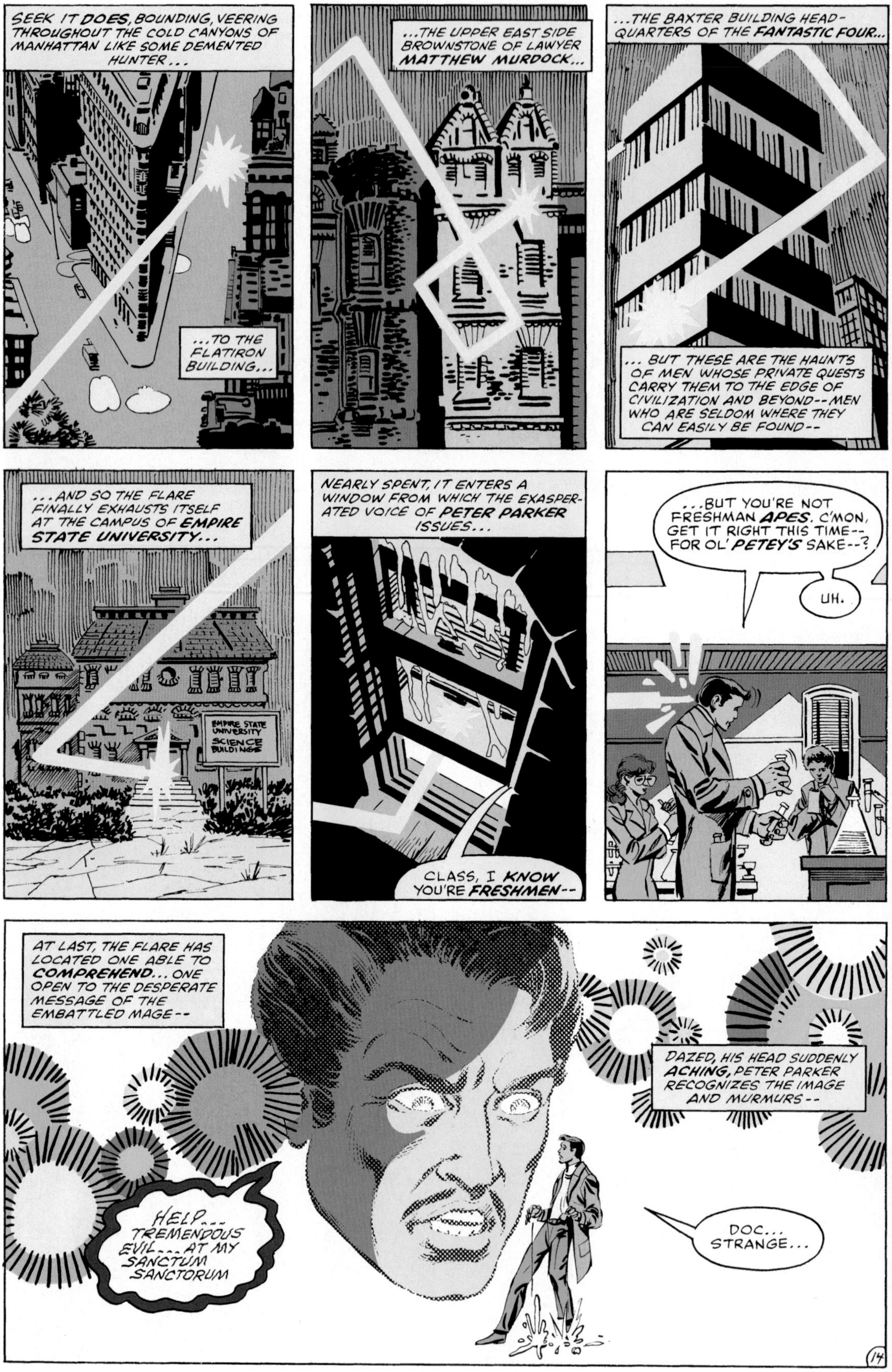
SEEK IT DOES, BOUNDING, VEERING THROUGHOUT THE COLD CANYONS OF MANHATTAN LIKE SOME DEMENTED HUNTER...
...TO THE FLATIRON BUILDING...
...THE UPPER EAST SIDE BROWNSTONE OF LAWYER MATTHEW MURDOCK...
...THE BAXTER BUILDING HEAD-QUARTERS OF THE FANTASTIC FOUR...
... BUT THESE ARE THE HAUNTS OF MEN WHOSE PRIVATE QUESTS CARRY THEM TO THE EDGE OF CIVILIZATION AND BEYOND-- MEN WHO ARE SELDOM WHERE THEY CAN EASILY BE FOUND--
...AND SO THE FLARE FINALLY EXHAUSTS ITSELF AT THE CAMPUS OF EMPIRE STATE UNIVERSITY...
EMPIRE STATE UNIVERSITY SCIENCE BUILDINGS
NEARLY SPENT, IT ENTERS A WINDOW FROM WHICH THE EXASPERATED VOICE OF PETER PARKER ISSUES...
CLASS, I KNOW YOU'RE FRESHMEN--
...BUT YOU'RE NOT FRESHMAN APES. C'MON, GET IT RIGHT THIS TIME-- FOR OL' PETEY'S SAKE--?
UH.
AT LAST, THE FLARE HAS LOCATED ONE ABLE TO COMPREHEND... ONE OPEN TO THE DESPERATE MESSAGE OF THE EMBATTLED MAGE--
DAZED, HIS HEAD SUDDENLY ACHING, PETER PARKER RECOGNIZES THE IMAGE AND MURMURS--
HELP... TREMENDOUS EVIL... AT MY SANCTUM SANCTORUM
DOC... STRANGE...
14

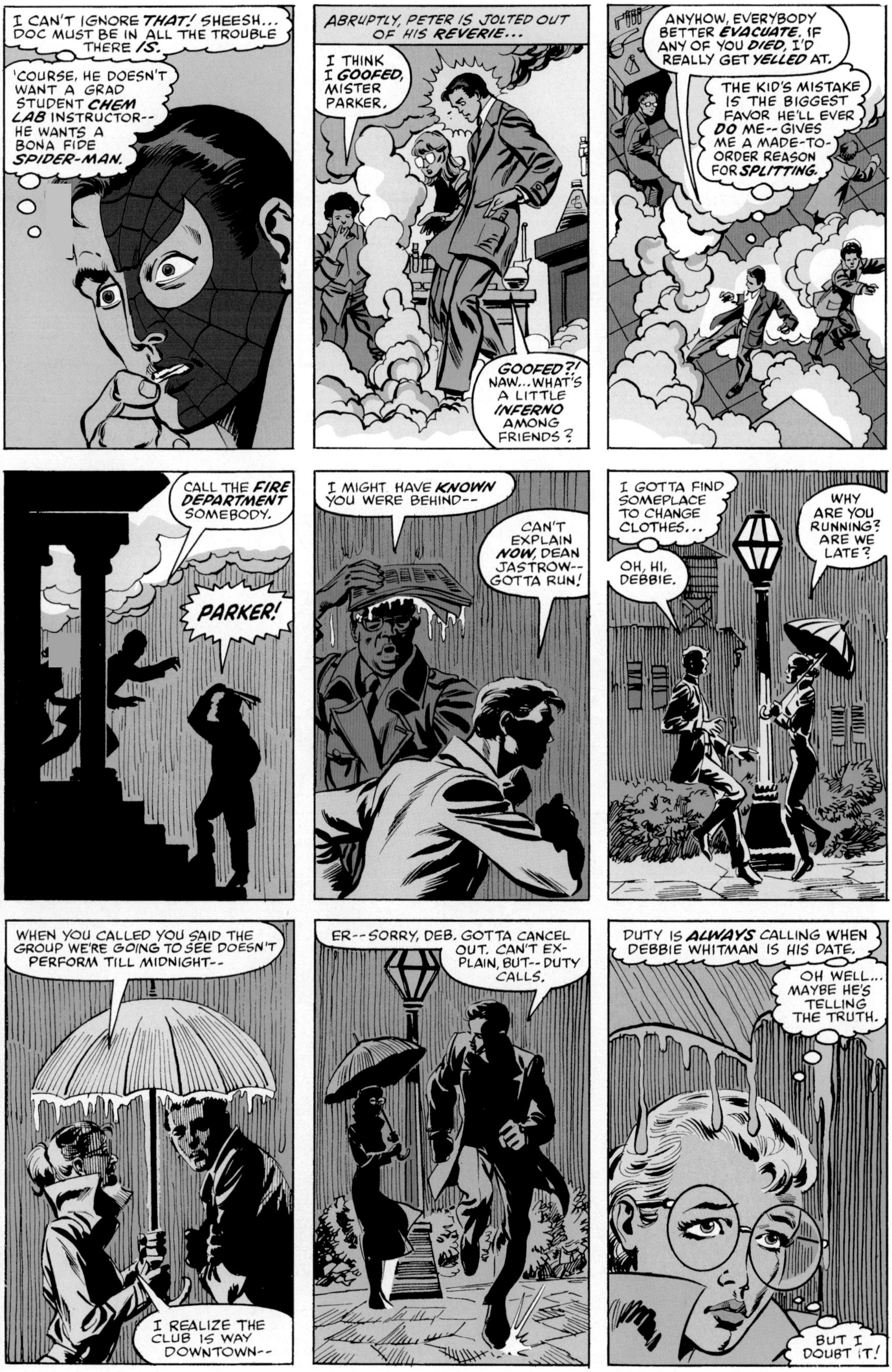

I CAN'T IGNORE THAT! SHEESH... DOC MUST BE IN ALL THE TROUBLE THERE IS.
'COURSE, HE DOESN'T WANT A GRAD STUDENT CHEM LAB INSTRUCTOR-- HE WANTS A BONA FIDE SPIDER-MAN.
ABRUPTLY, PETER IS JOLTED OUT OF HIS REVERIE...
I THINK I GOOFED, MISTER PARKER.
GOOFED?! NAW... WHAT'S A LITTLE INFERNO AMONG FRIENDS?
ANYHOW, EVERYBODY BETTER EVACUATE. IF ANY OF YOU DIED, I'D REALLY GET YELLED AT.
THE KID'S MISTAKE IS THE BIGGEST FAVOR HE'LL EVER DO ME-- GIVES ME A MADE-TO-ORDER REASON FOR SPLITTING.
CALL THE FIRE DEPARTMENT SOMEBODY.
PARKER!
I MIGHT HAVE KNOWN YOU WERE BEHIND--
CAN'T EXPLAIN NOW, DEAN JASTROW-- GOTTA RUN!
I GOTTA FIND SOMEPLACE TO CHANGE CLOTHES...
OH, HI, DEBBIE.
WHY ARE YOU RUNNING? ARE WE LATE?
WHEN YOU CALLED YOU SAID THE GROUP WE'RE GOING TO SEE DOESN'T PERFORM TILL MIDNIGHT--
I REALIZE THE CLUB IS WAY DOWNTOWN--
ER--SORRY, DEB. GOTTA CANCEL OUT. CAN'T EX-PLAIN, BUT--DUTY CALLS.
DUTY IS ALWAYS CALLING WHEN DEBBIE WHITMAN IS HIS DATE.
OH WELL... MAYBE HE'S TELLING THE TRUTH.
BUT I DOUBT IT!

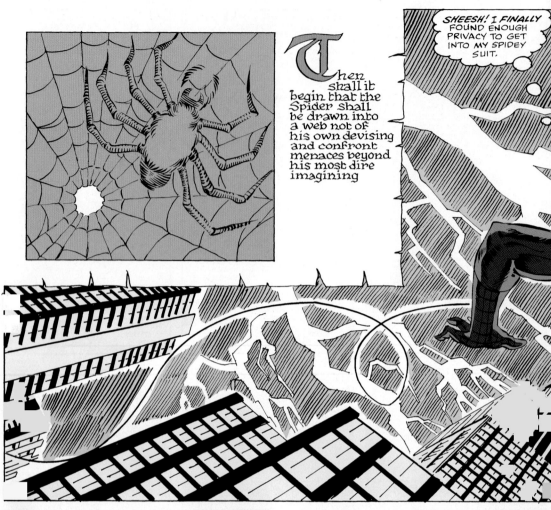

Then shall it begin that the Spider shall be drawn into a web not of his own devising and confront menaces beyond his most dire imagining

SHEESH! I FINALLY FOUND ENOUGH PRIVACY TO GET INTO MY SPIDEY SUIT.

YEAH, EXACTLY WHERE I REMEMBERED IT... THAT NUTTY UPPER WINDOW IS *UNMISTAKABLE.*

I DON'T SEE ANY SIGN OF TROUBLE, THOUGH.

MAYBE I *IMAGINED* THAT WEIRD MESSAGE...MAYBE I'VE BEEN WORKING TOO HARD.

MAYBE I'M CRACKING UP--

--AND I OUGHTTA SIGN MYSELF INTO THE *HAPPY HOUSE.*

BUT AS LONG AS I'M HERE, I MIGHT AS WELL CHECK THINGS OUT.

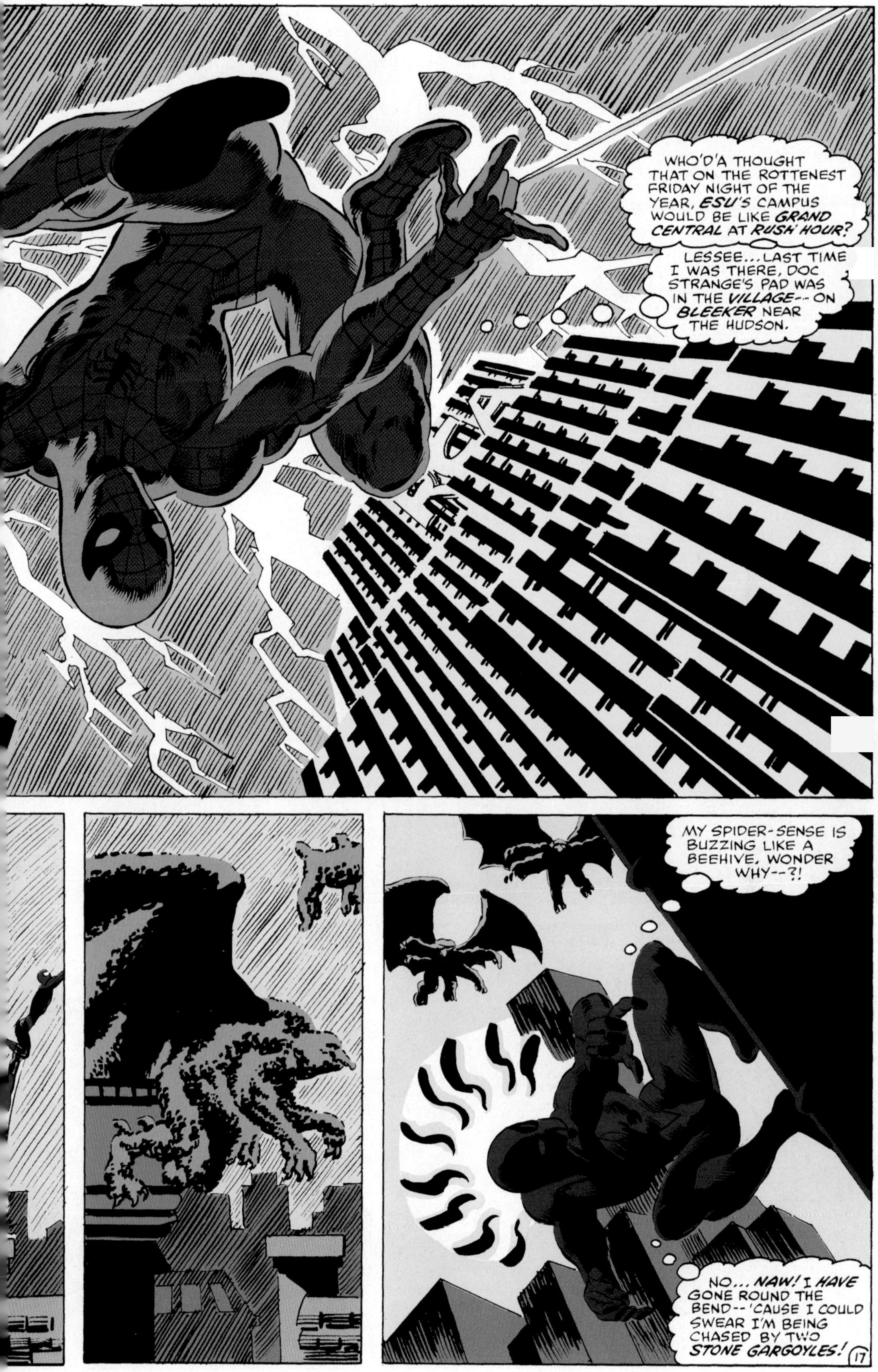
WHO'D'A THOUGHT THAT ON THE ROTTENEST FRIDAY NIGHT OF THE YEAR, ESU'S CAMPUS WOULD BE LIKE GRAND CENTRAL AT RUSH HOUR?
LESSEE... LAST TIME I WAS THERE, DOC STRANGE'S PAD WAS IN THE VILLAGE-- ON BLEEKER NEAR THE HUDSON.
MY SPIDER-SENSE IS BUZZING LIKE A BEEHIVE. WONDER WHY--?!
NO... NAW! I HAVE GONE ROUND THE BEND-- 'CAUSE I COULD SWEAR I'M BEING CHASED BY TWO STONE GARGOYLES!
17

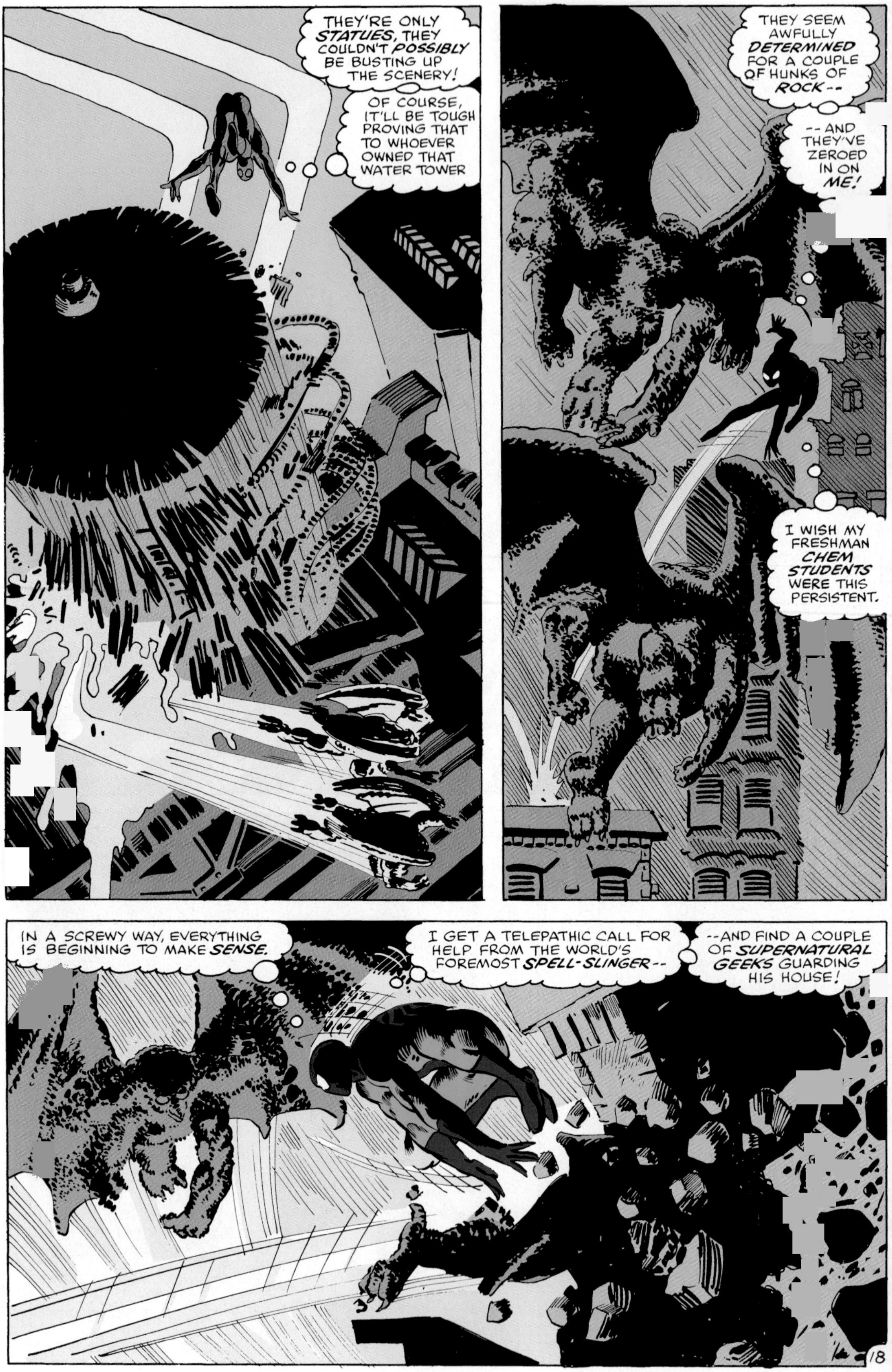
THEY'RE ONLY STATUES, THEY COULDN'T POSSIBLY BE BUSTING UP THE SCENERY!
OF COURSE, IT'LL BE TOUGH PROVING THAT TO WHOEVER OWNED THAT WATER TOWER
THEY SEEM AWFULLY DETERMINED FOR A COUPLE OF HUNKS OF ROCK--
--AND THEY'VE ZEROED IN ON ME!
I WISH MY FRESHMAN CHEM STUDENTS WERE THIS PERSISTENT.
IN A SCREWY WAY, EVERYTHING IS BEGINNING TO MAKE SENSE.
I GET A TELEPATHIC CALL FOR HELP FROM THE WORLD'S FOREMOST SPELL-SLINGER--
--AND FIND A COUPLE OF SUPERNATURAL GEEKS GUARDING HIS HOUSE!
18

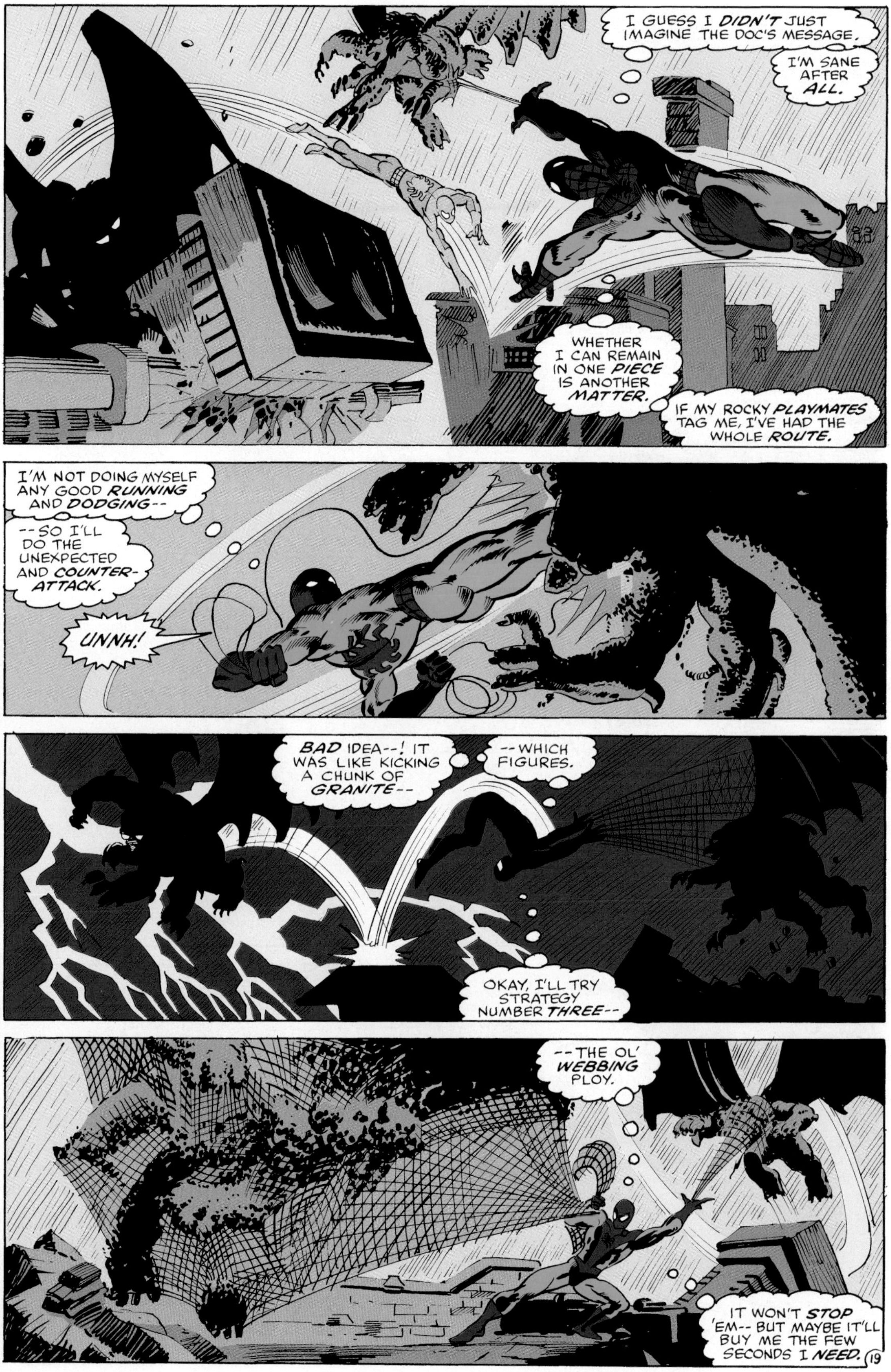
I GUESS I DIDN'T JUST IMAGINE THE DOC'S MESSAGE.
I'M SANE AFTER ALL.
WHETHER I CAN REMAIN IN ONE PIECE IS ANOTHER MATTER.
IF MY ROCKY PLAYMATES TAG ME, I'VE HAD THE WHOLE ROUTE.
I'M NOT DOING MYSELF ANY GOOD RUNNING AND DODGING--
--SO I'LL DO THE UNEXPECTED AND COUNTER-ATTACK.
UNNH!
BAD IDEA--! IT WAS LIKE KICKING A CHUNK OF GRANITE--
--WHICH FIGURES.
OKAY, I'LL TRY STRATEGY NUMBER THREE--
--THE OL' WEBBING PLOY.
IT WON'T STOP 'EM-- BUT MAYBE IT'LL BUY ME THE FEW SECONDS I NEED.
19

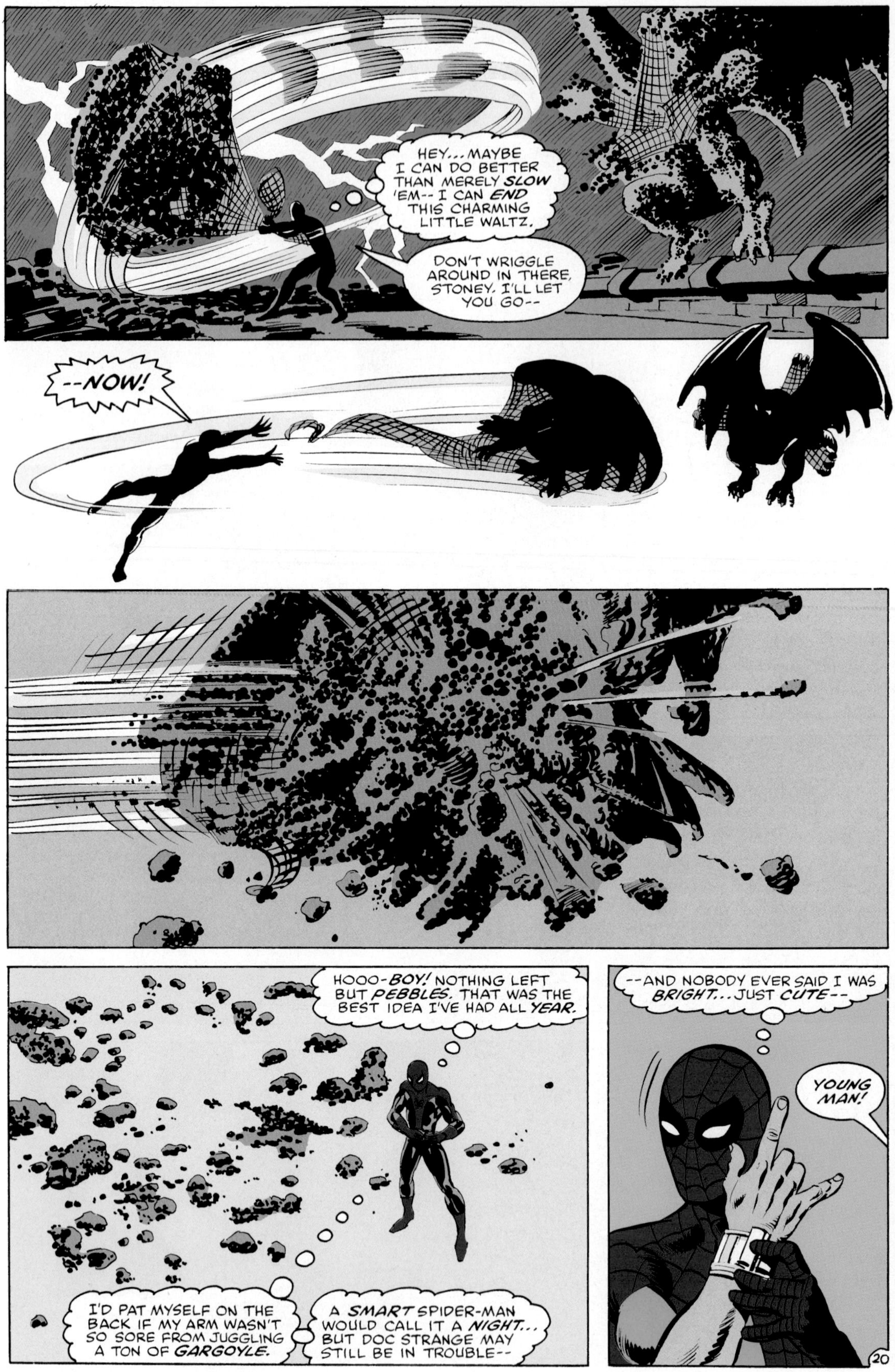
HEY... MAYBE I CAN DO BETTER THAN MERELY SLOW 'EM-- I CAN END THIS CHARMING LITTLE WALTZ.
DON'T WRIGGLE AROUND IN THERE, STONEY. I'LL LET YOU GO--
--NOW!
HOOO-BOY! NOTHING LEFT BUT PEBBLES. THAT WAS THE BEST IDEA I'VE HAD ALL YEAR.
I'D PAT MYSELF ON THE BACK IF MY ARM WASN'T SO SORE FROM JUGGLING A TON OF GARGOYLE.
A SMART SPIDER-MAN WOULD CALL IT A NIGHT... BUT DOC STRANGE MAY STILL BE IN TROUBLE--
--AND NOBODY EVER SAID I WAS BRIGHT... JUST CUTE--
YOUNG MAN!
20

WHAT IS THAT RACKET? DO YOU REALIZE THAT IT IS ELEVEN O'CLOCK? DECENT FOLKS HAVE BEEN IN BED FOR HOURS. THE PROBLEM WITH YOU YOUNG PEOPLE OF TODAY IS YOU HAVE ABSOLUTELY NO SENSE OF DECENCY OR PROPRIETY. WHEN I WAS YOUR AGE I KNEW HOW TO BEHAVE. WE DIDN'T HAVE HIPPIES OR DISCOTHEQUES IN THOSE DAYS, I CAN TELL YOU. DID YOU MAKE THAT MESS? WELL, GO GET YOURSELF A BROOM AND SWEEP IT UP, EVERY SINGLE BIT OF IT. DON'T STAND THERE. PAY ATTENTION WHEN I TALK TO YOU.

YOUNG M—

MMMPF

THAP

BETWEEN HER AND GARGOYLES, I'LL TAKE THE GARGOYLES.

MMMF

ANY DAY.

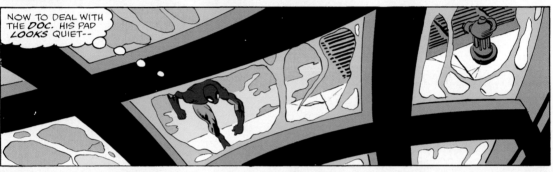

NOW TO DEAL WITH THE DOC. HIS PAD LOOKS QUIET—

—SO WHY IS MY SPIDER-SENSE JANGLING AGAIN?

HUH—? EITHER DOC HAS BIZARRE TASTE IN SIDEWALKS—

—OR I'M ABOUT TO MEET A NEW SET OF NASTIES!

LITTLE BUGGERS... SHOULDN'T BE TOO HARD TO SHAKE 'EM—

THEY'RE STICKING LIKE LEECHES... DRAGGING ME DOWN— AND WRINKLING MY COSTUME!

21

261

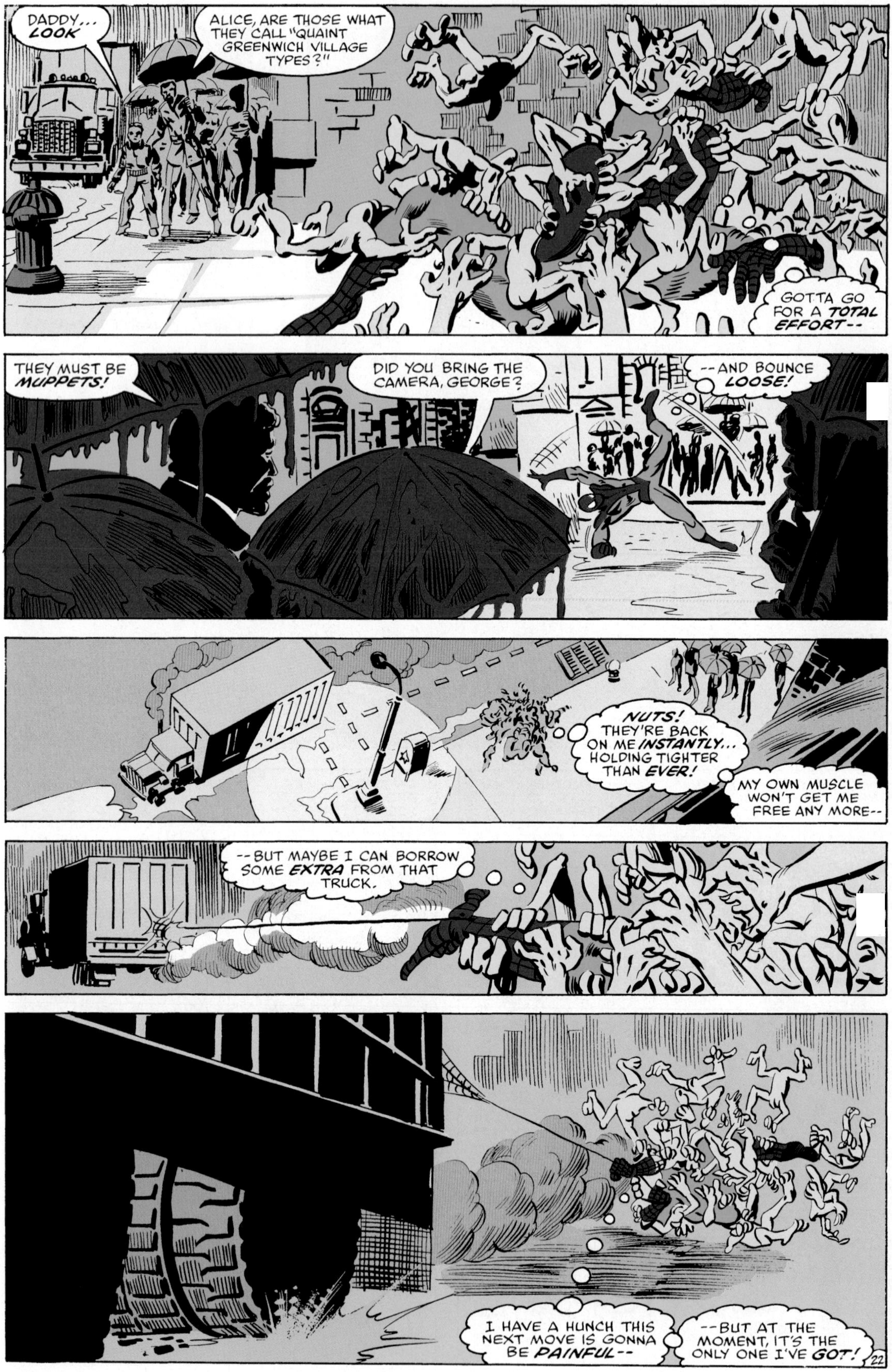
DADDY,... LOOK
ALICE, ARE THOSE WHAT THEY CALL "QUAINT GREENWICH VILLAGE TYPES?"
GOTTA GO FOR A TOTAL EFFORT--
THEY MUST BE MUPPETS!
DID YOU BRING THE CAMERA, GEORGE?
--AND BOUNCE LOOSE!
NUTS! THEY'RE BACK ON ME INSTANTLY... HOLDING TIGHTER THAN EVER!
MY OWN MUSCLE WON'T GET ME FREE ANY MORE--
--BUT MAYBE I CAN BORROW SOME EXTRA FROM THAT TRUCK.
I HAVE A HUNCH THIS NEXT MOVE IS GONNA BE PAINFUL--
--BUT AT THE MOMENT, IT'S THE ONLY ONE I'VE GOT!
22

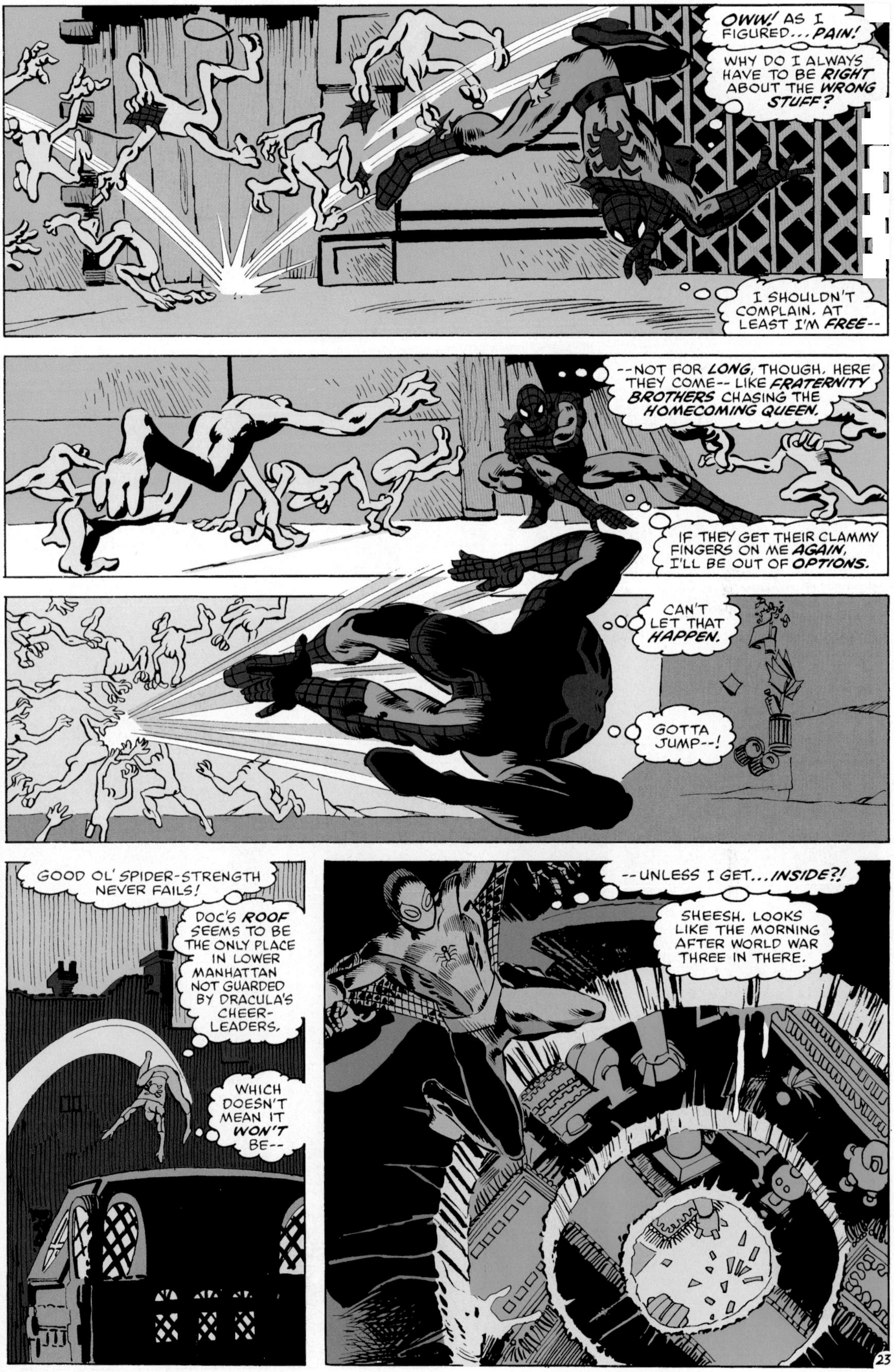
OWW! AS I FIGURED... PAIN!
WHY DO I ALWAYS HAVE TO BE RIGHT ABOUT THE WRONG STUFF?
I SHOULDN'T COMPLAIN. AT LEAST I'M FREE--
--NOT FOR LONG, THOUGH. HERE THEY COME-- LIKE FRATERNITY BROTHERS CHASING THE HOMECOMING QUEEN.
IF THEY GET THEIR CLAMMY FINGERS ON ME AGAIN, I'LL BE OUT OF OPTIONS.
CAN'T LET THAT HAPPEN.
GOTTA JUMP--!
GOOD OL' SPIDER-STRENGTH NEVER FAILS!
DOC'S ROOF SEEMS TO BE THE ONLY PLACE IN LOWER MANHATTAN NOT GUARDED BY DRACULA'S CHEER-LEADERS,
WHICH DOESN'T MEAN IT WON'T BE--
--UNLESS I GET... INSIDE?!
SHEESH. LOOKS LIKE THE MORNING AFTER WORLD WAR THREE IN THERE.
23

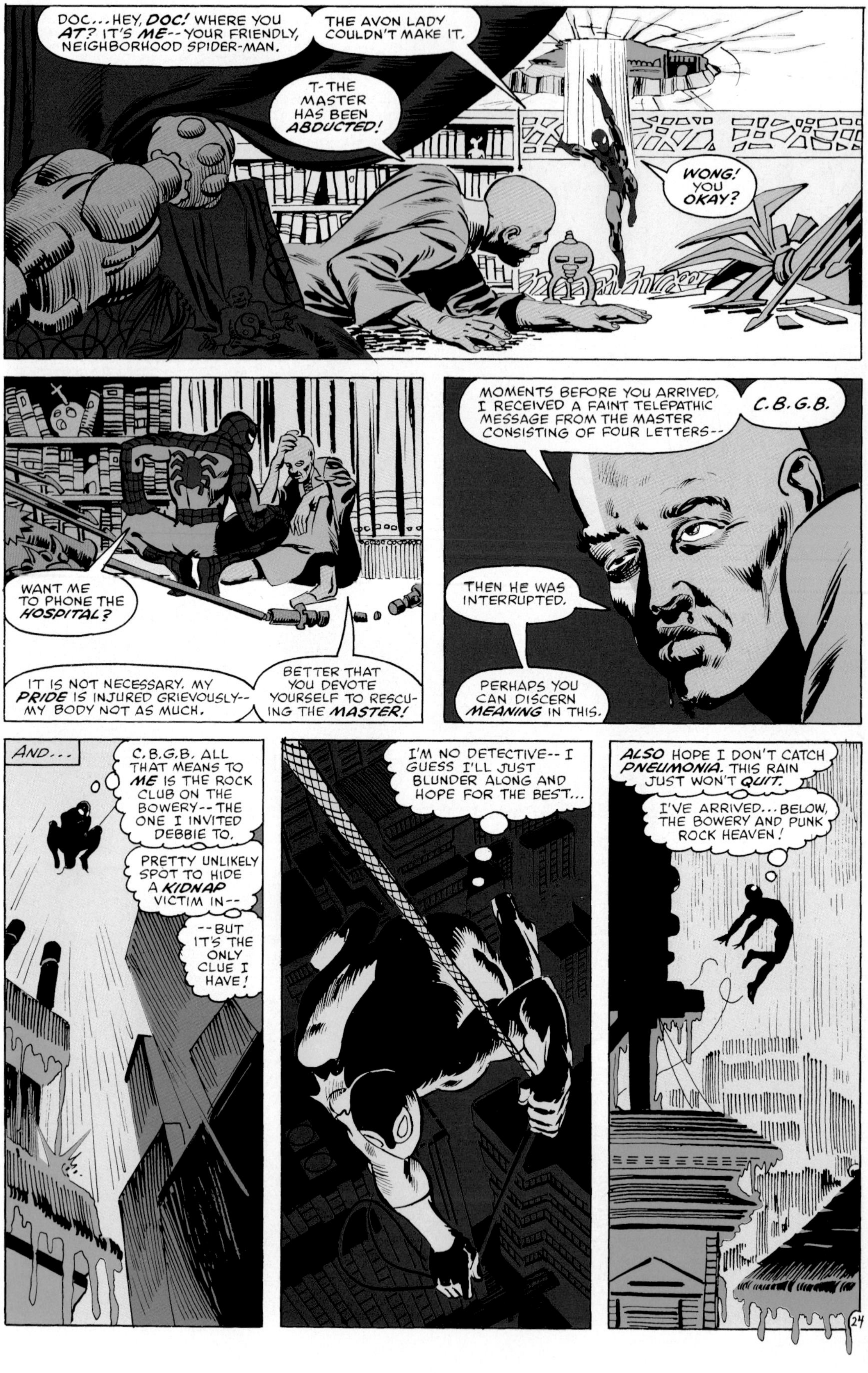

DOC...HEY, DOC! WHERE YOU AT? IT'S ME-- YOUR FRIENDLY, NEIGHBORHOOD SPIDER-MAN.
THE AVON LADY COULDN'T MAKE IT.
T-THE MASTER HAS BEEN ABDUCTED!
WONG! YOU OKAY?
WANT ME TO PHONE THE HOSPITAL?
IT IS NOT NECESSARY. MY PRIDE IS INJURED GRIEVOUSLY-- MY BODY NOT AS MUCH.
BETTER THAT YOU DEVOTE YOURSELF TO RESCUING THE MASTER!
MOMENTS BEFORE YOU ARRIVED, I RECEIVED A FAINT TELEPATHIC MESSAGE FROM THE MASTER CONSISTING OF FOUR LETTERS--
C.B.G.B.
THEN HE WAS INTERRUPTED.
PERHAPS YOU CAN DISCERN MEANING IN THIS.
AND...
C.B.G.B. ALL THAT MEANS TO ME IS THE ROCK CLUB ON THE BOWERY-- THE ONE I INVITED DEBBIE TO.
PRETTY UNLIKELY SPOT TO HIDE A KIDNAP VICTIM IN--
--BUT IT'S THE ONLY CLUE I HAVE!
I'M NO DETECTIVE-- I GUESS I'LL JUST BLUNDER ALONG AND HOPE FOR THE BEST...
ALSO HOPE I DON'T CATCH PNEUMONIA. THIS RAIN JUST WON'T QUIT.
I'VE ARRIVED... BELOW, THE BOWERY AND PUNK ROCK HEAVEN!
24

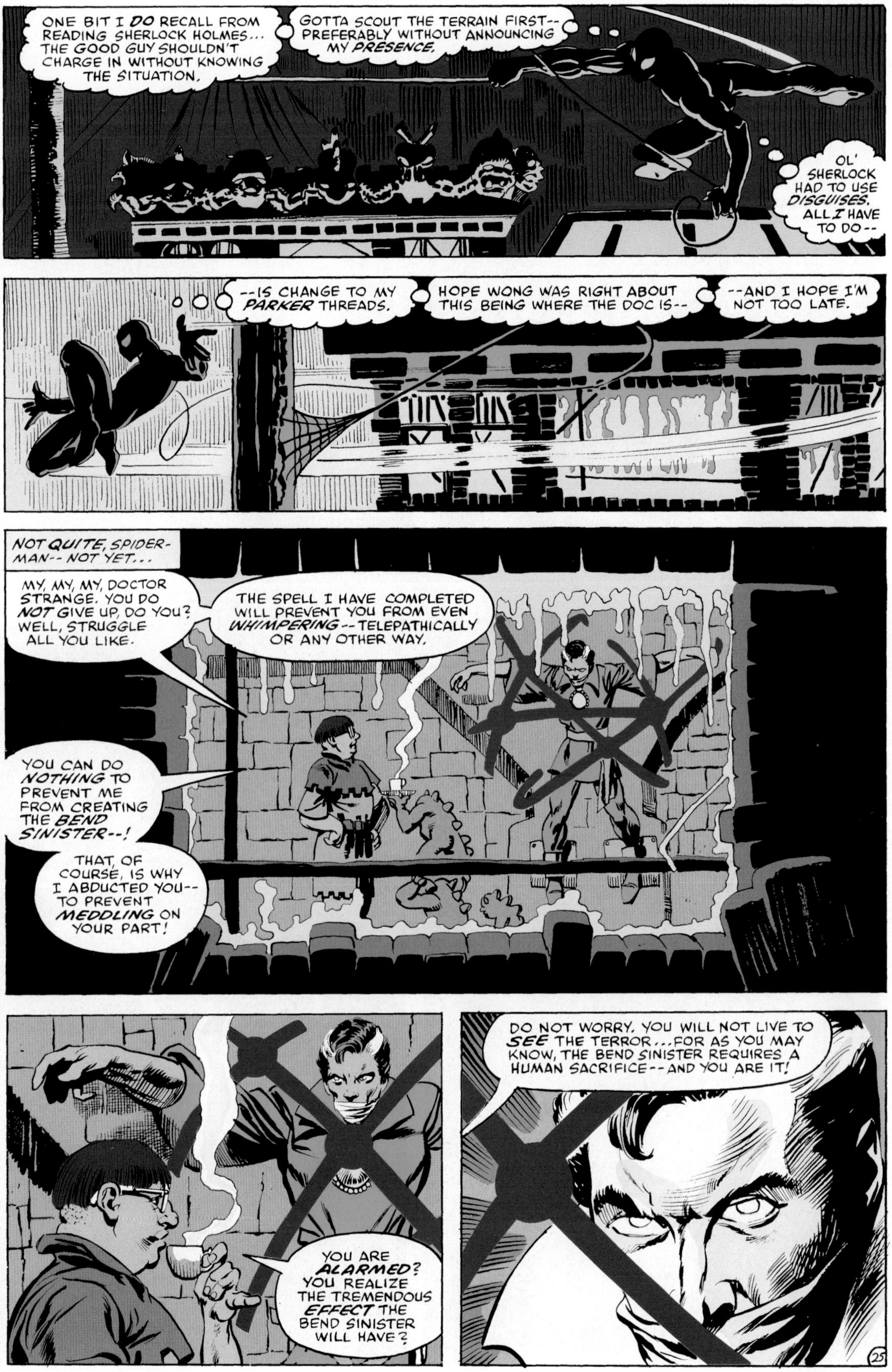
ONE BIT I DO RECALL FROM READING SHERLOCK HOLMES... THE GOOD GUY SHOULDN'T CHARGE IN WITHOUT KNOWING THE SITUATION.
GOTTA SCOUT THE TERRAIN FIRST-- PREFERABLY WITHOUT ANNOUNCING MY PRESENCE.
OL' SHERLOCK HAD TO USE DISGUISES. ALL I HAVE TO DO--
--IS CHANGE TO MY PARKER THREADS.
HOPE WONG WAS RIGHT ABOUT THIS BEING WHERE THE DOC IS--
--AND I HOPE I'M NOT TOO LATE.
NOT QUITE, SPIDER-MAN-- NOT YET...
MY, MY, MY, DOCTOR STRANGE. YOU DO NOT GIVE UP, DO YOU? WELL, STRUGGLE ALL YOU LIKE.
THE SPELL I HAVE COMPLETED WILL PREVENT YOU FROM EVEN WHIMPERING--TELEPATHICALLY OR ANY OTHER WAY.
YOU CAN DO NOTHING TO PREVENT ME FROM CREATING THE BEND SINISTER--!
THAT, OF COURSE, IS WHY I ABDUCTED YOU-- TO PREVENT MEDDLING ON YOUR PART!
YOU ARE ALARMED? YOU REALIZE THE TREMENDOUS EFFECT THE BEND SINISTER WILL HAVE?
DO NOT WORRY. YOU WILL NOT LIVE TO SEE THE TERROR...FOR AS YOU MAY KNOW, THE BEND SINISTER REQUIRES A HUMAN SACRIFICE--AND YOU ARE IT!
25

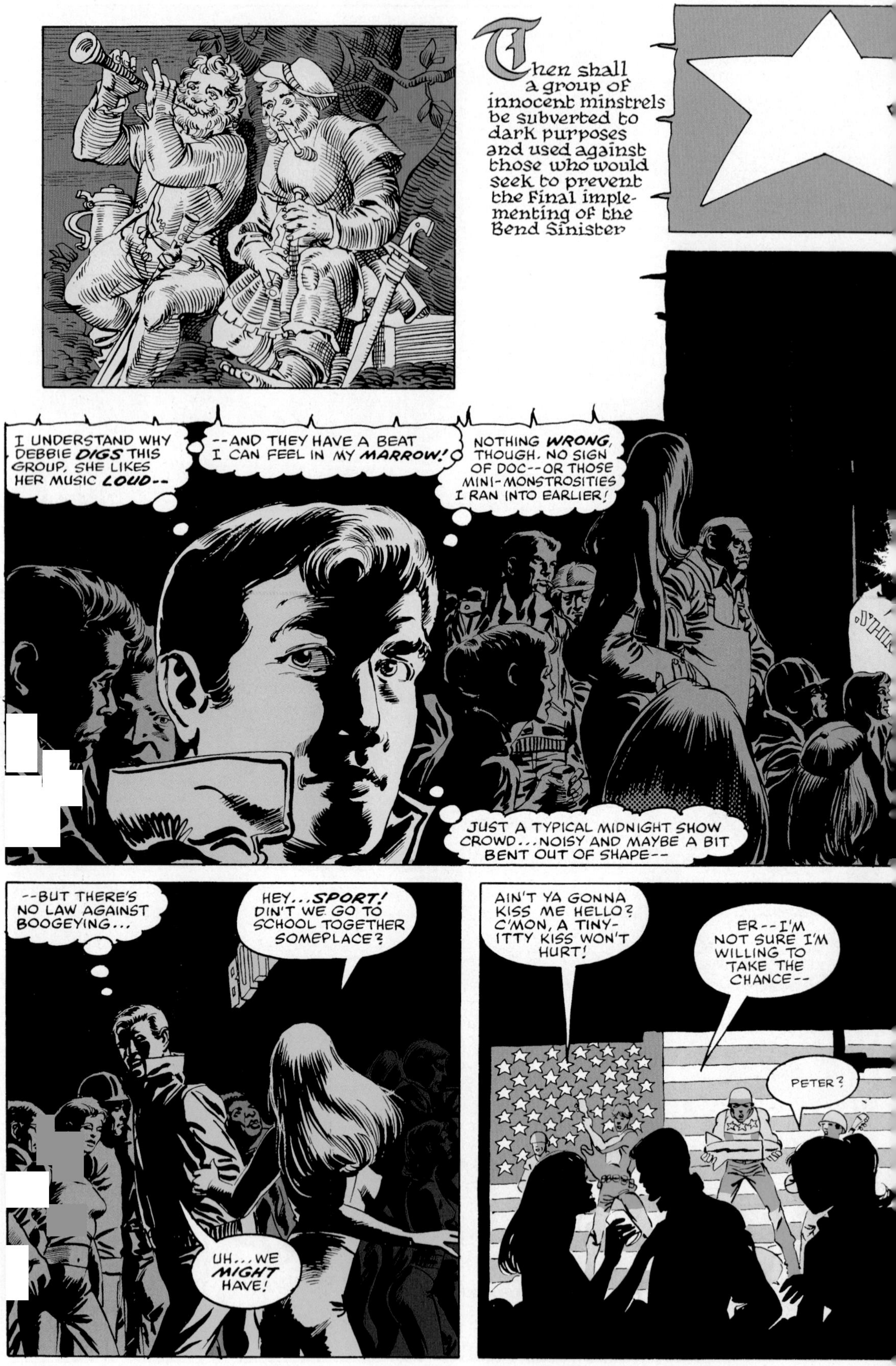
Then shall a group of innocent minstrels be subverted to dark purposes and used against those who would seek to prevent the Final implementing of the Bend Sinister
I UNDERSTAND WHY DEBBIE DIGS THIS GROUP. SHE LIKES HER MUSIC LOUD--
--AND THEY HAVE A BEAT I CAN FEEL IN MY MARROW!
NOTHING WRONG, THOUGH. NO SIGN OF DOC--OR THOSE MINI-MONSTROSITIES I RAN INTO EARLIER!
JUST A TYPICAL MIDNIGHT SHOW CROWD...NOISY AND MAYBE A BIT BENT OUT OF SHAPE--
--BUT THERE'S NO LAW AGAINST BOOGEYING...
HEY...SPORT! DIDN'T WE GO TO SCHOOL TOGETHER SOMEPLACE?
UH...WE MIGHT HAVE!
AIN'T YA GONNA KISS ME HELLO? C'MON, A TINY-ITTY KISS WON'T HURT!
ER--I'M NOT SURE I'M WILLING TO TAKE THE CHANCE--
PETER?

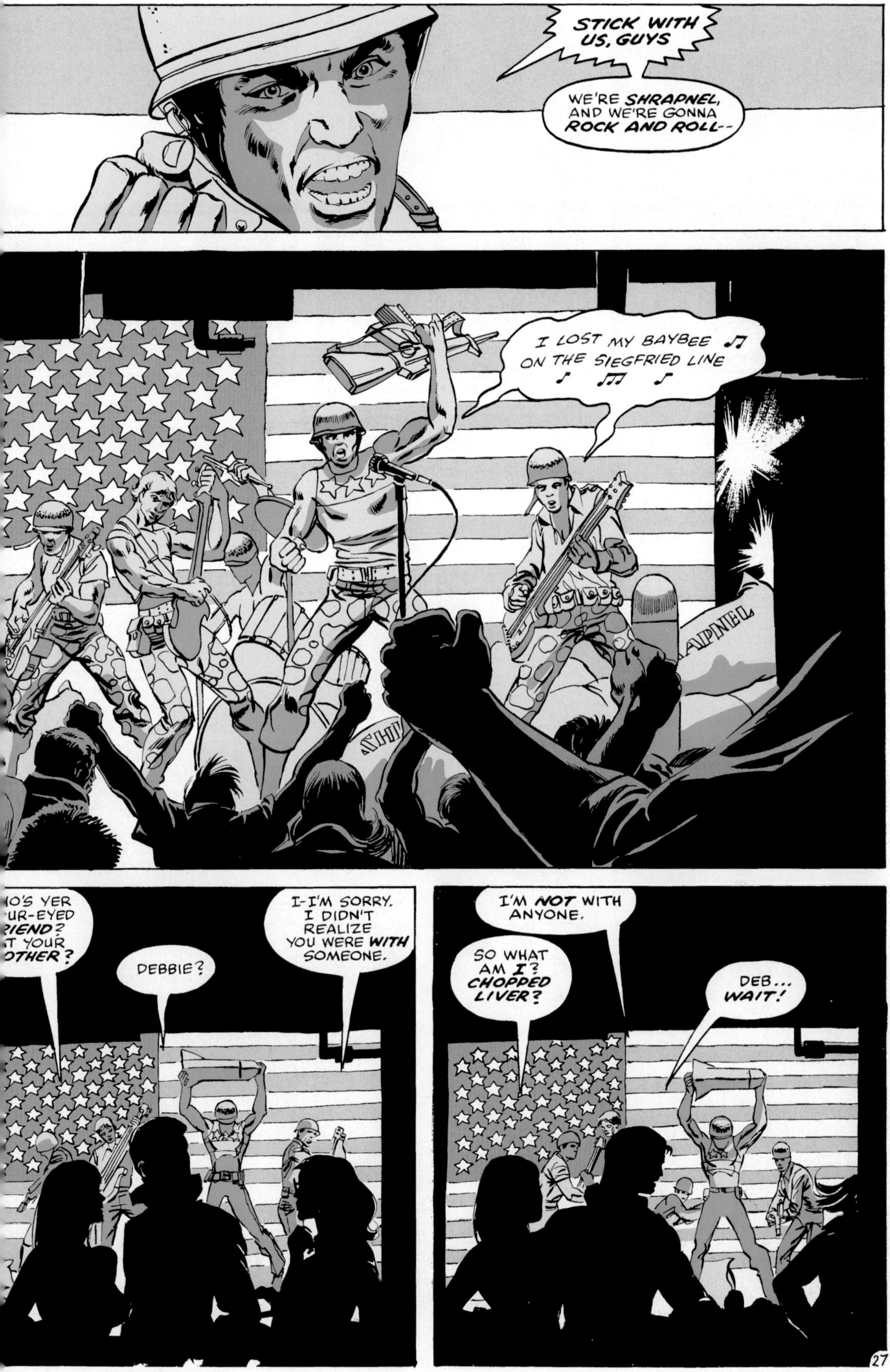
STICK WITH US, GUYS
WE'RE SHRAPNEL, AND WE'RE GONNA ROCK AND ROLL--
I LOST MY BAYBEE ON THE SIEGFRIED LINE
HO'S YER UR-EYED RIEND? T YOUR OTHER?
DEBBIE?
I-I'M SORRY. I DIDN'T REALIZE YOU WERE WITH SOMEONE.
I'M NOT WITH ANYONE.
SO WHAT AM I? CHOPPED LIVER?
DEB... WAIT!
27

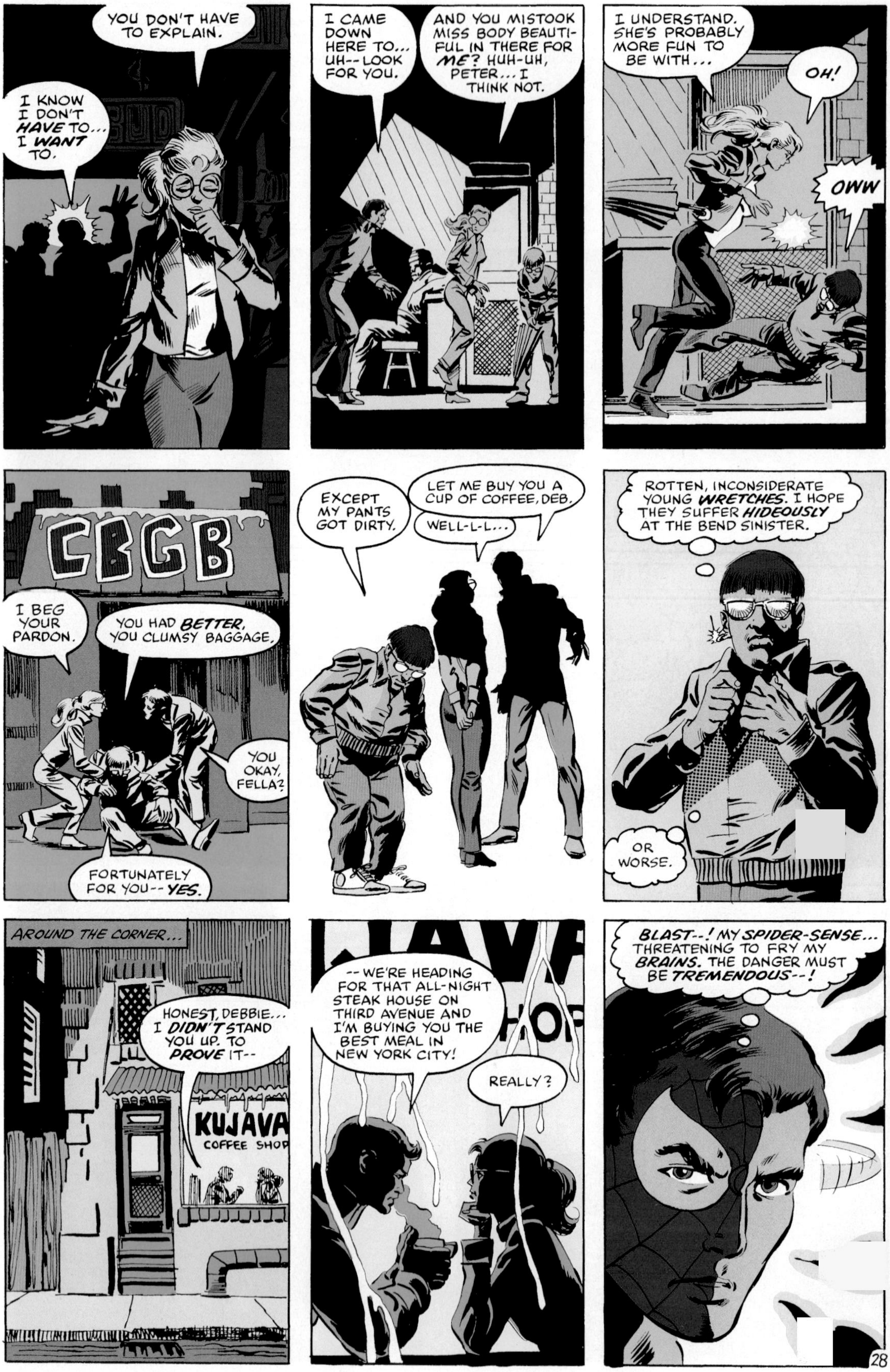

YOU DON'T HAVE TO EXPLAIN.
I KNOW I DON'T *HAVE* TO... I *WANT* TO.
I CAME DOWN HERE TO... UH-- LOOK FOR YOU.
AND YOU MISTOOK MISS BODY BEAUTIFUL IN THERE FOR *ME*? HUH-UH, PETER... I THINK NOT.
I UNDERSTAND. SHE'S PROBABLY MORE FUN TO BE WITH...
OH!
OWW
CBGB
I BEG YOUR PARDON.
YOU HAD *BETTER*, YOU CLUMSY BAGGAGE.
YOU OKAY, FELLA?
FORTUNATELY FOR YOU-- *YES*.
EXCEPT MY PANTS GOT DIRTY.
LET ME BUY YOU A CUP OF COFFEE, DEB.
WELL-L-L...
ROTTEN, INCONSIDERATE YOUNG *WRETCHES*. I HOPE THEY SUFFER *HIDEOUSLY* AT THE BEND SINISTER.
OR WORSE.
AROUND THE CORNER...
HONEST, DEBBIE... I *DIDN'T* STAND YOU UP. TO *PROVE* IT--
KUJAVA COFFEE SHOP
-- WE'RE HEADING FOR THAT ALL-NIGHT STEAK HOUSE ON THIRD AVENUE AND I'M BUYING YOU THE BEST MEAL IN NEW YORK CITY!
REALLY?
BLAST--! MY *SPIDER-SENSE*... THREATENING TO FRY MY *BRAINS*. THE DANGER MUST BE *TREMENDOUS*--!
28

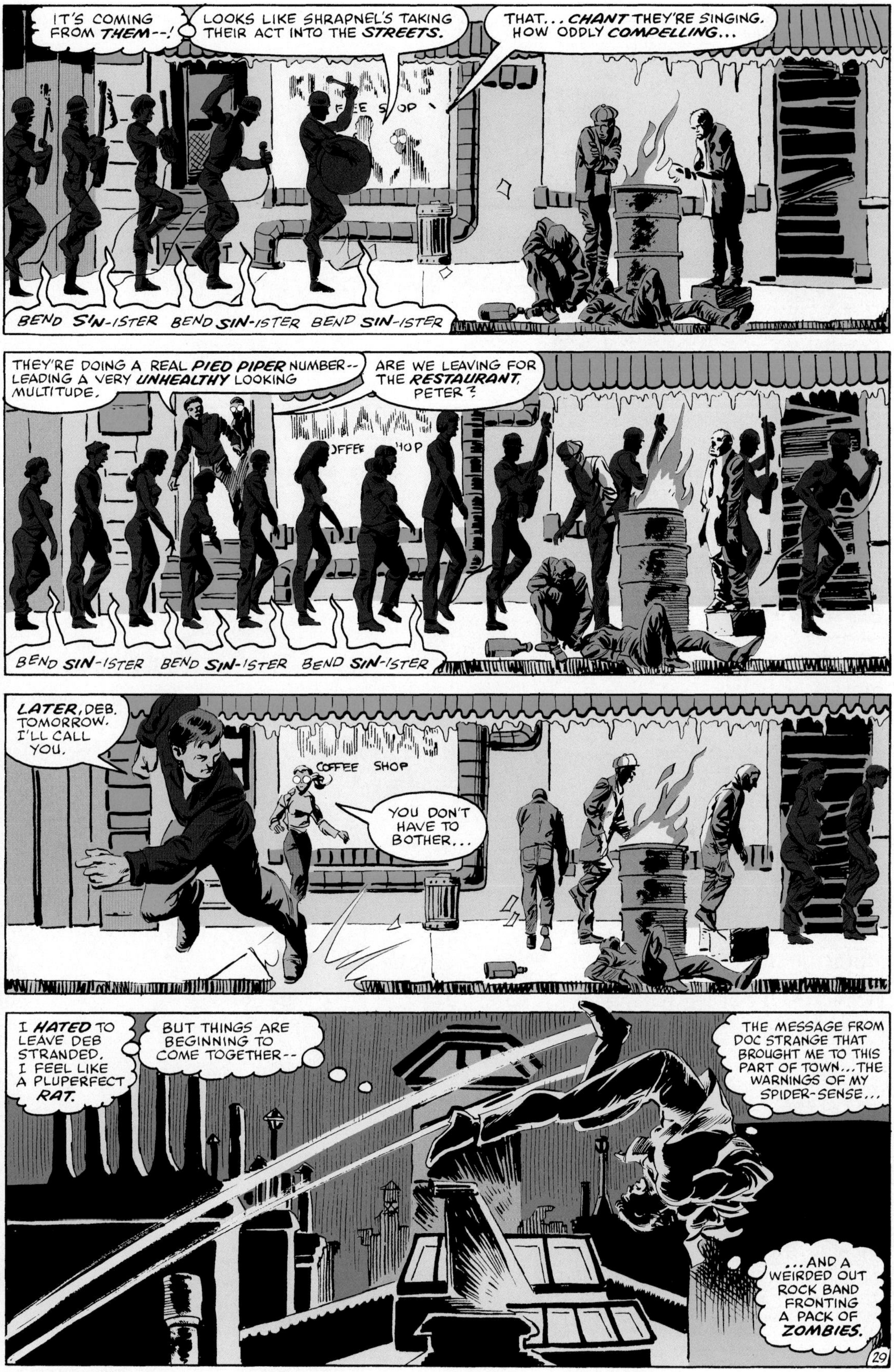
IT'S COMING FROM THEM--!
LOOKS LIKE SHRAPNEL'S TAKING THEIR ACT INTO THE STREETS.
THAT... CHANT THEY'RE SINGING. HOW ODDLY COMPELLING...
BEND S'IN-ISTER BEND SIN-ISTER BEND SIN-ISTER
COFFEE SHOP
THEY'RE DOING A REAL PIED PIPER NUMBER-- LEADING A VERY UNHEALTHY LOOKING MULTITUDE.
ARE WE LEAVING FOR THE RESTAURANT, PETER?
BEND SIN-ISTER BEND SIN-ISTER BEND SIN-ISTER
LATER, DEB. TOMORROW. I'LL CALL YOU.
COFFEE SHOP
YOU DON'T HAVE TO BOTHER...
I HATED TO LEAVE DEB STRANDED. I FEEL LIKE A PLUPERFECT RAT.
BUT THINGS ARE BEGINNING TO COME TOGETHER--
THE MESSAGE FROM DOC STRANGE THAT BROUGHT ME TO THIS PART OF TOWN... THE WARNINGS OF MY SPIDER-SENSE...
...AND A WEIRDED OUT ROCK BAND FRONTING A PACK OF ZOMBIES.
29

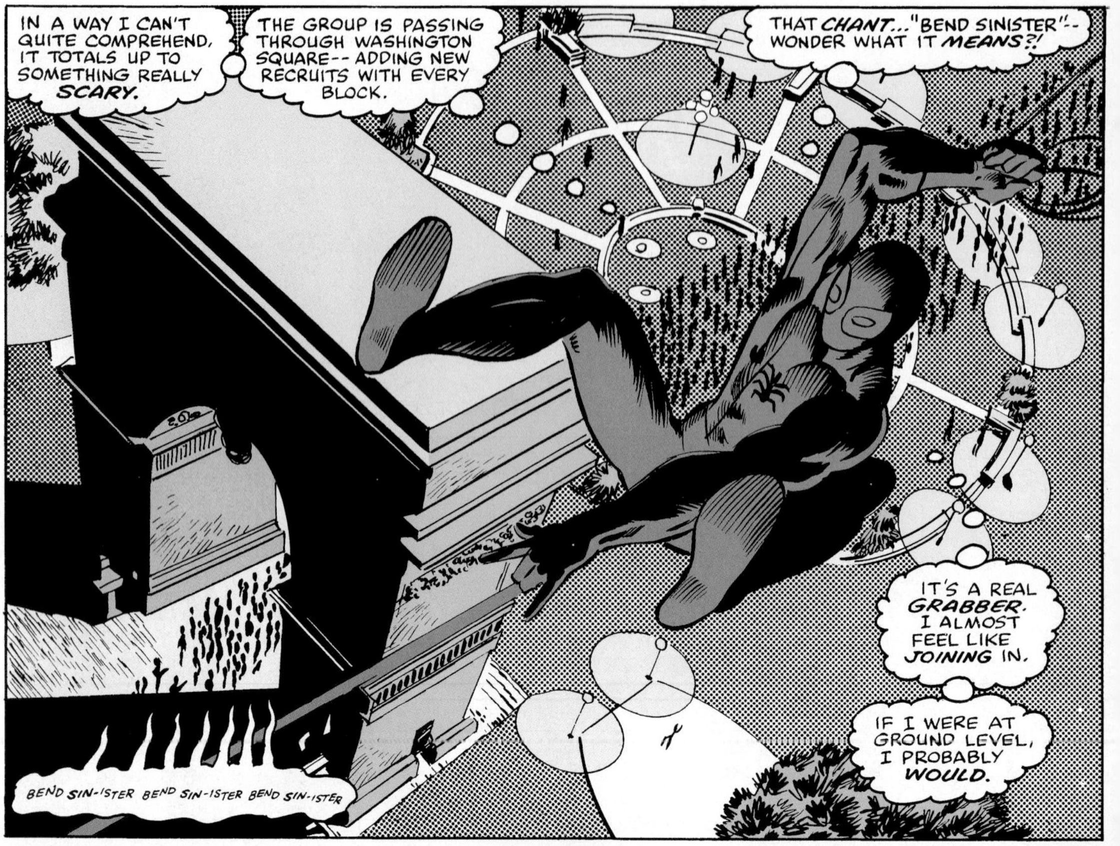
IN A WAY I CAN'T QUITE COMPREHEND, IT TOTALS UP TO SOMETHING REALLY SCARY.
THE GROUP IS PASSING THROUGH WASHINGTON SQUARE-- ADDING NEW RECRUITS WITH EVERY BLOCK.
THAT CHANT..."BEND SINISTER"-- WONDER WHAT IT MEANS?!
IT'S A REAL GRABBER. I ALMOST FEEL LIKE JOINING IN.
IF I WERE AT GROUND LEVEL, I PROBABLY WOULD.
BEND SIN-ISTER BEND SIN-ISTER BEND SIN-ISTER

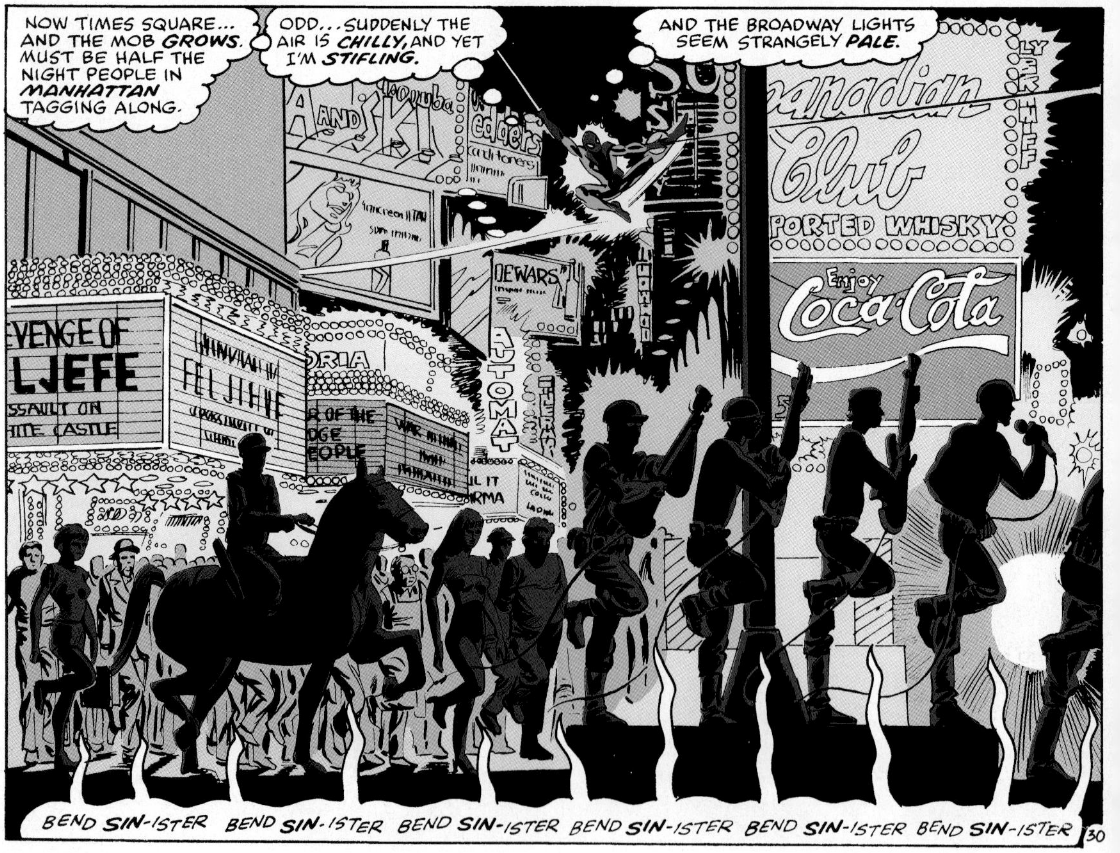
NOW TIMES SQUARE... AND THE MOB GROWS. MUST BE HALF THE NIGHT PEOPLE IN MANHATTAN TAGGING ALONG.
ODD... SUDDENLY THE AIR IS CHILLY, AND YET I'M STIFLING.
AND THE BROADWAY LIGHTS SEEM STRANGELY PALE.
Canadian Club
PORTED WHISKY
Enjoy Coca-Cola
DEWARS
AUTOMAT
EVENGE OF
LJEFE
SSAULT ON
HITE CASTLE
BEND SIN-ISTER BEND SIN-ISTER BEND SIN-ISTER BEND SIN-ISTER BEND SIN-ISTER BEND SIN-ISTER
30

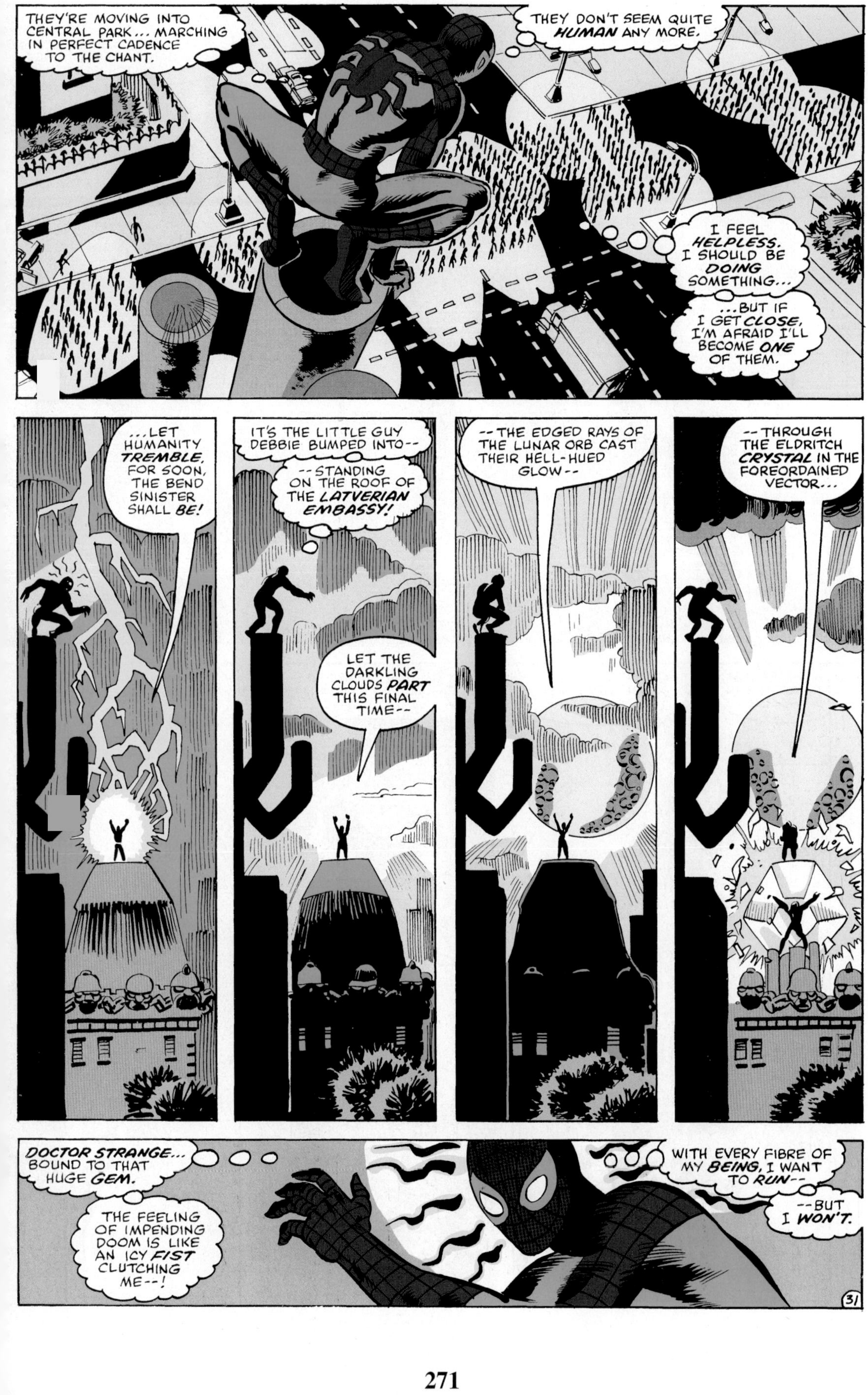
THEY'RE MOVING INTO CENTRAL PARK... MARCHING IN PERFECT CADENCE TO THE CHANT.
THEY DON'T SEEM QUITE HUMAN ANY MORE.
I FEEL HELPLESS. I SHOULD BE DOING SOMETHING...
...BUT IF I GET CLOSE, I'M AFRAID I'LL BECOME ONE OF THEM.
...LET HUMANITY TREMBLE, FOR SOON, THE BEND SINISTER SHALL BE!
IT'S THE LITTLE GUY DEBBIE BUMPED INTO--
--STANDING ON THE ROOF OF THE LATVERIAN EMBASSY!
LET THE DARKLING CLOUDS PART THIS FINAL TIME--
--THE EDGED RAYS OF THE LUNAR ORB CAST THEIR HELL-HUED GLOW--
--THROUGH THE ELDRITCH CRYSTAL IN THE FOREORDAINED VECTOR...
DOCTOR STRANGE... BOUND TO THAT HUGE GEM.
THE FEELING OF IMPENDING DOOM IS LIKE AN ICY FIST CLUTCHING ME--!
WITH EVERY FIBRE OF MY BEING, I WANT TO RUN--
--BUT I WON'T.
31

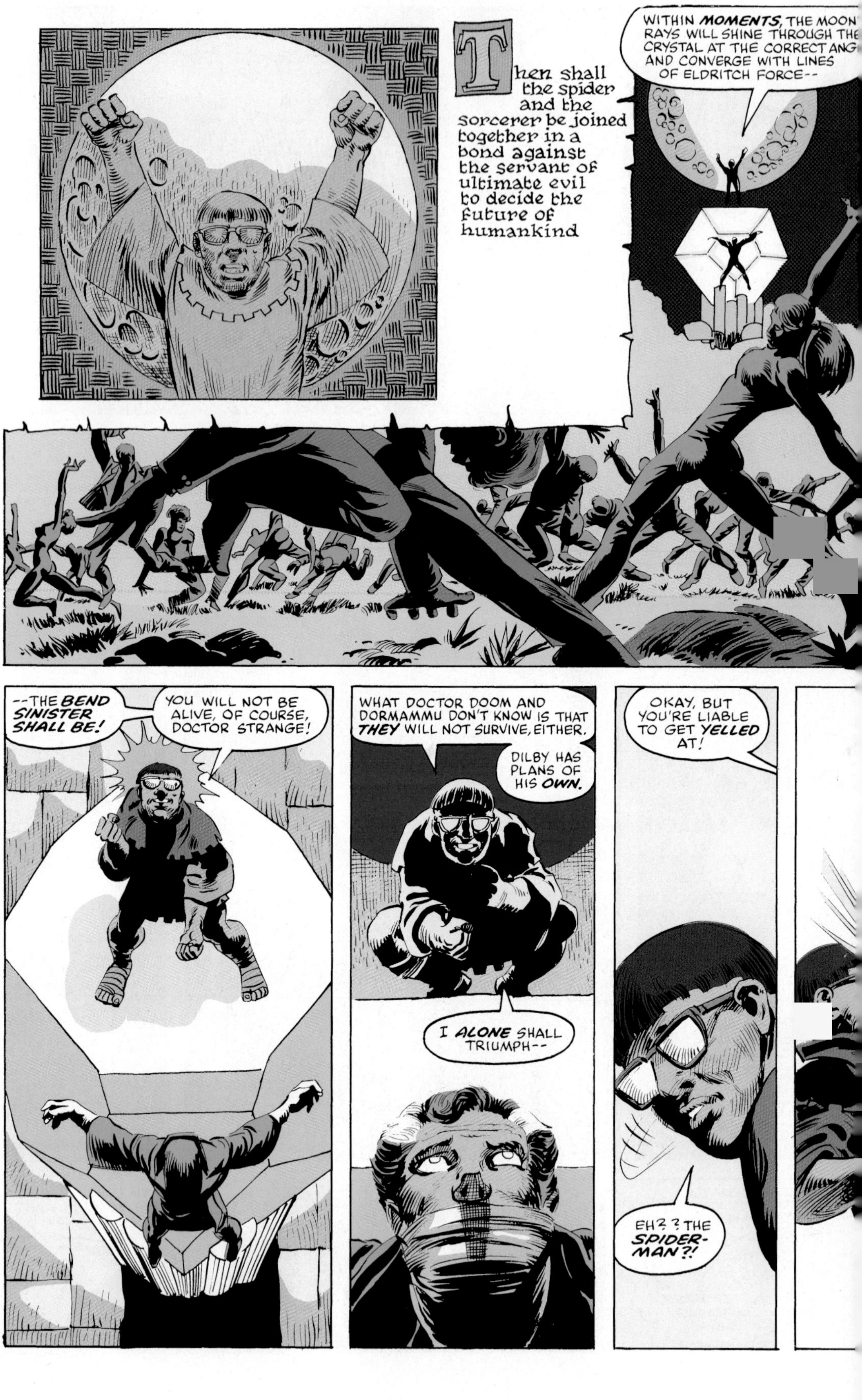
Then shall the spider and the sorcerer be joined together in a bond against the servant of ultimate evil to decide the future of humankind
WITHIN MOMENTS, THE MOON RAYS WILL SHINE THROUGH THE CRYSTAL AT THE CORRECT ANG AND CONVERGE WITH LINES OF ELDRITCH FORCE--
--THE BEND SINISTER SHALL BE!
YOU WILL NOT BE ALIVE, OF COURSE, DOCTOR STRANGE!
WHAT DOCTOR DOOM AND DORMAMMU DON'T KNOW IS THAT THEY WILL NOT SURVIVE, EITHER.
DILBY HAS PLANS OF HIS OWN.
I ALONE SHALL TRIUMPH--
OKAY, BUT YOU'RE LIABLE TO GET YELLED AT!
EH?? THE SPIDER-MAN?!

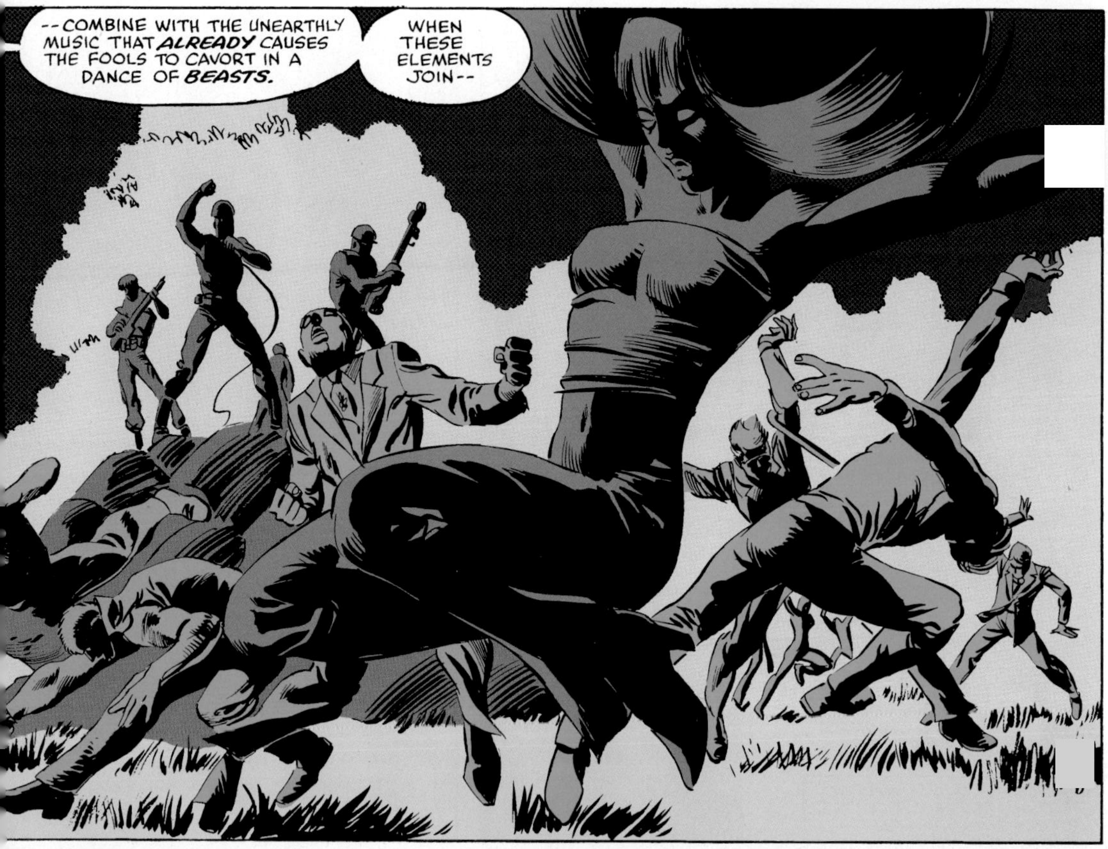
--COMBINE WITH THE UNEARTHLY MUSIC THAT ALREADY CAUSES THE FOOLS TO CAVORT IN A DANCE OF BEASTS.
WHEN THESE ELEMENTS JOIN--

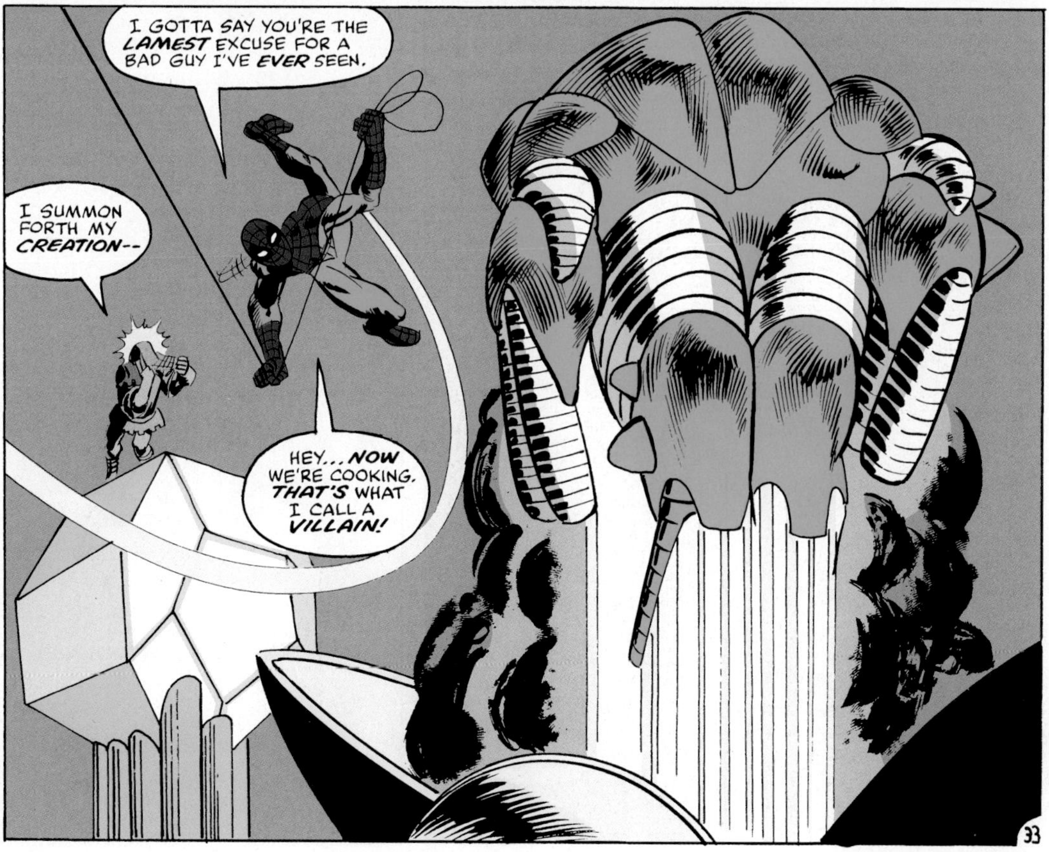
I GOTTA SAY YOU'RE THE LAMEST EXCUSE FOR A BAD GUY I'VE EVER SEEN.
I SUMMON FORTH MY CREATION--
HEY... NOW WE'RE COOKING. THAT'S WHAT I CALL A VILLAIN!
33

WHOSE TOY BOX DID **YOU** ESCAPE FROM?-- --AND HOW DO I PUT YOU **BACK**?

YOU'RE MORE THE **SLAUGHTER AND MAYHEM** TYPE!

NO ANSWER, HUH? I GUESS YOU'RE NOT PROGRAMMED FOR **SNAPPY PATTER.**

SPIDER-MAN'S KICK HAS NO EFFECT WHATSOEVER ON THE HURTLING JUGGERNAUT--

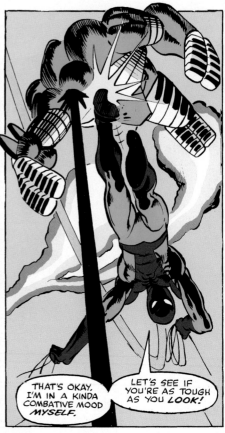

THAT'S OKAY. I'M IN A KINDA COMBATIVE MOOD **MYSELF.**

LET'S SEE IF YOU'RE AS TOUGH AS YOU **LOOK!**

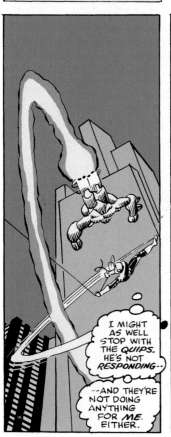

I MIGHT AS WELL STOP WITH THE **QUIPS.** HE'S NOT **RESPONDING--**

--AND THEY'RE NOT DOING ANYTHING FOR **ME,** EITHER.

USUALLY, THEY HELP ME TO FORGET TO BE **SCARED--** BUT NOT **NOW.**

MARTHA, IS THAT YOU?

MY, MY, MY, A **SHOW,** IS IT?

SPIDER-MAN IS PUTTING ON A **SHOW** FOR ME, TRYING TO REMAIN **ALIVE.**

WHEN THE BEND SINISTER **IS,** IT WILL NOT **MATTER** WHETHER OR NOT HE BREATHES.

THAT WILL BE IN MERE **SECONDS--**

34

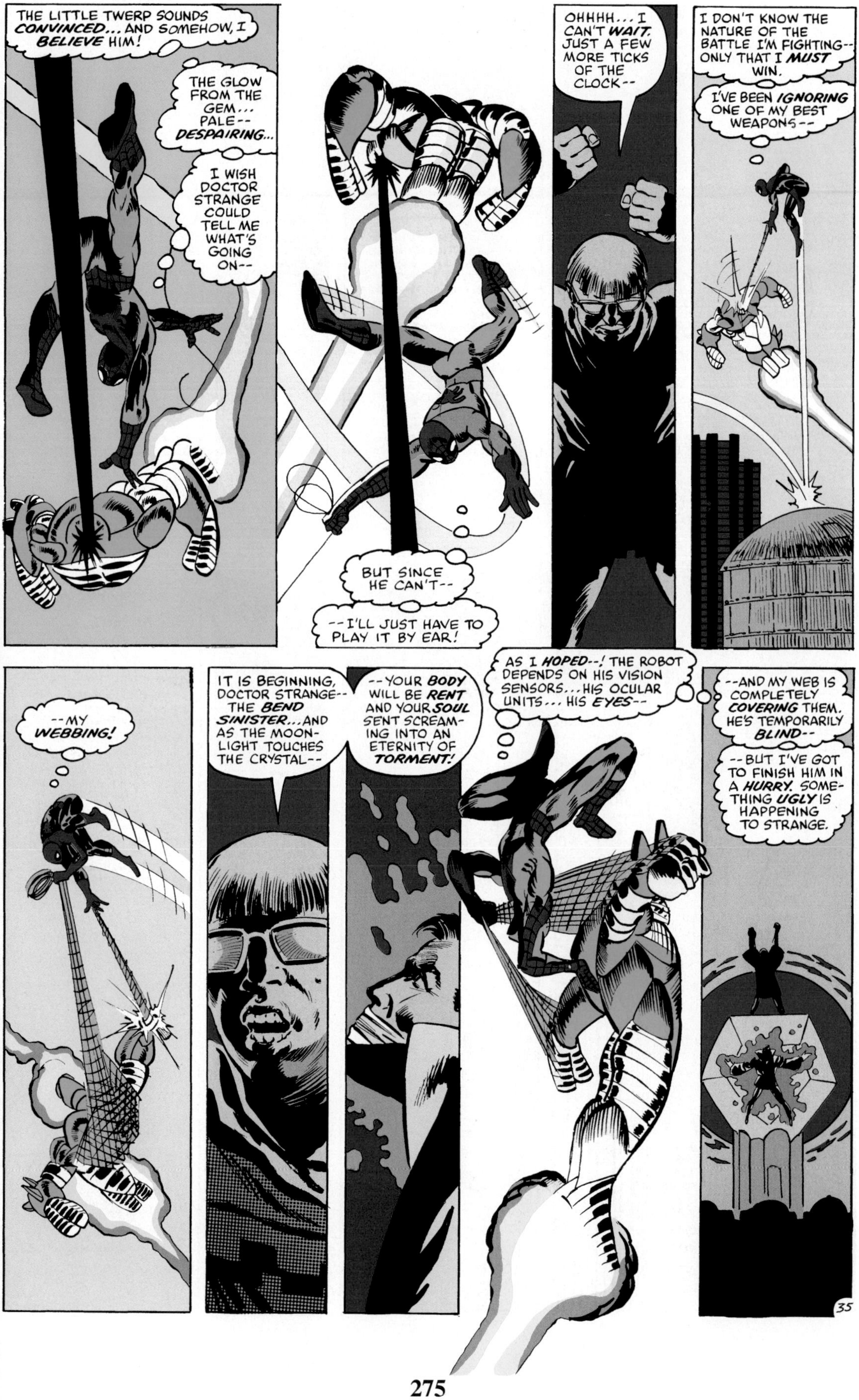
THE LITTLE TWERP SOUNDS CONVINCED... AND SOMEHOW, I BELIEVE HIM!
THE GLOW FROM THE GEM... PALE-- DESPAIRING...
I WISH DOCTOR STRANGE COULD TELL ME WHAT'S GOING ON--
BUT SINCE HE CAN'T--
--I'LL JUST HAVE TO PLAY IT BY EAR!
OHHHH... I CAN'T WAIT. JUST A FEW MORE TICKS OF THE CLOCK--
I DON'T KNOW THE NATURE OF THE BATTLE I'M FIGHTING-- ONLY THAT I MUST WIN.
I'VE BEEN IGNORING ONE OF MY BEST WEAPONS--
--MY WEBBING!
IT IS BEGINNING, DOCTOR STRANGE-- THE BEND SINISTER... AND AS THE MOON-LIGHT TOUCHES THE CRYSTAL--
--YOUR BODY WILL BE RENT AND YOUR SOUL SENT SCREAM-ING INTO AN ETERNITY OF TORMENT!
AS I HOPED--! THE ROBOT DEPENDS ON HIS VISION SENSORS... HIS OCULAR UNITS... HIS EYES--
--AND MY WEB IS COMPLETELY COVERING THEM. HE'S TEMPORARILY BLIND--
--BUT I'VE GOT TO FINISH HIM IN A HURRY. SOME-THING UGLY IS HAPPENING TO STRANGE.
35

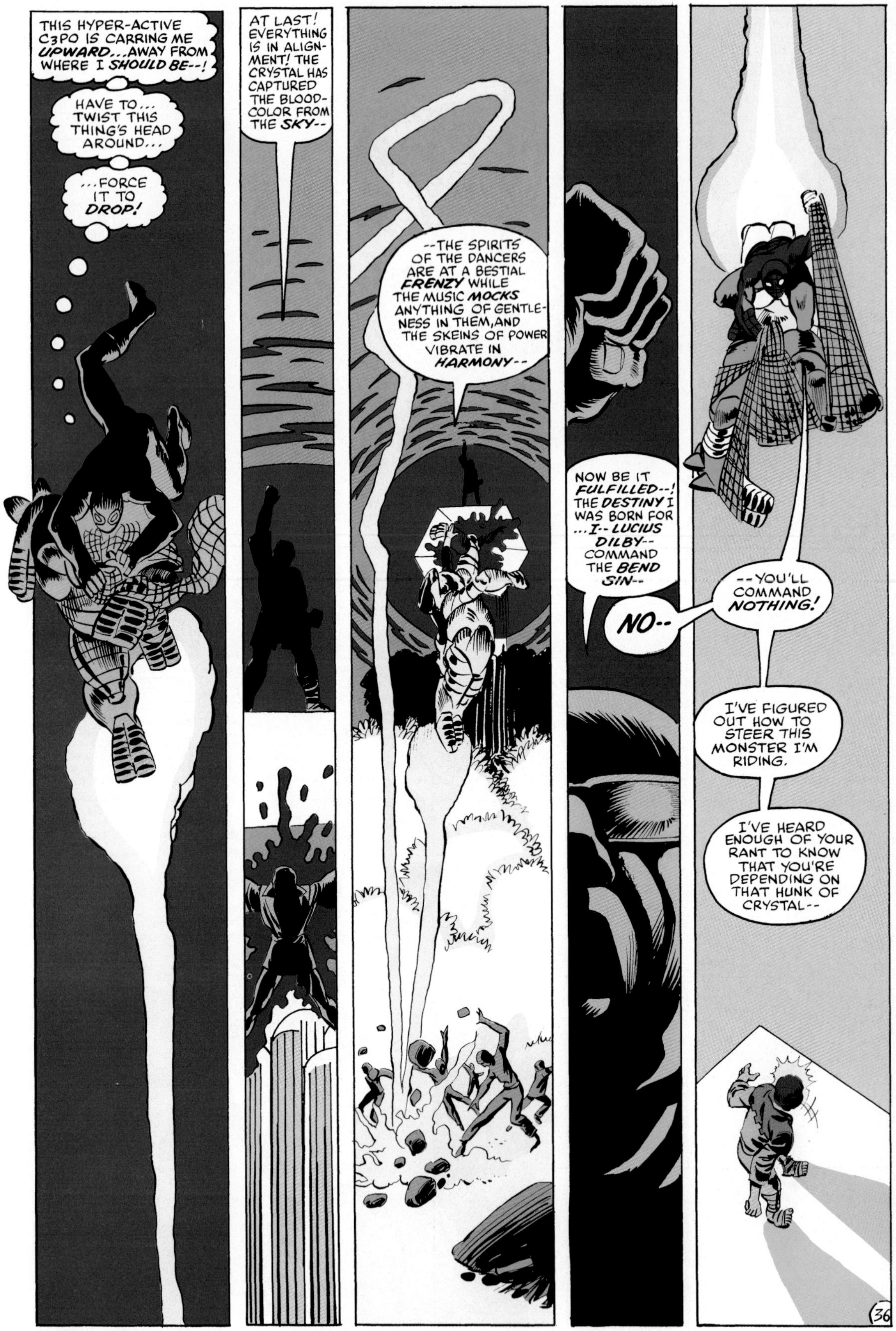
THIS HYPER-ACTIVE C3PO IS CARRING ME UPWARD... AWAY FROM WHERE I SHOULD BE--!
HAVE TO... TWIST THIS THING'S HEAD AROUND...
...FORCE IT TO DROP!
AT LAST! EVERYTHING IS IN ALIGNMENT! THE CRYSTAL HAS CAPTURED THE BLOOD-COLOR FROM THE SKY--
--THE SPIRITS OF THE DANCERS ARE AT A BESTIAL FRENZY WHILE THE MUSIC MOCKS ANYTHING OF GENTLENESS IN THEM, AND THE SKEINS OF POWER VIBRATE IN HARMONY--
NOW BE IT FULFILLED--! THE DESTINY I WAS BORN FOR ...I-- LUCIUS DILBY-- COMMAND THE BEND SIN--
NO--
--YOU'LL COMMAND NOTHING!
I'VE FIGURED OUT HOW TO STEER THIS MONSTER I'M RIDING.
I'VE HEARD ENOUGH OF YOUR RANT TO KNOW THAT YOU'RE DEPENDING ON THAT HUNK OF CRYSTAL--
36

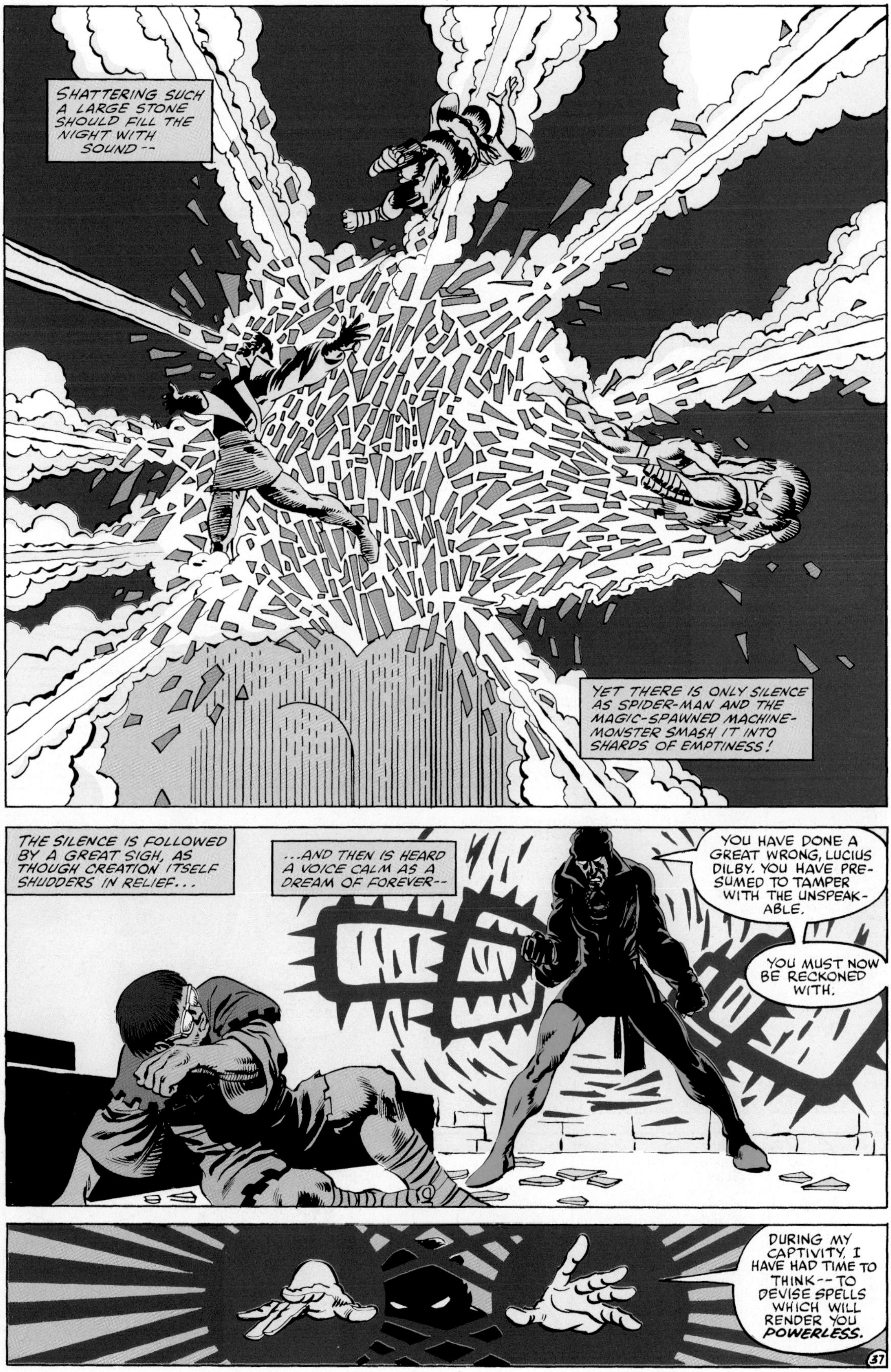
SHATTERING SUCH A LARGE STONE SHOULD FILL THE NIGHT WITH SOUND--
YET THERE IS ONLY SILENCE AS SPIDER-MAN AND THE MAGIC-SPAWNED MACHINE-MONSTER SMASH IT INTO SHARDS OF EMPTINESS!
THE SILENCE IS FOLLOWED BY A GREAT SIGH, AS THOUGH CREATION ITSELF SHUDDERS IN RELIEF...
...AND THEN IS HEARD A VOICE CALM AS A DREAM OF FOREVER--
YOU HAVE DONE A GREAT WRONG, LUCIUS DILBY. YOU HAVE PRESUMED TO TAMPER WITH THE UNSPEAKABLE.
YOU MUST NOW BE RECKONED WITH.
DURING MY CAPTIVITY, I HAVE HAD TIME TO THINK--TO DEVISE SPELLS WHICH WILL RENDER YOU POWERLESS.
37

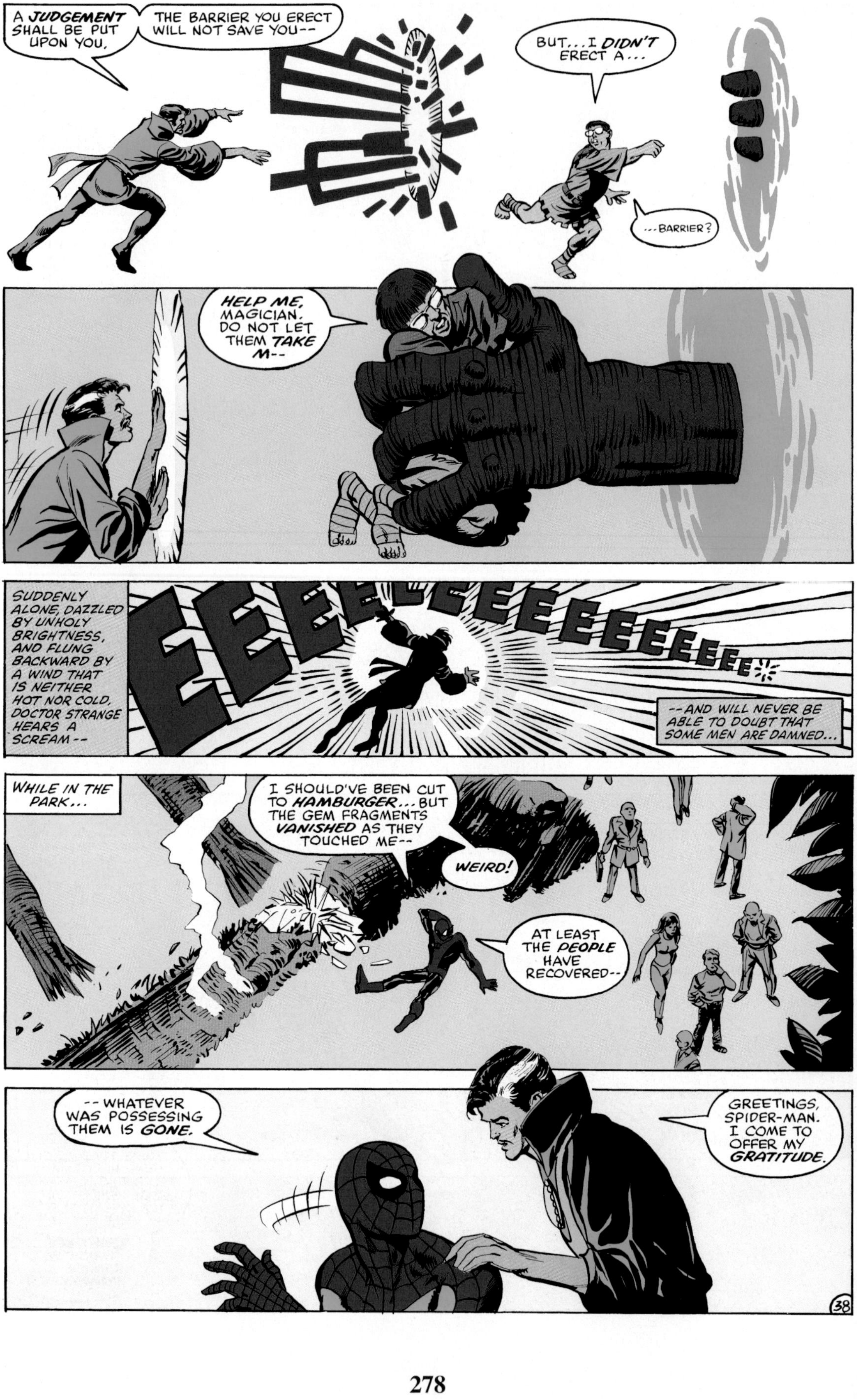
A JUDGEMENT SHALL BE PUT UPON YOU.
THE BARRIER YOU ERECT WILL NOT SAVE YOU--
BUT... I DIDN'T ERECT A...
...BARRIER?
HELP ME, MAGICIAN. DO NOT LET THEM TAKE M--
SUDDENLY ALONE, DAZZLED BY UNHOLY BRIGHTNESS, AND FLUNG BACKWARD BY A WIND THAT IS NEITHER HOT NOR COLD, DOCTOR STRANGE HEARS A SCREAM--
EEEEEEEEEEEEEEEEEE
--AND WILL NEVER BE ABLE TO DOUBT THAT SOME MEN ARE DAMNED...
WHILE IN THE PARK...
I SHOULD'VE BEEN CUT TO HAMBURGER... BUT THE GEM FRAGMENTS VANISHED AS THEY TOUCHED ME--
WEIRD!
AT LEAST THE PEOPLE HAVE RECOVERED--
--WHATEVER WAS POSSESSING THEM IS GONE.
GREETINGS, SPIDER-MAN. I COME TO OFFER MY GRATITUDE.
38

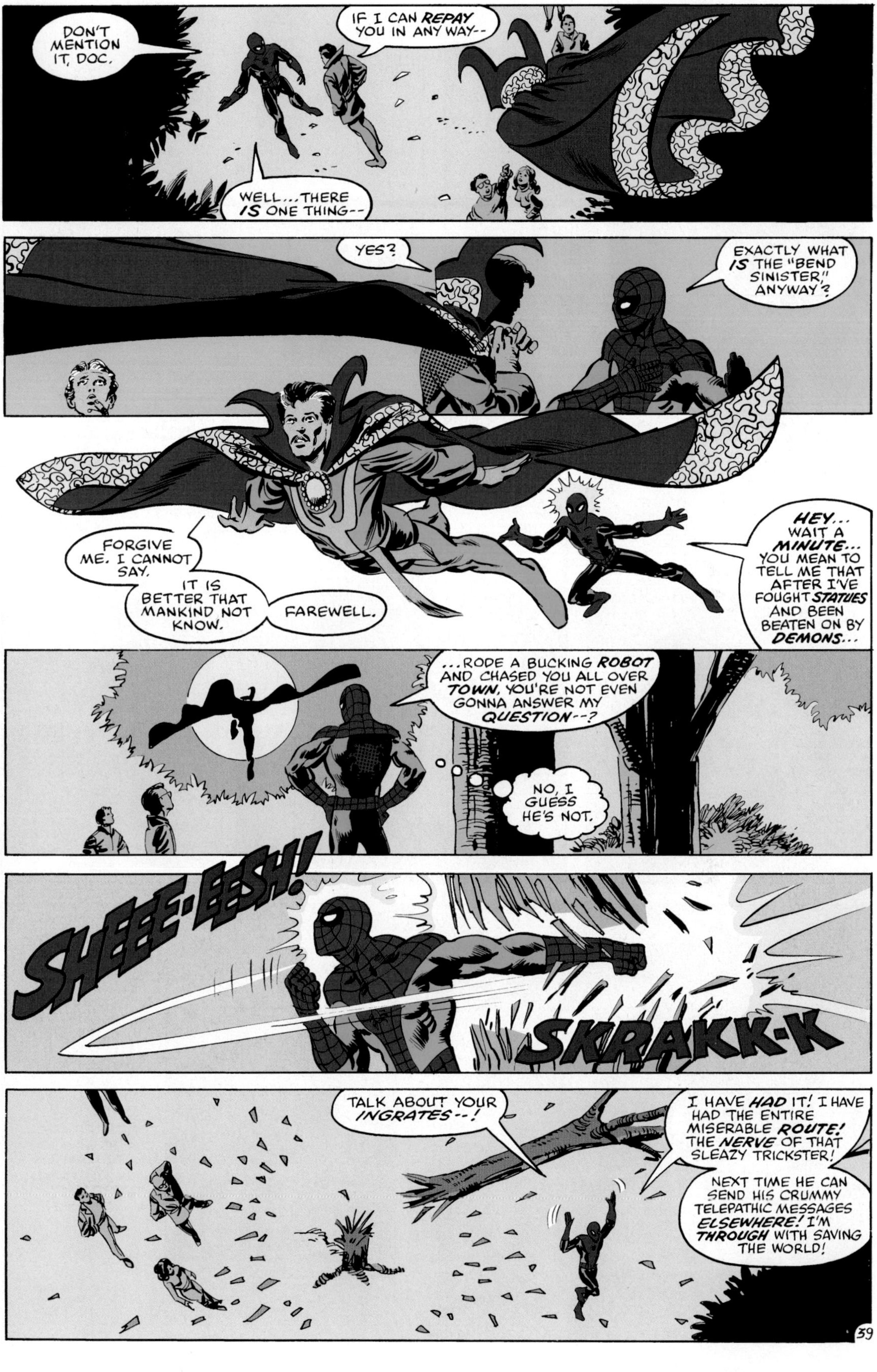
DON'T MENTION IT, DOC.
IF I CAN REPAY YOU IN ANY WAY--
WELL... THERE IS ONE THING--
YES?
EXACTLY WHAT IS THE "BEND SINISTER," ANYWAY?
FORGIVE ME. I CANNOT SAY.
IT IS BETTER THAT MANKIND NOT KNOW.
FAREWELL.
HEY... WAIT A MINUTE... YOU MEAN TO TELL ME THAT AFTER I'VE FOUGHT STATUES AND BEEN BEATEN ON BY DEMONS...
...RODE A BUCKING ROBOT AND CHASED YOU ALL OVER TOWN, YOU'RE NOT EVEN GONNA ANSWER MY QUESTION--?
NO, I GUESS HE'S NOT.
SHEEE-EESH!
SKRAKK-K
TALK ABOUT YOUR INGRATES--!
I HAVE HAD IT! I HAVE HAD THE ENTIRE MISERABLE ROUTE! THE NERVE OF THAT SLEAZY TRICKSTER!
NEXT TIME HE CAN SEND HIS CRUMMY TELEPATHIC MESSAGES ELSEWHERE! I'M THROUGH WITH SAVING THE WORLD!
39

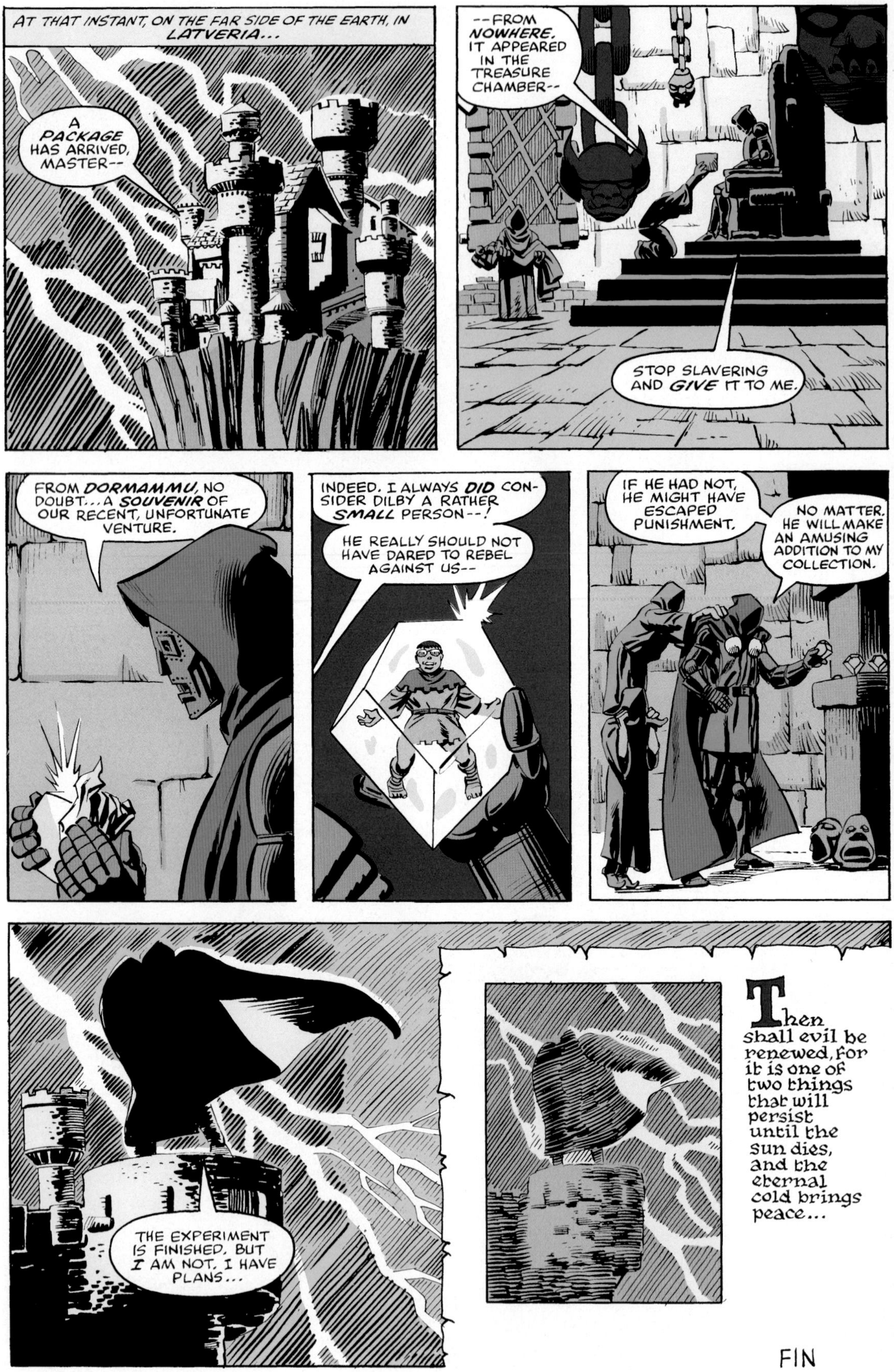

AT THAT INSTANT, ON THE FAR SIDE OF THE EARTH, IN LATVERIA...
A PACKAGE HAS ARRIVED, MASTER--
--FROM NOWHERE. IT APPEARED IN THE TREASURE CHAMBER--
STOP SLAVERING AND GIVE IT TO ME.
FROM DORMAMMU, NO DOUBT... A SOUVENIR OF OUR RECENT, UNFORTUNATE VENTURE.
INDEED. I ALWAYS DID CONSIDER DILBY A RATHER SMALL PERSON--!
HE REALLY SHOULD NOT HAVE DARED TO REBEL AGAINST US--
IF HE HAD NOT, HE MIGHT HAVE ESCAPED PUNISHMENT.
NO MATTER. HE WILL MAKE AN AMUSING ADDITION TO MY COLLECTION.
THE EXPERIMENT IS FINISHED. BUT I AM NOT. I HAVE PLANS...
Then shall evil be renewed, for it is one of two things that will persist until the sun dies, and the eternal cold brings peace...
FIN

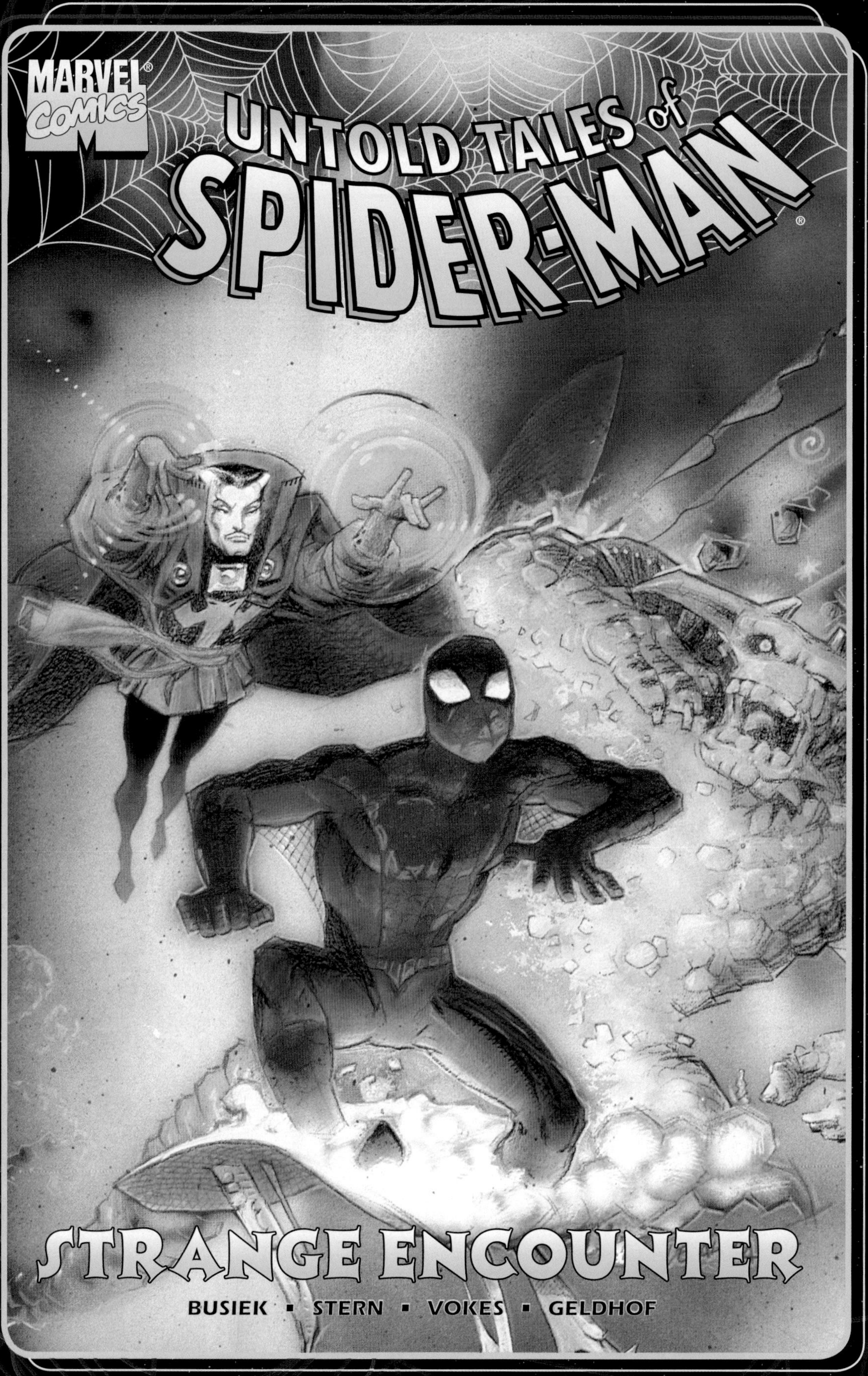
MARVEL COMICS
UNTOLD TALES of
SPIDER-MAN
STRANGE ENCOUNTER
BUSIEK ▪ STERN ▪ VOKES ▪ GELDHOF

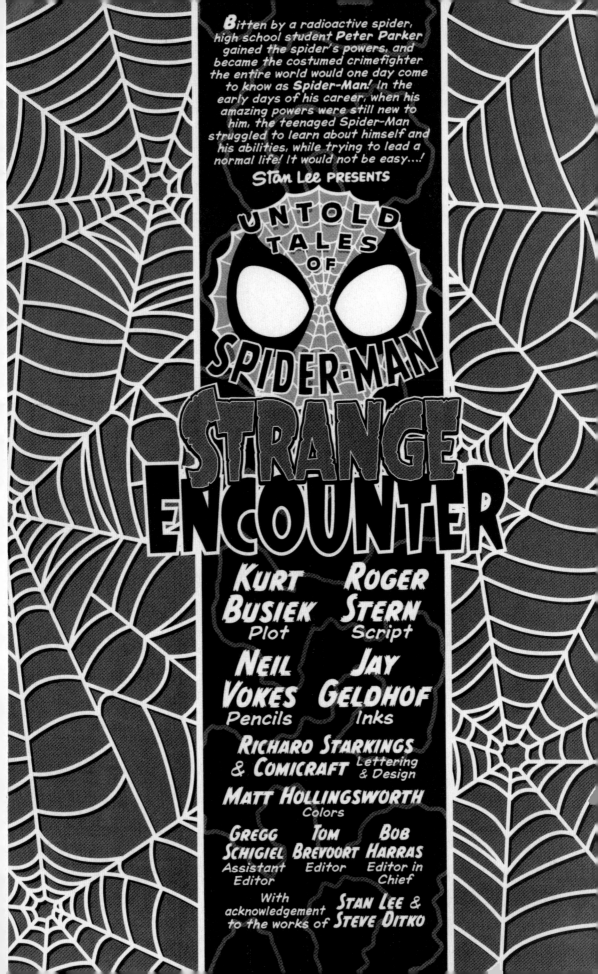

Bitten by a radioactive spider, high school student **Peter Parker** gained the spider's powers, and became the costumed crimefighter the entire world would one day come to know as **Spider-Man!** In the early days of his career, when his amazing powers were still new to him, the teenaged Spider-Man struggled to learn about himself and his abilities, while trying to lead a normal life! It would not be easy...!

Stan Lee PRESENTS

UNTOLD TALES OF SPIDER-MAN

STRANGE ENCOUNTER

Kurt Busiek
Plot

Roger Stern
Script

Neil Vokes
Pencils

Jay Geldhof
Inks

Richard Starkings & Comicraft
Lettering & Design

Matt Hollingsworth
Colors

Gregg Schigiel
Assistant Editor

Tom Brevoort
Editor

Bob Harras
Editor in Chief

With acknowledgement to the works of **Stan Lee & Steve Ditko**

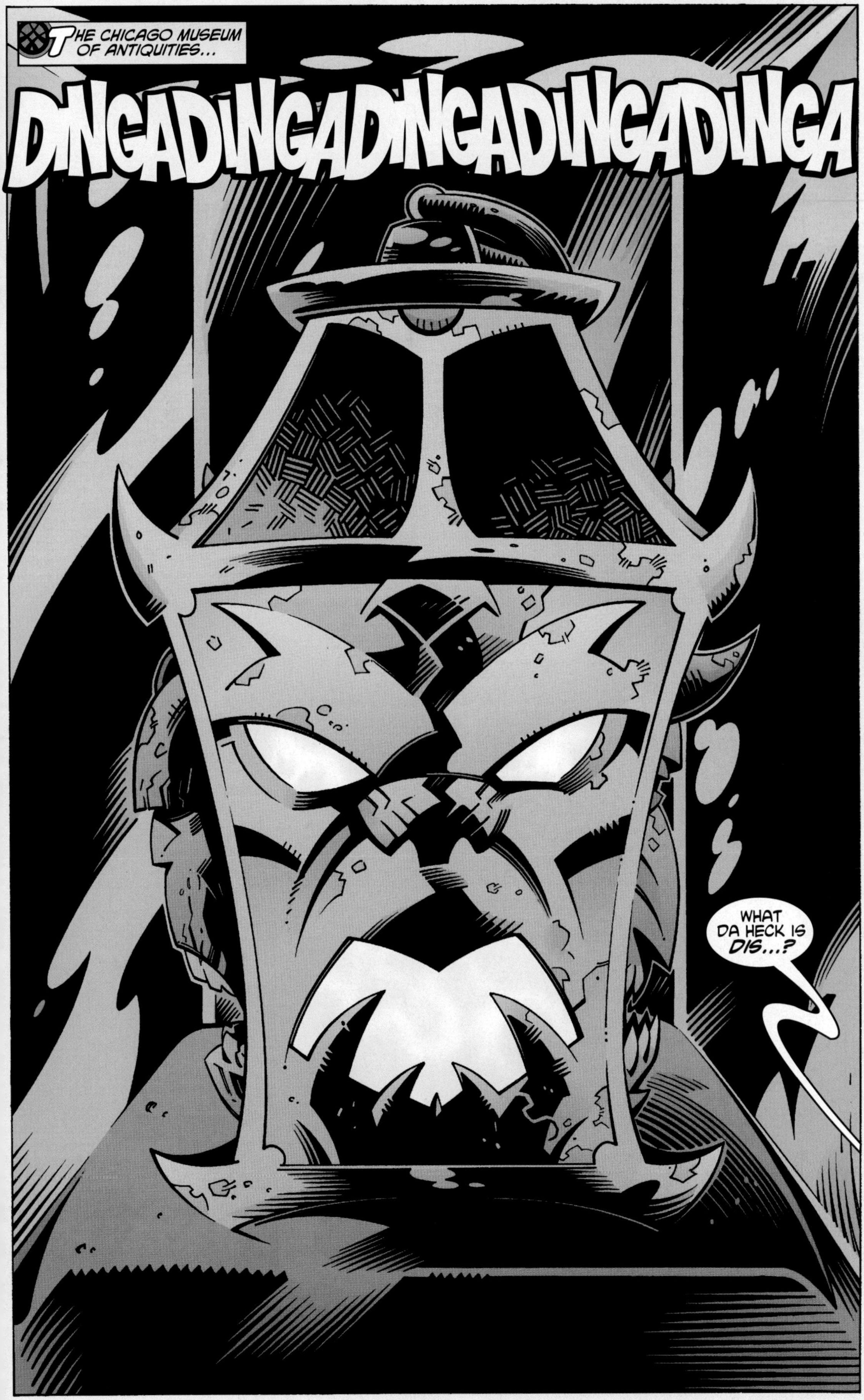
THE CHICAGO MUSEUM OF ANTIQUITIES...
DINGADINGADINGADINGADINGA
WHAT DA HECK IS DIS...?

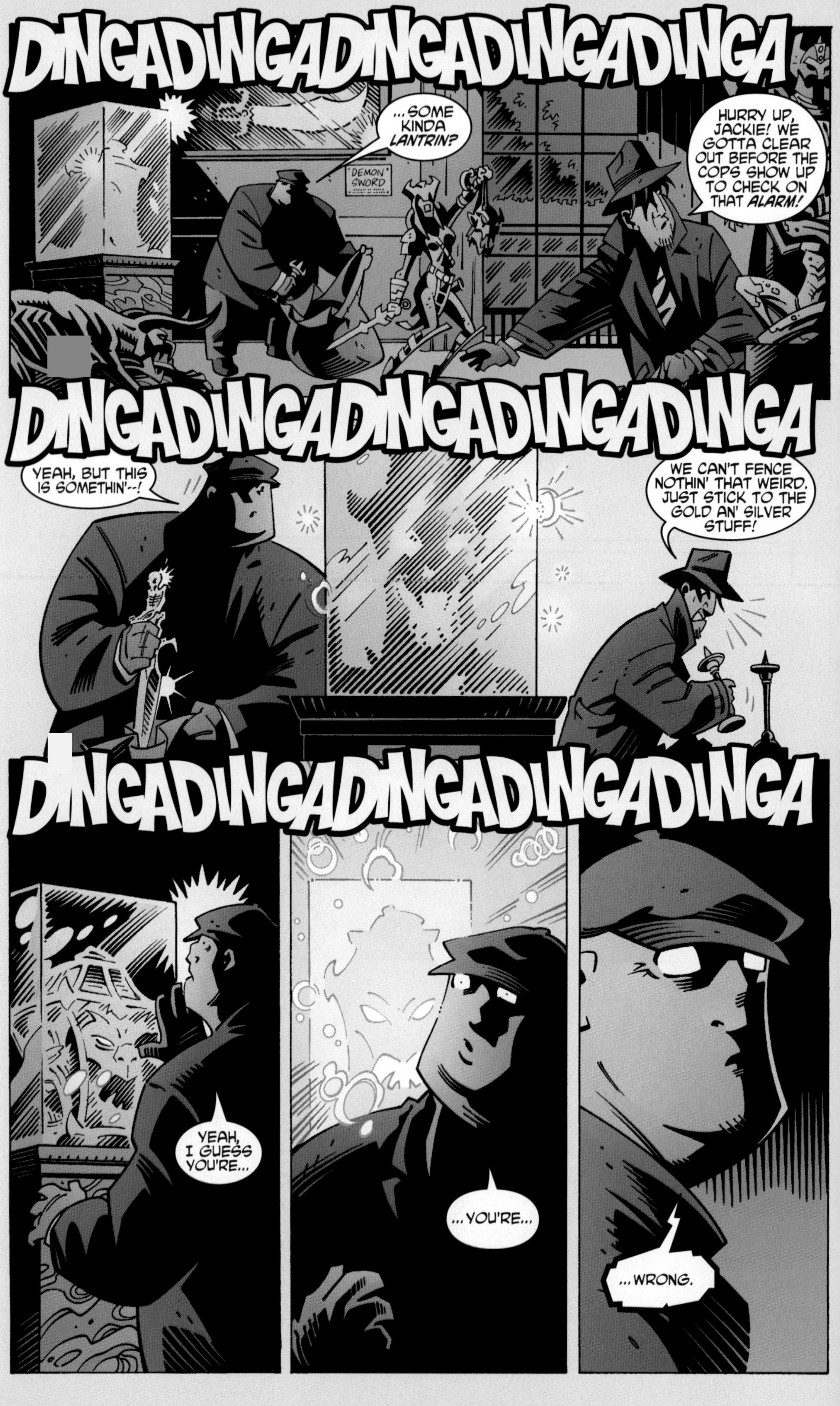
DINGADINGADINGADINGADINGA
...SOME KINDA LANTRIN?
"DEMON" SWORD
HURRY UP, JACKIE! WE GOTTA CLEAR OUT BEFORE THE COPS SHOW UP TO CHECK ON THAT ALARM!
DINGADINGADINGADINGADINGA
YEAH, BUT THIS IS SOMETHIN'--!
WE CAN'T FENCE NOTHIN' THAT WEIRD. JUST STICK TO THE GOLD AN' SILVER STUFF!
DINGADINGADINGADINGADINGA
YEAH, I GUESS YOU'RE...
...YOU'RE...
...WRONG.

ADINGADINGADING

"THIS IS BAD..."

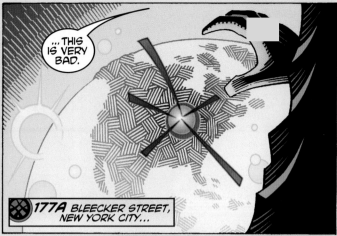

...THIS IS VERY BAD.

177A BLEECKER STREET, NEW YORK CITY...

SOMETHING IS AMISS, DOCTOR?

YES, WONG. THE *ORB OF AGAMOTTO* SHOWS A GREAT *WRONGNESS* IN THE CITY OF CHICAGO.

A SINGLE FLARE OF *TERRIBLE* POWER --!

AN ANCIENT *ARTIFACT* HAS FALLEN INTO UNSCHOOLED HANDS.

UNSCHOOLED...?

EXPERIENCED MYSTICS WOULD HAVE ATTEMPTED TO *MASK* THEIR ACQUISITION OF THE ARTIFACT.

AND YET, I CANNOT FURTHER TRACK THE ARTIFACT *ITSELF*... CLEARLY, IT CARRIES INNATE MYSTIC SHIELDS OF GREAT POWER.

THOSE WHO NOW HOLD THIS ARTIFACT DO NOT UNDERSTAND IT. THEY MUST BE FOUND, ELSE ITS POWER WILL THREATEN THE *ENTIRE WORLD!*

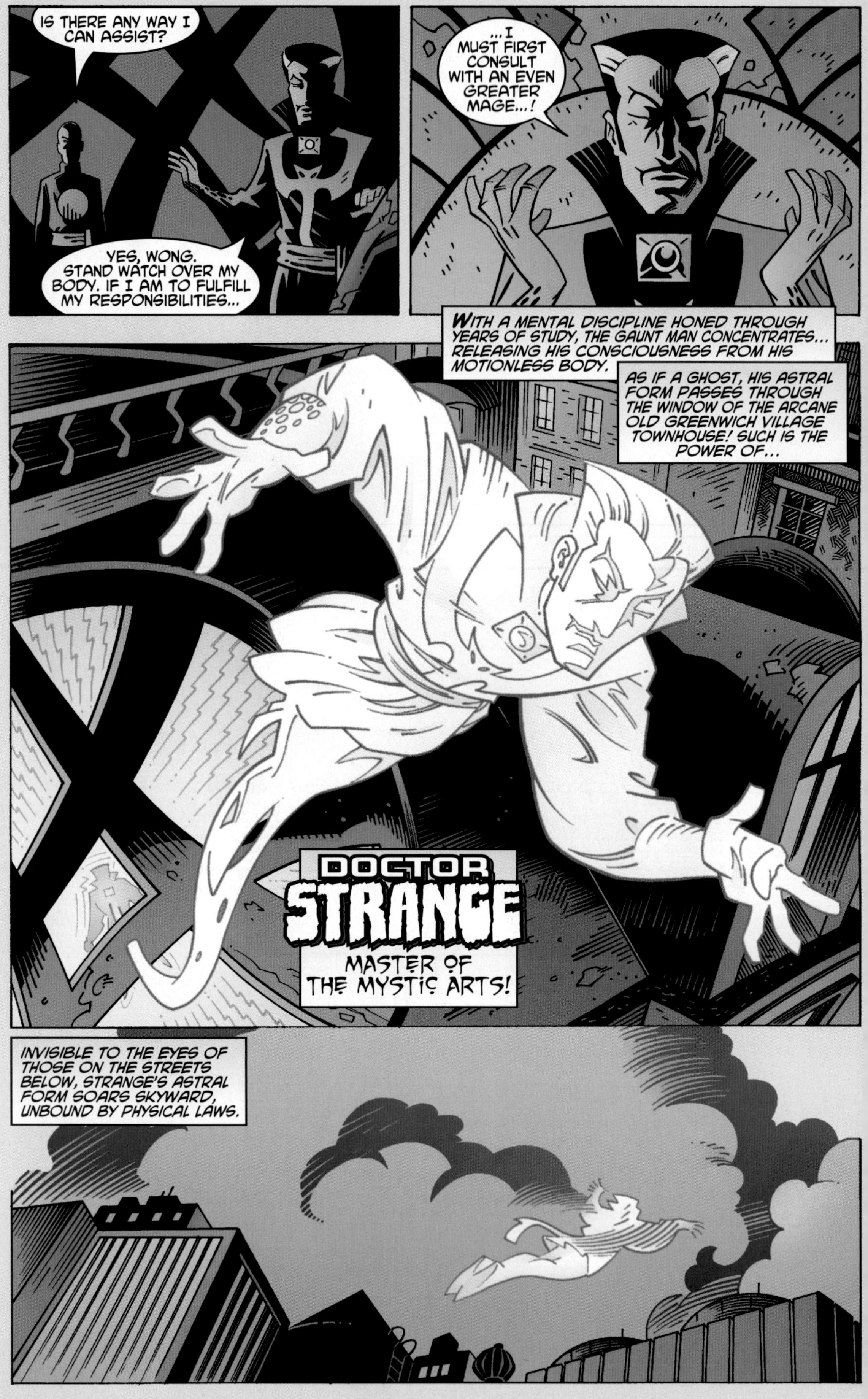
IS THERE ANY WAY I CAN ASSIST?
YES, WONG. STAND WATCH OVER MY BODY. IF I AM TO FULFILL MY RESPONSIBILITIES...
...I MUST FIRST CONSULT WITH AN EVEN GREATER MAGE...!
WITH A MENTAL DISCIPLINE HONED THROUGH YEARS OF STUDY, THE GAUNT MAN CONCENTRATES... RELEASING HIS CONSCIOUSNESS FROM HIS MOTIONLESS BODY.
AS IF A GHOST, HIS ASTRAL FORM PASSES THROUGH THE WINDOW OF THE ARCANE OLD GREENWICH VILLAGE TOWNHOUSE! SUCH IS THE POWER OF...
DOCTOR STRANGE
MASTER OF THE MYSTIC ARTS!
INVISIBLE TO THE EYES OF THOSE ON THE STREETS BELOW, STRANGE'S ASTRAL FORM SOARS SKYWARD, UNBOUND BY PHYSICAL LAWS.

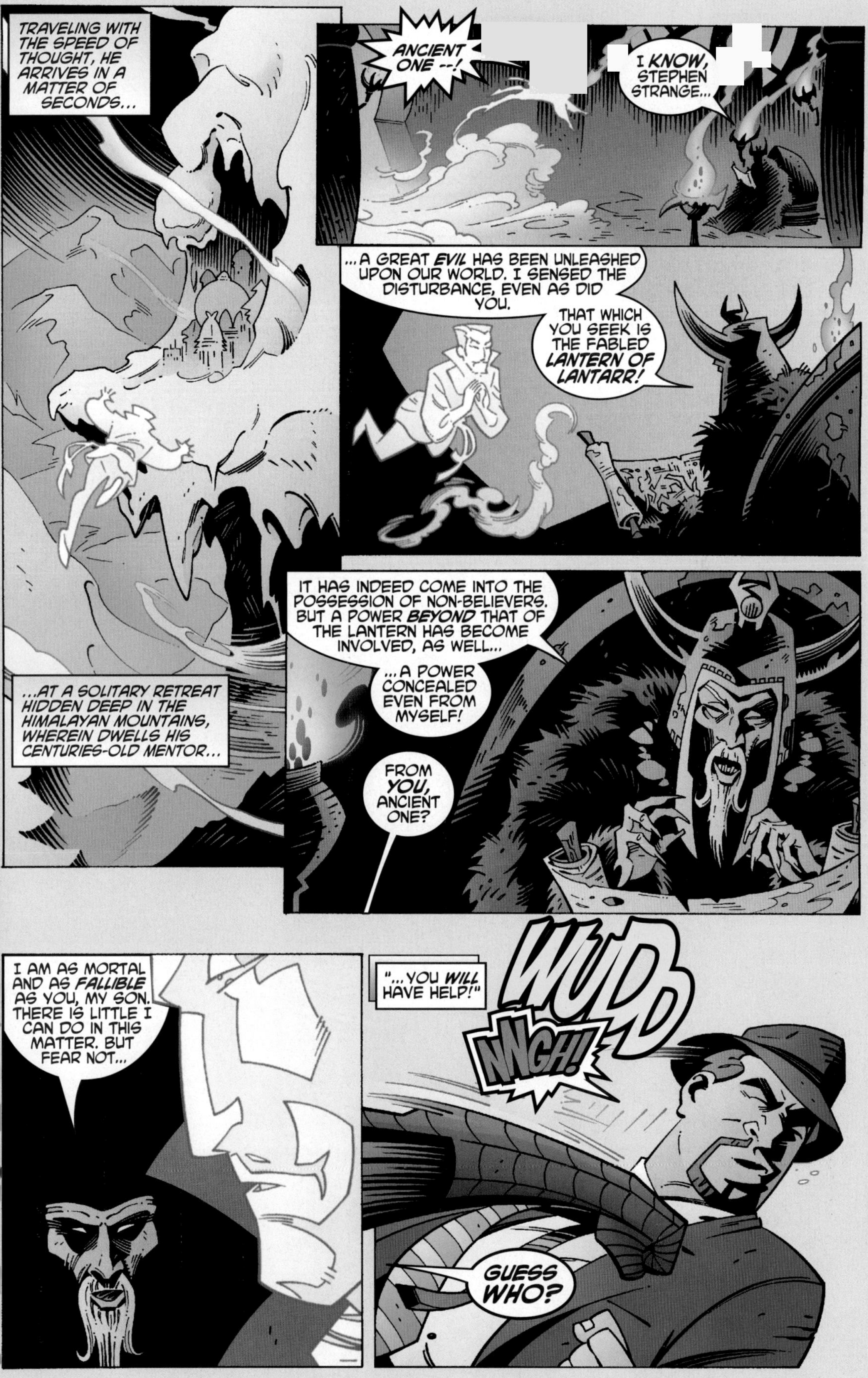
TRAVELING WITH THE SPEED OF THOUGHT, HE ARRIVES IN A MATTER OF SECONDS...
...AT A SOLITARY RETREAT HIDDEN DEEP IN THE HIMALAYAN MOUNTAINS, WHEREIN DWELLS HIS CENTURIES-OLD MENTOR...
ANCIENT ONE --!
I KNOW, STEPHEN STRANGE...
...A GREAT EVIL HAS BEEN UNLEASHED UPON OUR WORLD. I SENSED THE DISTURBANCE, EVEN AS DID YOU.
THAT WHICH YOU SEEK IS THE FABLED LANTERN OF LANTARR!
IT HAS INDEED COME INTO THE POSSESSION OF NON-BELIEVERS. BUT A POWER BEYOND THAT OF THE LANTERN HAS BECOME INVOLVED, AS WELL...
...A POWER CONCEALED EVEN FROM MYSELF!
FROM YOU, ANCIENT ONE?
I AM AS MORTAL AND AS FALLIBLE AS YOU, MY SON. THERE IS LITTLE I CAN DO IN THIS MATTER. BUT FEAR NOT...
"...YOU WILL HAVE HELP!"
WUDD
NNGH!!
GUESS WHO?

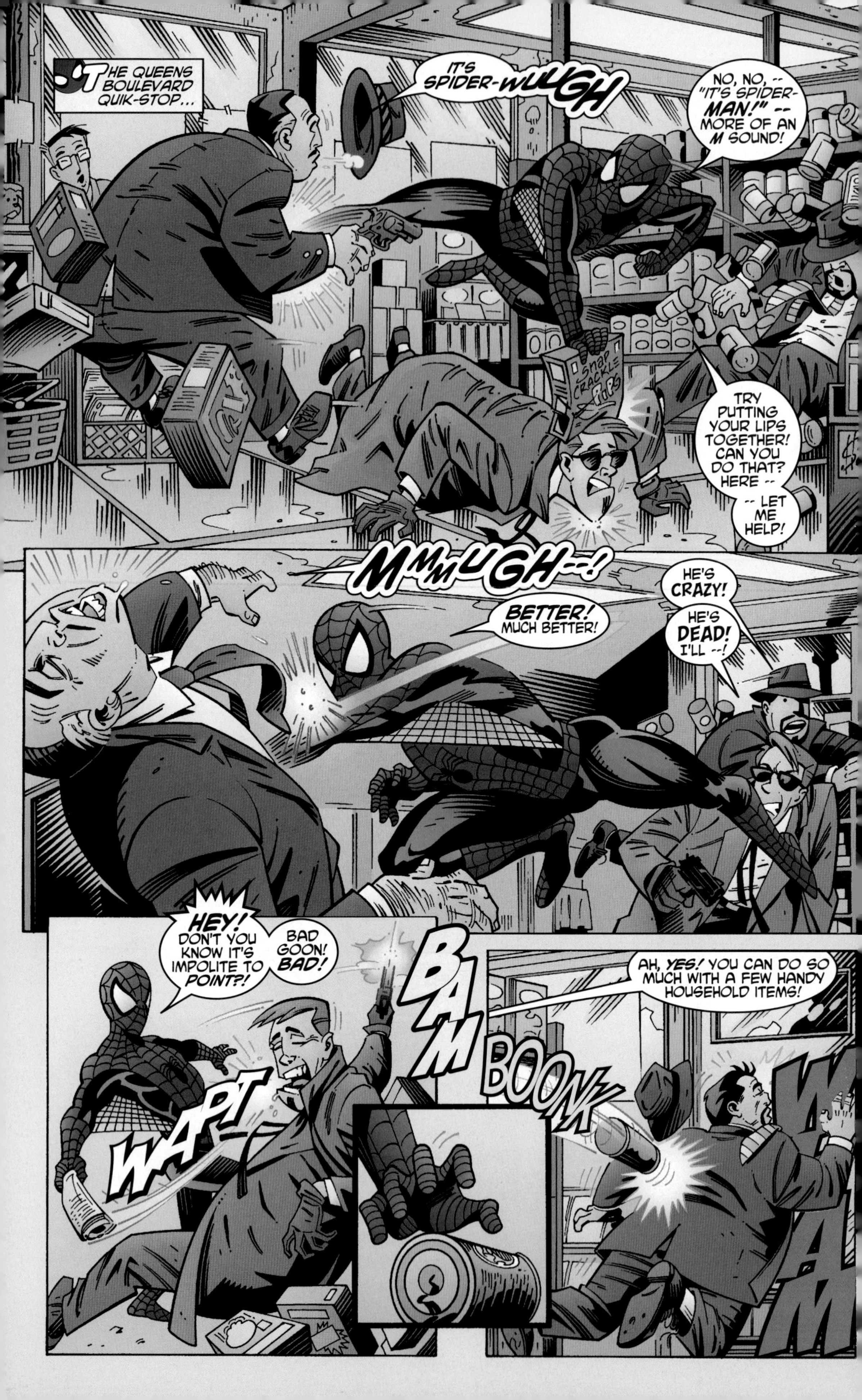
THE QUEENS BOULEVARD QUIK-STOP...
IT'S SPIDER-WUUGH
NO, NO, -- "IT'S SPIDER-MAN!" -- MORE OF AN M SOUND!
SNAP CRACKLE POPS
TRY PUTTING YOUR LIPS TOGETHER! CAN YOU DO THAT? HERE --
-- LET ME HELP!
MMMMUGH--!
BETTER! MUCH BETTER!
HE'S CRAZY!
HE'S DEAD! I'LL --!
HEY! DON'T YOU KNOW IT'S IMPOLITE TO POINT?!
BAD GOON! BAD!
BAM
AH, YES! YOU CAN DO SO MUCH WITH A FEW HANDY HOUSEHOLD ITEMS!
WAPT
BOONK
WAM

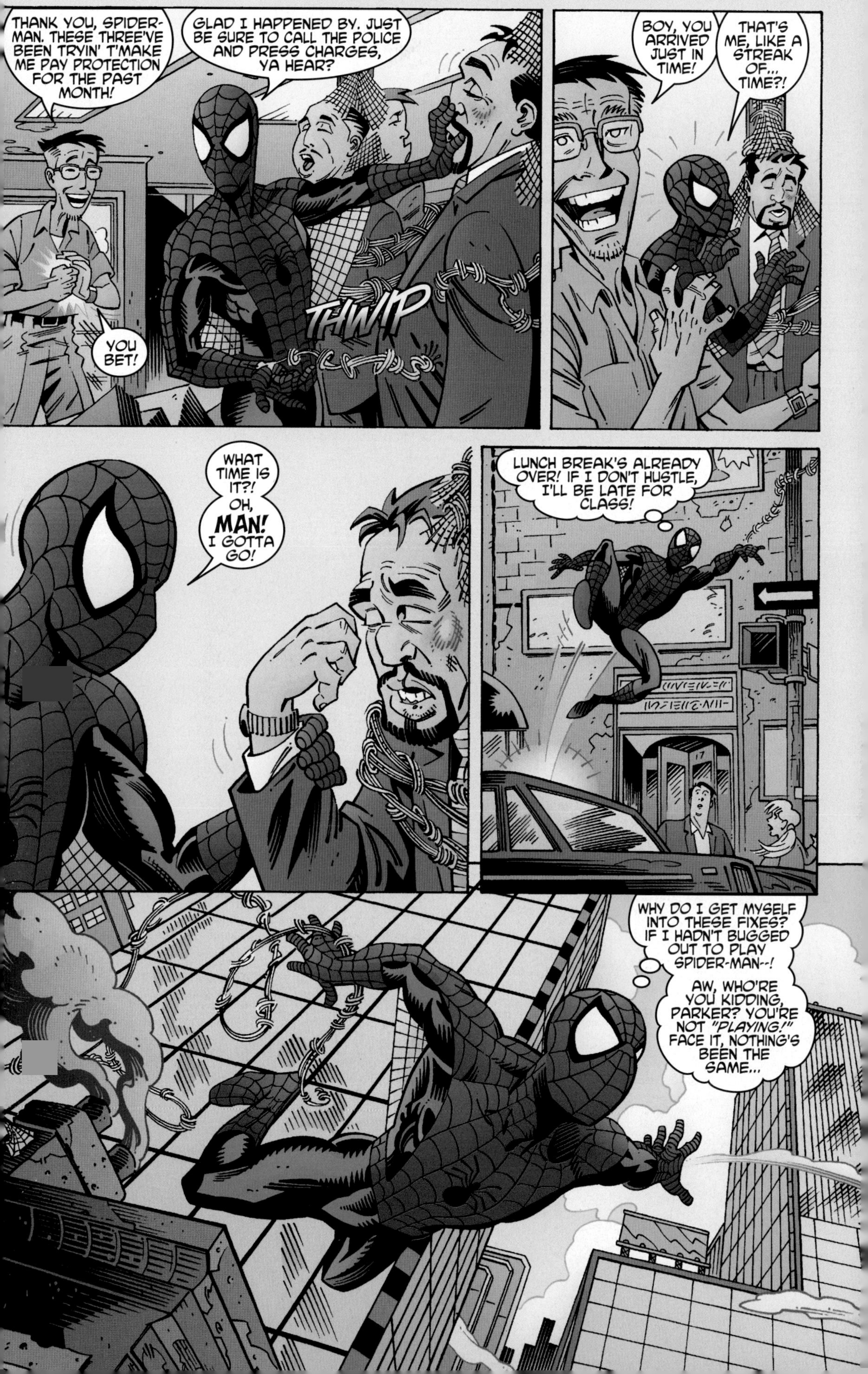
THANK YOU, SPIDER-MAN. THESE THREE'VE BEEN TRYIN' T'MAKE ME PAY PROTECTION FOR THE PAST MONTH!
GLAD I HAPPENED BY. JUST BE SURE TO CALL THE POLICE AND PRESS CHARGES, YA HEAR?
YOU BET!
THWIP
BOY, YOU ARRIVED JUST IN TIME!
THAT'S ME, LIKE A STREAK OF... TIME?!
WHAT TIME IS IT?! OH, MAN! I GOTTA GO!
LUNCH BREAK'S ALREADY OVER! IF I DON'T HUSTLE, I'LL BE LATE FOR CLASS!
WHY DO I GET MYSELF INTO THESE FIXES? IF I HADN'T BUGGED OUT TO PLAY SPIDER-MAN--!
AW, WHO'RE YOU KIDDING, PARKER? YOU'RE NOT "PLAYING!" FACE IT, NOTHING'S BEEN THE SAME...

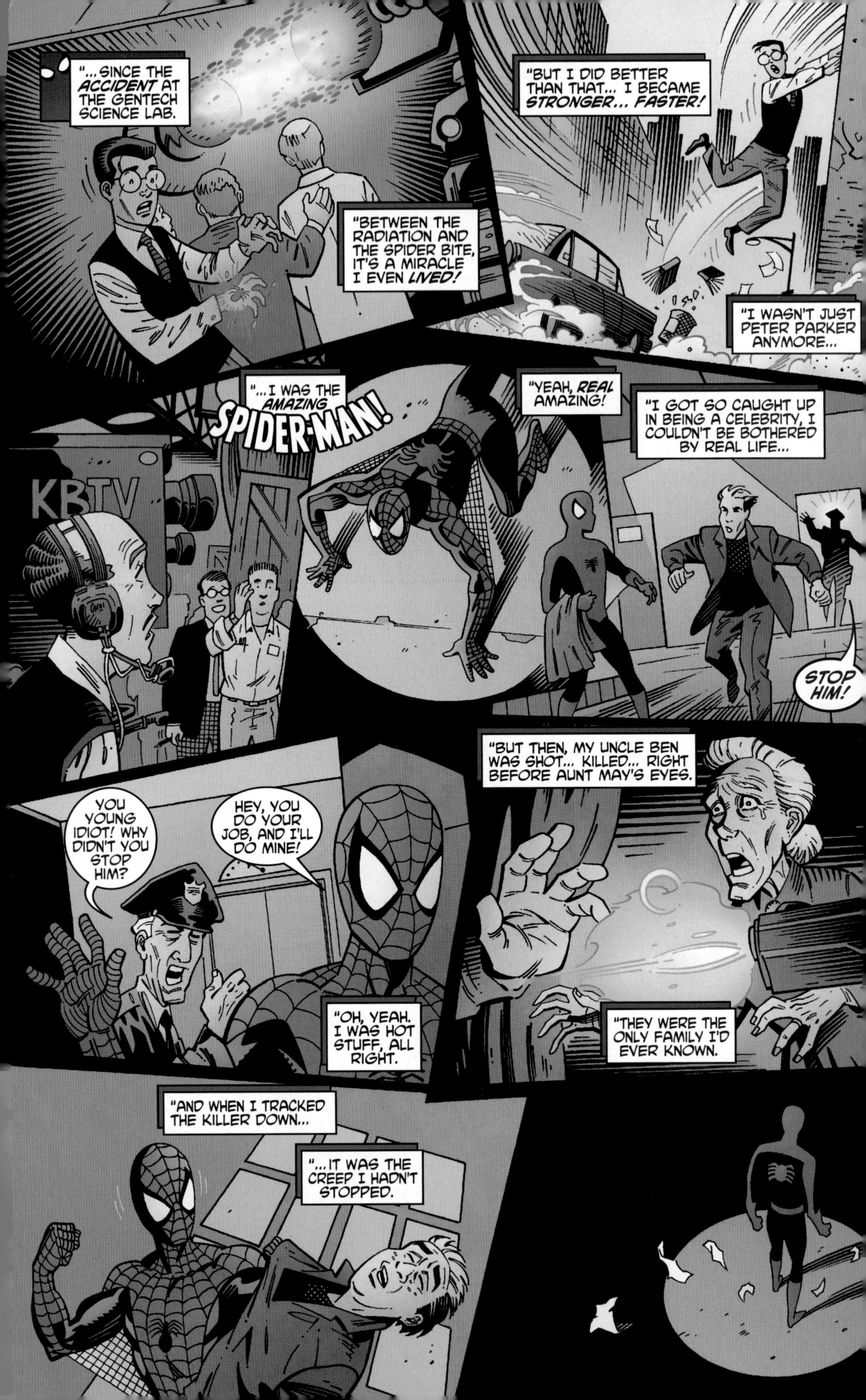
"...SINCE THE ACCIDENT AT THE GENTECH SCIENCE LAB.
"BETWEEN THE RADIATION AND THE SPIDER BITE, IT'S A MIRACLE I EVEN LIVED!
"BUT I DID BETTER THAN THAT... I BECAME STRONGER... FASTER!
"I WASN'T JUST PETER PARKER ANYMORE...
"...I WAS THE AMAZING
SPIDER-MAN!
KBTV
"YEAH, REAL AMAZING!
"I GOT SO CAUGHT UP IN BEING A CELEBRITY, I COULDN'T BE BOTHERED BY REAL LIFE...
STOP HIM!
YOU YOUNG IDIOT! WHY DIDN'T YOU STOP HIM?
HEY, YOU DO YOUR JOB, AND I'LL DO MINE!
"OH, YEAH. I WAS HOT STUFF, ALL RIGHT.
"BUT THEN, MY UNCLE BEN WAS SHOT... KILLED... RIGHT BEFORE AUNT MAY'S EYES.
"THEY WERE THE ONLY FAMILY I'D EVER KNOWN.
"AND WHEN I TRACKED THE KILLER DOWN...
"...IT WAS THE CREEP I HADN'T STOPPED.

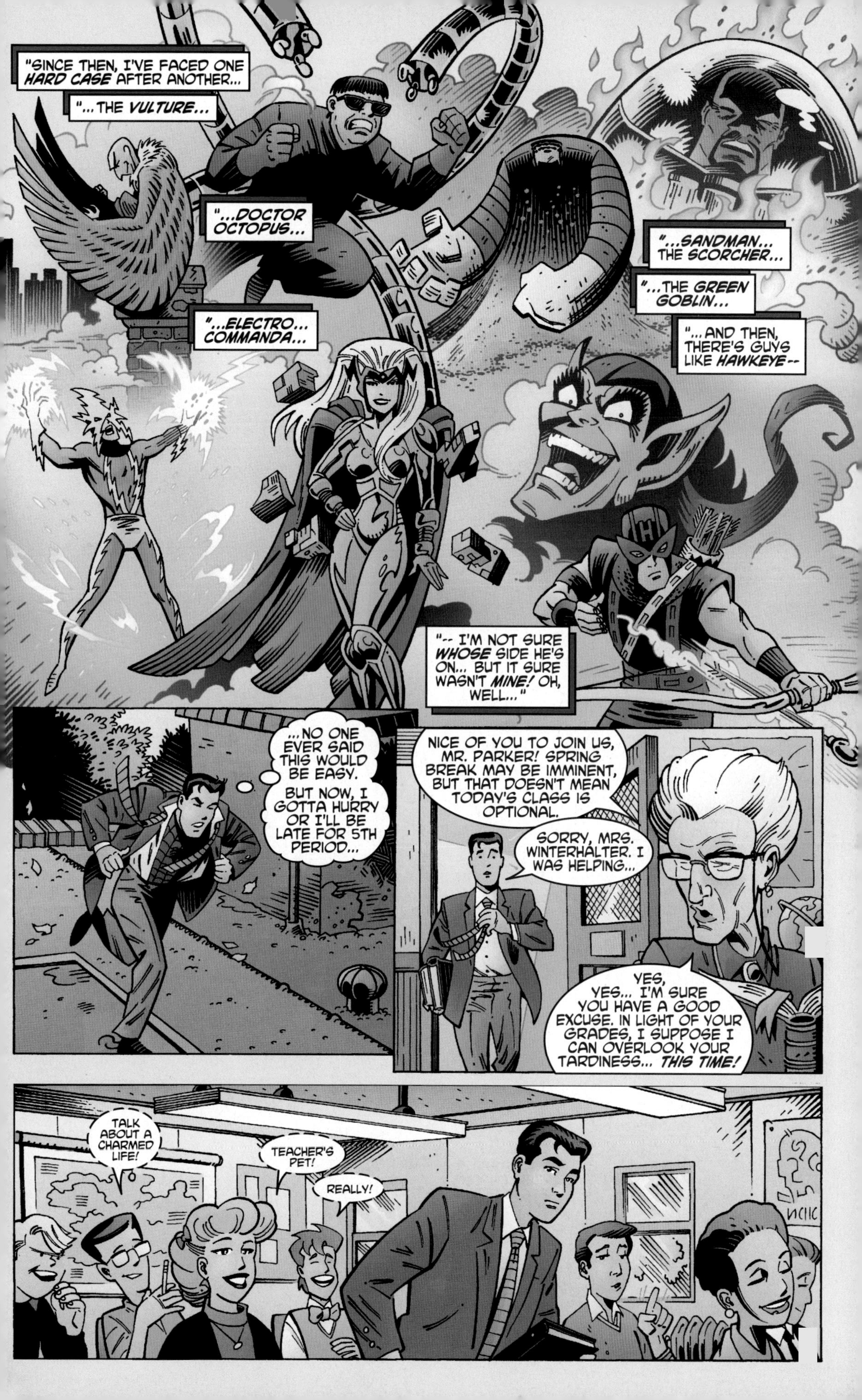
"SINCE THEN, I'VE FACED ONE HARD CASE AFTER ANOTHER...
"...THE VULTURE...
"...DOCTOR OCTOPUS...
"...ELECTRO... COMMANDA...
"...SANDMAN... THE SCORCHER...
"...THE GREEN GOBLIN...
"...AND THEN, THERE'S GUYS LIKE HAWKEYE--
"-- I'M NOT SURE WHOSE SIDE HE'S ON... BUT IT SURE WASN'T MINE! OH, WELL..."
...NO ONE EVER SAID THIS WOULD BE EASY.
BUT NOW, I GOTTA HURRY OR I'LL BE LATE FOR 5TH PERIOD...
NICE OF YOU TO JOIN US, MR. PARKER! SPRING BREAK MAY BE IMMINENT, BUT THAT DOESN'T MEAN TODAY'S CLASS IS OPTIONAL.
SORRY, MRS. WINTERHALTER. I WAS HELPING...
YES, YES... I'M SURE YOU HAVE A GOOD EXCUSE. IN LIGHT OF YOUR GRADES, I SUPPOSE I CAN OVERLOOK YOUR TARDINESS... THIS TIME!
TALK ABOUT A CHARMED LIFE!
TEACHER'S PET!
REALLY!

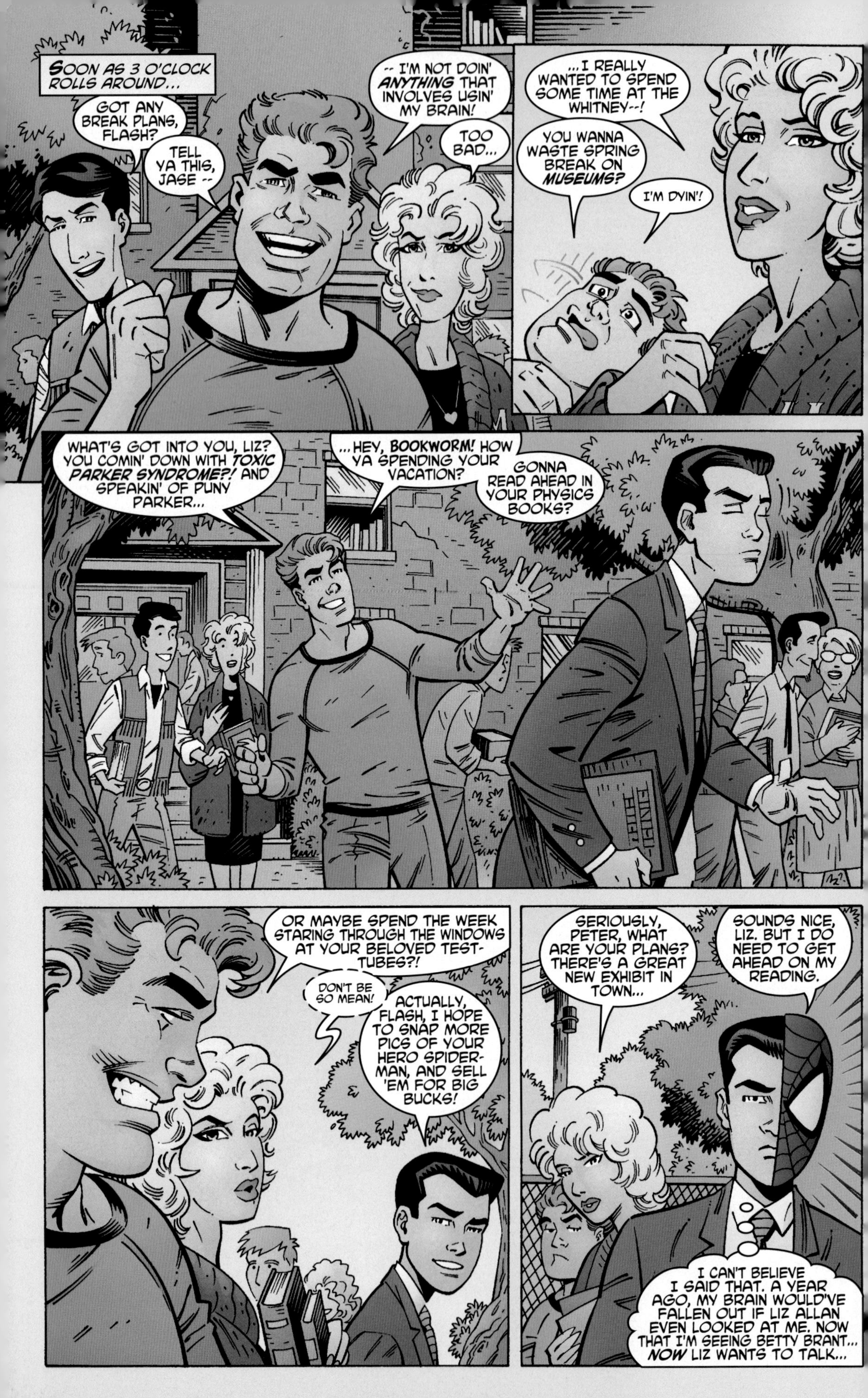
SOON AS 3 O'CLOCK ROLLS AROUND...
GOT ANY BREAK PLANS, FLASH?
TELL YA THIS, JASE --
-- I'M NOT DOIN' ANYTHING THAT INVOLVES USIN' MY BRAIN!
TOO BAD...
...I REALLY WANTED TO SPEND SOME TIME AT THE WHITNEY--!
YOU WANNA WASTE SPRING BREAK ON MUSEUMS?
I'M DYIN'!
WHAT'S GOT INTO YOU, LIZ? YOU COMIN' DOWN WITH TOXIC PARKER SYNDROME?! AND SPEAKIN' OF PUNY PARKER...
...HEY, BOOKWORM! HOW YA SPENDING YOUR VACATION?
GONNA READ AHEAD IN YOUR PHYSICS BOOKS?
OR MAYBE SPEND THE WEEK STARING THROUGH THE WINDOWS AT YOUR BELOVED TEST-TUBES?!
DON'T BE SO MEAN!
ACTUALLY, FLASH, I HOPE TO SNAP MORE PICS OF YOUR HERO SPIDER-MAN, AND SELL 'EM FOR BIG BUCKS!
SERIOUSLY, PETER, WHAT ARE YOUR PLANS? THERE'S A GREAT NEW EXHIBIT IN TOWN...
SOUNDS NICE, LIZ. BUT I DO NEED TO GET AHEAD ON MY READING.
I CAN'T BELIEVE I SAID THAT. A YEAR AGO, MY BRAIN WOULD'VE FALLEN OUT IF LIZ ALLAN EVEN LOOKED AT ME. NOW THAT I'M SEEING BETTY BRANT... NOW LIZ WANTS TO TALK...

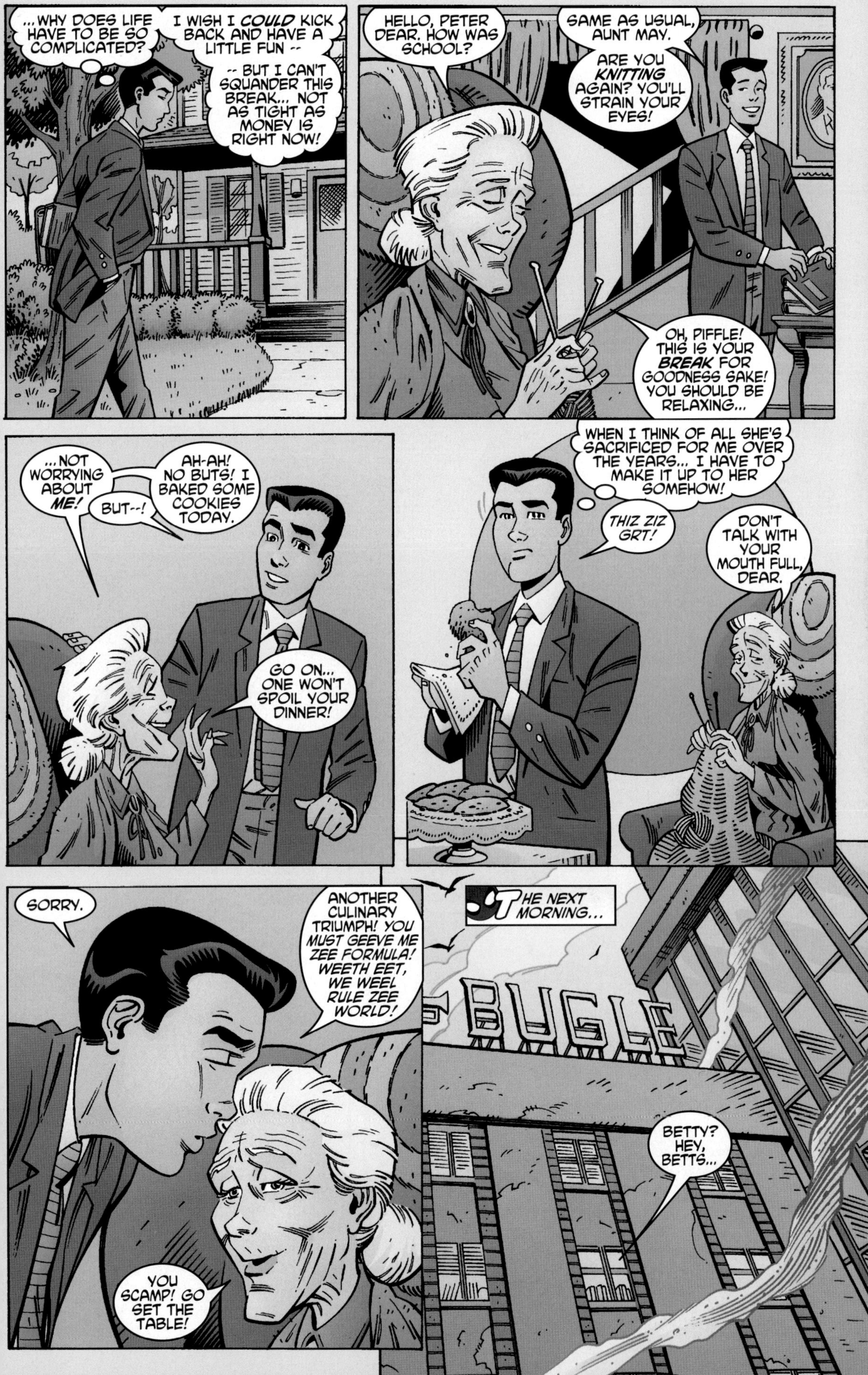
...WHY DOES LIFE HAVE TO BE SO COMPLICATED?
I WISH I COULD KICK BACK AND HAVE A LITTLE FUN --
-- BUT I CAN'T SQUANDER THIS BREAK... NOT AS TIGHT AS MONEY IS RIGHT NOW!
HELLO, PETER DEAR. HOW WAS SCHOOL?
SAME AS USUAL, AUNT MAY.
ARE YOU KNITTING AGAIN? YOU'LL STRAIN YOUR EYES!
OH, PIFFLE! THIS IS YOUR BREAK FOR GOODNESS SAKE! YOU SHOULD BE RELAXING...
...NOT WORRYING ABOUT ME!
BUT--!
AH-AH! NO BUTS! I BAKED SOME COOKIES TODAY.
GO ON... ONE WON'T SPOIL YOUR DINNER!
WHEN I THINK OF ALL SHE'S SACRIFICED FOR ME OVER THE YEARS... I HAVE TO MAKE IT UP TO HER SOMEHOW!
THIZ ZIZ GRT!
DON'T TALK WITH YOUR MOUTH FULL, DEAR.
SORRY.
ANOTHER CULINARY TRIUMPH! YOU MUST GEEVE ME ZEE FORMULA! WEETH EET, WE WEEL RULE ZEE WORLD!
YOU SCAMP! GO SET THE TABLE!
THE NEXT MORNING...
BUGLE
BETTY? HEY, BETTS...

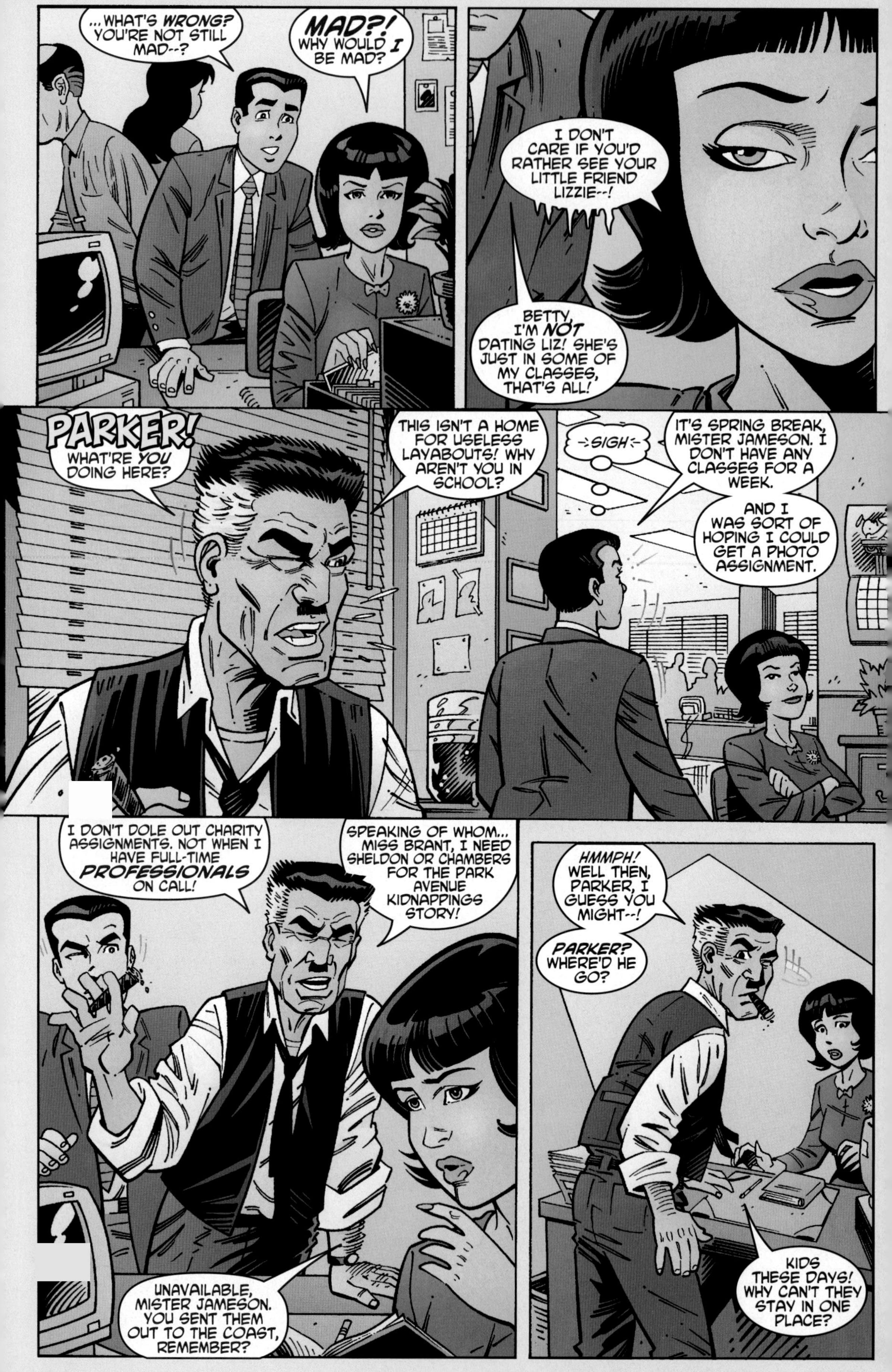
...WHAT'S WRONG? YOU'RE NOT STILL MAD--?
MAD?! WHY WOULD I BE MAD?
I DON'T CARE IF YOU'D RATHER SEE YOUR LITTLE FRIEND LIZZIE--!
BETTY, I'M NOT DATING LIZ! SHE'S JUST IN SOME OF MY CLASSES, THAT'S ALL!
PARKER! WHAT'RE YOU DOING HERE?
THIS ISN'T A HOME FOR USELESS LAYABOUTS! WHY AREN'T YOU IN SCHOOL?
SIGH
IT'S SPRING BREAK, MISTER JAMESON. I DON'T HAVE ANY CLASSES FOR A WEEK.
AND I WAS SORT OF HOPING I COULD GET A PHOTO ASSIGNMENT.
I DON'T DOLE OUT CHARITY ASSIGNMENTS. NOT WHEN I HAVE FULL-TIME PROFESSIONALS ON CALL!
SPEAKING OF WHOM... MISS BRANT, I NEED SHELDON OR CHAMBERS FOR THE PARK AVENUE KIDNAPPINGS STORY!
UNAVAILABLE, MISTER JAMESON. YOU SENT THEM OUT TO THE COAST, REMEMBER?
HMMPH! WELL THEN, PARKER, I GUESS YOU MIGHT--!
PARKER? WHERE'D HE GO?
KIDS THESE DAYS! WHY CAN'T THEY STAY IN ONE PLACE?

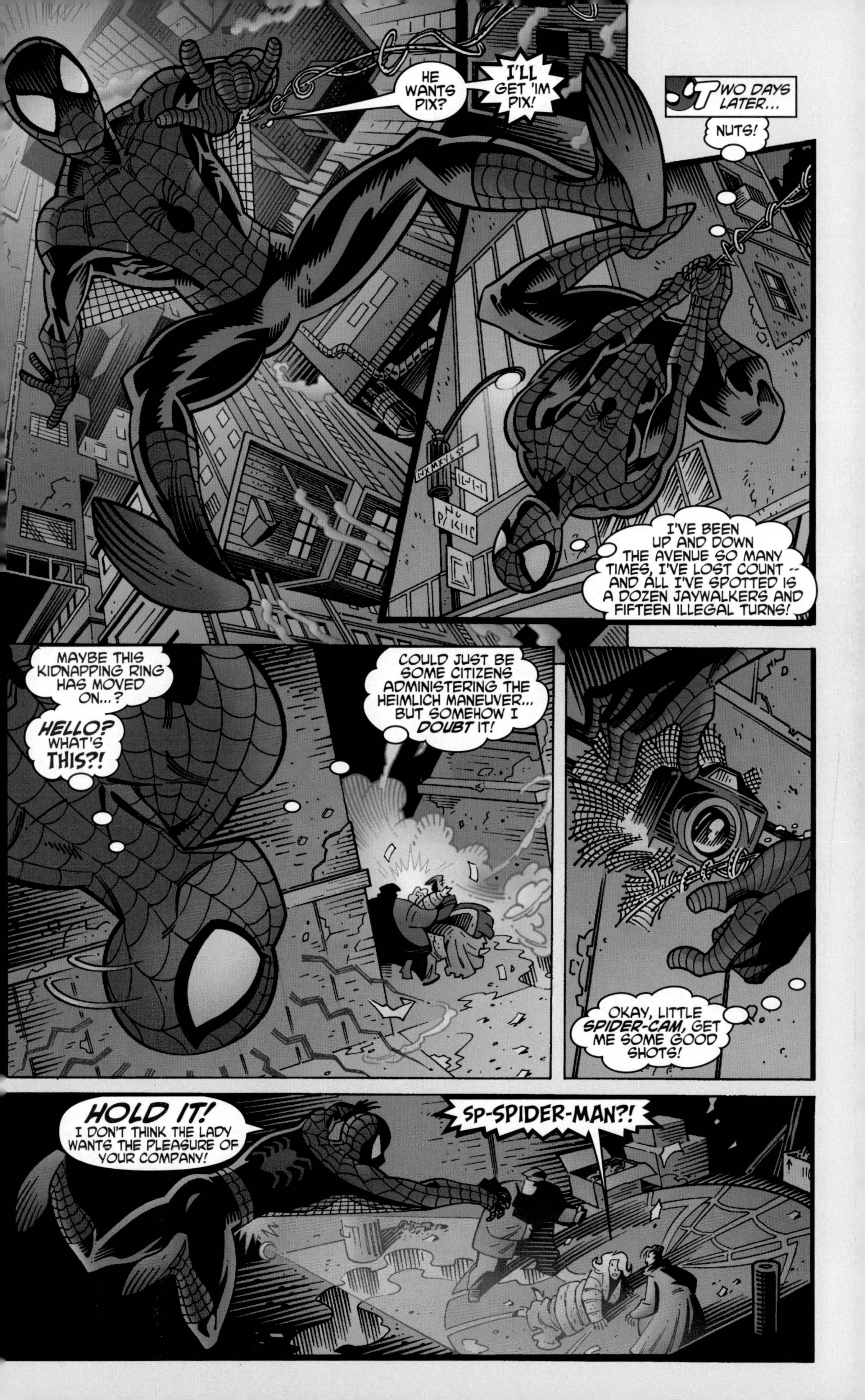

HE WANTS PIX?
I'LL GET 'IM PIX!
TWO DAYS LATER...
NUTS!
I'VE BEEN UP AND DOWN THE AVENUE SO MANY TIMES, I'VE LOST COUNT -- AND ALL I'VE SPOTTED IS A DOZEN JAYWALKERS AND FIFTEEN ILLEGAL TURNS!
MAYBE THIS KIDNAPPING RING HAS MOVED ON...?
HELLO? WHAT'S THIS?!
COULD JUST BE SOME CITIZENS ADMINISTERING THE HEIMLICH MANEUVER... BUT SOMEHOW I DOUBT IT!
OKAY, LITTLE SPIDER-CAM, GET ME SOME GOOD SHOTS!
HOLD IT! I DON'T THINK THE LADY WANTS THE PLEASURE OF YOUR COMPANY!
SP-SPIDER-MAN?!

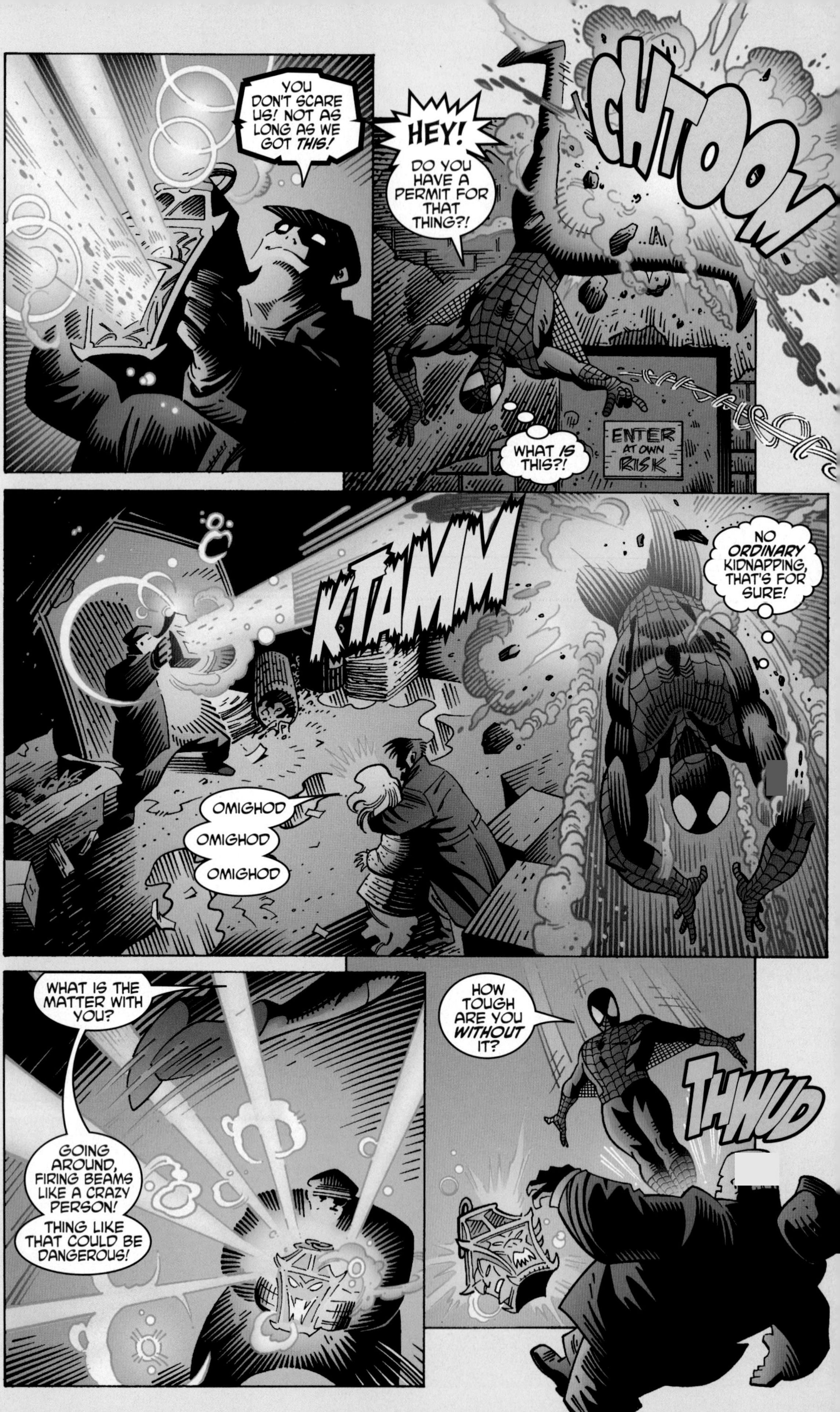
YOU DON'T SCARE US! NOT AS LONG AS WE GOT THIS!
HEY!
DO YOU HAVE A PERMIT FOR THAT THING?!
CHTOOM
WHAT IS THIS?!
ENTER AT OWN RISK
KTAMM
NO ORDINARY KIDNAPPING, THAT'S FOR SURE!
OMIGHOD
OMIGHOD
OMIGHOD
WHAT IS THE MATTER WITH YOU?
GOING AROUND, FIRING BEAMS LIKE A CRAZY PERSON!
THING LIKE THAT COULD BE DANGEROUS!
HOW TOUGH ARE YOU WITHOUT IT?
THWUD

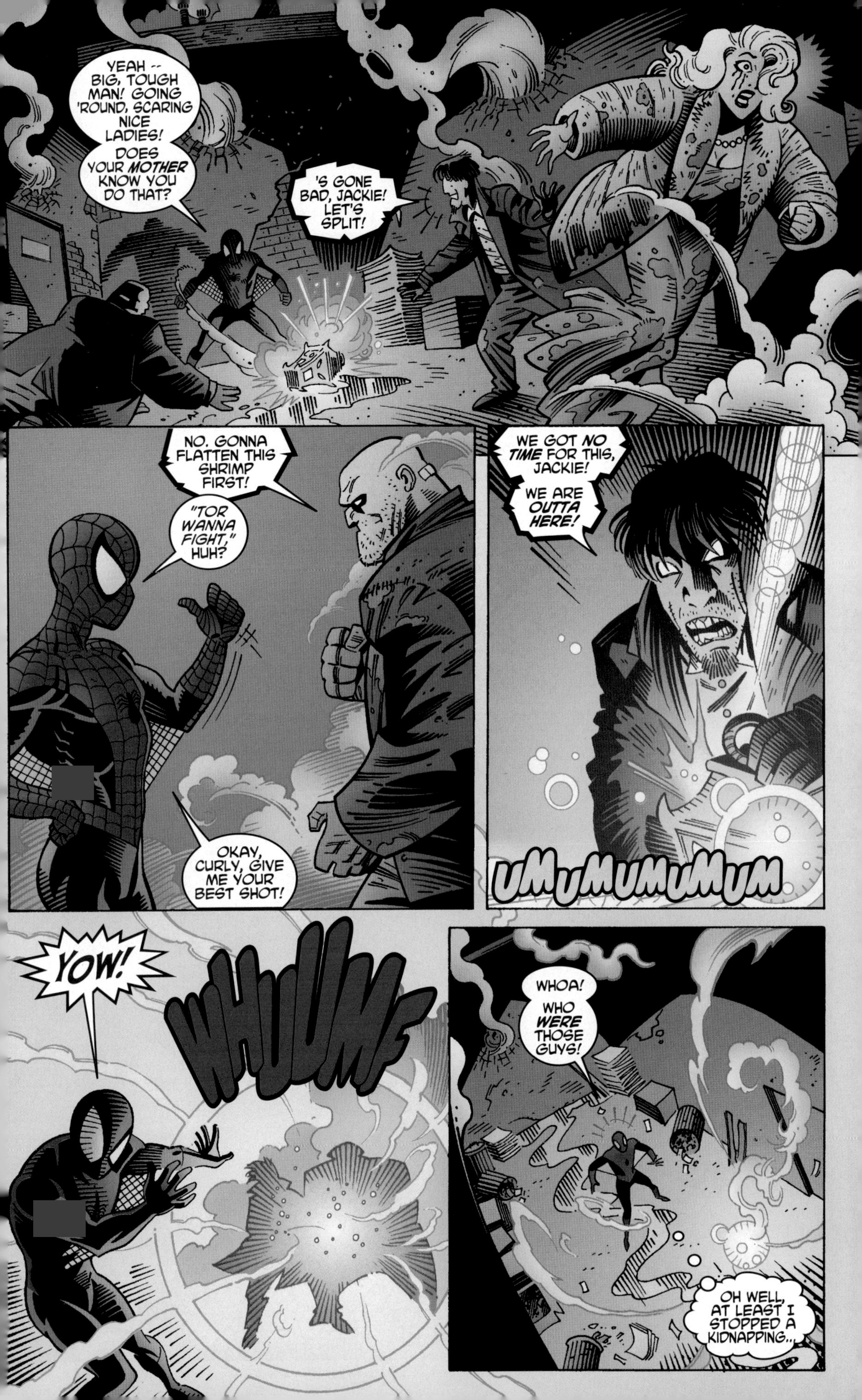
YEAH -- BIG, TOUGH MAN! GOING 'ROUND, SCARING NICE LADIES!
DOES YOUR MOTHER KNOW YOU DO THAT?
'S GONE BAD, JACKIE! LET'S SPLIT!
NO. GONNA FLATTEN THIS SHRIMP FIRST!
"TOR WANNA FIGHT," HUH?
OKAY, CURLY, GIVE ME YOUR BEST SHOT!
WE GOT NO TIME FOR THIS, JACKIE!
WE ARE OUTTA HERE!
UMMUMUMUMUMUM
YOW!
WHUUMF
WHOA!
WHO WERE THOSE GUYS!
OH WELL, AT LEAST I STOPPED A KIDNAPPING..

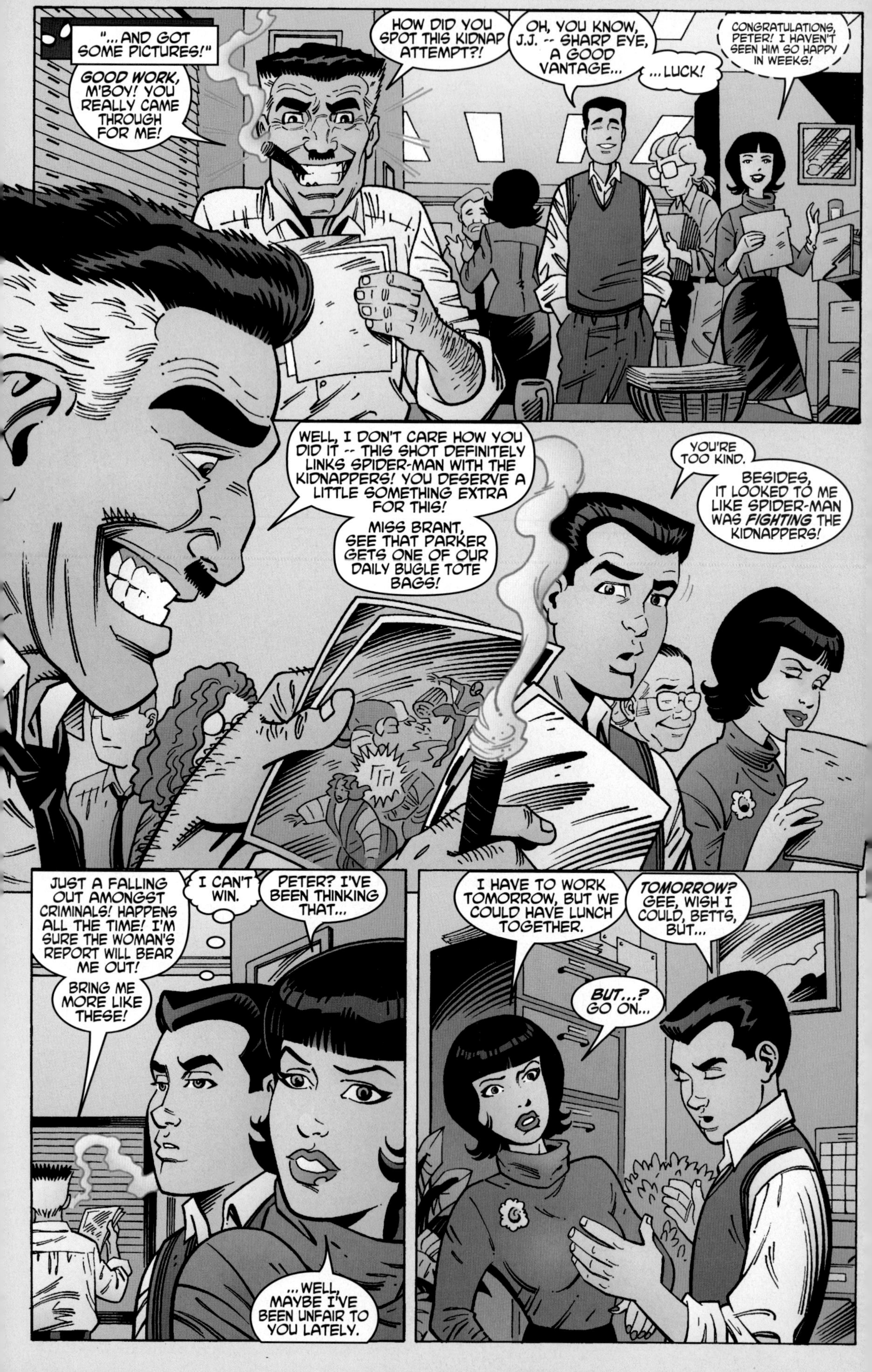
"...AND GOT SOME PICTURES!"
GOOD WORK, M'BOY! YOU REALLY CAME THROUGH FOR ME!
HOW DID YOU SPOT THIS KIDNAP ATTEMPT?!
OH, YOU KNOW, J.J. -- SHARP EYE, A GOOD VANTAGE...
...LUCK!
CONGRATULATIONS, PETER! I HAVEN'T SEEN HIM SO HAPPY IN WEEKS!
WELL, I DON'T CARE HOW YOU DID IT -- THIS SHOT DEFINITELY LINKS SPIDER-MAN WITH THE KIDNAPPERS! YOU DESERVE A LITTLE SOMETHING EXTRA FOR THIS!
MISS BRANT, SEE THAT PARKER GETS ONE OF OUR DAILY BUGLE TOTE BAGS!
YOU'RE TOO KIND.
BESIDES, IT LOOKED TO ME LIKE SPIDER-MAN WAS FIGHTING THE KIDNAPPERS!
JUST A FALLING OUT AMONGST CRIMINALS! HAPPENS ALL THE TIME! I'M SURE THE WOMAN'S REPORT WILL BEAR ME OUT!
BRING ME MORE LIKE THESE!
I CAN'T WIN.
PETER? I'VE BEEN THINKING THAT...
...WELL, MAYBE I'VE BEEN UNFAIR TO YOU LATELY.
I HAVE TO WORK TOMORROW, BUT WE COULD HAVE LUNCH TOGETHER.
TOMORROW? GEE, WISH I COULD, BETTS, BUT...
BUT...? GO ON...

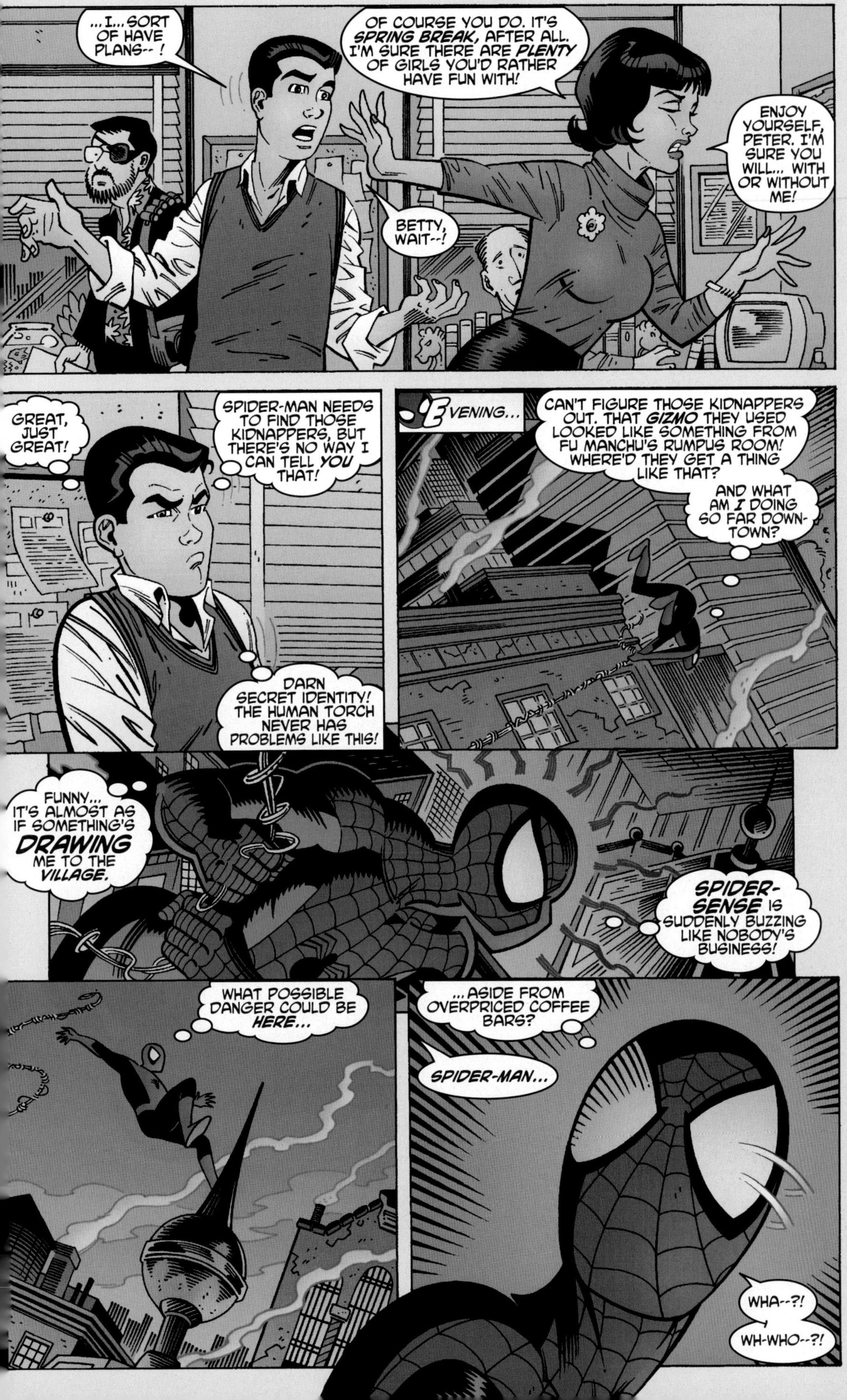

...I...SORT OF HAVE PLANS-- !
OF COURSE YOU DO. IT'S SPRING BREAK, AFTER ALL. I'M SURE THERE ARE PLENTY OF GIRLS YOU'D RATHER HAVE FUN WITH!
BETTY, WAIT--!
ENJOY YOURSELF, PETER. I'M SURE YOU WILL... WITH OR WITHOUT ME!
GREAT, JUST GREAT!
SPIDER-MAN NEEDS TO FIND THOSE KIDNAPPERS, BUT THERE'S NO WAY I CAN TELL YOU THAT!
DARN SECRET IDENTITY! THE HUMAN TORCH NEVER HAS PROBLEMS LIKE THIS!
EVENING...
CAN'T FIGURE THOSE KIDNAPPERS OUT. THAT GIZMO THEY USED LOOKED LIKE SOMETHING FROM FU MANCHU'S RUMPUS ROOM! WHERE'D THEY GET A THING LIKE THAT?
AND WHAT AM I DOING SO FAR DOWN-TOWN?
FUNNY... IT'S ALMOST AS IF SOMETHING'S DRAWING ME TO THE VILLAGE.
SPIDER-SENSE IS SUDDENLY BUZZING LIKE NOBODY'S BUSINESS!
WHAT POSSIBLE DANGER COULD BE HERE...
...ASIDE FROM OVERPRICED COFFEE BARS?
SPIDER-MAN...
WHA--?!
WH-WHO--?!

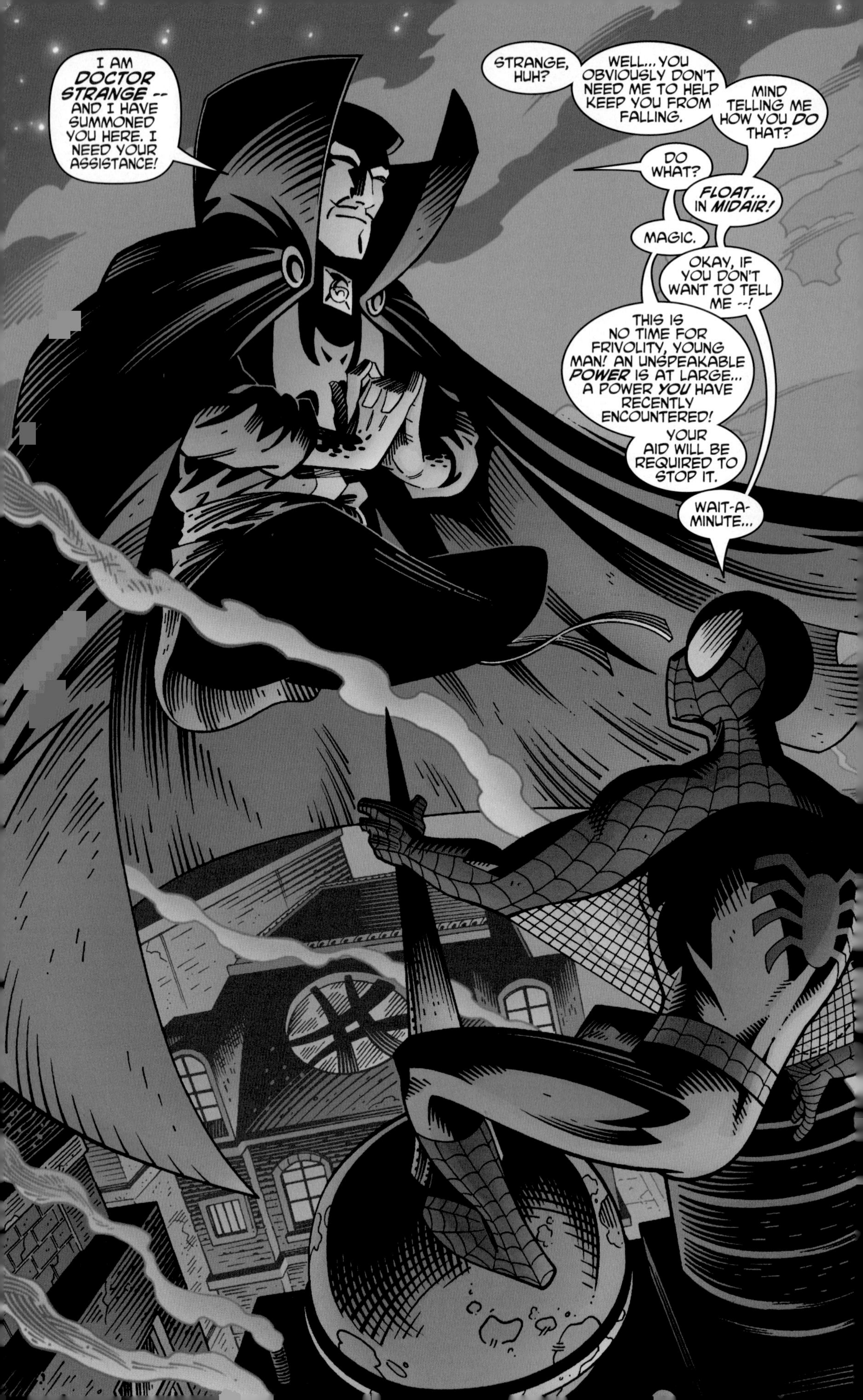
I AM DOCTOR STRANGE -- AND I HAVE SUMMONED YOU HERE. I NEED YOUR ASSISTANCE!
STRANGE, HUH?
WELL... YOU OBVIOUSLY DON'T NEED ME TO HELP KEEP YOU FROM FALLING.
MIND TELLING ME HOW YOU DO THAT?
DO WHAT?
FLOAT... IN MIDAIR!
MAGIC.
OKAY, IF YOU DON'T WANT TO TELL ME --!
THIS IS NO TIME FOR FRIVOLITY, YOUNG MAN! AN UNSPEAKABLE POWER IS AT LARGE... A POWER YOU HAVE RECENTLY ENCOUNTERED!
YOUR AID WILL BE REQUIRED TO STOP IT.
WAIT-A-MINUTE...

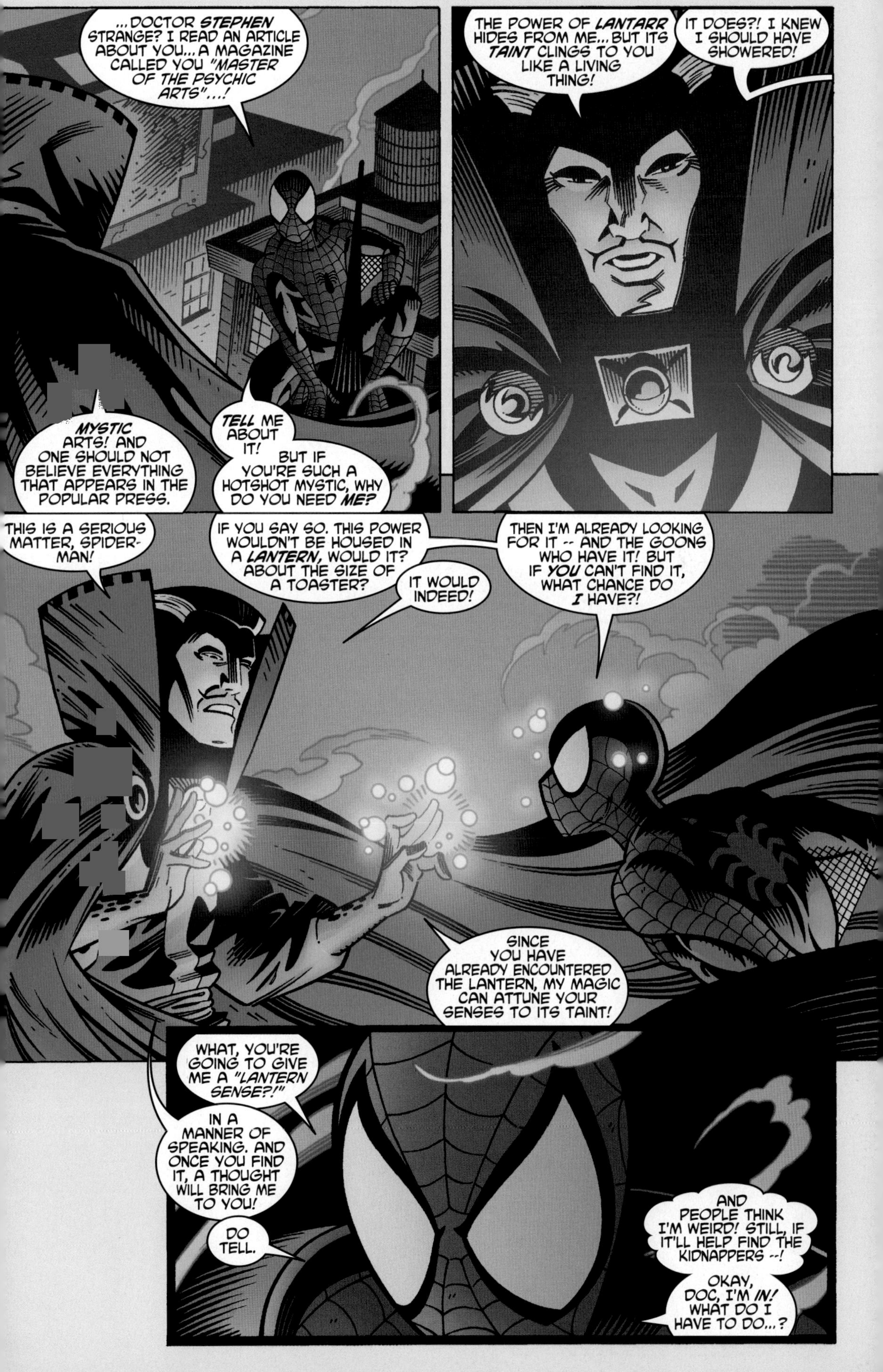

...DOCTOR STEPHEN STRANGE? I READ AN ARTICLE ABOUT YOU...A MAGAZINE CALLED YOU "MASTER OF THE PSYCHIC ARTS"...!
MYSTIC ARTS! AND ONE SHOULD NOT BELIEVE EVERYTHING THAT APPEARS IN THE POPULAR PRESS.
TELL ME ABOUT IT!
BUT IF YOU'RE SUCH A HOTSHOT MYSTIC, WHY DO YOU NEED ME?
THE POWER OF LANTARR HIDES FROM ME... BUT ITS TAINT CLINGS TO YOU LIKE A LIVING THING!
IT DOES?! I KNEW I SHOULD HAVE SHOWERED!
THIS IS A SERIOUS MATTER, SPIDER-MAN!
IF YOU SAY SO. THIS POWER WOULDN'T BE HOUSED IN A LANTERN, WOULD IT? ABOUT THE SIZE OF A TOASTER?
IT WOULD INDEED!
THEN I'M ALREADY LOOKING FOR IT -- AND THE GOONS WHO HAVE IT! BUT IF YOU CAN'T FIND IT, WHAT CHANCE DO I HAVE?!
SINCE YOU HAVE ALREADY ENCOUNTERED THE LANTERN, MY MAGIC CAN ATTUNE YOUR SENSES TO ITS TAINT!
WHAT, YOU'RE GOING TO GIVE ME A "LANTERN SENSE?!"
IN A MANNER OF SPEAKING. AND ONCE YOU FIND IT, A THOUGHT WILL BRING ME TO YOU!
DO TELL.
AND PEOPLE THINK I'M WEIRD! STILL, IF IT'LL HELP FIND THE KIDNAPPERS --!
OKAY, DOC, I'M IN! WHAT DO I HAVE TO DO...?

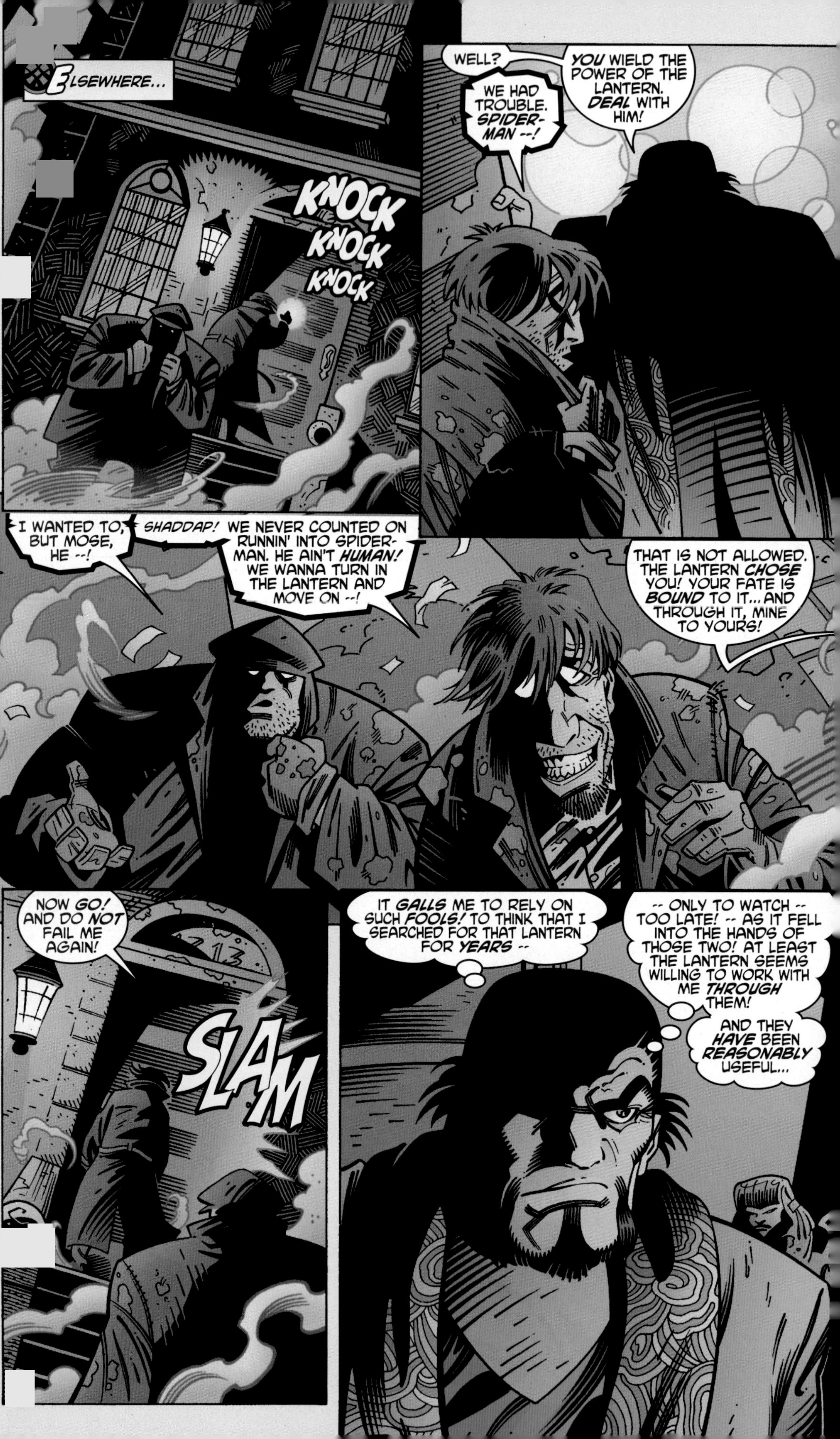
ELSEWHERE...
KNOCK KNOCK KNOCK
WELL?
WE HAD TROUBLE. SPIDER-MAN --!
YOU WIELD THE POWER OF THE LANTERN. DEAL WITH HIM!
I WANTED TO, BUT MOSE, HE --!
SHADDAP! WE NEVER COUNTED ON RUNNIN' INTO SPIDER-MAN. HE AIN'T HUMAN! WE WANNA TURN IN THE LANTERN AND MOVE ON --!
THAT IS NOT ALLOWED. THE LANTERN CHOSE YOU! YOUR FATE IS BOUND TO IT... AND THROUGH IT, MINE TO YOURS!
NOW GO! AND DO NOT FAIL ME AGAIN!
SLAM
IT GALLS ME TO RELY ON SUCH FOOLS! TO THINK THAT I SEARCHED FOR THAT LANTERN FOR YEARS --
-- ONLY TO WATCH -- TOO LATE! -- AS IT FELL INTO THE HANDS OF THOSE TWO! AT LEAST THE LANTERN SEEMS WILLING TO WORK WITH ME THROUGH THEM!
AND THEY HAVE BEEN REASONABLY USEFUL...

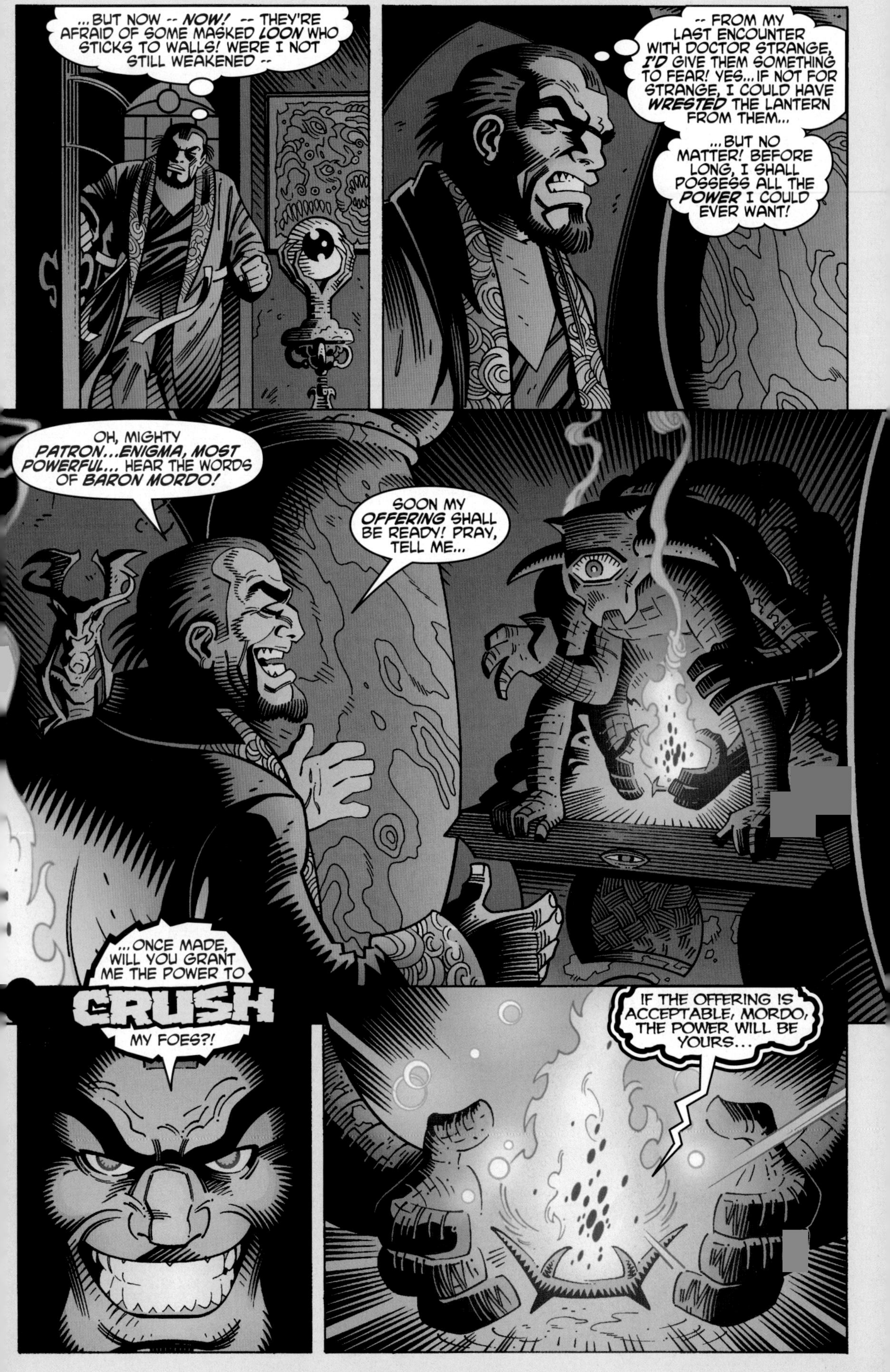
...BUT NOW -- NOW! -- THEY'RE AFRAID OF SOME MASKED LOON WHO STICKS TO WALLS! WERE I NOT STILL WEAKENED --
-- FROM MY LAST ENCOUNTER WITH DOCTOR STRANGE, I'D GIVE THEM SOMETHING TO FEAR! YES... IF NOT FOR STRANGE, I COULD HAVE WRESTED THE LANTERN FROM THEM...
...BUT NO MATTER! BEFORE LONG, I SHALL POSSESS ALL THE POWER I COULD EVER WANT!
OH, MIGHTY PATRON...ENIGMA, MOST POWERFUL... HEAR THE WORDS OF BARON MORDO!
SOON MY OFFERING SHALL BE READY! PRAY, TELL ME...
...ONCE MADE, WILL YOU GRANT ME THE POWER TO CRUSH MY FOES?!
IF THE OFFERING IS ACCEPTABLE, MORDO, THE POWER WILL BE YOURS...

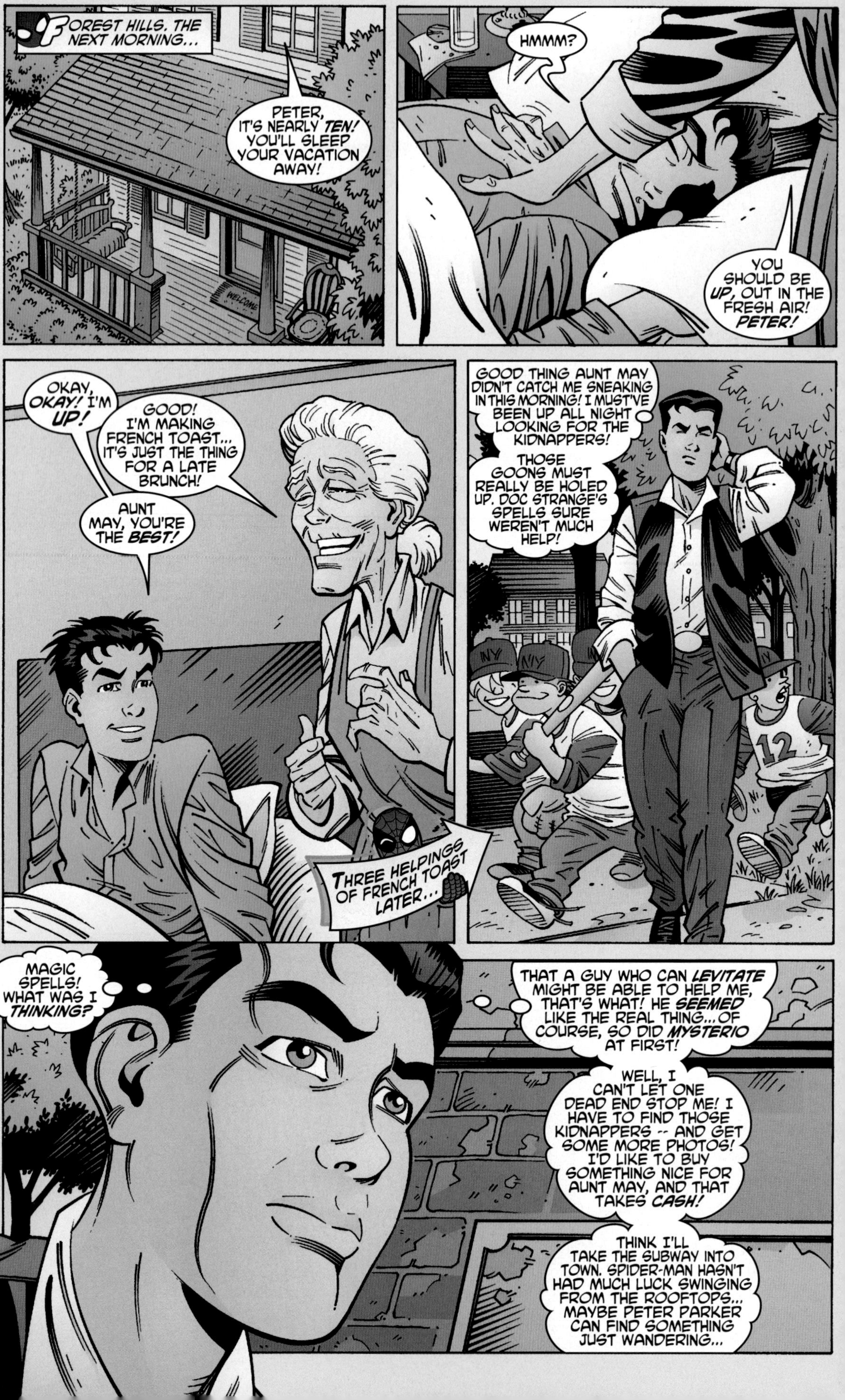
FOREST HILLS. THE NEXT MORNING...
PETER, IT'S NEARLY TEN! YOU'LL SLEEP YOUR VACATION AWAY!
HMMM?
YOU SHOULD BE UP, OUT IN THE FRESH AIR! PETER!
OKAY, OKAY! I'M UP!
GOOD! I'M MAKING FRENCH TOAST... IT'S JUST THE THING FOR A LATE BRUNCH!
AUNT MAY, YOU'RE THE BEST!
THREE HELPINGS OF FRENCH TOAST LATER...
GOOD THING AUNT MAY DIDN'T CATCH ME SNEAKING IN THIS MORNING! I MUST'VE BEEN UP ALL NIGHT LOOKING FOR THE KIDNAPPERS!
THOSE GOONS MUST REALLY BE HOLED UP. DOC STRANGE'S SPELLS SURE WEREN'T MUCH HELP!
MAGIC SPELLS! WHAT WAS I THINKING?
THAT A GUY WHO CAN LEVITATE MIGHT BE ABLE TO HELP ME, THAT'S WHAT! HE SEEMED LIKE THE REAL THING... OF COURSE, SO DID MYSTERIO AT FIRST!
WELL, I CAN'T LET ONE DEAD END STOP ME! I HAVE TO FIND THOSE KIDNAPPERS -- AND GET SOME MORE PHOTOS! I'D LIKE TO BUY SOMETHING NICE FOR AUNT MAY, AND THAT TAKES CASH!
THINK I'LL TAKE THE SUBWAY INTO TOWN. SPIDER-MAN HASN'T HAD MUCH LUCK SWINGING FROM THE ROOFTOPS... MAYBE PETER PARKER CAN FIND SOMETHING JUST WANDERING...

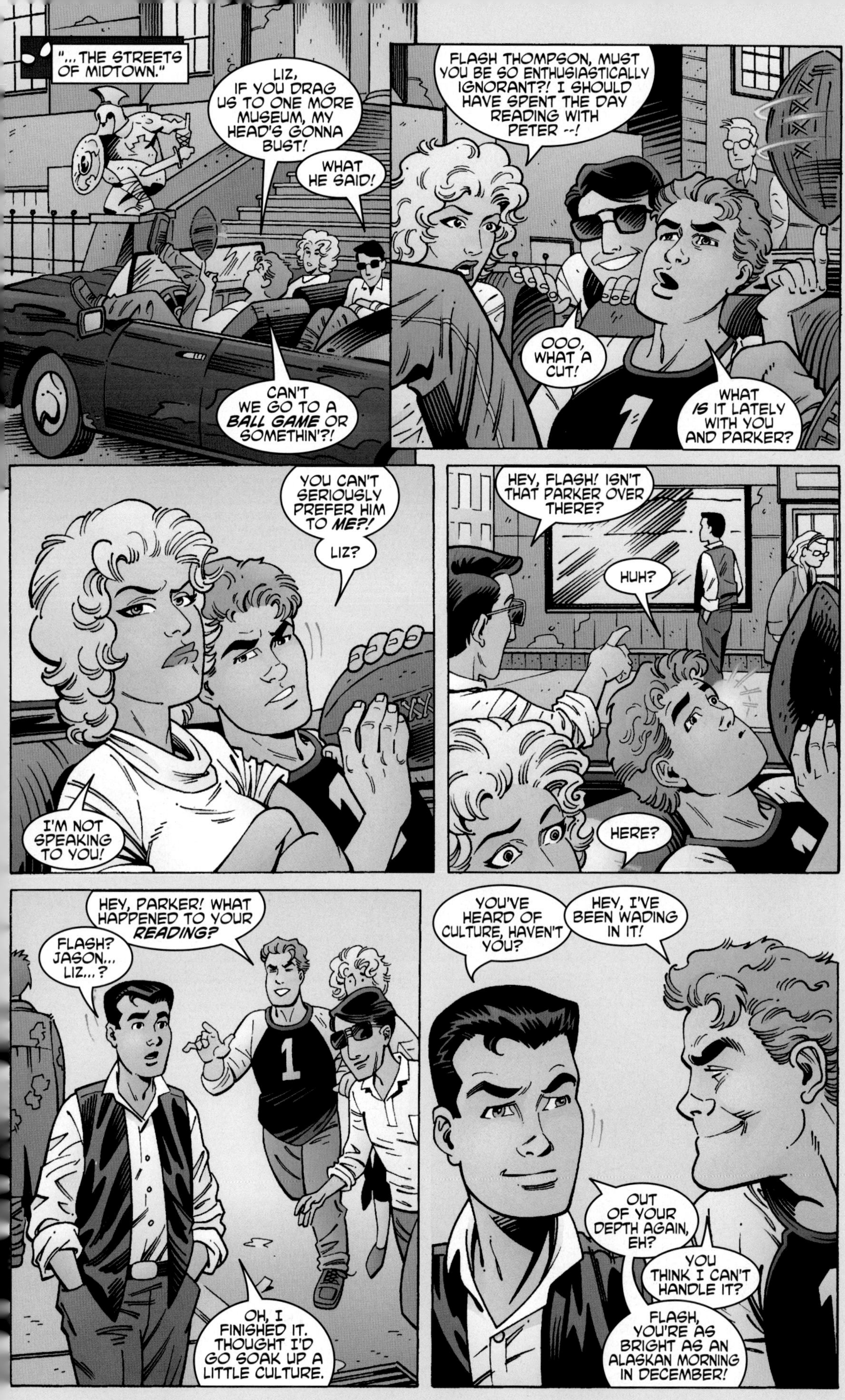
"...THE STREETS OF MIDTOWN."
LIZ, IF YOU DRAG US TO ONE MORE MUSEUM, MY HEAD'S GONNA BUST!
WHAT HE SAID!
CAN'T WE GO TO A BALL GAME OR SOMETHIN'?!
FLASH THOMPSON, MUST YOU BE SO ENTHUSIASTICALLY IGNORANT?! I SHOULD HAVE SPENT THE DAY READING WITH PETER --!
OOO, WHAT A CUT!
WHAT IS IT LATELY WITH YOU AND PARKER?
YOU CAN'T SERIOUSLY PREFER HIM TO ME?!
LIZ?
I'M NOT SPEAKING TO YOU!
HEY, FLASH! ISN'T THAT PARKER OVER THERE?
HUH?
HERE?
HEY, PARKER! WHAT HAPPENED TO YOUR READING?
FLASH? JASON... LIZ...?
OH, I FINISHED IT. THOUGHT I'D GO SOAK UP A LITTLE CULTURE.
YOU'VE HEARD OF CULTURE, HAVEN'T YOU?
HEY, I'VE BEEN WADING IN IT!
OUT OF YOUR DEPTH AGAIN, EH?
YOU THINK I CAN'T HANDLE IT?
FLASH, YOU'RE AS BRIGHT AS AN ALASKAN MORNING IN DECEMBER!

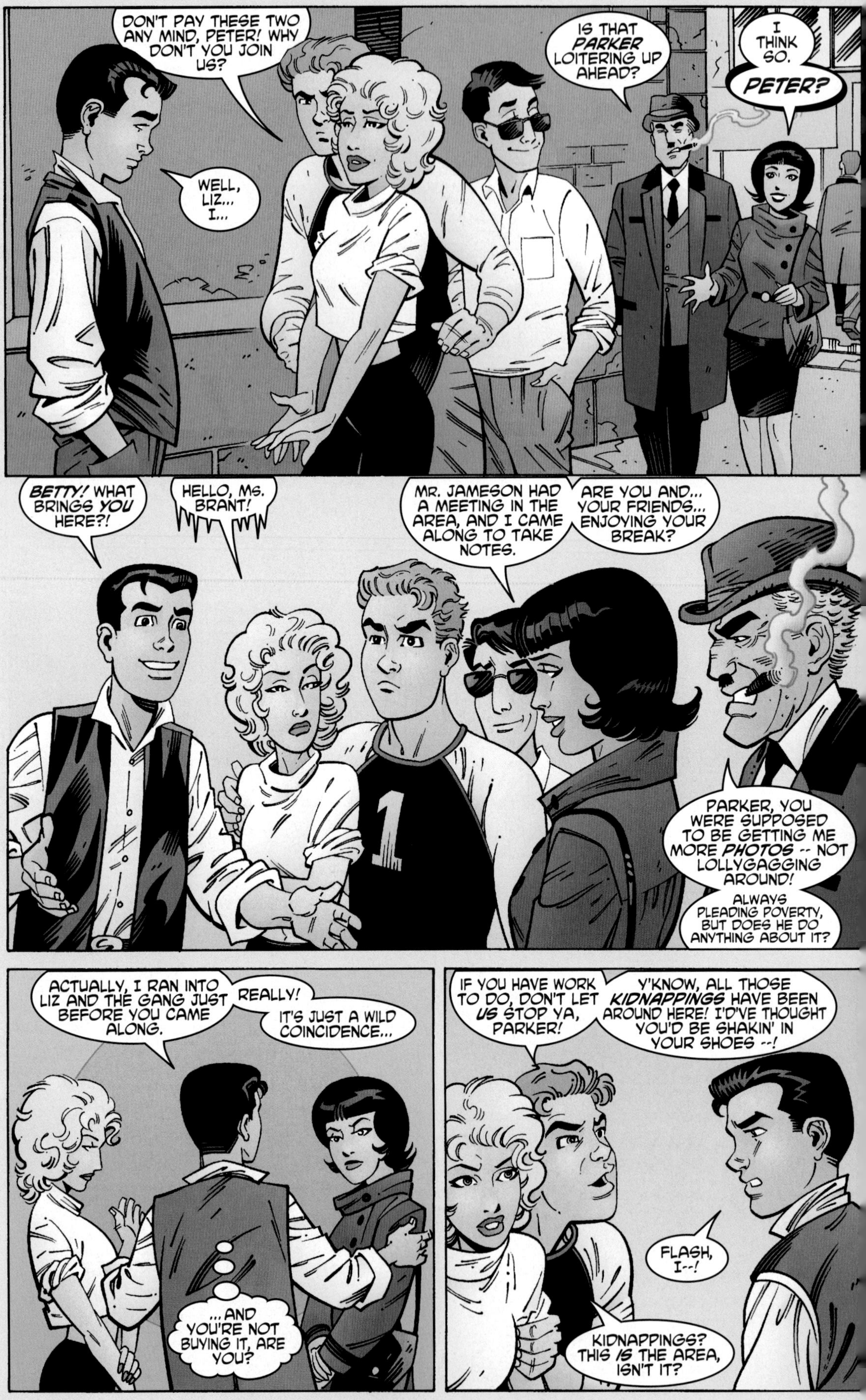

DON'T PAY THESE TWO ANY MIND, PETER! WHY DON'T YOU JOIN US?
WELL, LIZ... I...
IS THAT *PARKER* LOITERING UP AHEAD?
I THINK SO.
PETER?
BETTY! WHAT BRINGS *YOU* HERE?!
HELLO, MS. BRANT!
MR. JAMESON HAD A MEETING IN THE AREA, AND I CAME ALONG TO TAKE NOTES.
ARE YOU AND... YOUR FRIENDS... ENJOYING YOUR BREAK?
PARKER, YOU WERE SUPPOSED TO BE GETTING ME MORE *PHOTOS* -- NOT LOLLYGAGGING AROUND!
ALWAYS PLEADING POVERTY, BUT DOES HE DO ANYTHING ABOUT IT?
ACTUALLY, I RAN INTO LIZ AND THE GANG JUST BEFORE YOU CAME ALONG.
REALLY!
IT'S JUST A WILD COINCIDENCE...
...AND YOU'RE NOT BUYING IT, ARE YOU?
IF YOU HAVE WORK TO DO, DON'T LET *US* STOP YA, PARKER!
Y'KNOW, ALL THOSE *KIDNAPPINGS* HAVE BEEN AROUND HERE! I'D'VE THOUGHT YOU'D BE SHAKIN' IN YOUR SHOES --!
FLASH, I--!
KIDNAPPINGS? THIS *IS* THE AREA, ISN'T IT?

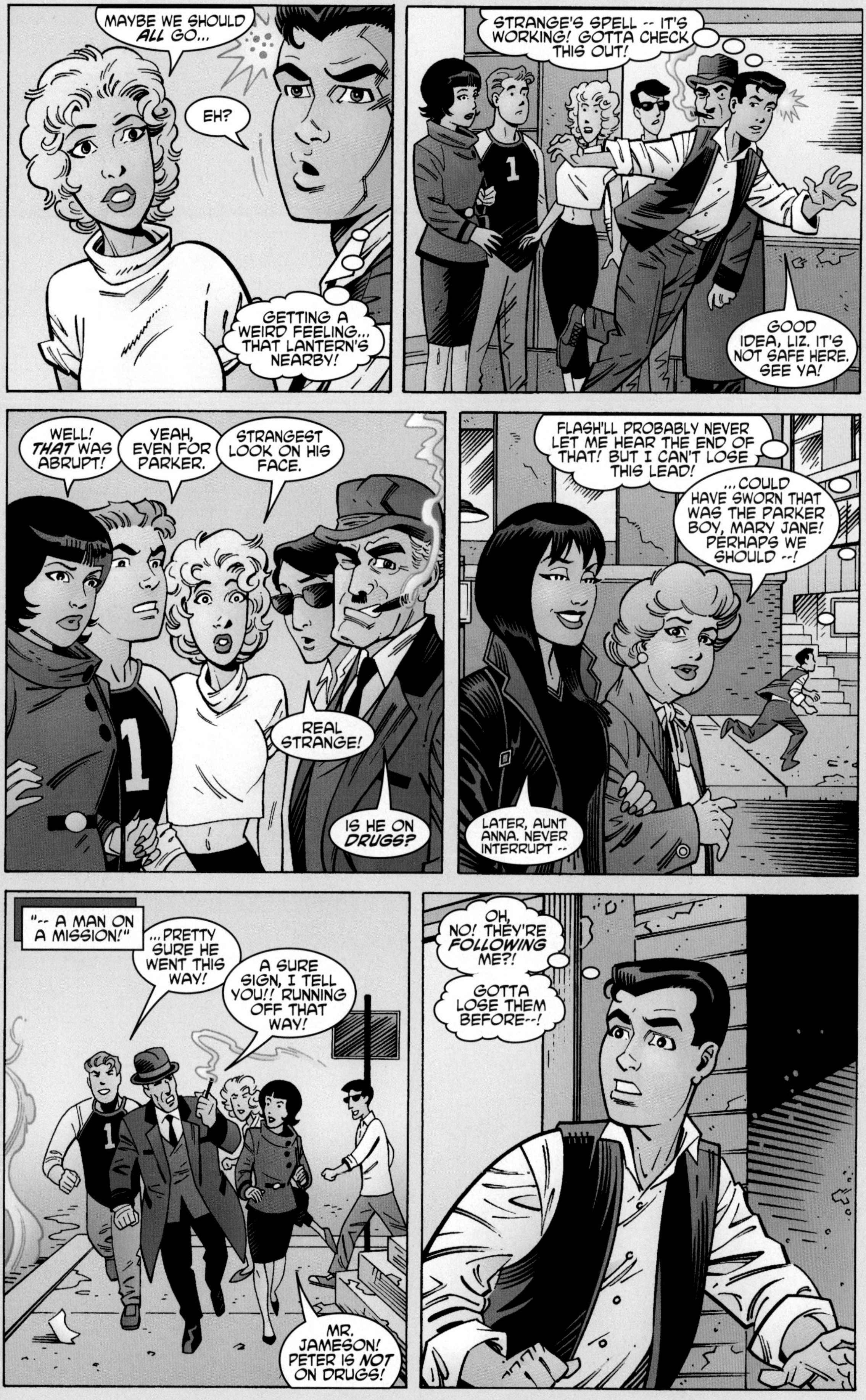
MAYBE WE SHOULD ALL GO...
EH?
GETTING A WEIRD FEELING... THAT LANTERN'S NEARBY!
STRANGE'S SPELL -- IT'S WORKING! GOTTA CHECK THIS OUT!
GOOD IDEA, LIZ. IT'S NOT SAFE HERE. SEE YA!
WELL! THAT WAS ABRUPT!
YEAH, EVEN FOR PARKER.
STRANGEST LOOK ON HIS FACE.
REAL STRANGE!
IS HE ON DRUGS?
FLASH'LL PROBABLY NEVER LET ME HEAR THE END OF THAT! BUT I CAN'T LOSE THIS LEAD!
...COULD HAVE SWORN THAT WAS THE PARKER BOY, MARY JANE! PERHAPS WE SHOULD --!
LATER, AUNT ANNA. NEVER INTERRUPT --
"-- A MAN ON A MISSION!"
...PRETTY SURE HE WENT THIS WAY!
A SURE SIGN, I TELL YOU!! RUNNING OFF THAT WAY!
MR. JAMESON! PETER IS NOT ON DRUGS!
OH, NO! THEY'RE FOLLOWING ME?!
GOTTA LOSE THEM BEFORE--!

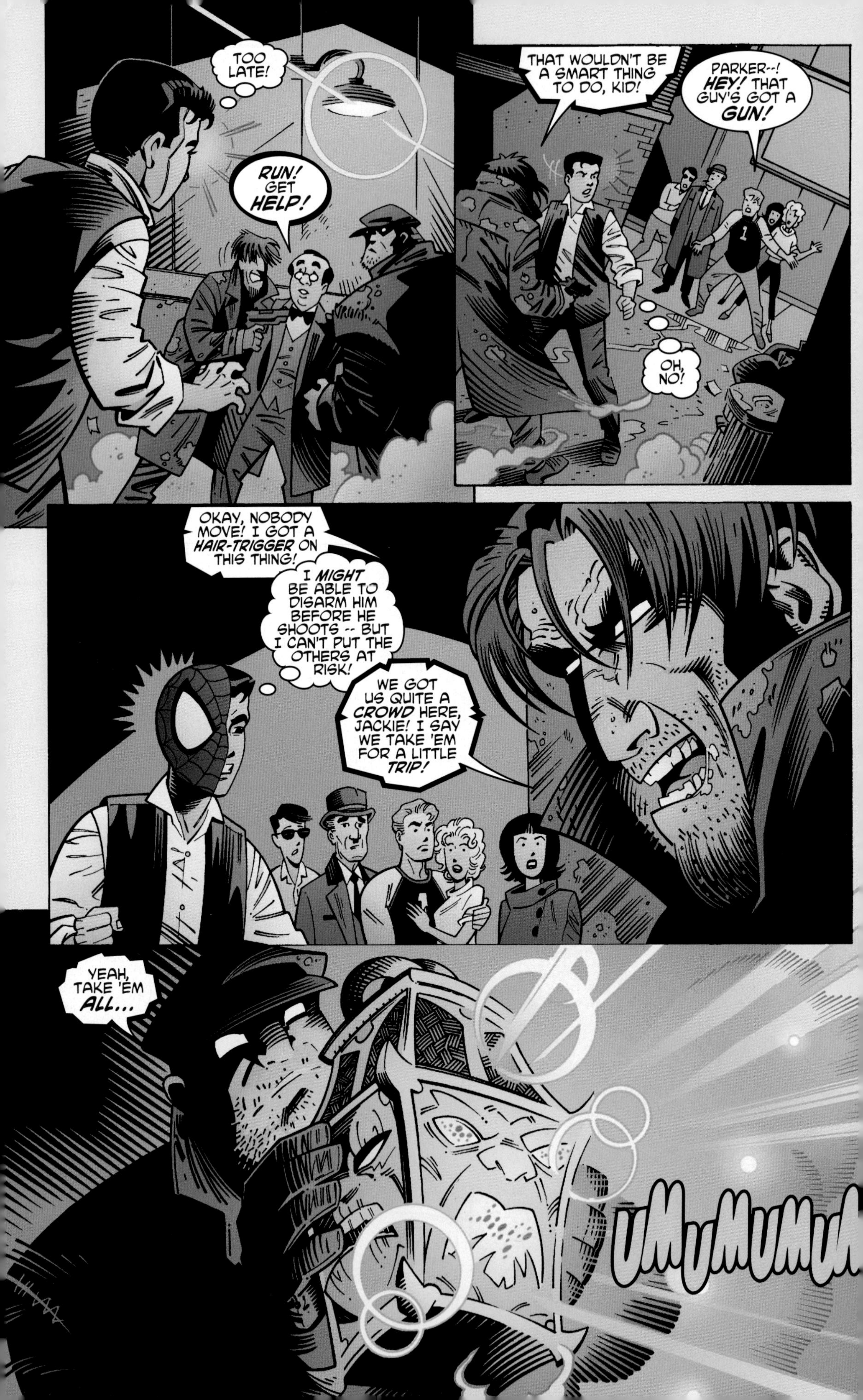
TOO LATE!
RUN! GET HELP!
THAT WOULDN'T BE A SMART THING TO DO, KID!
PARKER--! HEY! THAT GUY'S GOT A GUN!
OH, NO!
OKAY, NOBODY MOVE! I GOT A HAIR-TRIGGER ON THIS THING!
I MIGHT BE ABLE TO DISARM HIM BEFORE HE SHOOTS -- BUT I CAN'T PUT THE OTHERS AT RISK!
WE GOT US QUITE A CROWD HERE, JACKIE! I SAY WE TAKE 'EM FOR A LITTLE TRIP!
YEAH, TAKE 'EM ALL...
UMMUMMUM

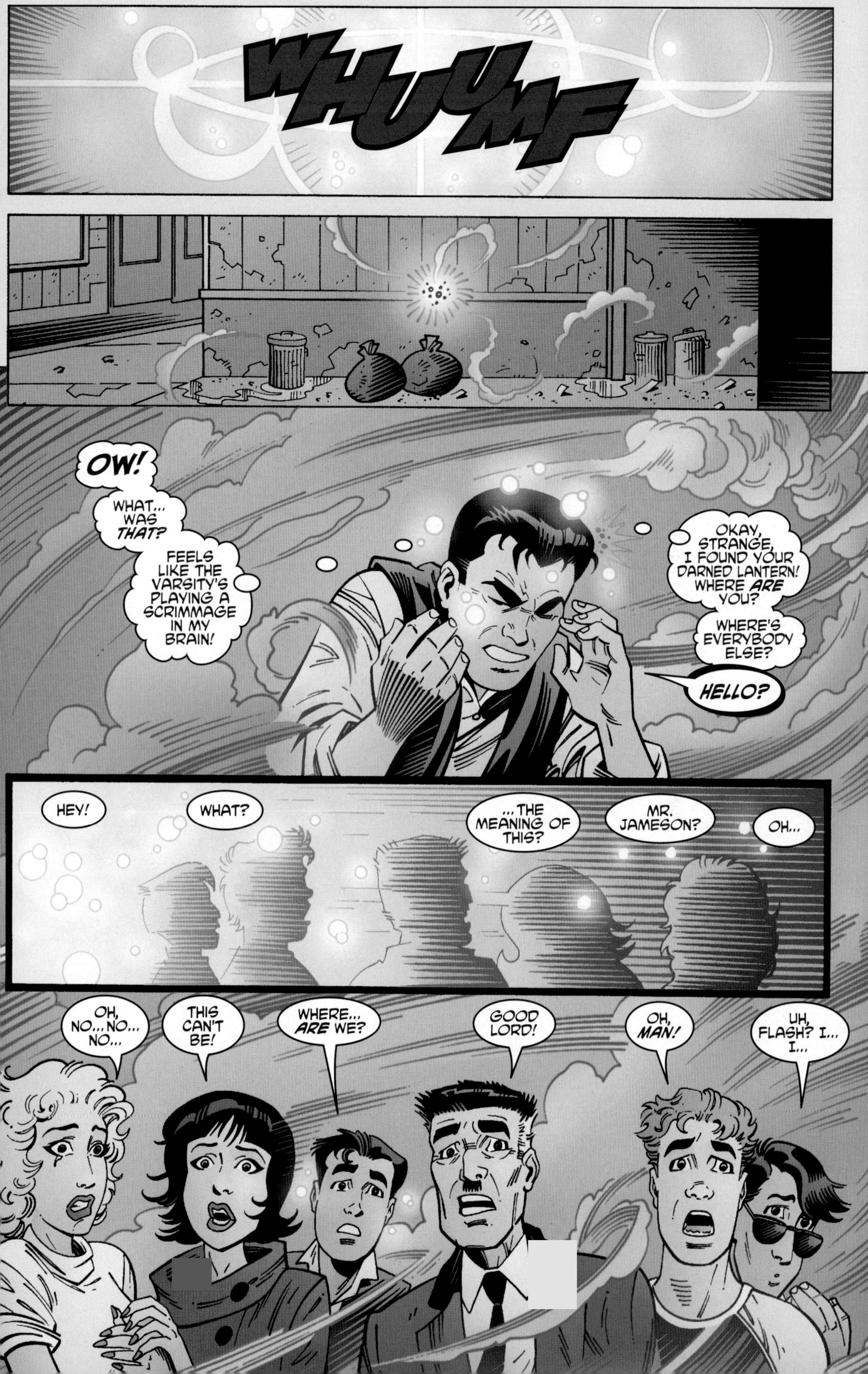
WHUUMF
OW!
WHAT... WAS THAT?
FEELS LIKE THE VARSITY'S PLAYING A SCRIMMAGE IN MY BRAIN!
OKAY, STRANGE, I FOUND YOUR DARNED LANTERN! WHERE ARE YOU?
WHERE'S EVERYBODY ELSE?
HELLO?
HEY!
WHAT?
...THE MEANING OF THIS?
MR. JAMESON?
OH...
OH, NO...NO... NO...
THIS CAN'T BE!
WHERE... ARE WE?
GOOD LORD!
OH, MAN!
UH, FLASH? I... I...

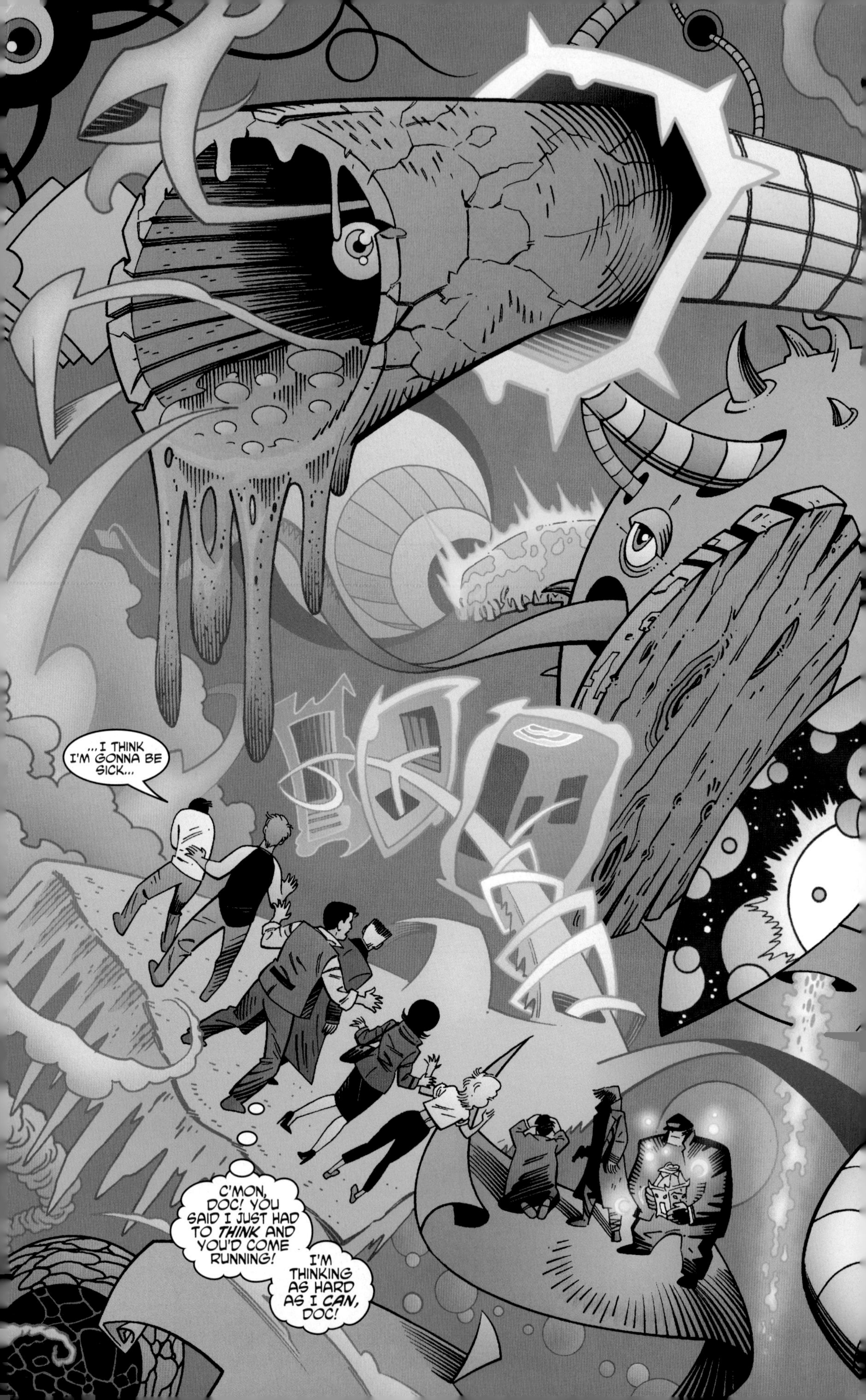
...I THINK I'M GONNA BE SICK...
C'MON, DOC! YOU SAID I JUST HAD TO *THINK* AND YOU'D COME RUNNING!
I'M THINKING AS HARD AS I *CAN*, DOC!

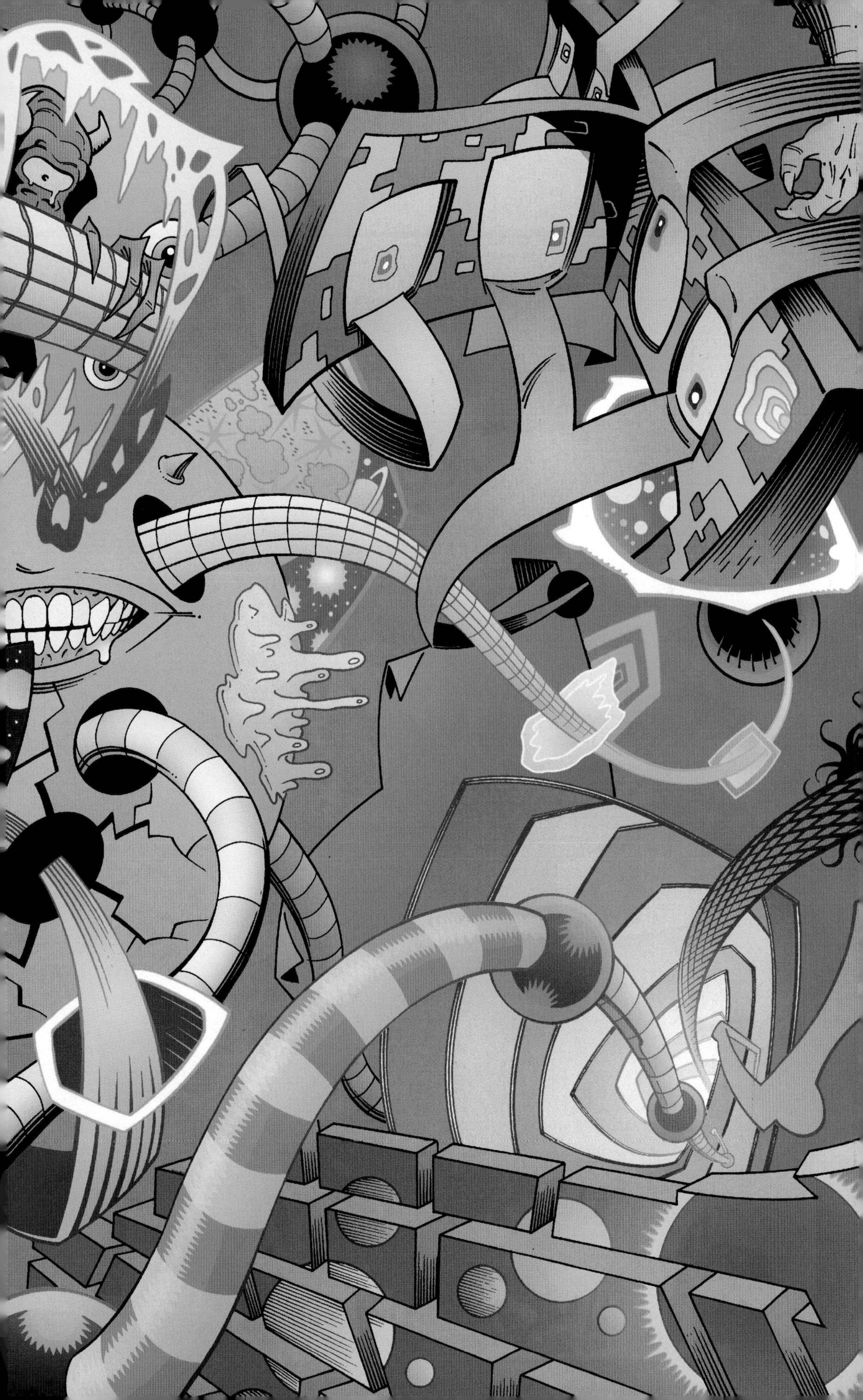

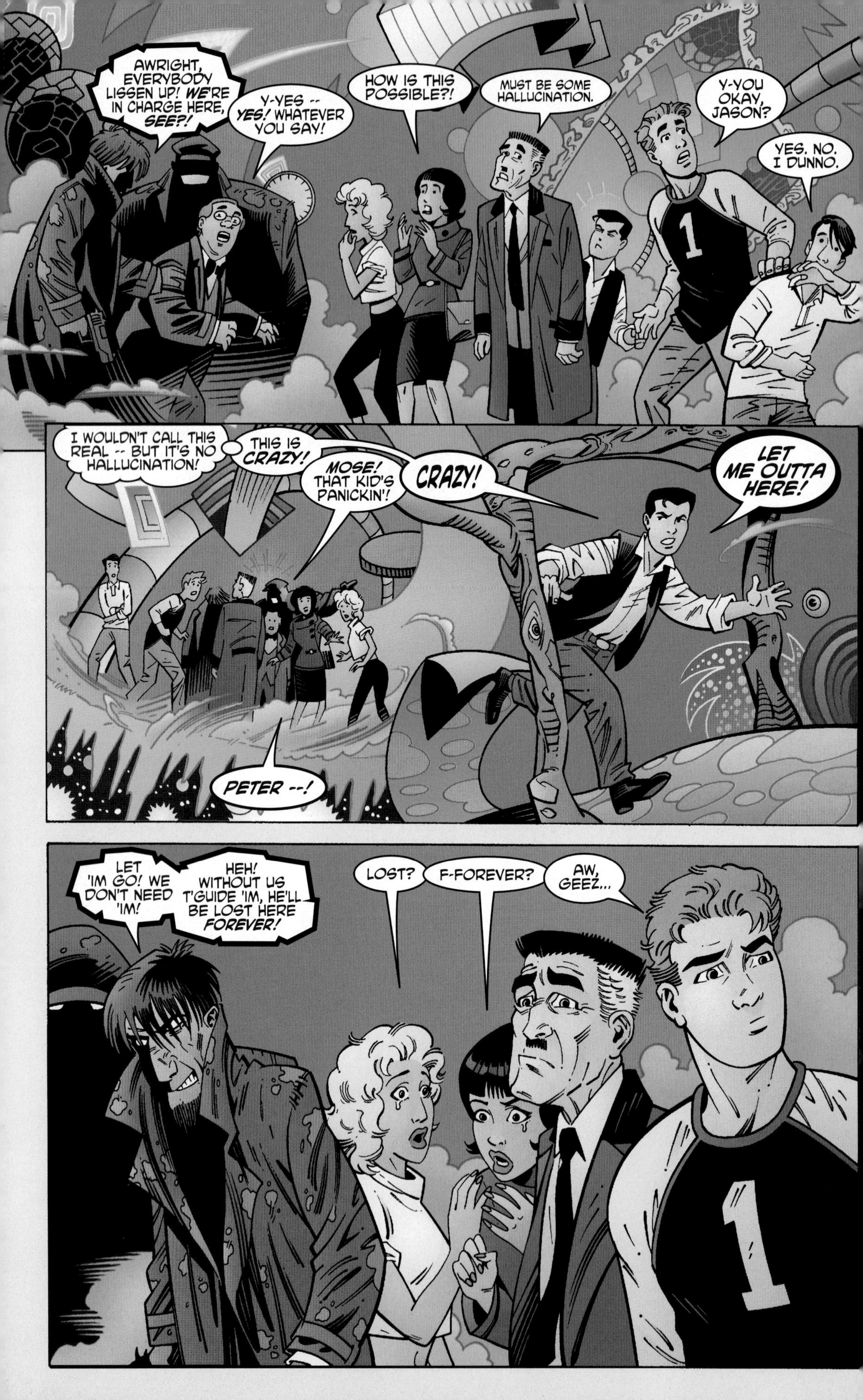
AWRIGHT, EVERYBODY LISSEN UP! WE'RE IN CHARGE HERE, SEE?!
Y-YES -- YES! WHATEVER YOU SAY!
HOW IS THIS POSSIBLE?!
MUST BE SOME HALLUCINATION.
Y-YOU OKAY, JASON?
YES. NO. I DUNNO.
I WOULDN'T CALL THIS REAL -- BUT IT'S NO HALLUCINATION!
THIS IS CRAZY!
MOSE! THAT KID'S PANICKIN'!
CRAZY!
LET ME OUTTA HERE!
PETER --!
LET 'IM GO! WE DON'T NEED 'IM!
HEH! WITHOUT US T'GUIDE 'IM, HE'LL BE LOST HERE FOREVER!
LOST?
F-FOREVER?
AW, GEEZ...

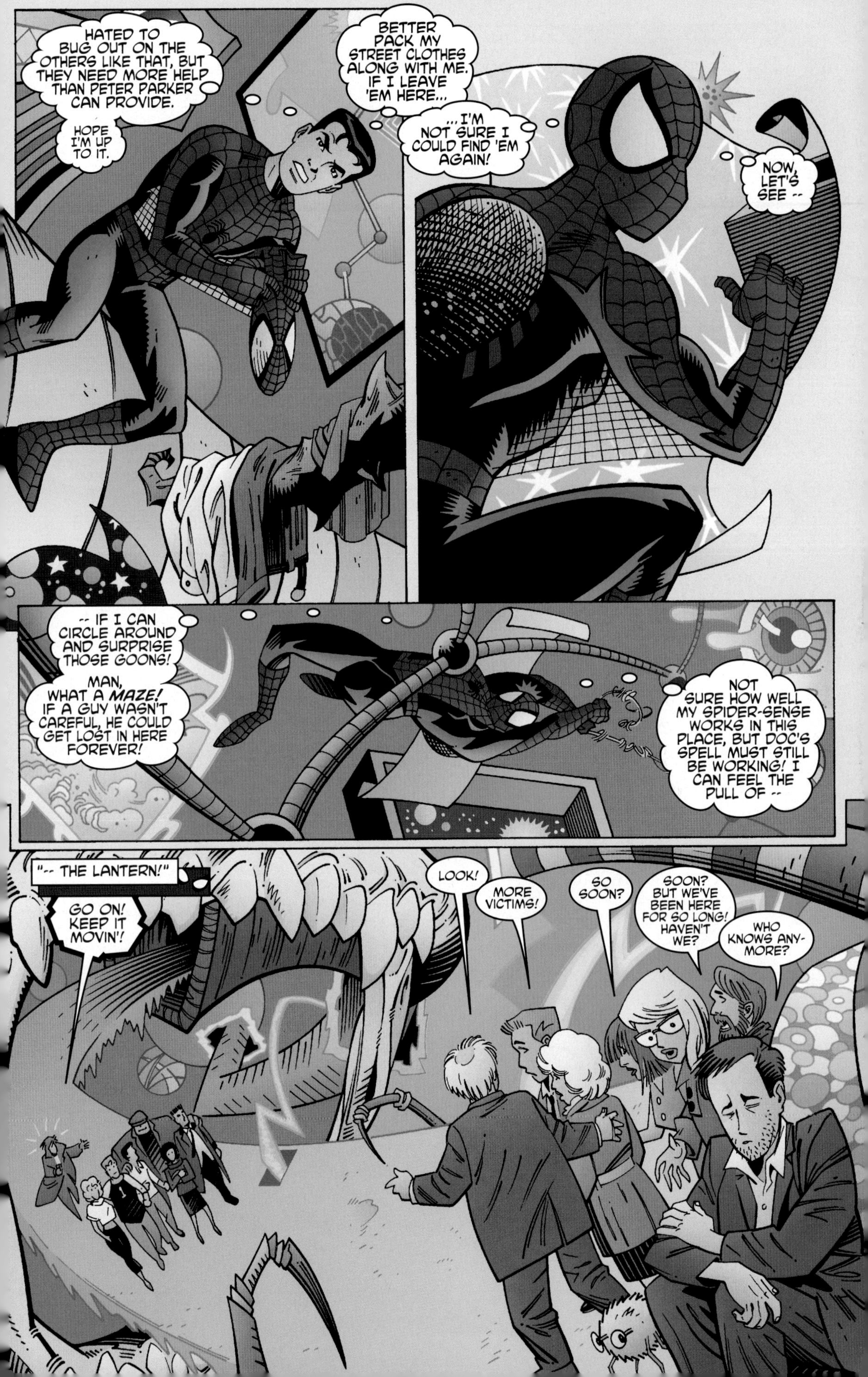
HATED TO BUG OUT ON THE OTHERS LIKE THAT, BUT THEY NEED MORE HELP THAN PETER PARKER CAN PROVIDE.
HOPE I'M UP TO IT.
BETTER PACK MY STREET CLOTHES ALONG WITH ME. IF I LEAVE 'EM HERE...
...I'M NOT SURE I COULD FIND 'EM AGAIN!
NOW, LET'S SEE --
-- IF I CAN CIRCLE AROUND AND SURPRISE THOSE GOONS!
MAN, WHAT A *MAZE!* IF A GUY WASN'T CAREFUL, HE COULD GET LOST IN HERE FOREVER!
NOT SURE HOW WELL MY SPIDER-SENSE WORKS IN THIS PLACE, BUT DOC'S SPELL MUST STILL BE WORKING! I CAN FEEL THE PULL OF --
"-- THE LANTERN!"
GO ON! KEEP IT MOVIN'!
LOOK!
MORE VICTIMS!
SO SOON?
SOON? BUT WE'VE BEEN HERE FOR SO LONG! HAVEN'T WE?
WHO KNOWS ANY-MORE?

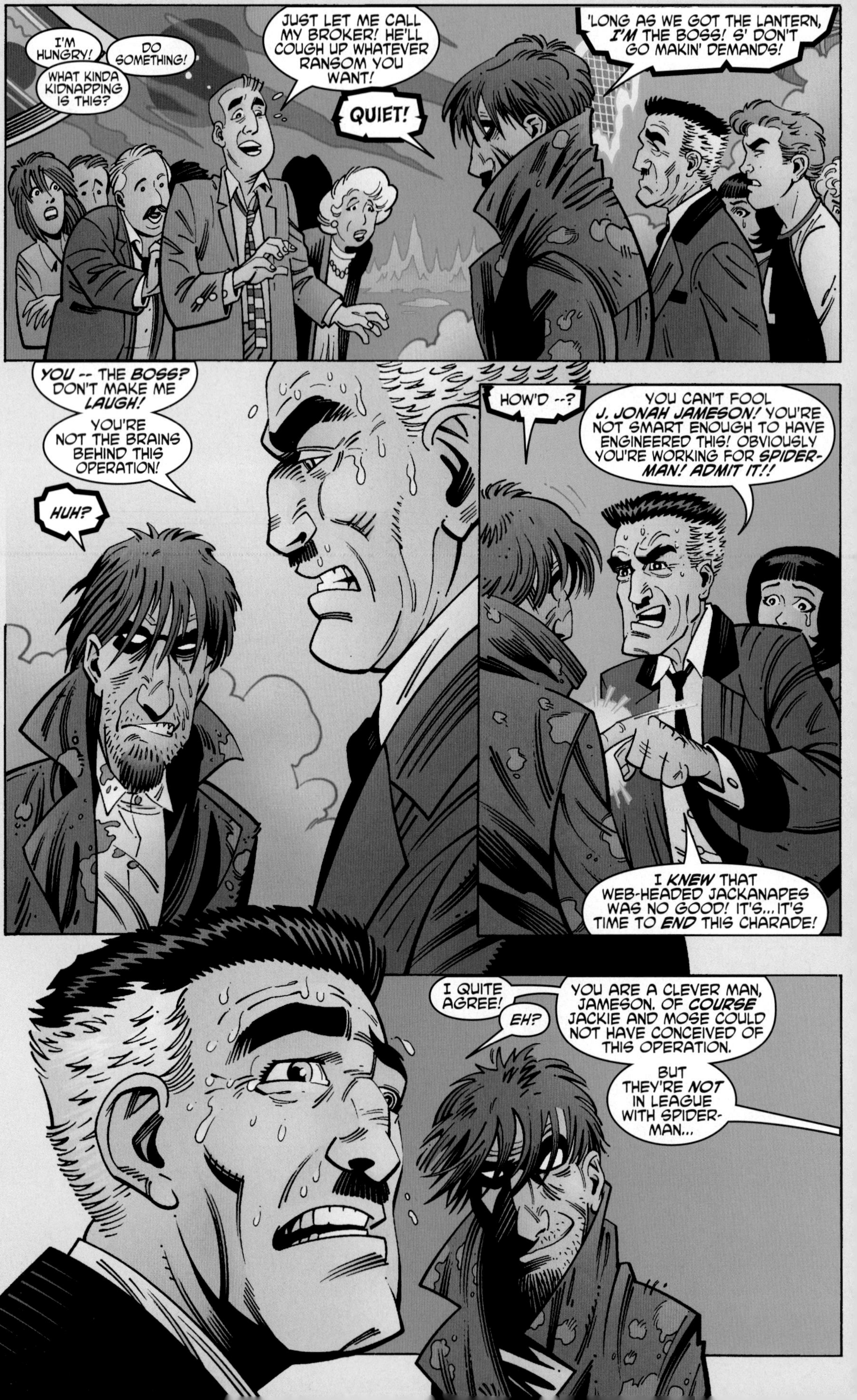

I'M HUNGRY!
DO SOMETHING!
WHAT KINDA KIDNAPPING IS THIS?
JUST LET ME CALL MY BROKER! HE'LL COUGH UP WHATEVER RANSOM YOU WANT!
QUIET!
'LONG AS WE GOT THE LANTERN, I'M THE BOSS! S' DON'T GO MAKIN' DEMANDS!
YOU -- THE BOSS? DON'T MAKE ME LAUGH!
YOU'RE NOT THE BRAINS BEHIND THIS OPERATION!
HUH?
HOW'D --?
YOU CAN'T FOOL J. JONAH JAMESON! YOU'RE NOT SMART ENOUGH TO HAVE ENGINEERED THIS! OBVIOUSLY YOU'RE WORKING FOR SPIDER-MAN! ADMIT IT!!
I KNEW THAT WEB-HEADED JACKANAPES WAS NO GOOD! IT'S...IT'S TIME TO END THIS CHARADE!
I QUITE AGREE!
EH?
YOU ARE A CLEVER MAN, JAMESON. OF COURSE JACKIE AND MOSE COULD NOT HAVE CONCEIVED OF THIS OPERATION.
BUT THEY'RE NOT IN LEAGUE WITH SPIDER-MAN...

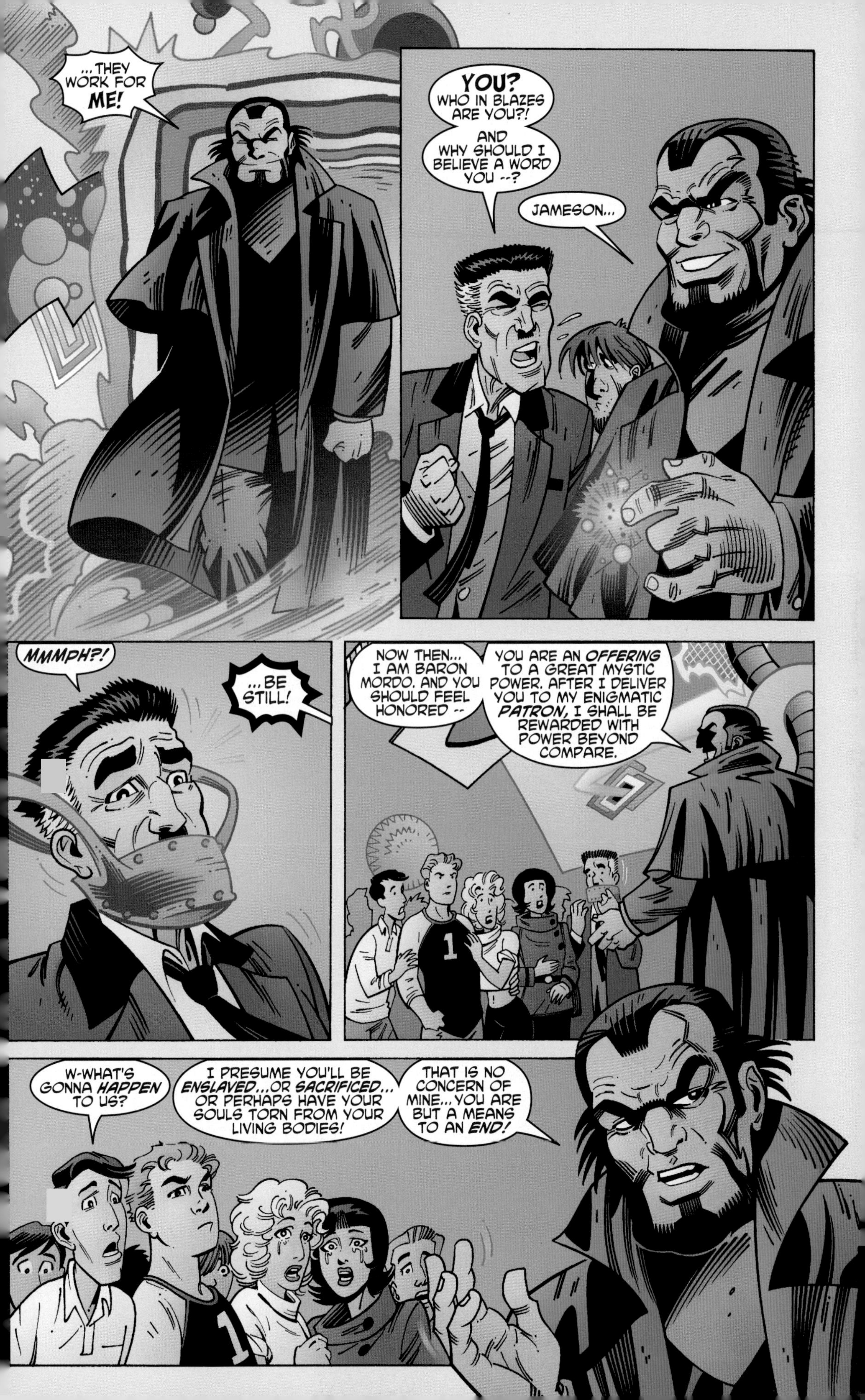
...THEY WORK FOR ME!
YOU? WHO IN BLAZES ARE YOU?!
AND WHY SHOULD I BELIEVE A WORD YOU --?
JAMESON...
MMMPH?!
...BE STILL!
NOW THEN... I AM BARON MORDO. AND YOU SHOULD FEEL HONORED --
YOU ARE AN OFFERING TO A GREAT MYSTIC POWER. AFTER I DELIVER YOU TO MY ENIGMATIC PATRON, I SHALL BE REWARDED WITH POWER BEYOND COMPARE.
W-WHAT'S GONNA HAPPEN TO US?
I PRESUME YOU'LL BE ENSLAVED...OR SACRIFICED... OR PERHAPS HAVE YOUR SOULS TORN FROM YOUR LIVING BODIES!
THAT IS NO CONCERN OF MINE...YOU ARE BUT A MEANS TO AN END!

OH, MAN... OH, MAN...

THIS CAN'T BE HAPPENING!

IT'S ALL MY FAULT! IF I HADN'T INSISTED ON GOING INTO THE CITY--!

NO WAY! IT'S NOTHING YOU'VE DONE! WE'LL GET OUTTA THIS SOMEHOW. IT'S GONNA BE OKAY! YOU'LL SEE.

IT'S GOTTA.

OF COURSE, IT SHALL... FOR *ME!*

HOLD THIS. AND TRY NOT TO SOIL IT!

YES, SIR.

PREPARING THEM FURTHER WILL BE SIMPLICITY ITSELF -- THEY ARE *FAR* TOO TERRIFIED TO PUT UP ANY FIGHT!

BY THE POWER UNDYING, BY THE FLAMES OF THE FALTINE, HEED THE WORDS NOW OF MORDO...

...CAN YOU SPARE ME A SALTINE?

WHAT?!?

NOT A *GREAT* RHYME -- BUT GIVE IT A GOOD BEAT AND YOU CAN *DANCE* TO IT!

WHO --?

IT'S JUST ME, YOUR FRIENDLY NEIGHBORHOOD *SPIDER-MAN!*

BUT I GOTTA SAY, THIS NEIGHBORHOOD AIN'T WHAT IT USED TO BE!

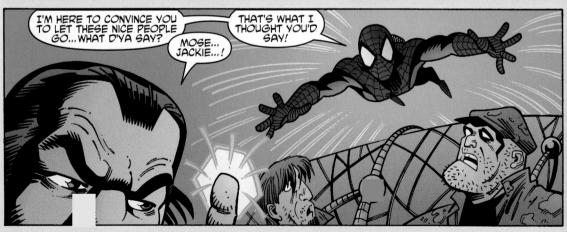

I'M HERE TO CONVINCE YOU TO LET THESE NICE PEOPLE GO...WHAT D'YA SAY?

MOSE... JACKIE...!

THAT'S WHAT I THOUGHT YOU'D SAY!

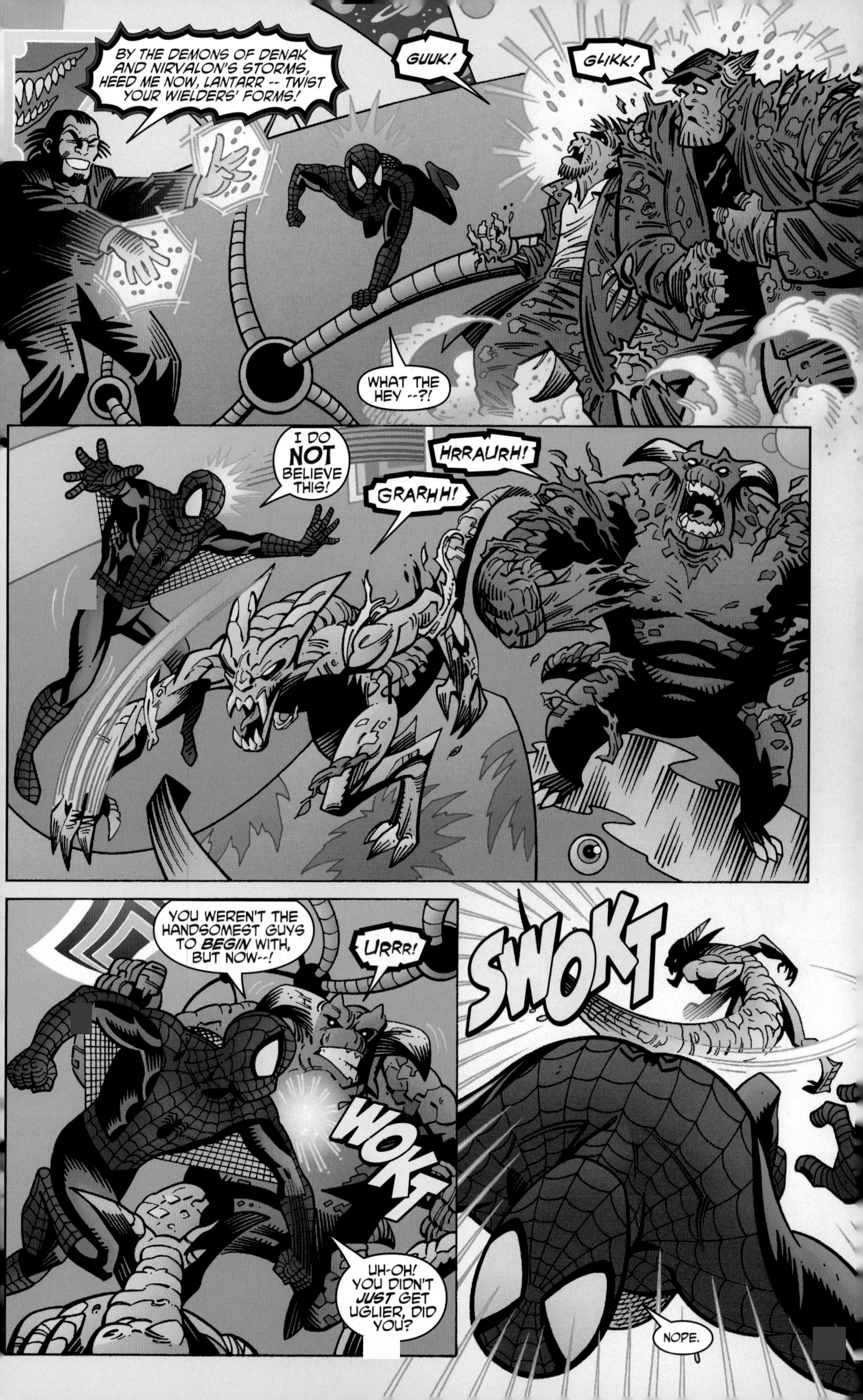
BY THE DEMONS OF DENAK AND NIRVALON'S STORMS, HEED ME NOW, LANTARR -- TWIST YOUR WIELDERS' FORMS!
GUUK!
GLIKK!
WHAT THE HEY --?!
I DO NOT BELIEVE THIS!
HRRAURH!
GRARHH!
YOU WEREN'T THE HANDSOMEST GUYS TO BEGIN WITH, BUT NOW--!
URRR!
SWOKT
WOKT
UH-OH! YOU DIDN'T JUST GET UGLIER, DID YOU?
NOPE.

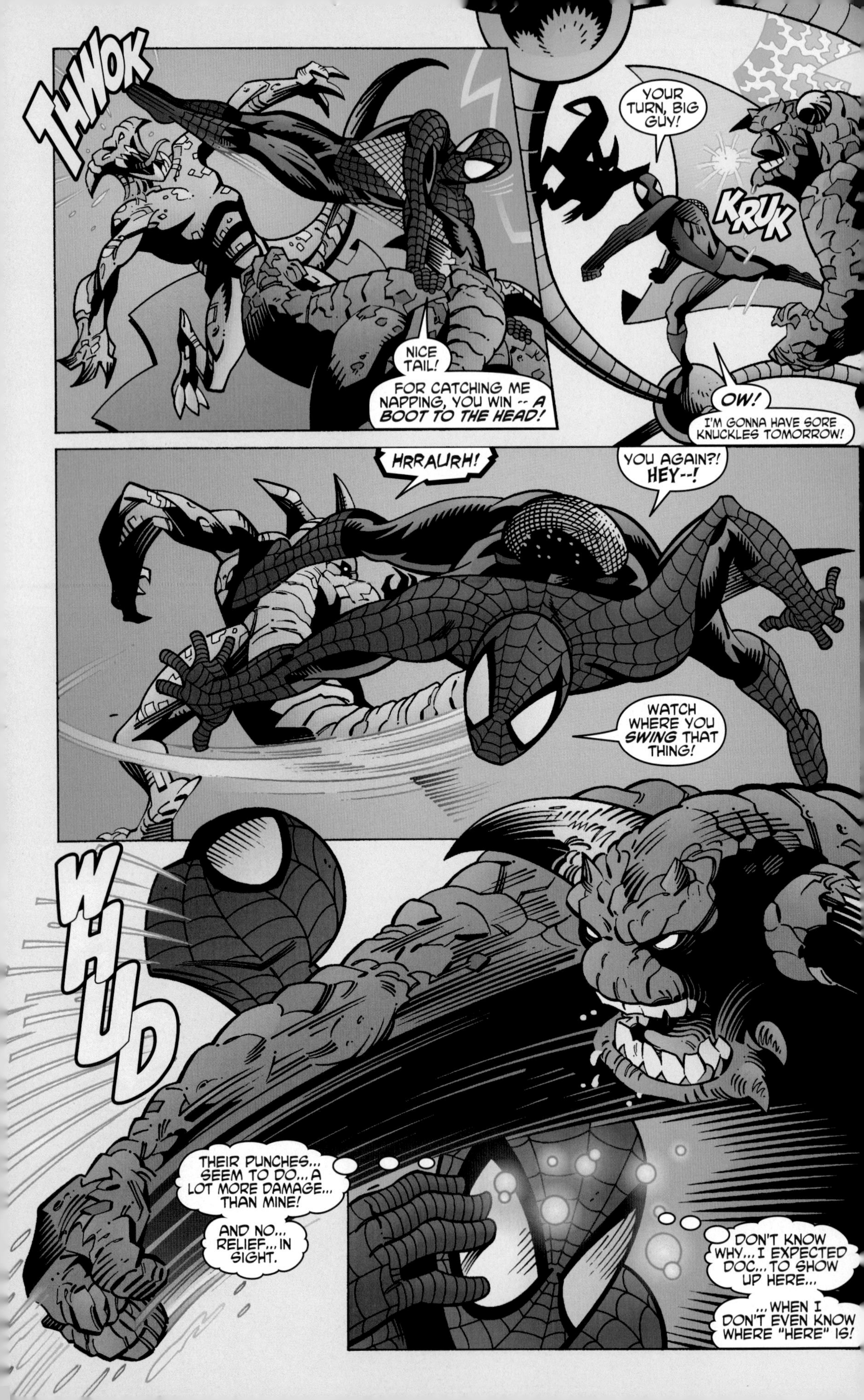
THWOK
NICE TAIL!
FOR CATCHING ME NAPPING, YOU WIN -- A BOOT TO THE HEAD!
YOUR TURN, BIG GUY!
KRUK
OW!
I'M GONNA HAVE SORE KNUCKLES TOMORROW!
HRRAURH!
YOU AGAIN?! HEY--!
WATCH WHERE YOU SWING THAT THING!
WHUD
THEIR PUNCHES... SEEM TO DO... A LOT MORE DAMAGE... THAN MINE!
AND NO... RELIEF... IN SIGHT.
DON'T KNOW WHY... I EXPECTED DOC... TO SHOW UP HERE...
...WHEN I DON'T EVEN KNOW WHERE "HERE" IS!

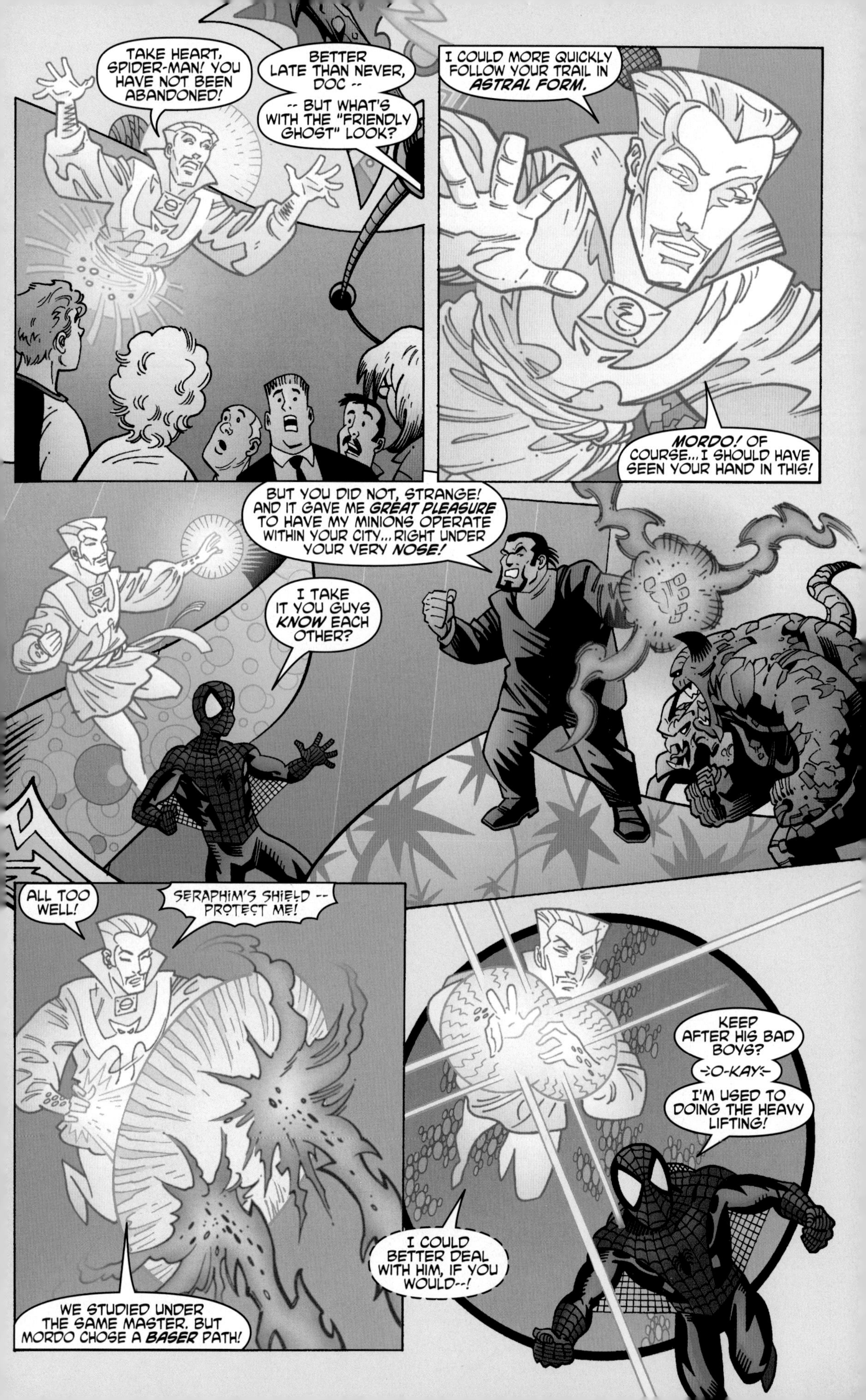
TAKE HEART, SPIDER-MAN! YOU HAVE NOT BEEN ABANDONED!
BETTER LATE THAN NEVER, DOC --
-- BUT WHAT'S WITH THE "FRIENDLY GHOST" LOOK?
I COULD MORE QUICKLY FOLLOW YOUR TRAIL IN ASTRAL FORM.
MORDO! OF COURSE... I SHOULD HAVE SEEN YOUR HAND IN THIS!
BUT YOU DID NOT, STRANGE! AND IT GAVE ME GREAT PLEASURE TO HAVE MY MINIONS OPERATE WITHIN YOUR CITY... RIGHT UNDER YOUR VERY NOSE!
I TAKE IT YOU GUYS KNOW EACH OTHER?
ALL TOO WELL!
SERAPHIM'S SHIELD -- PROTECT ME!
WE STUDIED UNDER THE SAME MASTER. BUT MORDO CHOSE A BASER PATH!
I COULD BETTER DEAL WITH HIM, IF YOU WOULD--!
KEEP AFTER HIS BAD BOYS?
O-KAY
I'M USED TO DOING THE HEAVY LIFTING!

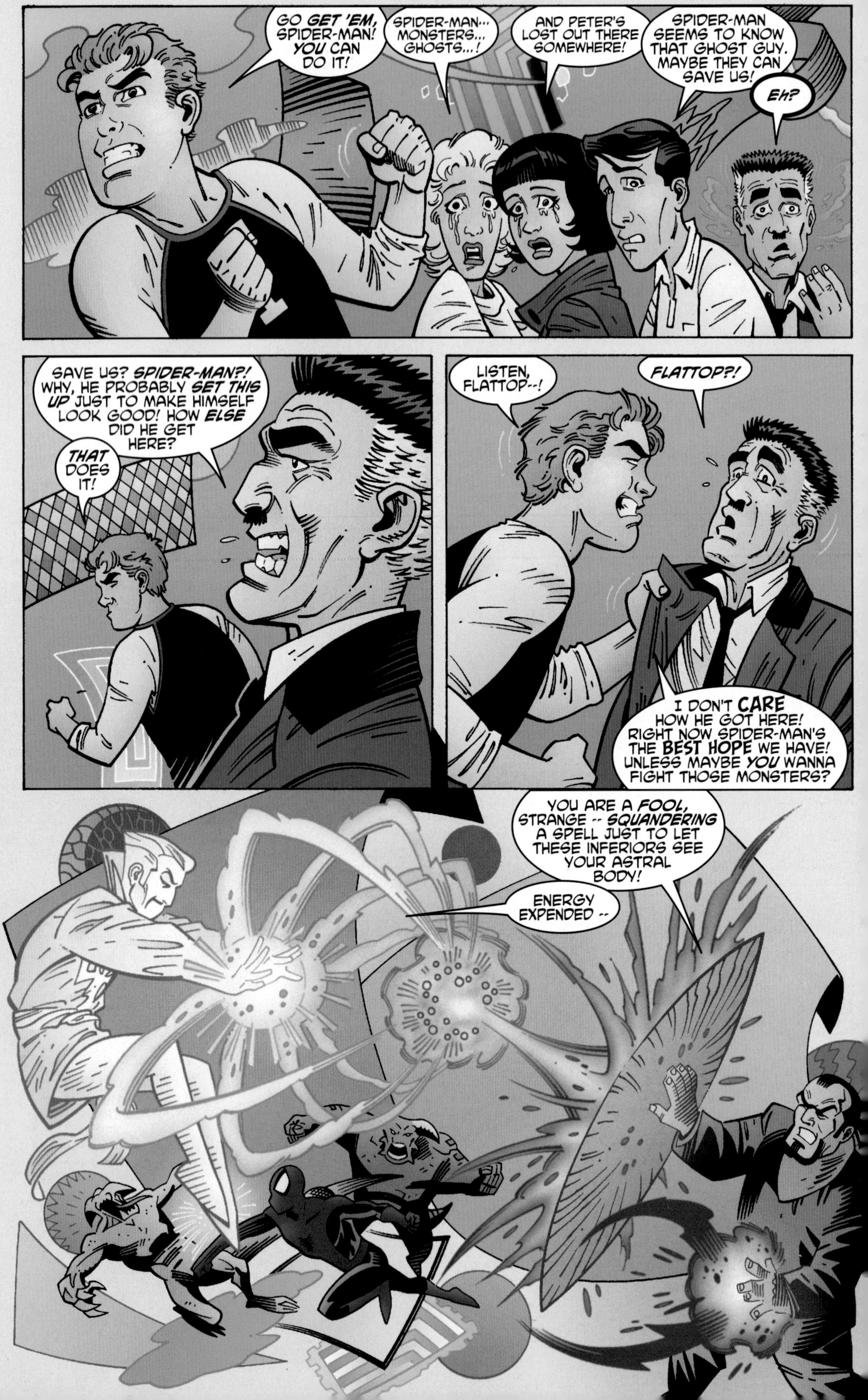

GO GET 'EM, SPIDER-MAN! YOU CAN DO IT!
SPIDER-MAN... MONSTERS... GHOSTS...!
AND PETER'S LOST OUT THERE SOMEWHERE!
SPIDER-MAN SEEMS TO KNOW THAT GHOST GUY. MAYBE THEY CAN SAVE US!
Eh?
SAVE US? SPIDER-MAN?! WHY, HE PROBABLY SET THIS UP JUST TO MAKE HIMSELF LOOK GOOD! HOW ELSE DID HE GET HERE?
THAT DOES IT!
LISTEN, FLATTOP--!
FLATTOP?!
I DON'T CARE HOW HE GOT HERE! RIGHT NOW SPIDER-MAN'S THE BEST HOPE WE HAVE! UNLESS MAYBE YOU WANNA FIGHT THOSE MONSTERS?
YOU ARE A FOOL, STRANGE -- SQUANDERING A SPELL JUST TO LET THESE INFERIORS SEE YOUR ASTRAL BODY!
ENERGY EXPENDED --

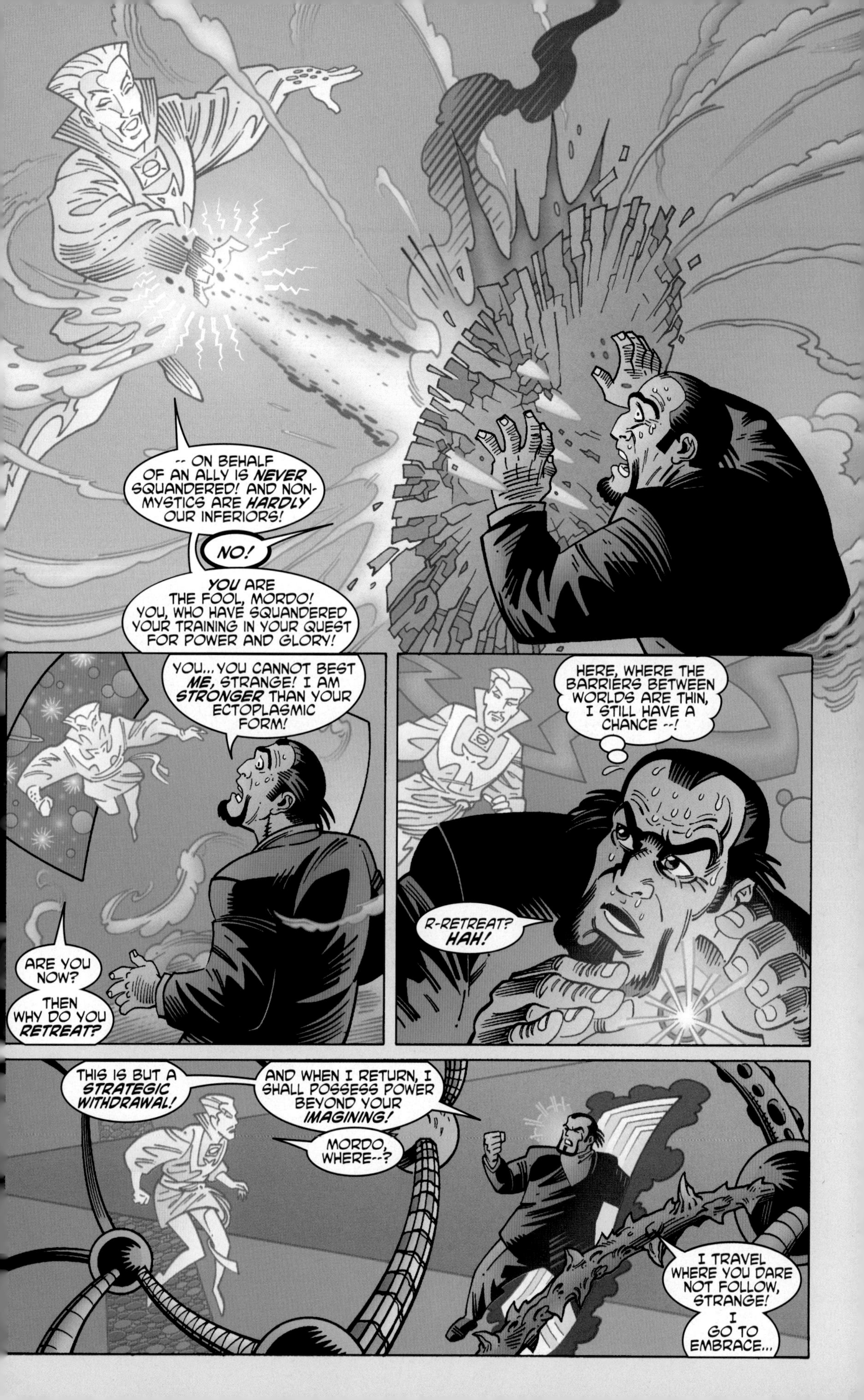
-- ON BEHALF OF AN ALLY IS NEVER SQUANDERED! AND NON-MYSTICS ARE HARDLY OUR INFERIORS!
NO!
YOU ARE THE FOOL, MORDO! YOU, WHO HAVE SQUANDERED YOUR TRAINING IN YOUR QUEST FOR POWER AND GLORY!
YOU... YOU CANNOT BEST ME, STRANGE! I AM STRONGER THAN YOUR ECTOPLASMIC FORM!
ARE YOU NOW?
THEN WHY DO YOU RETREAT?
HERE, WHERE THE BARRIERS BETWEEN WORLDS ARE THIN, I STILL HAVE A CHANCE --!
R-RETREAT? HAH!
THIS IS BUT A STRATEGIC WITHDRAWAL!
AND WHEN I RETURN, I SHALL POSSESS POWER BEYOND YOUR IMAGINING!
MORDO, WHERE--?
I TRAVEL WHERE YOU DARE NOT FOLLOW, STRANGE!
I GO TO EMBRACE...

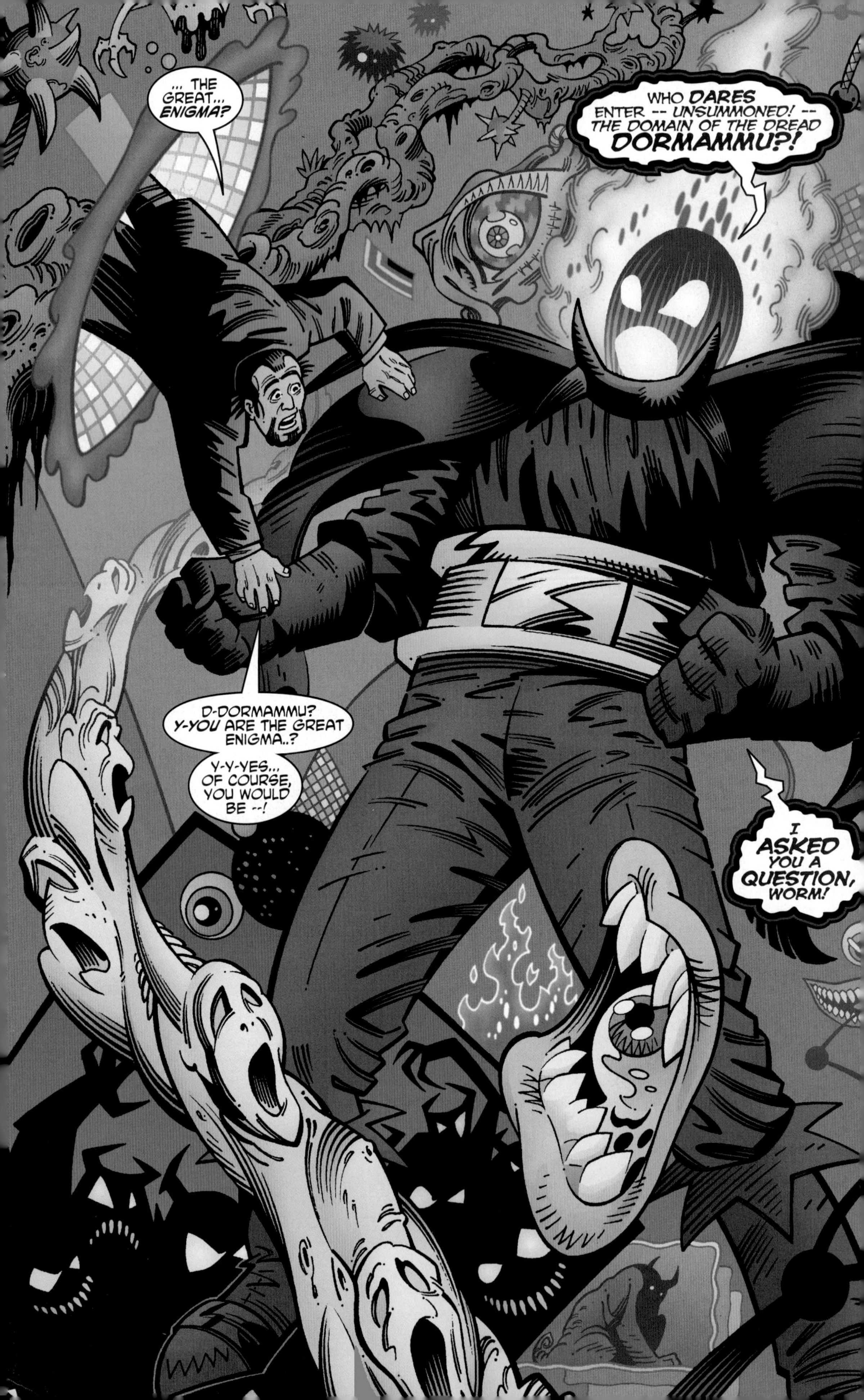
... THE GREAT... ENIGMA?
WHO DARES ENTER -- UNSUMMONED! -- THE DOMAIN OF THE DREAD DORMAMMU?!
D-DORMAMMU? Y-YOU ARE THE GREAT ENIGMA..?
Y-Y-YES... OF COURSE, YOU WOULD BE --!
I ASKED YOU A QUESTION, WORM!

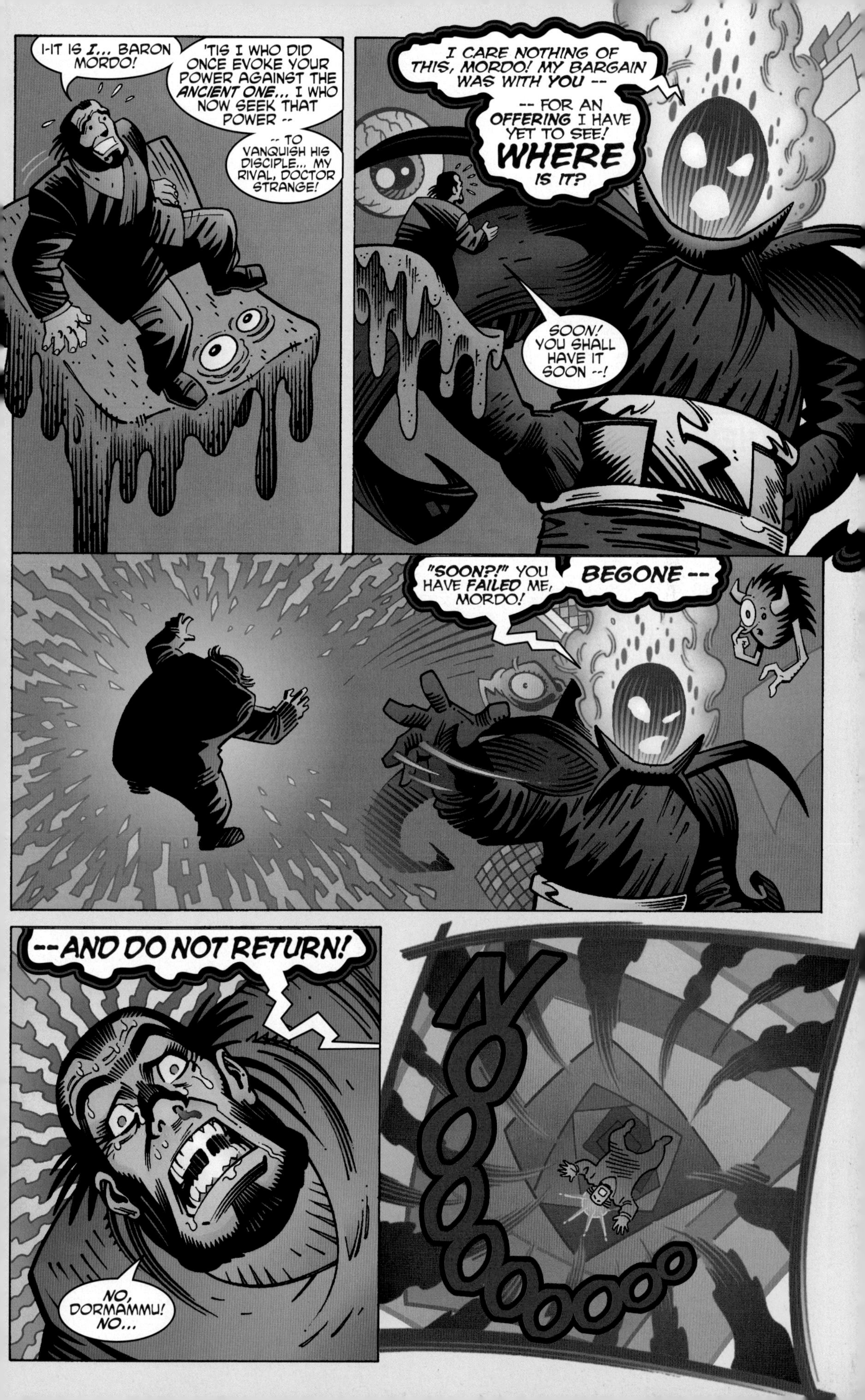
I-IT IS I... BARON MORDO!
'TIS I WHO DID ONCE EVOKE YOUR POWER AGAINST THE ANCIENT ONE... I WHO NOW SEEK THAT POWER --
-- TO VANQUISH HIS DISCIPLE... MY RIVAL, DOCTOR STRANGE!
I CARE NOTHING OF THIS, MORDO! MY BARGAIN WAS WITH YOU --
-- FOR AN OFFERING I HAVE YET TO SEE! WHERE IS IT?
SOON! YOU SHALL HAVE IT SOON --!
"SOON?!" YOU HAVE FAILED ME, MORDO!
BEGONE --
--AND DO NOT RETURN!
NO, DORMAMMU! NO...
NOOOOOOOOOOOO

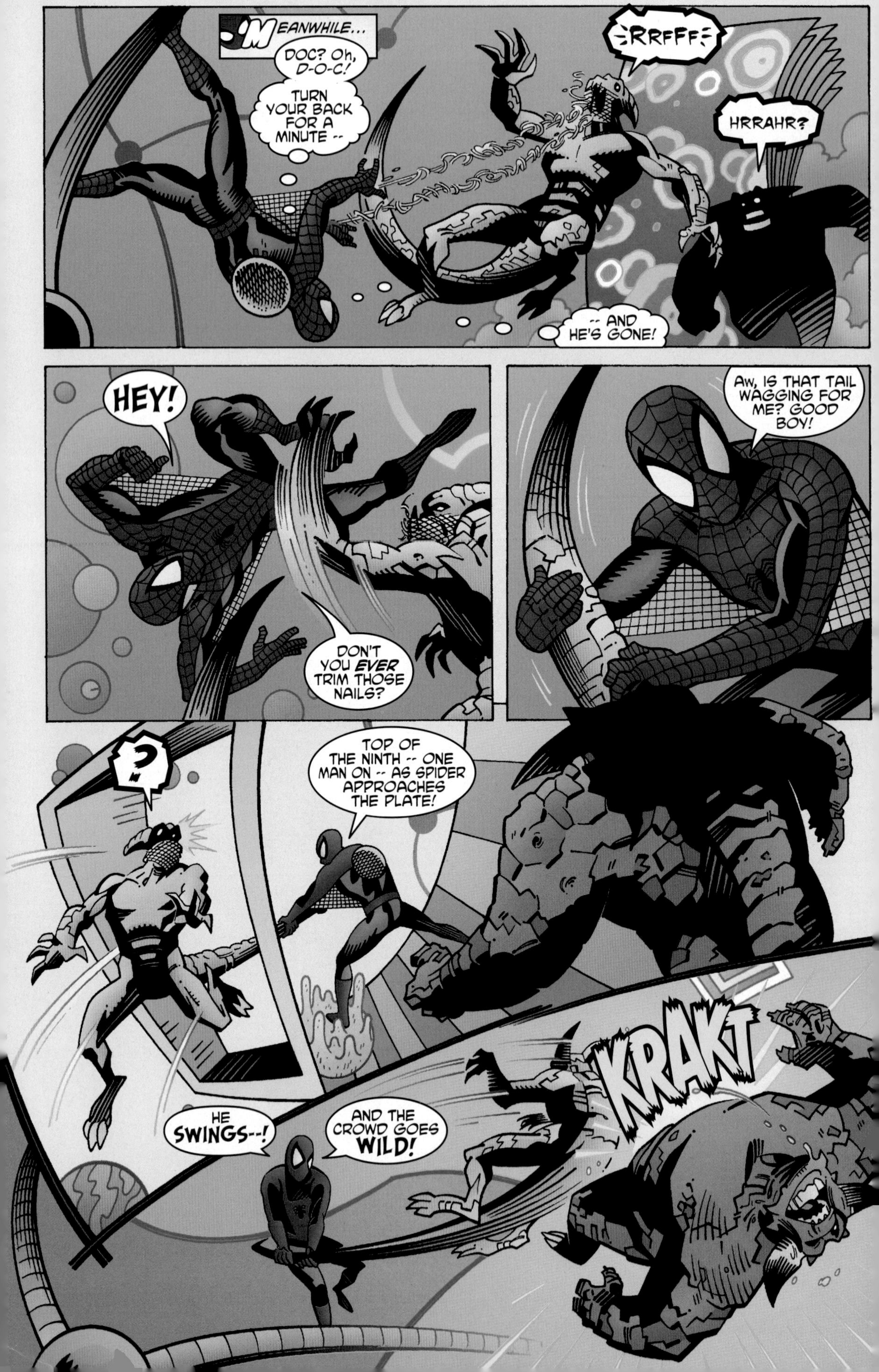

MEANWHILE...
DOC? OH, D-O-C!
TURN YOUR BACK FOR A MINUTE --
RRFFF
HRRAHR?
-- AND HE'S GONE!
HEY!
DON'T YOU EVER TRIM THOSE NAILS?
AW, IS THAT TAIL WAGGING FOR ME? GOOD BOY!
?
TOP OF THE NINTH -- ONE MAN ON -- AS SPIDER APPROACHES THE PLATE!
HE SWINGS--!
AND THE CROWD GOES WILD!
KRAKT

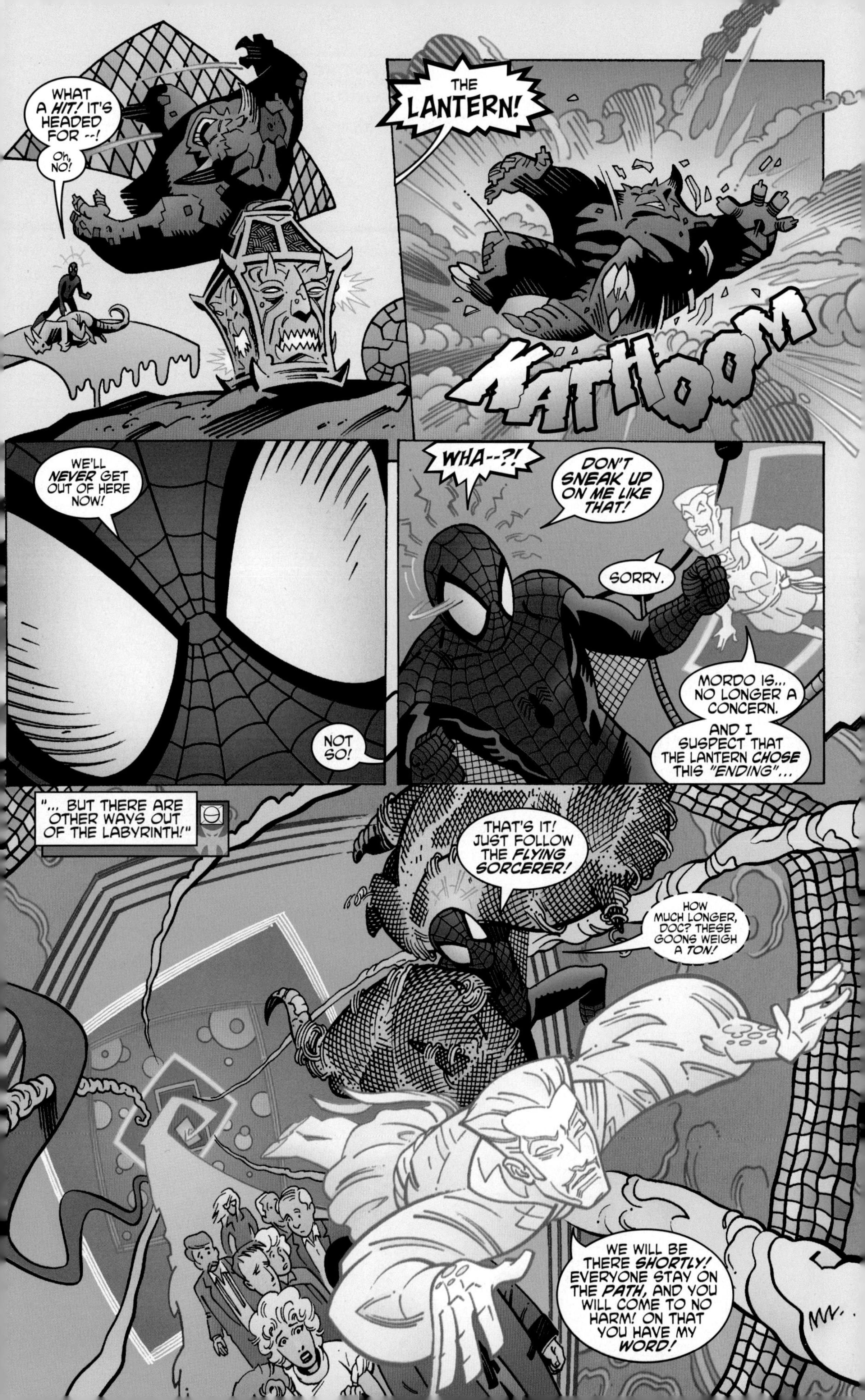

WHAT A HIT! IT'S HEADED FOR --!
Oh, NO!
THE LANTERN!
KATHOOM
WE'LL NEVER GET OUT OF HERE NOW!
NOT SO!
WHA--?!
DON'T SNEAK UP ON ME LIKE THAT!
SORRY.
MORDO IS... NO LONGER A CONCERN.
AND I SUSPECT THAT THE LANTERN CHOSE THIS "ENDING"...
"... BUT THERE ARE OTHER WAYS OUT OF THE LABYRINTH!"
THAT'S IT! JUST FOLLOW THE FLYING SORCERER!
HOW MUCH LONGER, DOC? THESE GOONS WEIGH A TON!
WE WILL BE THERE SHORTLY! EVERYONE STAY ON THE PATH, AND YOU WILL COME TO NO HARM! ON THAT YOU HAVE MY WORD!

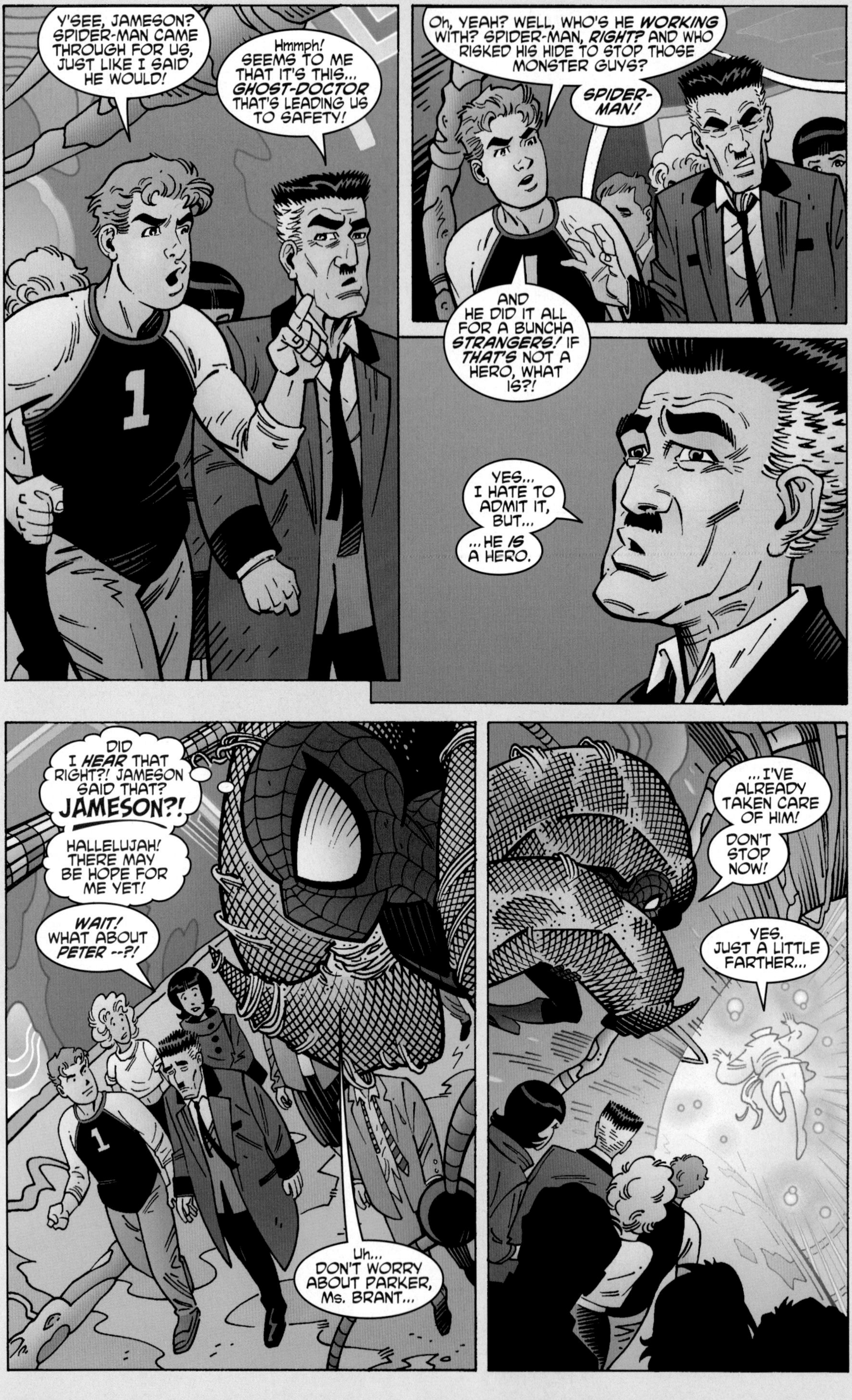

Y'SEE, JAMESON? SPIDER-MAN CAME THROUGH FOR US, JUST LIKE I SAID HE WOULD!
Hmmph! SEEMS TO ME THAT IT'S THIS... GHOST-DOCTOR THAT'S LEADING US TO SAFETY!
Oh, YEAH? WELL, WHO'S HE WORKING WITH? SPIDER-MAN, RIGHT? AND WHO RISKED HIS HIDE TO STOP THOSE MONSTER GUYS?
SPIDER-MAN!
AND HE DID IT ALL FOR A BUNCHA STRANGERS! IF THAT'S NOT A HERO, WHAT IS?!
YES... I HATE TO ADMIT IT, BUT...
...HE IS A HERO.
DID I HEAR THAT RIGHT?! JAMESON SAID THAT? JAMESON?!
HALLELUJAH! THERE MAY BE HOPE FOR ME YET!
WAIT! WHAT ABOUT PETER --?!
Uh... DON'T WORRY ABOUT PARKER, Ms. BRANT...
...I'VE ALREADY TAKEN CARE OF HIM!
DON'T STOP NOW!
YES. JUST A LITTLE FARTHER...

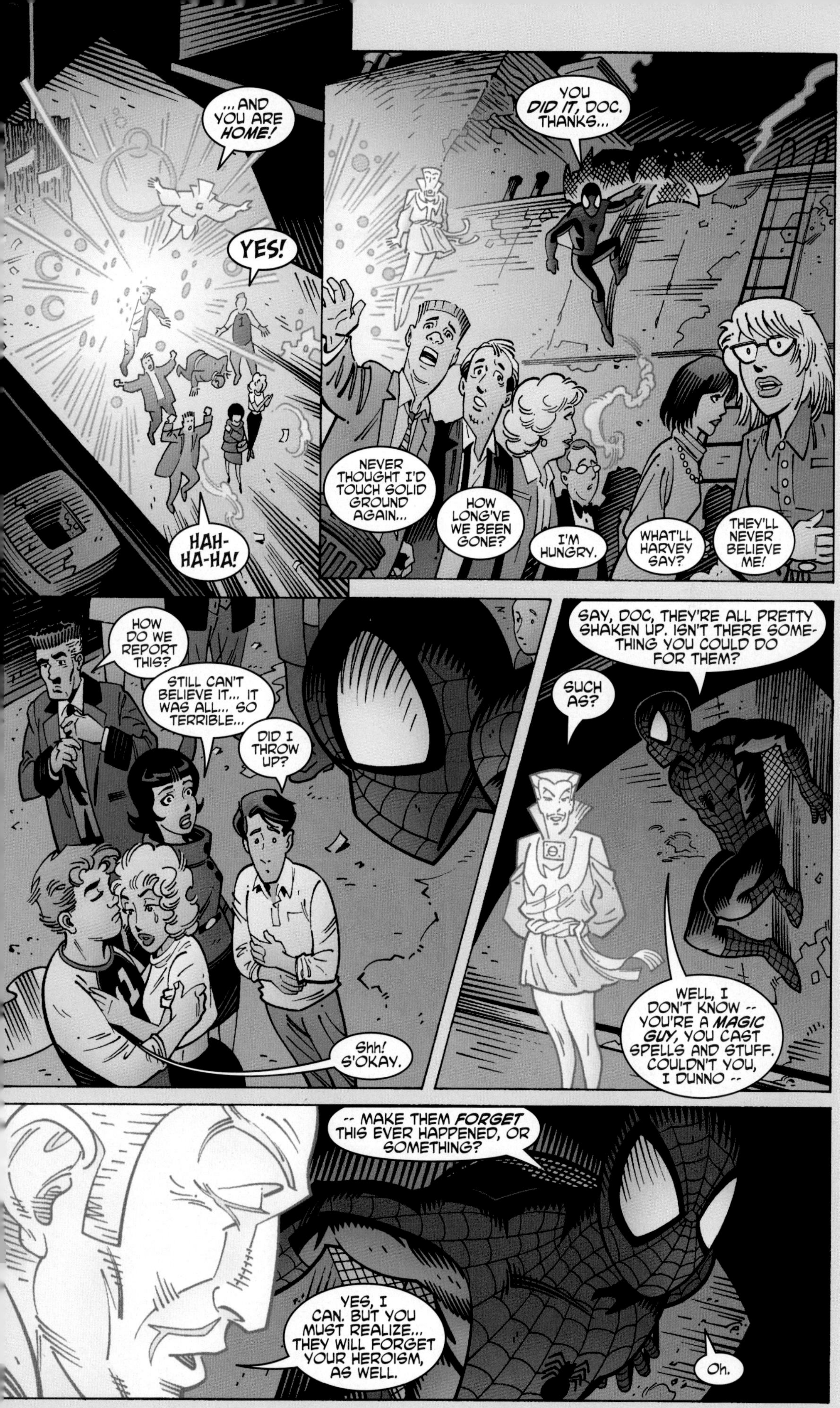
...AND YOU ARE *HOME!*
YES!
HAH-HA-HA!
YOU *DID IT*, DOC. THANKS...
NEVER THOUGHT I'D TOUCH SOLID GROUND AGAIN...
HOW LONG'VE WE BEEN GONE?
I'M HUNGRY.
WHAT'LL HARVEY SAY?
THEY'LL NEVER BELIEVE ME!
HOW DO WE REPORT THIS?
STILL CAN'T BELIEVE IT... IT WAS ALL... SO TERRIBLE...
DID I THROW UP?
Shh! S'OKAY.
SAY, DOC, THEY'RE ALL PRETTY SHAKEN UP. ISN'T THERE SOME-THING YOU COULD DO FOR THEM?
SUCH AS?
WELL, I DON'T KNOW -- YOU'RE A *MAGIC GUY*, YOU CAST SPELLS AND STUFF. COULDN'T YOU, I DUNNO --
-- MAKE THEM *FORGET* THIS EVER HAPPENED, OR SOMETHING?
YES, I CAN. BUT YOU MUST REALIZE... THEY WILL FORGET YOUR HEROISM, AS WELL.
Oh.

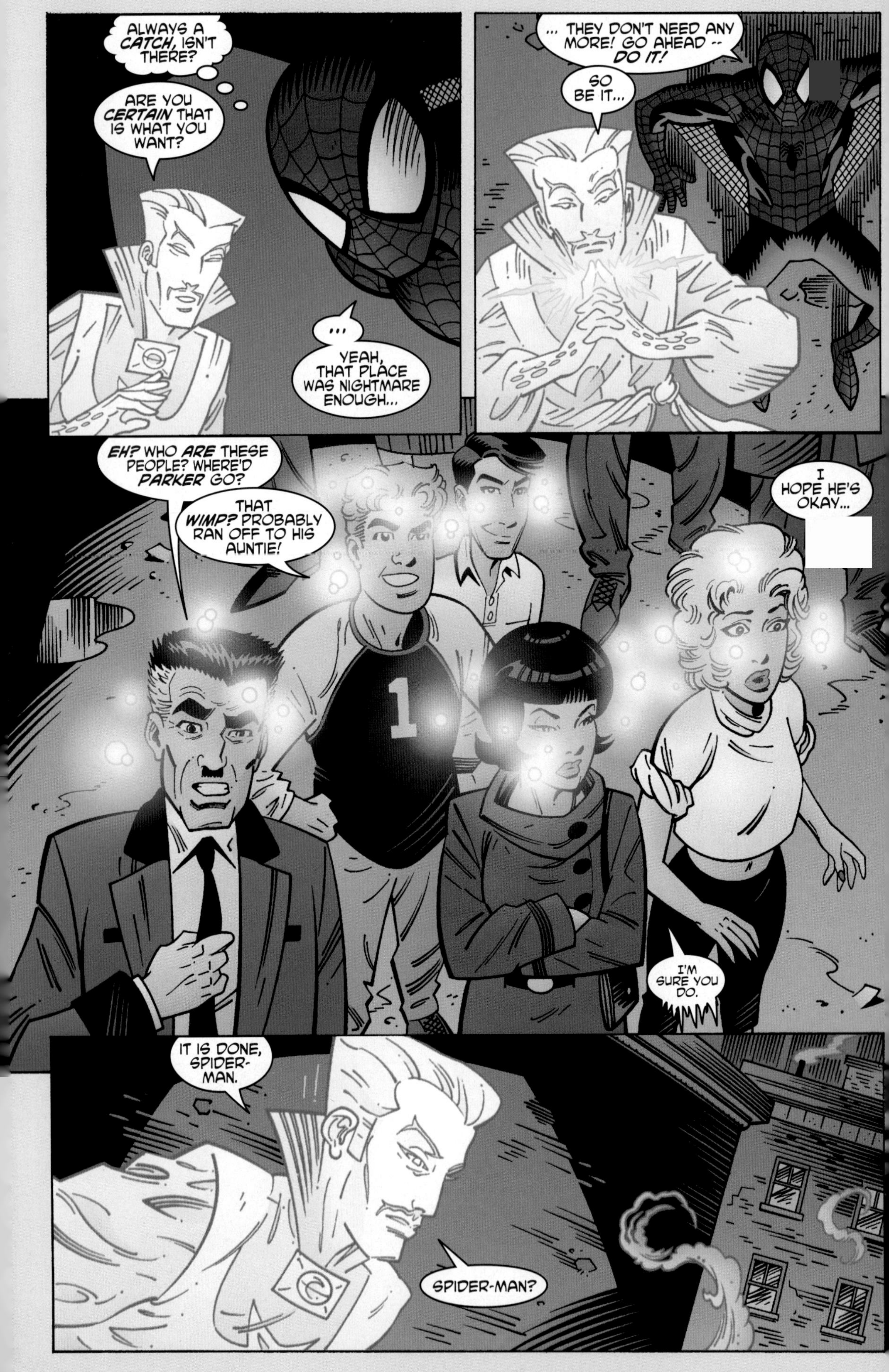
ALWAYS A CATCH, ISN'T THERE?
ARE YOU CERTAIN THAT IS WHAT YOU WANT?
...
YEAH, THAT PLACE WAS NIGHTMARE ENOUGH...
... THEY DON'T NEED ANY MORE! GO AHEAD -- DO IT!
SO BE IT...
EH? WHO ARE THESE PEOPLE? WHERE'D PARKER GO?
THAT WIMP? PROBABLY RAN OFF TO HIS AUNTIE!
I HOPE HE'S OKAY...
I'M SURE YOU DO.
IT IS DONE, SPIDER-MAN.
SPIDER-MAN?

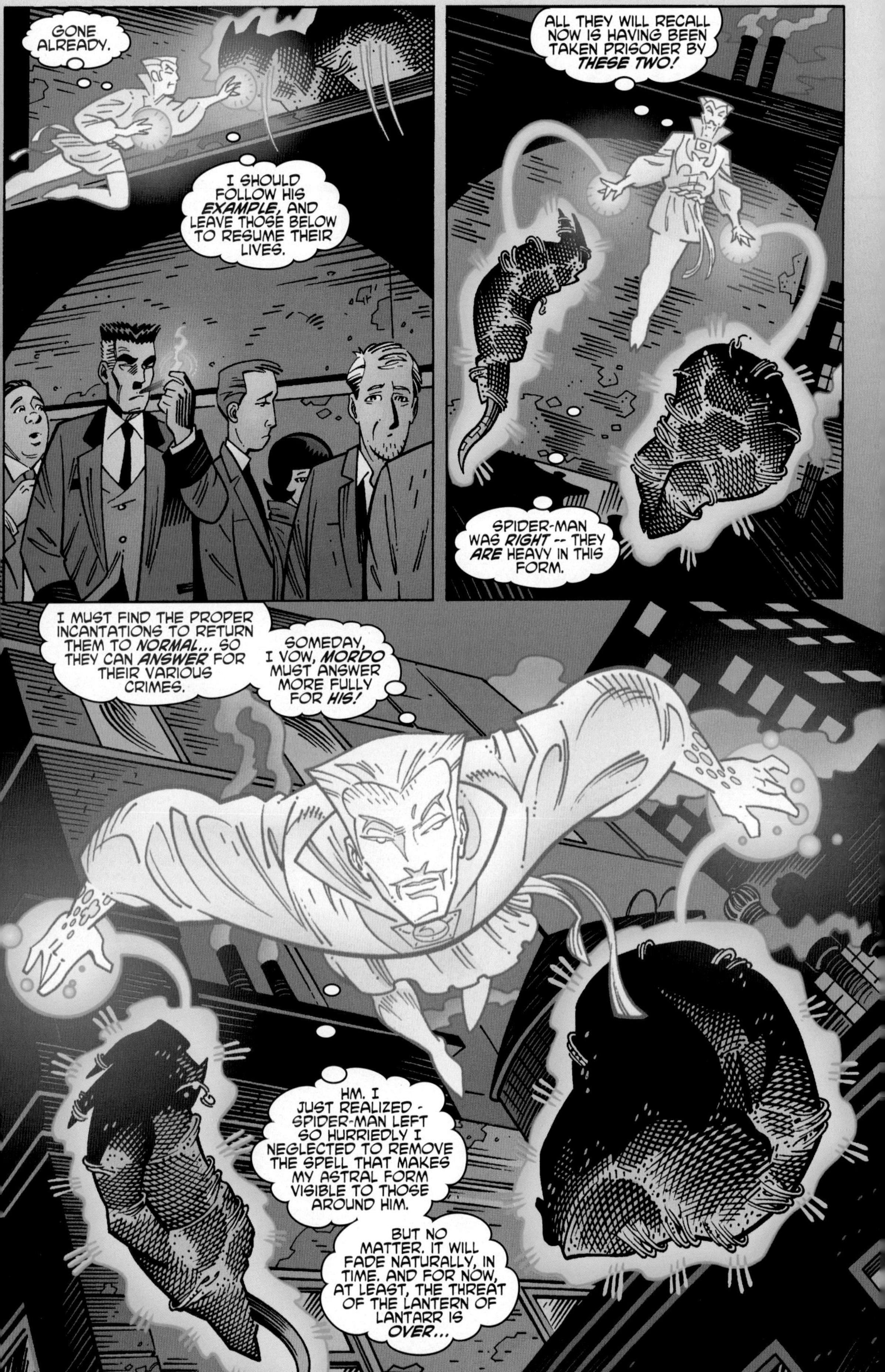
GONE ALREADY.
I SHOULD FOLLOW HIS EXAMPLE, AND LEAVE THOSE BELOW TO RESUME THEIR LIVES.
ALL THEY WILL RECALL NOW IS HAVING BEEN TAKEN PRISONER BY THESE TWO!
SPIDER-MAN WAS RIGHT -- THEY ARE HEAVY IN THIS FORM.
I MUST FIND THE PROPER INCANTATIONS TO RETURN THEM TO NORMAL... SO THEY CAN ANSWER FOR THEIR VARIOUS CRIMES.
SOMEDAY, I VOW, MORDO MUST ANSWER MORE FULLY FOR HIS!
HM. I JUST REALIZED - SPIDER-MAN LEFT SO HURRIEDLY I NEGLECTED TO REMOVE THE SPELL THAT MAKES MY ASTRAL FORM VISIBLE TO THOSE AROUND HIM.
BUT NO MATTER. IT WILL FADE NATURALLY, IN TIME. AND FOR NOW, AT LEAST, THE THREAT OF THE LANTERN OF LANTARR IS OVER...

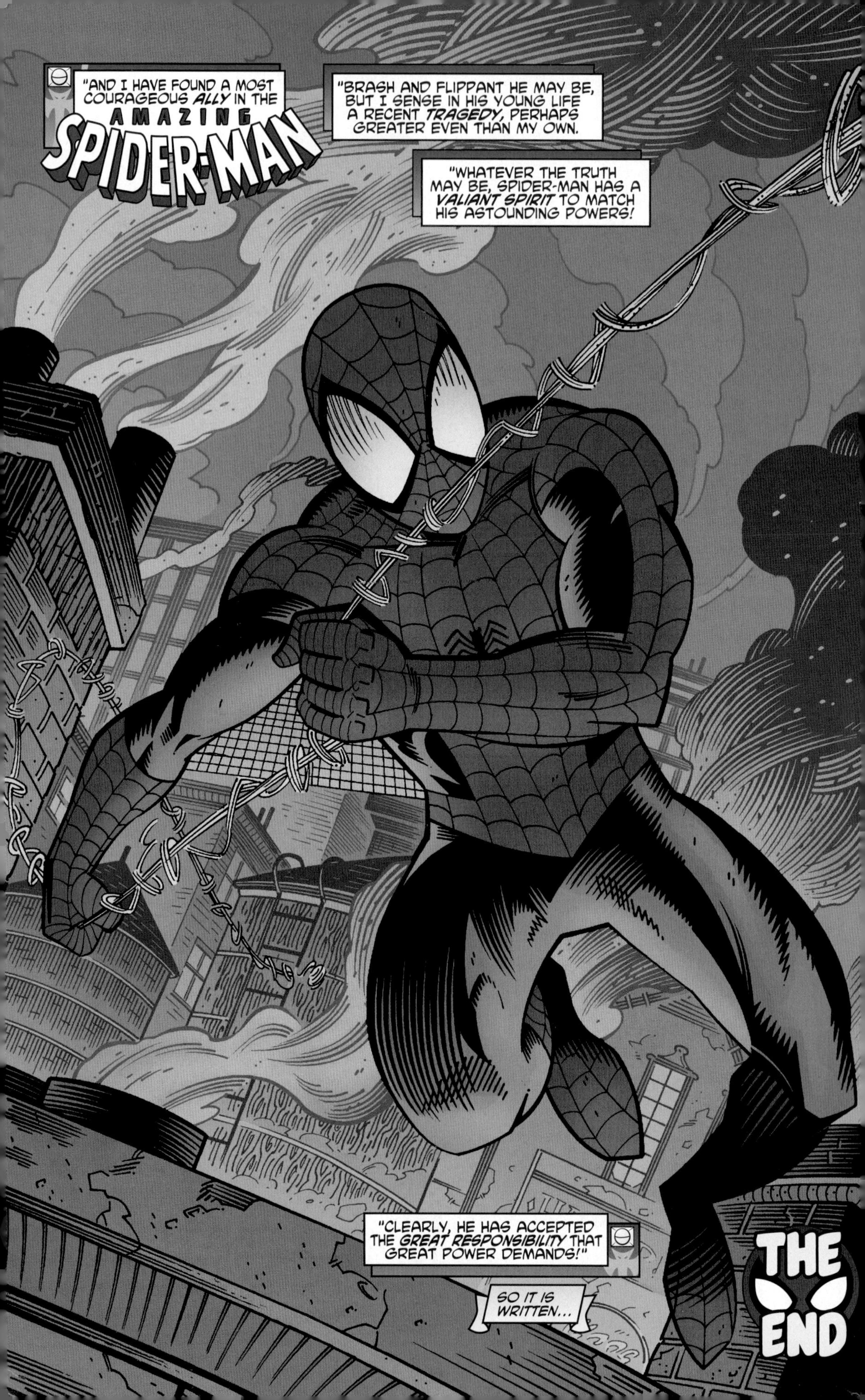
"AND I HAVE FOUND A MOST COURAGEOUS ALLY IN THE
AMAZING SPIDER-MAN
"BRASH AND FLIPPANT HE MAY BE, BUT I SENSE IN HIS YOUNG LIFE A RECENT TRAGEDY, PERHAPS GREATER EVEN THAN MY OWN.
"WHATEVER THE TRUTH MAY BE, SPIDER-MAN HAS A VALIANT SPIRIT TO MATCH HIS ASTOUNDING POWERS!
"CLEARLY, HE HAS ACCEPTED THE GREAT RESPONSIBILITY THAT GREAT POWER DEMANDS!"
SO IT IS WRITTEN...
THE END

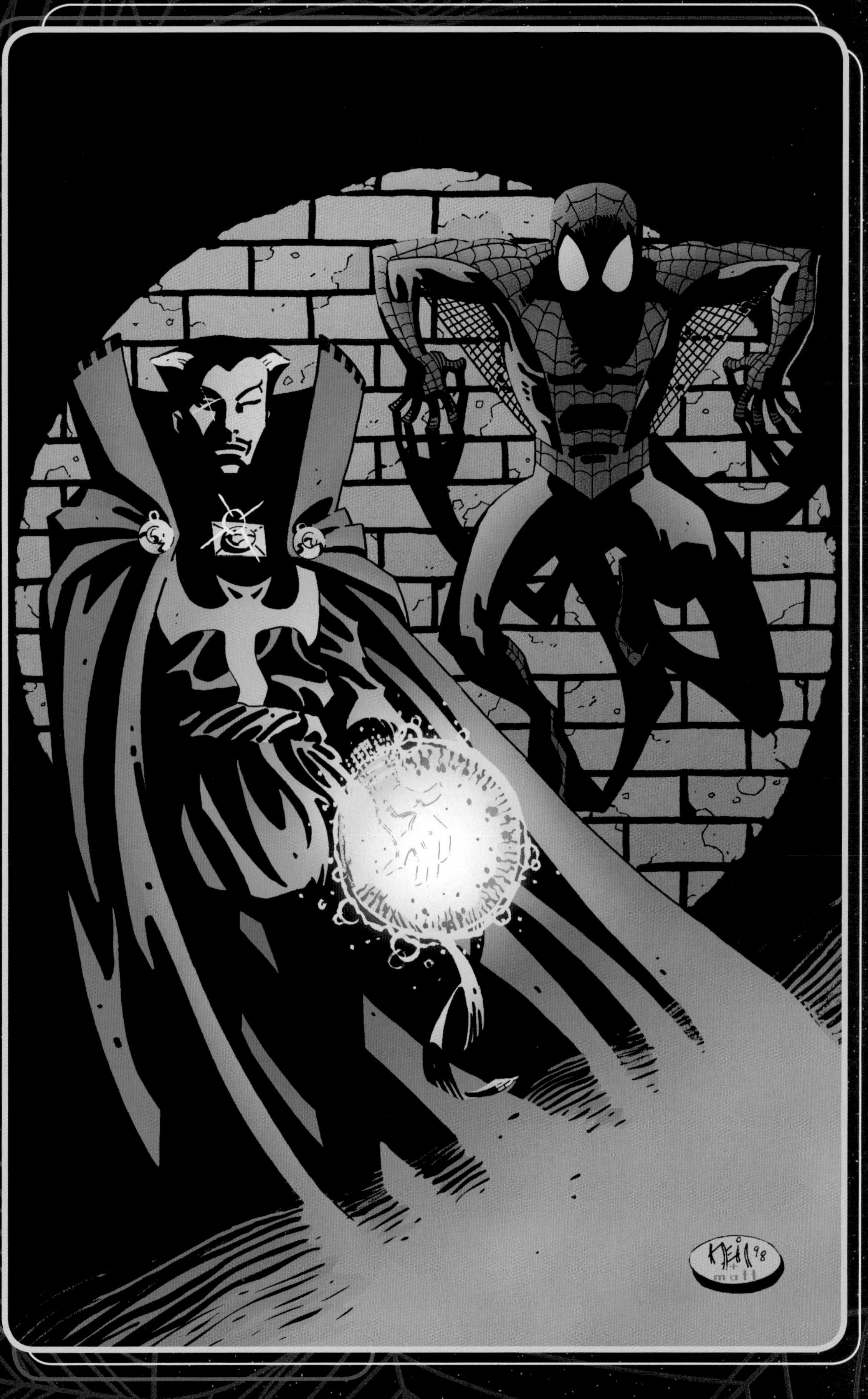

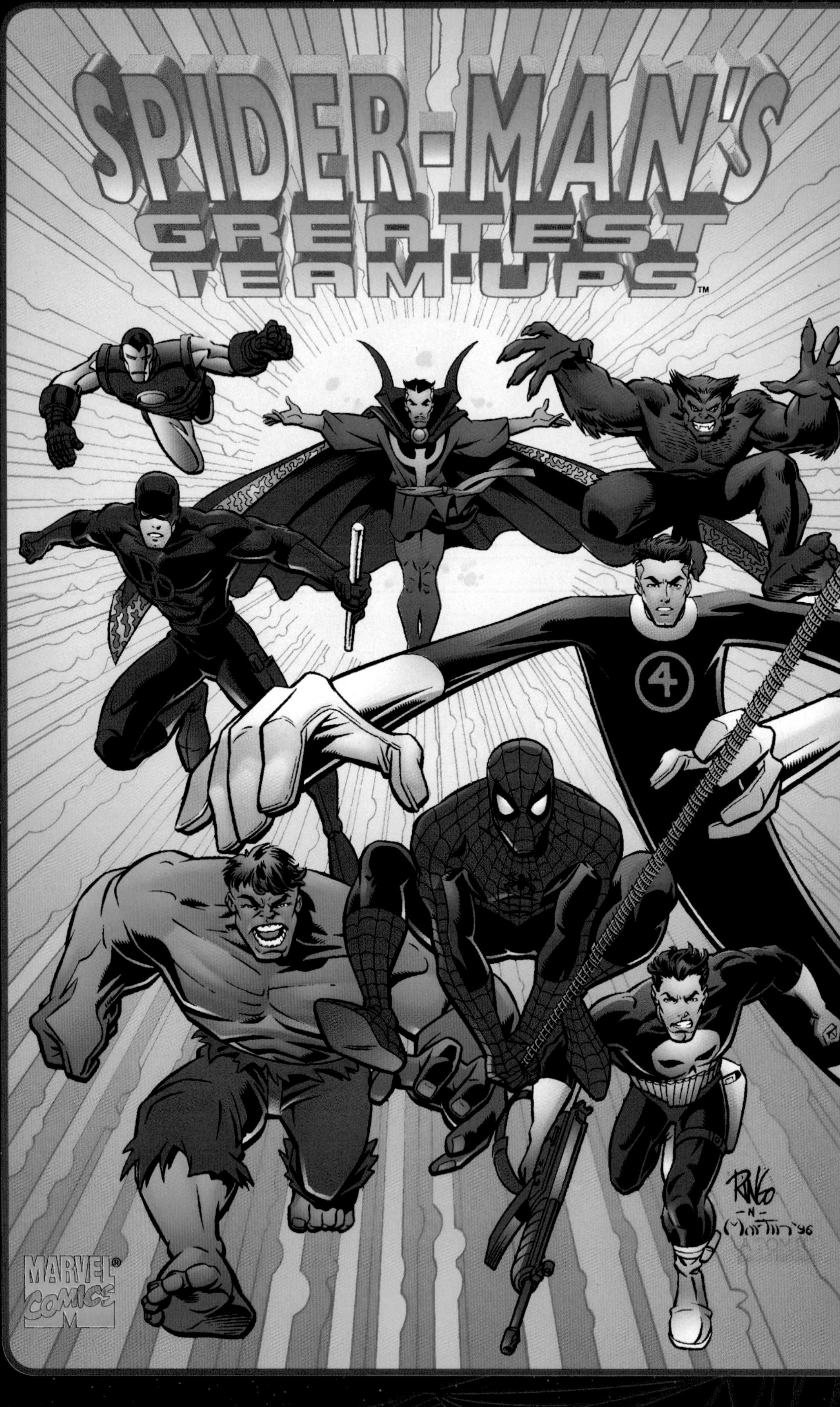
SPIDER-MAN'S
GREATEST
TEAM-UPS™
MARVEL® COMICS

SPIDER-MAN'S GREATEST TEAM-UPS TPB (1996) INCLUDED AMAZING SPIDER-MAN ANNUAL #2.
COVER ART BY MIKE WIERINGO, GARY MARTIN & ATOMIC PAINTBRUSH.

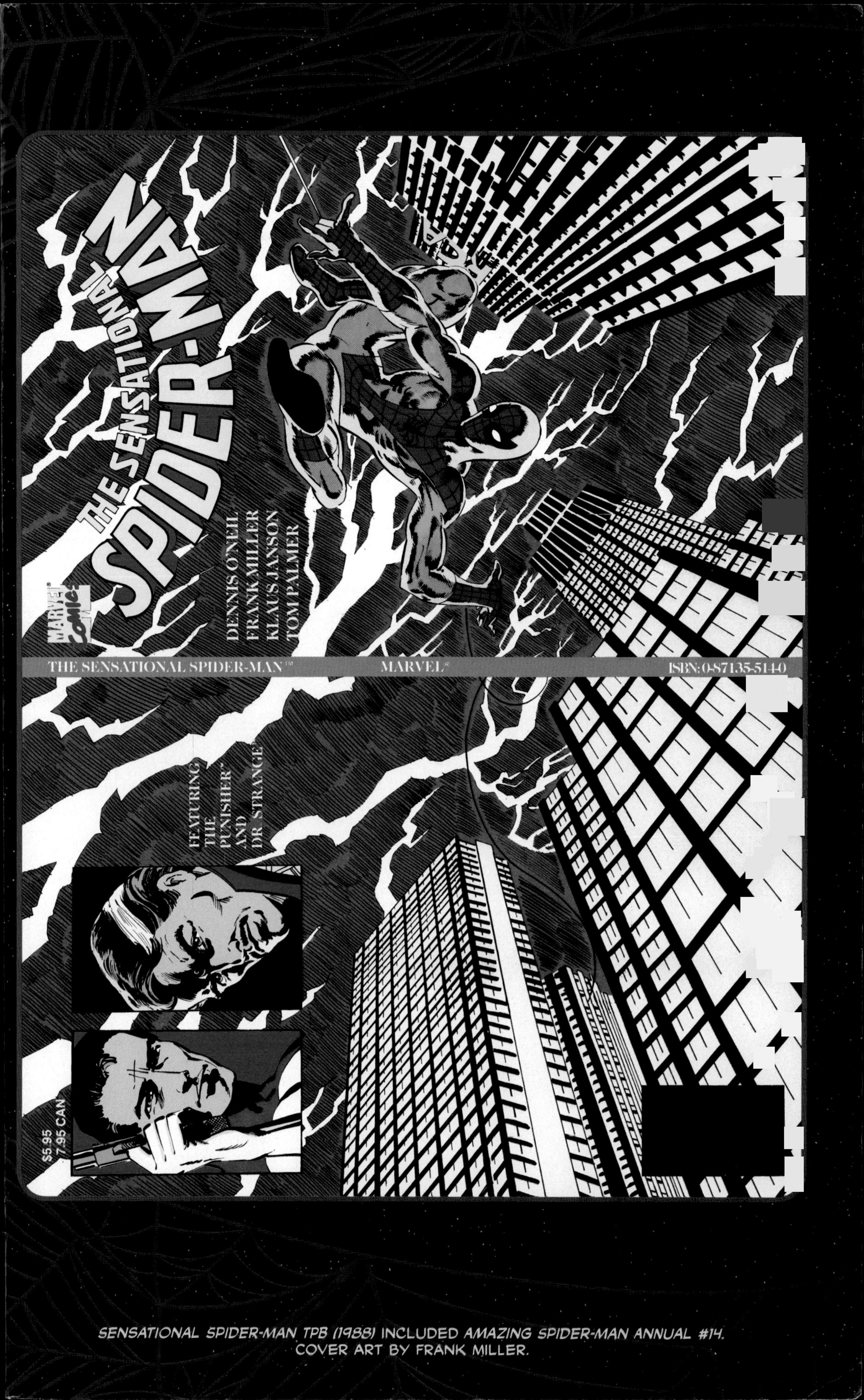
MARVEL COMICS
THE SENSATIONAL SPIDER-MAN
DENNIS O'NEIL
FRANK MILLER
KLAUS JANSON
TOM PALMER
THE SENSATIONAL SPIDER-MAN™
MARVEL®
ISBN: 0-87135-514-0
FEATURING
THE
PUNISHER®
AND
DR. STRANGE®
$5.95
7.95 CAN

SENSATIONAL SPIDER-MAN TPB (1988) INCLUDED *AMAZING SPIDER-MAN ANNUAL* #14.
COVER ART BY FRANK MILLER.

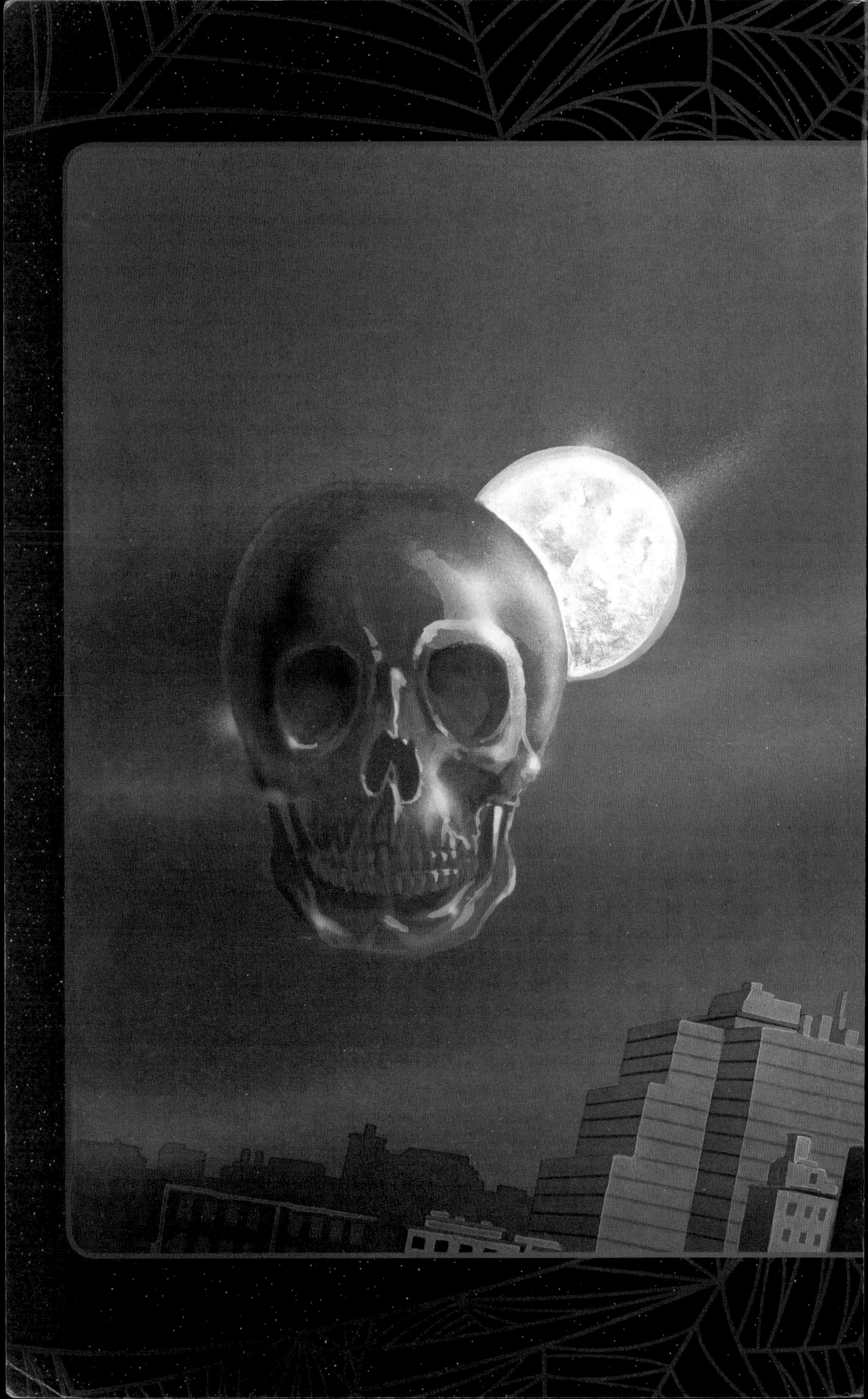

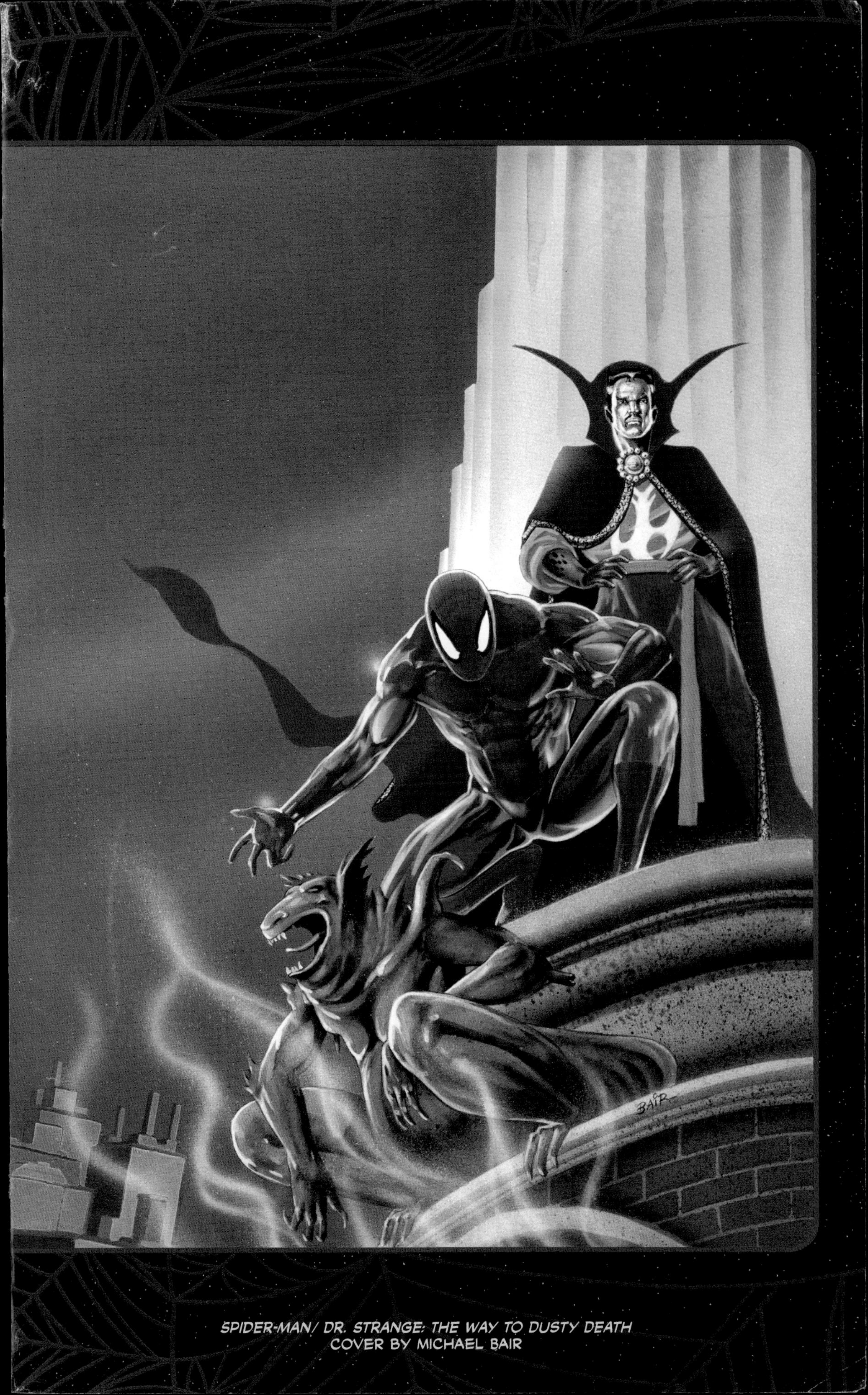
BAIR

SPIDER-MAN/ DR. STRANGE: THE WAY TO DUSTY DEATH
COVER BY MICHAEL BAIR

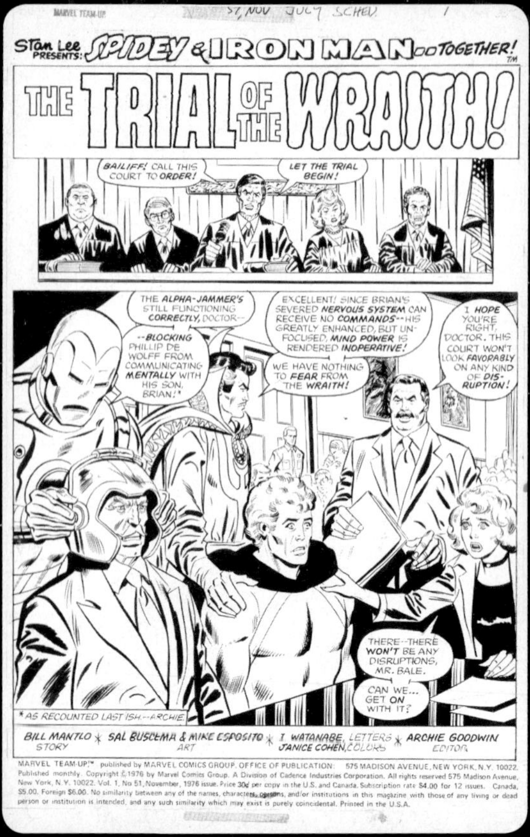

Stan Lee PRESENTS: SPIDEY & IRON MAN ..TOGETHER!
THE TRIAL OF THE WRAITH!
BAILIFF! CALL THIS COURT TO ORDER!
LET THE TRIAL BEGIN!
THE ALPHA-JAMMER'S STILL FUNCTIONING CORRECTLY, DOCTOR--
--BLOCKING PHILLIP DE WOLFF FROM COMMUNICATING MENTALLY WITH HIS SON, BRIAN!
EXCELLENT! SINCE BRIAN'S SEVERED NERVOUS SYSTEM CAN RECEIVE NO COMMANDS--HIS GREATLY ENHANCED, BUT UNFOCUSED, MIND POWER IS RENDERED INOPERATIVE!
WE HAVE NOTHING TO FEAR FROM THE WRAITH!
I HOPE YOU'RE RIGHT, DOCTOR. THIS COURT WON'T LOOK FAVORABLY ON ANY KIND OF DISRUPTION!
THERE--THERE WON'T BE ANY DISRUPTIONS, MR. BALE.
CAN WE... GET ON WITH IT?
*AS RECOUNTED LAST ISH.--ARCHIE
BILL MANTLO STORY * SAL BUSCEMA & MIKE ESPOSITO ART * I. WATANABE, LETTERS JANICE COHEN, COLORS * ARCHIE GOODWIN EDITOR
MARVEL TEAM-UP™ published by MARVEL COMICS GROUP. OFFICE OF PUBLICATION: 575 MADISON AVENUE, NEW YORK, N.Y. 10022. Published monthly. Copyright © 1976 by Marvel Comics Group. A Division of Cadence Industries Corporation. All rights reserved 575 Madison Avenue, New York, N.Y. 10022. Vol. 1, No 51, November, 1976 issue. Price 30¢ per copy in the U.S. and Canada. Subscription rate $4.00 for 12 issues. Canada, $5.00. Foreign $6.00. No similarity between any of the names, characters, persons, and/or institutions in this magazine with those of any living or dead person or institution is intended, and any such similarity which may exist is purely coincidental. Printed in the U.S.A.

MARVEL TEAM-UP #51, PAGE 1 ART BY SAL BUSCEMA & MIKE ESPOSITO

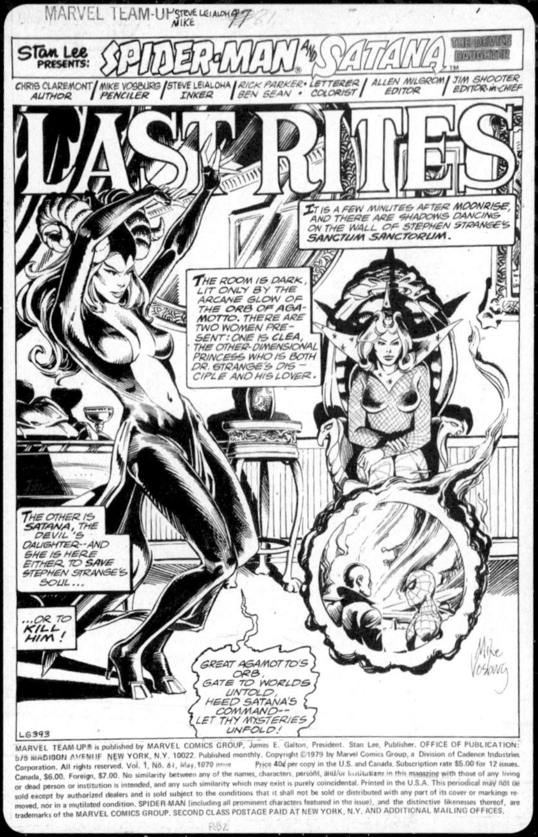

MARVEL TEAM-UP
Stan Lee PRESENTS: SPIDER-MAN AND SATANA THE DEVIL'S DAUGHTER
CHRIS CLAREMONT AUTHOR | MIKE VOSBURG PENCILER | STEVE LEIALOHA INKER | RICK PARKER • LETTERER BEN SEAN • COLORIST | ALLEN MILGROM EDITOR | JIM SHOOTER EDITOR-IN-CHIEF
LAST RITES
IT IS A FEW MINUTES AFTER MOONRISE, AND THERE ARE SHADOWS DANCING ON THE WALL OF STEPHEN STRANGE'S SANCTUM SANCTORUM.
THE ROOM IS DARK, LIT ONLY BY THE ARCANE GLOW OF THE ORB OF AGAMOTTO. THERE ARE TWO WOMEN PRESENT: ONE IS CLEA, THE OTHER-DIMENSIONAL PRINCESS WHO IS BOTH DR. STRANGE'S DISCIPLE AND HIS LOVER.
THE OTHER IS SATANA, THE DEVIL'S DAUGHTER--AND SHE IS HERE EITHER TO SAVE STEPHEN STRANGE'S SOUL...
...OR TO KILL HIM!
GREAT AGAMOTTO'S ORB, GATE TO WORLDS UNTOLD, HEED SATANA'S COMMAND--LET THY MYSTERIES UNFOLD!
Mike Vosburg
L6393
MARVEL TEAM-UP® is published by MARVEL COMICS GROUP, James E. Galton, President. Stan Lee, Publisher. OFFICE OF PUBLICATION: 575 MADISON AVENUE NEW YORK, N.Y. 10022. Published monthly. Copyright ©1979 by Marvel Comics Group, a Division of Cadence Industries Corporation. All rights reserved. Vol. 1, No. 81, May, 1979 issue. Price 40¢ per copy in the U.S. and Canada. Subscription rate $5.00 for 12 issues. Canada, $6.00. Foreign, $7.00. No similarity between any of the names, characters, persons, and/or institutions in this magazine with those of any living or dead person or institution is intended, and any such similarity which may exist is purely coincidental. Printed in the U.S.A. This periodical may not be sold except by authorized dealers and is sold subject to the conditions that it shall not be sold or distributed with any part of its cover or markings removed, nor in a mutilated condition. SPIDER-MAN (including all prominent characters featured in the issue), and the distinctive likenesses thereof, are trademarks of the MARVEL COMICS GROUP. SECOND CLASS POSTAGE PAID AT NEW YORK, N.Y. AND ADDITIONAL MAILING OFFICES.

MARVEL TEAM-UP #81, PAGE 1 ART BY MIKE VOSBURG & STEVE LEIALOHA

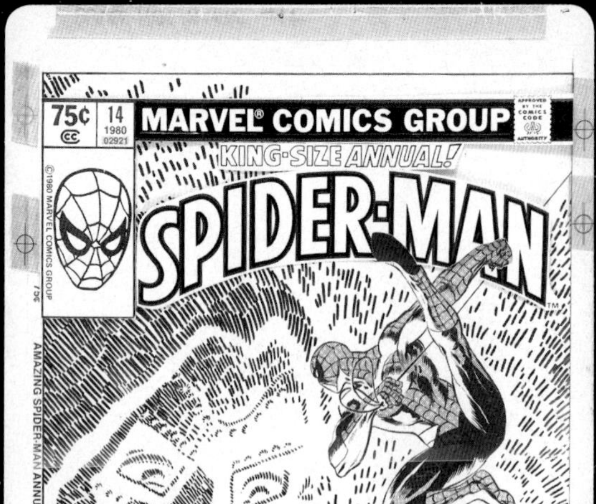

75¢
14
1980
02921
MARVEL® COMICS GROUP
KING-SIZE ANNUAL!
SPIDER-MAN
©1980 MARVEL COMICS GROUP
AMAZING SPIDER-MAN ANNUAL
MARVEL COMICS GROUP
SPIDEY and DOCTOR STRANGE versus DOCTOR DOOM and the DREAD DORMAMMU. 'nuff said!

AMAZING SPIDER-MAN ANNUAL #14 COVER ART BY FRANK MILLER & TOM PALMER COURTESY OF HERITAGEAUCTIONS.COM